Autonomy, Sovereignty, and Self-Determination

Autonomy, Sovereignty, and Self-Determination

THE ACCOMMODATION OF CONFLICTING RIGHTS

Hurst Hannum

upp

UNIVERSITY OF PENNSYLVANIA PRESS   Philadelphia

Library of Congress Cataloging-in-Publication Data

Hannum, Hurst.
    Autonomy, sovereignty, and self-determination : the accommodation of
conflicting rights / Hurst Hannum.
        p.   cm.—(Procedural aspects of international law)
    Includes bibliographical references.
    ISBN 0-8122-8206-X
    1. Self-determination, National. 2. Autonomy. I. Title.
    II. Series.
JX4054.H34   1990   89-40405
320.1'5—dc20   CIP

Correspondances

La Nature est un temple où de vivants piliers
Laissent parfois sortir de confuses paroles;
L'homme y passe à travers des forêts de symboles
Qui l'observent avec des regards familiers.

Comme de longs échos qui de loin se confondent
Dans une ténébreuse et profonde unité,
Vaste comme la nuit et comme la clarté,
Les parfums, les couleurs et les sons se répondent.

Il est des parfums frais comme des chairs d'enfants,
Doux comme les hautbois, verts comme les prairies,
—Et d'autres, corrompus, riches et triomphants,

Ayant l'expansion des choses infinies,
Comme l'ambre, le musc, le benjoin et l'encens,
Qui chantent les transports de l'esprit et des sens.

Charles Baudelaire, *Les Fleurs du Mal* (1857)

Contents

Acknowledgments

The present book is, in many respects, a logical progression from the author's early interests in human rights, minority rights, and constitutional law, which began at Boalt School of Law of the University of California at Berkeley. Subsequent work in Northern Ireland in the early 1970s, as a legal adviser to the Constitutional Conventions of Guam and the U.S. Virgin Islands in 1977 and 1978, and in preparing an initial study on autonomy in international law for the Procedural Aspects of International Law Institute in 1980 reinforced those earlier multidisciplinary interests.

However, mere interest is not sufficient to ensure that a project of such broad scope as the present one will be undertaken. Work on this issue has been possible only with the generous financial support of the Ford Foundation to the Procedural Aspects of International Law Institute, under whose auspices the present study has been written. In particular, I would like to thank Gary Sick and Stephen Marks of the Foundation for their early and continuing encouragement.

A great number of people have assisted in the project, some by direct contributions of research and writing, others by sharing with the author their perspectives on an extraordinarily diverse set of issues and situations. Comprehensive research and initial drafts of various case studies were prepared by several consultants to the Institute, including Enrique Armijo, Josiah Cobbah, Atle Grahl-Madsen, Virginia Leary, Dawn Martin, Amit Pandya, and Anna Tapay. Of course, the final choice and presentation of materials are solely that of the author, and only he is responsible for any errors or omissions.

The author traveled literally around the world in the course of research, including, among those situations addressed in the major case studies in Part II, to Hong Kong, India, Nicaragua, Norway, and Sri

Lanka. Numerous individuals, nongovernmental organizations, and government officials contributed to the success of these trips, and if most of them go unmentioned by name it is not because of any lack of appreciation for their efforts.

In addition, several international conferences in which the author was able to participate offered rich sources of information about problems of minority rights and autonomy in general and in the specific situations examined. Of particular value were meetings on Ethnicity and Rights, at Columbia University in June 1986; the State, Autonomy, and Indigenous Rights, in Managua in July 1986; Self-Determination in the Commonwealth Context, at the University of Edinburgh in July 1986; Ethnic Conflict, Human Rights, and Development, at the International Peace Research Institute in Oslo in October 1986; and the Fourth Seminar on the Small Nations of the North, in Qaqortoq, Greenland, in June 1988. Also of great value were discussions with knowledgeable colleagues and others at meetings in 1985 and 1987 of the Working Group on Indigenous Populations of the UN Sub-Commission on Prevention of Discrimination and Protection of Minorities.

Many people offered suggestions and corrections to earlier drafts of the manuscript, as well as provided essential factual information and documentation on ongoing situations. In this context, I would like to express my appreciation for their help in various ways to Gudmundur Alfredsson, Hon. S. De Alwis, Abdullahi Ahmed An-Na'im, Russel Barsh, Alegría Borrás Rodriguez, Kevin Boyle, Jens Brøsted, Georg Brunner, Christina Cerna, Roberta Cohen, Radhika Coomaraswamy, Tim Coulter, Władisław Czapliński, Jens Dahl, Shelton H. Davis, Shirley Dawson, Martin Diskin, Asbjørn Eide, Joseph T. Eldridge, K. Imani Ellis, William C. Gilmore, Dennis C. Ho, Abdeen M. Jabarra, Vivek Katju, Frank Koszorus, Tamara Kunanayakam, Peter Lo, Courtney O'Connor, Nicholas O'Neill, Natalino Ronzitti, Kumar Rupesinghe, Elsa Stamatopoulou-Robbins, Gary Stanley, Rodolfo Stavenhagen, Donald Tsang, Steven Tullberg, Michael van Walt, Tashi Wangdi, and Meredith Wilkie. A few people were kind (or foolish) enough to read substantial portions of the penultimate draft, and the observations of Gordon Christenson, Roger Clark, Justinia Dolgopol, Michael O'Boyle, Haciba Ounadjela, Danilo Türk, and Ben Whitaker were invaluable; particular thanks go out to Michael, Tina, and Haciba for their perserverance and perspicacity.

Hurst Hannum
Washington, DC
January 1989

Part I **The International Legal Context**

Chapter 1
Introduction

While this book is written from the perspective of an international lawyer, its focus is on individuals and groups rather than states, the traditional subjects and objects of international law.[1] Of course, the state
system is the context in which the discussion occurs, but the primary
concern is to examine the ways in which international law and domestic
constitutional arrangements can contribute to resolving disputes between minority and majority groups which, if not resolved, often lead
to violent conflicts.

Most of the situations examined in Parts II and III are examples of
ethnic conflict, a term which for the past two decades has been a popular
subject of investigation and discussion among social scientists. In an
introduction such as this, one formerly was expected to list the numerous
instances of ethnic or religious conflict around the world which justified
the particular scholarly work at hand; today, such conflicts are so widespread and well known that it seems superfluous to offer justifications
for addressing them.[2]

---

1 While lawyers, politicians, and the general public use the terms "state" and "nation" interchangeably, this book will adopt the distinction drawn by political scientists,
sociologists, and others between a recognized political entity that exercises the functions
of government, the "state," and a cultural or social grouping with certain shared characteristics (such as language or ethnicity), known as a "nation." While this practice runs
the risk of confusing American audiences for whom a state is a political subdivision of
the United States and does some injustice to terms such as "international" and "United
Nations," it seems the best available. See chap. 2 for a more detailed examination of
these and related concepts.

2 The problem of ethnic conflict has even reached the front page of the Washington
Post, which accurately observed that "[t]hese simmering conflicts, rooted in the most basic
forms of human identity, often do not command the headlines that rivet world attention
on international wars and guerrilla insurgencies, but they frequently prove more vicious
and intractable." The story went on to identify 25 current examples of ethnic and religious

While the designation of conflicts such as those in Northern Ireland, Sri Lanka, or Fiji as "ethnic" is convenient, it is important to understand the complexity of what in many situations would be more properly described as center-periphery, majority-minority, or powerful-powerless conflicts. There is no ethnic distinction between the inhabitants of Hong Kong and mainland China, but there are certainly differences; few of the cases studied herein reflect true racial differences, although cultural (linguistic, religious) distinctions may be substantial.[3]

While the need to protect shared individual and group interests against a more powerful society may thus arise because of many different factors, the solution sought in a great number of such instances is similar. The primary link among the specific situations discussed in this book is an expressed desire for greater political *autonomy* on the part of some segment of a larger society which is currently organized into a state. "Autonomy" is not a term of art in international or constitutional law,[4] and the present work does not seek to add yet another phrase to legal jargon. Personal and political autonomy is in some real sense the right to be different and to be left alone; to preserve, protect, and promote values which are beyond the legitimate reach of the rest of society.

In a few instances, demands for autonomy may be satisfied only by the emergence of a new, independent state in which the dissatisfied segment can exercise "sovereign" authority. In others, successful autonomy may imply no more than protection from discrimination and preservation of cultural, linguistic, or other values from majority assault. In many instances, adoption of a federal system or the devolution of meaningful power from the center to geographic, linguistic, or ethnic-based regions is sought.

Most minority or ethnic conflicts in the contemporary world have a substantial international or transnational component. This may be because members of the minority community in one state form part of

violence around the world, surely a modest listing. "Ethnic Conflicts: Toll Mounts," Wash. Post, 26 May 1987, at A1, col. 3.

3 While "racial" distinctions are popularly identified as those among the three classifications of Caucasoid, Mongoloid, and Negroid, the Convention on the Elimination of All Forms of Racial Discrimination encompasses "any distinction, exclusion, restriction or preference based on race, colour, descent, *or national or ethnic origin.*" [emphasis added] The U.S. Supreme Court recently has interpreted mid-nineteenth century federal statutes forbidding racial discrimination as protecting "identifiable classes of persons who are subjected to intentional discrimination solely because of their ancestry or ethnic characteristics," rejecting arguments for a narrower definition of race. Saint Francis College v. Al-Khazraji, 107 S.Ct. 2022, 2028 (1987).

4 *See* Hurst Hannum and Richard B. Lillich, "The Concept of Autonomy in International Law," 74 Am. J. Int'l L. 858 (1980); Frederik Harhoff, "Institutions of Autonomy," 55 Nordic J. Int'l L. 31 (1986).

the majority community in a neighboring state (e.g., Catholic nationalists in Northern Ireland, German-speakers in South Tyrol) or because a minority or ethnic community cuts across borders and thus involves more than one state (e.g., Kurds, Basques, Saamis). If ethnic or communal violence increases, geopolitical concerns often dictate the involvement of outside actors in the conflict, and central governments frequently allege (often correctly) that foreign governments encourage separatist conflicts.

Even in purely domestic situations where "autonomy" is advanced by one party as a solution to the conflict, each side commonly invokes international legal norms to support its claims. Sovereignty, self-determination, and human rights are the philosophical underpinnings claimed by one group or the other (or both), and such legal totems are the primary grounds of appeals for outside support. State and non-state groups define themselves as peoples or nations, not because these terms are necessarily descriptive or because they will contribute to a better understanding of a given situation, but rather because certain legal consequences are thought to flow from such designations.

These are the terms of international law, although to date international lawyers have expressed little interest in analyzing them in the context of political conflicts. Perhaps because concepts such as sovereignty and self-determination do have popular meanings, international lawyers have been content to leave their technical definition to the pens of academics and their political implications to the politicians. Similarly, there has been little legal (as opposed to philosophical) investigation into the relationship between human rights and the legitimacy of the state.

One difficulty in adopting a primarily legal approach to ethnic and other contemporary communal conflicts is that law, whether international or domestic, tends to assume a rational, egalitarian, individualistic structure. The sovereign equality of states—surely a fiction if ever there was one—reflects the Western conception of the internal polity of a state as being composed of "free-floating individuals, each of whom is endowed with a kit of basic rights and immunities and each of whom is available for those tasks and associations that fit his talents and preferences."[5] Ethnic conflicts, which are almost by definition based on ascriptive attributes, do not fit easily within the realm of a system of law which was created, in part, precisely to ignore those attributes.[6]

Nevertheless, law is the medium through which constitutions are

5 Donald L. Horowitz, *Ethnic Groups in Conflict* (Berkeley: Univ. of California Press, 1985) at 87.

6 *Cf. id.* at 86–89. Also see Stephen Ryan, "Explaining Ethnic Conflict: the neglected international dimension," 14 Rev. Int'l Studies 161 (1988).

developed and human rights defined and implemented. Insofar as legal norms might offer a framework for conflict resolution and legal techniques a means of facilitating formal agreement, the lawyer has an obligation to contribute his or her perspective to that of the political scientist, sociologist, economist, anthropologist, and military strategist.

The resurgence of ethnicity as a conflictual battle cry in part results from the understandable attempts by many post–1945 states, in particular, to substitute ideology or technocracy for ethnic identity in the multi-national societies which nearly all new states inherited. Where there is a dominant ethnic group, however, the assertion of *its* identity seems unavoidable, and ethnic minorities, if they are unsuccessful in securing basic human rights of non-discrimination and equality, may be driven to reinforce their own ethnic identity—or perish. Indeed, even guarantees of equality and non-discrimination may be insufficient, as freedom of movement and residence may allow dilution of minority strength through immigration of majority group members into the minority's traditional homeland; equal access to public administration may be insufficient to guarantee an effective minority voice.

There is a tendency in both developed and developing societies simply to ignore the existence of minority groups and their contribution to the development of a "national" (more often, state) identity. If a minority's essential cultural, religious, or linguistic values are seen as immaterial or contrary to those of the majority polity (as is the case for Irish Catholics in Northern Ireland, Tamils in Sri Lanka, and Kurds in Turkey), it should not be surprising that there is, in return, little acceptance by that minority of the values or legitimacy of the majority's state.

Despite assumptions about the desirability or inevitability of assimilation, whether in newly established or old states, "*it is the exact opposite which is true. The point about culturally divided societies . . . is that they wish to remain divided. . . .* Those who see division as a source of conflict overlook that conflict arises because of threats to the factors which make for that division."[7]

One common explanation of the apparent resurgence of ethnic conflict is that it offers a convenient vehicle for channeling political dissatisfaction into political organization. According to one well respected analyst, "ethnopolitics" seeks to address two sets of contradictions: the structural inequality of regions and groups, despite theoretically equal

---

7 Antony E. Alcock, "The Development of Governmental Attitudes to Cultural Minorities in Western Industrial States," in Antony E. Alcock, Brian K. Taylor, and John M. Welton (eds.), *The Future of Cultural Minorities* (London: Macmillan, 1979) at 108; emphasis in original.

development, and the failure of the state to implement the "normative promise" which is its *raison d'être*.[8] Given the complexity of modern life and the overlapping groups which demand attention from the existing power structure, ethnicity appears to be a rational organizational principle readily available to the political elite as well as to those who seek to replace it.[9]

[C]laims to group legitimacy provide alternative ways of measuring worth. If a group suffers by invidious comparison along the dimension of achievement motivation, it may nonetheless have a special connection with the land that furnishes an alternative basis for relative group evaluation. Groups that do suffer from such comparison tend, therefore, to make stronger claims to priority by virtue of legitimacy, so as to make up on one front what they have lost on another.

Relative group worth and relative group legitimacy thus merge into a politics of ethnic entitlement.[10]

Ethnicity is an even more obvious basis on which to assert political power when one considers that, under the guise of the "nation-state," ethnicity (or linguistic affinity or religion) became the foundation of political organization in the late nineteenth century.

The self-determination principle holds that any people, simply because it considers itself to be a separate national group, is uniquely and exclusively qualified to determine its own political status, including, should it so desire, the right to its own state. The concept, therefore, makes ethnicity the ultimate standard of political legitimacy.[11]

As demonstrated in chapter 3, this so-called ethnic principle of self-determination has never been seriously considered by the international community to be the sole, or even primary, factor in assessing claims to statehood. Nevertheless, the rhetoric of "one people, one state" echoes in the speeches of every dissatisfied minority.

A brief survey of ethnic conflicts suggests that economic or class aspects, while they may be important in many situations, cannot by

8 Joseph Rothschild, *Ethnopolitics* (New York: Columbia Univ. Press, 1981) at 4.
9 *Id*. at 213–27, 248–49.
10 Horowitz, *supra* note 5, at 186; see generally *id*. at 95–228.
11 Walker Connor, "The Political Significance of Ethnonationalism Within Western Europe," in Abdul Said and Luiz R. Simmons (eds.), *Ethnicity in an International Context* (New Brunswick, NJ: Transaction Books, 1976) at 111–12. This theme is developed in several other articles by Connor, e.g., "The Politics of Ethnonationalism", 27 J. Int'l Affairs 1 (1973); "Self-Determination, The New Phase," 20 World Politics 30 (1967).

themselves explain the existence or intensity of many conflicts.[12] Separatist or minority assertions are made by poor regions which complain of underdevelopment (e.g., the Tamil "homeland," southern Sudan) and rich regions complaining of exploitation or unequal treatment (e.g., the Basque country, Punjab); by regions which might well be economically better off after separation (e.g., Biafra), and those which would almost certainly be less well off (e.g., Quebec, Northern Ireland, Brittany); by economically deprived groups (e.g., Malays, Fijians) and economically advanced groups (e.g., Sikhs, Ibos). Indeed, one of the major political struggles within ethnic minority groups is often between those who adopt a more traditional or nationalist attitude and those who link ethnic solidarity with cross-ethnic class or economic issues.[13] While economic interests are perhaps the primary motivating factor in the concern of Hong Kong for autonomy within China, they are not as relevant to the Saamis in Norway or to the Turkish Kurds.

However, it is true that without perceived economic or political discrimination and the resulting weakening of the minority's position in society, the protection of purely cultural attributes might not become an issue. "[Nationalist] agitation acquires a mass basis, and hence takes on genuine significance, only when minority persons come to realize that the cultural persecution they suffer is accompanied by far more damaging discriminatory treatment in matters of economic opportunity, educational attainment, and social advancement."[14]

Many minority ethnic groups have retained their identity because of relative geographic isolation from the central government and culture, and peripheral regions are frequently less developed than those in the

---

12 One author has suggested that a more or less continuous process of secession, as a means of eliminating "transactions of decline" and the stagnation of cities, would be an extremely healthy economic development. However, she admits that this possibility would be "incredible" and exists only in theory: "The mystique of the nation is the powerful gruesome glamour of human sacrifice. To betray the nation and its unity is to betray all that shed blood; to do so to be better off economically would seem to render the most glorious pages of national history mere sound and fury. Virtually all national governments, it seems fair to say, and most citizens would sooner decline and decay unified, true to the sacrifices by which their unity was won, than seek to prosper and develop in division." Jane Jacobs, "The Dynamic of Decline," Atlantic Monthly, April 1984, at 98, 110.

13 Such splits can be seen between, e.g., the Provisional and Official I.R.A., pro- and anti-Sandinista Miskitos, and traditional and progressive Kurdish militants. *Cf.* the brief summary of Leninist and Stalinist views on nationalism and self-determination in chap. 3 at 51–53; Roxanne Dunbar Ortiz, *Indians of the Americas* (London: Zed Books, 1984) at 73–123; Hector Diaz-Polanco, "*Neoindigenismo* and the Ethnic Question in Central America," 14 Latin American Perspectives 87 (Winter 1987, No. 1).

14 Jack E. Reece, *The Bretons Against France* (Chapel Hill: Univ. of North Carolina Press, 1977) at 227.

center. The concept of "internal colonialism" has been used to describe the exploitation of politically and economically weaker regions and/or groups by the more powerful urban elite, as well as to suggest parallels between the rights of indigenous and other groups to self-determination and the recognized self-determination of formally colonized peoples.[15] However, the problem of internal colonialism seems to be as much a question of political marginalization as of economic disadvantage (although the two evidently tend to go hand in hand), and, as an economic analysis, it is no more successful than others in providing a general theory of ethnic or regional conflict over autonomy.

While modernization theories may not be applicable to conflicts in, for example, Burma, India, and Uganda, they should not be dismissed with respect, for instance, to separatist or regional movements in France or Great Britain.[16] The expansion of modern, technological, homogeneous, transnational "culture" and the loosening of traditional family ties often lead to a reassertion of minority cultural values with which members of local or regional communities can identify more easily;[17] it may be possible to protect these values only by acquiring political and economic power at the group or regional level.

Ethnic spokesmen are challenging the close connection of modernization and development. If modernity leads to alienation of the individual and to centralized injustice in the name of rational planning, then perhaps modernization is antithetical to genuine development. . . .
    Loss of a sense of boundaries, not just territorial but social and psychological, may be at the core of the current outbreak of communal versus nation-state tensions.[18]

15 See generally Rodolfo Stavenhagen, *Social Classes in Agrarian Societies* (New York: Doubleday Anchor, 1975). Stavenhagen has suggested the need for a new analysis of development that will take into account the reality of ethnic cohesiveness and its relevance to both economic and political development.
    16 Even this distinction between the "developed" and "developing" world may not hold much longer. *Cf.*, e.g., "Even Deep in Borneo, Civilization Intrudes in All Its Splendor," Wall Street Journal, 5 May 1987, at 1, col. 4, which describes the advent of shopping malls, videos, etc. in rural Borneo.
    17 *Cf.*, e.g., D. N. MacIver, "Ethnic Identity and the Modern State," in Colin H. Williams (ed.), *National Separatism* (Vancouver and London: Univ. of British Columbia Press, 1982) at 299–307.
    18 Cynthia H. Enloe, *Ethnic Conflict and Political Development* (Boston: Little, Brown, 1973) at 274. *Cf.* Ernest Gellner, *Culture, Identity, and Politics* (Cambridge: Cambridge Univ. Press, 1987) at 15–16:

    [M]odern society [is] literate, mobile, formally equal with a merely fluid, continuous, so to speak atomised inequality, and with a shared, homogeneous, literacy-carried, and school-inculcated culture. It could hardly be more sharply contrasted with a traditional society, within which literacy was a minority and specialised ac-

As the importance of transnational economic actors grows, individuals feel more and more distant from the political and economic centers of decision-making; Brussels and the headquarters of the International Monetary Fund are certainly less accessible to most citizens than is their country's capital, and such new international "centers" have increased their distance from the peripheries. Where political power has become concentrated in a large, centralized state government, even regular democratic elections may not be particularly meaningful to the individual voter who sees his single ballot as one largely empty gesture among millions. Returning power to the local or regional level is one way of increasing real and perceived participation in the political process.

Minority groups also may suffer discrimination and persecution simply because they are different. Racial prejudice and religious intolerance remain common in all regions of the world, and the fact that they may be deliberately exacerbated by those intent on gaining or retaining political dominance does not make them less real.[19] Even if individual members of minority groups may prefer to assimilate or participate in the larger society on the basis of equality and non-discrimination, they may be forced to defend their interests as part of the group if discrimination is sufficiently powerful or established.

Ethnic politics generally attack the very foundation of the state, in part because ethnic leaders may have little to gain by offering specific, non-ethnic alternatives to ameliorate the conditions that led to ethnic discontent. "[W]hile politicized ethnicity often erodes the legitimacy of a state and the effectiveness of the state's apparatus, . . . it ordinarily does not supply the follow-through conceptual model for major, historic, systemic social revolutions."[20]

If the minority/secessionist group does not have a very coherent program which negotiations could address, an escalating conflict soon comes to revolve around naked political power, and both sides find

complishment, where stable hierarchy rather than mobility was the norm, and culture was diversified and discontinuous, and in the main transmitted by local social groups rather than by special and centrally supervised educational agencies.

In such an environment, a man's culture, the idiom within which he was trained and within which he is effectively employable, is his most precious possession, his real entrance-card to full citizenship and human dignity, to social participation. . . . The wrong and alien culture becomes menacing. Culture, like prose, becomes visible, and a source of pride and pleasure to boot. The age of nationalism is born.

19 See, e.g., the annual *Report of the Committee on the Elimination of Racial Discrimination*, issued as a Supplement to the Official Records of the UN General Assembly, and *Report submitted by Mr. Angelo Vidal d'Almeida Ribeiro, Special Rapporteur appointed in accordance with resolution 1986/20 of the Commission on Human Rights* [concerning religious intolerance], UN Doc. E/CN.4/1988/45 (1988).

20 Rothschild, *supra* note 8, at 243.

themselves in positions where absolute stances—either separatism or forced unity on the majority's terms—are the only remaining options. Many of the case studies in Part II demonstrate that state repression of legitimate struggles against discrimination and human rights violations rapidly escalates the physical side of the conflict, until the return to the status quo ante—even after redressing prior discrimination and human rights violations—no longer suffices.

The resulting absolutist positions can be maintained indefinitely because of another component of contemporary reality essential to an understanding of ethnic and other conflict: the ready availability and sophisticated killing power of modern weapons. Neither small revolutionary cells nor external subversion have created the vast majority of the conflicts discussed in the present book (although they may exacerbate existing tensions). However, the rapid escalation of violence and simultaneous resort to state and opposition terrorism distort the underlying issues and make them much more difficult to resolve, even when majorities on both sides may be willing to compromise.

"Terrorism" is a much-maligned term these days, as governments and popular opinion pretend to distinguish between "their" terrorists and "our" freedom fighters. As used in this book, "terrorism" is the deliberate killing of randomly or arbitrarily selected non-combatants by any individual or group.[21] It is contrary to customary international laws of armed conflict and contemporary human rights norms. It is a perversion of ideological commitment, as the arguably respectable principle of dying for a cause has been replaced by the much more suspect one of killing for a cause.

Terrorism also is economical and sometimes seemingly effective, in terms of both human and financial costs. Modern state terrorism is made possible by continued diplomatic and often logistic support, primarily from other governments. Opposition terrorism is facilitated by continued financial and often logistic support, also primarily from governments. Both are encouraged by an international arms trade recently estimated as worth $900 billion annually.[22] A relatively small amount of money can purchase highly destructive automatic weapons, land mines, and explosives, which can be used by a relatively small number of people to devastating effect.

Foreign governments' initial tolerance of violence by minority "mil-

21 It is perhaps worth recalling that the concept of terrorism initially referred to state action. The *Oxford English Dictionary* (Oxford: Clarendon Press, 1933) gives as the first definition of "terrorism," "Government by intimidation as directed and carried out by the party in power in France during the Revolution of 1789–94." Vol. 11 at 216.

22 "Middle East Is Top Market for Arms, US Says," Wash. Post, 20 June 1987, at A19, col. 4.

itants" and massive human rights violations by security forces is quickly translated into the acquisition of weapons by those who now feel the need to defend themselves from armed attack. Allegations of human rights violations and terrorism become tools in the political and diplomatic struggle; governments are reluctant to condemn their friends, while nongovernmental organizations may be equally reluctant to condemn "defensive" killings by minority militants. Recalcitrant minorities on both sides often possess sufficient military strength to avoid "defeat," and violent stalemate results.

Indiscriminate repression by government security forces and politically motivated killings by opponents may discourage moderate or interim solutions which might otherwise be possible in the middle stages of an increasingly violent conflict. While there is nothing inherently desirable about compromise, the assassination of moderate political opponents by extremist opposition factions and the assumption of emergency powers by government forces acting with impunity may purposely deprive majorities on both sides of the conflict of an effective voice. It becomes difficult to break through the resulting stalemate simply through incremental shifts in political or military tactics, and either more repressive measures must be adopted or substantially more flexible solutions must be proposed by a government ready to face down its own internal opposition.

This book attempts to suggest ways in which norms of international law may be utilized to promote such flexible solutions, preferably before violence becomes widespread. First, the contemporary content of those norms is examined. Are human rights relevant to the group claims advanced by those who desire greater autonomy? Do such groups have valid claims that their rights as minorities and/or indigenous peoples are being denied? Can groups within existing states assert a legally colorable right to self-determination? Can the state deny all claims to greater political power-sharing by invoking its sovereignty?

"Since almost all politics are concerned with some form of majorities and minorities, reconciling their conflicting interests is an endemic as well as an inescapable problem in society."[23] The case studies in Parts II and III underscore the fact that demands for autonomy, self-government, or independence are universal. When one examines each conflict closely, it is apparent that any analysis must take into account a complex mosaic of history (often stretching back for centuries), economic development (or, more frequently, lack thereof), political manipulation

---

23 Ben Whitaker, "Minority Rights and Self-Determination," in Donald P. Kommers and Gilburt D. Loescher (eds.), *Human Rights and American Foreign Policy* (Notre Dame, IN: Notre Dame Univ. Press, 1979) at 63.

(by both sides to the conflict), and external interference (ranging from joint repression of minorities to active attempts at destabilizing the state). At the same time, however, the very absence of congruity among such very diverse situations makes the similar minority demands and state reactions more striking.

Part II examines in some detail claims for "autonomy" which have been advanced in nine very different contexts, from the protection of the traditional culture of the Saami in northern Scandinavia to a very modern assertion of political and economic autonomy by the inhabitants of Hong Kong.

Part III offers a survey of contemporary and historical "autonomous" entities, some of which may serve as models for future autonomy arrangements. The focus is not on conflicts but on solutions, both attempted and successful. These brief case studies demonstrate the kinds of flexible and creative structures that have been developed to respond to particular tensions; they also underscore the malleable nature of sovereignty and statehood.

Finally, a concluding chapter offers an analysis of the ways in which apparent conflicts among individual, group, and state rights can be reconciled. The legitimacy of the state will be seen to rest upon respect for human rights and the effective participation of all segments of the population in the economic and political decision-making process, commitments that go beyond mere rule by the numerical majority. The narrow limits within which the right of self-determination and secession has been recognized will be recalled, as will the obligations of a minority to accept legitimate decisions taken by the majority, which remain the fundamental basis of democracy.

Ultimately, one must resolve the inherent tension between the obligation of every society to recognize pluralism and diversity and the desire of every culture—whether majority, minority, or indigenous—to perpetuate its values and enforce conformity. The appropriate role of the state is to mediate between these competing forces, setting the parameters within which the resulting conflict will be creative rather than destructive.

Chapter 2
Sovereignty, Statehood, and Nationalism

SOVEREIGNTY AND STATEHOOD

"Sovereignty" and the accompanying corollary of the equality of states have been termed "the basic constitutional doctrine of the law of nations."[24] Sovereignty is the cornerstone of international rhetoric about state independence and freedom of action, and the most common response to initiatives which seek to limit a state's action in any way is that such initiatives constitute an impermissible limitation on that state's sovereignty.[25]

At the same time, however, the content of the term "sovereignty" is at best murky, whatever its emotional appeal. "[T]here exists perhaps no conception the meaning of which is more controversial than that of sovereignty. It is an indisputable fact that this conception, from the moment when it was introduced into political science until the present day, has never had a meaning which was universally agreed upon."[26]

[F]or the practical purposes of the international lawyer sovereignty is not a metaphysical concept, nor is it part of the essence of statehood; it is merely a term which designates an aggregate of particular and very extensive claims that states habitually make for themselves in their relations with other states. To the extent that sovereignty has come to imply that there is something inherent in

24 Ian Brownlie, *Principles of Public International Law* (Oxford: Clarendon Press, 3d. ed. 1979) at 287.

25 See, e.g., Alan James, *Sovereign Statehood* (London: Allen & Unwin, 1986) at 1.

26 L. F. E. Oppenheim, 1 *International Law* (London: Longman, 2 vols. 1905, 1906) at 103.

the nature of states that makes it impossible for them to be subjected to law, it is a false doctrine which the facts of international relations do not support.[27]

At least part of the difficulty in defining sovereignty lies in the fact that sovereignty traces its historical roots to sovereigns, in whose hands "absolute" spiritual and temporal power rested. Modern discussions of sovereignty have often addressed the question of whether one can speak of "absolute sovereignty" for states, a power above international law. Few, if any, would support such a view today, and the very concept of the equality of states at least implies that the sovereign rights of each state are limited by the equally sovereign rights of others.[28] " '[S]overeignty' in its original sense of 'supreme power' is not merely an absurdity but an impossibility in a world of States which pride themselves upon their independence from each other and concede to each other a status of equality before the law."[29]

Many writers essentially equate sovereignty with independence, the fundamental authority of a state to exercise its powers without being subservient to any outside authority.[30] Indeed, there is much to recommend the criterion of independence as the only one relevant in determining whether or not a state is fully sovereign. However, it is important to bear in mind that it is the authority or ability of a state to determine its relationship with outside powers that is significant; the actual delegation of certain powers to others—such as, for example, the retention by some fully sovereign countries of judicial appeals to the British Privy Council—will not detract from the sovereignty of the delegating state. James refers to this criterion as "constitutional independence," which he views as the essential determinant of whether or not a state is sovereign.[31]

One principle upon which there seems to be universal agreement is that sovereignty is an attribute of statehood, and that only states can be sovereign. The classic definition of a "state" is found in the 1933 Montevideo Convention on Rights and Duties of States, article I of which provides:

27 J. L. Brierly, *The Law of Nations* (Oxford: Clarendon Press, 4th ed. 1949) at 48–49; accord, James Crawford, *The Creation of States in International Law* (Oxford: Clarendon Press, 1979) at 26–27.

28 See generally Edwin DeWitt Dickinson, *The Equality of States in International Law* (Cambridge, MA: Harvard Univ. Press, 1920; New York: Klaus Reprint Co., 1972), esp. at 114–15, 150.

29 Jenks, in Arthur Larson, C. Wilfred Jenks, et al., *Sovereignty Within the Law* (Dobbs Ferry, NY: Oceana, 1965) at 11.

30 See, e.g., Brownlie, *supra* note 24, at 80; Crawford, *supra* note 27, at 27.

31 See generally James, *supra*, note 25.

The State as a person of international law should possess the following qualifications: (a) a permanent population; (b) a defined territory; (c) government;
and (d) capacity to enter into relations with other States.[32]

Other requirements for statehood have occasionally been advanced,
for example, that a certain degree of civilization necessary to maintain
international relations be allowed,[33] or that a state's government be
established consistently with the principle of self-determination.[34] The
former is unlikely to be acceptable or relevant today, while the latter
seems to be applicable only in the context of decolonization, such as
the refusal of the world community to concede statehood status to Southern Rhodesia from the time of Ian Smith's unilateral declaration of
independence in 1965 to the establishment of majority rule in 1980.

While the development of precise definitions or categories of state-
hood/sovereignty is largely irrelevant to the purposes of the present
work, it may nevertheless be useful to recall the wide range of governmental entities considered by international law as possessing some degree of international personality, if not full sovereignty.[35]

Guaranteed or neutralized states are independent states whose existence or neutrality is set forth in an international treaty. They are fully
sovereign, except for specific treaty restrictions imposed on neutral states
regarding war powers or implied restrictions on the exercise of foreign affairs powers which might jeopardize neutral status. Examples of guaranteed states would include Montenegro, Serbia, and Romania under the
terms of the 1878 Treaty of Berlin; neutralized states include Switzerland
since the 1815 Congress of Vienna, Belgium in 1839, and Norway in 1907.

A *protected independent state* has delegated certain of its powers by
treaty to a protecting or guardian state, but it retains full domestic
autonomy and its general right of control over foreign relations, except
insofar as that control has been delegated by specific treaty provisions.
Some retention of effective local authority even in the foreign relations
area may be necessary to retain "independent" status. Oppenheim refers
to such a state simply as a "protectorate," which has a greater international presence than a vassal state, is never part of the protecting

32 Signed 26 Dec. 1933, 165 L.N.T.S. 19.

33 Charles C. Hyde, 1 *International Law Chiefly as Interpreted and Applied by the
United States* (Boston: Little, Brown, 2 vols. 1922) at 17.

34 See, e.g., Crawford, *supra* note 27, at 102–06; Brownlie, *supra* note 24, at 593–
96; *cf.* chap. 3.

35 See generally W.W. Willoughby and C.G. Fenwick, *Types of Restricted Sover-
eignty and of Colonial Autonomy* (Washington, DC: U.S. Gov't Printing Office, 1919);
M. Ydit, *Internationalised Territories from the "Free City of Cracow" to the "Free City of
Berlin"* (London: Sithoff, 1961); Marjorie M. Whiteman, 1 *Digest of International Law*
(Washington, DC: Dept. of State, 1963) at 221–598.

state, and is not ipso facto bound by treaties of the protector.[36] Examples would include the "petty sovereignties" of Andorra, Liechtenstein, San Marino, and Monaco, as well as Cuba under the terms of the Platt Amendment and the Ionian Islands from 1815 to 1862.[37]

Associated statehood is a relatively modern concept that has arisen out of United Nations discussions with respect to the exercise of self-determination by non-self-governing territories. The modern associated state is perhaps closest to a protected independent state, with an essential attribute being the ability unilaterally to terminate the "association" with another state.[38]

An *internationalized territory* is somewhat analogous to the guaranteed state and is created under international supervision or control to respond to particular political situations. One author defines these territories as special state entities in which sovereignty is vested in a group of states or an international organization.[39] Such a territory may or may not be considered a "state," although it generally retains internal independence and is restricted only by its international statute. Examples would include the Free City of Cracow, the Free City of Danzig, and the unimplemented plans for a Free Territory of Trieste in 1954 and a Corpus Separatum of Jerusalem in the late 1940s.

A *vassal state* subject to the suzerainty of another state does have some international personality, but it is subject to greater control by the suzerain state than is the case for protected states. The status of vassals may be defined both by treaty and by rather vague customary and personal relations which originated within feudal law. "[A] distinctive element of the feudal suzerainty relationship is that the suzerain holds the source of the governmental authority of the vassal State whose ruler he grants the right to exercise the authority autonomously."[40] International treaties of the suzerain are automatically binding on the vassal, although the vassal does retain some capacity for independent international action, for instance, Bulgaria's war against sovereign Serbia while Bulgaria was at least a nominal vassal of Turkey. The term has most commonly been employed to describe various components of the Ottoman empire, and other examples might include the Native States in India under British "paramountcy," Outer Mongolia, and pre-1911 Tibet.

A *condominium* is a territory under the joint sovereignty of two or

---

36 Oppenheim, 1 *International Law*, *supra* note 26, at 137–39.

37 Willoughby and Fenwick, *supra* note 35, at 6–7.

38 See G.A. Res. 1541(XV) (Annex) of 15 Dec. 1960, 15 UN GAOR, Supp. (No. 14), UN Doc. A/4684 (1960) at 29.

39 Ydit, *supra* note 35, at 20–21.

40 Michael C. van Walt van Praag, *The Status of Tibet* (Boulder, CO: Westview Press, 1987) at 105–06.

more governing powers. While national legislation in such a situation is not automatically extended to the condominium, it does not generally have any independent international personality. The only modern examples are Andorra and the New Hebrides prior to its independence in 1980.

The *protected dependent state*, while called a state and often possessing nominal independence, is in fact dependent on the protecting power and has a very limited international status. Crawford observes that such "international protectorates" vary widely and generally evolve towards independence rather than annexation (citing Brunei as an example),[41] while Willoughby and Fenwick observe that they were usually considered to be "politically undeveloped" by the protecting power.[42]

The United Nations Charter recognizes as *non-self-governing territories* all those territories "whose peoples have not yet attained a full measure of self-government."[43] A sub-category of non-self-governing territories is the *international trusteeship*, an arrangement under which eleven territories were placed under the administration of a trusteeship power through agreements approved and supervised by the UN General Assembly and Trusteeship Council. The last remaining trust territory, the "strategic" Trust Territory of the Pacific Islands, is administered by the United States under the supervision of the Security Council; a slow, complex process of terminating the trusteeship through the acquisition of a form of commonwealth status by the Northern Marianas and quasi-"free association" by Palau, the Marshall Islands, and the Federated States of Micronesia had not been completed by the end of 1988.[44]

Similar is the *colonial protectorate*, which was subject to the plenary authority of the protecting power, although its citizens were not subjects of the metropolitan power. Under classic colonial domination, residents of the colony were often subjects of the colonizer; both forms of this kind of "protected" entity have now essentially disappeared.

This brief survey indicates only some of the complexities in describing the attributes of statehood, sovereignty, and international personality. The international order has now moved to a stage when the sovereign independent state is much more the norm than the exception, but it would be a mistake to conclude that there is little to learn from the international mosaic of the nineteenth century. While dependency was imposed rather than freely chosen prior to 1945, the sometimes

---

41 Crawford, *supra* note 27, at 197.

42 Willoughby and Fenwick, *supra* note 35, at 9.

43 G.A. Res. 1541(XV), *supra* note 38.

44 See *infra* note 111; see generally Roger S. Clark, "Self-Determination and Free Association—Should the United Nations Terminate the Pacific Islands Trust?" 21 Harvard Int'l L. J. 1 (1980).

misleading formal distinctions drawn in that era among international entities often mirror the complex web of relationships among independent states, international organizations, and private international actors that characterizes the twentieth century.

LIMITS ON SOVEREIGNTY

Whatever the different degrees of international personality accorded to such entities as protectorates or dependent states, international law has long imposed limitations on the permissible scope of the internal and external actions of independent sovereign states as well.[45] The nature of territorial sovereignty necessarily implies the fundamental limitation that no state has the right to impose its will on the territory of another, with the exception of certain narrow circumstances such as the protection of a state's own nationals. Since 1945, the prohibition against the threat or use of armed force would seem to have emerged as a norm of customary international law (if not *jus cogens*), although debates as to the precise meaning of article 2(4) of the UN Charter continue.[46]

State sovereignty also is limited by general and customary law, such as the right of innocent passage and freedom of navigation on the high seas and through international waterways.[47] While it may be premature to speak of an international customary "law of the commons," such law seems to be in the process of development with respect to the peaceful uses of outer space and economic exploitation of ocean resources.[48]

Even within their own territory, states have long been limited by international law in a manner which makes any argument in favor of "absolute" sovereignty difficult to maintain. Some of the limitations are

45 See generally Ingrid Delupis, *International Law and the Independent State* (New York: Crane Russak, 1974).

46 For rather different views of the application of art. 2(4) to the conflict in Central America, compare John Norton Moore, "The Secret War in Central America and the Future of World Order," 80 Am J. Int'l L. 43 (1986) with James P. Rowles, " 'Secret Wars,' Self-Defense and the Charter—A Reply to Professor Moore," *id.* at 568; also see International Court of Justice, Military and Paramilitary Activities in and against Nicaragua (Nicaragua v. United States of America), Judgment, I.C.J. Reports 1986, p. 14, and Harold G. Maier (ed.), "Appraisals of the ICJ's Decision: Nicaragua v. United States (Merits)," 81 Am. J. Int'l L. 77 (1987).

47 Delupis, *supra* note 45, at 29–44, American Law Institute, *Restatement (Third) of the Foreign Relations Law of the United States* (St. Paul, MN: American Law Institute, 2 vols. 1987) §§ 513, 521.

48 *Cf.*, e.g., *Restatement*, *supra* note 47, §§ 511–17, 523, 601–04; Marvin S. Soroos, *Beyond Sovereignty* (Columbia, SC: Univ. of South Carolina Press, 1986) at 261–93; Hugo Caminos and Michael R. Molitor, "Progressive Development of International Law and the Package Deal," 79 Am. J. Int'l L. 871 (1985); Kay Hailbronner, "Freedom of the Air and the Convention on the Law of the Sea," 77 *id.* 490 (1983); Stephen Gorove, "The Geostationary Orbit: Issues of Law and Policy," 73 *id.* 444 (1979).

related to the protection of other (equal) states, such as state responsibility for acts wholly within one state which cause damage to another state.[49] The equitable use of water resources upon which other states depend also is mandated by international law.[50]

State responsibility for injuries to aliens in general, and the principle of diplomatic immunity, in particular, constitute long-standing restrictions on the unfettered use of state power even within a state's own territory.[51] At least some fundamental human rights norms have achieved the status of customary international law or *jus cogens*, including the prohibition against genocide[52] and systematic racial discrimination.[53] It also is clearly legitimate for international bodies to consider the human rights situation in any country, as human rights cannot be said to fall "essentially within the domestic jurisdiction" of a state within the meaning of article 2(7) of the UN Charter.[54]

49 See, e.g., the Trail Smelter arbitration (1941), *Annual Digest of Public International Law Cases* (1938–40), no. 104, and the many commentaries thereon; 2 *Restatement*, *supra* note 47, § 601.

50 Delupis, *supra* note 45, at 95–97.

51 See generally Richard B. Lillich, *The Human Rights of Aliens in Contemporary International Law* (Manchester, UK: Manchester Univ. Press, 1984); *id.*, *International Law of State Responsibility for Injuries to Aliens* (Charlottesville: Univ. Press of Virginia, 1982); F.V. Garcia-Amador, *The Changing Law of International Claims* (Dobbs Ferry, NY: Oceana, 2 vols. 1984). On diplomatic immunity, see United States Diplomatic and Consular Staff in Tehran, Judgment, I.C.J. Reports 1980, p. 3. "But what has above all to be emphasized is the extent and seriousness of the conflict between the conduct of the Iranian State and its obligations under the whole corpus of the international rules of which diplomatic and consular law is comprised, rules the fundamental character of which the Court must here again strongly affirm." at 42.

52 See, e.g., Reservations to the Convention on the Prevention and Punishment of the Crime of Genocide, Advisory Opinion, I.C.J. Reports 1951, p. 15, at 23; Barcelona Traction, Light and Power Company, Limited, Second Phase, Judgment, I.C.J. Reports 1970, p. 3, at 33; 2 *Restatement*, *supra* note 47, § 702.

53 *Cf.*, e.g., Legal Consequences for States of the Continued Presence of South Africa in Namibia (South West Africa) notwithstanding Security Council Resolution 276 (1970), Advisory Opinion, I.C.J. Reports 1971, p. 16, at 57: "[T]o enforce . . . distinctions, exclusions, restrictions and limitations exclusively based on grounds of race, colour, descent or national or ethnic origin which constitute a denial of fundamental human rights is a flagrant violation of the purposes and principles of the Charter"; *Restatement*, *supra* note 47.

54 One has only to glance at the agendas of UN bodies such as the Commission on Human Rights, Economic and Social Council, and General Assembly to confirm this observation. As stated to the UN Commission on Human Rights by the Foreign Minister of Argentina, following the collapse of the military regime in 1983, "The preservation of human rights was a legitimate interest of individuals and groups that went beyond the sovereignties and powers of the States and was also of concern to the international community." UN Doc. E/CN.4/1984/SR.29 (1984) at 3, quoted in Howard Tolley, Jr., *The*

While it has been suggested that communist states do not recognize any legal limits on state sovereignty,[55] a leading Soviet writer does affirm the principles of noninterference in internal affairs and the equality of states and peoples, although these socialist principles supposedly "differ fundamentally from the corresponding principles of general international law."[56] According to Tunkin, it is only through socialist internationalism that states can exercise their sovereignty in practice as well as in theory.[57]

Even more significant today than those limits on state sovereignty which might be imposed by general or customary international law are the self-imposed or de facto restrictions which have resulted from the complex economic and political international order of the twentieth century.[58] Decisions made by international technocratic bodies with nearly universal membership (such as the International Telecommunications Union, World Meteorological Organization, Universal Postal Union, and International Civil Aviation Organization) are effectively binding on all states, whether or not such decisions are ultimately expressed in the form of multilateral conventions. The General Agreement on Trade and Tariffs obviously has major implications for the international economic system and the role that states play therein, whether or not any given state is a party to it.

States may by treaty limit their own sphere of action by delegating certain powers to other states, but this does not affect their status as sovereign states unless the delegation is essentially a cover for foreign control. Agreements for military protection or the stationing of foreign troops in one's territory are common; even reservation of a right of intervention by another state does not necessarily render a state nonsovereign, as demonstrated by the cases of Cyprus and the Federal Republic of Germany (the latter until 1968).

Sovereignty can be lost or ceded by agreement, as in the case of the federation of two formerly independent states. Creation of the

U.N. Commission on Human Rights (Boulder, CO and London: Westview Press, 1987) at 208.

55 See, e.g., John N. Hazard, "Soviet Law," in Larson, Jenks, et al., *supra* note 29, at 268–98.

56 G.I. Tunkin, *Theory of International Law* (Cambridge, MA: Harvard Univ. Press, Butler trans. 1974) at 438.

57 *Id.*, at 437–43.

58 For example, among the major issues which are beyond the scope of unilateral state action and have been addressed on a global basis in recent years are nuclear proliferation, economic development, human rights, exploitation of ocean resources through development of a new law of the sea, environmental pollution, and international telecommunications. See generally Soroos, *supra* note 48, for a discussion of these and other examples of modern international cooperation.

United Arab Republic in 1958 by the federation of Egypt and Syria and of Tanzania in 1964 through the federation of Tanganyika and Zanzibar were unquestioned. The re-division of the U.A.R. in 1961 into its constituent parts caused little debate, at least suggesting that such shifting sovereignty was of little import to the rest of the world so long as it was accepted by all the immediately concerned parties.

There are two other possible examples of sovereignty being lost since 1945, those of Sikkim and Tibet. Although there is some question whether the status of Sikkim under British protection could be termed sovereignty, it did enjoy at least semi-sovereign status until its absorption by India in the mid-1970s.[59] With respect to Tibet, there is also debate as to its sovereign status prior to the Chinese invasion in 1950, but there can be no disagreement that its incorporation within China was accomplished by force rather than by consent.[60]

Of course, adherence to a treaty is not a limitation on sovereignty; it is rather one of the ultimate sovereign acts. At the same time, however, the principle of *pacta sunt servanda* does suggest that states are not as free to denounce as they are to accede to treaties; article 56 of the Vienna Convention on Treaties, for example, recognizes only two exceptions to the general rule against unilateral denunciations, that is, if the parties intended to admit the possibility of a denunciation or withdrawal or if such a possibility "may be implied by the nature of the treaty."[61]

Of particular significance is the growth of multilateral economic and political treaties which seek to regulate a far greater range of issues among states than did earlier bilateral trade or diplomatic treaties or even earlier political-military alliances.[62] While neither the United Nations nor the European Community has become a world or regional government, respectively, their impact on the conduct of international relations has no doubt been greater than that of any preceding international organization. Although these and similar bodies are at great pains to emphasize the sovereign equality of states on which they are founded, there can be little doubt that, while legal equality has largely been maintained, the actual freedom of action of individual members has been reduced.

There is no longer any question that international organizations

---

59 See James, *supra* note 25, at 103–04.

60 See *infra* chap.18, at 420–27.

61 Adopted 22 May 1969, entered into force 27 Jan. 1980, 1155 U.N.T.S. 331. *Cf.* Ian Sinclair, *The Vienna Convention on the Law of Treaties* (Manchester, UK: Manchester Univ. Press, 2d. ed. 1984) at 185–202, *Restatement, supra* note 47, § 332, 336.

62 It has been estimated that over 40,000 treaties have been concluded in the twentieth century, which, *inter alia*, established some 280 international organizations. Richard B. Bilder, *Managing the Risks of International Agreement* (Madison and London: Univ. of Wisconsin Press, 1981) at 6.

themselves have some degree of international personality, including the capacity to enter into treaties, and the 1986 Vienna Convention on the Law of Treaties between States and International Organizations or between International Organizations[63] confirms the important role of international organizations in developing international law. The European Community has adopted an increasingly important political, if informal and non-binding, role, in addition to consolidating its supremacy in treaty-based economic areas.[64] It was the decision of an international organization, the Organization of African Unity, that effectively fixed the new state boundaries of Africa based on former colonial boundaries;[65] the OAU also has played an important role in attempting to determine the fate of the Western Sahara, although the resulting split in the organization demonstrates the limits of its authority.

The recognition for certain purposes of "national liberation movements" as international actors also might be thought to blur the edges of sovereignty, although such recognition is a political rather than a legal statement. One might also note the fact that many non-state entities, such as Greenland and Hong Kong, may be admitted to full or associate membership in various international governmental organizations.

NATIONALISM

If development of the notion of sovereignty partly reflected a shift from the sovereignty of the ruler to the sovereignty of the state, the growth of nationalism has been largely a reaction against states and empires which were unresponsive to the needs of the many communities of which they were composed.[66] "As an agency of destruction the theory of nationalism proved one of the most potent that even modern society has known."[67]

Scores of scholars have attempted to define and analyze nationalist movements, but they seem to have reached even less agreement than

63 Adopted 21 Mar. 1986, UN Doc. A/CONF.129/15 (1986), reprinted in 25 Int'l Legal Materials 543 (1986). The Preamble notes that treaties between states and international organizations are "a useful means of developing international relations and ensuring conditions for peaceful co-operation among nations . . . "

64 See generally, e.g., Mauro Cappelletti, Monica Seccombe, and Joseph Weiler, *Integration Through Law* (Berlin & New York: Walter de Gruyter, 3 vols. 1985, 1986), for an interesting comparison of developing European institutions with domestic federal systems.

65 OAU Resolution 16(1) of July 1964 declared that "all Member States pledge themselves to respect the frontiers existing on their achievement of national independence."

66 Cf. F.H. Hinsley, *Sovereignty* (New York: Basic Books, 1966) at 45–158; John Breuilly, *Nationalism and the State* (New York: St. Martin's Press, 1982) at 44–45.

67 Alfred Cobban, *The Nation State and National Self-Determination* (New York: Thomas Y. Crowell, rev. ed. 1969) at 36.

may be found among legal experts with respect to sovereignty.[68] "Nationalism" as a term did not appear in the Oxford English Dictionary until 1844, and it is commonly thought of as a phenomenon that did not exist or was not recognized until the end of the eighteenth century.[69] Early European usage of the term generally connoted efforts by a linguistic, religious, and/or ethnic group to gain political power in order to respond to the needs of its "nation." Particularly since 1945, however, nationalism has come to be equated with anti-colonial movements that rarely correspond to the nineteenth-century paradigm of a homogeneous community. Common use of the term "nation-state" by lawyers and others serves only to confuse the issue further.

The belief that every state is a nation, or that all sovereign states are national states, has done much to obfuscate human understanding of political realities. A state is a legal and political organisation, with the power to require obedience and loyalty from its citizens. A nation is a community of people, whose members are bound together by a sense of solidarity, a common culture, a national consciousness.[70]

Although awkward linguistically, a helpful distinction might be drawn between "nationalism," as a phenomenon which implies a demand for political power by an ethnically, linguistically, or otherwise homogeneous group, and "statism," as a similar demand for political power by a group which defines itself in terms of existing political and/or territorial boundaries rather than a more personally based sense of solidarity. Under these definitions, statism would more accurately describe the struggle against colonialism, although the frequent references to "nation-building" in newly independent states would still be relevant insofar as new states seek to build a politically homogeneous community to replace or complement existing ethnic and other communities.

A persuasive case can be made that nationalism is merely one among many tools designed to acquire political power, that it represents a search for political identity rather than a reaffirmation of cultural identity.[71] However, while it may be accurate to define nationalism as a demand for political power based on group identity, it would be wrong to suggest that all "nationalist" movements necessarily seek broad governmental or political power as their goal. For example, many "national" demands by minority groups described in the present book began with relatively

68 See, e.g., sources cited in the bibliographic essay in Breuilly, *supra* note 66, at 402–12.
69 Hans Kohn, *Nationalism: Its Meaning and History* (Princeton, NJ: Van Nostrand, rev. ed. 1965) at 9.
70 Hugh Seton-Watson, *Nations and States* (London: Methuen, 1977) at 1.
71 This thesis is presented by, e.g., Breuilly, *supra* note 66.

modest complaints about discrimination, violations of human rights, and economic underdevelopment, although some ultimately did encompass the acquisition of broad political power as well.

Politics may simply offer a vehicle through which greater group consciousness can be developed.

En effet, les mouvements nationalitaires actifs au sein de ces minorités veulent reconstituer des entités sociales vivantes, avec des morceaux d'héritage certes, mais surtout par une pratique nouvelle d'identité. . . . Cette opération idéologique . . . est une fuite en avant par laquelle on se masque que l'entité sociale n'a justement plus la cohérence et le dynamisme invoqués. L'idéologie de l'unité ne sert pas dans ce cas à légitimer une pratique instituée productrice d'identité, elle vise au mieux à reconstituer politiquement des conditions nouvelles pour une telle pratique.[72]

Another view gives greater credence to the proposition that nationalism does respond to a natural urge for community identity, apart from state power. "[S]tate and nation are now linked as servants of Man's highest ambitions. . . . [T]here is a sense in which the state has become a god-substitute; if so, nationalism is the religion-substitute."[73]

Such distinctions are perhaps essential to political scientists and historians who seek to analyze an infinite variety of political conflicts with a finite number of words; for our purposes, it is more important to underscore the inherent vagueness and unhelpfulness of terms such as "nationhood" and "sovereignty" in attempting to resolve legal and political conflicts. Both terms have been more frequently used to obscure questionable motives and defend existing privilege than to promote comprehension or compromise.

THE MODERN "NATION-STATE"

"It may well turn out that Europe's most enduring legacy to Africa [as well as to Asia and the rest of the world] is the nation-state,"[74] and one cannot deny the impact of the concept of the nation-state on the legal and political order of the world. Ignoring either component of this archaic political concept is to ignore reality, but to emphasize the theoretical rights of every "nation" or the immutable characteristics of

72 Alain Fenet, "La question des minorités dans l'ordre du droit," in Gérard Chaliand (ed.), *Les Minorités à l'Age de l'État-Nation* (Paris: Fayard & Minority Rights Group, 1985) at 60–61.

73 Tivey, "States, Nations and Economies," in Leonard Tivey, (ed.), *The Nation-State* (New York: St. Martin's Press, 1981) at 70.

74 Ali A. Mazrui and Michael Tidy, *Nationalism and New States in Africa* (London: Heinemann, 1984) at 373.

"sovereignty" is unlikely to resolve the inherent tension between these two components.

There are few, if any, nation-states in the world whose population reflects an entirely homogeneous ethnic, cultural community to the exclusion of all others. It is perhaps no coincidence that many that might claim such status are islands. As demonstrated in Parts II and III, the search for homogeneity may, in fact, be more likely to lead to repression and human rights violations than to promote the tolerance and plurality which many would claim to be essential values in the twentieth century and beyond.

As an artificial legal creation, the state continues to serve a purpose as the primary interlocutor among those who possess organized military power in the world. Other actors, however—whether international organizations, transnational corporations, or individuals asserting rights against all of the above—are also making their influence felt at the international level.[75] Their "intrusion" into the affairs of the state is as much of a fact as the continued viability of the state itself.

> The concept of sovereignty . . . is not in terms of its history or in terms of political science a concept which may properly be used to explain—let alone to justify —whatever the state or the political society does or may choose to do. It is a principle which maintains no more than that there must be a supreme authority within the political community if the community is to exist at all.[76]

"[T]he old religious mystical concept of sovereignty as being something which is 'absolute, sacred and inviolable' already has lost much of whatever relevance it once may have had. . . . The fact of the matter is that sovereignty today . . . is an extraordinarily flexible, manipulative concept."[77] The changing nature of state sovereignty in this context is to be welcomed rather than decried. An increasingly diverse set of "sovereign" state structures will not adversely affect formal sovereign equality at the international level, and such diversity is more likely to respond to the needs of the individuals and groups within each state who are theoretically the repositories of ultimate sovereign authority.

75 *Cf.*, e.g., Tivey, *supra* note 73, at 77–79, 84–94; James, *supra* note 25, at 174–79.

76 Hinsley, *supra* note 66, at 219.

77 Richard B. Lillich, "Sovereignty and Humanity: Can They Converge?" in Atle Grahl-Madsen and Jiri Toman (eds.), *The Spirit of Uppsala* (Berlin and New York: de Gruyter, 1984) at 413.

Chapter 3
Self-Determination

"The proposition (to begin by using a perfectly neutral word) that every people should freely determine its own political status and freely pursue its economic, social, and cultural development has long been one of which poets have sung and for which patriots have been ready to lay down their lives."[78] Perhaps no contemporary norm of international law has been so vigorously promoted or widely accepted as the right of all peoples to self-determination. Yet the meaning and content of that right remain as vague and imprecise as when they were enunciated by President Woodrow Wilson and others at Versailles.

The principle of self-determination by "national" groups developed as a natural corollary of developing nationalism in the eighteenth and nineteenth centuries.[79] As the central authorities of the Ottoman, Austrian, German, and Russian empires pursued increasingly assimilationist policies or began to weaken militarily and politically, initial demands for greater autonomy or local self-government often led to demands for total independence.[80] With the disintegration of the Austro-Hungarian and Ottoman empires during World War I, territory of the former empires required new sovereigns: the principle of self-determination be-

78 John P. Humphrey, "Political and Related Rights," in Theodor Meron (ed.), 1 *Human Rights in International Law: Legal and Policy Issues* (Oxford: Clarendon Press, 2 vols. 1984) at 193.

79 Numerous scholars have traced these developments, and many are referred to in the context of the rights of minorities in chap. 4. See generally, e.g., Cobban, *supra* note 67, at 34–56; C. A. Macartney, *National States and National Minorities* (London: Oxford Univ. Press, 1934) at 92–156.

80 On the other hand, it might be noted that the practice of what might be termed "empire nationalism" not only was prevalent throughout Europe in the late nineteenth century but also was expressed in British, French, German, Belgian, and Dutch colonialism in Asia and Africa, and United States hegemony in Latin America in the early twentieth century.

came the obvious vehicle for the re-division of Europe by the victorious powers. Self-determination was considered only for "nations" which were within the territory of the defeated empires; it was never thought to apply to overseas colonies.

Several of Wilson's "Fourteen Points" dealt with specific territorial settlements, including the creation of independent states out of the remnants of the Austro-Hungarian and Ottoman empires. Three of his subsequently enunciated four "principles" also concerned self-determination or territory: "peoples and provinces must not be bartered about from sovereignty to sovereignty as if they were chattels or pawns in a game"; territorial questions were to be settled "in the interests of the populations concerned"; and "well-defined national elements" were to be given "the utmost satisfaction that can be accorded them without introducing new, or perpetuating old, elements of discord and antagonism."[81]

The success or failure of assertions of minority rights or self-determination in the late nineteenth century depended to a great extent on external support from one or more of the Great Powers,[82] and that support was no less essential during the Paris Peace Conference. In most instances, the winners and losers were determined more by the political calculations and perceived needs of the Great Powers than on the basis of which peoples had the strongest claims to self-determination. For example,

[t]he brooding and unpredictable menace of Bolshevism persuaded the Allies . . . to create bastions of the West in eastern Europe, necessarily at the expense of smaller nationalities. As the much-trumpeted principle of national self-determination conjured up an impossible nationalist dream, so the compromises deemed necessary by Allied perceptions of practicality and strategy made disillusionment among the minorities all the keener.[83]

It should be underscored that self-determination in 1919 had little to do with the demands of the peoples concerned, unless those demands were consistent with the geopolitical and strategic interests of the Great Powers. With a few exceptions in frontier regions (and then only if the region was not an overly sensitive one), no plebiscites or referenda were

81 Quoted in Charles L. Mee, Jr., *The End of Order* (New York: E.P. Dutton, 1980) at 53–54.

82 See Raymond Pearson, *National Minorities in Eastern Europe 1848–1945* (London: Macmillan, 1983) at 84; Dimitrije Djordjevic and Stephen Fischer-Galati, *The Balkan Revolutionary Tradition* (New York: Columbia Univ. Press, 1981) at 160.

83 Pearson, *supra* note 82, at 136.

held to determine the wishes of the people affected by the Versailles map-making.[84]

This is perhaps best demonstrated by reference to the question of the Aland Islands, with respect to which two expert committees addressed the meaning of "self-determination" and whether it implied the possibility of secession from an existing state.[85] The first report noted:

Although the principle of self-determination of peoples plays an important part in modern political thought, especially since the Great War, it must be pointed out that there is no mention of it in the covenant of the League of Nations. The recognition of this principle in a certain number of international treaties cannot be considered as sufficient to put it upon the same footing as a positive rule of the Law of Nations. . . .

Positive International Law does not recognise the right of national groups, as such, to separate themselves from the State of which they form part by the simple expression of a wish, any more than it recognises the right of other States to claim such a separation. Generally speaking, the grant or refusal of the right to a portion of its population of determining its own political fate by plebiscite or by some other method, is, exclusively, an attribute of the sovereignty of every State which is definitively constituted.[86]

The second report considered the same issue, after having first determined that Finland (including the Aland Islands) became a fully constituted independent state following its declaration of independence from Russia in 1917. Despite its recognition that the vast majority of the Aland population would choose union with Sweden if a referendum were held, the Commission reached a similar conclusion as to the scope of self-determination—"a principle of justice and of liberty, expressed by a vague and general formula which has given rise to the most varied interpretations and differences of opinion."[87]

Is it possible to admit as an absolute rule that a minority of the population of a State, which is definitely constituted and perfectly capable of fulfilling its duties as such, has the right of separating itself from her in order to be incorporated in another State or to declare its independence? The answer can only

84 The classic works on plebiscites are Sarah Wambaugh, *A Monograph on Plebiscites* (New York: Oxford Univ. Press, 1920), and *id.*, *Plebiscites Since the World War* (Washington, DC: Carnegie Endowment for International Peace, 2 vols. 1933).

85 Also see discussion of the Aland Islands, *infra* chap. 17, at 370–75.

86 *Report of the International Committee of Jurists entrusted by the Council of the League of Nations with the task of giving an advisory opinion upon the legal aspects of the Aaland Islands question*, League of Nations Off. J., Spec. Supp. No. 3 (Oct. 1920) at 5. However, this and the subsequent report to the League, *infra* note 87, did suggest some theoretical circumstances which could lead to a different conclusion.

87 The Aaland Islands Question, *Report presented to the Council of the League by the Commission of Rapporteurs*, League of Nations Doc. B.7.21/68/106 (1921) at 27.

be in the negative. To concede to minorities, either of language or religion, or to any fractions of a population the right of withdrawing from the community to which they belong, because it is their wish or their good pleasure, would be to destroy order and stability within States and to inaugurate anarchy in international life; it would be to uphold a theory incompatible with the very idea of the State as a territorial and political unity.[88]

In supporting this conclusion, the Commission referred specifically to political considerations, including the need to recognize Finland's contribution "in repelling the attacks of Bolshevist Communism" and the opinions of the non-Aland Swedish population of Finland.[89]

In addition to its external aspect, self-determination also was felt by President Wilson and others to include an internal aspect, that of democracy.[90] If self-determination is "an expression in succinct form, of the aspiration to rule one's self and not to be ruled by others,"[91] then this self-rule implies meaningful participation in the processes of government. But while the equation of self-determination with democracy may have been the philosophical underpinning of Wilsonian principles, the states created in 1919 undertook no specific obligations to ensure a democratic form of government, although various minority guarantees were given.[92]

The obstacles that prevented universal application of the principle of self-determination at Versailles are similar to those that interfered with the protection of minorities: the limited application of the post-Versailles treaties to only the defeated or new states; the failure of border adjustments to eliminate minorities (including those which desired national self-determination); and the continuing political instability of Europe during the inter-war period. In addition, it was obviously difficult, if not impossible, to identify those criteria which a national group should fulfill in order to legitimize its aspirations for self-determination and/or statehood.

Most discussions of "self-determination" begin with an attempt to break the concept into its component parts: what constitutes the relevant "self," and in what manner should its fate be determined? The former includes subjective and objective components, in that it is necessary for

88 *Id.* at 28.

89 *Id.* at 29–31.

90 See, e.g., Cobban, *supra* note 67, at 63–64; *cf.* Lee C. Buchheit, *Secession* (New Haven, CT: Yale Univ. Press, 1978) at 14–16; Antonio Cassese, "Political Self-Determination—Old Concepts and New Developments," in Antonio Cassese (ed.), *UN Law/Fundamental Rights* (Alphen aan den Rijn: Sijthoff & Noordhoff, 1979) at 137–65.

91 Dov Ronen, *The Quest for Self-Determination* (New Haven, CT: Yale Univ. Press, 1979) at 7.

92 See chap. 4.

members of the group concerned to think of themselves as a distinctive group, as well as for the group to have certain objectively determinable common characteristics, for example, ethnicity, language, history, or religion. Of course, everyone belongs to many different groups at the same time, and the difficulty arises in determining which are the relevant groups for purposes of respecting the principle of self-determination. In the world of geopolitics, it should not be surprising that well-defined boundaries are rare.

[I]t was not only the intermingling of racial, linguistic, and religious groups which presented obstacles to solutions acceptable to all the elements involved [at the end of the First World War]. Even more dangerous to peace than the conflicting "natural" rights of the nationalities were their "historical rights." Each nationality claimed the frontiers as they existed at the time of its greatest historical expansion, frontiers which disregarded the ethnic and historical development of intervening centuries. . . . The awakening of the peoples released collective passions which became in the century after 1848 the most potent factor in arousing hatreds and fomenting wars.[93]

A glance at contemporary conflicts is all that is needed to expose these difficulties, many of which appear during attempts to define the relevant borders. Within the two islands of Ireland and the United Kingdom, for example, the relevant "self" might be both islands taken together, despite their ethnic mix of English, Scots, Welsh, and Irish; each island separately, despite the mix of the first three in Great Britain and of Irish and Scots in Ireland; the two existing states; or each ethnic/geographic group, which would include at least the four separate entities of England, Scotland, Wales, and Ireland, with from zero to two additional groups (Irish Catholics and "British" Protestants) in Northern Ireland. Citing a multitude of equally irreducible situations will not advance our thinking very far, but their existence does underscore the fact that the assertion by one "self" of political auto-determination almost necessarily entails the denial of auto-determination to another "self" which may be either greater or smaller; as is the case with minorities, selves can never be wholly eliminated.

The Czech leader Jan Masaryk stated that self-determination does not carry with it an unconditional right to political independence,[94] and the League of Nations scheme for minority protections was in part designed to provide what might be termed cultural self-determination to those groups whose demands for fuller political recognition were denied by the Great Powers. Obviously, this did not satisfy the basic

93 Kohn, *supra* note 69, at 45–46.
94 Cited in Cobban, *supra* note 67, at 69.

quest for the "nation-state" which pervaded the rhetoric of the period surrounding 1919.

Wilson proposed that the principle of self-determination be recognized in the Covenant of the League of Nations. His draft stated:

The Contracting Powers unite in guaranteeing to each other political independence and territorial integrity but it is understood between them that such territorial adjustments, if any, as may in future become necessary by reason of changes in present racial and political relationships, pursuant to the principle of self-determination, and also such territorial adjustments as may in the judgement of three-fourths of the Delegates be demanded by the welfare and manifest interest of the people concerned, may be effected if agreeable to those peoples; and that territorial changes may in equity involve material compensation. The Contracting Powers accept without reservation the principle that the peace of the world is superior in importance to every question of political jurisdiction or boundary.[95]

Even this modest formulation was dropped before adoption of the Covenant, but the focus on peace in its final sentence accurately reflects the priorities of the Peace Conference, even in the mind of its most public proponent of self-determination.

Both Lenin and Stalin saw self-determination in the context of the "national question" which surrounded World War I and the Peace Conference. They were strong proponents of the principle of national self-determination, but only insofar as its exercise would promote the interests of the class struggle; secession (the primary form of self-determination in the post-1919 period) was to be promoted as a tactic to fight oppressor nations, not to support bourgeois nationalists in oppressed nations.[96]

The right of nations to self-determination implies exclusively the right to independence in the political sense, the right to free political separation from the oppressor nation. Specifically, this demand for political democracy implies complete freedom to agitate for secession and for the decision on secession to be made by a referendum of the seceding nation. This demand, therefore, is not the equivalent of a demand for separation, fragmentation and the formation of small states. It implies only a consistent expression of struggle against all national oppression.[97]

---

95 Quoted in Karl Josef Partsch, "Fundamental Principles of Human Rights: Self-Determination, Equality and Non-Discrimination," in Karel Vasak and Philip Alston, 1 *The International Dimensions of Human Rights* (Paris: Unesco and Westport, CT: Greenwood Press, 2 vols. 1982) at 63.

96 See V.I. Lenin, *Questions of National Policy and Proletarian Internationalism* (Moscow: Foreign Languages Publishing House, n.d.) at 78–83, 203–05.

97 *Id.* at 138–39.

Thus, communist support for national self-determination and de-colonization was a tactical rather than a philosophical decision; "an abstract presentation of the question of nationalism is of no use at all. ... [and therefore] the fundamental interest of proletarian solidarity ... requires that we never adopt a formal attitude to the national question."[98]

In the Russian context, exercise of the theoretical right of secession of border areas would be firmly rejected, "because it is fundamentally opposed to the interests of the mass of the peoples both of the centre and of the border regions."[99] But while secession was thus dismissed in practice, the Soviet Union did recognize national cultural and linguistic rights in a meaningful way.[100]

In part because of the inconsistent manner in which the principle of self-determination was applied following the First World War, it was not initially recognized as a fundamental right of the United Nations regime established in 1945. There is probably a consensus among scholars that, whatever its political significance, the principle of self-determination did not rise to the level of a rule of international law at the time the UN Charter was drafted.[101]

The "principle" of self-determination is mentioned only twice in the Charter of the United Nations, both times in the context of developing "friendly relations among nations" and in conjunction with the principle of "equal rights ... of peoples."[102] Self-determination is not mentioned in the 1948 Universal Declaration of Human Rights, even though there is a preambular reference to developing friendly relations between nations.

Before the moral and political imperative of decolonization, how-ever, the vague "principle" of self-determination soon evolved into the "right" to self-determination.[103] This evolution culminated in the adop-

98 *Id.* at 201, 202.

99 Josef Stalin, "The Policy of the Soviet Government on the National Question in Russia" (1920), *reprinted in* Josef Stalin, *Marxism and the National and Colonial Question* (London: Lawrence & Wishart, Eng. ed. 1936) at 79.

100 See, e.g., Oscar I. Janowsky, *Nationalities and National Minorities* (New York: Macmillan, 1945) at 69–104; *infra* chap. 16, at 358–69.

101 See, e.g., Hanna Bokor-Szegő, *New States and International Law* (Budapest: Akadémiai Kiadó, 1970), who describes the right to self-determination as "lex imperfecta" in 1945; Partsch, *supra* note 95, at 62–63; Wambaugh (1933), *supra* note 84, at 490 ("Unquestionably the view is gaining that a people suffering persecution under an alien sovereign have a just claim to decide their own fate. However, such a claim has, as yet, no status in international law.").

102 United Nations Charter, arts. 1(2), 55.

103 See generally Buchheit, *supra* note 90; Cassese, *supra* note 90; Yassin El-Ayouty, *The United Nations and Decolonization: The Role of Afro-Asia* (The Hague:

tion by the UN General Assembly in 1960 of the Declaration on the Granting of Independence to Colonial Countries and Peoples (herein-after cited as the "Declaration on Colonial Countries").[104] Premised, *inter alia*, on the need for stability, peace, and respect for human rights, the Declaration on Colonial Countries "[s]olemnly proclaims the ne-cessity of bringing to a speedy and unconditional end colonialism in all its forms and manifestations" and declares that "[a]ll peoples have the right to self-determination; by virtue of that right they freely determine their political status and freely pursue their economic, social and cultural development."[105] It also declares that "[i]nadequacy of political, eco-nomic, social or educational preparedness should never serve as a pretext for delaying independence."[106]

Paragraph 6 of the declaration sets forth another fundamental prin-ciple, without which one almost never (at least in UN forums) finds a reference to self-determination: "Any attempt aimed at the partial or total disruption of the national unity and the territorial integrity of a country is incompatible with the purposes and principles of the Charter of the United Nations." The seventh and final paragraph reiterates "the sovereign rights of all peoples and their territorial integrity."

The obvious questions raised by the Declaration on Colonial Coun-tries—for instance, the definition of "peoples" and the larger issue of whether the right to self-determination exists outside the context of decolonization—were addressed, if not necessarily clarified, ten years later in the Declaration on Principles of International Law concerning Friendly Relations and Co-operation among States in accordance with the Charter of the United Nations (hereinafter cited as "Declaration on Friendly Relations").[107] As might be presumed from the scope of its title, the Declaration on Friendly Relations considers a wide range of issues, including reiteration of the prohibition against intervention in the internal affairs of a state; the duty of states to promote human rights in accordance with the Charter; and the principle of sovereign equality of states. Among those sections relevant to the issue of self-determination, the declaration includes the following:

Martinus Nijhoff, 1971); Michla Pomerance, *Self-Determination in Law and Practice* (The Hague: Martinus Nijhoff, 1982); A. Rigo Sureda, *The Evolution of the Right of Self-Determination: A Study of United Nations Practice* (Leyden: Sijthoff, 1973); Umo-zurike Oji Umozurike, *Self-Determination in International Law* (Hamden, CT: Archon Books, 1972).

104 G.A. Res. 1514, 15 UN GAOR, Supp. (No. 16), UN Doc. A/4684 (1960) at 66.
105 *Id.*, Preamble, para. 2.
106 *Id.*, para. 3.
107 G.A. Res. 2625, Annex, 25 UN GAOR, Supp. (No. 28), UN Doc. A/5217 (1970) at 121.

The use of force to deprive peoples of their national identity constitutes a violation of their inalienable rights and of the principle of non-intervention. . . .

By virtue of the principle of equal rights and self-determination of peoples enshrined in the Charter of the United Nations, all peoples have the right freely to determine, without external interference, their political status and to pursue their economic, social and cultural development, and every State has the duty to respect this right in accordance with the provisions of the Charter.

Every State has the duty to promote . . . realization of the principle of equal rights and self-determination of peoples . . . in order:

(a) To promote friendly relations and co-operation among States; and

(b) To bring a speedy end to colonialism, having due regard to the freely expressed will of the peoples concerned; and bearing in mind that subjection of peoples to alien subjugation, domination and exploitation constitutes a violation of the principle [of self-determination], as well as a denial of fundamental human rights, and is contrary to the Charter. . . .

Nothing in the foregoing paragraphs shall be construed as authorizing or encouraging any action which would dismember or impair, totally or in part, the territorial integrity or political unity of sovereign and independent States conducting themselves in compliance with the principle of equal rights and self-determination of peoples as described above and thus possessed of a government representing the whole possible belonging to the territory without distinction as to race, creed or colour.

Every State shall refrain from any action aimed at the partial or total disruption of the national unity and territorial integrity of any other State or country. . . .

The territorial integrity and political independence of the State are inviolable.

Returning to the two issues raised above (the definition of peoples and the application of self-determination to non-colonial situations), we find that the Declaration on Friendly Relations does nothing to clarify the first and may, in fact, further confuse the second.

A long-time member of the Human Rights Committee has identified five different uses of the term "peoples" in the 1919–1945 period, to which the political principle of self-determination applied: a people living entirely within a state ruled by another people (e.g., the Irish before 1920); peoples living as minorities in various countries without controlling a state of their own (e.g., Poles in Russia before 1919); a people living as a minority group in a state but understanding themselves as forming part of the people of a neighboring state (e.g., Hungarians in Romania); a people dispersed throughout many separate states (e.g., the German people in various European states); and a people who constitute a majority in a territory under foreign domination (e.g., colonial regimes).[108] Self-determination in its pre-United Nations sense took different forms in different contexts, ranging from national independence (for the Poles but

108 Partsch, *supra* note 95, at 63.

not for the Armenians or Kurds) to placing vulnerable yet strategic minorities under direct international protection (e.g., Danzig and Memel) to the provision of domestic constitutional protections to guarantee minority rights (e.g., for the Germans in Czechoslovakia).

In the context of post-1945 decolonization, it soon became evident that the primary, and often sole, definition of "peoples" was that of non-European inhabitants of former colonies, without further regard for ethnicity, language, religion, or other objective characteristics of such colonized peoples (apart from the fact of colonization itself). Territory, not "nationhood," was the determining factor.[109] Despite the lack of cultural, political, or other homogeneity, however, in most colonies a subjective feeling of belonging to a people—even if defined only by shared anti-colonialism—did exist

Despite UN affirmations of "the necessity of scrupulously respecting the national unity and territorial integrity of a colonial territory at the time of its accession to independence,"[110] exceptions have not been uncommon. Partition—and thus redefined "selves"—was recognized in British India, Ruanda-Urundi, the Northern Cameroons, and the Gilbert and Ellice Islands, and it will probably be approved (though not without dissent) for the U.S. Trust Territory of the Pacific Islands.[111] On the other hand, the continued preference of the island of Mayotte to remain associated with France rather than with the now independent Comorros Islands has been regularly criticized by the General Assembly as a violation of the Comorros' sovereignty.[112]

109 *Cf.* Pomerance, *supra* note 103, at 18–19.

110 G.A. Res. 34/91, GAOR, Supp. (No. 46), UN Doc. A/34/46 (1979) at 82 [regarding the French islands of Glorieuses, Juan de Nova, Europa, and Bassas da India].

111 In 1986, the Trusteeship Council agreed (over Soviet objections) that it was appropriate to terminate the U.S. trusteeship, TC Res. 2183 (LIII), 53 UN TCOR Supp. (No.3), UN Doc. T/1901 (1986) at 14. The Soviet dissent was based on, *inter alia*, accusations of the "illegal fragmentation" of the territory. See "Trusteeship Council calls termination of Micronesia Agreement 'appropriate,' " 23 UN Chronicle (No. 4, Aug. 1986) at 67–71; "Trusteeship Council recommends early approval of Compact for Palau," 25 *id.* (No. 3, Sept. 1988) at 49–51. No action formally terminating the trusteeship had been taken by the Security Council by the end of 1988.

Plebiscites, some monitored by the UN, approving compacts of free association (or, in the case of the Northern Marianas, commonwealth status) with the United States were held in the four component parts of the Trust Territory, and the agreements with the Marshall Islands, Federated States of Micronesia, and Northern Mariana Islands entered into force in late 1986. As of the end of 1988, incompatibility between the Palau compact and the Palau constitution, despite a series of referenda, had prevented final resolution of that situation. See Clark, *supra* note 44; compare Marian Nash Leich, "Contemporary Practice of the United States Relating to International Law," 81 Am. J. Int'l L. 405 (1987), with Roger S. Clark, letter to the Editor-in-Chief, *id.* at 927.

112 See, e.g., G.A. Res. 42/17, 42 UN GAOR, Supp. (No. 49), UN Doc. A/42/49

It is also interesting to note the numerous instances where former European colonies have been recognized not as entities with any right to self-determination, but rather as fair prey for neighboring, non-European states with real or purported historical claims to the territories in question. In some cases (e.g., annexation by India of Goa, the cession of certain French enclaves to India, and Dahomey's incorporation of the Portuguese enclave of Sao Joao Batista de Ajuda), absorption might have been the only logical result, although it has become an article of faith that small size or lack of economic viability cannot detract from the right of a former colony to achieve independence.[113] In other cases, however (e.g., India's annexation of Hyderabad and Sikkim, Indonesia's invasion of West Irian and East Timor, and the assumption by China of control over Hong Kong and Macao), it is much more difficult to see why the "peoples" of such well-defined colonial territories were not viewed as having any rights to self-determination.[114] As noted by Judge Nagendra Singh in the *Western Sahara* case,

the consultation of the people of the territory awaiting decolonization is an inescapable imperative whether the method followed on decolonization is integration or association or independence. . . . Thus even if integration of territory was demanded by an interested State, as in this case, it could not be had without ascertaining the freely expressed will of the people—the very *sine qua non* of all decolonization.[115]

(1987) at 39 (reaffirming the sovereignty of the Comorros over Mayotte), and resolutions cited therein. *Cf.* Pomerance, *supra* note 103, at 30–31.

113 A Sub-Committee on Small Territories was established by the special Committee on the Situation with regard to the Implementation of the Declaration on the Granting of Independence to Colonial Countries and Peoples [the "Committee of 24"]. It currently has the status of 13 small, non-self-governing island territories under review: American Samoa, Anguilla, Bermuda, the British and U.S. Virgin Islands, Cayman Islands, Pitcairn, the Turks and Caicos, Guam, Tokelau, Montserrat, St. Helena, and the U.S. Trust Territory of the Pacific Islands.

114 It has been suggested that different rules apply to "colonial enclaves," which are restricted in their exercise of self-determination "to the one solution of the return of the territory to the sovereign of the surrounding territory", but the criteria for assigning "enclave status" to a territory remain unclear. Malcolm Shaw, "The *Western Sahara* Case," 49 Brit. Y.B. Int'l L. 119, 123 (1978). *Cf.* Rigo Sureda, *supra* note 103, at 214.

In fairness, it should be noted that the UN General Assembly and Security Council called for the withdrawal of Indonesian troops from East Timor and reaffirmed East Timor's right of self-determination. G.A. Res. 3485, 30 UN GAOR, Supp. (No. 34) 118, UN Doc. A/10034 (1975); SC Res. 384, 30 UN SCOR, Resolutions and Decisions 10, UN Doc. S/Res./384 (1975). *See* Roger S. Clark, "The 'Decolonization' of East Timor and the United Nations Norms on Self-Determination and Aggression," 7 Yale J. World Public Order 2 (1982).

115 Western Sahara, Advisory Opinion, I.C.J. Reports 1975, p. 12, at 81.

One might compare, for example, the situation of Belize, which was welcomed into the UN as an independent state despite Guatemala's claims of sovereignty.

The claims of Morocco and Mauritania to the former Spanish Sahara were rejected in 1975 by the International Court of Justice, which indicated that the wishes of the inhabitants needed to be taken into account despite the purported Spanish cession of the territory and historical claims of Morocco and Mauritania.[116] The Court reaffirmed the validity of the principle of self-determination, although it did not explicitly affirm its existence as a binding rule of international law.[117] The Court did note that the General Assembly retained "a measure of discretion with respect to the forms and procedures by which that right is to be realized."[118] It found that various legal ties existed between Western Sahara and both the Sultan of Morocco and the "Mauritanian entity" which existed in the pre-colonial era, but it held that those ties were not "of such a nature as might affect the application of resolution 1514(XV) in the decolonization of Western Sahara and, in particular, of the principle of self-determination through the free and genuine expression of the will of the peoples of the Territory."[119] The Court did not decide between the competing priorities to be accorded to the principles of self-determination and national integrity advanced respectively by Algeria and Morocco, although it did suggest that previous sovereign ties could be disregarded if the inhabitants of the territory concerned did not constitute a "people" or in other "special circumstances."[120]

[I]ts attitude appeared to be to regard decolonization as the basic framework and self-determination as the most important relevant principle. . . . The principle of decolonization is composed to a large extent of the principle of self-determination, while self-determination has operated in international law primarily in the sphere of decolonization.[121]

Finally, the issue of the impact of "settler" populations on a colonial territory also has been dealt with in a somewhat inconsistent manner. Where the settlers constitute a dominant minority—as in Zimbabwe or

---

116 Western Sahara, Advisory Opinion, *supra* note 115.

117 Shaw, *supra* note 114, at 147.

118 Western Sahara, Advisory Opinion, *supra* note 115, at 36.

119 *Id.* at 68. In August 1988 an agreement was reached between Morocco and Saharawi Polisario guerrillas for a UN-supervised referendum in Western Sahara. Sixty-eight states had recognized the Saharawi Republic as of early 1987, despite the fact that the Saharawi "government" has never exercised effective control within its claimed territory.

120 Western Sahara, Advisory Opinion, *supra* note 115, at 37.

121 Shaw, *supra* note 114, at 147.

South Africa—there has been no difficulty in upholding the right to self-determination of the indigenous majority. Contrary to the consistent practice in Africa, however, Indian settlers (initially brought by the British) in Fiji were considered to constitute a part of the Fijian people for the purposes of the principle of one person-one vote.[122] On the other hand, the disenfranchisement of several hundred thousand Indian "estate Tamils" by newly independent Ceylon was unchallenged by all but India, although the Tamils had been brought to Ceylon in circumstances that are difficult to distinguish from those in Fiji.[123] Serious questions have been raised regarding the legitimacy of British settler populations in Gibraltar and the Falkland (Malvinas) Islands, and the General Assembly in 1986 returned New Caledonia, a majority of whose residents are non-indigenous, to the list of non-self-governing territories.[124] In light of these inconsistencies, one highly critical commentator has concluded that,

[f]rom whichever angle the question of defining the "self" within the new "UN Law of Self-Determination" is approached . . . the Wilsonian dilemmas have persisted. Except for the most obvious cases of "decolonization", objective criteria have not been developed or applied for preferring one claim over another or for delimiting which population belongs to which territory.[125]

Once the "self" has been identified, it is abundantly clear that full independence is considered to be the "normal" result of the exercise of self-determination. While this has been the result in all but a handful of cases of decolonization thus far, it is equally clear, however, that independence is not a necessary result.

Three days after adoption of the Declaration on Colonial Countries in 1960, the General Assembly adopted Resolution 1541, the Annex to which sets forth "principles which should guide members in determining whether or not an obligation exists to transmit the information called for under article 73e of the Charter," that is, whether or not a territory is non-self-governing.[126] This resolution clarifies that a non-self-governing territory under Chapter XI of the Charter can achieve "a full measure of self-government" by emergence as a sovereign independent

122 *Cf.* Pomerance, *supra* note 103, at 122 and esp. n.122; see discussion of Fiji, *infra*, chap. 18, at 427–32.

123 *Cf.* chap. 14.

124 G.A. Res. 41/41A, 41 UN GAOR, Supp. (No. 53), UN Doc. A/41/53 (1986) at 49. See *Report of the Special Committee on the Situation with regard to the Implementation of the Declaration on the Granting of Independence to Colonial Countries and Peoples*, 41 UN GAOR, Supp. (No. 23), UN Doc. A/41/23 (1986).

125 Pomerance, *supra* note 103, at 23.

126 G.A. Res. 1541, *supra* note 38.

state, free association with an independent state, or integration with an independent state.[127]

The clear preference for independence as the normal result of exercise of the right to self-determination is evidenced by detailed requirements for the free and informed consent of the peoples concerned if either free association or integration is chosen.[128] Free association requires a "free and voluntary choice . . . through informed and democratic processes" and must include the right of unilateral modification of the association by the peoples of the territory.[129] Integration must be on the basis of "complete equality" between peoples of the territory and the independent country to which they are adhering, and it can only come about if the territory has attained "an advanced stage of self-government with free political institutions" and if the option of integration is chosen with "full knowledge" through democratic processes,

127 *Id.*, Principle VI; see Clark, *supra* note 44, at 38–66, for an excellent discussion of the evolution of the concept of free association.

128 One hundred and five territories have been designated by the General Assembly as non-self-governing, and nineteen (Namibia, Western Sahara, East Timor, Gibraltar, New Caledonia, Anguilla, Pitcairn, Montserrat, British Virgin Islands, Turks and Caicos Islands, Tokelau, Cayman Islands, St. Helena, Bermuda, Guam, American Samoa, U.S. Virgin Islands, the Trust Territory of the Pacific Islands, and the Falkland [Malvinas] Islands) remained in that category as of 1988. *Report of the Special Committee on the Situation with Regard to the Inplementation of the Declaration on the Granting of Independence to Colonial Countries and Peoples*, 43 UN GAOR, Supp. (No. 23), UN Doc. A/43/23 (1988), chaps. 8–10.

Of the remaining number, only eleven were deleted from the list of non-self-governing territories by attaining a status of less than full independence: Goa and other Portuguese dependencies in India, which were incorporated into India in 1961; Sao Joao Batista de Ajuda, incorporated into Dahomey in 1961; the Netherlands New Guinea (West Irian), incorporated into Indonesia in 1963; North Borneo, Sarawak, and Singapore, which federated with Malaya to form the new state of Malaysia in 1963; the Cook Islands, which entered into free association with New Zealand in 1965; Ifni, ceded to Morocco by Spain in 1969; Macao and Hong Kong, which were removed from the list at the request of China, on the grounds that they were integral parts of the Chinese state illegally occupied by Portugal and the United Kingdom, respectively; and Niue Island, which entered into free association with New Zealand in 1974.

Despite adoption of the West Indies Act of 1967 by the United Kingdom, which provided for a kind of free association between the Windward and Leeward Islands and the U.K., the British Caribbean territories were not removed from the non-self-governing list, although the U.K. unilaterally ceased reporting on them. Following the demise of the West Indies Associated States, Grenada, Dominica, Saint Lucia, Saint Vincent and the Grenadines, Antigua and Barbuda, and Saint Christopher and Nevis became independent. *Cf.* William C. Gilmore, "Legal Perspectives on Associated Statehood in the Eastern Caribbean," 19 Va. J. Int'l L. 489 (1979).

With respect to the status of the U.S. Trust Territory of the Pacific Islands, see *supra* note 111.

129 G.A. Res. 1541, *supra* note 38, Principle VII.

"impartially conducted and based on universal adult suffrage."[130] There are no procedural requirements to be fulfilled for a non-self-governing territory to emerge as a sovereign independent state.

The options are slightly, if significantly, expanded in the Declaration on Friendly Relations, which provides:

> The establishment of a sovereign and independent State, the free association or integration with an independent State *or the emergence into any other political status freely determined by a people* constitute modes of implementing the right of self-determination by that people.[131]

This flexibility has not yet been utilized to justify emergence from dependent status to any unusual constitutional or other arrangements, but it does represent a rare and welcome recognition of the potential for new inter- and intra-state relations.

The two international covenants on human rights adopted by the UN General Assembly in 1966 entered into force a decade later, and there are now more than 80 parties to each.[132] Common article 1 in both Covenants states:

> All peoples have the right of self-determination. By virtue of the right they freely determine their political status and freely pursue their economic, social and cultural development.

States are required under article 40 of the Covenant on Civil and Political Rights to submit periodic reports to a body of experts, the Human Rights Committee, on their implementation of the rights guaranteed under the Covenant. These reports and the subsequent discussions between Committee members and government representatives could suggest the Committee's interpretation of both the internal and external aspects of self-determination. Unfortunately, most countries either have not specifically addressed article 1 or have done so in such general terms that nothing is added to an understanding of its content.

The Indian reservation to article 1 of the Covenant, made at

---

130 *Id.*, Principles VIII and IX.

131 *Supra* note 107; emphasis added.

132 International Covenant on Economic, Social and Cultural Rights, adopted 16 Dec. 1966, entered into force 3 Jan. 1976, 999 U.N.T.S. 3; International Covenant on Civil and Political Rights, adopted 16 Dec. 1966, entered into force 23 Mar. 1976, 999 U.N.T.S. 171. For a summary of the debates during the drafting process, including reference to the protection of minority rights in art. 27, see Buchheit, *supra* note 90, at 76–85; Marc J. Bossuyt, *Guide to the "Travaux Préparatoires" of the International Covenant on Civil and Political Rights* (Dordrecht, Boston, Lancaster: Martinus Nijhoff, 1987) at 493–98.

the time of India's ratification, represents in direct terms the view of many countries which support a restricted interpretation of "self-determination":

> With reference to article 1 [of both Covenants] . . . , the Government of the Republic of India declares that the words "the right of self-determination" appearing in those articles apply only to the peoples under foreign domination and that these words do not apply to sovereign independent States or to a section of a people or nation - which is the essence of national integrity.[133]

In a subsequent appearance before the Human Rights Committee, India stated more explicitly that the UN Charter applies "the right to self-determination in the international context only to dependent Territories and peoples."[134]

There are frequent references to popular participation in the political process as the way in which internal self-determination is assured; these are discussed in greater detail in chapter 6, although it is not clear what the consequence of failure to guarantee such participation would be in terms of self-determination.[135] Jordan has stated that "the principle of self-determination is a continuous process and does not end with the declaration of independence."[136]

The British government has declared, rather ambiguously, that "in the event of any conflict between their obligations under Article 1 of the Covenant and their obligations under the Charter (in particular,

133 Centre for Human Rights, *Human Rights, Status of International Instruments* (New York: United Nations, 1987), UN Sales No. E.87.XIV.2, at 9. Three states filed objections to the Indian reservation. The Netherlands stated that "the right of self-determination as embodied in the covenants is conferred upon all peoples. . . . Any attempt to limit the scope of the right or to attach conditions not provided for in the relevant instruments would undermine the concept of self-determination itself and would thereby seriously weaken its universally acceptable character." *Id.* at 19. France objected because the Indian reservation "attaches conditions not provided for by the Charter of the United Nations." *Id.* at 50. The Federal Republic of Germany "strongly object[ed]" to the Indian reservation, stating: "The right of self-determination . . . applies to all peoples and not only to those under foreign domination. . . . The Federal Government cannot consider as valid any interpretation of the right of self-determination which is contrary to the clear language of the provisions in question. It moreover considers that any limitation of their applicability to all nations is incompatible with the object and purpose of the Covenants." *Id.* at 18–19.
134 Statement by the representative of India to the Human Rights Committee, UN Doc. CCPR/C/SR.498 (1984) at 3.
135 Cassese, *supra* note 90, suggests that there may be a growing recognition, at least at the nongovernmental level, that denial of fundamental human rights, including those of democratic participation in government, constitutes a denial of the right of internal self-determination.
136 Jordan, art. 40 CCPR Report, UN Doc. CCPR/C/1/Add.55 (1981) at 2.

under Articles 1, 2 and 73 thereof) their obligations under the Charter shall prevail."[137] The initial British report to the Committee, submitted in 1978, contained a detailed report on the manner in which self-determination or self-government was being promoted in the British dependencies of Belize (now independent), Bermuda, British Virgin Islands, Cayman Islands, Channel Islands, Gibraltar, Gilbert Islands (now independent), Hong Kong (to be transferred to China in 1997), Montserrat, Pitcairn, St. Helena, and the Turks and Caicos Islands.[138]

The U.S.S.R. and Byelorussian S.S.R. emphasize the right of secession as essential to self-determination within the Soviet context, as the right to secede is the "legal expression of national sovereignty."[139] The Soviet Union representative stated that it is "inconceivable that a republic would want to secede, since there [is] a solid and unshakable bond uniting all the peoples and nations of the State."[140]

At least two attempts have been made through individual applications to the Committee under the Optional Protocol to the Covenant to raise the issue of whether Indian bands in Canada enjoy a right to self-determination.[141] However, the Committee decided in both cases that, since only "individuals . . . who claim to be victims" of violations have standing to raise complaints under the Optional Protocol, the issue of an alleged violation of the right of a "people" to self-determination under article 1 could not be raised through the Optional Protocol procedure.[142]

The Human Rights Committee has issued "general comments" on several provisions of the Covenant, dealing with both substantive questions and procedural issues related to states' reporting requirements.[143] Its general comment on article 1 was not published until 1984, and it does nothing to clarify the meaning of "self-determination" or the scope of state obligations under article 1.[144]

The discussions surrounding adoption of the general comment on

137 *Staus of International Instruments, supra* note 133, at 46.
138 United Kingdom, art. 40 CCPR Report, UN Doc. CCPR/C/1/Add.37 (1978), Annexes.
139 Byelorussian S.S.R., art. 40 CCPR Report, UN Doc. CCPR/C/1/Add.27 (1978) at 5.
140 Statement by the representative of U.S.S.R. to the Human Rights Committee, UN Doc. CCPR/C/SR.108 (1900) at 4; *cf.* discussion of the Soviet Union, *infra,* chap. 16, at 358–69.
141 See United Nations, *Report of the Human Rights Committee,* 42 UN GAOR, Supp. (No. 40), UN Doc. A/42/40 (1987) at 106.
142 *Id.*
143 Covenant on Civil and Political Rights, art. 40(4).
144 United Nations, *Report of the Human Rights Committee,* 39 UN GAOR, Supp. (No. 40), UN Doc. A/39/40 (1984) at 142–43.

article 1 reveal the difficulties in drafting a text which would, in fact, add some degree of interpretive insight to the plain words of the Covenant.[145] The Committee's chairman correctly noted that the right to self-determination is "one of the most awkward to define, since the abuse of that right could jeopardize international peace and security in giving states the impression that their territorial integrity was threatened."[146] Some Committee members suggested that the concept of self-determination was not limited to the colonial context,[147] but the lack of consensus made it impossible to define with more precision the extent of the right.

Neither the European[148] nor the American[149] convention on human rights includes specific recognition of the right of self-determination. The African Charter on Human and Peoples' Rights[150] refers to the equality of peoples in article 19, including the statement that "[n]othing shall justify the domination of a people by another," and article 20 sets forth the right to self-determination:

1. All peoples shall have the right to existence. They shall have the unquestionable and inalienable right to self-determination. They shall freely determine their political status and shall pursue their economic and social development according to the policy they have freely chosen.
2. Colonized or oppressed peoples shall have the right to free themselves from the bonds of domination by resorting to any means recognized by the international community.
3. All peoples shall have the right to the assistance of the States Parties to the present Charter in their liberation struggle against foreign domination, be it political, economic or cultural.

A continuing debate among international lawyers is whether or not there exists a *right* to self-determination in customary international law. and, if so, whether or not it is limited to colonial situations. Professors Brownlie and Gros Espiell submit that the right to self-determination

145 See discussions of the Human Rights Committee, UN Docs. CCPR/C/SR.476, 478, 503, 504, 513, 514, 516 (1984).
146 UN Doc. CCPR/C/SR.503 (1984) at 32.
147 See, e.g., remarks of Mr. Tomuschat, UN Doc. CCPR/C/SR.478 (1983) at 2, 6; Mr. Ermacora, *id.* at 5; Mr. Aguilar, *id.* at 7; Mr. Graefrath (as Chairman), *id.* at 8; Sir Vincent Evans, UN Doc. CCPR/C/SR.503 (1984) at 5; and Mr. Dimitrijevic, *id.* at 8.
148 European Convention for the Protection of Human Rights and Fundamental Freedoms, signed 4 Nov. 1940, entered into force 3 Sept. 1953, 312 U.N.T.S. 222.
149 American Convention of Human Rights, signed 22 Nov. 1969, entered into force 18 July 1978, O.A.S.T.S. No. 36, p. 1, O.A.S. Off Rec. OEA/Ser.L/V/II.23, doc. 21, rev. 6.
150 African Charter on Human and Peoples' Rights, adopted 27 June 1981, entered into force 21 Oct. 1986, O.A.U. Doc. CAB/LEG/67/3 Rev. 5.

constitutes *jus cogens*, a peremptory norm of international law,[151] while Professor Verzijil represents the other extreme in holding that self-determination is "unworthy of the appellation of a rule of law."[152]

Without entering into the debate of whether the right to self-determination is *jus cogens*, it would seem difficult to question its status as a "right" in international law. While General Assembly resolutions do not of themselves make law, the unanimous adoption of Resolutions 1514, 2625, and numerous others reiterating the "right" to self-determination is significant, as is the fact that more than half of the world's states have formally accepted the right of self-determination through their adherence to one or both of the Covenants.

Governments and scholars from all regional and political perspectives also accept the right of peoples to self-determination.[153] While the definition of "peoples" and the means by which it is appropriate or necessary to ensure that the right to self-determination is respected will undoubtedly remain controversial in the context of specific situations,[154] the fundamental question is whether the international right to self-

151 Brownlie, *supra* note 24, at 515; United Nations, *The Right to Self-Determination, Implementation of United Nations Resolutions* (Hector Gros Espiell, Special Rapporteur), UN Doc. E/CN.4/Sub.2/405/Rev.1 (New York: United Nations, 1980) at para. 50; Hector Gros Espiell, "Self-Determination and Jus Cogens," in Cassese, *supra* note 90, at 167–73. But compare United Nations, *The Right to Self-Determination, Historical and Current Developments on the Basis of United Nations Instruments* (Aurelieu Cristescu, Special Rapporteur), UN Sales No. E.80.XIV.3 (1981) at para. 154: "No United Nations instrument confers such an imperative character [as that of *jus cogens*] to the right of peoples to self-determination."

152 J.H.W. Verzijil, 1 *International Law in Historical Perspective* (Leiden: Sijthoff, 1968) at 325.

153 Among the many sources which could be cited are Bokor-Szego, *supra* note 101, at 10–51. Brownlie, *supra* note 24, at 513; Crawford, *supra* note 27, at 101; Gros Espiell, *supra* note 151, at 13; Humphrey, *supra* note 78, at 195; Branimir M. Jankovic, *Public International Law* (Dobbs Ferry, NY: Transnational Publishers, 1984) at 220; and Partsch, *supra* note 95, at 66.

154 The International Court of Justice seemed to concede in the Northern Cameroons case that the modalities of self-determination were essentially political questions within the purview of the General Assembly. "Whatever the motivation of the General Assembly in reaching the conclusions [endorsing the plebiscites in the Northern Cameroons]..., whether or not it was acting wholly on the political plane and without the Court finding it necessary to consider here whether or not the General Assembly based its action on a correct interpretation of the Trusteeship Agreement, there is no doubt—and indeed no controversy—that the resolution had definitive legal effect.... The Applicant has expressly said it does not ask the Court to revise or reverse those conclusions of the General Assembly or those decisions as such, and it is not therefore necessary to consider whether the Court could exercise such an authority." Case concerning the Northern Cameroons (Cameroon v. United Kingdom), Preliminary Objections, Judgment of 2 Dec. 1963, I.C.J. Reports 1963, p. 15, at 32.

determination has been recognized as applicable outside the context of decolonization.

Despite the references in General Assembly Resolutions 1514 and 2625 and in the two Covenants to the self-determination of "all" peoples, in practice the right of self-determination has been limited to colonial situations or, if one prefers, to colonial "peoples."[155] "No State has accepted the right of *all* peoples to self-determination. . . . Of course, no one any longer *claims* to be denying self-determination; but whether this establishes the normative character of 'self-determination' remains debatable."[156]

In fact, it is the principle of national unity that has been almost universally followed by the international community—which, after all, is composed of states whose interest is to maintain themselves. With the single exception of Bangladesh, whose independence was due more to the Indian army than to the precepts of international law, no secessionist claim has been accepted by the international community since 1945.

> The express acceptance in . . . [relevant UN resolutions] of the principles of the national unity and the territorial integrity of the State implies nonrecognition of the right of secession. The right of peoples to self-determination, as it emerges from the United Nations, exists for peoples under colonial and alien domination, that is to say, who are not living under the legal form of a State. The right to secession from an existing State Member of the United Nations does not exist as such in the instruments or in the practice followed by the Organization, since to seek to invoke it in order to disrupt the national unity and the territorial integrity of a State would be a misapplication of the principle of self-determination contrary to the purposes of the United Nations Charter.[157]

African states, which were among the leaders in developing the post-1945 "right" to self-determination in the context of decolonization, have adopted a very narrow interpretation of the right in the post-colonial context of independence. Because of the extreme ethnic het-

---

155 *Cf.* R.P. Dhokalia, "International Recognition of the Human Right of Collective Self-Determination," 11 Banaras L. J. 20 (1975) at 27–33. "These [General Assembly] resolutions have in fact again and again reiterated the right of self-determination of people with reference to only colonial people and have not conceived of the minorities or even majorities of heterogeneous populations within generally accepted political units which do not share in common values and are struggling for realization of the right of self-determination." *Id.* at 31–32. In the context of the I.C.J.'s decision in the Western Sahara case, Shaw states simply, "The principle of self-determination is clearly recognized as a legal right in the context of decolonization." Shaw, *supra* note 114 , at 153.

156 Pomerance, *supra* note 103, at 68.

157 Gros Espiell, *The Right to Self-Determination, supra* note 151, para. 90. Cristescu arrives at a similar conclusion, also citing Res. 2625, *supra* note 151, para. 279.

erogeneity of most African states and the resulting difficulties in developing a sense of statehood in the immediate post-independence period, the principles of territorial integrity and national unity have been determined to be more fundamental than that of self-determination.[158] Whether in the context of minority secession or even the adjustment of borders,

the idea of ethnical self-determination or the creation of new nations out of the existing States was rejected categorically [by African states]. . . . The whole task of national integration and nation building may require the denial of the right to ethnic self-determination in most territories as they emerge from dependency.[159]

Africa may simply be more honest than the rest of the world in admitting that self-determination *of the state* has replaced the theoretical self-determination of peoples that, if taken to its logical conclusion, could result in some instances in secession.[160] Even the promotion of regionalism may be prohibited in countries sensitive to maintaining "national unity."[161]

Sanction suprême dans la société traditionelle, la sécession est devenue aujourd'hui la faute suprême de lèse-unité africaine. Aussi est-elle sanctionée avec une extrême vigueur, au nom de l'unité africaine, elle-même conditionnée par le principe étatique.

Le principe étatique est l'idée que l'Etat doit être facteur dynamique en même temps que limite transcendante de l'exercice du droit des peuples à disposer d'eux-mêmes. . . .

En somme on pourrait dire qu'en Afrique, de même que l'individu se définit

158 See generally Ibou Ibrahima Fall, *Contribution à l'étude du Droit des Peuples à Disposer d'Eux-Mêmes en Afrique* (Paris: Univ. de Paris I, doctoral thesis 1972) at 265–340.

159 Yilma Makonnen, *International Law and The New States of Africa: A Study of the International Legal Problems of State Succession in the Newly Independent States of Eastern Africa* (Paris: Unesco, 1983) at 462. Makonnen identifies only Somalia, which has made irredentist claims on behalf of ethnic Somalis, as pressing for the "self-determination of peoples" rather than the "self-determination of colonial territories."

160 One Algerian lawyer is quoted as observing, "Après les indépendances, l'idée chère au général de Gaulle du droit des peuples à disposer d'eux-mêmes s'est transformée en droit des Etats à disposer de leurs peuples." Ali Yayia, quoted in Jeune Afrique, 2 Sept. 1987, at 19.

161 *Cf.*, e.g., Constitutional Act No. 63–22 of 7 Mar. 1963 (Senegal), which prohibits "[a]ny act of racial, ethnic or religious discrimination and any regionalist propaganda prejudicial to the internal security of the State or to the integrity of the territory of the Republic." Cited in Senegal, Report to Committee on the Elimination of Racial Discrimination, UN Doc. CERD/C/131/Add.5 (1985) at para. 11.

par et dans la société, c'est par et dans l'Etat que doit s'exercer le droit des peuples à disposer d'eux-mêmes.[162]

While Latin American states have been supportive of decolonization efforts, they tend to view issues of self-determination as largely irrelevant to the Western Hemisphere (except with respect to the principle of non-intervention as an essential principle of national sovereignty and independence). "Since irredentist minorities do not exist in Latin America, it is quite clear that political self-determination could not be a claim put forward by any group on the continent."[163]

Professor Gros Espiell believes that the right to self-determination is *jus cogens*, but only in a very limited form:

> The United Nations has established the right of self-determination as a right of peoples under colonial and alien domination. The right does not apply to peoples already organized in the form of a State which are not under colonial and alien domination, since resolution 1514 (XV) and other United Nations instruments condemn any attempt aimed at the partial or total disruption of the national unity and the territorial integrity of a country. If, however, beneath the guise of ostensible national unity, colonial and alien domination does in fact exist, whatever legal formula may be used in an attempt to conceal it, the right of the subject people concerned cannot be disregarded without international law being violated.[164]

The internal aspect of self-determination means that states and their peoples have the right to independence from foreign domination. Thus, existing states which have been invaded or which are otherwise clearly controlled by foreign powers have a right to self-determination, i.e., the right to overthrow the invaders and re-establish independence.[165]

This does not imply, however, that any non-colonial "people" or minority *within an existing state* has yet acquired the right to independ-

---

162 Fall, *supra* note 158, at 388–89, 390.

163 Natan Lerner, "Self-Determination: The Latin American Perspective," in Yonah Alexander and Robert A. Friedlander (eds.), *Self-Determination: National, Regional, and Global Dimensions* (Boulder, CO: Westview Press, 1980) at 67. *Cf.* Frank Griffith Dawson, "Contributions of Lesser Developed Nations to International Law: The Latin American Experience," 13 Case Western Reserve J. Int'l L. 37 (1981), which contains no reference to self-determination in the course of a fairly detailed exposition of Latin American legal theory.

164 *The Right to Self-Determination, supra* note 151, at 10.

165 Similarly, one also might find an inherent "right of revolution" within the right of a people to self-determination, but this does not necessarily imply a right for part of a state's "people" to secede. See S. Chowdhury, "The Status and Norms of Self-Determination in Contemporary International Law," in Frederick E. Snyder and Surakiat Sathirathai, *Third World Attitudes Toward International Law* (Dordrecht: Martinus Nijhoff, 1987) at 87–99; Cassese, *supra* note 90, at 148–53.

ence or self-determination under international law. Although several authors have argued that some form of a "right to secession" *should* be recognized as part of the right to self-determination,[166] constant state practice and the weight of authority require the conclusion that such a right does not yet exist.[167] Attempts to assert that a given minority or other group is, in effect, under alien or colonial domination have not been successful, except insofar as they relate to the internal self-determination of a recognized state under foreign occupation or control.

Thus, while self-determination may have become "a shibboleth that all pronounce to identify themselves with the virtuous,"[168] UN and state practice since 1960 provides evidence that the international community recognizes only a very limited right to 1) external self-determination, defined as the right to freedom from a former colonial power, and 2) internal self-determination, defined as independence of the whole state's population from foreign intervention or influence.

Despite this limited contemporary definition of the *right* to self-determination—a definition created primarily by states[169]—the *principle* of self-determination will continue to be a major political force both internationally and domestically. Indeed, developing concepts of human rights, minority rights, and indigenous rights may contribute directly to strengthening the principle of self-determination, even as state-developed law is seeking to minimize its post-colonial impact.

---

166 The most comprehensive treatise is Buchheit, *supra* note 90; also *cf.*, e.g., Cassese, *supra* note 90, at 155–57; Crawford, *supra* note 27, at 247–70; Ved P. Nanda, "Self-Determination Outside the Colonial Context: The Birth of Bangladesh in Retrospect," in Alexander and Friedlander, *supra* note 163, at 193–220; Pomerance, *supra* note 103; "Klingenthal Symposium: Peoples' Rights and Human Rights," in 7 Human Rights L. J. 410, 410–12, 421–22 (1986); discussion of the Algiers Declaration, *infra* at 116. Various Marxist writers also support the right of secession in theory, but none has offered any specific example of when such a right might exist in a non-colonial context. See, e.g., Bokor-Szegő, *supra* note 101, at 34–35 (rejecting the right of minority groups to secede).

167 Even those who do assert that there is or should be a right of secession have not yet succeeded in identifying any but the most general criteria for determining when secession is permissible. "The complexity of the factors involved in claims for separation makes it impossible to recommend rules which would automatically determine the applicability of the right of self-determination." Eisuke Suzuki, "Self-Determination and World Public Order: Community Response to Territorial Separation," 16 Va. J. Int'l L. 779, 861 (1976).

168 Vernon Van Dyke, "Self-Determination and Minority Rights," 13 Int'l Studies Q. 223 (1969) at 223.

169 However, "[a]s the lion in Aesop said to the Man, 'There are many statues of men slaying lions, but if only the lions were sculptors there might be quite a different set of statues.'" Barbara W. Tuchman, *Practicing History* (New York: Alfred A. Knopf, 1981) at 19.

Chapter 4
The Rights of Minorities

All but the smallest and most cohesive of societies include numerically inferior groups which may be distinguished—and which may distinguish themselves—from the majority. As noted below, no proposed definition of "minority" has yet been widely accepted by international lawyers, but a common-sense definition of a numerically smaller, non-dominant group distinguished by shared ethnic, racial, religious, or linguistic attributes will suffice for present purposes.[170]

One can trace the international protection of minorities at least to the Treaty of Westphalia in 1648, under the terms of which the parties agreed to respect the rights of certain (not all) religious minorities within their jurisdiction. However, given the historical congruence of religious and secular authority prior to this period, such agreements could as easily be seen as recognizing the power of certain political groups rather than religious rights per se.[171] Religion was certainly the most significant distinction among most groups until at least the eighteenth century, and most of the early provisions for the protection of minorities were concerned with what today might be viewed as freedom of religion rather than group rights.

A distinctive system of ensuring a certain degree of cultural and religious autonomy was the "millet" system developed by the Ottoman empire. The millets generally followed religious lines, with each religious

170 While many commentators define minority status in terms of powerlessness as opposed to numerical inferiority, non-dominant majority situations would be in most instances more appropriately considered in the context of self-determination. *Cf.*, e.g., Charles Wagley and Marvin Harris, *Minorities in the New World* (Unesco, 1958; New York: Columbia Univ. Press ed., 1964) at 4–5; Jay A. Sigler, *Minority Rights, A Comparative Analysis* (Westport, CT: Greenwood Press, 1983) at 5.

171 An excellent survey of earlier treatment of minorities is James B. Muldoon, "The Development of Group Rights," in Sigler, *supra* note 170, at 31–66.

community (the most important being the Orthodox, Armenian, and Jewish) having the authority to regulate such matters as personal status, inheritance, and other intra-communal relationships; each millet also was responsible for collecting taxes due the central Ottoman government.

Although some millets acquired a more geographic or political character in the later Ottoman period,[172] the system has been described as essentially "the solution devised by a government that did not know what nationality meant and, therefore, was unfamiliar with the majority-minority concept."[173] The development of autonomous, religous-based communities also was consistent with Quranic injunctions of tolerance for other religions, and large non-Muslim communities continued to flourish throughout the Ottoman empire.[174]

The Congress of Vienna, which dismembered the Napoleonic empire in 1815, also considered the rights of national minorities to some extent. With the exception of Belgium's secession from the united Netherlands, the Congress' borders lasted essentially without change for the next 30 years. The German Confederation was based on ethnicity and language, and the rights of what was then considered to be the Polish ethnic minority within Russia were guaranteed through creation of the "Kingdom of Poland," although this lasted only until a Polish revolt was crushed by Russia in 1830–31. The 1876 Treaty of Berlin included protections for the "traditional rights and liberties" enjoyed by the religious community of Mount Athos in Greece.

The Bulgarian constitution of 1878 also contained guarantees for its Greek and Turkish minorities, but the most conscious and comprehensive attempts to protect ethnic and other minorities through international legal means were the so-called minority treaties adopted at the end of the First World War and subsequently overseen by the League of Nations.[175] "The national minorities which had been contained, controlled

---

172 Eleven non-Muslim millets were recognized in the Ottoman empire by the end of the nineteenth century, although all but the Orthodox, Armenian, Bulgarian, and Jewish constituted less than one percent of the empire's population. S. J. Shaw, 2 *History of the Ottoman Empire and Modern Turkey* (Cambridge: Cambridge Univ. Press, 2 vols. 1976) at 240.

173 Peter F. Sugar, *Southeastern Europe under Ottoman Rule, 1354–1804* (Seattle: Univ. of Washington Press, 1977) at 274.

174 *Cf.*, e.g., Farooq Hassan, *The Concept of State and Law in Islam* (Lanham, MD, and London: University Press of America, 1981) at 45–46, 225–41. Christians and Jews, as monotheistic "people of the Book," occupy a special position in an Islamic state, and it is on this basis that the millets were allowed to develop their own culture and civil administration. *Id.* at 45.

175 Perhaps the best and most detailed treatment of the adoption and implementation of the treaties is Macartney, *supra* note 79, at 212–423; also see United Nations,

or repressed by imperial authority had an unprecedented (and many believed unrepeatable) opportunity for what was now called 'self-determination',"[176] although it is fair to say that the exceptions to the much vaunted "self-determination" of Woodrow Wilson's Fourteen Points were sufficiently numerous to cast doubt on the acceptance of the "nation-state" as an immutable (or even necessarily desirable) principle of international relations.[177]

These treaties fell within three categories, although the substantive protections included in each were relatively similar.[178] The first group of treaties included those imposed upon the defeated states of Austria, Hungary, Bulgaria, and Turkey. The second included either new states created out of the dissolution of the Ottoman Empire or states whose boundaries were altered specifically to respond to what President Wilson referred to as self-determination; in this group were Czechoslovakia, Greece, Poland, Romania, and Yugoslavia. Finally, special provisions relating to minorities were included in the regimes established in Aland, Danzig, the Memel Territory, and Upper Silesia.

Among the protections commonly included in the first two categories of treaties were the right to equality of treatment and non-discrimination; the right to citizenship, although a minority group mem-

Study on the rights of persons belonging to ethnic, religious and linguistic minorities (F. Capotorti, Special Rapporteur), UN Sales No. E.78.XIV.1 (1979) at 16–26.

176 Pearson, *supra* note 82, at 134.

177 See chap. 3. The Great Powers were well aware of the potentially disruptive nature of the proposals regarding minority rights. A memorandum prepared for the British government by Jan Smuts warned that

> efforts will doubtless be made to embody provisions in the [Paris Peace] treaty safeguarding the rights of racial, religious and other minorities and, further, to interpret the doctrine of 'national self-determination' as entitling such minorities, if they can claim to be nations, to present their case to the Peace Conference and to subsequent Inter-State Conferences. On both these points the best course would seem to be to leave as much discretion as possible in the hands of each of the Associated Powers. It would clearly be inadvisable to go even the smallest distance in the direction of admitting the claim of the American negroes, or the Southern Irish, or the Flemings or Catalans, to appeal to an Inter-State Conference over the head of their own Government. Yet if a right of appeal is granted to the Macedonians or the German Bohemians it will be difficult to refuse it in the case of other nationalist movements.

Quoted in L.C. Green, "Protection of Minorities in the League of Nations and the United Nations," in Allan Gotlieb (ed.), *Human Rights, Federalism and Minorities* (Toronto: Canadian Institute of International Affairs, 1970) at 193.

178 The unilateral declarations to guarantee minority rights made by states before the League of Nations might be considered to constitute a fourth category. See Capotorti Study, *supra* note 175, at 18; Felix Ermacora, "The Protection of Minorities before the United Nations," 182 Recueil des Cours 251 (1984) at 258–59.

ber could opt to retain another citizenship if desired; the right to use one's own language; the right of minorities to establish and control their own charitable, religious, and social institutions; a state obligation to provide "equitable" financial support to minority schools (in which instruction at the primary level would be in the minority language) and other institutions; and recognition of the supremacy of laws protecting minority rights over other statutes.[179] A certain degree of territorial autonomy was provided for the Aland Islands,[180] Ruthenia in Czechoslovakia,[181] the Valachs of Pindus in Greece,[182] and the Transylvanian Saxons and Szeklers in Romania.[183]

Extensive critiques of the minority treaties have been written and need not be repeated here, and there can be little doubt about their ultimate failure.[184] Nevertheless, the result of the Versailles Treaty was a map of Europe that did more closely approach the theoretical goal of a collection of true "nation-states" than did pre-war Europe. While approximately half of the population of Europe were "minorities" in 1914, only one-fourth were minorities in 1919. Albania, Bulgaria, Estonia, Hungary, Latvia, Lithuania, Poland, and Romania had ethnic majorities, while the more artificial states of Czechoslovakia and Yugoslavia had dominant, if not majority, ethnic groups.[185]

The minority guarantees built into the various post-1919 treaties were not inserted to redress earlier depredations by empires (despite such atrocities as the Armenian genocide in 1915–16), but rather to

179 See generally Inis L. Claude, Jr., *National Minorities* (Cambridge, MA: Harvard Univ. Press, 1955; reprinted, New York: Greenwood Press, 1969) at 17–20; Janowsky, *supra* note 100, at 112–15; Macartney, *supra* note 79, at 273–94, 502–06 (text of the Polish Minorities Treaty); Capotorti Study, *supra* note 175, at 18–19; United Nations Sub-Commission on Prevention of Discrimination and Protection of Minorities, *Treaties and international instruments concerning the protection of minorities 1919–1951*, UN Doc. E/CN.4/Sub.2/133 (1951) at paras. 2–12.

180 See *infra*, chap. 17, at 370–75.

181 The Treaty of St. Germain-en-Laye provided for the "fullest degree of self-government compatible with the unity of Czechoslovakia" in Ruthenia, including local legislative power over all linguistic, scholastic, and religious questions, local adminstration, and such other matters as might be delegated by the Czechoslovakian government. *Cf. Treaties and international instruments concerning the protection of minorities 1919–1951*, *supra* note 179, at para. 16.

182 The 1920 Treaty of Sèvres granted the Valachs authority over religious, charitable, and scholastic matters and also confirmed Greece's recognition of the autonomy of Mt. Athos guaranteed under the Treaty of Berlin. *Id.* at para. 14.

183 Article 11 of the Treaty of Paris granted local autonomy in scholastic and religious matters, "subject to control of the Romanian State." *Id.* at para. 17.

184 See, e.g., Claude, *supra* note 179, at 31–50; Pearson, *supra* note 82, at 142–46; Capotorti Study, *supra* note 175, at 25–26.

185 Pearson, *supra* note 82, at 148–49.

assuage and protect those "national" minorities whose claims to self-determination were not recognized by the victorious Great Powers.

In practice, the threat to religious minorities came not from the Ottomans, whose millet system had always provided an acceptable minimum measure of protection for Christian communities, but from the ebullient new states, which distrusted any and all minorities within their domains. The toleration clauses reluctantly accepted by the new states of Serbia, Greece, Rumania, Bulgaria and Albania as the price of their diplomatic recognition were inserted to protect minorities not against the faltering authority of empire but the raw power of nationalism.[186]

The supervisory mechanisms established by the League of Nations were cumbersome and began with the filing of a petition by a minority group with the League's Secretariat.[187] The petition was forwarded to the government concerned for comment, and it was then considered by the "Committee of Three," which consisted of the president of the League Council and two other Council members. Neither the Committee nor the Council had any powers of enforcement, and it appears that there was a bias in favor of governments—although these weaknesses were no greater than those from which many contemporary oversight mechanisms also suffer.

Despite the failures of the League system, the principle of international supervision over treaty obligations relating to minority rights was significant. While one of the most widespread criticisms of the minority treaties was that they applied only to weak or defeated states, the appropriate remedy would have been to expand rather than abandon the system of minority protections. The minority treaties were unable to protect Jews and others from the Holocaust; however, the life of the League of Nations and of the international order which it attempted to maintain was so brief that is unfair to draw many conclusions about the efficacy of international remedies for the protection of minorities from the League precedent.

The fate of the League minority system was largely determined by its international political context. The problem of minorities was not a technical matter which could be handled in routine fashion by an agency isolated from the vicissitudes of political conflicts; it was a political problem of great moment, and it could be solved only in conjunction with other political problems. When the League failed to cope with the factors making for the disintegration of the world order, the collapse of the minority system was inevitable; it was an integral

---

186 *Id*. at 131–32.

187 See generally Macartney, *supra* note 79, at 308–69; Capotorti Study, *supra* note 175, at 20–24; Louis B. Sohn and Thomas Buergenthal, *International Protection of Human Rights* (Indianapolis, IN: Bobbs-Merrill, 1973) at 213–306.

part of the League, and its destiny could not be divorced from that of the League.[188]

Three aspects of the League of Nations treaties should be under-scored. First, the minority protections set forth therein were imposed only on a few selected states; no suggestion was made that the Great Powers should be bound by similar obligations. Secondly, the treaties guaranteed what by that time had come to be viewed as traditional minority rights dealing with religion, language, and cultural activities. They did not imply any broader economic or political autonomy, except in the special cases of Danzig, Memel, and Upper Silesia.[189] Third, the purported "self-determination" of certain nationalities resulted, in fact, from the dictates of the Great Powers; the minorities involved were permitted to lobby in Paris, but not to vote at home.

Even had the minorities treaties been wholly successful, they would not have eliminated the "minority problem." In Eastern Europe, for example, minorities continued to represent from roughly 15% to over 50% (in Czechoslovakia and Yugoslavia) of the new states. "The First World War and Versailles Settlement together only converted eastern Europe from an area dominated by a select number of extensive empires to an area quarrelled over by an extensive number of select empires."[190]

Irredentist disputes arose almost immediately and continued throughout the short inter-war period. The post-Versailles map of Europe no longer contained great empires to divide, and minorities in avowedly "nationalist" states were perhaps even less welcome than they had been under the empires.

[I]n the nation-states of the interwar era, a minority seemed fated, short of a war and a redrawing of frontiers, to remain a minority forever, not simply in the neutral statistical sense, but also in terms of political if not civil deprivation. Hence it tended to seek succor from its ethnic and cultural 'mother country' against the pressures of the 'host' state, and thus the dispute was internation-alized. . . . The 'host' government, in turn, was committed to the cultivation of the specific national culture of its state-nation throughout its territory; otherwise, it reasoned, the achievement of national independence would have been purposeless.[191]

It was primarily in the European arena that concepts of minority rights and nationalism developed in the nineteenth and early twentieth

188 Claude, *supra* note 179, at 49–50.

189 Fuller discussions of the Free City of Danzig and Memel Territory and Free City of Danzig may be found *infra*, chap. 17, at 375–84.

190 Pearson, *supra* note 82, at 148–49.

191 Joseph Rothschild, *East Central Europe between the Two World Wars* (Seattle: Univ. of Washington Press, 1974) at 12.

centuries. The colonial empires were notorious for ignoring ethnic, linguistic, or other "national" considerations, leaving such complexities to be dealt with by the independent states that emerged from decolonization.[192] Although African and Asian nations or ethnic groups may often have been set against one another by colonial powers, there seems to have been no concern for the protection of "minorities"—unless it was the consolidation and protection of the privileges of the white colonist.

The individualistic orientation of anglophone countries such as Australia, Canada, and the United States left little room for concern with the rights of minority groups, and the American "melting pot" was concerned only (and rarely) with individual equality and non-discrimination. Indigenous groups were given no recognition in the Western Hemisphere by the settler populations.[193]

One of the few examples of non-European legal provisions relating to minorities can be found in the 1926 Lebanese constitution, which provided for proportional legislative representation for seven religious groups, including one labeled "minorities"; in some ways this might be considered as a natural extension of the Ottoman millet system. Religious and linguistic differences in Switzerland led not to "national self-determination" for each community but to a complex federal system which became more rather than less centralized with the new constitution adopted in 1874.[194]

Thus, it is difficult to conclude that "minority rights" were relevant to much of the world outside Europe, prior to the new emphasis on "human rights" that became one of the founding principles of the United Nations. Neither the concept of protecting the culture and traditions of numerical minorities nor that of conceding statehood to ethnic or linguistic "nations" is evident outside the geographical setting of European (including the Ottoman) empires, and the new United Nations had little difficulty in essentially ignoring the preoccupation with minority issues that was the hallmark of its predecessor.

192 *Cf.* Mazrui and Tidy, *supra* note 74, at 373–84. But compare Horowitz, *supra* note 5, at 75–76: "The boundary-drawing process [in colonial territories] frequently took ethnic interests into account, and boundaries were often redrawn later by colonial powers in response to ethnic demands. . . . What the colonialists did that was truly profound, and far more important for ethnicity, was to change the scale of the polity by several fold. The colonies were artificial, not because their borders were indifferent to their ethnic composition, but because they were, on the average, many times larger than the political systems they displaced or encapsulated." *Cf. id.* at 149–60.
193 See chap. 5.
194 See *infra*, chap. 16, at 352–58.

The United Nations Charter contains no provision specifically addressing the issue of minority rights. The existence of German-speaking minorities had provided one excuse for Hitler's aggression, and one heard little about the rights of "national minorities" from the victorious allies after the Second World War. Rather, the emphasis was placed on (individual) human rights and the collective right of all "peoples" to self-determination.[195]

Instead of adopting the League of Nations approach of attempting to resolve the territorial-political problems posed by the existence of minority groups within a state (particularly those which had linguistic or ethnic ties to neighboring states) by boundary adjustments which might more accurately reflect a true nation-state, the drafters of the UN Charter seemed to assume 1) that European and other minorities would be satisfied if their individual rights, particularly those of equality and non-discrimination, were respected; and 2) that reference to the principle of self-determination would be adequate to resolve the problem of colonialism. Despite the disastrous consequences for the individual victims of, e.g., the Greek-Turkish population "exchange" of 1920–22, migration became the preferred solution for post-1945 European minorities; it was largely the people (especially Germans) who moved, not the boundaries.[196]

There were occasional exceptions where minority interests were protected in a fashion similar to that adopted in the post-World War I period, although these lacked the international supervision offered by the League of Nations. The German-speaking minority in the South Tyrol, for example, was the subject of a 1946 agreement between Italy and Austria.[197] The Austrian State Treaty, which re-established Austria to its pre-1938 borders, contains specific provisions for the protection

195 Cf. Treaties and international instruments concerning the protection of minorities, supra note 179, paras. 114–33.

196 See generally Alfred M. de Zayas, Nemesis at Potsdam (London & Boston: Routledge & Kegan Paul, 1977). Population transfer also was considered as the most desirable solution to deal with discrimination against the Turkish minority in Bulgaria in the 1960s, although in practice only 50,000 ethnic Turks (out of 600,000 who had originally applied to leave Bulgaria) were able to afford the customs duties imposed on those emigrating. See Agreement between the Peoples' Republic of Bulgaria and the Republic of Turkey concerning Emigration from the People's Republic of Bulgaria to the Republic of Turkey of Bulgarian Nationals of Turkish Origin whose Close Relatives Emigrated to Turkey before 1952, signed 22 Mar. 1968, 759 U.N.T.S. 223.

Renewed repression of the Turkish minority in Bulgaria in the mid-1980s led to the migration of large numbers of Muslims from Bulgaria to Turkey in 1989.

197 See infra, chap. 18, at 432–40.

of the Slovene and Croat minorities, including guarantees of non-discrimination and linguistic and educational rights.[198]

There was at least one other important post-war example of the recognition of the vulnerability of minority groups to majority repression. Contemporaneous with the earliest days of the United Nations and more responsive to the violations of the rights of minorities which had occurred during the Second World War were the activities of the International Military Tribunal at Nuremberg and the subsequent drafting of the International Convention on the Prevention and Punishment of the Crime of Genocide.[199] The Genocide Convention is directed specifically against the destruction of national, racial, ethnic, and religious groups *per se*, as opposed to violations of the rights of individuals. However, a proposal to include political groups within the coverage of the Genocide Convention was defeated on the grounds, *inter alia*, that such groups did not have permanent characteristics and would thus be difficult to define; the convention's scope therefore is limited to those more traditionally defined minority groups which had been of concern in the late nineteenth century and under the League of Nations.[200]

The Universal Declaration of Human Rights adopted by the UN General Assembly in 1948 makes no specific mention of minority rights,[201] but the United Nations was nevertheless actively involved in minority issues during the 1950s. The ultimately unimplemented proposal for a Free Territory of Trieste[202] and the UN-approved establishment of an autonomous Eritrea federated with Ethiopia[203] both addressed minority situations, although each envisioned a greater degree

---

198 217 U.N.T.S. 223 (1955), art. 7. These provisions were reinforced by a 1975 treaty between Austria and Yugoslavia, under the terms of which both governments agreed to "respect faithfully the principle of the protection of minorities not only in accordance with their respective Constitutions and domestic laws but also in accordance with the Charter of the United Nations, the Universal Declaration of Human Rights, the International Convention on the Elimination of All forms of Racial Discrimination and the Covenants on human rights." Quoted in Italy, art. 40 CCPR Report, UN Doc. CCPR/C/6/Add.4 (1980) at 61.

199 Opened for signature 9 Dec. 1948, entered into force 12 Jan. 1951, 78 U.N.T.S. 277.

200 *Cf.*, e.g., Hurst Hannum, "Genocide in Cambodia: The Sounds of Silence," 11 Human Rights Q. 82, 103–12 (1989); Lawrence J. LeBlanc, "The Intent to Destroy Groups in the Genocide Convention: The Proposed U.S. Understanding," 78 Am. J. Int'l L. 369 (1984).

201 UN G.A. Res. 217A(III), UN Doc. A/810 (1948) at 71. A separate part of the same resolution noted accurately, if somewhat disingenuously, that "it was difficult to adopt a uniform solution for this complex and delicate question [of minorities], which had special aspects in each State in which it arose." G.A. Res. 217C(III). *id.*

202 See *infra*, chap. 17, at 400–06.

203 See *infra*, chap. 16, at 337–41.

of political autonomy than would traditionally have been reserved to a minority group. The UN Commission on Human Rights soon established a Sub-Commission on Prevention of Discrimination and Protection of Minorities, although (except as noted below) early attempts by the Sub-Commission to address minority issues were essentially rebuffed by the Commission.[204]

In 1960, the UN Educational, Scientific and Cultural Organization (Unesco) adopted the Convention Against Discrimination in Education, which generally recognized the right of members of national minorities to carry on their own educational activities, including the maintenance of schools and the use or teaching of their own language.[205] However, the latter right was dependent upon "the educational policy of each State," and the general right to minority education was not to prevent minority group members "from understanding the culture and language of the community as a whole and from participating in its activities, or ... prejudice national sovereignty."[206]

Drafting of binding international agreements to implement the Universal Declaration began soon after the Declaration's adoption, and article 27 of the Covenant on Civil and Political Rights[207] does specifically address the issue of minority rights. It provides:

In those States in which ethnic, religious or linguistic minorities exist, persons belonging to such minorities shall not be denied the right, in community with the other members of their group, to enjoy their own culture, to profess and practise their own religion, or to use their own language.

The Covenant addresses only minimal, although traditional, minority rights, that is, cultural, religious, and linguistic rights.[208] In ad-

---

204 It requires only two pages of a 400-page report on the UN's human rights activities to describe the UN's work in the area of minority rights (apart from questions of discrimination). See United Nations, *United Nations Action in the Field of Human Rights*, UN Sales No. ST/HR/2/Rev.2 (1983) at 210–12; also see Capotorti Study, *supra* note 175, at paras. 141–48; Humphrey, "The United Nations Sub-Commission on Prevention of Discrimination and Protection of Minorities," 62 Am. J. Int'l L. 869 (1968). However, the Sub-Commission was responsible for publication of a very helpful booklet which contains excerpts from international texts for the protection of minorities and an analytical survey of the kinds of protection provided, United Nations, *Protection of Minorities*, UN Sales No. 67.XIV.3 (1967). Also see United Nations Sub-Commission on Prevention of Discrimination and Protection of Minorities, *Activities of the United Nations Relating to the Protection of Minorities*, UN Doc. E/CN.4/Sub.2/194 (1958).

205 Adopted 14 Dec. 1960, entered into force 22 May 1962, 429 U.N.T.S. 93, art. 6.

206 *Id.*

207 *Supra* note 132.

208 *Cf.* Sohn, "The Rights of Minorities," in Louis Henkin (ed.), *The International*

dition, rights are granted to "persons belonging to such minorities" rather than to minority groups themselves. Although this latter distinction may not be important in practice, it indicates the individualistic orientation of the Covenant on Civil and Political Rights, as well as the reluctance to recognize the rights of groups which have yet to be satisfactorily defined.[209]

The UN Sub-Commission on Prevention of Discrimination and Protection of Minorities finally was able to address the issue of minorities in some depth in the mid-1970s. Its Special Rapporteur, Francesco Capotorti, completed in 1978 what has remained the leading study on discrimination against minorities.[210] The Sub-Commission subsequently suggested preparation of a Declaration on the Rights of Minorities, and a draft declaration was submitted to the Commission by Yugoslavia in 1979.[211] A revised Yugoslav draft was put forward in 1981,[212] and since 1979 the Commission has considered the draft declaration in an "open-ended" working group which meets during the Commission's annual sessions.

The Commission's working group foundered upon, *inter alia*, lack of consensus on a definition of "minority," and in 1984 it requested the Sub-Commission to prepare such a definition.[213] After surveying various national and international precedents, Sub-Commission member Jules Deschenes submitted the following definition to the Sub-Commission:

A group of citizens of a State, constituting a numerical minority and in non-dominant position in that State, endowed with ethnic, religious or linguistic characteristics which differ from those of the majority of the population, having a sense of solidarity with one another, motivated, if only implicitly, by a col-

Bill of Rights, The Covenant on Civil and Political Rights (New York: Columbia Univ. Press, 1981) at 270–75, 282–87.

209 It should perhaps be noted that neither the American nor the European Convention on Human Rights refers to minority rights; the African Charter on Human and Peoples' Rights, which entered into force in 1986, contains several references to "peoples," but none to minorities or groups.

210 *Supra* note 175.

211 UN Doc. E/CN.4/L.1367/Rev.1 (1979).

212 UN Doc. E/CN.4/Sub.2/L.734 (1981).

213 Comm. on Human Rights Res. 1984/62, UN ESCOR, Supp. (No. 4), UN Doc. E/1984/14 (1984) at 99. A list of UN studies and discussions which address the question of a definition of "minority" may be found in United Nations Sub-Commission on Prevention of Discrimination and Protection of Minorities, *Note by the Secretary-General*, UN Doc. E/CN.4/Sub.2/1984/31 (1984). Also *cf.*, e.g., Ermacora, *supra* note 178 at 269–73, 287–98.

lective will to survive and whose aim is to achieve equality with the majority in fact and in law.[214]

This definition occasioned considerable debate within the Sub-Commission, and the Deschenes proposal was forwarded to the Commission without having been approved by the Sub-Commission.[215] Perhaps in recognition of the serious, if inconclusive, debate in the Sub-Commission (or its own lack of progress in preceding years), the Commission's working group decided in 1986 to postpone further consideration of definitional questions and to proceed to elaborate the substantive articles of the draft declaration.[216]

Thus far, the working group has tentatively approved a ten-paragraph Preamble and three articles of the declaration itself.[217] The

214 United Nations Sub-Commission on Prevention of Discrimination and Protection of Minorities, *Proposal concerning a definition of the term "minority" submitted by Mr. Jules Deschenes*, UN Doc. E/CN.4/Sub.2/1985/31 & Corr. 1 (1985) at 30.

Capotorti defined a minority as "[a] group numerically inferior to the rest of the population of a State, in a non-dominant position, whose members—being nationals of the State—possess ethnic, religious or linguistic characteristics differing from those of the rest of the population and show, if only implicitly, a sense of solidarity, directed towards preserving their culture, traditions, religion or language." Capotorti Study, *supra* note 175, at 96.

While the Permanent Court of International Justice issued several judgments and advisory opinions dealing with minority issues, it never formally defined the word "minority." It did, however, offer a definition of the word "community" as used in a Greco-Bulgarian convention encouraging emigration and population exchange between the two countries: "[T]he 'community' is a group of persons living in a given country or locality, having a race, religion, language and traditions of their own and united by this identity of race, religion, language and traditions in a sentiment of solidarity, with a view to preserving their traditions, maintaining their form of worship, ensuring the instruction and upbringing of their children in accordance with the spirit and traditions of their race and rendering mutual assistance to each other." Greco-Bulgarian "Communities", Advisory Opinion, 1930, P.C.I.J., Series B, No. 17, at 21.

A rather different perspective is expressed in the definition adopted by one of the few recent works which specifically addresses the question of minority rights: a minority is deemed to be "any group category of people who can be identified by a sizable segment of the population as objects for prejudice or discrimination or who, for reasons of deprivation, require the positive assistance of the state. A persistent nondominant position of the group in political, social, and cultural matters is the common feature of the minority." Sigler, *supra* note 170, at 5.

215 Sub-Commission on Prevention of Discrimination and Protection of Minorities Res. 1985/6, UN Doc. E/CN.4/1986/5 (1985) at 85.

216 See *Report of the Working Group on the Rights of Persons Belonging to National, Ethnic, Religious and Linguistic Minorities*, UN Doc. E/CN.4/1986/43 (1986).

217 The text approved through 1988 by the working group and proposals submitted concerning the remainder of the declaration may be found in the working group's 1988 report to the Human Rights Commission, UN Doc. E/CN.4/1988/36 (1988), Annexes I and II.

provisions adopted through the working group's 1988 session are as follows (provisions upon which consensus has not yet been reached are in brackets):

Article 1
   1. [Persons belong to] [national or] ethnic, linguistic and religious minorities (hereinafter referred to as minorities) have the right to respect for, and the promotion of, their ethnic, cultural, linguistic and religious identity without any discrimination.
   2. [Persons belong to] minorities have the right to life, liberty and security of person and all other human rights and freedoms without discrimination.

Article 2
   1. In accordance with the Charter of the United Nations and other relevant international instruments, [persons belonging to] minorities have the right to be protected against any activity, including propaganda, [directed against minorities] which:
   (i) may threaten their existence [or identity];
   (ii) [interferes with their freedom of expression or association] [or the development of their own characteristics]; or
   (iii) otherwise prevents their full enjoyment and exercise of universally recognized human rights and fundamental freedoms.
   2. In accordance with their respective constitutional processes [and in accordance with the relevant international treaties to which they are parties], all States shall undertake to adopt legislative or other appropriate measures to prevent and combat such activities, with due regard to the principles embodied in this Declaration and in the Universal Declaration of Human Rights.

Article 3
   1. [Persons belonging to] minorities have the right, individually or in community with the other members of their group, to enjoy their own culture, to profess and practice their own religion, and to use their own language, freely and without interference or any form of discrimination.
   2. All States [which have not yet done so] shall [take measures to create favourable conditions to enable (persons belonging to) minorities to freely] [ensure that (persons belonging to) minorities are freely able to] express their characteristics, to develop their [education,] culture, language, religion, traditions and customs, and to participate on an equitable basis in the cultural, religious, social, economic and political life in the country where they live.
   3. To the same ends, persons belonging to minorities shall enjoy, without any discrimination, the right to establish and maintain contacts with other members of their group [and with other minorities], especially by exercise of the right to freedom of association, the right to freedom of movement and residence within the borders of each State, and the right to leave any country, including their own, and to return to their countries. [This right shall be exercised in accordance with national legislation and relevant international human rights instruments.]

The Preamble recognizes that protecting minority rights will "contribute to the political and social stability of States in which they live" and, in turn, "contribute to the strengthening of friendship and co-operation among peoples and States."

Among the unresolved issues still facing the Commission's working group, in addition to the bracketed question of whether the rights of minority groups *per se* or of their members should be recognized, are whether any further definition of "minority" will be required and the extent (if any) of a state's positive obligations to promote minority cultures. There seems to be little interest in expanding the scope of the declaration to address issues of minority political or economic rights, such as the right to participate in governance and development.

Unfortunately, neither the country reports filed with the Human Rights Committee under article 40 of the Covenant on Civil and Political Rights, the discussion of those reports by the Committee, nor its consideration of individual complaints filed under the Optional Protocol to the Covenant is of much help in defining the current content of minority rights under article 27 of the Covenant. Thus far, the Committee has been unable to agree on formulation of a "general comment" with respect to article 27, again underscoring the sensitivity of the subject.[218]

A number of countries admit the existence of various minorities, and all proclaim that minorities have equal rights with members of the majority population. In many instances, reference is made to specific promotional activities in the areas of minority language and culture.[219] Some states do not consider indigenous populations to fall within the category of "ethnic" minorities,[220] while others discuss in detail the situation of indigenous groups.[211] Iraq states that separate religious courts have authority over the personal status of Assyrians, Jews, Armenians, and Chaldeans,[222] while Iran (in 1977) provided for parliamentary representation for the four principal minorities.[223]

The one case arising under article 27 of the Covenant thus far considered on its merits by the Human Rights Committee under the Optional Protocol held that provisions of the Indian Act of Canada violated

---

218 See e.g., summary records of the Committee's discussions contained in UN Docs. CCPR/C/SR.607, 618, 624 (1985).

219 See, e.g., art. 40 CCPR reports of Canada, UN Doc. CCPR/C/1/Add.43 (1979); Finland, UN Doc. CCPR/C/1/Add.32 (1978); German Democratic Republic, UN Doc. CCPR/C/1/Add.13 (1977); and Mauritius, UN Doc. CCPR/C/1/Add.21 (1978).

220 See, e.g., art. 40 CCPR reports of Chile, UN Doc. CCPR/C/32/Add.1 (1984); Colombia, UN Doc. CCPR/C/1/Add.50 (1979); El Salvador, UN Doc. CCPR/C/14/Add.5 (1983); and Kenya (distinguishing between "minor ethnic groups" and "tribes"), UN Doc. CCPR/C/1/Add.59 (1982).

221 See, e.g., art. 40 CCPR reports of Canada, UN Doc. CCPR/C/1/Add.62 (1983), and Panama, UN Doc. CCPR/C/1/Add.9 (1985).

222 Iraq, art. 40 CCPR Report, UN Doc. CCPR/C/1/Add.45 (1978) at 112.

223 Iran, art. 40 CCPR Report, UN Doc. CCPR/C/1/Add.16 (1977) at 4.

the protections of article 27, insofar as they interfered with the complainant's cultural rights by denying her right to reside on an Indian reserve following marriage to a non-Indian.[224] Without discussion, the Committee assumed that "[p]ersons who are born and brought up on a [Indian] reserve, who have kept ties with their community and wish to maintain these ties must normally be considered as belonging to that minority within the meaning of the Covenant."[225]

The International Convention on the Elimination of All Forms of Racial Discrimination entered into force in 1969 and has been ratified by over 100 states.[226] States are obligated under article 9 to submit periodic reports on their implementation of the convention to the Committee on the Elimination of Racial Discrimination (CERD), and some of these reports discuss issues related to minorities in some detail. "Racial discrimination" under the convention is defined in article 1 as any distinction "based on race, colour, descent, *or national or ethnic origin*" which impairs the exercise of human rights (emphasis added). Article 2 of the convention requires, *inter alia*, that parties take, in appropriate circumstances, "special and concrete measures to ensure the adequate development and protection of certain racial groups or individuals belonging to them, for the purpose of guaranteeing them the full and equal enjoyment of human rights and fundamental freedoms."

Most state reports to CERD are concerned with issues such as legal and other measures to promote equality and non-discrimination or prohibitions against racist propaganda; many reports also consider indigenous peoples in the context of the convention.[227] However, others do consider the protection or promotion of minority rights as they are discussed in the present book, that is, in the context of cultural, linguistic, or other rights which go beyond mere non-discrimination.[228]

Among European countries, for example, several have reported on special measures taken with respect to the gypsy or Romany population. Most seem to have an ultimate goal of integrating the gypsies into national society, with varying degrees of respect for gypsy culture and language.

---

224 Views of the Human Rights Committee, Lovelace v. Canada, Communication No. 24/1977, *Report of the Human Rights Committee*, 36 UN GAOR, Supp. (No. 40), UN Doc. A/36/40 (1981) at 166, reprinted in Human Rights Committee, *Selected Decisions under the Optional Protocol*, UN Sales No. E.84.XIV.2 (1985) at 83; *cf.* Note, "The Human Rights Committee and the Case of Sandra Lovelace," 20 Canadian Yearbook Int'l L. 244 (1982).

225 *Report of the Human Rights Committee, supra* note 224, at 173.

226 Adopted 21 Dec. 1965, entered into force 4 Jan. 1969, 660 U.N.T.S. 195.

227 See chap. 5.

228 *Cf.* Theodor Meron, *Human Rights Law-Making in the United Nations* (Oxford: Clarendon Press, 1986) at 36–44.

In Czechoslovakia, legal restrictions on nomads "are not used in practice," but at the same time "it has been achieved that Gypsy citizens have permanently settled."[229] A similar policy of integration exists in Hungary, where the policy up to the late 1970s "was based primarily on the effort to have them [Gypsies] exercise the same rights and comply with the same duties as those of the rest of the citizens."[230] Italy also emphasizes integration and education through "Operi Nomadi," which, *inter alia*, permits gypsy children to choose among complete integration in an ordinary school class, attendance at an ordinary school with special assistance, or attendance at special classes.[231]

Sinti and Romany gypsies are eligible for social security payments on an equal basis with other citizens of the Federal Republic of Germany, but a special cultural and documentation center has been proposed "as a contribution towards preserving their cultural identity."[232] In Finland, special provisions regarding social assistance for the gypsy (Romany) population were discontinued in 1984, but there is a permanent commission for gypsy affairs under the Ministry for Social Affairs and Health.[233] A 1982 Finnish report on cultural policy recommended that "public measures and funds for the protection and development of gypsy culture should be intensified," and the primary endeavor is to promote the Romany language.[234]

Spain has adopted measures to promote educational opportunities for gypsies and plans to adopt an administrative organ for the gypsy community and a "National Plan for the Advancement of Gipsies."[235] "The social principle underlying such action must be cultural independence and social integration, so that the members of the Gipsy community can continue to be Gipsies, yet at the same time become full citizens of the nation and of Spanish society."[236]

Other countries have reported on their efforts to both integrate and respect minority cultures and groups. Australia, for example, has a government Department of Immigration and Ethnic Affairs, which pro-

229 Czechoslovakia, art. 9 CERD Report, UN Doc. CERD/C/149/Add.2 (1986) at 3; *cf.* Government Decrees Nos. 279/1970 and 231/1972.

230 Hungary, art. 9 CERD Report, UN Doc. CERD/C/149/Add.9 (1986) at 11; in the previous Hungarian report, UN Doc. CERD/C/118/Add.2 (1984), there was no reference to gypsies, who are not considered to constitute a "nationality."

231 Italy, art. 9 CERD Reports, UN Docs. CERD/C/R.95/Add.1 (1977), CERD/C/46/Add.1 & Corr.1 (1979), CERD/C/104/Add.2 (1983).

232 Federal Republic of Germany, art. 9 CERD Report, UN Doc. CERD/C/149/Add.21 (1986) at 3–4.

233 Finland, art. 9 CERD Report, UN Doc. CERD/C/107/Add.3 (1984) at 4–5; also see *id.*, UN Doc. CERD/C/132/Add.1 (1986) at 4.

234 *Id.* (1984 report) at 4.

235 Spain, art. 9 CERD Report, UN Doc. CERD/C/149/Add.14 (1986) at 5–11.

236 *Id.* at 7.

vides adult education services for recent immigrants; the educational system has developed multicultural curricula and is said to promote cultural diversity.[237] Rwanda notes that it has adopted special measures in education and housing to assist the "backward" Batwa minority, in order to integrate them more fully into the national community.[238]

The official policy of Canada is "multiculturalism within a bilingual framework."[239] In 1985, a Federal-Provincial-Territorial Conference on Multiculturalism was held, and many Canadian provinces have adopted special measures to address multiculturalism in schools and through the establishment of government bodies to deal specifically with issues of multiculturalism.[240]

The reassertion of the rights of French-speaking Quebec throughout the 1970s and 1980s is well known, and, in May 1987, Quebec agreed to sign the 1982 Canadian constitution under the terms of the "Meech Lake agreement," which includes amending the 1982 constitution to recognize *inter alia*, "that Quebec constitutes within Canada a distinct society."[241] The agreement also recognizes "that the existence of French-speaking Canadians . . . and English-speaking Canadians . . . constitutes a fundamental characteristic of Canada"; grants the provinces greater control over immigration; and requires that at least three of the nine justices of the Canadian Supreme Court be appointed from the civil (as opposed to common law) bar.[242]

Somewhat similar to the official Canadian policy is that of Mauritius, which describes its national philosophy as "pluricultural Mauritianism". This includes the "preservation of all positive cultural traits specific to all the cultural sections of the population," but there are no specific legal provisions for the support or protection of minority groups.[243]

237 See, e.g., Australia, art. 9 CERD Report, UN Doc. CERD/C/115/Add.3 (1985) at 9–10.

238 Rwanda, art. 9 CERD Report, UN Doc. CERD/C/115/Add.2 (1985) at 4.

239 Canada, art. 9 CERD Report, UN Doc. CERD/C/107/Add.8 (1985) at 6.

240 For example, the Alberta Cultural Heritage Act 1984 established a Department of Culture which is, *inter alia*, "to encourage the preservation, enhancement and development of artistic, historical and language resources by ethno-cultural groups in Alberta." Canada, art. 9 CERD Report, UN Doc. CERD/C/132/Add.3 (1986) at 16. In Manitoba, an Intercultural Council has a similar mandate. *Id.* at 22–23. The school curriculum in Saskatchewan includes "the study of a variety of cultures so as to establish an understanding of types of cultural variation and to gain an appreciation of and tolerance for differences." Canada, art. 9 CERD Report, UN Doc. CERD/C/107/Add.8 (1985) at 65.

241 Constitution Amendment Act 1987, s. 2(1)(b).

242 *Id*, §2(1)(a), 3, 6.

243 Mauritius, art. 9 CERD Report, UN Doc. CERD/C/131/Add.8 (1986) at 5–6. A commentary on the 1987 elections in Mauritius noted that, despite the fact that electoral appeals along communal lines are common, "Mauritians make a virtue of their religious

Major religious groups (the three largest are Roman Catholic, Hindu, and Muslim) are subsidized by the state.

China's 1985 report to CERD discusses in some detail Chinese provisions for its "minority nationalities," who constitute 6.7% of the Chinese population but inhabit over 50% of the country's total area.[244] Mongolia has identified over 20 national minorities within its borders; one, the Kazakhs, resides in an administrative region in which the minority language is used in education, the press, and business.[245]

In addition to the two major ethnic groups of Czechs and Slovaks, Czechoslovakia has recognized special rights for its Hungarian, German, Polish and Ukrainian/Ruthenian minorities in Constitutional Act No. 144 of 27 Oct. 1968.[246] The act provides for proportional representation of these ethnic groups in government bodies and guarantees other rights[247] "to the extent appropriate to the interests of their ethnic development and under conditions specified by law."[248] Ethnic identity is self-selected.[249]

In the German Democratic Republic, there is a national Sorb organization, the Domowina, and assistance is given to Sorb publications and a small number of films; "the equal participation of the Sorbs in the exercise of political power was one of the essential characteristics of the German Democratic Republic's nationality policy."[250] The Sorbs are the only national minority recognized in the GDR. In Hungary, there are "special, independent social organizations of citizens" for ethnic Slavs, Germans, Slovaks, and Romanians, which promote minority cultures in co-operation with the state.[251] Similar associations exist in Poland, and schools in ethnic communities are reported to offer classes in either Polish or the local language.[252]

---

and liguistic complexity." Larry W. Bowman, "Amity on Mauritius—a noteworthy election," Christian Science Monitor, 16 Sept. 1987, at 13, col. 1.

244 China, art. 9 CERD Report, UN Doc. CERD/C/126/Add.1 (1985) at 2; China's autonomous regions are discussed in greater detail in chap. 18, at 420–27.

245 Mongolia, art. 9 CERD Report, UN Doc. CERD/C/91/Add.10 (1983), and earlier reports.

246 Reprinted in Czechoslovakia, art. 9 CERD Report, *supra* note 229, Annex; see generally Czechoslovakia's Fifth Periodic Report to CERD, UN Doc. CERD/C/20/Add.12 (1978).

247 Including the right to education in one's own language, to "all-round cultural development," to associate in ethnic cultural and social organizations, and to publish and receive information in one's own language.

248 Constitutional Act No. 144 of 27 Oct. 1968, art. 3, reprinted in Czechoslovakia, art. 9 CERD Report, *supra* note 229, Annex, p. 1.

249 *Id.*, art. 4.

250 German Democratic Republic, art. 9 CERD Report, UN Doc. CERD/C/116/Add.1 (1984) at 3; also see *id.*, UN Doc. CERD/C/147/Add.1 (1986) at 6–8.

251 See Hungary, art. 9 CERD Report (1984), *supra* note 230, at 8–9.

252 Poland, art. 9 CERD Report, UN Doc. CERD/C/118/Add.21 (1985) at 12–13.

The Italian constitution envisages special protections for linguistic minorities and territorial autonomy for those in border regions, such as the German-speaking minority in the South Tyrol,[253] the French-speaking minority in the Valle d'Aosta, the Slovene minority in Friuli-Venezia Giulia, and the Ladin-speaking minority in Trentino-Alto Adige.[254] Italy also has small, integrated Albanian and Greek minorities which retain certain linguistic, religious, and other customs but which have no special protections.[255]

Article 36 of the Pakistan constitution provides that "the State shall safeguard the legitimate rights and interests of minorities, including their due representation in the Federal and Provincial Services." Pakistan identifies only 3.32% of the population as constituting minorities and states that there are no linguistic minorities; at the same time, it recognizes that Punjabi, Sindhi, Pushto, Baluchi, and other languages are spoken in different parts of the country.[256] The lack of census data on ethnic origin is said to be "a striking illustration of the non-existence of racial prejudice,"[257] although widely reported incidents of human rights violations against religious minorities, such as the Ahmadiyyas,[258] and the resignation of the entire federal cabinet following ethnic riots in Karachi in 1986 between Pathans and Muhajirs[259] would seem to suggest that Pakistan's report to CERD is disingenuous, at best.

There are over 50 ethnic minorities in Viet Nam, constituting 12.3% of the population.[260] The 1980 constitution declares that Viet Nam is "a unitary State belonging to all the ethnic groups living on Vietnamese territory, which are equal in their rights and their duties. The State shall preserve, develop and consolidate the great unified block of all the ethnic minorities in the country and shall strictly forbid any act of discrimination towards them and any act likely to divide them." A 1955 decree, still in force, grants ethnic minorities the rights, *inter alia*, to develop their own languages, preserve or change their manners and customs, and practice a religion.[261] There is a state Central Committee of Nationalities, but no specific body which represents ethnic minorities at the local or national level.

---

253 See *infra* chap. 18, at 432–40.

254 See Italy, art. 9 CERD Report, UN Doc. CERD/C/104/Add.2 (1983) at 7–9.

255 *Id.* at 9–10.

256 Pakistan, art. 9 CERD Report, UN Doc. CERD/C/149/Add.12 (1986) at 2.

257 Pakistan, art. 9 CERD Report, UN Doc. CERD/C/118/Add.15 (1984) at 2.

258 *Cf.*, e.g., UN Sub-Commission on Prevention of Discrimination and Protection of Minorities Res. 1985/21, UN Doc. E/CN.4/1986/5 (1985) at 102.

259 "Pakistani Cabinet Resigns Following Riots," Wash. Post, 21 Dec. 1986, at A40, col. 3.

260 Viet Nam, art. 9 CERD Report, UN Doc. CERD/C/101/Add.5 (1983) at 2.

261 Decree No. 229/SL, reprinted in *id.*, Annex IV.

Several countries assert that they pursue a policy of non-discrimination with respect to minorities, sometimes supplemented by advisory or other bodies representative of the major minority groups.[262] Many countries in which minority groups have asserted rights, such as France and Sudan, simply ignore such issues in their reports to CERD. Nevertheless, as the above survey demonstrates, CERD is developing a certain record of international oversight of minority rights, even though these rights may be only indirectly protected under the Convention on the Elimination of All Forms of Racial Discrimination.

Other recent UN initiatives of relevance to developing standards for the protection of minorities include adoption by the General Assembly in 1982 of a Declaration on the Elimination of All Forms of Intolerance and Discrimination Based on Religion or Belief;[263] appointment of special rapporteurs by the Commission on Human Rights and its Sub-Commission to consider more concrete aspects of religious intolerance and discrimination;[264] and a 1988 decision by the Sub-Commission to ask one of its members to prepare a working paper on "the possibile mechanisms and procedures which the Sub-Commission might establish to facilitate the peaceful and constructive resolution of situations involving racial, national, religious, and linguistic minorities."[265]

Although there has been relatively little substantive development of international law related to minorities since 1945, there is nevertheless a consensus over at least the minimum content of international minority rights. Fundamental, of course, are the principles of equality before the law and non-discrimination, which have by now acquired the status of customary international law binding on all states.[266]

Article 27's reference to the right "to profess and practise their own religion" has probably been subsumed for all practical purposes into the

262 *Cf.*, e.g., Israel, art. 9 CERD Report, UN Doc. CERD/C/144/Add.2 (1986); Netherlands, art. 9 CERD Report, UN Doc. CERD/C/106/Add.11 (1984); Tanzania, art. 9 CERD Report, UN Doc. CERD/C/75/Add.10 (1981); Tunisia, art. 9 CERD Report, UN Doc. CERD/C/118/Add.27 (1985); United Kingdom, art. 9 CERD Report, UN Doc. CERD/C/149/Add.7 (1986).

263 36 UN GAOR, Supp. (No. 51), UN Doc. A/36/51 (1982) at 171. *Cf.* Donna J. Sullivan, "Advancing the Freedom of Religion or Belief Through the UN Declaration on the Elimination of Religious Intolerance and Discrimination," 82 Am. J. Int'l L. 487 (1988).

264 See Comm. on Human Rights Res. 1986/20, UN ESCOR, Supp. (No. 2), UN Doc. E/1986/22 (1986) at 66; Sub-Commission Res. 1983/31, UN Doc. E/CN.4/1984/2 (1983) at 98.

265 Sub-Commission Res. 1988/36, UN Doc. E/CN.4/1989/3 (1988) at 63–64.

266 See, e.g., Richard B. Lillich, "Civil Rights," in 1 Meron, *supra* note 78, at 132–33; Ramcharan, "Equality and Nondiscrimination," in Henkin, *supra* note 208, at 249–50.

guarantees of religious freedom included in other human rights instruments. While the growing attention to the issue of religious intolerance in recent years is sad testimony to violations of the right to practice one's religion, the right's legal status has not been questioned.

The right to enjoy one's own culture also seems to be well accepted, although its meaning is less clear. One leading commentator concludes that this "includes the right to have schools and cultural institutions,"[267] but the extent of protection for other cultural manifestations and of any positive obligation on states to promote or support minority cultures is rather murky.[268] While societies vary greatly in their degree of cultural tolerance, most do forbid cultural and/or religious practices which offend fundamental community beliefs (e.g., polygamy, divorce, use of alcohol) or which are deemed to be outweighed by health or safety concerns (e.g., restrictions on Sikhs' carrying of the short dagger known as the *kirpan*, or on the provision of medical treatment to minors despite the religious objections of their parents).[269]

Use of language is one of the most divisive issues in minority-majority relations, although the right to use one's own language is perhaps the most widely guaranteed minority right in international law.[270] "Many factors have to be taken into account in the formulation of a language policy and the question is so complex that any solution given to it may contain in itself the seeds of a potential conflict."[271] Restrictions

267 Sohn, *supra* note 208, at 284.

268 The Caportorti study, *supra* note 175, at 36–37, concludes that there is a positive obligation on states to intervene on behalf of or provide support to minorities, and the Norwegian government has accepted that it has affirmative obligations with respect to aiding the preservation and development of Saami culture; see Statement by the Observer Delegation of Norway to the Fifth Session of the UN Working Group on Indigenous Populations (n.d. [Aug. 1987]) and chap. 12. "The reading is logical, but has not as yet become part of any subsequent instrument, nor does it command universal assent." Patrick Thornberry, *Minorities and Human Rights Law* (London: Minority Rights Group Report No. 73, 1987) at 7. *Cf.* Sohn, *supra* note 208, at 284–85; Wolfgang Burtscher, "Les lacunes de l'ordre juridique international en matière de protection de minorités," 5 Europa Ethnica 57, 130 (1986) at 131–32.

269 See generally Thomas M. Franck, 1 *Human Rights in Third World Perspective* (New York: Oceana, 1982) at 455–510; John E. Nowak, Ronald D. Rotunda and J. Nelson Young, *Constitutional Law* (St. Paul, MN: West Publishing, 2d ed. 1983) at 1053–81; Sebastian M. Poulter, *English Law and Ethnic Minority Customs* (London: Butterworths, 1986); Paul Sieghart, *The International Law of Human Rights* (Oxford: Clarendon Press, 1983) at 321–26.

270 See the list of "special protective measures of an international character" dealing with language, in United Nations, *Protection of Minorities*, *supra* note 204, at 50–55; a compilation of constitutional provisions relating to linguistic rights may be found in Albert P. Blaustein and Dana Blaustein Epstein, *Resolving Language Conflicts: A Study of the World's Constitutions* (Washington, DC: U.S. English, 1986).

271 Capotorti Study, *supra* note 175, at 39.

on the private use of language would seem to be clearly unjustifiable, and specific provisions for use of minority languages in court also are common.

At least four socio-political realities have contributed to the difficulties in defining minorities and minority rights at the international level.

First, the concept of "minorities" does not fit easily within the theoretical paradigm of the state, whether that state is based on the individual social-contract theory of Western democracies or the class-based precepts of Marxism. The state is seen as a collection of shifting coalitions founded on self-interest or of economic classes, yet the reality is that ethnic or linguistic ties are often much more influential than considerations of class or individual interest in provoking or dampening many conflicts. Thus, the existence of minorities (and, by extension, minority rights) may contradict the philosophical basis of at least democratic and Marxist societies (although the existence of group or community rights and obligations is often better recognized in African and Asian societies).[272]

Second, the reality of minorities and largely heterogeneous states in the contemporary world is also at odds with the theory of the nation-state as it developed in the nineteenth century, and the rhetoric of one people-one state has carried over into the concept of self-determination in the post-1945 period.[273] At the same time, however, the paradigm of the "nation-state" has been conveniently ignored, as former colonies have accepted without question the boundaries drawn by the colonial powers, despite the fact that those boundaries often bear no relevance to ethnic, religious, or linguistic realities.

Third, there is a fundamental fear on the part of *all* countries, and especially newer states, that the recognition of minority rights will encourage fragmentation or separatism and undermine national unity and the requirements of national development. The "natural hypersensitivity of new states about their sovereignty and the imperfect implementation of the principle of national self-determination" noted in the post-Versailles period[274] has been at least as problematic in the post-colonial era.

272 "The concepts of natural law, the social contract, and individualism provide the ideological basis for granting sovereignty to the nation-state. . . . As the measure of all things, it was the individual who became the relevant political and legal unit. Nationalism was a way of democratically linking autonomous individuals to the nation-state." Marguerite Ross Barnett, *The Politics of Cultural Nationalism in South India* (Princeton, NJ: Princeton Univ. Press, 1976) at 7, 8.

273 See chap. 3.

274 Pearson, *supra* note 82, at 185.

Finally, one also must recognize the unpleasant social reality of widespread discrimination and intolerance based on religion and ethnicity. Such intolerance is found in all regions of the world and in states at all stages of economic development; it is fanned by dictators and democrats alike to serve narrow political interests, as suggested by several of the case studies in Part II. While the often violent conflicts that result from such psychological hatreds may well have strong political and economic components, it would be a mistake to conclude (as some analysts would prefer) that ethnic and religious discrimination is not often a major factor.

The difficulties faced by states in recognizing minority rights have their counterpart in increasing fears among minority groups themselves.[275] These fears are in part a reaction to the non-recognition of minority rights as such since the Second World War, as the concept of minorities has been sacrificed to state-building despite the fact that ethnicity and/or religion continues to define many internal conflicts.

There has been a cultural resurgence among ethnic or linguistic groups, who fear a loss of identity due to increased, often unintended, social pressures from dominant modern (often, though not necessarily, Western) society, intensified by developments in telecommunications and other technologies. At the same time, there is an increasing sense of isolation from centralized decision-makers in the economic and political spheres; Catalans and Bretons, for example, may feel even more estranged from power-centers in Brussels and Luxembourg than from traditional dominance by Madrid or Paris.

The result of this confrontation between the reassertion of rights by minority groups and the resistance of states to meaningful pluralism has been that many minority groups today seek broader political and economic goals than the more limited cultural and linguistic rights traditionally accorded to them. The violence that has ensued from these

---

275 As noted in a background paper prepared for a UN Interregional Consultation on Developmental Social Welfare Policies and Programmes, in typically understated fashion:

> In many countries there are ethnic or religious groups that feel that they are being discriminated against indirectly, for instance; through inadequate resources being directed to their part of the country; in the award of government jobs or housing; or through a failure by society to make every allowance for their customs and traditions. Even though the justice of their grievances might not be apparent to neutral observers, to those involved the supposed injustices can be sufficient to justify violence and terrorism. It has proved difficult for society to deal with these internal problems while continuing to safeguard the human rights of all their [sic] members. *Report of the Secretary-General on Social Policy in the Context of Changing Needs and Conditions*, UN Doc. E/CONF.80/2 (1987) at 31.

broader political confrontations has engulfed new states, where it has grown out of ethnic conflicts unresolved at the time of independence (e.g., Sri Lanka, India, Nigeria), as well as older states whose minorities are becoming more self-aware and assertive or who are renewing former claims (e.g., Spain, France, Canada, Nicaragua).

By refusing to recognize even the limited "traditional" rights of minorities to religion, language, and culture, states have been themselves primarily responsible for the resurgence of minority demands in recent years. Without underestimating the role that domestic and foreign political opponents may play in fanning minority discontent, that discontent need rarely be fabricated. In many states, a new partnership must now be created between minorities and the majority, and it may be too late for that partnership to be founded solely on a few minority schools and newspapers.

Chapter 5
Indigenous Rights[276]

Genocide has been committed against indigenous, Indian, or tribal peoples[277] in every region of the world, and it is in this context that any

276 Parts of this chapter are drawn from United Nations, *Study of the Problem of Discrimination Against Indigenous Populations* (José R. Martinez Cobo, Special Rapporteur), UN Doc. E/CN.4/Sub.2/1986/7 & Adds.1–4 (1986) [hereinafter cited as "UN Indigenous Study"], one of the most comprehensive surveys in recent years of the status of indigenous communities in all regions of the world. The five volumes are reprints of a series of partial reports issued by the UN Sub-Commission on Prevention of Discrimination and Protection of Minorities from 1981 to 1983 and prepared largely by Augusto Willemsen Diaz of the UN Center for Human Rights; the final installment is available as a UN publication (Sales No. E.86.XIV.3) and contains the conclusions and recommendations of the study [hereinafter cited as "UN Indigenous Study Conclusions"]. As the reissued set of documents is not widely available, the original documents also might be consulted; they are, in order of their original appearance, UN Docs. E/CN.4/Sub.2/476/Adds.1–6 (1981); E/CN.4/Sub.2/1982/2/Adds.1–7 (1982); and E/CN.4/Sub.2/1983/21/Adds.1–7 (1983).

The UN study is largely based on information received concerning 37 countries: Argentina, Australia, Bangladesh, Bolivia, Brazil, Burma, Canada, Chile, Colombia, Costa Rica, Denmark (including Greenland), Ecuador, El Salvador, Finland, France (including French Guyana), Guatemala, Guyana, Honduras, India, Indonesia, Japan, Laos, Malaysia, Mexico, New Zealand, Nicaragua, Norway, Pakistan, Panama, Paraguay, Peru, Philippines, Sri Lanka, Suriname, Sweden, United States, and Venezuela.

An excellent review of recent writings on indigenous questions may be found in Bernadette Kelly Roy and Gudmundur Alfredsson, "Indigenous Rights: The Literature Explosion," 13 Transnational Perspectives 19 (1987). Also see Russel L. Barsh, Note, "Indigenous Peoples: An Emerging Object of International Law," 80 Am. J. Int'l L. 369 (1986).

277 Governments, UN Secretariat employees, and NGO lawyers often carefully distinguish between "peoples" and "populations," on the theory that designation as a "people" automatically entitles the group so characterized to assert a right to self-determination (i.e., "All peoples have the right of self-determination."). As shown in chap. 3, such a simplistic equation is meaningless in UN practice as well as everyday speech, and the attempt to sneak in references to indigenous "peoples" (or carefully to

discussion of indigenous rights must occur. The general perspective of the state towards indigenous peoples—that they are either to be conquered by or converted to the beliefs of the dominant, more "advanced" society—has remarkable similarities, wherever the state is found. If there are few "problems" with indigenous people in contemporary Europe, it is because most of the conquests or assimilation of the original inhabitants occurred hundreds rather than scores of years ago. However, just as concern with "genocide" itself is of relatively recent origin, the consideration of indigenous rights per se by the international community dates primarily from the past three decades.

CURRENT STATUS OF INDIGENOUS RIGHTS UNDER INTERNATIONAL AND DOMESTIC LAW

Most indigenous peoples have not only been attacked militarily but have subsequently seen their way of life systematically assaulted. Colonial powers and nineteenth-century states in the Americas attempted to conquer and exterminate hostile tribes, force the assimilation of more acculturated indigenous groups, erode traditional culture and landholdings, and expand private property at the expense of the collective or communal holdings of indigenous peoples. Early European colonists in Latin America, for example, used indigenous laborers first as slaves and subsequently as forced wage laborers.[278] Religious missionaries often played a prominent role, frequently intervening to protect indigenous populations from abuse and lobbying for more effective protective measures. At the same time, however, they saw their own role as one of "civilizing" and "converting" the "heathen" natives and showed relatively little concern for preserving indigenous culture.

In the late nineteenth and early twentieth centuries, the expansion of colonialism greatly increased the number and diversity of indigenous populations under colonial rule. A gradual policy of guardianship de-

---

avoid such references) exalts form over substance to such a degree that even the author rebels. Therefore, unless the context makes it clear that a distinction is intended, the present work will utilize the terms "indigenous peoples," "indigenous populations," and "indigenous communities" interchangeably.

278 It is, of course, impossible to generalize about an entire continent or to enter into much detail given the limited focus and length of the present chapter. In addition to the UN Indigenous Study, reference might be made to several reports by the Minority Rights Group [MRG] on indigenous groups in the Western Hemisphere: Hugh O'Shaughnessy and Stephen Corry, *What Future for the Amerindians of South America?* (London: MRG Report No. 15, rev.ed. 1977); James Wilson, *Canada's Indians* (London: MRG Report No. 21, rev. ed. 1982); James Wilson, *The Original Americans: U.S. Indians* (London: MRG Report No. 31, rev. ed. 1980); Ian Creery, *The Inuit (Eskimo) of Canada* (London: MRG Report No. 60, 1983); and David Stephen and Phillip Wearne, *Central America's Indians* (London: MRG Report No. 62, 1984).

veloped, which often led to segregation of some indigenous groups under colonial administration.[279] This presented problems in the post-colonial period, as many indigenous groups which had been under separate colonial administration, and which had little contact or affinity with the new dominant culture, made vigorous attempts to secede from the new state.

The fact that many North American Indian nations entered into treaties with various governments, including Canada, France, Great Britain, and the United States, made little difference in terms of the discrimination and land seizures to which they were subjected. While the existence of treaties has had some significant domestic legal impact in recent years, their breach has been of no more concern to the international community than the breach of countless treaties among European states, many of which were created or destroyed by acts of so-called Great Powers irrespective of treaty obligations.[280]

The North American Indian nations which entered into treaties with the European settler states from the seventeenth to nineteenth centuries obviously were subjects of international law, but their status as "indigenous" nations or states had no international legal relevance.[281] Indigenous rights, unlike the rights of religious and other minorities, were never recognized as separate issues of international concern. In fact, apart from treaties to which Indian nations themselves were parties and the agreement which established the Inter-American Indian Institute in 1940,[282] no multilateral treaty or agreement addressed the issue of indigenous rights per se prior to the adoption of International Labour Organisation (ILO) Convention No. 107 in 1957.[283]

279 For the early legal development of indigenous rights in North America, *cf.* Gordon I. Bennett, "Aboriginal Title in the Common Law: A Stony Path Through Feudal Doctrine," 27 Buffalo L. Rev. 617 (1978); Howard R. Berman, "The Concept of Aboriginal Rights in the Early Legal History of the United States," *id.* at 637.

280 In 1987, the UN Sub-Commission on Prevention of Discrimination and Protection of Minorities proposed a study of indigenous-state treaties and their contemporary significance. A discussion of the proposed study, with a slightly altered scope, may be found in UN Sub-Commission on Prevention of Discrimination and Protection of Minorities, *Report of the Working Group on Indigenous Populations on its sixth session*, UN Doc. E/CN.4/Sub.2/1988/24 (1988) at 25–30.

281 But compare John Howard Clinebell and Jim Thomson, "Sovereignty and Self-Determination: The Rights of Native Americans Under International Law," 27 Buffalo L. Rev. 669 (1978).

282 Convention providing for the creation of the Inter-American Indian Institute, opened for signature 1 Nov. 1940, 56 Stat. 1303, TS No. 978.

283 Convention Concerning the Protection and Integration of Indigenous and Other Tribal and Semi-Tribal Populations in Independent Countries (I.L.O. No. 107), signed 26 June 1957, 328 U.N.T.S. 247 [hereinafter cited as "ILO Convention No. 107"]. Several other ILO conventions (Nos. 50, 58, 59, 64, and 65), do refer to indigenous workers in

The ILO has been a significant exception among international organizations in addressing the particular issue of indigenous peoples, within its mandate of workers' rights and working conditions.[284] As early as 1921, the ILO carried out a series of studies on indigenous workers, and a Committee of Experts on Native Labour was established in 1926. The latter's recommendations led to the adoption of a number of conventions and recommendations in the 1930s, concerned with, *inter alia*, forced labor and recruitment practices. Another Committee of Experts on Indigenous Labour first met in 1951; the instruments which followed from its recommendations were largely concerned with encouraging states to extend legislative provisions generally to all segments of their population, including indigenous communities, and calling for improved education, vocational training, social security, and protection in the field of labor for indigenous peoples. In 1953, the ILO published a comprehensive reference book entitled *Indigenous Peoples: Living and Working Conditions of Aboriginal Populations in Independent Countries*, which surveyed indigenous populations throughout the world and summarized national and international action to aid them.[285]

ILO Convention No. 107, and its accompanying Recommendation 104, reflect the common view of the 1940s and 1950s, insofar as their primary goals are assimilation/integration and non-discrimination. Despite its shortcomings, Convention No. 107 does recognize the right of collective and individual indigenous land ownership, indigenous customary laws, and the right to compensation for land taken by the government. The ILO monitors compliance with the convention through its normal oversight procedures, in particular through the Committee of Experts on the Application of Conventions and Recommendations.[286]

non-metropolitan territories. See *Analytical compilation of existing legal instruments and proposed draft standards relating to indigenous rights*, prepared by the Secretariat in accordance with Sub-Commission resolution 1985/22, UN Doc. M/HR/86/36 (n.d.[1986]), at 3 n.1.

284 See 1 UN Indigenous Study at 42–70; ILO Working Document entitled *International Standards and Indigenous and Tribal Populations*, presented to the ILO Meeting of Experts on the Revision of the Indigenous and Tribal Populations Convention, 1957 (No. 107), Geneva,1–10 Sept. 1986, at 4–10.

285 Studies and Reports, New Series, No. 35 (Geneva: ILO, 1953).

286 See generally the annual *Report of the Committee of Experts on the Application of Conventions and Recommendations (General Report and Observations concerning Particular Countries)*, which is submitted to the International Labour Conferences. *Cf.* Lee Swepston, "Human Rights Complaint Procedures of the International Labor Organization," in Hurst Hannum (ed.), *Guide to International Human Rights Practice* (Philadelphia: Univ. of Pennsylvania Press, 1984) at 59–73. In recent years, the Committee of Experts has made comments on the situations in Argentina, Bangladesh, Bolivia, Brazil, Colombia, Ecuador, India, Panama, Pakistan, Paraguay, and Peru.

Pressure to revise Convention No. 107 grew, particularly with the increasing activity of indigenous NGOs at the United Nations, and in November 1986 the ILO Governing Body approved initiation of the process for such a revision.[287] The draft proposed following the 1988 International Labor Conference would, *inter alia*, refer to the communities concerned as "peoples" rather than "populations";[288] eliminate the convention's present advocacy of integration; provide that governments should "seek the consent" of indigenous peoples regarding legislative and administrative measures which affect them, including the exploitation of natural resources; call for the involvement of indigenous peoples "to the extent possible" in development plans; provide that "[s]pecial measures should be taken to safeguard the control of the peoples concerned over natural resources pertaining to their traditional territories"; and recommend that "due regard" be given to customary indigenous law, in the application of national laws to indigenous peoples.[289] Following preliminary approval and the solicitation of the views of governments, it is anticipated that a revised convention will be adopted at the ILO General Conference in 1989.

Other international human rights instruments are relevant to indigenous peoples, although none considers indigenous rights specifically.[290] In particular, one might note adoption of the Genocide Convention in 1948 and various UN activities directed against racial discrimination and slavery. For example, country reports under article 9 of the Convention on the Elimination of All Forms of Racial Discrimination frequently refer to a state's treatment of indigenous peoples within its jurisdiction.[291] The Working Group on Slavery, established in 1974 by the UN Sub-Commission on Prevention of Discrimination and Protection of Minorities, has recognized that "a special problem exists in countries with indigenous populations who might be vulnerable to exploitation, such as debt bondage and other slavery-like practices."[292]

---

287 For a summary of the 1986 meeting of experts which preceded the Governing Board's decision, see Russell L. Barsh, "Revision of ILO Convention No. 107," 81 Am. J. Int'l L. 756 (1987); Scott Leckie, "Indigenous Peoples, Recent Developments in the International Labour Organization," SIM [Studie- en Informatiecentrum Mensenrechten/ Netherlands Institute of Human Rights] Newsletter (No. 16, Nov. 1986) at 22, 25–39.

288 See discussion *infra*, at 95–103.

289 See International Labour Conference, 75th sess., Report VI(2), *Partial revision of the Indigenous and Tribal Populations Convention, 1957 (No. 107)* (Geneva: ILO, 1988) at 105–12. A summary of the major issues involved in the revision, including lengthy excerpts from the report of the 1986 meeting of experts, may be found in *id.*, Report VI(1) (1988).

290 *Cf.* 1 UN Indigenous Study at 7–24.

291 See *infra* note 308.

292 1 UN Indigenous Study at 17.

The Organization of American States (OAS), within the jurisdiction of whose members many of the world's indigenous peoples are found, has adopted no formal instrument concerned with indigenous rights, although it did establish the Inter-American Indian Institute in 1940. The Inter-American Indian Institute is now a specialized agency of the OAS; it acts as a standing committee to organize periodic Inter-American Indian Conferences (which are considered organs of the OAS) and also provides advisory services and technical services to OAS member states.[293] The Inter-American Commission on Human Rights expressed some concern over indigenous rights in the early 1970s[294] and has considered serious violations of human rights against indigenous individuals and communities in cases or reports concerning, for example, Brazil, Colombia, Guatemala, Nicaragua, and Paraguay.[295]

One explanation for this lack of international attention to indigenous rights until recent years is the diversity of indigenous groups and of the domestic legal regimes under which they live.[296] The status of indigenous groups and particular policies affecting them are set forth in constitutional provisions, statutes, and judicial decisions. In many cases, general provisions concerning equality and non-discrimination may be supple-

293 *Cf.* 1 UN Indigenous Study at 140–45; Inter-American Commission on Human Rights, *Inter-American Yearbook on Human Rights 1969–1970* (Washington, DC: OAS, 1976) at 73–83.

294 See Inter-American Comm. Human Rights, *Report on the Work Accomplished by the Inter-American Commission on Human Rights during its 29th Session* (Oct. 16–27, 1972), OAS Doc. OAS/Ser.L/V/II.29 doc. 40 rev. 1 (1973) at 63–65; *id.*, *Ten Years of Activities 1971–1981* (Washington, DC: OAS, 1982) at 328–29.

295 See, e.g., Case No. 7615 (Brazil), Inter-American Commission on Human Rights, *Annual Report 1984–1985*, OAS Doc. OEA/Ser.L/V/II.66, doc. 10 rev.1, at 24–34; Case No. 1690 (Colombia), *id.*, *Report on the Work Accomplished by the Inter-American Commission on Human Rights during Its 29th Session*, *supra* note 294, at 26–28; *id.*, *Report on the Situation of Human Rights in the Republic of Guatemala*, OAS Doc. OEA/Ser.L/V/II.61, doc. 47 rev. 1 (1983) at 60–70; *id.*, *Report on the Situation of Human Rights of a Segment of the Nicaraguan Population of Miskito Origin*, OAS Doc. OEA/Ser.L/V/II.62, doc.26 (1984) [hereinafter cited as "IACHR Miskito Report"]; Case 1802 (Paraguay), reprinted in *Ten Years of Activities*, *supra* note 294, at 151–52. The Brazilian, Colombian, and Paraguayan cases are examined in Shelton H. Davis, *Land Rights and Indigenous Peoples* (Cambridge, MA: Cultural Survival Report 29, 1988); also see discussion of Brazil, *infra* chap. 18, at 412–19.

296 *Cf.* 2 UN Indigenous Study at 107–38. A good general survey of the current position of many indigenous communities may be found in Independent Commission on International Humanitarian Issues, *Indigenous Peoples, A Global Quest for Justice* (London and New Jersey: Zed Books, 1987) [hereinafter cited as "*Global Quest*"]. For a summary of the legal status of indigenous peoples in ten Latin American countries in the late 1970s, see Lee Swepston, "The Indian in Latin America: Approaches to Administration, Integration, and Protection," 27 Buffalo L. Rev. 715 (1978).

mented by exceptions for measures intended to promote "backward," "tribal," or "aboriginal" peoples; other provisions may impose a general legal obligation on the state to assist or promote the economic and social development of indigenous groups. For example, the constitutions of India and Pakistan contained detailed provisions regarding "scheduled tribes" and "tribal areas," respectively, which establish semi-autonomous areas under the direct administration of the central government;[297] India also reserves seats for tribal representatives in the central or state (provincial) legislatures.[298]

It is not clear whether a special legal status exists for indigenous peoples in many countries, despite obvious distinctions in many instances between indigenous and other peoples within a state's jurisdiction. In general, domestic treatment of indigenous peoples falls into two categories. In the first category, the state accords a special legal status which seeks to protect indigenous inhabitants and free them from certain civil obligations, but which also limits their enjoyment of certain rights. The second approach recognizes that indigenous inhabitants possess all the rights and obligations of other nationals of a country, but it also takes account of their special needs as is done with respect to other "disadvantaged" groups.

The legal status accorded indigenous populations within the first group of states varies widely. In Paraguay, for example, there was no general law on indigenous peoples prior to the 1980s; the great majority of Indians were not considered to be full citizens.[299] Canada and the United States consider that Indians, at least those on reservations or reserves, are self-governing for certain purposes, although Indian activities remain ultimately subject to federal jurisdiction. Brazil and Colombia recognize different categories of indigenous peoples, depending on their degree of integration into the dominant society.

Among the second group of countries, which generally provide certain special services or programs for indigenous groups within an overall context of legal equality, are Argentina, Australia, Costa Rica, Finland, Guatemala, Guyana, Indonesia, Japan, Malaysia, New Zealand, Norway, Philippines, and Sweden.[300] However, "in all countries, whether developed or developing, unitary or federal and wherever they may be located and whatever their background may be, there is discrimination in fact even when full equality may have been formally proclaimed in

---

297 Indian Const., arts. 338–340; Pakistani Const., Part XI, chap. 3.
298 Indian Const., arts. 330 and 332.
299 2 UN Indigenous Study at 120–21.
300 *Id*. at 128–38.

law. . . . Actual behaviour is often very far from what has been foreseen in juridical norms."[301]

Many governments have established administrative agencies to deal with indigenous affairs and/or special programs to deal with health, housing, education, employment, and other issues of concern to indigenous communities, as indigenous people are often among the poorest members of society, living either in isolated rural areas or in urban slums. Nevertheless, indigenous peoples consistently assert that "none of the forms of autonomy and self-determination which the indigenous populations require as essential to their adequate development is applied satisfactorily in practice."[302]

"The policies followed in a great many States were based on the assumption that indigenous populations, cultures and languages would disappear naturally or by absorption into other segments of the population and the 'national culture'."[303] Thus, states often have been aggressively hostile to indigenous languages and indigenous-controlled education and have attempted to stimulate state unity through "acts of imposition and cultural intolerance, and even 'forced' conversion to the religions of the dominant groups and pressure or intimidation to abandon the practice of certain rites and ceremonies."[304]

One consistent feature of these various domestic arrangements is that the central state government retains ultimate authority over indigenous peoples. Since indigenous peoples (unlike some minorities) have not enjoyed the support of ethnically related neighboring states, the lack of international attention to the situation of indigenous peoples until the mid-1970s is hardly surprising (although there has always been a certain interest in Indian affairs in Latin America).

RECENT DEVELOPMENTS

In 1949, Bolivia proposed establishing a sub-commission of the UN Social Commission to study "the social problems of the aboriginal populations of the American continent," but the resolution ultimately adopted only called upon the Economic and Social Council to undertake a study on the situation of indigenous peoples. Even this was too much for some countries (including the United States, Brazil, Peru, and Venezuela), and a subsequent resolution effectively barred any such studies unless requested by affected member states.[305] No requests were forth-

---

301 *Id.* at 140.
302 UN Indigenous Study Conclusions at 8.
303 *Id.* at 17.
304 *Id.* at 20.
305 *Cf.* 1 UN Indigenous Study at 25–27.

coming, and this initiative ended UN concern with the general problems of indigenous peoples for two decades.

In 1971, the UN Sub-Commission on Prevention of Discrimination and Protection of Minorities appointed a Special Rapporteur to study the problem of discrimination against indigenous populations. His voluminous report,[306] which was not completed until 1983, served as a vehicle for increasing international interest in indigenous problems and involvement by indigenous nongovernmental organizations at the international level.

During the 1970s, international human rights standards and procedures also became increasingly visible and relevant. Indigenous peoples were victims of many of the worst human rights violations, and indigenous organizations and other NGOs were able to link their specific concerns regarding indigenous rights with more general human rights developments.

UN activities in the area of racial discrimination also highlighted the situation of indigenous peoples. A 1969 Sub-Commission study on racial discrimination included a chapter on indigenous peoples,[307] and numerous state reports under the Convention on the Elimination of All Forms of Racial Discrimination (which entered into force in 1969) also contain references to the treatment of indigenous peoples.[308] The con-

306 *Supra* note 276.

307 United Nations, *Special Study on Racial Discrimination in the Political, Economic, Social and Cultural Spheres* (Hernan Santa Cruz, Special Rapporteur), UN Sales No. E.71.XIV.2 (New York: United Nations, 1971), chap. IX. In light of the pending study by Martinez Cobo, *supra*, note 276, this chapter was deleted in the 1976 revision. See *id.*, *Racial Discrimination*, UN Sales No. E.76.XIV.2 (New York: United Nations, 1977) at v–vi.

308 Those reports which make specific reference to indigenous populations include (only the most recent report available is cited): Argentina, art. 9 CERD Report, UN Doc. CERD/C/149/Add.1 (1986) at 3; Australia, art. 9 CERD Report, UN Doc. CERD/C/115/Add.3 (1985) at 3 (referring to "special and concrete measures" to assist Aboriginal Australians); Bolivia, art. 9 CERD Report, UN Doc. CERD/C/107/Add.1 (1983); Brazil, art. 9 CERD Report, UN Doc. CERD/C/149/Add.3 (1986) at 3, 8–12 (referring to the work of FUNAI); Canada, art. 9 CERD Report, UN Doc. CERD/C/132/Add.3 (1986) at 10; Central African Republic, art. 9 CERD Report, UN Doc. CERD/C/117/Add.5 (1985) at 3; Chile, art. 9 CERD Report, UN Doc. CERD/C/117/Add.3 (1985) at 3–10 (referring to the ownership rights of the Mapuche); China, art. 9 CERD Report, UN Doc. CERD/C/126/Add.1 (1985) (referrring to "national minorities"); Colombia, art. 9 CERD Report, UN Doc. CERD/C/112/Add.1 (1984) at 6–8 (referring to a program to maintain indigenous reserves); Costa Rica, art. 9 CERD Report, UN Doc. CERD/C/118/Add.31 (1985) at 3; Cyprus, art. 9 CERD Report, UN Doc. CERD/C/118/Add.13 (1984) at 14–15 (referring to Turkish racial discrimination against the indigenous Greek Cypriot population); Ecuador, art. 9 CERD Report, UN Doc. CERD/C/118/Add.4 (1984) (referring to land reform); Finland, art. 9 CERD Report, UN Doc. CERD/C/132/Add.1 (1985) (referring to the Saami "ethnic minority"); India, art. 9 CERD Report, UN Doc.

cluding declaration of the 1978 World Conference to Combat Racism and Racial Discrimination refers specifically to both minorities and indigenous peoples, endorsing "the right of indigenous peoples to maintain their traditional structure of economy and culture, including their own language, and also recogniz[ing] the special relationship of indigenous peoples to their land and stress[ing] that their land, land rights and natural resources should not be taken away from them."[309]

Perhaps the most significant international activity has been the convening of several major NGO conferences, notable in particular for the fact that they were largely gatherings of indigenous peoples themselves and their representatives.[310] Among the most important of these conferences were two Inuit Circumpolar Conferences (Alaska, 1977, and Greenland, 1980), three General Assemblies of the World Council of Indigenous Peoples (Sweden, 1977; Australia, 1981; and Panama, 1984), the International NGO Conference on Discrimination against Indigenous Populations in the Americas (Geneva, 1977), the First Congress of Indian Movements of South America (Peru, 1980), and the International NGO Conference on Indigenous Peoples and the Land (Geneva, 1981).

CERD/C/20/Add.34 (1980) (referring to the Scheduled Tribes, which India denies are "indigenous"); Luxembourg, art. 9 CERD Report, UN Doc. CERD/C/128/Add.2 (1986) at 3–4 (referring to promoting understanding between immigrant groups and the "indigenous" population of Luxembourg); Mexico, art. 9 CERD Report, UN Doc. CERD/C/115/Add.1 (1984); New Zealand, art. 9 CERD Report, UN Doc. CERD/C/131/Add.9 (1986) (referring to programs to assist the Maori); Nicaragua, art. 9 CERD Report, UN Doc. CERD/C/128/Add.1 (1985) at 6–7; Norway, art. 9 CERD Report, UN Doc. CERD/C/107/Add.4 (1984) at 13 (referring to the Saami); Pakistan, art. 9 CERD Report, UN Doc. CERD/C/149/Add.12 (1986) at 4–7 (referring to "tribals"); Panama, art. 9 CERD Report, UN Doc. CERD/C/149/Add.4 (1986) at 14–20 (referring to the Cuna, Guaymi, and Embera); Papua New Guinea, art. 9 CERD Report, UN Doc. CERD/C/101/Add.4 (1983) at 6–11 (referring to the abolition of colonial laws which discriminated against the indigenous population); Peru, art. 9 CERD Report, UN Doc. CERD/C/90/Add.7 (1983) at 2; Philippines, art. 9 CERD Report, UN Doc. CERD/C/118/Add.30 (1985) at 3–8 (referring to "cultural minorities"); Rwanda, art. 9 CERD Report, UN Doc. CERD/C/115/Add.2 (1985) at 4 (referring to the "backward" Batwa "minority"); Sri Lanka, art. 9 CERD Report, UN Doc. CERD/C/126/Add.2 (1985), Annex 2; Sweden, art. 9 CERD Report, UN Doc. CERD/C/131/Add.2 (1985) at 7–9 (referring to the Saami); Trinidad and Tobago, art. 9 CERD Report, UN Doc. CERD/C/116/Add.3 (1986) at 2; Tunisia, art. 9 CERD Report, UN Doc. CERD/C/118/Add.27 (1985) at 4; U.S.S.R., art. 9 CERD Report, UN Doc. CERD/C/149/Add.8 (1986) at 6 (referring to "indigenous nationalities"); and Venezuela, art. 9 CERD Report, UN Doc. CERD/C/118/Add.24 (1985) at 4–6. Also see discussion of various CERD Reports on gypsy and other "minorities" in chap. 2.

309 Quoted in 1 UN Indigenous Study at 31.

310 For a summary of these and other meetings, see 1 UN Indigenous Study at 148–201.

Partly in response to recommendations contained in the UN Indigenous Study and the 1981 Geneva Conference on Indigenous Peoples and the Land, creation of a pre-sessional Working Group on Indigenous Populations of the UN Sub-Commission on Prevention of Discrimination and Protection of Minorities was approved by the Economic and Social Council; the group's first annual meeting was held in August 1982.[311] The mandate of the Working Group extends to the review of developments pertaining to the protection of the human rights of indigenous populations and to the development of international standards for indigenous rights.[312]

The Working Group has become the primary focus of international activities by both governments and nongovernmental organizations concerned with indigenous peoples, and its sessions are now held in the same large conference room at the Palais des Nations in Geneva in which the Commission on Human Rights meets. Its five members are drawn from different regions, according to standard UN practice, and all serve in their individual capacity (as do other members of the Sub-Commission).

At its first session, the Working Group took the almost unprecedented step of allowing oral (and written) interventions from all indigenous organizations which wished to participate in its work, not limiting such participation to those with formal consultative status. Approximately 380 persons took part in its sixth session in 1988, including representatives from over 70 indigenous organizations and observers from 33 countries.[313] As a result of this wide participation, the Working Group has provided a meaningful forum for the exchange of proposals regarding indigenous rights and for the exposition of indigenous reality throughout the world. While the Working Group reiterates at each session that it is not a "chamber of complaints" and has no authority to hear allegations of human rights violations, it has nevertheless permitted very direct criticisms of government practices by NGOs, as a means of gathering data upon which standards will eventually be based.[314]

311 See generally Gudmundur Alfredsson, "Fourth Session of the Working Group on Indigenous Populations," 55 Nordic J. Int'l L. 22 (1986); Barsh, *supra* note 276.

312 ESC Res. 1982/34, UN ESCOR, Supp. (No. 1), UN Doc. E/1982/82 (1982) at 26–27.

313 *Report of the Working Group on Indigenous Populations on its sixth session*, *supra* note 280, at 3–5.

314 See, e.g., *Report of the Working Group on Indigenous Populations on its fourth session*, UN Doc. E/CN.4/Sub.2/1985/22 (1985) at 6; *id.* (second session), UN Doc. E/CN.4/Sub.2/1983/22 (1983) at 8, 17. The Working Group's other reports to date may be found in UN Docs. E/CN.4/Sub.2/1982/33 (1982), E/CN.4/Sub.2/1984/20 (1984), and E/CN.4/Sub.2/1987/22 (1987).

The early sessions of the Working Group were devoted largely to collecting data, that is, receiving information from indigenous and other NGOs as to the actual situation of indigenous peoples under assault from dominant societies. While neither an exhaustive nor a specific catalog of allegations can be included here, the most common violations alleged concerned arbitrary arrests, torture, and killings, which constituted genocide or "ethnocide" in the view of some; seizure of indigenous lands, either through settlement or pursuant to state-defined development projects, such as hydroelectric projects or large-scale mining or agricultural projects; and the attempted destruction of indigenous culture and identity through, *inter alia*, desecration or destruction of religious sites. Frequent references have been made to the economic gap between indigenous and dominant populations, both in terms of existing social services provided by the government and the exploitation of natural resources on indigenous lands without either indigenous consent or adequate compensation.

The review of developments related to the human rights of indigenous peoples continues to form an important segment of the Working Group's activity, but since 1985 it has begun to focus on developing a draft declaration on the rights of indigenous populations. From the perspective of international law, this declaration will probably be the most significant development to date in the area of indigenous rights.

The Working Group developed fourteen "draft principles" based on discussions through its first five sessions,[315] and it subsequently requested its Chairman/Rapporteur to prepare a full draft declaration. Although this draft "Universal Declaration on Indigenous Rights" was described as "a very preliminary first draft" when presented to the Working Group in 1988,[316] the principles it sets forth are worth quoting in full:

1. The right to the full and effective enjoyment of all fundamental rights and freedoms, as well as the observance of the corresponding responsibilities, which are universally recognized in the Charter of the United Nations and in existing international human rights instruments.
2. The right to be free and equal to all the other human beings in dignity and rights to be free from adverse distinction or discrimination of any kind.
3. The collective right to exist and to be protected against genocide, as well as the individual rights to life, physical integrity, liberty and security of person.
4. The collective right to maintain and develop their ethnic and cultural

315 *Report of the Working Group on Indigenous Populations on its fifth session, supra* note 314, Annex II.

316 *Report of the Working Group on Indigenous Populations on its sixth session, supra* note 280, at 17.

characteristics and identity, including the right of peoples and individuals to call themselves by their proper names.

5. The collective right to protection against ethnocide. This protection shall include, in particular, prevention of any act which has the aim or effect of depriving them of their ethnic characteristics or identity, of any form of forced assimilation or integration, of imposition of foreign life styles and of any propaganda directed against them.

6. The right to preserve their cultural identity and traditions and to pursue their own cultural development. The rights to the manifestations of their cultures, including archeological sites, artifacts, designs, technology and works of art, lie with the indigenous peoples or their members.

7. The duty of States to grant—within the resources available—the necessary assistance for the maintenance of their identity and their development.

8. The right to manifest, teach, practise and observe their own religious traditions and ceremonies, and to maintain, protect and have access to sacred sites and burial grounds for these purposes.

9. The right to maintain and use their own languages, including for administrative, judicial and other relevant purposes.

10. The right to all forms of education, including in particular the right of children to have access to education in their own languages, and to establish, structure, conduct and control their own educational systems and institutions.

11. The right to promote intercultural information and education, recognizing the dignity and diversity of their cultures, and the duty of States to take the necessary measures, among other sections of the national community, with the object of eliminating prejudices and of fostering understanding and good relations.

12: The right of ownership and possession of the lands which they have traditionally occupied. The lands may only be taken away from them with their free and informed consent as witnessed by a treaty or agreement.

13. The right to recognition of their own land-tenure systems for the protection and promotion of the use, enjoyment and occupancy of the land.

14. The right to special measures to ensure their control over surface resources pertaining to the territories they have traditionally occupied, including flora and fauna, waters and sea ice.

15. The right to reclaim land and surface resources or where this is not possible, to seek just and fair compensation for the same, when the property has been taken away from them without consent, in particular, if such deprival has been based on theories such as those related to discovery, *terra nullius*, waste lands or idle lands. Compensation, if the parties agree, may take the form of land or resources of quality and legal status at least equal to that of the property previously owned by them.

16. The right to protection against any action or course of conduct which may result in the destruction, deterioration or pollution of their land, air, water, sea ice, wildlife or other resources without free and informed consent of the indigenous peoples affected. The right to just and fair compensation for any such action or course of conduct.

17. The duty of States to seek and obtain their consent, through appropriate mechanisms, before undertaking or permitting any programmes for the exploration or exploitation of mineral and other subsoil resources pertaining to their traditional territories. Just and fair compensation should be provided for any such activities undertaken.

18. The right to maintain within their areas of settlement their traditional economic structures and ways of life, to be secure in the enjoyment of their own traditional means of subsistence, and to engage freely in their traditional and other economic activities, including hunting, fresh- and salt-water fishing, herding, gathering, lumbering and cultivation, without adverse discrimination. In no case may an indigenous people be deprived of its means of subsistence. The right to just and fair compensation if they have been so deprived.

19. The right to special State measures for the immediate, effective and continuing improvement of their social and economic conditions, with their consent, that reflect their own priorities.

20. The right to determine, plan and implement all health, housing and other social and economic programmes affecting them, as far as possible through their own institutions.

21. The right to participate fully in the political, economic and social life of their State and to have their specific character duly reflected in the legal system and in political institutions, including proper regard to and recognition of indigenous laws and customs.

22. The right to participate fully at the State level, through representatives chosen by themselves, in decision-making about and implementation of all national and international matters which may affect their life and destiny.

23. The collective right to autonomy in matters relating to their own internal and local affairs, including education, information, culture, religion, health, housing, social welfare, traditional and other economic activities, land and resources administration and the environment, as well as internal taxation for financing these autonomous functions.

24. The right to decide upon the structures of their autonomous institutions, to select the membership of such institutions, and to determine the membership of the indigenous people concerned for these purposes.

25. The right to determine the responsibilities of individuals to their own community, consistent with universally recognized human rights and fundamental freedoms.

26. The right to traditional contacts and co-operation, including cultural and social exchanges and trade, with their own kith and kin across State boundaries in accordance with established laws and practices.

27. The duty of States to honour treaties and other agreements concluded with indigenous peoples.

28. The individual and collective right to access to and prompt decision by mutually acceptable and fair procedures for resolving conflicts or disputes between States and indigenous peoples, groups or individuals. These procedures should include, as appropriate, negotiations, mediation, national courts and international human rights review and complaints mechanisms.[317]

This preliminary draft declaration will no doubt undergo substantial revision before it is ultimately submitted through the appropriate channels to the UN General Assembly, and final adoption of a Universal Declaration on Indigenous Rights should not be expected before the mid-1990s.

317 *Id.*, Annex II (preamble omitted).

SUBSTANTIVE ISSUES OF INDIGENOUS RIGHTS

Defining "indigenous"

As is true for the concepts of "minority" and "people," it has thus far proved impossible to arrive at a commonly accepted definition of "indigenousness." Among the criteria which have been utilized in defining indigenous groups or individuals are ancestry, culture (including religion, dress, livelihood, and living as a member of a tribal system), language, residence, group consciousness or self-identification, and acceptance by an indigenous community.[318]

Indigenous groups emphasize their right to define themselves, both in terms of individual self-identification and with respect to the community's right to define its members. This "subjective" criterion has been widely accepted, although it is not clear whether it would be sufficient if other "objective" criteria (e.g., ancestry) were not also present.[319] It is also uncertain whether an ethnically indigenous individual would lose whatever legal rights and obligations accrue to an "indigenous" person, if, for example, he or she were expelled from the indigenous community or chose to become fully assimilated into the dominant society.

The UN Indigenous Study eventually offered the following definition "for the purposes of international action that may be taken affecting their [indigenous populations'] future existence":

318 See 2 UN Indigenous Study at 3–70; also see *Global Quest, supra* note 296, at 5–11.

319 In the United States, for example, a non-Indian adopted into an indigenous group cannot participate in federal programs designed for indigenous groups; in Malaysia, adoption and membership in an indigenous community *do* create indigenous status. 2 UN Indigenous Study at 65. In the only international decision to address this question, the Human Rights Committee has found that withdrawal of an Indian woman's right to reside on a Canadian Indian reserve because of her marriage to a non-Indian (despite a subsequent divorce) violated her right, "in community with the other members of [her] group, to enjoy [her] own culture," guaranteed by art. 27 of the Covenant on Civil and Political Rights. Lovelace v. Canada, *supra* note 224. Canada's defense with respect to charges that the Indian Act also was discriminatory on the grounds of sex (the same provision did not apply to Indian men who married non-Indian women) relied on, *inter alia*, the patrilineal nature of Indian society and the fact that a "change in the law could only be sought in consultation with the Indians themselves who, however, were divided on the issue of equal rights." The Committee did not directly address the question of whether Ms. Lovelace had lost her status as an Indian, although it seems to have implicitly decided that the Maliseet Indian band from which she came remained the group of which she was a part; there was no evidence presented that the band objected to her residing on the reserve.

Indigenous communities, peoples and nations are those which, having a historical continuity with pre-invasion and pre-colonial societies that developed on their territories, consider themselves distinct from other sectors of the societies now prevailing in those territories, or parts of them. They form at present non-dominant sectors of society and are determined to preserve, develop and transmit to future generations their ancestral territories, and their ethnic identity, as the basis of their continued existence as peoples, in accordance with their own cultural patterns, social institutions and legal systems. . . .

On an individual basis, an indigenous person is one who belongs to these indigenous populations through self-identification as indigenous (group consciousness) and is recognized and accepted by these populations as one of its members (acceptance by the group).[320]

The Working Group grappled with the question of defining "indigenous" during its second and third sessions, and there was particular interest on the part of some governments (such as India and Bangladesh) in limiting the definition to those peoples in the Western Hemisphere and Australasia.[321] Ultimately, the working group opted for a "flexible" approach which would not require formal adoption of a definition, although some governments (e.g., China and the U.S.S.R., in addition to India and Bangladesh) continue to maintain a questionable equation between colonization and indigenousness, denying that there are any "indigenous" peoples within their territories.[322]

The contemporary movement for the international recognition of indigenous rights originated largely with North American Indians, aboriginal peoples from Australia, and northern indigenous groups such as the Inuit and Saami. Despite some efforts to impose a "blue water" criterion in defining pre-invasion indigenous peoples, it seems clear that Asian "hill tribes," such as the Karen and Hmong, and Arab and African nomadic tribes who pursue traditional life-styles, also should be included in a common-sense understanding of "indigenous." Less certain would be the inclusion of central Asian peoples such as the Armenians, Baluchis, Tatars, and Kurds, or survivors of overland invasions by peoples of similar race, such as occurred in Africa and much of Asia.

Another difficulty in arriving at an acceptable definition is the extraordinarily wide variety of groups that most observers would concede are "indigenous." The traditions, life-style, and political structure of

320 UN Indigenous Study Conclusions at 50, 51.

321 *Report of the Working Group on its second session, supra* note 314, at 22–23; *cf.* Barsh, *supra* note 276, at 373–76.

322 See Barsh, *supra* note 311, at 375; statement by the representative of India to the Working group, 6 Aug. 1987, at 6 (on file with author); *cf. Report of the Working Group on its third session, supra* note 314, at 18–20; *Report of the Working Group on its fourth session, supra* note 314, at 15–16.

sophisticated North American Indian nations such as the Haudenosaunee would seem to have little in common with Brazilian forest-dwellers, despite the similarities in the attacks on each by the dominant societies. However, these seemingly disparate societies may well share spiritual values associated with living communally and in harmony with nature. The existence of a continuing government is characteristic of many indigenous peoples in the Western Hemisphere, but it is hardly applicable to the small, isolated tribes of Papua New Guinea (although every society, no matter its size, obviously has some social structure which exercises governmental or quasi-governmental authority).

The most significant characteristic of indigenous peoples may be what might be termed their pre-modern or pre-industrial life-styles, including a communally oriented economic system. This designation connotes no positive value judgment on modernity, but it is the centralized, urban, technologically sophisticated character of twentieth-century society that is most at odds with the decentralized, rural, technologically traditional societies of the Maori, Inuit, or Hmong. In particular, the impact of technology on culture cannot be underestimated; while it is reasonable to conclude, for example, that reindeer-herding by snowmobile should be considered as "traditional" a Saami activity as reindeer-herding on foot, this technological innovation will change parts of Saami culture as surely as the steam engine and machine gun altered that of Western Europe.

Indigenous groups themselves generally reject the need for definition, on the grounds that only indigenous communities have the right to determine their own members.[323] "At the same time, indigenous groups have reacted vigorously to any suggestion that they are simply a special case of 'minorities.' "[324]

In the end, definitional questions become truly important only if inclusion in or exclusion from a particular definition has legal implications. China does not object to referring to its "national minorities" as "indigenous peoples" on semantic grounds, but because of fears that rights may be developed for indigenous peoples which China does not

323 See, e.g., the Declaration of Principles adopted at the Fourth General Assembly of the World Council of Indigenous Peoples in Panama, September 1984 [hereinafter "WCIP Principles"], reprinted in *Report of the Working Group on its fourth session, supra* note 314, at Annex III, Principle 5; Draft Declaration of Principles proposed by the Indian Law Resource Center, Four Directions Council, National Aboriginal and Islander Legal Service, National Indian Youth Council, Inuit Circumpolar Conference, and the International Indian Treaty Council [hereinafter "NGO Principles"], reprinted in *id.* at Annex IV, Principle 2.

324 Barsh, *supra* note 276, at 376. But compare, e.g., Wagley and Harris, *supra* note 170, who include in their broad survey the cases of Indians in Brazil and Mexico.

believe to be appropriate for "its" ethnic-national minority-indigenous populations. No state objects to complete self-definition by indigenous peoples for social or cultural purposes; many *would* object to such a practice if it necessarily implied state obligations towards the persons or groups so designated or the recognition of certain rights which could be asserted against other public or private parties.

The decision of the Sub-Commission's Working Group not to adopt a formal definition seems appropriate. As demonstrated by the inaction of the Human Rights Commission's working group on minorities,[325] definitional debates can occupy great amounts of time and often add little to the protection of rights—the professed goal of such efforts. As noted by many, the United Nations has made meaningful contributions to the international protection of rights without defining terms such as "peoples" or "self-determination." While this has led to some confusion or inconsistency in difficult cases, there seems to be no need, at least at the present stage, to allow definitional technicalities to stand in the way of addressing the problems admittedly faced by indigenous populations around the world.

Land rights[326]

Indigenous peoples universally emphasize the spiritual nature of their relationship with the land or earth, which is basic to their existence and to their beliefs, customs, traditions, and culture.[327] While the economic benefits that may be obtained from exploitation of natural resources are of increasing importance to many indigenous communities, land is not merely a possession or means of production.

> [A]ll indigenous communities have, and uphold, a complete code of rules of various kinds which are applicable to the tenure and conservation of land as an important factor in the production process, the foundation of family life and the territorial basis for the existence of their people as such. The whole range of emotional, cultural, spiritual and religious considerations is present where the relationship with the land is concerned. . . . The land forms part of their existence. . . .
>
> Between man and the land there was a relationship of a profoundly spiritual and even religious nature. They spoke of Mother Earth and its worship. For all those reasons it was in no way possible to regard it as a mere possession or still less as a commodity. . . . The only rights that were available, and could be granted, to them by tradition and legal custom were usufruct and priority of

325 See chap. 4, at 60–63.

326 See generally 4 UN Indigenous Study at 4–203; *Global Quest, supra* note 296, at 43–67.

327 See, e.g., Dean B. Suagee, "American Indian Religious Freedom and Cultural Resources Management: Protecting Mother Earth's Caretakers," 10 Am. Indian L. Rev. 1 (1982) at 7–12, and sources cited therein.

use of the ancestral plot, with the consequent obligation to make use of it in the manner required by ecology and custom and not to leave it unused indefinitely.

The expropriation, erosion, pillage, improper use and abuse of, and the damage inflicted on, indigenous land are tantamount to destroying the cultural and spiritual legacy of indigenous populations. Forcing them to hand over such land is tantamount to allowing them to be exterminated. In a word, it is ethnocide.[328]

The Chairman of Yarrabah, an aboriginal community in Queensland, Australia, put it aptly when he asked this question: "If we haven't got land rights, what've we got to manage anyway?"[329]

The history of indigenous peoples is, to a large extent, the chronicle of their unsuccessful attempts to defend their land against invaders. While some land was lost through treaties, often accepted by the indigenous parties because of misplaced trust or fraud,[330] much was lost through defeats in war. Morality aside, war was an accepted component of foreign policy at least through the nineteenth century, and conquest has been the common means of acquiring territory from time immemorial. The "manifest destiny" of many states expressed itself through territorial expansion and overseas colonization, and the nature of the conquered or colonized nations was of little concern to the victors.

Land was important to colonial powers only if it could be settled; when the settlers, in turn, formed states, they expanded territorially as European and Asian nations and empires had expanded centuries earlier—by conquering neighboring peoples and seizing their land. While both colonialism and national territorial expansion may have been fa-

328 4 UN Indigenous Study at 28–29, 32.
329 Barbara Miller, *The aspirations of Aborigines living at Yarrabah in relation to local management and human rights* (Canberra: Human Rights Commission, Discussion Paper No. 7, 1986) at 78.
330 *Cf.*, e.g., House of Commons, *Report of the Special Committee on Indian Self-Government in Canada* (Ottawa: House of Commons, Issue No. 40, 1983) [the "Penner Report"] at 105–06: "Indian people see treaties as affirming rights and establishing the sharing of land and resources, while non-Indian governments view treaties as extinguishing Indian rights to land and resources. . . . Indian witnesses considered the non-Indian view of reserves as property provided to Indians by the government to be historically inaccurate. Rather these were areas that Indians reserved for themselves under treaties, or were part of lands that they never surrendered:

> When we established those reserves, . . . they were . . . reserved with sovereignty intact for generations by our people. They were not lands that were acquired by the Crown and granted to us later. The Crown did not have any land to give to us at the time of treaty; we had all the lands. We granted you conditional access to those lands. [Federation of Saskatchewan Indian Nations]"

cilitated by theories of cultural superiority or the need to "civilize" the "natives," the underlying motivations were economic and political.

The legal veneer for the seizure of Indian lands in the Americas was generally provided by the imposition of notions of private property ownership that were unknown and irrelevant to indigenous societies. There was no "title" to indigenous lands, and, even where aboriginal title was recognized, it was often effectively bypassed by collusion between governments and private parties which resulted in the "legal" alienation of vast tracts of indigenous land. In many instances, lands inhabited by indigenous peoples were presumed to be vacant and were claimed by the government on the theory of discovery of a "terra nullius."

The physical genocide of the nineteenth century has largely given way to continuing assaults by governments and private parties on indigenous lands and their sub-soil mineral and oil deposits.[331] These conflicts almost invariably arise in the context of national development plans, and they will undoubtedly remain the major concern of many indigenous groups. While even ILO Convention No. 107 recognizes indigenous rights to collective ownership of land and to compensation for land expropriated by government, its provisions regarding forcible relocation are weak. In addition, many states assert ownership of all rights to sub-soil resources, even if indigenous (or private) ownership of the land itself is recognized.[332] Another common assertion of states to justify incursions onto traditional indigenous land is that such actions are necessary to ensure national security, especially where the indigenous populations are on border areas.[333]

331 Unfortunately, "old-fashioned" massacres and forced colonization of indigenous areas have not entirely ceased, as evidenced most vividly by allegations of massive attacks by Bangladesh against inhabitants of the Chittagong Hill Tracts, in order to promote Bengali settlement in the area. See generally, e.g., Amnesty International, *Torture in Bangladesh 1983–1986* (London: Amnesty International, AI Index ASA 13/14/86, 1986) and sources cited in the bibliography; "In the Hills of Bangladesh, a Conflict Gathers Fury," New York Times, 23 Oct. 1986; "Racism in Bangladesh," Inside Asia (July-Aug. 1986, No. 9) at 28; "Shattered Lives," India Today (15 Mar. 1987) at 76. The U.S. State Department estimates that "close to 300,000" Bengalis have been settled in the Chittagong Hill Tracts in the past decade. U.S. State Dept., *Country Reports on Human Rights Practices for 1986* (Washington, DC: U.S. Gov't Printing Office, 1987) at 1122.

Amnesty International regularly forwards information on human rights violations within AI's mandate to the Sub-Commission's Working Group on Indigenous Populations; a recent submission noted concerns in Bangladesh, Brazil, Chile, Colombia, El Salvador, Guatemala, Iran, Iraq, Mexico, Nicaragua, Peru, Philippines, Turkey, and the United States. UN Doc. E/CN.4/Sub.2/AC.4/1985/WP.4/Add.2 (1985) at 2–5.

332 *Cf.* Leckie, *supra* note 287, at 32–37.

333 This argument is of particular concern in the Amazon basin today. The government of Ecuador has stated, "The first basic reason for colonising the Amazon region

Another issue is that of restitution of indigenous land, whether taken by conquest, in violation of treaty obligations, or through "legal" alienation where indigenous peoples have been unable to prove formal title. It is far beyond the scope of the present chapter even to summarize the land claim cases pending in U.S. and Canadian courts, but one issue that may arise in the course of drafting an international declaration on indigenous rights is whether its provisions—particularly those related to land, restitution, and compensation—will be retroactive.

Indigenous proposals relating to land are clear and absolute, although no state has yet recognized indigenous land rights to the extent proposed. For example, the WCIP Principles submitted to the Sub-Commission's Working Group in 1985 state:

> Indigenous people shall have exclusive rights to their traditional lands and its resources. . . . [W]here the lands and resources of the indigenous peoples have been taken away without their free and informed consent such lands and resources shall be returned.
> The land rights of an indigenous people include surface and subsurface rights, full rights to interior and coastal waters and rights to adequate and exclusive coastal economic zones within the limits of international law.
> No action or course of conduct may be undertaken which, directly or indirectly, may result in the destruction of land, air, water, sea ice, wildlife, habitat or natural resources without the free and informed consent of the indigenous peoples affected.[334]

A similar position is advanced in the NGO Principles submitted to the same session:

> Indigenous nations and peoples are entitled to the permanent control and enjoyment of their aboriginal ancestral-historical territories. This includes surface and subsurface rights, inland and coastal waters, renewable and non-renewable resources, and the economies based on these resources. . . .
> Discovery, conquest, settlement on a theory of *terra nullius* and unilateral legislation are never legitimate bases for States to claim or retain the territories of indigenous nations or peoples.
> In cases where lands taken in violation of these principles have already been settled, the indigenous nation or people concerned is entitled to immediate restitution, including compensation for the loss of use, without extinction of

of the country is to maintain the integrity of the national territory. The best defense which can be given to this part of the national patrimony and to its natural resources . . . is colonisation since this provides the human potential which is necessary for the national security." Quoted in Note by the International Labour Office, *Indigenous and Tribal Peoples and Land Rights*, submitted to the third session of the Working Group on Indigenous Populations, at 68. Also see discussion of Brazil, *infra* chap. 18, at 412–19.

334 WCIP Principles 9 and 10, *supra* note 323.

original title. Indigenous peoples' desire to regain possession and control of sacred sites must always be respected.[335]

Self-determination

There is constant reference by indigenous communities and organizations to the concept of self-determination, which they consider essential in order to be able to control their own destiny. The most straightforward formulation simply asserts that indigenous populations are "peoples" in the internationally recognized sense of that term:

> All indigenous peoples have the right of self-determination. By virtue of this right they may freely determine their political status and freely pursue their economic, social, religious and cultural development.[336]

Other formulations are more specific and, perhaps, more expansive:

> All indigenous nations and peoples have the right to self-determination, by virtue of which they have the right to whatever degree of autonomy or self-government they choose. This includes the right to freely determine their political status, freely pursue their own economic, social, religious and cultural development, and determine their own membership and/or citizenship, without external interference.
>
> No State shall assert any jurisdiction over an indigenous nation or people, or its territory, except in accordance with the freely expressed wishes of the nation or people concerned. . . .
>
> Indigenous nations and peoples may engage in self-defence against State actions in conflict with their right to self-determination.[337]

The content of this asserted right to self-determination varies tremendously, reflecting the diversity of situations in which indigenous peoples find themselves and the diverse character of indigenous groups themselves. Some do aspire to complete independence and statehood, while many others demand autonomy or self-government only in specific areas of competence (such as full control over land and natural resources). A statement prepared by indigenous groups prior to the 1987 session of the Sub-Commission working group emphasizes that freedom of choice is the "most fundamental element of the right to self-determination" and recognizes that indigenous self-determination "may be realized in many ways ranging from the choice of full independence

---

335 NGO Principles 4, 6, and 7, *supra* note 323.
336 WCIP Principle 1, *supra* note 323.
337 NGO Principles 2, 3, and 28, *supra* note 323.

to various forms of autonomy, self-government and participation in the political processes of the state."[338]

Governments tend to equate all demands for "self-determination" with independence and secession, and insistence on this formulation, even when an indigenous group desires a status less than full independence, may inhibit the resolution of claims that are not as wholly incompatible as they first appear. As noted in chapter 3, "self-determination," as that term has been defined thus far by the United Nations, does imply the right (although not the necessity) of independent statehood; it also has been restricted in practice to the colonial context. Thus, negative government reactions to indigenous demands for self-determination are not surprising.[339]

The Inter-American Commission on Human Rights (IACHR) of the Organization of American States is the only international body to have directly addressed the issue of whether indigenous peoples have the right to self-determination. In the context of Miskito Indian complaints of various human rights violations by Nicaragua, primarily in 1981 and 1982, the IACHR considered "whether or not ethnic groups also have additional rights [beyond those set forth in article 27 of the Covenant on Civil and Political Rights], particularly the rights to self-determination or political autonomy."[340]

The present status of international law does recognize observance of the principle of self-determination of peoples, which it considers to be the right of a people to independently choose their form of political organization and to freely establish the means it deems appropriate to bring about their economic,

338 "Statement on Self-Determination by the participants at the Indigenous Peoples Preparatory Meeting", para. 5 [Geneva, Aug. 1987] (on file with author). Underscoring a particular concern with the internal aspects of self-determination, the statement goes on to reject "[s]tate imposition of governmental or organizational systems and forms without consent by the indigenous people concerned . . . even where the ostensible purpose is to provide a measure of self-rule or autonomy." *Id.*, para. 8. *Cf.* Clinebell and Thomson, *supra* note 281.

339 For example, while 26 of the 33 governments which responded to an ILO questionnaire on proposed revisions to ILO Convention No. 107 supported use of the term indigenous "peoples" rather than "populations," Australia, Ecuador, and Sweden specified that this does not imply recognition of an indigenous right to self-determination; Canada and the Netherlands opposed the designation "peoples" on similar grounds. See ILO Report VI(2), *supra* note 289, at 12–14. In the view of the Australian government, Aboriginal self-determination implies only the wish "to put Aboriginals in the position of making decisions about their own future, at the same time accepting responsibility and being accountable for those decisions." *Aboriginal Affairs 1983–1987* (Commonwealth of Australia, 1987) at 10.

340 IACHR Miskito Report, *supra* note 295, at 78.

social and cultural development. This does not mean, however, that it recognizes the right to self-determination of any ethnic group as such.[341]

Citing, *inter alia*, UN General Assembly resolutions 1514 (XV)[342] and 2625 (XXV),[343] the IACHR concluded that the right to self-determination could never justify disrupting the territorial integrity of a sovereign state. It went on to note, however, that the absence of any right to autonomy or self-determination does not grant to Nicaragua "an unrestricted right to impose complete assimilation on those Indians."[344]

> Although the current status of international law does not allow the view that the ethnic groups of the Atlantic zone of Nicaragua have a right to political autonomy and self-determination, special legal protection is recognized for the use of their language, the observance of their religion, and in general, all those aspects related to the preservation of their cultural identity. To this should be added the aspects linked to productive organization, which includes, among other things, the issue of the ancestral and communal lands. . . . [I]t is funda-mental to establish new conditions for coexistence between the ethnic minorities and the Government of Nicaragua, in order to settle historic antagonisms and the serious difficulties present today. In the opinion of the IACHR, the need to preserve and guarantee the observance of these principles in practice entails the need to establish an adequate institutional order as part of the structure of the Nicaraguan state.[345]

Semantics should not obscure the complexity of the issues involved in addressing indigenous calls for sufficient control over their lives to ensure the continuation and development of their own cultures. For example, internal self-determination, or self-government, is likely to be much more significant than external self-determination, or recognition as a state or formal independence.[346] Non-interference with traditional indigenous political institutions has been termed "of supreme impor-tance for the orderly and harmonious existence of indigenous commu-nities. . . . Any interference in such matters has disastrous consequences, which disorganize and destabilize indigenous communities by preventing them from functioning normally as such."[347]

One sensitive issue that arises in this context is whether international

341 *Id*. at 78–79.
342 *Supra* note 104.
343 *Supra* note 107.
344 IACHR Miskito Report, *supra* note 295, at 81.
345 *Id*. at 81–82.
346 See, e.g., Erica-Irene Daes, "Native People's Rights," 27 Les Cahiers de Droit 123, 126–27 (no. 1, 1986).
347 4 UN Indigenous Study at 244.

human rights norms do or should apply to indigenous governments. Were an indigenous people to establish its own state, it would be appropriate for NGOs and others to encourage that state to ratify relevant international conventions.[348] On the other hand, recognition that the desire on the part of an indigenous nation to preserve traditional structures may not be compatible with the full panoply of internationally recognized human rights creates no greater problems than are encountered with respect to other states or cultures.

Even if a community enjoys full internal self-government and autonomy, the surrounding or dominant state might still be internationally responsible for human rights within that autonomous community.[349] In any event, customary international law would be applicable to any indigenous state and to indigenous or other autonomous communities within states. As developed further in chapter 6, rights such as that of effective popular participation in governmental decision-making might also be relevant, particularly where indigenous peoples have asserted rights to autonomy or self-government based on, *inter alia*, international human rights norms.

Indigenous authority vis à vis the dominant society and state in which indigenous peoples live involves external self-determination. In this context, one encounters complexities similar to those which might be raised in any negotiation between parties relating to federation, autonomy, or the development of other political structures. For example, assuming a relationship short of complete separation, issues arise regarding the "negative" powers and "positive" rights of an autonomous indigenous community. The former might include the veto by an indigenous com-

---

348 The Mikmaq nation in northeastern North America ratified the two international covenants on human rights in 1987, although, since it is not a state, its ratifaction has not been internationally recognized. See UN Commission on Human Rights, Written Statement submitted by the Four Directions Council, UN Doc. E/CN.4/1987/NGO/37 (1988).

349 See art. 27 of the Vienna Convention on the Law of Treaties, *supra* note 61: "A party may not invoke the provisions of its internal law as justification for its failure to perform a treaty." *Cf.* Tyrer v. U.K., App. No. 5856/72, Eur. Court Human Rights, Judgment of 25 Apr. 1978, Ser. A No. 26 (discussing the responsibility of the U.K. for birching in the autonomous Isle of Man); Case 9647 (United States), *Annual Report of the Inter-American Commission on Human Rights 1986–1987* (Washington, DC: Organization of American States, 1987) at 147 (decision of the Inter-American Comm. Human Rights that U.S. federal government has an obligation to prevent the arbitrary application of the death penalty by states to juveniles); Gordon A. Christenson, "The Doctrine of Attribution in State Responsibility," in Richard B. Lillich (ed.), *International Law of State Responsibility for Injuries to Aliens* (Charlottesville: Univ. Press of Virginia, 1983) at 333–35; Andrew Byrnes and Hilary Charlesworth, "Federalism and the International Legal Order: Recent Developments in Australia," 79 Am. J. Int'l L. 622 (1985).

munity of a particular national development project within its territory, while the latter might include the right to receive certain social services from the central government or to be represented at various political levels in the larger state.

There are few examples of indigenous communities filling a role as local political or administrative bodies, although some states may recognize indigenous entities for purposes of consultation.[350] Three countries (Canada, Colombia, and the United States) discussed in the UN Indigenous Study do recognize Indian communities as performing certain local governmental functions. Colombia apparently grants authority over all matters relating to the financial administration of the community to traditionally selected indigenous councils or *cabildos*. In Canada and the United States, officially recognized Indian councils are elected according to provisions of federal law rather than indigenous traditions. There are "indigenous municipalities" in southern Mexico, which appear to have powers similar to those of other Mexican municipalities and simply represent territory in which a large proportion of indigenous people live.[351]

While indigenous authority in areas such as social customs and religion is generally recognized,[352] effective grants of even limited governmental power are extremely rare.[353] In addition to the developing situations in Nicaragua and Norway (discussed in Part II), one might cite Finland, where a Lappish Parliament was established in 1973, and New Zealand, where district Maori Councils have very limited powers to regulate the conduct of Maori people, for instance, in minor criminal matters, within their districts.

Panama has had a special regime for the Cuna Indians since 1934, although the basic law (now in the process of amendment) dates from 1953. In 1983, a law establishing the Embera *Comarca* (the term for the indigenous region) was adopted, and a draft for the Guaymi *Comarca* was submitted to the legislature in 1986.[354] Each new law seems to represent an advance in indigenous autonomy, although the Guaymi draft has been very controversial and was rejected by the Panamanian legislature in 1987.[355] The Cuna and Embera arrangements essentially

350 *Cf.* 4 UN Indigenous Study at 247–56.
351 4 UN Indigenous Study at 262.
352 An important exception to this observtion is when land-use policies of the dominant culture are inconsistent with indigenous religious values, in which case the latter are often ignored. *Cf.* Suagee, *supra* note 327.
353 *Cf.* 4 UN Indigenous Study at 257–69.
354 See Panama, art. 9 CERD Report, *supra* note 308, at 14–20.
355 The main substantive criticisms were that the draft legislation reduced the orig-

establish parallel indigenous and central authorities; the Guaymi proposal would fuse these authorities into the single person of the traditional
leader elected by the Guaymi General Congress, who would still be
appointed and subject to removal by the central government.

The Embera and draft Guaymi acts commit the state "to guarantee
the necessary items in the annual budget" for the effective administration
of the *Comarcas*, and the *Comarcas* may "plan and execute comprehensive development projects" and assess municipal taxes.[356] The collective ownership of indigenous lands is guaranteed under article 123 of
the 1972 Panama constitution. However, while there is an obligation on
the central government to consult and negotiate with, and provide compensation to, the indigenous *Comarcas* with respect to the exploitation
of natural resources, ultimate decisions as to whether or not exploitation
will be permitted remain within the central government's jurisdiction.

The similarities between the *Comarcas* and other municipalities suggest that the former are not truly "self-governing" regions, but the
Panamanian provisions do recognize indigenous rights to a greater extent
than is the case in most of Latin America.

In the United States, there are 167 Indian reservations covering
over 51 million acres.[357] Indian tribes have been described as "sovereign,
domestic dependent nations that have entered into a trust relationship
with the United States Government. Their unique status as distinct
political entities within the United States federal system is acknowledged
by the United States Government in treaties, statutes, court decisions and executive orders, and recognized in the United States
Constitution."[358]

Indian nations were recognized by the U.S. Supreme Court in 1832
as "distinct political communities having territorial boundaries within
which their authority is exclusive, and having a right to all the lands

inal Guaymi land claim by over 40%, eroded the political autonomy which the Guaymi
leadership claims was accepted during negotiations with the government, and did not
provide sufficient Guaymi control over natural resource development.

356 Panama, art. 9 CERD Report, *supra* note 308, at 16.

357 Clinebell and Thomson, *supra* note 281, at 674 (1976 figures). The Australian
government estimates that Indians have "secure title" to 2.3% of the land in the U.S.,
compared to 0.3% of the land in Canada and 12% of the land in Australia. *Aboriginal
Affairs 1983–1987, supra* note 339, at 5–6.

358 Quoted in 2 UN Indigenous Study at 57. See generally, e.g., William C. Canby,
Jr., *American Indian Law in a Nutshell* (St. Paul, MN: West Publishing Co., 1981).
Federal, as opposed to state (i.e., provincial) authority over Indian matters stems in part
from general foreign relations powers and in part from the specific reference in the
Commerce Clause to Congressional power "[t]o regulate Commerce with foreign Nations,
and among the several States, and with the Indian Tribes." U.S. Constitution, art. I,
sec. 8(3).

within those boundaries."[359] However, U.S. legislation has consistently eroded Indian authority and sovereignty. The 1830 Removal Act forced tribes to abandon ancestral lands; the Major Crimes Act in 1885 removed jurisdiction over serious crimes committed on reservations from the tribal to federal authorities; and the 1887 General Allotment Act effectively abolished Indian communal land holding and distributed "surplus" land to white settlers. The 1934 Indian Reorganization Act returned some powers to tribal governments, but only on condition that "modern" forms of democratic government were adopted.

As demonstrated by the scope of the above acts, relations between the U.S. government and Indian tribes are within the "plenary powers" of the U.S. Congress. Indian governments have "sovereign" powers to legislate with respect to their own territory, including powers of taxation, but only if there is no superseding federal legislation.[360] For example, Indian tribes have no criminal jurisdiction over non-Indians for acts committed on reservations.[361] The internal sovereignty of Indian tribes is generally exempt from the provisions of the U.S. constitution, but Congress has imposed most of the provisions of the federal Bill of Rights upon the tribes.[362] Indians in the United States are full citizens and cannot be discriminated against by the states, and state and local governments have no jurisdiction over Indian tribes unless it is specifically granted by federal law.

The Canadian-Indian relationship is perhaps equally complex, but, in the 1980s, a process of re-defining the relationship between "Indian First Nations" and Canada began.[363] The 1982 Canadian constitution states that "existing aboriginal and treaty rights of the aboriginal peoples of Canada are hereby recognized and affirmed," although the extent of those rights—in particular, those relating to self-government—is not entirely clear.[364] A bill based on a 1983 House of Commons Special Committee report on Indian self-government[365] was introduced in June 1984 but not adopted. It would have granted to Indian First Nation governments legislative authority over, *inter alia*, education, membership, law enforcement, real property taxation, and other matters which would have been decided upon at the time an Indian nation was rec-

359 Worcester v. Georgia, 31 U.S. 515 (1832) at 577.

360 *Cf.* Merrion v. Jicarilla Apache Tribe, 455 U.S. 130 (1982) (regarding tribal taxation of oil and gas leases).

361 Oliphant v. Suquamish Indian Tribe, 435 U.S. 191 (1978).

362 Indian Civil Rights Act of 1968, 25 U.S.C. sec. 1301 et seq.

363 See generally Peter A. Cumming and Diana Ginn, "First Nations Self-Government in Canada," 55 Nordic J. Int'l L. 86 (1986).

364 *Cf.* Wilson, *Canada's Indians, supra* note 278, at 19–20.

365 Penner Report, *supra* note 330.

ognized, such as land-use planning, public health and safety, the environment and resources, public order and the administration of justice, family law, property rights, and local matters relating to good government.[366] Provincial laws would not have applied to Indian nations, and general federal laws would have applied only to the extent that they were not inconsistent with Indian laws.[367]

The 1984 Cree-Naskapi Act grants rights over the use, administration, and regulation of land and natural resources to certain Indian bands, and a band council may adopt local bylaws concerning, *inter alia*, public health, safety, and order; protection of the environment; provision of local services; taxation (other than income tax); and the operation of businesses and trades. However, it has been observed that this may not be an appropriate model for a new country-wide act, as it does not reflect even notional equality or entrenched power-sharing among the federal, provincial, and indigenous governments. "[A]lthough it does give the bands a much greater say in resource development, and greater powers of local government, the authority exercised by the new band councils is delegated from the federal government. The form of band local government is [only] that of a municipal government."[368] It is not yet clear whether this observation too broadly exalts form over substance.

Without entering further into a detailed analysis of the complex relations between Indian nations and the Canadian and U.S. governments, respectively, there can be no hesitancy in concluding that implementation of this "trust" by both governments has been woefully inadequate and duplicitous. Indian treaty rights were violated and governmental obligations to defend those rights ignored. Indeed, it is the reaffirmation and implementation of those treaties that are a major arena of conflict today.[369]

Despite the automatically negative reaction of governments to the term "self-determination," there is some evidence that the issue can be considered with flexibility. At an early session of the Working Group on Indigenous Populations, some government observers noted

366 Cumming and Ginn, *supra* note 363, at 105.
367 *Id*. at 107.
368 *Id*. at 108. For a highly critical view of the process which led to adoption of the Cree-Naskapi Act, see the statement of the Grand Council of the Crees (of Quebec) to the Working Group on Indigenous Populations, July 1985 (on file with author).
369 The litigation successes since the 1970s of several Indian tribes in reasserting treaty-based hunting and fishing rights in the United States have led to a non-Indian backlash in some areas, and there have been calls (thus far unheeded) for unilateral Congressional amendment or abrogation of Indian treaty rights. See, e.g., "Indian treaty rights under attack," Christian Science Monitor, 8 Sept. 1987, at 1, col. 4.

that their Governments had come to realize that the policies applied in the past seeking to assimilate the indigenous populations had failed to meet the needs and to respect the rights of the indigenous populations. Governments had therefore revised those policies recognizing their distinct identity and adapting them with a view to allow an increased degree of self-determination for the indigenous populations in their relations with the respective Governments. Such a revision had taken place in different ways, in accordance with the historical background, the specific needs of the indigenous populations and the orientation of the specific and general policies of the countries.[370]

It is not clear whether international recognition of an undefined indigenous right to "self-determination" would make governments more or less willing to enter into meaningful negotiations with indigenous peoples, in order to guarantee the preservation and development of indigenous societies as those societies see fit. However, abandonment of coercive assimilationist or integrationist policies which inevitably subordinate indigenous to state interests is essential, and control by indigenous peoples over their own destiny must be a part of any policy which claims to be consistent with human rights principles.

The unique position of most indigenous societies, their relative powerlessness in real political and military terms, and the increasing coordination of their efforts at the international level offer a rare opportunity to advance international legal norms and respond to real needs at the same time. Not only will these activities by indigenous peoples benefit their own members, but their success may also point the way for the negotiated resolution of other conflicts among states, groups, and individuals.

---

370 *Report of the Working Group on its second session, supra* note 314, at 13.

Chapter 6
Human Rights

With the exception of the somewhat questionable doctrine of humanitarian intervention and a state's long-standing responsibility for injuries to aliens, the treatment by a state of those within its jurisdiction was not generally considered to be a legitimate concern of international law until the post-World War II period.[371] The development of an international law of human rights has been one of the most significant aspects of the post-1945 international legal order, along with decolonization and the resulting independence of scores of new states.[372]

The United Nations Charter contains several references to "human rights and fundamental freedoms." Perhaps the most frequently cited are article 1, which lists among the purposes of the United Nations the achievement of international co-operation "in promoting and encouraging respect for human rights and for fundamental freedoms for all without distinction as to race, sex, language, or religion," and article 55, which states that "the United Nations shall promote... universal respect for, and observance of, human rights and fundamental freedoms for all without distinction as to race, sex, language, or religion." Article

371 Earlier protections of minority rights, as opposed to rights of individuals per se, are discussed in chap. 4.

372 See generally John Carey, *UN Protection of Civil and Political Rights* (Syracuse, NY: Syracuse Univ. Press, 1970); Hannum, *Guide to International Human Rights Practice*, *supra* note 286; Henkin, *The International Bill of Rights, The Covenant on Civil and Political Rights*, *supra* note 208; Richard B. Lillich and Frank C. Newman, *International Human Rights: Problems of Law and Policy* (Boston: Little, Brown, 1979); Meron, *Human Rights in International Law: Legal and Policy Issues*, *supra* note 78; Meron, *Human Rights Law-Making in the United Nations*, *supra* note 228; Sieghart, *The International Law of Human Rights*, *supra* note 269; Sohn and Buergenthal, *International Protection of Human Rights*, *supra* note 187; Howard Tolley, Jr., *The U.N. Commission on Human Rights* (Boulder, CO and London: Westview Press, 1987); Vasak and Alston, *The International Dimensions of Human Rights*, *supra* note 95.

55's injunction is made binding by article 56, which provides that "[a]ll Members pledge themselves to take joint and separate action in cooperation with the Organization for the achievement of the purposes set forth in Article 55."

While the Universal Declaration of Human Rights,[373] adopted unanimously by the UN General Assembly in 1948, was only proclaimed as "a common standard of achievement for all peoples and all nations," many of its provisions have subsequently become binding either as expressions of customary international law or as an authoritative interpretation of the UN Charter. To codify the Declaration, the UN Commission on Human Rights began discussions which led to the drafting of two international covenants on human rights and their promulgation by the General Assembly in 1966.[374]

The era of UN standard-setting in human rights lasted through the 1970s and saw the adoption of many other multilateral treaties which deal with specific human rights concerns. The most significant and widely ratified of these treaties include, *inter alia*, the Convention on the Prevention and Punishment of the Crime of Genocide,[375] Convention and Protocol Relating to the Status of Refugees,[376] Convention on the Political Rights of Women,[377] International Convention on the Elimination of All Forms of Racial Discrimination,[378] International Convention on the Suppression and Punishment of the Crime of Apartheid,[379] Convention on the Elimination of All Forms of Discrimination against Women,[380] and Convention against Torture and Other Cruel, Inhuman or Degrading Treatment or Punishment.[381]

At the regional level, effective implementation of new human rights norms began well before the entry into force of the two covenants in

373 G.A. Res. 217A(III) of 10 Dec. 1948, UN Doc. A/810 (1948) at 71, Preamble.

374 International Covenant on Economic, Social and Cultural Rights, *supra* note 132; International Covenant on Civil and Political Rights, *supra* note 132. In addition to sources cited *supra* note 372, see *United Nations Action in the Field of Human Rights*, *supra* note 204, at 5–15.

375 *Supra* note 52.

376 Convention opened for signature 28 July 1951, entered into force 22 April 1954, 189 U.N.T.S. 137, amended by the Protocol Relating to the Status of Refugees, signed 21 Jan. 1967, entered into force 4 Oct. 1967, 606 U.N.T.S. 267.

377 Opened for signature 31 Mar. 1953, entered into force 7 July 1954, 193 U.N.T.S. 135.

378 *Supra* note 226.

379 Adopted 30 Nov. 1973, entered into force 18 July 1976, G.A. Res. 3068(XXVIII), 28 UN GAOR, Supp. (No. 30), UN Doc. A/9030 (1974) at 166.

380 Adopted 18 Dec. 1979, entered into force 3 Sept. 1981, G.A. Res. 34/180, UN GAOR, Supp. (No. 46), UN Doc. A/34/46 (1981) at 193.

381 Adopted 10 Dec. 1984, entered into force 26 June 1987, G.A. Res. 39/46, 39 UN GAOR, Supp. (No. 51), UN Doc. A/39/51 (1984) at 197.

1976 and the development of other UN mechanisms to promote human rights in the 1970s and 1980s. All 21 members of the Council of Europe are now parties to the European Convention for the Protection of Human Rights and Fundamental Freedoms,[382] and all have accepted the optional right of individuals to submit petitions alleging human rights violations. The European Social Charter, which sets forth in detail various economic, social, and cultural rights, entered into force in 1965.[383] In 1975, 35 European and other nations gave their political assent to the Final Act of the Conference on Security and Cooperation in Europe (the "Helsinki Accord"), important sections of which set forth various human rights obligations.[384]

In the Americas, adoption of the American Declaration of Rights and Duties of Man[385] actually pre-dated that of the Universal Declaration by several months. Subsequently, the Inter-American Commission on Human Rights began its activities in the late 1960s, under competence granted through decisions of the General Assembly of the Organization of American States; in 1978, the entry into force of the American Convention on Human Rights[386] expanded the Commission's jurisdiction and also established the Inter-American Court of Human Rights.[387]

The third major regional initiative, the African Charter on Human and Peoples' Rights, entered into force only in 1986.[388]

382 *Supra* note 148. See generally Council of Europe, *Digest of Strasbourg Case-Law relating to the European Convention on Human Rights* (Cologne: Carl Heymanns, 6 vols. 1984–1985); European Commission of Human Rights, *Stock-Taking on the European Convention on Human Rights, The first thirty years: 1954 until 1984* (Strasbourg: Council of Europe, 1984).

383 Signed 18 Oct. 1961, entered into force 26 Feb. 1965, 529 U.N.T.S. 89. See generally David Harris, *The European Social Charter* (Charlottesville: Univ. Press of Virginia, 1984).

384 Signed 1 Aug. 1975, 37 Dep't State Bull. 323 (1975).

385 Signed 2 May 1948, O.A.S. Off. Rec. OEA/Ser.L/V/II.23, doc. 21, rev. 6 (Eng. 1979).

386 *Supra* note 149.

387 See generally Thomas Buergenthal and Robert Norris, *Human Rights: The Inter-American System* (Dobbs Ferry, NY: Oceana, 3 vols. 1982–83); Thomas Buergenthal, Robert Norris, and Dinah Shelton, *Protecting Human Rights in the Americas, Selected Problems* (Kehl, Fed. Rep. of Germany: N.P. Engel, 2d. rev. ed. 1986).

388 *Supra* note 150. See generally International Commission of Jurists, *Human and Peoples' Rights in Africa and the African Charter* (Report of a Conference held in Nairobi from 2–4 Dec. 1985) (Geneva: International Commission of Jurists, 1986); Richard Gittleman, "The African Charter on Human and Peoples' Rights: A Legal Analysis," 22 Va. J. Int'l L. 667 (1982); B. Obinna Okere, "The Protection of Human Rights in Africa and the African Charter on Human and Peoples' Rights: A Comparative Analysis with the European and American Systems," 6 Human Rights Q. 141 (1984).

Specialized agencies, such as the UN Educational, Social, and Cultural Organization (Unesco) and the International Labor Organization (ILO), also have adopted a number of international treaties directly relevant to human rights. Among those adopted by the ILO, for example, are conventions dealing with freedom of association,[389] indigenous peoples,[390] and discrimination in employment.[391]

In addition to these conventional developments, the United Nations has become increasingly active in the promotion and protection of human rights, particularly since the early 1970s. In 1971, it became possible for individuals to complain to the UN regarding situations which evidenced "a consistent pattern of gross violations of human rights and fundamental freedoms," although the confidential mechanisms established have been justifiably criticized.[392] The overthrow of the government of Salvador Allende in Chile in 1973 led to a broadening of UN discussions on human rights, and human rights issues in particular countries are now regularly raised at the Commission on Human Rights, its Sub-Commission on Prevention of Discrimination and Protection of Minorities, the Economic and Social Council, and the General Assembly and its Third Committee.[393]

In addition to considering violations of human rights in particular countries, the United Nations has examined human rights issues

389 Convention Concerning Freedom of Association and Protection of the Right to Organize (ILO No. 87), adopted 9 July 1949, entered into force 11 July 1951, 96 U.N.T.S. 257.

390 *Supra* note 283.

391 Convention Concerning Discrimination in Respect of Employment and Occupation (ILO No. 111), adopted 25 June 1958, entered into force 15 June 1960, 362 U.N.T.S. 32.

392 Esc. Res. 1503(XLVIII), 48 UN ESCOR, Supp. (No. 1A), UN Doc. E/4832/Add.1 (1970) at 8. Among many critical analyses of the "1503 procedure," see Lillich and Newman, *supra* note 372, at 316–87; Dinah L. Shelton, "Individual Complaint Machinery under the United Nations 1503 Procedure and the Optional Protocol to the International Covenant on Civil and Political Rights," in Hannum, *supra* note 286, at 59; Maxime Tardu, 1 *Human Rights: The International Petition System* (Dobbs Ferry, NY: Oceana, 3 vols. 1979), sec. 1A, at 25–40; *id.*, "United Nations Response to Gross Violations of Human Rights: The 1503 Procedure," 20 Santa Clara L. Rev. 559 (1980).

393 In a marked departure from earlier practice, for example, a major UN publication on human rights refers specifically to the question of human rights in Afghanistan, Bolivia, Chile, Cyprus, El Salvador, Guatemala, Iran, Kampuchea, Malawi, Mauritania, Nicaragua, and Poland, in addition to Southern Africa, Palestine, and "assistance" in the human rights field to the Central African Republic, Equatorial Guinea, and Uganda. *United Nations Action in the Field of Human Rights*, *supra* note 204, at 220–33. At the 1988 session of the UN Commission on Human Rights, 22 countries felt obliged to exercise their right of reply to allegations of human rights violations raised during the session. Commission on Human Rights, *Report on the Forty-Fourth Session*, UN Doc. E/1988/12, E/CN.4/1988/88 (1988) at 229.

through, for example, the undertaking of expert studies, the appointment of special rapporteurs, and the establishment of working groups.
Among the themes examined in recent years are torture, "disappearances," arbitrary and summary executions, the right to development,
the right to food, religious intolerance, indigenous populations, genocide, the right to leave and return, slavery, migrant workers, and the
protection of human rights during states of emergency.[394] The situations
in southern Africa, Chile, and the Middle East are regularly considered
throughout the UN system.

At least since the decision was reached to draft two separate international covenants on human rights (one dealing with civil and political
rights and the other with economic, social, and cultural rights), jurists,
scholars, and others have attempted to draw various distinctions among
rights.[395] However, the various categories suggested—civil, political,
economic, social, cultural, individual, collective, positive, negative,
first-, second-, or third-generation, etc.—are often misleading and rarely
lead to greater protection for individuals or groups.[396] Indeed, the most
common purpose for identifying such categories is to deny the status of
"right" to one or more of them, rather than to expand international or
domestic protections.[397]

---

394 See, e.g., David Weissbrodt, "The Three 'Theme' Special Rapporteurs of the
UN Commission on Human Rights," 80 Am. J. Int'l L. 685 (1986); *United Nations Action
in the Field of Human Rights*, *supra* note 204, at 125–214.

395 *Cf.*, e.g., Theodor C. van Boven, "Distinguishing Criteria of Human Rights,"
in 1 Vasak and Alston, *supra* note 95, at 43–59; Stephen P. Marks, "Emerging Human
Rights: A New Generation for the 1980s?" 33 Rutgers L. Rev. 435 (1981).

396 Critiques of "categorizations" of rights should not imply an insensitivity to
regional and/or cultural variations that may well be essential to the effective implementation of "universal" human rights norms. However, while one cannot deny the Western
influence in drafting the two UN covenants, a majority of the state parties to the covenants
are from the Third World; this formal adherence to purportedly universal norms cannot
be ignored without accusing such states of blatant hypocrisy. In fact, the suggestion that
non-Western cultures are not (or were not historically) as concerned as Western cultures
with such basic societal requirements as ensuring justice, stability, and a government
based in some meaningful sense on consent cannot be sustained and has frequently been
rejected by Third World commentators. *Cf.*, e.g., Hurst Hannum, "The Butare Collo-
quium on Human Rights and Economic Development in Francophone Africa: A Summary
and Analysis," 1 Universal Human Rights 63 (no. 2, 1979); Maqbut Ilaha Malik, "The
Concept of Human Rights in Islamic Jurisprudence," 3 *id.* 56 (no. 3, 1980); Keba M'Baye,
"Human Rights in Africa," in 2 Vasak and Alston, *supra* note 95, at 583; Abdul Aziz
Said, "Precept and Practice of Human Rights in Islam," 1 Universal Human Rights 63
(no. 1, 1979); Albert Tevoedjre, "Human Rights and Democracy in Africa" (Tokyo:
United Nations Univ., 1986).

397 In this context, particular note should be taken of GA Res. 32/130, 32 UN
GAOR, Supp. (No. 45), UN Doc. A/32/45 (1977) at 150, on alternative approaches and
ways and means for improving the effective enjoyment of human rights. The resolution

A cursory analysis of those rights which would seem to fit clearly into one category or another demonstrates the futility of drawing meaningful conclusions from such distinctions. The prohibition against torture, for example, is generally considered to be a "negative" (i.e., requiring no affirmative government action) "civil" right, yet it is clear that the mere passage of a statute is insufficient to guarantee that torture is not used by police or security forces. Also required is training and education (which require positive steps by government) and adequate detention facilities (which must compete with other government priorities for funding). Freedom of the press (a classic "civil" right) means little in a country of illiterates (who have a "social" or "cultural" right to education). Trade union rights are included in both covenants and are perhaps one of the most obviously "mixed" rights.

Human beings are organized in societies, and few rights can be thought of as purely "individual." As noted below, rights to religion, education, and language generally have meaning only if they can be exercised in concert with others. "Political" rights, such as the right to participate in government and to self-determination, presume the existence of a collectivity.

Conversely, many so-called "collective" rights, often referred to as "third-generation" rights, have little meaning unless individual members of the collectivity benefit from them. Many, particularly Western, commentators deny the existence of such "peoples' rights" as the rights to development, control over natural resources, peace, and a healthful environment, on the grounds, *inter alia*, that no entity can be identified which has the obligation to see that such rights are protected.[398] Yet unless one is to equate such rights of "peoples" with the rights of "states," it is clear that those who should peacefully develop their natural resources in a clean environment are the individuals who make up so-

lists a number of concepts which should be taken into account in the human rights work of the UN, including, as the first principle, that "[a]ll human rights and fundamental freedoms are indivisible and interdependent; equal attention and urgent consideration should be given to the implementation, promotion and protection of both civil and political, and economic, social and cultural rights." This principle has been frequently reiterated in subsequent resolutions, e.g., GA Res. 41/131, adopted in 1986, which, *inter alia*, "underlin[es] the need for the creation of conditions at the national and international levels for the promotion and full protection of the human rights of individuals and peoples, ... affirm[s] that the ultimate aim of development is the constant improvement of the well-being of the entire population, on the basis of its full participation in the process of development and a fair distribution of the benefits therefrom, ... [and affirms] that the promotion and protection of one category of rights should never exempt or excuse States from the promotion and protection of the others." 41 UN GAOR, Supp. (No. 53), UN Doc. A/41/53 (1986) at 189.

398 See, e.g., Sieghart, *supra* note 269, at 367–76.

ciety, not some abstract "people" reflected in statistical measurements of Gross Domestic Product. Thus, individuals must be the ultimate beneficiaries of collective rights if the latter are to have real meaning.

Excluding such disputed "collective" rights, international human rights law has only infrequently been applied to protect the interests of groups per se. Rather, its provisions have extended to individual *members* of groups even in those few instances—such as article 27 of the Covenant on Civil and Political Rights—where the protection of groups is clearly the primary concern. At the same time, however, certain human rights are of particular importance in the protection of group or community rights.

While *freedom of religion* is commonly considered to be a classic "civil" or "individual" right, religious rights are fundamental to the protection of the rights of minority, indigenous, and other groups. As the cornerstone of many cultures, religious practices often have been the object of discrimination by the majority; state or majority intolerance of religious diversity has perhaps surpassed racial prejudice as the primary motivation behind human rights violations in the world today.

The UN Declaration on the Elimination of All Forms of Intolerance and of Discrimination Based on Religion or Belief notes that

the disregard and infringement of human rights and fundamental freedoms, in particular of the right to freedom of thought, conscience, religion or whatever belief, have brought, directly or indirectly, wars and great suffering to mankind, especially where they serve as a means of foreign interference in the internal affairs of other States and amount to kindling hatred between peoples and nations.[399]

Article 6 of the Declaration sets forth in some detail the rights to maintain places of worship and religious education, to write and disseminate relevant publications, and "[t]o establish and maintain communications with individuals and communities in matters of religion or belief at the national or international levels."

The UN Commission on Human Rights decided to appoint a Special Rapporteur to monitor implementation of the Declaration on Religious Intolerance,[400] and his first report concluded:

[I]t is apparent that intolerance and discrimination based on religion or belief is [sic] a common phenomenon throughout the world. . . . Occurrences such as the forced assimilation of religious minorities, confrontations between

399 *Supra* note 263, Preamble.
400 Comm. Human Rights Res. 1986/20, UN Doc. E/1986/22 (1986) at 66.

supporters of different ideologies or beliefs and persecution and discrimination for reasons of religion or belief are unfortunately very widespread. . . .

The outcome of the savage repression in certain countries, of the supporters of a particular faith or belief, and the heavy toll taken by armed conflicts in which ideological considerations are involved is that the victims of intolerance can be counted in hundreds of thousands. The atmosphere of instability fostered by such confrontations is a real threat to international peace and security.[401]

The second report summarized allegations of religious intolerance sent by the Rapporteur to the governments of Albania, Bulgaria, Burundi, Iran, Pakistan, Turkey, and U.S.S.R.; it concluded that there was "a persistence of incidents and governmental measures inconsistent with the Declaration [on Religious Intolerance] . . . , with infringements of freedom of religion or belief being committed in various forms and in practically all regions of the world."[402]

Does it matter to these victims whether it is their individual rights or their rights as members of a minority or indigenous group which are being violated?

Linguistic and educational rights also are of particular significance to groups, as they constitute the vehicles through which culture is transmitted. The recognition (or non-recognition) of a language as "official" or "national" has contributed to violent conflicts in countries as diverse as Sri Lanka, Belgium, Canada, Bulgaria, and Turkey. Even where the free use of minority languages is permitted, the obligation (if any) of the state to support the propagation or maintenance of such languages through the provision of educational or other facilities is unclear.

Linguistic rights are not specifically protected under international human rights law, except in a relatively restricted manner. The two covenants do prohibit discrimination on the basis of language,[403] and it is clear that no one can be, for example, imprisoned, denied the right to enter or leave, or forbidden from participating in public affairs on the grounds that he or she speaks a particular language. On the other hand, is there a right for every citizen to have an election ballot in a language he or she understands? Is the right to a free, compulsory primary education dependent on the ability to speak the majority language in which that education may be offered? Does the prohibition of discrimination on the basis of language mean that there can be no "official" national language?

401 *Report submitted by Mr. Angelo Vidal d'Almeida Ribero, supra* note 19, at 26, 27.

402 *Id.,* at 26.

403 Covenant on Economic, Social and Cultural Rights, art. 2(2); Covenant on Civil and Political Rights, arts. 2(1), 24(1) [rights of children to necessary protections], 26, 27 [rights of linguistic minorities].

The answers to these and similar questions would seem to be no, at least if those answers are based on state practice and the jurisprudence of international human rights bodies. Many countries have an "official" language, and all have a de facto one. Proficiency in that language is a reasonable requirement for, e.g., employment in the civil service. On the other hand, the European Court of Human Rights has held that denying the opportunity for education in one's own language based on residence may interfere with a parent's right to have his or her child educated in conformity with the family's beliefs.[404]

Some commentators have suggested that there may be an affirmative obligation on the part of the state to enable a minority language or educational system to survive.[405] Whether or not this is a legal obligation, many states conduct business in more than one language in order to recognize minority cultures and rights. The distinction between state-wide "official" languages and regional or "national" languages is common, as is the de facto provision of government services in whatever language may be most appropriate in a particular section of the country.[406]

With few exceptions, a *territorial base* also is essential to the preservation of a group's culture. Seizure of land, for population expansion or the exploitation of natural resources, is perhaps the most common complaint of indigenous peoples; those European "minorities" which were not able to maintain a separate territory are in the process of disappearing. However, no specific right to land is mentioned in any major human rights instrument, perhaps reflecting state desires to retain absolute control over their territory.

The provision in article 17 of the Universal Declaration of Human Rights that everyone has the right to own property and that no one shall be arbitrarily deprived of his or her property was not reiterated in the subsequent covenants, although similar provisions are found in the American Convention on Human Rights (art. 21) and European Con-

404 *Case Relating to Certain Aspects of the Laws on the Use of Languages in Education in Belgium*, Eur. Court Human Rights, Judgment of 23 July 1968, Series A No. 6.

405 See, e.g., Patrick Thornberry, "Is There a Phoenix in the Ashes?—International Law and Minority Rights," 15 Texas Int'l L. J. 421 (1980) at 449–50; *Study on the rights of persons belonging to ethnic, religious and linguistic minorities, supra* note 175, at 98–99.

406 On the other hand, reactions against the "intrusion" of a "foreign" language can be powerful, as demonstrated by the designation of English as the "official" language in at least eight states in the United States; one of the most recent laws, an amendment to the California constitution, was adopted by a popular referendum in November 1986. *Cf.* Note, " 'Official English': Federal Limits on Efforts to Curtail Bilingual Services in the States," 100 Harv. L. Rev. 1345 (1987).

vention on Human Rights (art. 1 of Protocol No. 1). The American Convention permits deprivation of property "upon payment of just compensation, for reasons of public utility or social interest," while the European provisions prohibit deprivation of possessions "except in the public interest and subject to the conditions provided for by law and by the general principles of international law."

The European system has developed extensive jurisprudence relating to, *inter alia*, the definition of adequate compensation or public interest,[407] but the protection of private property also could be ensured by resort to international norms of non-discrimination or to a fair and impartial hearing in the determination of rights and obligations. Nevertheless, the protection of group rights to traditional homelands or large tracts of communally held land is much more precarious. Even if one could eliminate extra-legal land seizures by public and private entities, the conflict between central development plans and local, regional, or group rights over land and natural resources would remain one of the most significant and serious disputes in the years to come.

The right to *popular participation* in government, as expressed in article 21 of the Universal Declaration of Human Rights and article 25 of the Covenant on Civil and Political Rights, should be interpreted as implying more than simple majority rule through the electoral process. In many respects, this right reflects the "internal" aspect of self-determination,[408] and it can be viewed as fundamental to both political democracy and economic development.

Popular participation was first discussed within the United Nations in the context of the need to consult those who are most directly affected (generally the rural poor) by national development plans.[409] Soon, however, the political aspects of participation also were recognized, and in 1983 the Commission on Human Rights requested the Secretary-General to prepare a comprehensive analytical study on "popular participation in its various forms as an important factor in development and in the full realization of human rights."[410]

This study, submitted to the Commission in 1985, contains a detailed exposition of the principle of popular participation.[411] It concludes that

407 See, e.g., excerpts collected in 5 *Digest of Strasbourg Case-Law relating to the European Convention on Human Rights*, *supra* note 382, at 631–741.

408 *Cf.* chap. 3; Cassese, *supra* note 90.

409 See, e.g., United Nations, *Popular Participation in Decision Making for Development*, UN Sales No. E.75.IV.10 (1975); *id.*, *Popular Participation as a Strategy for Promoting Community-level and National Development*, UN Sales No. E.81.IV.2 (1981).

410 Comm. on Human Rights Res. 1983/14, UN Doc. E/1983/13, E/CN.4/1983/60 (1983) at 138.

411 United Nations, *Study by the Secretary-General on Popular Participation in its*

the right to popular participation, in its most general terms, does not appear to be expressly established as such by universal instruments having binding legal value. On the other hand, a number of international texts of varying legal natures contain elements of popular participation, and some of these texts go so far as to enunciate a global right to participation.[412]

Among these "elements" of popular participation recognized at the international level are the right to self-determination; the right to education; the right to take part in cultural life and the conduct of public affairs; minority rights; trade union rights; family rights; the right of association and peaceful assembly; and freedom of thought, conscience, religion, opinion, expression, and information.[413] A broad definition of popular participation might simply require the involvement of citizens in public affairs, "with the fullest respect for human rights, without any discrimination and giving special attention to groups which have so far been kept apart from genuine participation."[414] The Secretary-General's study notes the importance of freedom of information and suggests, in particular, that "minority groups should have the possibility of making known their diverging opinions, as repression of such views may run counter to the dynamics of society and to desirable change and renewal in national life."[415]

The 1986 Declaration on the Right to Development adopted by the UN General Assembly underscores the importance of the right to popular participation.[416] The Declaration notes, *inter alia*:

The human person is the central subject of development and should be the active participant and beneficiary of the right to development. . . .

States have the right and the duty to formulate appropriate national development policies that aim at the constant improvement of the well-being of the entire population and of all individuals, on the basis of their active, free and meaningful participation in development and in the fair distribution of the benefits resulting therefrom. . . .

Various Forms as an Important Factor in Development and in the Full Realization of Human Rights, UN Doc. E/CN.4/1985/10 (1984). Also see generally Henry J. Steiner, "Political Participation as a Human Right," 1 Harv. Human Rights Y.B. 77 (1988).

412 *Study by the Secretary-General*, *supra* note 411, at 36.

413 *Id.* at 34.

414 *Id.* at 6.

415 *Id.* at 18.

416 Declaration on the Right to Development, G.A. Res. 41/128, Annex, 41 UN GAOR, Supp. (No. 53), UN Doc. A/41/53 (1986) at 186. *Cf.* Commission on Human Rights, *International Dimensions of the Right to Development*, UN Doc. E/CN.4/1334 (1979); *id.*, UN Doc. E/CN.4/1488 (1981).

States should encourage popular participation in all spheres as an important factor in development and in the full realization of all human rights.[417]

The African Charter on Human and Peoples' Rights declares, "All peoples shall have the right to their economic, social and cultural development with due regard to their freedom and identity and in the equal enjoyment of the common heritage of mankind."[418]

The need for effective participation in development by groups has been underscored by some indigenous organizations, but facilitating mass participation (e.g., by disadvantaged groups such as migrant workers, women, the elderly, and the disabled[419]) will not necessarily promote participation by or recognition of groups such as ethnic minorities or indigenous peoples. States tend to pay more attention to the involvement of the citizenry as a whole in development than to that of particular segments of the society.[420]

Despite the Secretary-General's conclusion that the right to popular participation per se is not yet included in universal human rights instruments, the essential components of the right to effective participation in the political and economic decision-making processes of government are guaranteed through related rights and freedoms. If an identifiable segment of society is consistently excluded from any real share in economic or political life, alternative means of ensuring participation may be required. Where persistent denial of the opportunity for participation occurs, the population concerned may ultimately have recourse to the

417 Declaration on the Right to Development, *supra* note 416, arts. 2(1), 2(3), and 8(2). Query whether this leaves room for ethnic, indigenous, or regional minorities to influence or control development at the local level, even if local goals may conflict with national development plans?

418 *Supra* note 150, art. 22(1). The Preamble notes that it is "essential to pay particular attention to the right to development and that civil and political rights cannot be dissociated from economic, social and cultural rights in their conception as well as universality."

419 See, e.g., *Study by the Secretary-General*, *supra* note 411, at 11–14.

420 See, e.g., statement by the U.S.S.R. in response to a Note Verbale from the UN Secretary-General: "Thus, the pattern for the development both of the public and of the State constituents of the political system in the USSR is, fundamentally, the same: it consists in the maximum promotion of the activity and initiative of the working masses. . . . In view of the legal status of the individual in the Soviet Union and of the unity of the fundamental interests of socialist society and its members, mass participation by the population in the conduct of the entire range of social and political affairs is effectively guaranteed." UN Doc. E/CN.4/1987/11 (1986) at 8, 9. The government of Rwanda indicated, in the context of popular participation, that "[t]he Rwandese people is politically organized within the national Revolutionary Movement for Development, a political grouping outside which no political activity may take place." Statement by Rwanda in response to Ecosoc Res. 1983/31, UN Doc. E/CN.4/1985/10/Add.1 (1984) at 12.

principle of self-determination in order to ensure meaningful participation in the society in which it lives.

This position is essentially that adopted in the Universal Declaration
of the Rights of Peoples, adopted at a nongovernmental meeting in
Algiers in 1976 (hereinafter cited as "Algiers Declaration").[421] After
reiterating the right of every people to self-determination, the Algiers
Declaration states:

> Every people has the right to have a democratic government representing
> all the citizens without distinction as to race, sex, belief or colour, and capable
> of ensuring effective respect for the human rights and fundamental freedoms
> for all.

The declaration goes on to provide that "[a]ny people whose fundamental rights are seriously disregarded has the right to enforce them,
. . . even, in the last resort, by the use of force," perhaps consciously
reflecting the right "to rebellion against tyranny and oppression" mentioned in the Preamble of the Universal Declaration of Human Rights.

The Algiers Declaration also implicitly supports the right of a minority group to secede from the larger political entity if its human rights
are denied, if one reads the above-cited articles in conjunction with
article 21, which provides:

> These rights [of minorities] shall be exercised with due respect for the
> legitimate interests of the community as a whole and cannot authorise impairing
> the territorial integrity and political unity of the State, *provided the State acts
> in accordance with all the principles set forth in this Declaration.*[422]

Recognition of this interlocking of human rights, minority participation, and self-determination is essential if these concepts are to be
more than mere slogans. As noted by a Sudanese observer:

> Liberal democracy presupposes a framework characterized by a broad con-
> sensus on the fundamental principles of nationhood, the structure of govern-
> ment, and the shaping and sharing of power, wealth, and other national
> resources. Where consensus on these fundamentals is lacking, and people lack
> even a shared sense of belonging to the nation, even the concepts of majority
> and minority cannot apply. Parliamentary democracy under those circumstances
> becomes the rule of a numerical majority imposed on an alienated minority,
> whether numerically determined or otherwise marginalized. Such a structure
> cannot enjoy legitimacy or stability. This means that we must address the pending

---

421 The text of the declaration is reprinted in Cassese, *supra* note 90, at 219–23.
422 Emphasis added. See generally the discussion in Cassese, *supra* note 90.

fundamental issues of nationhood before we can legitimately invoke majority votes as a justification for imposing any decisions on the minority.[423]

Another fundamental human right, one that is widely accepted as constituting a general principle of international law (and possibly *jus cogens*), is the *prohibition against racial discrimination*.[424] This "individual" right obviously is relevant to members of racial, ethnic, and indigenous groups, and allegations of racial discrimination are at the heart of many complaints filed by minority groups at the United Nations and elsewhere. However, the prohibition of discrimination and the concomitant guarantee of equality before the law may not be sufficient to enable a minority to maintain its distinctive characteristics. As noted by the Permanent Court of International Justice, "Equality in law precludes discrimination of any kind; whereas equality in fact may involve the necessity of different treatment in order to attain a result which establishes an equilibrium between different situations."[425]

Demands for increased political power, autonomy, or self-determination are the primary concern of the present work, but most groups are threatened primarily by gross violations of *rights to personal security* rather than more subtle violations of rights to political or economic representation. Mass and individual killings; torture; arbitrary and indefinite arrests; induced starvation; illegal expropriation of land; and discrimination in employment, housing, and public services are the most common *causes* of the assertion of group rights by the powerless.[426] In addition, they constitute the most common *responses* by central governments to perceived threats to national unity and territorial integrity. Such violations are often linked to imposition of states of siege or emergency,[427] and the violation of human rights by members of the security

423 Francis Mading Deng, "Myth and Reality in Sudanese Identity," in Francis Mading Deng and Prosser Gifford (eds.), *The Search for Peace and Unity in the Sudan* (Washington, DC: Wilson Center Press, 1987) at 69.

424 See, e.g., *Legal Consequences for States of the Continued Presence of South Africa in Namibia (South West Africa) supra* note 53, para. 131 (discrimination based on race, colour, descent or national or ethnic origin "is a flagrant violation of the purposes and principles of the Charter."); Ian Brownlie, *Principles of Public International Law* (Oxford: Clarendon Press, 3rd ed. 1979) at 596–98; B.G. Ramcharan, "Equality and Nondiscrimination," in Henkin, *supra* note 208, at 249; United Nations, *Racial Discrimination* (rev. ed. 1977), *supra* note 307, para. 919; 1 *Restatement (Third) of the Foreign Relations Law of the United States, supra* note 52, sec. 702.

425 Minority Schools in Albania, Advisory Opinion, 1935, P.C.I.J., Series A/B, No. 64, p. 4, at 19.

426 *Cf.*, e.g., Suzuki, *supra* note 167, at 798–812 (citing Biafra and Bangladesh as examples).

427 See generally Lawless v. Ireland, App. No. 332/57, Eur. Court H.R., Judgment of 14 Nov. 1960 (preliminary objections), Ser. A No. 1; *id.*, Judgment of 1 July 1961

forces almost universally renders the resolution of conflicting assertions of rights impossible through normal legal or political processes.

Both central government and minority leaders may have a vested interest in portraying conflicts as reflecting deep communal or other divisions rather than fears based on persistent human rights violations. In such situations, the central authorities are able to shift international attention from alleged human rights violations to supposed attacks on the state's sovereignty and territorial unity, while minority leaders may acquire much greater personal power if they demand political concessions rather than merely seeking the implementation of guaranteed rights.

It is nevertheless essential to recognize how many ethnic and other conflicts have originated and been exacerbated by the gross violation of what one might term "ordinary" human rights. Where discrimination and violent assaults on the minority by majority mobs and/or government security forces escalate a conflict to the level where survival of the minority becomes an issue, it is hardly surprising that political compromises become impossible "sell-outs" thousands of deaths later.

(merits), Ser. A No. 3; Ireland v. U.K., App. No. 5310/71, Eur. Court H.R., Judgment of 18 Jan. 1978, Ser. A No. 25; Denmark et al v. Greece, Apps. Nos. 3321/67 et al, Eur. Comm. H.R., Report of 5 Nov. 1969, 12 *Y.B. Eur. Conv. on Human Rights* (1969); Inter-Am. Court H.R., Habeas Corpus in Emergency Situations (Arts. 27(2), 25(1) and 7(6) American Convention on Human Rights), Advisory Opinion OC-8/87 of 30 Jan. 1987, Ser. A No. 8, at 38–48; Inter-Am. Court H.R., Judicial Guarantees in States of Emergency (Arts. 27(2), 25 and 8 American Convention on Human Rights), Advisory Opinion OC-9/87 of 6 Oct. 1987, Ser. A No. 9; Buergenthal, Norris & Shelton, *supra* note 387, at 217–39; International Commission of Jurists, *States of Emergency, Their Impact on Human Rights* (Geneva: Int'l Comm. of Jurists, 1983); Sieghart, *supra* note 269, at 110–18; *The Individual's Duties to the Community and the Limitations on Human Rights and Freedoms under Article 29 of the Universal Declaration of Human Rights* (E. Daes, Special Rapporteur), UN Doc. E/CN.4/Sub.2/432/Rev.2 (1983); *Study of the implications for human rights of recent developments concerning situations known as states of siege or emergency* (N. Questiaux, Special Rapporteur), UN Doc. E/CN.4/Sub.2/1982/15 (1982); Buergenthal, "To Respect and Ensure: State Obligations and Permissible Derogations," in Henkin, *supra* note 208, at 80–91; "Derogation from Guarantees Laid down in Human Rights Instruments," in *Protection of Human Rights in Europe: Limits and Effects* (I. Maier ed. 1982) at 123–60; "Symposium: Limitation and Derogation Provisions in the International Covenant on Civil and Political Rights," 7 Human Rights Q. 1 (1985); International Law Association, Committee on the Enforcement of Human Rights Law, *Interim Report of the Committee* (presented to the Seoul Conference, 1986); *id.*, *Second Interim Report of the Committee* (presented to the Warsaw Conference, 1988).

Part II Searching for Solutions: Nine Case Studies

[A]ny strictly rational approach to history distorts it much as a road map distorts reality. The most sophisticated theories of why what happens suffer from a flat-earth syndrome; missing are the dimensions of fear, centuries of hate gathering in poisoned pools, the darkness of bigotry, ignorance, despair. The irrational, by definition, eludes the reasoned unraveling of causal connections, slips through the mesh of logic, and locks men into its own version of the truth. Hunger is the result of maldistribution and economic inequities; being hungry is a rage in the belly.

Ernst Pawel, *The Nightmare of Reason, A Life of Franz Kafka* (1984)

MAN

Kick him—he'll forgive you. Flatter him—he may or may not see through you.

But ignore him, and he'll hate you, even if he conceals it until he dies.

Idries Shah, *Caravan of Dreams* (1968)

INTRODUCTION

The themes discussed in the preceding chapters—national unity and integrity, the right to self-determination, the human rights of minorities and indigenous peoples, sovereignty—have been raised, often stridently, in each of the case studies which follow. In each of the nine situations, autonomy, self-government, or self-determination is demanded by a group within an existing state, in order to protect the group's culture. In most cases, the minority group is a minority which has felt disadvantaged and discriminated against.

To the casual observer, it may appear that there are greater differences than similarities between, for example, Hong Kong and the Kurds or between Northern Ireland and Nicaragua. Certainly the range of demands is diverse, as is the political and social majority from which each smaller group seeks to distance itself. It is precisely this range of political, economic, geographic, and social factors that has led to the selection of the following situations for more detailed examination than those considered in Part III. The thesis is that, despite the very different origins of the conflicts and the superficially different solutions sought, there is an underlying similarity in potential resolutions that may be instructive. Also noteworthy are the similar ways in which several of the conflicts deteriorated from essentially political disagreements to increasingly violent confrontations (with the exception, thus far, of the Saamis and Hong Kong).

The cases selected include established European states (Spain, the United Kingdom, the Nordic countries), newly independent multi-ethnic societies in Asia or Africa (India, Sri Lanka, Sudan), a non-state society (the Kurds), indigenous peoples (Saamis, Miskitos), and a dependent colony (Hong Kong). It is largely a coincidence that those states discussed which gained their independence since 1945 are former British colonies, as ethnic or other conflicts in which autonomy has been an issue certainly exist in former French, Belgian, Portuguese, and Spanish colonies, as well.

Some of the most well-known situations in which ethnic conflict is paramount are not included in the present work, primarily because of the ready availability of other materials and the necessity of limiting an already lengthy book. Thus, there are only passing references, if any, to significant contemporary or historical conflicts in Bangladesh, Canada (Quebec), Cyprus, or Nigeria. Neither are conflicts in which the primary issue is one of decolonization, such as in Palestine, Western Sahara, East Timor, and the U.S. Trust Territory, discussed in any detail. Finally, the otherwise relevant federal systems of Switzerland and Yugoslavia have been extensively analyzed elsewhere, although the latter, in particular, remains an important microcosm in which both ethnic and autonomous problems as well as possible solutions can be examined.[428]

Hong Kong is not normally included in discussions of autonomy or "ethnic" conflict, one supposes because the conflict is obviously not "ethnic": approximately 98% of the population of Hong Kong is ethnically Chinese, and the autonomy Hong Kong seeks to assert is not against the British but against the People's Republic of China. The primary motivations on both sides are economic and political, although the differences between the two social and economic systems may be sufficiently great that one can speak of separate "cultures" as well. The situation also is distinguished by the fact that all parties agree on the ultimate goal, i.e., maintenance of Hong Kong's capitalist economy and a personality separate, to some extent, from that of China.

India is one of the most ethnically diverse countries in the world, and it has been beset by insurgencies and demands for greater linguistic and/or regional autonomy since partition. When the concept for the present study was being developed, the situation in the Punjab had not yet escalated to its post-1984 heights of violence; Indira Gandhi was still alive; and the hope was that a case study of the Punjab would provide an example of the relatively peaceful resolution of a difficult situation. However, despite the political flexibility inherent in the Indian constitutional system and the relatively privileged traditional position of the Sikh community, initially moderate demands for regional autonomy and certain economic adjustments have given way to terrorism, repression, . and demands by extremist elements for secession. The central government of Rajiv Gandhi has seen its national authority erode, at least in part because of its inability to resolve the Punjab conflict.

Kurdistan has been a concern of the international community since the early twentieth century. Despite the fact that they would appear to have all the external attributes necessary for statehood, the Kurds have been singularly unsuccessful in achieving recognition as a single entity. The reaction of those states in which Kurds are found ranges from repression and denial in Turkey to at least formal recognition of Kurdish identity in Iraq. Unlike the Sikhs, the Kurdish community is poor and not well organized, and, perhaps more than any other situation discussed herein, its fate has been closely entwined with geopolitical developments in the strategic part of the world which it inhabits.

---

428 Indeed, ethnic and other conflicts in Yugoslavia in the late 1980s only reconfirmed the continuing importance of autonomy and minority rights issues in the contemporary political world.

Nicaragua in many respects resembles a newly independent state, as the 1979 revolution reversed decades of authoritarian rule and now seeks to consolidate a new statism. Yet the Sandinista revolution co-incided with a new assertiveness by indigenous peoples of their rights of self-government, and the historic division between Indian (and other) communities on Nicaragua's Atlantic Coast and the much larger Spanish population in the western half of the country has intensified as both "nations" seek to assert their identity. Intervention by the United States in an attempt to draw the Miskito and other Indian communities into a larger anti-Sandinista war certainly complicated the political and military equation in Nicaragua, but in many respects the differences between Indians and the central Nicaraguan government represent classic disputes between indigenous peoples and central governments around the world.

Northern Ireland is perhaps the oldest conflict among the cases examined in this section, although the most recent incarnation of the conflict dates only from the partition of Ireland in 1920. Northern Ireland evidences the fact that ethnic conflict and minority dissatisfaction are very much a part of the developed world, as well as of developing countries, and it also offers a perspective on the limits of autonomy and the difficulty of drawing political, as well as geographical, borders. Majorities and minorities overlap, and the need to recognize the legitimacy of the two communities which compose Northern Ireland today may suggest lessons for other polities.

The *Saami* or Lapp people of Norway, Sweden, Finland, and the Soviet Union are an indigenous people whose history of isolation and attempted assimilation parallels, in some respects, those of Western Hemisphere Indians and Australian Aborigines. Their strategic trans-national location is reminiscent of the Kurdish situation. Nordic governments have, in recent years, been more sympathetic to efforts to reassert and protect Saami culture than have many other governments faced with indigenous demands, and there is reason to be somewhat optimistic about the development of Saami self-government.

Spain is a modern European state which has radically transformed its constitutional structure in the years following the death of General Franco, devolving substantial powers to regional governments. Regional autonomy has long been sought by the Basques and Catalans, in particular, although Basque extremists have continued a violent struggle for independence despite the recent constitutional changes. Like the Punjab, the Basque country and Catalonia have traditionally been more economically developed than the rest of Spain, although complaints of regional disparity and inequality are also heard. Like other minorities, the Basques feel culturally threatened by the larger Spanish and even

European society, as demographic changes in their homeland alter Basque numerical dominance.

Sri Lanka presents many of the attributes of a classic ethnic conflict and is undoubtedly one of the most widely studied countries in this context. There are many parallels with Northern Ireland, as well as with other dual-language societies such as Belgium and Canada; a major question is how a manageable, if difficult, political situation in the 1960s deteriorated into a communal civil war by the 1980s, despite economic and other advantages not possessed by many other developing countries.

The situation in the *Sudan* reflects the ethnic and religious complexity of many other African states. To some extent, the Sudanese case study is historical, in that it focuses on the initial success of the 1972 constitutional arrangements in ending the civil war and the weaknesses in those arrangements which contributed to the resumption of war in 1983. It also chronicles the consequences of religious intolerance (or its manipulation for political purposes), and the particular difficulties faced by large, relatively poor states in satisfying both the legitimate demands of minorities and the necessities of state development.

If a little knowledge is dangerous, then moderate understanding may need to be treated with even greater circumspection. Books have been written on all of the situations addressed in the following pages, and the reader should turn to such sources for a deeper comprehension of, in particular, the social and economic aspects of the conflicts. As noted by historian Barbara Tuchman, "The contemporary has no perspective; everything is in the foreground and appears the same size. Little matters loom big, and great matters are sometimes missed because their outlines cannot be seen."[429] The inevitable delay between writing and publication will mean that political developments may have rendered some of the specific descriptions less accurate, although the analyses should remain largely valid. The information in the following pages is generally accurate up to mid-1988, and later developments have been taken into account where possible.

At the same time, however, the studies do address in some detail the practical difficulties in trying to fashion an appropriate degree of "autonomy" in a highly charged, emotional, often violent context. These somewhat fuller descriptions also may enable the reader to arrive at a clearer understanding of the real issues involved and the role played by political ambition, apart from questions of ethnicity. "The degree of conviction nationalism conveys to outsiders depends partly on the distance between them and the conflict. Those closely concerned in disputes

---

429 Tuchman, *supra* note 169, at 28.

involving nationalism are more likely to be fully aware of the gulf between rhetoric and reality."[430]

While it is perhaps too much to expect "statesmen" to conduct
reasoned negotiations in the midst of massacres, the absence of prin-
cipled leadership in most of the studies which follow is notable. Even
more striking are the long-term schisms caused by the pursuit of short-
term political goals, which are often of as little significance as winning
the next election. If the selfless dedication claimed by both opposition
and government leaders is somewhat blurred in the following pages by
reality, one can only hope that greater clarity may result.

430 Breuilly, *supra* note 66, at 372.

Chapter 7
Hong Kong

Hong Kong's 5.7 million people live in an area of 1,071 square kilometers, making Hong Kong one of the most densely populated areas of the world; approximately 98% are of Chinese origin, and by the mid-1980s nearly 60% had been born in Hong Kong.[431] Administered by the United Kingdom since 1842, the territory of Hong Kong consists of Hong Kong and the Lan Tau Islands, the Kowloon Peninsula, and more than 200 smaller islands. It is a major trading and manufacturing hub and the world's third largest financial center, with total banking deposit liabilities of over US$80 billion and a generally unfettered free-market economy.[432] Its annual per capita income of approximately US$8,300 is surpassed in Asia only by Singapore and Japan and is almost fifteen times greater than that of the People's Republic of China. Average annual growth in Gross Domestic Product in 1976–1985 was 7.6%, with increases of over 11% in 1986 and 1987.[433]

The British acquired authority over Hong Kong in a series of three nineteenth-century treaties: the 1842 Treaty of Nanking,[434] which ceded the island of Hong Kong (an area of 75.6 square kilometers) to Great Britain following the "Opium War"; the 1860 Treaty of Peking,[435] which ceded 11.1 square kilometers in the southern part of the Kowloon Pen-

---

431 Hong Kong Government, *Hong Kong 1988* (Hong Kong: Government Information Services, 1988) at 302–03.

432 *Id.* at 49.

433 *Id.* at 46; Government Information Services, "An Overview of Hong Kong's Economy" (n.d.).

434 Sino-British Treaty of Nanking, signed 29 Aug. 1842, 93 Consolidated Treaty Series 467.

435 Convention of Friendship between China and Great Britain, signed 24 Oct. 1860, 123 Consolidated Treaty Series 73.

insula; and a 99-year lease in 1898 of an additional 965.1 square kilometers adjacent to Kowloon, the area which has subsequently become known as the "New Territories."[436]

The British have consistently maintained that the first two treaties ceded sovereignty over Hong Kong and Kowloon to Britain, while China has, as consistently, rejected British occupation as illegal and based on the imposition of unequal treaties.[437] In any event, the expiration in 1997 of the 1898 lease on the New Territories—which constitute over 90% of the total territory of Hong Kong and provide much of the water and electricity to Kowloon and Hong Kong Island—was the motivating force behind the agreement of the British and Chinese governments to alter the status of the entire territory of Hong Kong in 1997.

POLITICAL/CONSTITUTIONAL STRUCTURE[438]

"Hong Kong has often been described as a place with freedom but no democracy,"[439] and formal structures of self-government were not developed until very recently. It is often said that this lack of democratic development was due to British recognition of Chinese sensitivities over any changes which might be interpreted as "decolonizing" Hong Kong or preparing it for a status unrelated to China; an equally valid observation might be that Hong Kong's economic success made authorities reluctant to tamper with the political as well as economic status quo.

Hong Kong is a British Dependent Territory (formerly known as a Crown Colony). The head of the Hong Kong government is the Gov-

See generally Peter Wesley-Smith, *Unequal Treaty 1898–1997* (Hong Kong: Oxford Univ. Press, 1980).

436 Convention between China and Great Britain respecting an Extension of Hong Kong Territory, signed 9 June 1898, 186 Consolidated Treaty Series 310.

437 See, e.g., Yu Shengwu and Yang Shihao, "Three Unequal Treaties," in *The Hong Kong Solution* (Beijing: Beijing Review Foreign Affairs Series, China & the World (6), 1985) at 123–36. Following admission of the People's Republic of China to the United Nations, China requested that Hong Kong and Macao be removed from the UN's list of non-self-governing territories, on the grounds that "Hong Kong and Macao are a part of Chinese territory occupied by British and Portuguese authorities. The settlement of these questions is completely within the scope of China's sovereignty, as these areas do not [at] all belong to the general category of colonies." "Report on the Hongkong Accord," in *id.* at 52–53. The Chinese position was subsequently accepted by the UN General Assembly. GA Res. 2978 (XXVII), 27 UN GAOR, Supp. (No. 30) at 80, UN Doc. A/8730 (1972). Also see Joseph Y.S. Cheng (ed.), *Hong Kong In Search of a Future* (Hong Kong: Oxford Univ. Press, 1984) at 45–74.

438 See generally Hong Kong Government, *Hong Kong 1985* (Hong Kong: Government Information Services, 1985) at 52–70; the situation as of December 1987 is described in United Kingdom, art. 40 CCPR Report, UN Doc. CCPR/C/32/Add.14 (1988), at 77–81.

ernor, who is appointed by the Queen and has traditionally been a career member of the British colonial service. He is ultimately responsible for the government of Hong Kong, and his authority is derived from Letters Patent and Royal Instructions issued in the name of the Queen (i.e., the British government in London). Members of the civil service are appointed by the Governor, as were all members of the Executive Council and Legislative Council prior to 1985.

The Executive and Legislative Councils (commonly referred to as "Exco" and "Legco," respectively) have consisted of "official" and "unofficial" members. While all were appointed until the election of some Legco members beginning in 1985, the former are members of the Hong Kong civil service, while the latter are normally drawn from among well-known business, banking, professional, and other local leaders. The unofficial members of the Executive and Legislative Councils, known collectively as "Omelco," participate actively in the government of Hong Kong; the Omelco Office is funded by the government, although it is not a government department.

Prior to 1985, the Legco had a maximum membership of 61, comprised of 29 official and 32 unofficial members. The Legco enacts legislation, which cannot beome law until the Governor gives his assent; while the Queen has reserve powers to disallow Legco laws (ordinances), these powers have not been used in recent years.

The Hong Kong legal system generally follows that of England and Wales. The extent to which English law is in force in the colony is determined by the 1966 Application of English Law Ordinance, which provides that English common law and rules of equity shall be in force in Hong Kong "so far as they are applicable to the circumstances of Hong Kong or its inhabitants subject to such modifications as such circumstances may require."[440] The power to make any laws, through order of Her Majesty in Council, "as may appear necessary for the peace, order and good government of the territory" is reserved to the British government by the Letters Patent.[441]

The United Kingdom is responsible for the foreign relations of Hong Kong, but the latter "in practice now enjoys a considerable degree of autonomy, particularly regarding trade matters."[442] Hong Kong negotiates bilateral restraint agreements with textile-importing countries under the Multi-Fibre Arrangement and is a separate contracting party to the General Agreement on Tariffs and Trade (GATT). Hong Kong is

439 Emily Lau, "The News Media," in Joseph Y.S. Cheng (ed.), *Hong Kong in Transition* (Hong Kong: Oxford Univ. Press, 1986) at 420.
440 *Hong Kong 1985, supra* note 438, at 63.
441 *Id.*
442 *Id.* at 69.

represented in international trade forums by its own delegation, separate from that of Britain, and may take different positions from the latter.[443]

The judiciary in Hong Kong is headed by a Court of Appeal, from which appeal may be taken to the British Privy Council. While such appeals are rare, decisions of the Privy Council and House of Lords are binding on the Hong Kong courts. Eighty per cent of the judges and lawyers in Hong Kong are expatriates.[444] Chinese and English are official languages in Hong Kong, although only the latter is generally used for legal matters.[445]

Initial reforms towards democratizing the political system in Hong Kong began in 1982, with the creation of local District Boards in each of eighteen administrative districts. Their role is primarily advisory, and since the March 1985 elections a majority of the Board members have been directly elected. An Urban Council deals with health, recreational, and cultural matters for the 80% of the population which lives in urban areas; half of its 30 members are appointed by the Governor and half elected from district constituencies. A Regional Council to deal with the rest of Hong Kong was introduced in 1986; its 36 members are divided equally among directly elected members, appointed members, and members indirectly elected by district boards and other representatives in the New Territories.

At the height of the negotiations which ultimately resulted in the Joint Declaration discussed below, the Hong Kong government presented a Green Paper for public discussion on "The Further Development of Representative Government in Hong Kong."[446] The subsequent White Paper[447] was published after the Sino-British agreement in September 1984, and it adopted several modest reforms to increase popular participation in the government of Hong Kong. The generally conservative nature of the Hong Kong government (and at least a large segment of the population) is reflected in many of the White Paper's conclusions:

Public reaction was generally in favour of the aims of the Green Paper and the gradual and progressive nature of the proposals made in it. The need to ensure that the prosperity and stability of Hong Kong are not put at risk by

443 *Id.* at 70.
444 Albert H.Y. Chen, "Hong Kong's Legal System: Adaptations for 1997 and Beyond," in Y.C. Jao, Leung Chi-Keung, Peter Wesley-Smith and Wong Siu-Lun (eds.), *Hong Kong and 1997, Strategies for the Future* (Hong Kong: Univ. of Hong Kong, 1985) at 247.
445 *Cf. id.* at 241–42.
446 *Green Paper: The Further Development of Representative Government in Hong Kong* (Hong Kong: Gov't. Printer, July 1984).
447 *White Paper: The Further Development of Representative Government in Hong Kong* (Hong Kong: Gov't. Printer, Nov. 1984).

introducing too many constitutional changes too rapidly was widely recognized. . . .

The main aims [of the reforms] are to develop progressively a system of representative government at the central level which is more directly accountable to the people of Hong Kong and is firmly rooted in Hong Kong; to base this system on our existing institutions, as far as possible, and to preserve their best features; and to allow for further development later on.[448]

The primary change was in the composition of the Legislative Council, which, beginning in 1985, would consist of 57 members: 12 unofficial members elected by an electoral college; 12 unofficial members elected by functional constituencies; 22 unofficial members appointed by the Governor; 10 official members, ex officio or appointed by the Governor; and the Governor himself. No changes were made in the Executive Council or the office of Governor.

The concern for "stability and prosperity" is strongly reflected in this system of indirect elections. The electoral college consists of all members of the District Boards, the Urban Council, and the Regional Council (many of whom are themselves appointed). The remaining indirectly elected members of Legco are selected by nine functional constituencies, representing the major economic and professional interests.[449]

The failure to provide for the direct election of any Legco members was criticized by many groups in Hong Kong and was the primary issue debated during another review of the political structure conducted during 1987. The resulting White Paper, issued in February 1988, is an extraordinarily conservative document which was "greeted with almost universal disappointment among political leaders in Hong Kong."[450] While the White Paper recognized that "there is a strong desire among the community for the system of representative government to be developed further,"[451] the only modest changes it proposed were an increase by two of the Legco members indirectly elected by functional constituencies (with a concomitant reduction in the number of appointed

448 *Id*. at paras. 4, 46.

449 One Legco member is selected, respectively, by the Hong Kong General Chamber of Commerce, Chinese General Chamber of Commerce, Federation of Hong Kong Industries, Chinese Manufacturers Association, Hong Kong Association of Banks, Hong Kong Council of Social Services, Hong Kong Medical Association, and through electoral rolls of the education, legal, and engineering professions; the All Registered Employee Trade Unions select two members. *Id*. at Appendix B.

450 "U.K. Plan Saddens Hong Kong Leaders," Int'l Herald Tribune, 11 Feb. 1988, at 1, col. 2.

451 *White Paper: The Development of Representative Government: The Way Forward* (Hong Kong: Gov't. Printer, 1988) at para. 75.

members) and the direct election of ten Legco members (out of 56) in the 1991—not 1988—elections.

The present political system has been described as "a duopoly which consists of government officials and a narrowly-based coalition of private interests."[452] Whether and how that duopoly should be changed or rendered more representative is the fundamental political debate in Hong Kong that will doubtless continue until at least the late 1980s.[453]

THE HONG KONG SPECIAL ADMINISTRATION REGION AFTER 1997

The agreement between China and the United Kingdom on the future of Hong Kong after 1997[454] was described by Premier Zhao Ziyang as "a task of historic significance."[455] Prime Minister Thatcher referred to the agreement as "a landmark in the life of the territory, in the course of Anglo-Chinese relations, and in the history of international diplomacy."[456] For once, neither politician may have exaggerated the significance of the occasion.

Negotiations between China and the United Kingdom were secret, although statements by government leaders were closely analyzed for

---

452 Miron Mushkat and Elfed V. Roberts, "Towards Adversarial Decision-Making in the Pre-1997 Hong Kong Government," in *Hong Kong and 1997, supra* note 444, at 177.

453 See generally *Hong Kong and 1997, supra* note 444, at 9–100, 177–98; *Hong Kong in Transition, supra* note 439, at 1–87; David Bonavia, *Hong Kong 1997, The Final Settlement* (Hong Kong: South China Morning Post, 1985) at 1–18, 151–61; LAU Siu-kai and KUAN Hsin-chi, *Hong Kong after the Sino-British Agreement: Limits to Institutional Change in a Dependent Polity* (Hong Kong: Centre for Hong Kong Studies, Occasional Paper No. 9, Chinese Univ. of Hong Kong, Sept. 1985).

454 The agreement [hereinafter cited as "Joint Declaration"] consists of a "Joint Declaration of the Government of the United Kingdom of Great Britain and Northern Ireland and the Government of the People's Republic of China on the Question of Hong Kong," three accompanying Annexes setting forth the agreement in more specific terms (entitled, respectively, "Elaboration by the Government of the People's Republic of China of Its Basic Policies regarding Hong Kong," "Sino-British Joint Liaison Group," and "Land Leases"), and an Exchange of Memoranda between the two governments concerning nationality and travel documents; the Declaration was initialled on and is dated 26 Sept. 1984, while the undated memoranda were signed at the formal signing of the declaration on 19 Dec. 1984. The text may be found in White Paper, *A Draft Agreement on the Future of Hong Kong*, Cmnd. 9352 (London: HMSO, 1984); *The Hongkong Solution, supra* note 437, at 5–42; and *Hong Kong 1985, supra* note 438, at 1–16; page references in the present work are to the first-cited document.

455 Statement by Chinese Premier Zhao Ziyang at the signing ceremony of the Sino-British joint declaration on the question of Hong Kong, reprinted in *The Hongkong Solution, supra* note 437, at 43.

456 Statement by Prime Minister Margaret Thatcher at the signing ceremony of the Sino-British joint declaration on the question of Hong Kong, *id.* at 45.

hints as to the progress of the talks.[457] An initial hurdle was the mutually exclusive positions on sovereignty over Hong Kong (with respect to those portions ceded to Britain in 1842 and 1860). Initially, the United Kingdom proposed to recognize Chinese sovereignty over Hong Kong after 1997 but to continue British administration; China was unwilling to recognize any formal British role in the post-1997 era. The ultimate concern stated by both sides was to maintain "the prosperity and stability of Hong Kong,"[458] and the United Kingdom soon agreed that this would be accomplished under Chinese sovereignty.

Despite the British government's assertion that it "sought to take into account the view of the people of Hong Kong to the maximum extent possible during the negotiations,"[459] there was no formal consultation with or participation by Hong Kong residents in the negotiation process. However, members of the Hong Kong Executive Council were consulted and informed of progress in the talks by the British government, and the Hong Kong Governor (a British appointee) participated in the negotiations as part of the British delegation.

The British government made clear that, once the text was adopted, neither Hong Kong nor Parliament could alter it:

[A]s is normal with international agreements negotiated between nations there is no realistic possibility of amending the text. The agreement must be taken as a whole. . . .

The alternative to acceptance of the present agreement is to have no agreement. In this case the Chinese Government has made it plain that negotiations could not be reopened and that it would publish its own plan for Hong Kong. . . . Hong Kong, including the New Territories, has since 1898 become an integral whole and Her Majesty's Government are satisfied that there is no possibility of dividing the New Territories which revert to China on 1 July 1997 from the remainder. The choice is therefore between reversion of Hong Kong to China under agreed, legally binding international arrangements or reversion to China without such arrangements. This is not a choice which Her Majesty's Government have sought to impose on the people of Hong Kong. It is a choice imposed by the facts of Hong Kong's history.[460]

While there was understandably a great deal of anxiety in Hong Kong during the negotiations, the Joint Declaration was generally

457   The best source with respect to the negotiations is *Hong Kong In Search of a Future*, *supra* note 437, which is a collection and analysis of official documents and semi-official statements from the 1982–83 period; it includes a particularly useful chronology through the thirteenth round of negotiations in April 1984. Also see Bonavia, *supra* note 453.

458   Joint Declaration, Preamble.

459   *Draft Agreement*, Cmnd. 9352, Introduction, *supra* note 454, at 7.

460   *Id.* at 9–10.

greeted with relief. An Assessment Office was appointed by the Governor to analyze public response to the agreement, and it concluded that

although anxieties and reservations have been expressed by many who have submitted their views, the detailed provisions of the draft agreement have been welcomed, whilst the assurances that they will be implemented have been noted. . . . The calmness with which the draft agreement was received and the reasoned response to it underlines its overall acceptability. There is a general feeling of relief and a wish to build Hong Kong's future on the foundation provided by the draft agreement.[461]

Members of Omelco and other Hong Kong government officials also supported the agreement,[462] and it was formally ratified in Beijing by the British and Chinese Prime Ministers on 19 December 1984.

The debate within Hong Kong quickly turned to developing a more representative government in the period prior to 1997 and ensuring that the 1997 transition would be as smooth as possible. "Prosperity and stability" remain the key concerns of all involved.

Sovereignty

The Sino-British agreement took the rather unusual form of a "joint declaration" rather than a treaty because of the issue of sovereignty; the Chinese position, that the status of Hong Kong is an internal matter, was not consistent with conclusion of a treaty on the subject. Nevertheless, there is no doubt that the "declaration" and annexes constitute a binding international agreement. "Each part of the agreement has the same status. The whole makes up a formal international agreement, legally binding in all its parts. An international agreement of this kind is the highest form of commitment between two sovereign states."[463] "A joint declaration was seen as a more appropriate form for presenting matters concerning sovereignty and administration, with relevant details explained in annexes. In a broad sense, a joint declaration is an international treaty in a different form, and is legally binding under international law."[464]

---

461 *Report by the Commissioner, Assessment Office, on the views expressed in Hong Kong on the Draft Agreement . . . on the Future of Hong Kong* (Hong Kong: Gov't. Printer, Nov. 1984) at paras. 3.2 and 3.26.

462 See Statement issued by the Unofficial Members of the Hong Kong Executive and Legislative Councils on 29 Nov. 1984, reprinted in *Hong Kong 1985, supra* note 438, at 39–41.

463 *Draft Agreement*, Introduction, *supra* note 454, at 7.

464 Chinese Foreign Minister and State Councillor Wu Xueqian, "Report on the Hongkong Accord," in *The Hongkong Solution, supra* note 437, at 59.

The conflicting British and Chinese positions regarding sovereignty over Hong Kong are not directly addressed in the agreement, in tacit recognition that the settlement of historic legal disputes had little relevance to developing a workable future for Hong Kong. The Joint Declaration states that China "has decided to resume the exercise of sovereignty over Hong Kong," while the United Kingdom "declares that it will restore Hong Kong to . . . China," thus preserving both positions.[465]

Within the context of undisputed Chinese sovereignty, the essential characteristic of the agreement is the theory of "one country, two systems" upon which it is based.[466] Hong Kong will become the first "Special Administrative Region" (SAR) under article 31 of the Chinese constitution,[467] retaining "a high degree of autonomy, except in foreign and defence affairs."[468] The basic Chinese policies for an autonomous Hong Kong will remain unchanged for 50 years and include, *inter alia*, the vesting of executive, legislative, and independent judicial power in the Hong Kong SAR; retaining laws currently in force in Hong Kong "basically unchanged," including the current social and economic systems and life-style; protection of human rights; retaining Hong Kong's independent financial status and exempting the SAR from central government taxation; maintenance of Hong Kong's status as a free port and separate customs territory; and granting to Hong Kong control over entry and exit from the SAR.[469] These policies will be implemented through enactment by the Chinese National People's Congress of a "Basic Law" for Hong Kong.[470]

Executive powers

The Hong Kong SAR government is to be composed of local inhabitants, and the chief executive "shall be selected by election or through consultations held locally and be appointed by the Central People's Government."[471] While the executive authorities "shall be accountable to

465 Joint Declaration at 11; *cf*. Roda Mushkat, "The Transition from British to Chinese Rule in Hong Kong: A Discussion of Salient International Legal Issues," 14 Den. J. Int'l L. & Pol'y 171 (1986) at 174–89.

466 See, e.g., Qian Junrui, "One Country, Two Systems—Key To Settling Hongkong Issue," in *The Hongkong Solution, supra* note 437, at 105–12.

467 Art. 31 provides: "The state may establish special administrative regions when necessary. The systems to be instituted in special administrative regions shall be prescribed by law enacted by the National People's Congress in the light of the specific conditions."

468 Joint Declaration at 11.

469 Joint Declaration at 11–12.

470 Joint Declaration, Annex I, §I.

471 *Id*.

the legislature,"[472] this does not necessarily envisage a parliamentary system of government. Principal cabinet officials also will be appointed by the Chinese government, upon nomination by the Hong Kong chief executive. The agreement specifically permits employment of British and other foreign nationals in the SAR civil service and the continuance in office of those public servants, including police, employed on 1 July 1997.[473]

The maintenance of public order is within the responsibility of Hong Kong, and Chinese military forces stationed in Hong Kong for defense purposes "shall not interfere in the internal affairs" of the SAR. Of course, the question arises as to whether there is any restriction on the introduction of Chinese forces if, in the opinion of the central government, public order is no longer being maintained.

Legislative powers

The Hong Kong legislature is to be composed of local inhabitants and "shall be constituted by elections," although there is no indication that this would require direct rather than indirect elections. Legislative competence extends to all subjects "in accordance with the provisions of the [Chinese] Basic Law and legal procedures," and laws adopted by the SAR are to be reported to the Standing Committee of the National People's Congress "for the record."[474] As noted above, all laws in Hong Kong not inconsistent with the Basic Law will remain in force, unless they are subsequently amended by the SAR legislature.

It is unclear which body has the power to determine whether a law adopted by the SAR is in conformity with the Basic Law. Article 67 of the Chinese constitution grants the authority to "interpret statutes" to the Standing Committee of the National People's Congress and specifically authorizes the Standing Committee "to annul those local regulations or decisions of the organs of state power of . . . autonomous regions . . . that contravene the Constitution, the Statutes or the administrative rules and regulations." However, an "autonomous region" is not identical with the "special administrative regions" provided for in article 31 of the constitution and referred to in the agreement.[475] In addition, interpretation of Hong Kong statutes by the Standing Committee might be considered to interfere with the principle of an independent SAR judiciary with the power of final judgment, which is set forth in the agreement.[476]

472 *Id.*
473 *Id.*, §IV.
474 *Id.*, §II.
475 *Cf.* discussion of autonomous regions in China, *infra* chap. 18, at 420–27.
476 Joint Declaration, Annex I, §III.

This issue will undoubtedly be one of the most important to be addressed in the Basic Law. It has been suggested that the Standing Committee may retain "legislative power of interpretation," while Hong Kong courts will have "judicial power" to interpret the Basic Law in the context of specific cases,[477] but this does not necessarily advance our understanding of where ultimate power lies. In most autonomous situations, final authority to interpret the constitution or other basic law of the autonomous community rests with the central government or a joint central-autonomous body, although Hong Kong's unique status may make adherence to the minority view of autonomous competence more reasonable.[478]

Judicial powers

With the exception of determining the compatibility of SAR statutes with the Basic Law, the Hong Kong judiciary appears to be wholly independent of the central government. Judges are appointed by the Hong Kong chief executive upon the recommendation of an independent local commission, and appointment or removal of "principal judges" must receive the approval of the Hong Kong legislature; the latter are reported to the central government for the record only.[479]

The present judicial system in Hong Kong is to be maintained, except for changes made necessary by vesting in Hong Kong courts the power of final adjudication, which presumably extends to all acts of the SAR authorities.

Finances and economy

It is not surprising that several sections of the agreement deal with specific questions vital to Hong Kong's continuing existence as a major financial and trading center after 1997. There will be essentially no formal financial ties between the SAR and central governments, and Hong Kong is to "deal on its own with financial matters, including disposing of its financial resources and drawing up its budgets and its final accounts."[480] The central government has no authority to levy taxes on the SAR, and the latter "shall use its financial revenues exclusively for its own purposes."[481] These provisions are unusual in autonomous-

477 Mushkat, *supra* note 465, at 181 n.55.

478 Among other situations examined in the present work, Eritrea (prior to annexation by Ethiopia) retained authority to interpret its basic law; disputes between Danzig and Poland were submitted to the League of Nations; and disputes concerning interpretation of the statute of the Free Territory of Trieste were to be submitted to an ad-hoc commission.

479 Joint Declaration, Annex I, §III.

480 *Id.*, §V.

481 *Id.*

central relations, and they underscore the special position occupied by Hong Kong both in the international and Chinese financial contexts.

Hong Kong also has full autonomy in decisions as to economic and trade policies, under the general limitation that it "shall maintain the capitalist economic and trade systems previously practised in Hong Kong."[482] Present monetary and financial systems are to be maintained and remain within the competence of the SAR government, and the Hong Kong dollar will remain the freely convertible currency of Hong Kong.[483] A separate shipping register may be maintained, under the name of "Hong Kong, China," and the SAR has the authority to regulate access of shipping to the ports of Hong Kong (with the exception of foreign warships, access for which will require the permission of the central government).[484] Civil aviation also remains largely within Hong Kong's jurisdiction, including the negotiation and conclusion of air service agreements (under authorization from China) with foreign states for services which do not operate to, from, or through mainland China.[485]

Foreign relations

Along with the "one country, two systems" philosophy of an autonomous capitalist Hong Kong within a communist China, perhaps the most distinctive feature of the agreement is the extensive authority granted to the Hong Kong SAR in the area of foreign relations and participation in international organizations. While residual competence in foreign affairs is reserved to China,[486] the specific grants of competence to Hong Kong are significant.

As noted above, Hong Kong currently participates in the activities of several international organizations, subject to the constitutional preeminence of the British government. It is treated as a separate territory within GATT; it is a member of, *inter alia*, the UN Economic and Social Commission for Asia and the Pacific, the Asian Productivity Organization, and the Asian Development Bank. "[A]cting with the consent of" the British government, Hong Kong has negotiated agreements directly with foreign governments concerning, for example, textile quotas, and has concluded agreements with the Chinese provincial government of Guandong.[487]

In general, this autonomous international participation is to continue after 1997. The Joint Declaration states that, "[u]sing the name of 'Hong Kong, China', the Hong Kong Special Administrative Region

482 *Id.*, §VI.
483 *Id.*, §VII.
484 *Id.*, §VIII.
485 *Id.*, §IX.
486 Joint Declaration at 11; Annex I, §XI.
487 Mushkat, *supra* note 465, at 172–73.

may on its own maintain and develop economic and cultural relations and conclude relevant agreements with states, regions and relevant international organisations."[488] In particular, specific authority is granted to the SAR to participate in international trade agreements, such as GATT, and to continue to enjoy its own export quotas, tariff preferences, and other similar arrangements. The SAR also may establish official and semi-official economic and trade missions in foreign countries, reporting such missions to the central government for the record.[489] As noted above, the conclusion of bilateral foreign air service agreements also falls mainly within Hong Kong's competence, although any agreements involving air services between other parts of China with stops in Hong Kong are to be concluded by the central government.[490]

Hong Kong may "on its own, . . . maintain and develop relations and conclude and implement agreements with states, regions and relevant international organisations *in the appropriate fields*, including the economic, trade, financial and monetary, shipping, communications, touristic, cultural and sporting fields."[491] Members of the SAR government also may participate, as members of the Chinese delegation, in diplomatic negotiations which directly affect the SAR and in international organizations or conferences limited to states which affect the SAR. The SAR may participate independently in international organizations and conferences *not* limited to states, under the name "Hong Kong, China."

The Chinese government will decide, in consulation with the SAR, whether to apply to Hong Kong treaties to which China is a party; treaties to which China is not a party but which are implemented in Hong Kong shall continue to be implemented in the latter. China is to "take the necessary steps" to ensure that Hong Kong retains its status "in an appropriate capacity" in international organizations of which China is a member and in which Hong Kong now participates.[492]

Foreign consular and other missions may be established in the SAR with China's permission; such permission is specifically granted for the establishment of a British Consulate-General.

Human rights

Although a majority of today's Hong Kong residents were born in the territory, a large proportion of the older population of Hong Kong consists of refugees or immigrants from mainland China. Insofar as many

---

488 Joint Declaration at 12.
489 Joint Declaration, Annex I, §VI.
490 *Id.*, §IX.
491 *Id.*, §XI (emphasis added).
492 *Id.*

had fled communist China for political as well as economic reasons, serious concern has been expressed over the protection of human rights—particularly freedom of the press, religion, and travel[493]—following reunification in 1997. In part to meet these anxieties, the agreement specifies that the Hong Kong SAR

shall maintain the rights and freedoms as provided for by the laws previously in force in Hong Kong, including freedom of the person, of speech, of the press, of assembly, of association, to form and join trade unions, of correspondence, of travel, of movement, of strike, of demonstration, of choice of occupation, of academic research, of belief, inviolability of the home, the freedom to marry and the right to raise a family freely.[494]

The explanatory notes attached to the agreement by the British government underscore that this list is not intended to be exhaustive.[495]

The agreement also refers to the rights to counsel and judicial remedies, including a statement that "[e]very person shall have the right to challenge the actions of the executive in the courts."[496] The right of religious organizations to maintain schools and other institutions, as well as the competence of the SAR to determine educational policies and continue the present educational system, also are guaranteed.[497]

Detailed provisions regarding the right of abode or residence, travel, and nationality are contained in section XIV of the agreement and in the appended memoranda exchanged by the two governments.[498] The SAR has the right to issue SAR passports to all Chinese nationals who are permanent residents of Hong Kong and travel documents to other lawful residents, guaranteeing the bearers' right to return to Hong Kong. Hong Kong may regulate immigration to the SAR by "persons of foreign states and regions," and entry into Hong Kong by persons from other parts of China is to be regulated in accordance with present practice.

Questions of nationality are important primarily in determining whether Hong Kong residents might have the right to enter and reside in the United Kingdom or to avail themselves of British diplomatic protection, and the memoranda dealing with these issues have been among the most widely criticized portions of the agreement.[499] The

493 *Report of the Assessment Office, supra* note 461, paras. 4.48–4.51.
494 Joint Declaration, Annex I, §XIII.
495 *Draft Agreement, supra* note 454, at 37.
496 Joint Declaration, Annex I, §XIII.
497 *Id.*, §X and §XIII.
498 *Id.*, §XIV.
499 See, e.g., *Report of the Assessment Office, supra* note 461, paras. 4.65–4.71. Others have questioned whether the two unilateral memoranda by the United Kingdom and China, respectively, are internationally binding; unlike the Annexes, they are not

Chinese memorandum sets out the consistent Chinese position that all Hong Kong Chinese are Chinese nationals, whether or not they are considered by the British to be "British Dependent Territories citizens" (BDTCs). However, it also permits former BDTCs to use British travel documents after 1997, "[t]aking account of the historical background of Hong Kong and its realities."[500]

The United Kingdom Memorandum states that BDTC status will lapse on 1 July 1997, but that it will be replaced by "an appropriate status which, without conferring the right of abode in the United Kingdom [which is not currently possessed by BDTCs], will entitle them to continue to use passports issued by the Government of the United Kingdom."[501] The new status (that of British Nationals [Overseas] or "BNO") will not be transferable by descent, and its holders will be able to avail themselves of British diplomatic protection overseas, except in Hong Kong or China.

With respect to non-Chinese BDTCs, it appears that the British actions may have the effect of rendering them (and their children) stateless, as they would be neither Chinese nor British nationals after 1997. The British have sought to address this problem by utilizing yet another category of nationality, British Overseas Citizens, a non-transferable status that will include post-1997 babies born to BNO parents and non-Chinese BDTCs who do not obtain or qualify for BNO passports.[502]

The Joint Declaration states that private property and ownership of enterprises will be protected by law, and the final Annex to the agreement considers in detail the issue of land leases; implementation of the Annex is to be monitored by a joint British-Chinese Land Commission during the period up to 30 June 1997.[503]

One of the most interesting undertakings in the agreement is that "[t]he provisions of the International Covenant on Civil and Political Rights and the International Covenant on Economic, Social and Cultural Rights as applied to Hong Kong shall remain in force."[504] China was not a party to either Covenant at the time of the Joint Declaration, nor had it become a party by the end of 1988. Certainly the United Kingdom's responsibility for Hong Kong will be extinguished in 1997, and

---

referred to specifically in the Joint Declaration itself. See Mushkat, *supra* note 465, at 202 n.169. For support for the proposition that unilateral declarations can have binding legal effect, see International Court of Justice, Nuclear Tests (Australia v. France; New Zealand v. France), Judgments, I.C.J. Reports 1974, pp. 253, 457.
   500 Joint Declaration, Chinese Memorandum, at 29.
   501 *Id.*, United Kingdom Memorandum, at 28.
   502 *Cf.* Mushkat, *supra* note 465, at 203–05.
   503 Joint Declaration at 12; Annex III.
   504 *Id.*, Annex I, §XIII.

China can have no obligation thereafter unless it does become a party to the Covenants. While separate ratification or accession by "Hong Kong, China" might present an attractive alternative, participation in both Covenants appears to be limited to states.[505]

Were China to become a party to the Covenants, the agreement's reference to provisions "as applied to Hong Kong" might limit China's obligations to those previously accepted by the United Kingdom.[506] The United Kingdom has recognized the competence of the Human Rights Committee to receive interstate complaints under article 41 of the Covenant on Civil and Political Rights. This surely is a provision of the Covenant applicable to Hong Kong; is China obligated under the agreement not only to ratify the Covenant but to make a corresponding declaration under article 41?[507]

Observations

"I approach the subject of political development in Hong Kong with trepidation, for never before in the history of Hong Kong is the political scene so muddled that statements about its future can hardly be made

---

505 Covenant on Civil and Political Rights, art. 48; Covenant on Economic, Social and Cultural Rights, art. 26.

506 Query whether this formulation would oblige China to adopt the United Kingdom reservations, even if it wished to extend the full scope of the Covenants to the Hong Kong SAR? With respect to the Covenant on Civil and Political Rights, the latter has made reservations affecting Hong Kong to articles 12(1) (considering each territory as a separate entity for purposes of recognizing freedom of movement and residence), 12(4) (regarding immigration), 13 (regarding the right of review of a decision to deport an alien and to be represented for this purpose before the competent authority), 20 (regarding propaganda for war or advocacy of national, racial, or religious hatred, on the grounds that existing British legislation is sufficient not to require additional legislation), 24 (reserving the right to enact such nationality legislation as the government "may deem necessary"), and 25 (reserving the right not to establish an elected Executive or Legislative Council).

With respect to the Covenant on Economic, Social and Cultural Rights, reservations applicable to Hong Kong refuse to extend the provisions of articles 7(a)(i) (regarding equal pay to men and women for equal work in the private sector) and 8(1)(b) (the right of trade unions to establish national federations or confederations and to form or join international trade-union organizations).

For the texts of the reservations, see *Human Rights, Status of International Instruments, supra* note 133, at 16–17, 47–48; Richard B. Lillich (ed.), *International Human Rights Instruments* (Buffalo, NY: William S. Hein, 1985) at 170.28–170.30, 180.14–180.15.

507 A suggestion by the Governor of Hong Kong (during a speech to the National Press Club, Washington, DC, 21 Oct. 1987) that the human rights provisions of the Covenants may be preserved through their inclusion in the law of the Hong Kong SAR hardly seems sufficient to meet the letter of the Agreement, as international oversight by the Human Rights Committee constitutes an essential part of the "provisions" of the Covenants.

with certitude."[508] Yet while the specifics may remain muddled, there is a consensus that the goal of the next decade is to develop institutions that will preserve stability and prosperity in Hong Kong and ensure the smoothest possible transition between 30 June and 1 July 1997.

It is this shared goal, the desire not to tamper with a system that most feel has worked well in the past, that gives cause for optimism when one considers whether the Sino-British agreement on autonomy for Hong Kong will succeed in establishing a viable "one country, two systems" and preserve the essential economic, political, and social characteristics of Hong Kong within the larger Chinese communist state. At the same time, however, it is clear that changes will be necessary in order for things to stay the same.[509]

The economic (and perhaps political) success of Hong Kong in the past must be understood in a colonial context: the lack of representative democratic institutions in Hong Kong was of little concern in light of the benign authoritarianism of British rule, informal conventions of consultation (at least with the elites), and laissez-faire capitalism which characterized the territory's political life. However, these informal practices cannot simply be transferred to the very different authority of Beijing. Thus, the feeling has grown that Hong Kong must develop into a more solidly based participatory democracy, in order to assert its autonomy effectively in the post-1997 era.

Reform is constrained by several factors, the most important of which are the generally passive or even apathetic attitude towards politics of the vast majority of Hong Kong's population, and the desire of China, the United Kingdom, and the current Hong Kong elites not to rock the thus far successful boat unnecessarily. This conservative climate has been disturbed by relatively small numbers of democratic activists, who have focused on issues such as direct election of at least some members of the Legislative Council and ensuring broad competence for Hong Kong courts to interpret local laws and determine their compatibility with the Chinese Basic Law.

A 1987 opinion poll found that 42% of Hong Kong residents were uninterested in election procedures for the Legislative Council or proposed changes thereto,[510] despite the fact that this is the most widely discussed component of reforms to increase the representative nature of government. In the 1985 District Board elections, only 32% of those

508 Lau Siu-kai, "Political Reform and Political Development in Hong Kong: Dilemmas and Choices," in *Hong Kong and 1997, supra* note 444, at 23.

509 *Cf.* Lau and Kuan, *supra* note 453, at 3–4.

510 "Direct polls win support of 39pc," South China Morning Post, 31 Jan. 1987, at 1, col. 2.

eligible to vote were registered, and only 38% of this number actually voted.[511] Given the limited powers of the District Boards, the low turn-out is perhaps unsurprising, but it also may reflect the lack of any electoral tradition in Hong Kong.

The Hong Kong political system is often described as consensual, and one area of disagreement among those seeking to determine the territory's political future is whether adversarial politics would disrupt the "stability and prosperity" which has developed under a colonial system dominated by the executive and the bureaucracy. No true political parties have developed since the announcement of the agreement and the beginnings of more representative government. Many factors will probably militate against the growth of strong parties, including the institutional weakness of the legislature compared with the executive; the lingering political apathy noted above; the fragmentation of power which has resulted from the current system of indirect elections and functional representation; the absence of strong ideological issues, in light of the broad pro-capitalist consensus in Hong Kong; the semi-dependent image of many political leaders, who have been ultimately subservient to the British and will be similarly overshadowed by the mainland Chinese; and the apparent opposition of both British and Chinese governments to the "dangers" of openly competing political forces.[512]

While some have criticized the British government for moving too slowly on political reforms, the attitude of the Chinese government obviously increases in importance as 1997 approaches. This is explicitly recognized in the 1988 White Paper on representative government, which notes that the post-1997 framework of government in Hong Kong will be incorporated into the Chinese Basic Law to be promulgated in 1990 and then goes on to state: "Decisions will therefore need to be taken during the period up to 1997 to enable Hong Kong's system of government to evolve in a way that is compatible both with the aspirations of the Hong Kong community and with the framework set out in the Basic Law."[513]

China might contend, with some justification, that its agreement in 1984 to maintain the laws in force in Hong Kong "basically unchanged" implies no major alterations to the political or economic structure of Hong Kong in the post-1984 period. Following the 1985 Legco elections,

---

511 Joseph Y. S. Cheng, "The 1985 District Board Elections in Hong Kong," in Cheng, *supra* note 439, at 67, 68.

512 *Cf.*, e.g., Lau Siu-kai, "Political Reform and Political Development in Hong Kong: Dilemmas and Choices," in *Hong Kong and 1997, supra* note 444, at 40–43; "Real 'Party Politics' Still Appear Unlikely," Int'l Herald Tribune, 23 Oct. 1986, at 10, col. 5.

513 *White Paper, supra* note 451, para. 77.

for example, senior Beijing officials warned against "unnecessary chaos" if political reforms were too dramatic.[514] The removal of Chinese Communist party chief Hu Yaobang in January 1987 and the accompanying campaign against "bourgeois liberals" caused great anxiety in Hong Kong, as the permissible limits of disagreement with the party line became more evident. The massacre of pro-democracy demonstrators by Chinese troops in Beijing's Tiananmen Square in June 1989 stunned Hong Kong, which had seen the largest demonstrations in its history in support of the Chinese democracy movement.

At least prior to June 1989, not all the signs had been negative. Local opposition forced the Hong Kong government to modify legislation (the Legislative Council Powers and Privileges Bill) which lawyers and journalists had denounced as an attempt to stifle dissent. The Sino-British Joint Liaison Group, created by the agreement to facilitate various transitional issues (such as reviewing international agreements applicable to Hong Kong and the actions which must be taken by both governments to ensure their continued application),[515] has generally functioned well, and agreement has been reached on issues which include travel and identification documents, air service agreements, and establishment of a shipping register.[516] There is active (if minority) participation by Hong Kong residents in the Chinese Basic Law Drafting Committee.

An initial draft of the Basic Law was published in April 1988 and opened for public comment.[517] Many of its 172 articles parallel the language of the Joint Declaration, including the latter's ambiguities. Reflecting the lack of consensus among members of the Drafting Committee, several different alternatives are presented for election of the SAR's Chief Executive and Legislative Council.[518] The human rights provisions of the draft[519] also are problematic and appear to permit much greater limitations on rights than might be permissible under the two international covenants, the provisions of which, under the Joint Declaration, are to "remain in force." The draft Basic Law provides only

514 "Colony's Quest For Confidence Shadows Upturn," Int'l Herald Tribune, 23 Oct. 1986, at 9, col. 5.

515 Joint Declaration, Annex II.

516 Speech by Hong Kong Governor Sir David Wilson, National Press Club, Washington, DC, 21 Oct. 1987.

517 Drafting Committee for the Basic Law, *The Draft Basic Law of the Hong Kong Special Administrative Region of the People's Republic of China (for solicitation of opinions)* (April 1988).

518 *Id.*, Annexes I and II. A second draft of the Basic Law, adopted in February 1989, provides for direct election, by district, of one-half of the Legco members in the third and fourth legislative terms. Direct election of all Legco members may begin thereafter if approved by referendum and the Chinese government.

519 *Id.*, arts. 23–42.

that the covenants are to be implemented "through legislation by the Hong Kong Special Administrative Region."[520]

Articles 169 and 170 of the draft specify that the powers of interpreting and amending the Basic Law rest with the Standing Committee of the National People's Congress.[521] However, the SAR courts may interpret the Basic Law in adjudicating cases before them, subject to mandatory reference to the Standing Committee for the interpretation of provisions concerning defense, foreign affairs, "and other affairs which are the responsibility of the Central People's Government."[522]

Comments on the draft were received through September 1988, and public opinion was again solicited following approval in February 1989 of a second draft by the Standing Committee of the National People's Congress. The Basic Law then will be formally submitted to the full People's Congress for adoption, presumably no later than 1990, although calls for delaying the process followed the Tiananmen Square massacre.

There is no question that life in Hong Kong will be different after 1997, and it is evident that no society—let alone one as dynamic as that of Hong Kong—will remain unchanged for fifty years, as promised by the Sino-British agreement. While the economic situation has remained generally positive, there have been flights of capital, companies, and businesses from Hong Kong. Not everyone would share the following harsh analysis, but neither is it unique:

The plain fact is that, ever since the British began negotiations with Peking over the 1997 issue, standards have plummeted in every area of Hongkong life, both public and private. The hugely successful city which once encapsulated capitalist optimism and confidence is dwindling into a third-rate place where worries are paramount, the profit motive has been superceded by myopic greed and men and women of principle feel at odds with the rest of society.[523]

520 *Id.*, art. 38.

521 Art. 170 states that no amendment to the Basic Law "shall contravene the established basic policies of . . . China regarding Hong Kong."

522 *Id.*, art. 169.

523 Derek Davies, "Stopping the rot," Far Eastern Economic Review, 16 Apr. 1987, at 39. Similar sentiments were expressed a few months earlier, following the death of Sir Edward Youde, Governor of Hong Kong.

There is a very distinct feeling here that we are all standing on a bridge that may be about to collapse. No one wants to start a stampede, because then it very definitely will collapse. No one wants to be seen to be trying to get off, because that would start a stampede. So people are sliding off quietly, edging away, and hoping that no one will notice them.

Simon Winchester, "A Funeral in Hong Kong," Wash. Post, 16 Dec. 1986, at A19, col. 1. *Cf.* "A New Wave for Hong Kong: Young Professionals Fleeing," N.Y. Times, 9 Nov. 1987, at A1, col. 1.

The strong traditional role of the executive and bureaucracy in Hong Kong will render it more susceptible to influence from Beijing, particularly since the power to appoint the Hong Kong chief executive rests with the central Chinese government. However, it is essential in analyzing Hong Kong's internal political reforms to remember that one is not examining an independent state or even an entity in the process of decolonization. Hong Kong has been a "dependent territory" and will become a "special administrative region," and it should not be expected that it will have all (or most) of the attributes of independence.

In fact, the extensive grants of autonomous powers to the Hong Kong SAR make a certain degree of informal or indirect control by the central government almost inevitable. The most striking aspect of Hong Kong after 1997 will not be any limits on direct electoral politics but the autonomous development of the SAR in economic, trade, and international affairs. In light of the broad powers described in the agreement and the fact that no one can accuse the People's Republic of China of not taking sovereignty seriously, the example of Hong Kong undermines the arguments of other governments which view much less extensive autonomy arrangements as threats to national unity.

The one area in which Hong Kong's autonomy may be somewhat less extensive than that of other situations discussed in the present book is with respect to future changes in the relationship between the SAR and the mainland, in that the People's National Congress has the power to amend the Basic Law unilaterally. The provisions of the agreement can be safeguarded only indirectly by the British government between 1997 and 2047, and it would be helpful if the Basic Law itself contained a dispute-settlement or consultative mechanism in the event of disagreements over its implementation or amendment.

The Joint Declaration's autonomy arrangements were essentially imposed upon the Hong Kong population, without formal consultation or provision for a referendum. While the subsequent "assessment" conducted by the Hong Kong government is undoubtedly correct in its conclusion that the agreement was generally supported by Hong Kong residents, that support could be expressed only on a take-it-or-leave-it basis. While the peculiar position of Hong Kong as a colony or occupied territory (depending on which theory one adopts) rendered Sino-British negotiations more defensible legally, the resolution of the situation from above rather than from below recalls efforts by London and Dublin to address the Northern Irish conflict and by Colombo and Delhi to deal with the conflict in Sri Lanka. More local consultation occurred in Hong Kong than in the other two situations, but the ultimate success or failure of each will depend on the substantive reasonableness of the agreements and the will to implement them in the face of possible extremist opposition, rather than on the manner in which they were adopted.

Underlying the Hong Kong experiment and the concept of "one country, two systems" is the Chinese desire for eventual "reintegration" of Macao and, in particular, Taiwan with the mainland. In March 1987, Portugal and China agreed that Macao will revert to China in 1999, and its status is widely expected to resemble closely that of Hong Kong, on which Macao depends heavily. Taiwan has not publicly responded to Chinese overtures, but there is no question that any eventual negotiations between China and Taiwan can occur only if the Hong Kong agreement can be seen to be a success.

On its side, China has persistently refused to link the autonomy granted to Hong Kong with other autonomous regions within China, such as Tibet. Chinese repression of Tibetan demonstrations for independence or autonomy may serve as a warning to Hong Kong, and one can fairly accuse China of inconsistency, at least, in its tolerance of a separate system in Hong Kong but not in Tibet. However, a successful (from Beijing's perspective) Hong Kong SAR would surely offer a valuable precedent to Tibetans and others who wish to preserve their lifestyle from destruction by the Han Chinese majority.

One of the most difficult challenges to the "one country, two systems" formulation will be in the area of human rights and political freedoms, as demonstrated only too clearly by China's crushing of the pro-democracy movement in 1989. The "two systems" envisaged are based on fundamentally different approaches, and it will be particularly difficult for them to co-exist if a free and democratic Hong Kong is only an island in a totalitarian and repressive China.[524] However, just as one should not expect Hong Kong to remain unchanged for fifty years, it is equally inconceivable that mainland society will be static. There will no doubt be constant pressures on each system to become more compatible with the other, and it remains to be seen which combination of communism, capitalism, authoritarianism, and democracy will prevail. While this uncertainty is a source of anxiety to many in Hong Kong, it might also be viewed as an opportunity for Hong Kong to influence the wider development of Chinese society.

---

524 *Cf.* the discussion of the Sudan, chap. 15.

Chapter 8
India and the Punjab

Problems of national unification and of religious and linguisic rights have been fundamental to modern Indian politics and history. India has experienced not only the partition of British India into India and Pakistan, but also insurgencies in Nagaland and other parts of the northeast and a long-standing sentiment on the part of some in favor of Kashmiri independence or accession to Pakistan.[525]

Although most ethnic conflicts in India do not raise the specter of secession, many ethnic and linguistic groups fear the loss of their homelands and cultural identities in the face of the modernization of Indian society and the internal migration which almost inevitably follows.[526] For example, the state[527] of Maharashtra claims a district in neighboring Karnataka, on the grounds of linguistic affinity; the Chief Minister of Sikkim has demanded that the central government recognize the rights of Nepali speakers, who constitute 70% of Sikkim's population; and the Nepali-speaking Gurkhas of West Bengal fought for two years for an autonomous Gurkhaland. The crisis in Assam, which was partially resolved in August 1985, has now shifted from the grievances of the Assamese to the grievances of the tribal and Bengali people of the state who feel prejudiced by restrictions on illegal immigration from Bangladesh and the disenfranchisement of foreign nationals in Assam.

These challenges to national unity are not new phenomena. The

525 Cf., e.g., Neville Maxwell, *India, the Nagas and the Northeast* (London: Minority Rights Group, 1980); Dilip Hiro, *Inside India Today* (New York: Monthly Review Press, 1976), chap. 17; and M.J. Akbar, *India: The Siege Within* (London: Penguin Books, 1985).

526 See, e.g., Myron Weiner, *Sons of the Soil* (Princeton, NJ: Princeton Univ. Press, 1978).

527 Following Indian usage, "state" in this chapter refers to the sub-federal constituent parts of the larger Indian Union.

pre-independence period was characterized by demands for special consideration or even sovereignty by various groups, such as the larger
princely states and the populous Tamil and other Dravidian peoples in
southern India. Indeed, the devolution of provincial autonomy under
the Government of India Act of 1935 was intended to be the first step
in a process whereby the provincial governments and the princely states
would enter into an undetermined form of federation.[528]

The Indian Independence Act of 1947 was the legal basis for the
transfer of sovereignty from the British crown to the Dominion governments of India and Pakistan. However, since the crown had had
treaty relations with the nominally sovereign rulers of the Indian princely
states outside the provincial structure of British India, a further act of
accession to India or Pakistan by these nominal sovereigns was necessary. In most instances, these accessions by the princely states brought
the relations between them and the central government into line with
the distribution of powers between "the center" and the provinces provided for in the Government of India Act.

The large and wealthy princely state of Hyderabad maintained that
it was sovereign at the time of independence in 1947, and its ruler placed
his case before the UN Security Council in August 1948.[529] While the
Security Council was considering the matter, India invaded Hyderabad,
and the latter's complaint was withdrawn in favor of a negotiated compromise with the Indian government.[530]

In Kashmir, the ruling Maharajah was a Hindu, descended from a
family which had provided advisers and military leaders to the Punjab
empire, while the vast majority of the state's population was Muslim.
Nevertheless, the Muslim League, which led the struggle for partition
of India and Pakistan, failed to win the support of the Kashmiri Muslim
masses, who instead opted for a program of social reform and economic
development similar to that offered elsewhere by the Congress party.

The Maharajah of Kashmir refused to accede to either Pakistan or
India. When irregular troops from Pakistan invaded Kashmir, the Maharajah appealed to the Indian government for assistance, but he was
rebuffed on the grounds that such assistance would be improper in the
absence of a valid instrument of accession. On 26 October 1947 the
Maharajah signed an instrument acceding to India, precipitating the first
Indo-Pakistani war.[531]

---

528 Ayesha Jalal, *The Sole Spokesman* (Cambridge: Cambridge Univ. Press) at 15
et seq.

529 3 UN SCOR, Supp., UN Doc. S/986 (1948) at 5; *cf.* Whiteman, *supra* note 35,
at 502–05.

530 See Whiteman, *supra* note 35, at 504–05.

531 See generally Josef Korbel, *Danger in Kashmir* (Princeton, NJ: Princeton Univ.
Press, rev. ed. 1966); Whiteman, *supra* note 35, at 505.

The instrument of accession granted only defense, foreign affairs, and communications powers to the central government, a much narrower grant than the instruments of accession executed by the other princely rulers. It was arguable that the Maharajah retained some elements of sovereignty, and the 1950 constitution of India recognizes the special status of Kashmir in article 370.[532]

CONSTITUTIONAL FRAMEWORK

The political context in which the Constituent Assembly met to draft the constitution of independent India made creation of a federal solution almost inevitable. Even without the violence which surrounded and followed independence, a federal system was compelling in a nation which has fifteen major languages and hundreds of minor ones; numerous ethnic, cultural, and religious identities; and vast economic and geographic disparities. On the other hand, as a desperately poor country in need of rapid development, India also desired a strong central government which would be able to coordinate capital investment, allocate scarce raw materials, and integrate marginal groups into the process of economic development.

The Congress party had a strong centralist orientation and a geographically and culturally diverse base of support which made it a genuinely all-India party. It was committed to an autarchic model of government-led economic development and took the position that provincial autonomy without a strong central government was only a British manoeuvre to derail the independence movement and to reward conservative loyalist elites in the provinces.[533] Following the trauma of partition, there was a compelling case for stemming the centrifugal tide, and the Congress party did support the principle of linguistically based provinces.

The constitution of India declares in Article 1 that "India . . . shall be a Union of States." However, this is a far cry from, for example, the U.S. model of federalism, under which the national government is granted enumerated powers while undelegated powers and residual sovereignty remain with the states. Article 3 of the Indian constitution— under which Parliament may form new states by partition or merger, increase or diminish the area of any state, and alter the boundaries or name of any state—makes clear the extent to which sovereignty remains with the central government. Unlike the United States, which is an indestructible union of indestructible states, the Indian union is an indestructible union of destructible states.

---

532 *Cf.* Magher Singh v. Principal Secretary, Jammu & Kashmir Government, AIR 1953, J&K 25, 27–28.

533 Jalal, *supra* note 528, at chap. 2.

The procedure for amending the constitution also evidences India's strongly unitary nature. Article 368 provides that a two-thirds majority of Parliament is all that is required to amend the Constitution, with the exception of those articles which relate to the election of the President (Articles 54 & 55), the extent of executive power of the central and state governments (Articles 73 & 162), the composition and jurisdiction of the High Courts of the states (Article 241 and Chapter V of Part VI), the Supreme Court's composition and jurisdiction (Chapter IV of Part V), the demarcation of legislative jurisdiction between the states and the Center (Chapter I of Part XI and the Seventh Schedule to the Constitution), the manner of representation of the states in Parliament, and the provisions of Article 368 itself.[534] Section 5 of Article 368 explicitly declares that the constituent power of Parliament is unlimited.

Articles 245–255 of the constitution divide legislative competence between Parliament and the state legislatures by defining three categories of laws. The first category (the "Union List") enumerates the subjects which are within the exclusive competence of the central Parliament; the second ("State List") enumerates the areas of exclusive state powers; and the third ("Concurrent List") enumerates areas which are subject to concurrent jurisdiction. However, Article 249 allows Parliament to legislate with respect to the subjects in the state list if it is determined by the Upper House of Parliament (which is largely elected indirectly by the state legislatures) that it is "necessary or expedient in the national interest." Article 250 allows Parliament to legislate with respect to any matter on the state list during a proclaimed state of emergency, and Article 248 confers residual legislative powers upon Parliament.

The legislative hegemony of the central government is mirrored by executive hegemony, and the executive power of the states is subject to direction by the central executive in order to ensure compliance with national laws (Article 256). Article 257, which is considerably enhanced by the emergency powers available to the central government under Articles 352–360, provides that a state may not "impede or prejudice the executive power of the Union."

Article 356 allows the President of India to assume executive and legislative power over a state if the government of the state "cannot be carried on in accordance with the provisions of this Constitution." This power has been invoked on approximately 70 occasions since independence, and it has often been used in a partisan manner by central governments against opposition parties which have managed to form state governments.

---

534 For these matters, the constitution requires the concurrence of half of the state legislatures.

The Indian Supreme Court has done little to preserve the scope of state competence. In 1963, the court extensively discussed the consistently unitary nature of the Indian state since the assumption of power by the British crown and concluded that the Indian constitution had effected no change in that essentially unitary nature.[535] In a case which arose in Punjab shortly after its creation as a Sikh majority state, the court upheld the power of the centrally-appointed Governor to prorogue the state legislature even though it was not in session, in order to acquire the authority to promulgate an ordinance.[536] A 1977 case seemed to confirm in dictum the power of the central government to intervene in state politics by instructing the chief minister of a state to dissolve the state legislature and call new elections.[537]

THE PUNJAB

By virtue of its geographical position, Punjab has always been a stage for conflict between political powers based in the subcontinent and invading armies from Afghanistan and central Asia.[538] The Sikh religion, which arose in the Punjab and has always been limited to Punjabis, itself reflects both Islamic values carried into the subcontinent by Muslim invaders and what may broadly be considered "Hindu" social and religious values.

With the ascension of Maharajah Ranjit Singh to the leadership of a small Punjabi kingdom, the former victims of expanding empires became themselves the architects of one of the most powerful empires in Asia.[539] At its height, the empire of Ranjit Singh extended from Tibet to the Arabian Sea and from Afghanistan to the vicinity of Delhi.

The Sikhs, who constituted only a small minority of the population of the empire, clearly benefited from their common religious identity with the Maharajah, and many provincial Sikh families held prominent positions. However, all religious groups within the empire participated in its administration; Muslims were important in the conduct of foreign policy and Hindus in financial affairs. Thus, at its height, Sikh political power was exercised in the context of a multicultural empire, the ma-

---

535 State of West Bengal v. Union of India, AIR 1963 S.C. 1241. See generally Pannalal Dhar, *National Integration and Indian Constitution* (New Delhi: Deep & Deep Publ., 1986) at 121–67.

536 State of Punjab v. Satpal Dang, appeal of Civil Writ no. 1226 of 1968, Punjab and Haryana High Court.

537 State of Rajasthan v. Union of India, AIR 1977 S.C. 1361.

538 The word Punjab means "five rivers," and in geographical rather than political terms it refers to the river plains of the Ravi, Beas, Sutlej, Jhelum, and Indus rivers.

539 The standard reference on the history of the Sikhs from the fifteenth through the twentieth centuries is the two-volume work by Kushwant Singh, *A History of the Sikhs* (Princeton, NJ: Princeton Univ. Press, 1963, 1966).

jority of whose subjects were Muslims. Sikhs themselves were scattered throughout the empire, and their culture and religion were a source of prestige and power even where they constituted minuscule minorities.

For ten years following the death of Ranjit Singh in 1839, the British kept close watch on events in the Punjabi court at Lahore, as the late Maharajah's family and courtiers engaged in bloody intrigues to determine the succession and distribution of power among the various provinces of the empire. Following two wars between the Lahore court and the British, who by now had entered into alliances with several notables within and outside the pale of the empire, the British annexed Punjab.

Despite the two wars and mutual mistrust, subsequent developments led to a strong identification between Sikh and British interests. During the Indian Mutiny of 1857, less than a decade after the subjugation of Punjab, the Sikhs remained loyal to British interests and refused to participate in the rebellion (although to some extent this was because of the Sikh perception of the mutiny as a Muslim attempt to reestablish the Mughal empire). The British soon came to depend upon the Sikhs as the backbone of their military presence in the subcontinent, while the Sikhs came to see the British as guarantors against the perceived threat from other Indian communities. Punjabis came to predominate in the armed forces of British India, with Sikhs having the most disproportionate representation.

While a central tenet of the Sikh religion is adherence to the teaching of the faith's founder, Guru Nanak, and to the holy book, Guru Granth Sahib, many Sikhs continued simultaneously to follow Hindu social customs and practices. By the beginning of the seventeenth century, however, partly in response to religious persecution by the Muslim rulers in Delhi, the leaders of the Sikh community began to propound a more clearly defined and militant Sikh identity. The tenth and last Guru, Gobind Singh (who died in 1708), founded the Khalsa brotherhood, whose members adopted the common surname of Singh (lion) and wore five symbols of their dedication: *Kes* (uncut hair), *Kirpan* (a short sword), *Kanga* (a comb), *Kara* (a steel bracelet), and *Kachcha* (a kind of breeches).[540]

The struggle to save the Punjab empire led to a consolidation of this militant Sikh identity. The British encouraged Sikhs to manifest their separate identity, for example, by requiring that persons wishing to fill Sikh recruitment quotas in the Army be unshorn.[541]

While the revival of a distinct Sikh, as opposed to Punjabi, identity

---

540 See generally *id.*; Rajiv A. Kapur, *Sikh Separatism* (London: Allen & Unwin, 1986), chaps. 1 and 2.

541 See Kapur, *supra* note 540, at chaps. 1 and 2.

coincided with the establishment and consolidation of British power, Sikh militancy would soon be directed against the British. After World War I, many Sikhs were dissatisfied with the economic situation they found upon their return to Punjab. A more militant, culturally based nationalism developed among Sikhs, as it did among other communities throughout India.

A militant unarmed army was formed to recapture Sikh holy places from what were considered to be corrupt priests who had contaminated Sikh observances with Hindu polytheism and ritual. After a long struggle, the British authorities passed the Sikh Gurdwaras Act in 1925, which granted management of Sikh temples to the Shiromani Gurdwara Prabhandak Committee (SGPC). To this day, the SGPC administers Sikh temples and shrines throughout Punjab and collects substantial sums of money from the faithful. The Akali Dal, which led the fight for the Gurdwaras Act, soon captured control of the SGPC, and the SGPC retained a preeminent position in Sikh political life until weakened by internal divisions in the 1980s.

However, it was precisely the theocratic orientation of the Akali Dal which prevented it from becoming the exclusive political spokesman for the Punjab. Most Punjabis were Muslim, and the bulk of its rich agricultural lands were in the overwhelmingly Muslim areas of what is now the Pakistani province of Punjab. Moreover, when the British crown assumed jurisdiction over India from the East India Company in 1858, the Hindu, Hindi-speaking province of Haryana had been joined to the Punjab.

Thus, the politics of (undivided) Punjab came to be dominated by a Muslim-led Unionist coalition which included Sikhs and Hindus. The Unionists, conservative and dominated by landed elites, pressed for provincial autonomy as opposed to a strong central government, for they opposed the land reform and other redistributive programs to which the Congress party was committed.

The decade between the enactment of the Government of India Act in 1935, which provided limited provincial self-government, and the end of World War II saw a profound change in the Punjabi political landscape. The Unionists collapsed, and the Muslim League, which after 1940 supported an independent Muslim state of Pakistan, came to dominate Muslim politics in Punjab.

The Sikhs had everything to lose if Punjab were partitioned, as inevitably would be the case if Muslim majority areas were separated from areas with non-Muslim majorities. The richest Sikh agricultural lands were in predominantly Muslim West Punjab and were sure to go to Pakistan in the event of partition. The Sikhs were scattered throughout Punjab and could only hope to maintain their political power as a group in the context of a united Punjab and a united India. As a community which constituted no more than 12–13% of greater Punjab's total population, their interests would be best served by a plural provincial government which would recognize the special needs of the Sikhs as a religious minority.

The ultimate acquiescence of the Congress party to the partition of India and Pakistan in 1947 confirmed Sikh mistrust of Congress' secular nationalism. While an Akali Dal meeting in August 1944 had rejected a resolution which demanded a "Sikh independent sovereign state," the possibility of a separate Sikh entity remained an issue during the constitutional and political negotiations leading to Indian independence.[542] When a British Cabinet mission visited India to ascertain the wishes of the Indian people, the Akali Dal's representatives pressed for a Sikh nation—but in terms that marked that demand as a negotiating tactic to resist the idea of a separate Pakistan.[543] On 18 July 1946, Sir Stafford Cripps, leader of the mission, addressed the British Parliament:

It was a matter of great distress to us that the Sikhs should feel they had not received the treatment which they deserved as an important section. The difficulty arises, not from anyone's underestimation of the importance of the Sikh community, but from the inescapable geographical facts of the situation. What the Sikhs demand is some special treatment analogous to that given to the Muslims. The Sikhs, however, are a much smaller community, 5,500,000 against 90,000,000, and are not geographically situated so that any area as yet desired ... can be carved out in which they would find themselves in a majority.[544]

Nor did the prospect of becoming a minority within Pakistan offer much to the Sikhs. Expressing views that are common to many separatist movements, one of the leaders of the pro-Pakistan movement counseled his supporters:

Avoid minorityism, which means that we must not leave our minorities in Hindu lands, even if the British and the Hindus offer them the so-called constitutional safeguards. For no safeguards can be substituted for the nationhood which is their birthright. Nor must we keep Hindu and/or Sikh minorities in our lands, even if they themselves were willing to remain with or without any special safeguards. For they will never be of us. Indeed, while in ordinary times they will retard our national reconstruction, in times of crisis they will betray us and bring about our redestruction.[545]

542 See Kushwant Singh, *supra* note 539, at 252–53.

543 Vapal P. Menon, *The Transfer of Power in India* (Princeton, NJ: Princeton Univ. Press, 1957) at 242.

544 The Statesman, 19 July 1946, cited in Khushwant Singh, *supra* note 539, at 262.

545 Rahmat Ali, *The Millat and its Mission; Muslim League Attack on Sikhs and Hindus*, at 8.

The consequences of partition for the Sikh community were terrible, as they were for many others in India and Pakistan. Widespread violence against the Sikhs of West Punjab, which became part of Pakistan, compelled their flight to Indian Punjab. The richest Sikh agricultural lands were lost forever to those who fled. Also lost through inclusion in Pakistan were many of the most important Sikh shrines, including the birthplace of the religion's founder.

Partition created profound economic and demographic changes within Indian Punjab, where a ceiling of 30 acres was fixed on landholdings in order to accommodate the influx of refugees. Thus, while Sikhs from Pakistani Punjab lost all their lands, Sikhs in Indian Punjab also were partially dispossessed. Urban Sikhs who were forced to migrate to India found that they had to compete with Hindu refugees from Pakistan, as well as with established Hindu traders.

Equally important was the change in the political configuration of the Sikh community. The exodus from Pakistan dispersed the followers of Sikh leaders, which encouraged cooperation with the governing Congress party in Indian Punjab, since the population of Indian Punjab remained predominantly non-Sikh. Only in PEPSU (the Patiala and East Punjab States Union, formed by the merger of the Sikh princely states) were the Sikhs in a majority. PEPSU offered the possibility of Sikh "self-determination" within the Indian federal system. At the same time, however, the practical integration of Sikh and secular politics in Punjab encouraged development of a larger and more plural model of party politics.

Events in India in the first decade of independence heightened Sikh distrust of the larger Indian political system. The Congress party had committed itself repeatedly to the principle of linguistically defined provinces, and the Constituent Assembly appointed a commission to examine the feasibility of redrawing state boundaries. However, Punjab was specifically excluded from the commission's terms of reference. In any event, the commission recommended against any boundary revisions, on the grounds, *inter alia*, that such revisions would encourage claims by the Sikhs and others.

In the early 1950s, a movement arose in south India for the creation of a separate Telugu-speaking state out of the state of Madras. In an attempt to settle the issue, the Indian government created the States Reorganization Commission in 1953, which did recommend the reorganization of the Indian states on the basis of language. Its recommendations were embodied in the States Reorganization Act of 1956; however, the commission had no Sikh member, and it specifically recommended against creation of a Punjabi-speaking state.

While Punjabi is the language of many Hindus as well as Sikhs, the

Sikhs' attachment to it is reinforced by the fact that Punjabi is the language of the Sikh scriptures. As Punjabi Hindus frequently spoke Hindi in addition to Punjabi, the demand for a Punjabi-speaking state was universally understood as a demand for a Sikh-majority State.

The Sikhs were outraged at the rejection of the possibility of a Punjabi-speaking state. Moreover, PEPSU, the only state in which Sikhs constituted a majority of the population, was merged into Punjab in 1956. The Akali Dal subsequently began a long campaign of civil disobedience, which culminated, in 1966, in the division of Indian Punjab into two new states of Punjab, with a 60% Punjabi-speaking Sikh majority, and Haryana, with a Hindu and Hindi-speaking majority.

This settlement might have resolved the most serious conflict between Sikhs and the larger Indian state, but deep animosities and distrust had developed between some Sikhs and the Congress party during the struggle for a Punjabi-speaking state. Economic development also created new social realities which would provide fertile ground for a revival of the traditional ideal of Sikh greatness.

It has frequently been noted that modern Punjab is the Indian success story par excellence in terms of economic development. Even before the "Green Revolution" in grain production, the growth of agricultural output in Punjab was well above the national norm.[546] Nationwide production of wheat nearly doubled from 1966–67 to 1969–70, due primarily to the Punjab. Between 1964–65 and 1969–70, 66% of total increases in grain output occurred in the three northern states of Punjab, Haryana, and Uttar Pradesh. This development increased disparities between the Punjab and other regions of India and gave Punjabi farmers, who were primarily Sikhs, a heightened sense of their importance. At the same time, however, economic disparities within Punjab also widened. Between 1964 and 1974, the number of landless peasants doubled, while the number of marginal farmers tripled. These negative consequences fell disproportionately on the more agricultural Sikh community.

In a heavily regulated economy such as India's, it is understandably tempting to blame "the government" or "the center" for economic problems. Moreover, seasonal laborers, who had previously been encouraged to emigrate from other parts of India, contributed to growing Sikh fears of unfair competition and inundation by "the Hindus."

The Green Revolution had, to some extent, reached a plateau by the 1980s. In addition, individual land holdings had diminished with every generation as family size increased, creating a class of young rural Sikhs with high expectations but limited economic opportunity. Emi-

---

546 This and the following statistics are taken from Biswapriya Sanyal, "How Revolutionary Was India's Green Revolution?" South Asia Bulletin (Fall 1983) at 37.

gration, historically an important factor in Sikh prosperity, became more difficult, as the United Kingdom implemented increasingly restrictive immigration policies. Meanwhile, the perception grew among many Sikhs that they have not received a fair proportion of industrial development assistance from the Indian government.

This economic context is important not only to a general understanding of Sikh grievances, but also to an understanding of the alliance between the Akali Dal and Sikh fundamentalist forces. The Akali Dal primarily represents the interests of the relatively prosperous Sikh agriculturalists. Its goals have been to wrest power from the Congress party and to implement pro-Punjab policies with respect to use of river waters, the production of electricity, and development of local industries. These economic goals assume participation in the larger national economy, if only to ensure access to the gigantic Indian market.

The fundamentalists emphasize Sikh separateness from the larger world of "Hindu" and modern Indian culture and draw their recruits primarily from the dispossessed youths who have been the victims of prosperous farmers. At the same time, the fundamentalists have been willing to enter into tactical alliances with the Congress party against the Akali Dal.

The Akali Dal appears to have calculated that the fundamentalists offered the basis for an ideological mobilization which could be co-opted in a struggle against the central government and the Congress party, while the fundamentalists apparently hoped to legitimize their position by association with the traditional political leadership. As long as both factions supported the reestablishment of a strong religious and cultural identity, neither could challenge the other without drawing into question its own ideological commitment.

The present phase of the Punjab crisis can perhaps be dated from the adoption by the Akali Dal in April 1973 of the Anandpur Sahib Resolution, which has become the charter of modern Sikh political demands. In addition to demanding greater political autonomy, the resolution demanded transfer of the city of Chandigarh (which became the joint capital of Punjab and Haryana in 1966 and is administered by the central government as a "Union Territory") to the exclusive jurisdiction of Punjab; adjustment of state boundaries to include within Punjab certain Punjabi-speaking areas of the neighboring states of Haryana and Rajasthan; and a larger allocation to Punjab of the waters of the Ravi, Sutlej, and Beas rivers, including control over canal headworks and hydroelectric installations.

The failure of the Akali Dal to pursue the resolution's demands during the period in which it controlled the state government in 1977–1980 might have consigned those demands to history. However, that period coincided with the development of a fundamentalist political movement which challenged the Akali Dal's credentials as the representative of Sikh aspirations.

This religious fundamentalism was actively encouraged by the pre-1977 Congress party government of Punjab, led by the later President of India, Giani Zail Singh.[547] The Congress party questioned the religious or pro-Sikh commitment of the Akali Dal, and Zail Singh supported attempts by a fundamentalist village preacher to challenge the Akali Dal's control of the Sikh Temple Management Committee, the SGPC.

That preacher was Jarnail Singh Bhindranwale. In the late 1970s, he had established a reputation as an itinerant preacher who sought to encourage Sikh youth, in particular, to return to a pure Sikh faith and eschew modern habits such as drinking, smoking, and cutting of hair.

Bhindranwale and his followers soon began to attack Sikh sects which did not share their definition of the original faith.[548] Among the many assassinations attributed to Bhindranwale's supporters were those of the leader of the Nirankari Sikh sect, Baba Gurbachan Singh, in April 1980, and Lala Jagat Narain, owner of the most powerful chain of vernacular newspapers in Punjab, in September 1981. Narain's son was murdered in May 1984.

That a fundamentalist movement should eventually have taken a secessionist direction is hardly remarkable, but that direction was rendered more likely by political manipulation and knowing rejection of compromise solutions in favor of short-term political goals. The failure of moderate political options in the 1979–1984 period led inexorably to more radical demands by Sikh politicians, and these demands were eventually supported by large segments of the Sikh population in the Punjab. The failure of the authorities in Punjab or Delhi to take meaningful action against the violence of Bhindranwale's followers gave the impression that Bhindranwale was above the law, increasing both pride in and fear of his power on the part of the average Sikh. As violence increased, compromise became more difficult and did not seem to be seriously pursued by Bhindranwale's militants, Akali Dal politicians, or Indian Prime Minister Indira Gandhi.

A new version of the Anandpur Sahib Resolution adopted by the Akali Dal in 1978 proposed that the central government retain authority

547 See Kuldip Nayar and Khushwant Singh, *The Tragedy of Punjab* (New Delhi: Vision Books, 1984), chaps. 1 and 2.

548 The rise of Bhindranwale is chronicled in all contemporary accounts of the Punjab conflict; see, e.g., Mark Tully and Satish Jacob, *Amritsar* (London: Pan Books and Calcutta: Rupa and Co., 1985) at 52–72, and Nayar & Kushwant Singh, *supra* note 547, at 27–90.

only over defense, foreign affairs, posts and telegraphs, railways, and currency. It spoke of "progressive decentralization of power" and reiterated the demand for the incorporation of Punjabi-speaking areas into Punjab, although the Akali Dal has never supported secession.

The Akali Dal's demands were not met by the Janata central government during the latter's tenure between 1977 and 1979, following the end of the national state of emergency declared by Mrs. Gandhi. In the 1979 elections, the Congress party won practically all the national parliamentary seats from Punjab and later won an absolute majority in the Punjab Legislative Assembly.

The Congress party's subsequent strategy contributed to a growing sense of alienation between Sikh opinion and the political system which the Congress party had again come to dominate. Several attempts to resolve differences foundered on both the intransigence of Congress party negotiators and the reluctance of Akali negotiators to condemn the fundamentalists. Punjabi Hindus, who constituted approximately 40% of the population, were increasingly concerned about the attempt to remake Punjabi politics in an exclusively Sikh mold. The Congress party also may have resisted Akali demands in order to increase its political appeal outside Punjab, as Hindu opinion in the rest of India has become increasingly critical of what are perceived to be special concessions to militant minorities.

The early 1980s saw the simultaneous development of a mass civil disobedience campaign led by the Akali Dal, in support of the demands contained in the Anandpur Sahib Resolution, and a campaign of terrorism led by Bhindranwale fundamentalists. On 16 June 1980, formation of a sovereign Sikh state of Khalistan was announced in Taran in the Amritsar district of Punjab, although little support for this purported declaration of independence was evident at the time.

Four hundred ten people were killed in Punjab between August 1982 and June 1984, including nearly 300 in the first six months of 1984.[549] Assassinations of moderate Sikhs, government officials, and randomly chosen Hindus occurred on a nearly daily basis; retaliatory killings of Sikhs occurred in neighboring Haryana. To prevent threatened demonstrations at the 1982 Asian Games in Delhi, thousands of Sikhs were stopped, searched, and humiliated by the police; over 1,500 were arrested.[550] Negotiations between the Akali Dal and Prime Minister Gandhi's government failed, and the central government dismissed the state government and assumed direct rule over Punjab in October 1983.

549 Government of India, *White Paper on the Punjab Agitation, A Summary* (New Delhi, 10 July 1984) at 18.
550 Tully and Jacob, *supra* note 548, at 87.

The Golden Temple in Amritsar, the holiest of Sikh temples, had been heavily fortified and provided a sanctuary for Bhindranwale and his followers. On 5 June 1984 the Indian Army launched Operation Bluestar and entered the Golden Temple by force, three days after a speech by the Prime Minister in which she stated, "the reality that has emerged is not the adequacy or otherwise of the terms of the settlement offered by the government on the various demands of the Akali Dal but the fact that the agitation is now in the hands of a few who have scant regard for the unity and integrity of our country or concern for communal peace and harmony or the continued economic progress of the Punjab."[551]

There seems to have been ample justification for action against the arsenal stockpiled by Bhindranwale's terrorist followers, but the invasion of the Golden Temple outraged the vast majority of the Sikh population, even those who opposed Bhindranwale and his goals. Several Sikh units of the Indian Army mutinied and began to march toward Punjab.

Bhindranwale was killed in the assault. His followers quickly turned their erstwhile leader into a martyr and vowed to assassinate Prime Minister Indira Gandhi and her son Rajiv. Moderate Sikh nationalists committed to a united India felt obliged, by both personal conviction and the state of Sikh political opinion, to condemn the assault on the Temple and the subsequent arrests of thousands of Sikhs, including the leaders of the Akali Dal.

Five months later, in November 1984, Mrs. Gandhi was assassinated by Sikh members of her bodyguard. This was immediately followed by four days of rioting in Delhi, in which at least 2,000 Sikhs were killed; some Congress party leaders and members allegedly planned and participated in the riots.[552] With these events, the mutual alienation of the Sikh community and the larger national polity seemed to be complete.

When national parliamentary elections were held throughout India in December 1984, they were not held in Punjab because of the security situation. The same was true when the rest of the country went to the polls in early 1985 for state legislative elections. Having consolidated his authority in both elections, Prime Minister Rajiv Gandhi, Indira Gandhi's son and successor, proceeded to seek a solution to the seemingly intractable problem of Punjab. As a first step, he released the leadership of the Akali Dal.

551 Quoted in *id*. at 142–43.

552 See People's Union for Democratic Rights and People's Union for Civil Liberties, *Who are the Guilty? Report of a Joint Inquiry into the Causes and Impact of the Riots in Delhi from 31 October to 10 November* (Delhi, 1984).

It is a symptom of how deep the alienation had become that these leaders immediately adopted rhetoric which seemed indistinguishable from that of the extremists. Harchand Singh Longowal, the preeminent Akali leader and a professed follower of the non-violent methods of Mahatma Gandhi, visited Bhindranwale's village and paid respect to his memory. At the same time, however, he condemned acts of violence and reiterated that the Akali Dal did not favor establishment of an independent Sikh state.

Negotiations between Longowal and the Gandhi government finally led to the signing of an accord between Longowal and Rajiv Gandhi on 24 July 1985. The accord included, *inter alia*, the following points: The city of Chandigarh would be given to Punjab; in exchange, several Hindi-speaking areas of Punjab would be transferred to the state of Haryana. The existing division of river water among Punjab, Haryana, and Rajasthan was frozen, while other questions relating to water shares would be referred to a tribunal to be presided over by a Supreme Court judge. Those points in the Anandpur Sahib Resolution concerning center-state relations would be referred to a Commission on Center-State Relations, which had been empaneled in 1983 to consider such issues throughout India. The Akali Dal in turn confirmed that the Anandpur Sahib Resolution "is entirely within the framework of the Indian Constitution; that it attempts to define the concept of Center-State relations in a manner which may bring out the true federal characteristics of our unitary constitution; and that the purpose of the Resolution is to provide greater autonomy to the state with a view to strengthening the unity and integrity of the country, since unity in diversity forms the cornerstone of our national unity."[553]

The accord also provided that the 1983 Armed Forces (Punjab and Chandigarh) Special Powers Act would no longer be applied to Punjab and that the special courts set up to try security offenses would thenceforth try only offenses such as waging war or hijacking. Other provisions promised efforts to rehabilitate those discharged from the Army for their role in the mutinies which followed the attack on the Golden Temple and reaffirmed that recruitment into the armed forces would continue to be on the basis of merit (a concession to those who had feared the implications of a central government policy to reduce the disproportionate representation of Sikhs in the armed forces).

The accord was widely welcomed, both because it promised to end a longstanding conflict which had sapped the political resources of the

---

553 *Memorandum of Settlement signed by Shri Rajiv Gandhi, Prime Minister, and Sant Harchand Singh Longowal, President, Shiromani Akali Dal, on July 24, 1985,* sec. 8.1.

country and caused extreme suffering in Punjab and because it seemed to have been reached with a party which could legitimately claim to represent Sikh grievances. The Indian government moved quickly to hold elections for the Punjab Legislative Assembly and for the Punjabi seats in the national Parliament.

Within a month, Akali leader Longowal was assassinated by Sikh extremists. Despite a boycott urged by a breakaway section of the Akali Dal, headed by the aged father of Jarnail Singh Bhindranwale, the subsequent Punjab elections brought a higher than usual voter turnout, and the mainstream Akali Dal received an absolute majority for the first time in its history.

Unfortunately, implementation of the Gandhi-Longowal accord lagged, and Chandigarh was not exchanged for certain Punjab territory on 1 January 1986, as had been stipulated. In February 1986, approximately half of the Akali Dal's members in the state Legislative Assembly withdrew their support for the government of Longowal's successor, Surjit Singh Barnala, claiming that the Barnala government had failed to pursue implementation of the July 1985 accord sufficiently forcefully. They also condemned a second and much more limited assault on the Golden Temple, which had been ordered to dislodge terrorists who apparently had reestablished a base there. The Barnala government was subsequently forced to rely on Congress party support in order to continue governing.

Reliance on Congress support weakened the Barnala government's legitimacy in the eyes of at least a segment of the Sikh community and rendered consensus almost impossible. The Congress party continued to be perceived by most Sikhs as the instrument of central government interference in the affairs of Punjab and as the perpetrator of a repressive and overly broad anti-terrorist campaign.

Throughout 1986, political divisions within the Sikh community deepened, and support for an independent "Khalistan" probably increased. Killings, many directed against moderates who oppose an independent Sikh state, also increased, with an official toll in 1986 of 640 deaths.[554] The Akal Takht, the group of five head priests who exercise ultimate authority in the Sikh religion, purported to dissolve the five existing factions of the Akali Dal party in February 1987, in order to create a new United Akali Dal more sympathetic to the demands of the militants. Those who refused to submit to the priests' edict, including Akali Chief Minister Barnala, were excommunicated, amidst allegations of the improper extension of religion into politics.

In May 1987, the central government again dissolved the state gov-

554 "Courts Bombed in India's Punjab," Wash. Post, 20 Feb. 1988, at A19, col. 1.

ernment of Punjab and instituted direct "President's rule" from Delhi, which has been regularly renewed. The death toll reached 1,230 in 1987, and 2,400 killings, including that of the head priest of the Golden Temple, were attributed to terrorism in 1988.[555] Another raid of the Golden Temple by the Indian Army occurred in April 1988.

The 1985 Gandhi-Longowal accord has yet to be fully implemented, and few would agree with Prime Minister Gandhi's assertions that the central government has done everything required of it.[556] At the same time, however, several of the remaining issues are complex and cannot be resolved in a manner which will be equally satisfactory to all parties.

OUTSTANDING ISSUES[557]

Apportionment of river waters[558]

Section 9 of the Gandhi-Longowal accord provided for a tribunal to adjudicate "within six months" the respective claims of Punjab and Haryana to river waters, a procedure which is generally consistent with the Inter-State Water Disputes Act intended to address similar conflicts between other states. The subsequently established Eradi Commission did not issue its decision until mid-1987, although at least part of the delay may be attributable to the Punjab government, which failed to complete construction of a planned canal. The Akali Dal party led by former Chief Minister Barnala rejected the commission's report, claiming that it violated the terms of reference set forth in the Gandhi-Longowal accord and would ruin Punjab's economy.

Territorial disputes and the transfer of Chandigarh

Following the Gandhi-Longowal accord, the central government appointed the Mathews Commission to arrange for the transfer of land from Punjab to Haryana in exchange for the transfer of exclusive control of Chandigarh to Punjab. The commission was instructed to follow three principles: the village as a unit, linguistic affinity, and contiguity of territory. However, the commission concluded that it could not identify suitable land and comply with the requirement of contiguity of territory,

---

555 *Id.*; "Sikhs Kill Hindus After Hangings," Wash. Post, 8 Jan. 1989.

556 Transcript of Prime Minister's Press Conference (uncorrected), Indian Press Information Bureau, 20 Jan. 1987. Compare the analysis in "Tall Talk, Small Mercies," India Today, 15 Feb. 1987, at 48–49.

557 A good, brief exposition of the main Sikh grievances may be found in "Khalistan: The politics of passion," Overseas Hindustan Times, 15 Oct. 1981, at 8–10. It is perhaps significant that most of the disputes outlined therein were still unresolved several years later.

558 See generally S. Krishnaswamy, "An Approach to Inter-State River Water Disputes in India," 17 Indian Yearbook Int'l Affairs 372 (1974).

presumably because the intermingling of Sikh and Hindu populations makes the contiguous division of villages impossible.

Two subsequent commissions, known respectively as the Venkatra-maiah and Desai commissions, also were empaneled and recommended the transfer of specific lands pursuant to the Gandhi-Langowal accord. However, these recommendations have been rejected by one or both of the parties concerned, although the legal justification for so doing seems at best questionable. The binding nature of the adjudications with respect to land is fundamental to implementation of the Gandhi-Longowal accord, as it is clear that a "mutually acceptable exchange between the two states has become an impossibility."[559]

Additional conflicting claims between Punjab and Haryana, apart from the transfer of Punjabi land in exchange for Chandigarh, were to be considered by yet another commission, whose findings also were to be binding on both states. Again, the terms of reference require recognition of the village as a unit, linguistic affinity, and contiguity.

Personal status

The demand for a separate personal law for the Sikhs grows out of Section 10 of the Anandpur Sahib Resolution, which proposes amendment of the Hindu Succession Act (to which Sikhs are subject) so that a Sikh widow would inherit property from her father-in-law rather than her father. While unexceptionable on its face, this does present certain problems.

Articles 25 and 26 of the Indian constitution guarantee the free exercise of religion, subject to the preservation of public order, morality, and health. In early 1984, copies of article 25 of the constitution were burned by Sikh demonstrators to protest their alleged inclusion as part of the Hindu community. The language objected to is found in an explanation of terms used in the body of article 25:

Explanation II. In sub-clause (b) of clause (2), the reference to Hindus shall be construed as including a reference to persons professing the Sikh, Jaina or Buddhist religion, and the reference to Hindu religious institutions shall be construed accordingly.

The sub-clause to which this refers provides:

Nothing in this Article shall affect the operation of any existing law or prevent the state from making any law . . . providing for social welfare or reform, or the throwing open of Hindu religious institutions of a public character to all classes of Hindus.

---

559 India Today, *supra* note 556, at 48.

This provision is designed to permit the government to prohibit the exclusion of persons of low caste from attending temples or otherwise participating in their chosen religion. Since the religious groups referred to in Explanation II have maintained the supposedly Hindu caste system, the protection of people of low caste is also extended to members of these minority religions.

Explanation I, which precedes the language just quoted, negates the inference that article 25 identifies the Sikh religion as merely a subset of Hinduism. Explanation I provides, "The wearing and carrying of kirpans [i.e., the dagger required to be carried at all times as a sign of Sikh identity] shall be deemed to be included in the profession of the Sikh religion." Sikhism thus seems to be clearly recognized as a distinct religion, deserving of special protection.

In any event, the provision of separate personal laws for certain religious communities was a matter of short term expediency and was intended to be phased out over time. Article 44 of the constitution directs the development of a uniform civil code for citizens, and one might question whether provision of a separate Sikh personal law at this time would be consistent with the intent of this article.[560]

Human rights

A major factor in the continuing resentment by Sikhs of the central government is the suspension of personal liberties and continuing violations of human rights.[561] Thousands of persons were detained in 1984 and 1985, following the assault on the Golden Temple, and amendments to the National Security Act enable the government to detain persons in Punjab and Chandigarh without trial for two years for acts alleged to be prejudicial to the defense or security of the state. Persons may be detained for six months even without review by the Advisory Boards which ordinarily review National Security Act detentions. Other amendments, applicable throughout India, provide that a court may only re-

560 A controversy over Muslim personal law and women's rights erupted throughout India following the Supreme Court's 1985 decision in Md. Ahmed Khan v. Shah Bano Begum, AIR 1985 S.C. 945, in which the Court granted post-divorce maintenance to a former wife despite contrary Muslim customary law. In response to objections to the decision expressed by conservative Muslims, the government subsequently adopted the Muslim Women (Protection of Rights on Divorce) Act 1986, nullifying the legal impact of the Supreme Court's judgment—thereby alienating other segments of Muslim and non-Muslim opinion alike.

561 See generally Amnesty International, *Report 1986* (London: Amnesty International Publications, 1986) at 219–24; *id., Report 1985* at 209–13; Chr. Michelsen Institute and Norwegian Human Rights Project, *Human Rights in Developing Countries 1986* (Oslo: Norwegian Univ. Press, 1986) at 166–96; People's Union for Civil Liberties, *Black Laws 1984–85* (Delhi: PUCL, June 1985).

lease a detainee if it finds that all grounds of detention are invalid, rather than specified ones, and that authorities need not disclose to a detainee for up to fifteen days the reason for his arrest.

The Terrorist Affected Areas (Special Courts) Ordinance of 1984 allows the government to try persons *in camera*, and, upon a minimal showing by the government, shifts the burden of proof to the accused. Appeals are possible only to the Supreme Court, rather than to the High Courts, and must be lodged within thirty days. In response to increasing violence and terrorism, the government in 1985 adopted the Terrorist and Disruptive Activities (Prevention) Act, amended in 1987 and applicable nationwide. It includes penalties for a wide range of "disruptive activities" deemed to undermine India's unity, including provision that confessions made to a Superintendent of Police shall be admissible in a court, "which shall presume the crime has been committed unless proved otherwise."[562]

Some emergency powers were abrogated following the Gandhi-Longowal Accord in May 1985, although over 350 persons remained imprisoned, apparently under the National Security Act, in the Jodhpur jail in Rajastan after Operation Bluestar in 1984.[563] Charges eventually were brought against all the Jodhpur detainees under the Indian penal code, for insurrection and various firearms offenses. By the end of 1988, charges against approximately half of the accused had been dropped and the detainees released, while the trial of the 194 persons charged and still imprisoned had not been completed. In March 1989, Prime Minister Gandhi announced that most of those imprisoned following the 1984 Golden Temple raid would be released and that legislation allowing detention without trial would be repealed.

No prosecutions followed the massacre of thousands of Sikhs in Delhi and elsewhere in India after the 1984 assassination of Indira Gandhi, and the government delayed establishing a commission of inquiry to investigate the causes of the riots.[564] When the commission finally issued its report in February 1987, it was widely criticized for rejecting the allegations of Congress-party organization of the riots; it did, however, condemn the "total passivity, callousness and indifference" of the police.[565] The commission's report referred to the filing of 240 charges

562 "New Anti-Terrorism Law," Overseas Tribune (Wash., DC), 29 Aug. 1987, at 1, col. 4; Brahma Chellaney, "Tough Indian security laws draw fire from civil-rights groups," Christian Science Monitor, 8 Sept. 1987, at 14, col. 1.

563 *Amnesty International Report 1988* (London: Amnesty International, 1988) at 158–59.

564 See sources cited *supra* note 561.

565 N.Y. Times, 24 Feb. 1987, at A10, col. 1. The report, known as the Misra report, had not been publicly released by the end of 1988.

arising out of the riots, and Prime Minister Rajiv Gandhi created two more committees to prosecute those accused of participating in the riots.

Political killings by extremist Sikh terrorists continue in Punjab, and government forces under the best of circumstances would have a difficult time reestablishing order. The Golden Temple complex has been entered twice since July 1984 to arrest suspected terrorists, although in both instances with considerably less violence. Nevertheless, the use of detention without trial and alleged security force excesses evidently do not contribute to restoring the trust of Sikhs in the central government. In 1986, almost 1,600 Sikh extremists were arrested and 80 killed in "encounters" with the police; over 200 Sikhs were killed by the police in the first nine months of 1987.[566]

At the same time, there is no doubt that political killings of opponents of "Khalistan" and terrorism against Punjabi Hindus have made any political compromise much less likely. Whatever the percentage of the non-Sikh population of Punjab, it can hardly be sanguine about its safety in an independent Sikh Khalistan, as Sikh extremists have made it clear that their desire is to replace the present Hindu population in the Punjab with Sikhs who would be encouraged to immigrate to Punjab from the rest of India. The attempted mutual genocide which accompanied partition remains fresh in the minds of many Punjabis, both Sikh and Hindu, and Sikh terrorism remains a serious obstacle to any settlement.

OBSERVATIONS

India may be the most culturally, ethnically, and religiously diverse state in the world, and perhaps nowhere else has this diversity led to as many violent clashes. Communal and other tensions continue to be a matter of constant political, social, and economic concern, and the Punjab conflict—while perhaps unusually important due to the Punjab's strategic and economic significance—must be viewed in the overall context of Indian politics. In a roughly two-month period in early 1987, for example, the Indian and foreign press reported stories concerned with a new state created after a twenty-year insurgency (Mizoram, discussed further below); conflict over languages in Goa, which led to adoption of a three-language bill by the Goa state legislature; talks between the central government and those seeking a separate state of Ghurkaland; criticism of the Assam accord for ignoring the tribal population; an insurgency in Manipur, on the Burmese border; declaration of certain

566 Figures from Rajiv A. Kapur, " 'Khalistan': India's Punjab problem," 9 Third World Q. 1206, 1221 (No. 4, Oct. 1987), and "Sikh Violence in Punjab A Threat to Indian Unity," N.Y. Times, 5 Oct. 1987, at A1, col. 3.

border areas in Tripura as "disturbed areas"; and objections by China to the incorporation of allegedly Chinese territory in the new Indian state of Arunachal Pradesh.

In these circumstances, credit should be given to the Indian political system for a generally flexible approach in dealing with this diversity. Indeed, the Indian constitution is replete with references to various arrangements for special status for states and regions within the country.

Article 370 of the constitution limits the applicability of the constitution in the state of Jammu and Kashmir, which is the only state in the Indian Union with its own constitution. The power of Parliament with respect to Kashmir is limited by this article to the matters specified in the 1947 instrument of accession, and jurisdiction over other matters by the central government may occur only with the concurrence of the state legislature.

In practical terms, however, this autonomy is more apparent than real. Article 370 is entitled "Temporary Provisions with respect to the state of Jammu and Kashmir," and, with a few insignificant exceptions, the Indian constitution has been progressively applied to the state in accordance with the procedure laid down in article 370; the most significant act was the first, the Constitution (Application to Jammu and Kashmir) Order of 1954.

Other constitutional provisions relate to Maharashtra and Gujarat (Article 371), Nagaland (Article 371A), Assam (Article 371B), Manipur (Article 371C), Andhra Pradesh (Article 371D), and Sikkim, which enjoyed autonomy under its own monarch until 1974 (Article 371F).

With respect to Nagaland, article 371A provides that, notwithstanding any other constitutional provision, no law shall apply to Naga religious or social practices, customary law and procedure, criminal justice administration, or ownership or transfer of land, unless the state assembly approves. A similar provision may be found in the recently concluded Mizoram accord, which led to Mizoram's creation as India's twenty-third state and the assumption of state power by the former insurgents through elections in February 1987. Resolution of the Mizoram conflict is generally acknowledged to be one of Rajiv Gandhi's significant successes, as both sides respected the agreement reached in mid-1986 for ending hostilities and holding elections.

Other constitutional provisions reflect a concern to ensure effective participation by minority groups in society. For example, article 371D permits the President to provide, "having regard to the requirements of the State [of Andhra Pradesh] as a whole, for equitable [education and public employment] opportunities and facilities for the people belonging to different sections of the population." The Fifth and Sixth

Schedules to the constitution make special provision for the administration of "scheduled areas" and "scheduled tribes."

Unfortunately, these provisions are of only limited guidance in resolving the question of Sikh autonomy. Kashmir is an integral part of the Indian Union, and its unique status (perhaps more theoretical than real) has historical antecedents unavailable to the Punjab. Nagaland, which achieved statehood by being carved out of the state of Assam, and Mizoram present special cases. The Mizos and Nagas were among the last groups to be incorporated into India, after long periods of armed resistance, as their tribal cultures had always successfully resisted encroachment by the social and economic forces of the subcontinent to their south and west. The British "protected" them even after their incorporation into British India, by appointing administrators sensitive to Mizo and Naga fears of inundation by the burgeoning Hindu and Muslim populations of Bengal and Assam, and by restricting access to these areas.

In addition, the Mizos and Nagas inhabit well demarcated areas where they constitute a clear majority, while the Sikh population of Punjab constitutes only a relatively weak majority within the present Punjab boundaries and was a minority in historic Punjab. The Sikhs also have played a major role in the history and culture of the larger Indian nation, as distinguished from the separate cultural history of the Mizos and Nagas. Almost half of the Sikh population in India lives outside Punjab, and Sikhs participate vigorously in the economic, military, cultural, and political life of the national society.

Self-determination in the form of an independent Khalistan will not be obtained by the Sikhs without a civil war. In addition to the universal rejection of the legitimacy of secession, the strategic location of Punjab on the Indo-Pakistani border ensures that the Indian government will never negotiate away its ultimate authority over Punjab.[567]

Calls for independence in Punjab gained strength only after the assault on the Golden Temple, and the 1985 electoral success of the Akali Dal suggests that, even then, the majority of the population of Punjab would be willing to accept an arrangement which guarantees meaningful autonomy and the resolution of certain outstanding economic grievances. While many Sikhs remain distrustful of the central government, there is not widespread support for an independent state

---

567 The saber-rattling and troop movements along the Punjab border by India and Pakistan in early 1987 is only one recent example of the sensitivity of that region, although it is doubtful that infiltration from Pakistan plays a significant role in the Punjab conflict. See, e.g., "A Fragile Frontier," India Today, *supra* note 556, at 112–15.

of Khalistan. Why, then, has a settlement thus far proved to be unobtainable?

First, the complexity of issues such as the distribution of river waters and the adjustment of territorial disputes between Punjab and Haryana should not be underestimated. Nevertheless, both of these issues are capable of settlement (if not to the entire satisfaction of either side), and the central government and Akali Dal effectively agreed to binding arbitration under the Gandhi-Longowal accord. In addition, these issues also underscore the Punjabi, as opposed to Sikh, character of many demands; the cultural-religious ideology of extremist Sikh elements should not obscure the fact that many of the differences between the state and central governments are classically political and economic and do not reflect specifically ethnic or religious distinctions.

There can be no doubt that the failure to resolve these issues within the time frame set out in the Gandhi-Longowal accord dealt a serious, and perhaps fatal, blow to the prospects of achieving a settlement on the basis of that agreement. It is difficult to imagine that greater political effort could not have been expended by Prime Minister Gandhi to prevent the delays that plagued practically every aspect of the accord's implementation. Fears of antagonizing other political factions by insisting that difficult decisions be reached no doubt led to acquiescence in the delays and a return to tactics of blaming the intransigence of the other party for the ultimate failure.[568]

To many Sikhs, failure to implement the 1985 accord is simply one more example of the duplicity of the Indian government. They recall promises made by Nehru at the time of independence that the Sikhs were entitled to special consideration, on the basis of which Sikh leaders

---

568 For example, political motivations clearly were behind the postponement of elections anticipated in Haryana in March 1987 (although others were held as scheduled in Kerala, West Bengal, and Jammu and Kashmir). As noted editorially in one of Delhi's leading English-language newspapers,

> [there is] ample reason to fear that the elections are being delayed for the sake of political expedience and in the interest of the ruling party. The Congress-I's calculations are obvious. Punjab acts as a bugbear and the Congress-I fears that the voters will remain discontented so long as Haryana does not get a fair deal in the wake of the Punjab accord. . . .
>
> Delay in the Haryana elections will further postpone the start of a meaningful political dialogue in Punjab at a time when everyday [sic] that passes reduces the chance of a peaceful settlement in that strife-torn State. "An Unwise Decision," Hindustan Times, 6 Feb. 1987, at 9, col. 1.

When elections were finally held, in June 1987, the Congress-I party was badly defeated, winning only 5 seats in the 90-seat legislature; the new Haryana Prime Minister campaigned primarily on a platform opposing Gandhi's alleged concessions to the Punjab.

did not pursue either independence or autonomous association with Pakistan.[569] As noted above, the twin blows of the Golden Temple assault and the massacres which followed Indira Gandhi's assassination have also shaken faith in Delhi. While there were at least plausible justifications for the former, the unrestrained and apparently organized murder of thousands of Sikhs by Hindu mobs raised fundamental questions as to whether Sikhs would ever be accepted as full partners in the Indian polity. As in Sri Lanka, issues of political or religious autonomy may now be secondary to those of personal security.

Even if communal and ethnic conflict is to some degree inevitable in a multi-cultural society such as India, the violence and extremism now prevalent in the Punjab are not. And, indeed, there seems to be consensus as to where the blame lies for the deterioration of the Punjab conflict in the past decade.

It is very tempting to blame Sant Jarnail Singh Bhindranwale and his brand of Sikh fundamentalism which was nurtured by hatred of Hindus, but fundamentalism does not exist in a vacuum. No Shah, no Khomeni; no Indira and no Bhindranwale. . . . Mrs Gandhi was in no way a tyrant or an autocrat. However she *was* responsible for the political atmosphere which made the fundamentalism of Bhindranwale relevant. The Akali Dal Trinity [of Badal, Longowal, and Torah] must also bear their share of the responsibility. Badal and Longowal lacked the courage to stand out against a force they knew was evil. Torah tried to use it for his own ends.[570]

I hold Akali leaders chiefly responsible for the Hindu-Sikh divide and the sorry pass to which they have brought their community. They are a short-sighted, self-seeking group of men of limited political ability and lack of foresight with a penchant for over-playing the game of brinksmanship.[571]

President Singh played a key role in creating a monster out of an unknown village priest. . . . That has led to the Golden Temple assault, the murder of Indira Gandhi and the continuing turmoil in the Punjab.

The Punjab crisis cannot be settled because too many Sikh leaders want the job of chief minister in the state. . . .

Most thinking Indians believe that India's sorrow is their [sic] politicians. President Singh and Mr. Gandhi appear equally determined to confirm this view.[572]

Unfortunately, there are too many politicians and too few statesmen in the subcontinent. . . .

The only way to deal with internal problems, such as the problem of Sikh

---

569 See, e.g., "An Accord which is Faltering," (editorial), The Sikh Herald (Toronto), Sept. 1986 at 2.

570 Tully and Jacob (Indian ed.), *supra* note 548, at 218 (emphasis in original).

571 Kushwant Singh, in Nayar and Kushwant Singh, *supra* note 547, at 12.

572 "Crisis looms over Indian sub-continent," (editorial), Hongkong Standard, 19 Jan. 1987, at 6, col. 1.

extremism, the Chittagong Hill Tracts problem or the Sri Lankan conflict, is to meet legitimate demands so that the mainstream of the community does not feel hurt.[573]

In most of the studies included in the present book, politicians deservedly share much of the responsibility for the positive or negative outcomes of what are fundamentally political problems. In India, however, which possesses a flexible political system capable of adopting creative approaches to regional or ethnic conflicts, politicians must bear a particularly heavy burden for having pursued largely partisan goals rather than utilizing that flexibility in good faith.

At the same time, the increase in terrorist murders by Sikh extremists cannot be ignored. Killings have escalated sharply since 1986, reaching 2,400 in 1988.[574] In July 1987 alone, 72 Hindus were killed after buses in Punjab and Haryana were stopped by Sikh gunmen.[575] In such circumstances, political agreements are obviously even more difficult to conclude and implement —although this is precisely what Prime Minister Gandhi has attempted to achieve in Sri Lanka.[576]

There have been some positive developments since the Gandhi-Longowal accord in 1985, despite the increasing violence. For example, the use or recognition of the Punjabi language is no longer a major issue in Punjab. While Article 351 of the Indian constitution imposes a duty on the central government to promote the spread of Hindi, Article 345 provides that the legislature of a state may adopt one or more of the languages in use in the state for any or all official purposes. Article 350 provides that a person may submit a representation for the redress of grievances in any of the languages used in the state or the Union, as the case may be, and Schedule 8 to the constitution formally recognizes Punjabi among the languages used in the Union.

There also is evidence that some Sikh religious leaders, including the SGPC, are seeking to deprive separatist terrorism of the religious legitimacy it claims. For example, in October 1988, the SGPC banned the carrying of firearms into Sikh temples under its control, including the Golden Temple premises. This action followed an initial refusal by the SGPC to support a similar ban imposed by the government in May 1988 under the Religious Institutions (Prevention of Misuse) Ordinance and reportedly reflects a desire "to close the 'old chapter' and . . . restore the temple as a 'center of spiritual solace.' "[577]

573 "Politics of Murder," (ed.) Overseas Tribune (Wash., DC), 14 June 1986, at 2.
574 *Supra* note 555.
575 N.Y. Times, *supra* note 47.
576 See chap. 14.
577 Overseas Tribune (Wash., DC), 22 Oct. 1988, at 2, col. 5.

A related development is the resolution of a two-year insurgency by Nepali-speaking Gurkhas, centered in Darjeeling, a strategic area which controls a vital 12-mile-wide corridor connecting the northeast of India with the rest of the country. At least 300 people were killed during the insurgency, which ended in August 1988 when the central government engineered a compromise between the Gurkhas and the West Bengal state government. While the Gurkhas did not achieve their goal of a separate state, an autonomous hill council with control over local matters was created. Despite opposition to the accord by more extremist Gurkha elements, the Gurkha National Liberation Front, which led the insurgency and accepted the August 1988 compromise, swept nearly all the available seats for the new council elected in December 1988.

While the Darjeeling settlement cannot be seen as offering a substantive precedent for resolution of the Punjab conflict, it does evidence the positive role that can be played by Delhi and the flexibility of potential solutions. Changes may be necessary in the legal, constitutional, and, most importantly, political culture, so as to infuse the Indian federal system with the true spirit of federalism. Some of these changes may be suggested in the long-awaited report of the Sarkaria Commission on Centre-State Relations; indeed, the frequent extensions of time granted the commission reflect the extreme sensitivity with which its subject matter is viewed.

Sikh terrorism must be rejected, but the central government cannot rely on Sikh support for the government's anti-terrorism efforts until the Sikh community has regained some degree of faith in the ability of Delhi to implement a fair and lasting solution. The reassertion of Sikh identity does not require violence and intolerance of other cultures and religions, and the central government must recognize that true federalism requires that it abandon attempts to manipulate and control the states. One should not underestimate the difficulty of arriving at the necessary compromises after years of violence, but a resolution will be possible only in an atmosphere which reaffirms the multi-ethnic nature of Indian and Punjabi society and the respect due to each of its members.

Chapter 9
The Kurds[578]

THE KURDISH PEOPLE

The largest concentration of Kurds live in the mountains which connect Iraq, Iran, and Turkey, while smaller Kurdish communities are also found in Syria, Lebanon, and the U.S.S.R. Despite severe repression over the centuries, the Kurdish culture remains dominant in this region, which has been referred to as Kurdistan since the early thirteenth century. "[A]lthough the term Kurdistan appears on a few maps, it is clearly more than a geographical term since it refers also to a human culture which exists in that land. To this extent Kurdistan is a social and political concept."[579]

Throughout successive invasions, Kurdish identity has remained distinct for nearly two thousand years. Although the origins of the Kurds are uncertain, it is unlikely that they are truly indigenous to Kurdistan or that their ancestors came from a single source. It is believed that some Kurds are rooted in Turkic, Armenian, or Assyrian tribes, but most probably are descendants of Indo-European groups. Their language is in the Indo-European tradition, and, by the seventh century A.D., the ethnic term "Kurd" had been applied to an amalgam of Iranian tribes.

The exact size of the Kurdish population is controversial, as governments tend to minimize and nationalists to exaggerate the numbers. One problem in obtaining reliable information is that many Kurds still remember brutal anti-Kurd repression during the past half-century and

---

578 This chapter is drawn primarily from David McDowall, *The Kurds* (London: Minority Rights Group Report No. 23, rev. ed. 1985), and Gerard Chaliand (ed.), *People Without a Country* (London: Zed Press, 1980) [first published as *Les Kurdes et le Kurdistan* (Paris: Francois Maspero, 1978)].

579 McDowall, *supra* note 578, at 5.

are cautious about declaring themselves to be Kurds. A 1970 estimate placed the total number of Kurds in Turkey, Iran, Iraq, Syria, and the U.S.S.R. at approximately 14.5 million.[580] More recent estimates range from 16.3 million to just over 20 million, constituting 19–24% of the population of Turkey, 23–27% of Iraq, 10–16% of Iran, and 8–9% of Syria.[581]

Although Kurds share a north-western Iranian linguistic origin, they do not have a single systematized written or spoken language. There are two major dialects, each with considerable localized variation and a number of sub-dialects. While limited comprehension is possible, there is often a lack of clear understanding. This inability to speak to one another easily obviously renders internal cohesion more difficult.

In the 1830s and 1840s, the Yazidis emigrated to the Caucasus in order to escape persecution. Today, the nearly 100,000 Kurdish Yazidis remain a persecuted community, and, as a result, many Yazidis now identify themselves as Kurds and have joined the Kurdish nationalist movement.

While it is difficult to classify or define Kurdish tribalism, there is a strong cohesion based on family and territorial loyalties. Confederations are the largest form of tribal groupings and were originally created or fostered by various states in order to guard the borders. Each confederation is composed of smaller groups, such as tribal subsections and village groupings. Loyalties of this type are not immutable, however, and can be severed in response to the political or economic climate of the time. Although most tribes form confederations, the most effective source of political power remains with the aghas, or chiefs.

There also are differences between the Kurds that live in the plains and foothills, and those that live in the mountainous regions. Although kinship ties exist among the former group, they are not as strong as those among the mountain tribes. Mountain lands were traditionally controlled by individual tribes, with the agha responsible for the equitable allocation of pastoral rights. The plains and foothills were controlled by landlords who shared neither common lineage nor common economic interests with those who actually worked the land. The transition from a subsistence economy to a market economy, which began in the mid-nineteenth century, intensified the common interests of the landlords and the mountain chiefs, as both were co-opted into the state establishment.

---

580 Kendal, "The Kurds in the Soviet Union," in Chaliand, *supra* note 578, at 220–22.
581 See McDowall, *supra* note 578, at 7; Christiane More, *Les Kurds aujourd'hui, mouvement nationale et partis politiques* (Paris: Ed. Harmatlan, 1984).

In the 1920s, individual aghas in Iraq and Iran began to register land in their own name, further increasing their power; many tribes-people became little more than cultivators. The former nomadic pattern of many tribes continued to decline, thus indirectly consolidating the new international borders established after World War I. In Iran, many nomads were forcibly resettled.

As farming has become more mechanized, agricultural work for Kurds has become largely seasonal. As a result, there have been large migrations to urban areas in search of full-time employment. Other problems, such as land scarcity and general economic underdevelopment in Kurdish areas, also have contributed to an exodus of working males from the villages. Such socio-economic factors have further eroded the position of the agha, while increased urbanization also has weakened traditional tribal ties.

Parts of Kurdistan are rich in natural and mineral resources. Of particular importance are the oil fields around Kirkuk, and oil is also found in commercial quantities in Khanaqin, Iraq; Batman, Turkey; and Rumeylan, Syria. Significant quantities of chrome, copper, iron, coal, and lignite can also be found within Kurdistan.

As the original nomadic culture of the Kurds gradually declined, strong religious loyalties developed, often in competition with existing territorial and kinship ties. As a result, many Kurdish religious leaders, known as sheikhs, have been in the forefront of Kurdish rebellions.

Unlike many other mountain inhabitants, the majority of the Kurds converted to the Sunni form of Islam after the Arab conquests in the seventh century. Small pockets of Kurds in various regions also adhere to Shi'ite Islam (the established faith of Iran), other Islamic sects, and Yazidism.

Kurdish loyalty to the sheikhs has remained strong and is considered to be one of the strongest obstacles to attempts to mobilize the Kurds along class lines. Traditional tribal ties and in-fighting remain a major, if perhaps declining, factor in Kurdish politics.

Through the centuries, the Kurdish national movement has consistently manifested itself somewhat belatedly compared to the movements of the majority peoples of the surrounding areas. This is attributable to the economic, social, political and cultural level attained by Kurdish society. A mountain people, and, like nearly all mountain peoples, relatively backward, with a very small elite, the Kurds have historically been overtaken and crushed by the old, well-established statist tradition of the Persians and, to an even greater extent, by that of the Turks. . . .

Combined with the severe geopolitical handicaps, this is the crucial point which underlies the main weaknesses of the Kurdish national movement: *its elites were backward*, and this historical inheritance has perpetuated the crisis of Kurdish society and weighed heavily on the course of its national destiny. A traditionalism in values, mentality and behaviour has still not been replaced by an alternative conception of things. . . . The fundamental values are still those of yesterday: tactical cunning instead of political mobilization, and a few revolutionary slogans instead of a real radical practice.[582]

HISTORY TO 1923

Early Kurdish relationships with government were based primarily on trade, and successive regional governments accorded at least semi-autonomous status to the Kurdish aghas throughout the medieval period. As in most situations of indirect rule, the aghas found themselves linked to the regional governing establishment; they cooperated in creating a governing class of feudal lords, with a formal hierarchy within Kurdish society and ties to the outside world.

During the fourteenth century, a military aristocracy was organized to control the nomadic Kurdish tribes, as was a provincial nobility, civil service, and religious class. By the seventeenth century, the Kurdish tribes and their chiefs formalized their status even further as a result of conflicts between the Ottoman and Persian Safavid empires. Under a 1639 treaty, the Kurds undertook to guard the border between the two empires, after a majority of the Kurdish tribes had supported the Ottomans in return for promises of Kurdish fiefdoms and principalities to some aghas.

As a result of this agreement, fifteen main principalities were established, the ruling families of which were granted hereditary titles by the government. This political structure remained in place until the nineteenth century, when the regular Ottoman administration was extended into Kurdistan. While this system allowed the Kurds a great deal of autonomy, it also gave the state an important hold on key positions, for another family member was always available to replace an overly independent agha.

The Safavid Shahs of Iran used Kurdish tribes to defend their border in Khorasan, and these tribes eventually became permanently established in the area. The Safavids dealt ruthlessly with unsubmissive Kurdish princes, but they were not as successful in consolidating their power by direct rule as the Ottoman rulers were through indirect rule. Most of the Kurds were Sunni and may therefore have been less amenable to defending the Shi'ite Persian empire, and the ruling families were often split between pro-Ottoman and pro-Iranian factions. During the nineteenth century, Kurdistan was the site of armed struggles among Ottomans, Persians, and Russians, with Kurdish tribes often fighting on different sides.

582 Gerard Chaliand, "Introduction," in Chaliand, *supra* note 578, at 15, 16 (emphasis in original).

The abolition of the Kurdish principalities had a profound effect on Kurdish society and politics. In the absence of a recognized structure of arbitration, there was frequent rivalry among the aghas, and eventually the traditional power bases were weakened. As a result, the religious sheikhs were increasingly called upon to act as arbiters in disputes among aghas, villages, and tribes. The sheikhs worked together and often cut across tribal lines, thereby becoming a powerful and coherent force in an otherwise fragmented society.

The first important Kurdish revolt against the Ottoman Empire occurred in 1806, but this and subsequent efforts were unsuccessful.[583] The next major revolt, in 1880, was led by one of these religious leaders, Sheikh Ubaydallah, who called for an autonomous Kurdistan. Two years prior to the revolt, he had written to the British Vice-Consul:

> The Kurdish nation is a people apart. Their religion is different and their laws and customs are distinct. . . . The chiefs and rulers of Kurdistan, whether Turkish or Persian subjects, and the inhabitants of Kurdistan one and all are agreed that matters cannot be carried on in this way with the two governments.[584]

Ubaydallah enjoyed wide support among Kurds on both sides of the Persian-Ottoman border. However, his rebellion was defeated by the combined efforts of the Sultan and the Shah, aided by hostile Kurdish tribes who profited from the established Ottoman order.

Armenians and Kurds had long been intermingled or shared ill-defined borders, but Russian encouragement of Armenian separatism presented a threat to the relatively privileged position of the Kurds, who were co-religionists of the Ottoman Turks. Therefore, the Kurdish aghas assisted in the Ottoman repression and massacres of Armenian communities, which reached its climax in 1895–96. Soon thereafter, Kurdish families moved into many of the villages which were once occupied by Armenians.

As a larger Kurdish urban class developed around the turn of the century, Kurdish nationalism also increased. After the Young Turk revolution of 1908, Kurdish intellectuals, aghas, and officers established a number of political clubs, a few Kurdish schools, and the first Kurdish newspaper. However, these activities served not to unify the Kurdish people, but to create a new source of tension between urban intellectuals and the aghas, as the latter feared that political education and literacy would threaten their own position in the community.

583 See generally Kendal, "The Kurds under the Ottoman Empire," in Chaliand, *supra* note 578, at 25–32.

584 Quoted in Derk Kinnane, *The Kurds and Kurdistan* (London: Oxford Univ. Press, 1964) at 24.

After the outbreak of World War I, other concerns became much more pressing. As Ottoman citizens, most Kurds served in the war, and many participated in the genocide against the Armenians. Nevertheless, the government soon began to persecute the Kurds as well, fearing that they might collaborate with the Russians on the north-eastern front.

The Ottoman empire capitulated on 30 October 1918, and the Kurds had their greatest opportunity to establish a Kurdish state or autonomous region. However, foreign armies were encamped in much of Kurdistan, and struggles continued between the military powers in the region.

At the end of the war, the Kurds were unorganized, and many were more concerned with tribal loyalty than with creating a Kurdish nation. Soon a split developed between those who were willing to accept autonomy within Turkey and those who wanted complete independence. Nevertheless, the Kurds were able to cooperate with the Armenians in presenting a joint memorandum to the Peace Conference in Paris in 1919.

Point 12 of Woodrow Wilson's Fourteen Points stated that the non-Turkish minorities within the Ottoman empire should be "assured of an absolute unmolested opportunity to autonomous development."[585] On 10 August 1920, the Allies and the Turkish government signed the Treaty of Sèvres, which provided for local autonomy for the Kurds. The treaty stated that a commission composed of Allied appointees would

prepare for local autonomy in those regions where the Kurdish element is preponderant lying east of the Euphrates, to the south of the still-to-be established Armenian frontier and to the north of the frontier between Turkey, Syria and Mesopotamia. . . .

The plan [for autonomy] must provide complete guarantees as to the protection of the Assyro-Chaldeans and other ethnic or religious minorities in the area. . . .

If, after one year has elapsed since the implementation of the present treaty, the Kurdish population of the areas designated in Article 62 calls on the Council of the League of Nations and demonstrates that a majority of the population in these areas wishes to become independent of Turkey, and if the Council then estimates that the population in question is capable of such independence and recommends that it be granted, then Turkey agrees, as of now, to comply with this recommendation and to renounce all rights and titles to the area.[586]

Unfortunately for the Kurds, the Treaty of Sèvres was never implemented.

With the creation of modern Turkey, Mustafa Kemal Ataturk led a revolt in Anatolia which received the support of a significant number

585 Quoted in McDowall, *supra* note 578, at 11.
586 Treaty of Sèvres, arts. 62, 64.

of Kurds, who preferred to support other Muslims of Anatolia rather than fall within a Christian Armenian state. Ataturk soon established undisputed leadership in the west, following his defeat of the Greeks and the elimination of virtually all Christians remaining in Anatolia.

Ataturk refused to recognize the Treaty of Sèvres, and the Allies either had to renegotiate that settlement with an empire which no longer existed or attempt to implement the treaty by force. So long as the essential interests of the Great Powers were safeguarded, there was no interest in exercising the latter option on behalf of minorities such as the Kurds and Armenians.

The Allies therefore convened a new peace conference in November 1922, enabling Turkey to impose terms on the war's purported victors under the Treaty of Lausanne, which was signed in July 1923.[587] The treaty re-established complete Turkish sovereignty over eastern Thrace and all of Anatolia, totally ignored the claims of the Kurds and Armenians which had been recognized in the Treaty of Sèvres, and divided the remaining Kurdish territory between Iraq and Iran.[588] The Treaty of Lausanne did include certain guarantees for non-Muslim minorities in Turkey (e.g., for free use of their own language), but Turkey has subsequently refused to apply these guarantees to the Muslim Kurds.

Kurds who had supported the Ottoman empire did not look forward to the specifically Turkish, secular state envisaged by Ataturk. Despite some early official statements recognizing the national and social rights of the Kurds, they soon lost their special status as fellow Muslims. The Ottoman Caliphate was abolished on 3 March 1924, thus removing the temporal and spiritual foundation of the Kurdish aghas and sheikhs, and on the same day Kurdish schools, associations, publications, religious fraternities, teaching foundations, and all public vestiges of a separate Kurdish identity were banned in Turkey.[589]

In Iran, Reza Khan replaced the last of the Qajar Shahs in 1923, with the support of the British, and proclaimed himself Shah two years later. His deepest concern was to ensure the unity of a state composed of several minority groups, and he feared that the successful separation of any one of these communities could prove fatal to the integrity of the rest.

Among the many separatist risings occurring within Iran, the most

587 28 L.N.T.S. 11, signed 24 July 1923, entered into force 31 March 1924.

588 The primary concern of the Allies was oil, not the national aspirations of the Kurds. In 1926, the oil-rich area around Mosul was attached to the British Mandate, despite the fact that an enquiry conducted by the Council of the League of Nations found that the local population favored establishment of an independent Kurdish state. Kendal, *supra* note 583, at 58–60.

589 McDowall, *supra* note 578, at 12.

serious was in Kurdistan. In 1921, Kurdish chief Isma'il Shakkah Simko began the first of several revolts in which he attempted to overthrow the government authorities.[590]

Tehran's initial response was to offer Simko limited autonomy, as the government actually welcomed any attempt to provide authority in this sensitive region threatened by Turkish, Russian, and British forces. However, the Shah later led an expedition which drove Simko into Iraq, and Simko was assassinated in 1930. Reza Shah continued to suppress any separatist tendencies by confiscating land and often uprooting entire tribes from their ancestral lands.

The state of Iraq emerged from the Ottoman provinces in Mesopotamia, initially as a British League of Nations mandatory. During the dispute over the Turkish-Iraqi border, a commission appointed by the League of Nations noted that the disputed territory was primarily Kurdish, and that the Kurds lived separately from the Arab population. Among the commission's observations was that "[i]f one was to base oneself on ethnic arguments, one would have to conclude that the best solution would be to set up an independent Kurdist State, seeing as the Kurds account for five-eighths of the population."[591] However, the commission ultimately suggested that this Kurdish area be attached to Iraq, in order to ensure the latter's economic viability.[592]

Although the British served only in a supervisory capacity, they initiated a system of direct administration through the use of Kurdish officials, which served to strengthen Kurdish national sentiments. The Iraqi government pledged to honor the recommendations of the League of Nations that the Kurdish language be allowed in schools and that the administration of the region be comprised primarily of Kurds. However, no substantive steps were ever taken on the language issue, and these pledges were not included in the 1930 Anglo-Iraqi treaty which formally ended the British mandate.

Thus, as was the case with several Balkan and other "nations," Kurdish nationalist aspirations were essentially ignored in the post-war border adjustments of 1919–1923. While the Kurds had never been united within a single state or empire, in the 1920s they found themselves divided among four countries: Turkey, Iraq, Iran, and Syria (with small minorities in the Soviet Union and Lebanon). The Kurds, like the Armenians, were not sufficiently strong militarily or politically to forge

---

590 See Martin van Bruinessen, "Kurdish Tribes and Simko's Revolt," in R. Tapper, *The Conflict of Tribe and State in Iran and Afghanistan* (London: Croom-Helm, 1983) at 364–396.

591 Quoted in Ismet Sheriff Vanly, "Kurdistan in Iraq," in Chaliand, *supra* note 578, at 162.

592 *Id.*

their own state out of the disintegrating empires, and the Allied Powers had no need for buffer states to contain the Ottoman remains. Kurdish communities have continued to struggle, often with each other, to establish a new national identity.

TURKEY

Despite initial Kurdish support for the Ataturk revolution that established modern Turkey, the unyielding secularization and Turkification of the country has meant constant repression, not only of Kurdish desires for political autonomy but of Kurdish identity. The 1924 prohibition of Kurdish schools, associations, and publications established a policy that has been followed by successive Turkish governments, whether military or civilian, and the Kurds have sporadically attempted to resist this expurgation of their culture.

The first revolt, led by Naqshbandi, Sheikh Said of Piran, erupted in 1925, but it was crushed relatively quickly by Turkish troops; ruthless suppression of the dervish orders followed. Soon thereafter, the local aghas, supported by a new Kurdish liberation organization, Khoyboun, led another revolt. Khoyboun, which was based in Lebanon and Syria, brought together all the leading Kurdish groups and enjoyed the support of the Shah of Iran. The Kurds gained control of a sizeable area, but the sudden decision of the Shah to cut off assistance to the Kurds allowed the Turks to move through Iranian territory and encircle the Kurdish forces.

The extent of the subsequent persecution of the Kurds is evidenced by Law No. 1850, which legalized "[m]urders and other actions committed individually or collectively, from the 20th of June 1930 to the 10th of December 1930, . . . during the pursuit and extermination of the revolts" in Kurdish areas.[593] The then Minister of Justice was quoted as stating that "[w]e live in a country called Turkey, the freest country in the world. . . . I believe that the Turk must be the only lord, the only master of this country. Those who are not of pure Turkish stock can have only one right in this country, the right to be servants and slaves."[594]

Over one million Kurds were forcibly relocated between 1925 and 1938. Kurdish villages were closely policed, and the use of Kurdish language, dress, folklore, and names was prohibited. A revolt in Dersim was finally crushed in 1938, and martial law remained in force in Kurdish areas until 1946.

In 1950, the first free general election in Turkey was held, and the

593 Quoted by Kendal, *supra* note 583, at 65.
594 *Id.* at 65–66.

Democratic Party was swept to power in reaction to almost 25 years of authoritarian rule. Some Kurds were elected to Parliament, and schools, roads, and hospitals began to appear in the region. In 1961, a new constitution was introduced which allowed freedom of expression, press, and association. The large urban Kurdish population, which had been scattered throughout Turkey by relocation and deportations, soon became aware of other Kurds seeking to assert their identity. In 1965, the separatist Kurdistan Democratic Party (KDP) was established, which acted in solidarity with Barzani's movement in Iraqi Kurdistan.[595]

As Kurdish and leftist groups became more vocal, the Turkish government increased its efforts to silence all cultural and political activity of which it did not approve. In January 1967, the Demirel government prohibited many of the bilingual Kurdish-Turkish journals that had appeared in the mid-1960s, and their editors were arrested. Repression increased after 1967, with the introduction of special commando groups to patrol Kurdistan and intimidate the population.

In March 1971, the army overthrew the Demirel government, and Kurdish political parties were banned. Throughout the 1970s, oppression of the Kurds continued sporadically, and martial law was again imposed in the Kurdish provinces in 1979. The Turkish President was quoted as saying that "there is no room for liberated regions and activities aimed at language, racial, class or sectarian differences in our homeland. The government will defeat the disease and heads will be crushed."[596]

Another military coup d'état, similar to those in 1960 and 1971, took place in September 1980. Tens of thousands of leftist activists and Kurds were arrested, interrogated, and tortured, and the excesses of the military were widely condemned.[597] In 1982, France, Denmark, the Netherlands, Norway, and Sweden filed a complaint with the European

595 See *infra* at 190–93.

596 Quoted in Edmund Ghareeb, *The Kurdish Question in Iraq* (Syracuse, NY: Syracuse Univ. Press, 1981) at 10.

597 See generally Hrair Balian, *Turkey—Continued Violations of International Human Rights and Humanitarian Law* (Berkeley, CA: Human Rights Advocates, 1987) and sources cited therein (particularly various reports by Amnesty International and Helsinki Watch) for a summary of the major allegations of human rights violations in Turkey during and since the military coup. A succinct statement of the Turkish government's position may be found in Michael M. Gunter, "The Kurdish Problem in Turkey," paper delivered at the 20th Annual Meeting of the Middle East Studies Association of North America, Boston, MA, 20–23 Nov. 1986, at 42–45. Gunter observes that "it might have been necessary to amputate a limb in order to save the body politic. . . . [I]t is difficult to fault the Turkish government for taking the necessary steps to maintain the territorial integrity of its state." *Id.* at 44.

Commission of Human Rights alleging widespread human rights violations in Turkey, although it contained no specific reference to discrimination or other acts directed against the Kurds.[598]

The restoration of civilian authority in 1984 seems to have had no effect on the conflict between the government and the Kurds. Using the rationale of protecting Western strategic interests and responding to the needs of the North Atlantic Treaty Organization (NATO), militarization of the eastern and southern provinces has been intensified, and two of Turkey's four armies are now permanently based in the east. In 1984, Turkey and Iraq agreed to establish a joint six-mile-wide security zone along their border, and Turkish forces have crossed the border to attack Kurdish guerrilla bases in Iraq. Clashes in the border region between armed Kurdish groups and the Turkish army have continued, and attacks on Turkish civilians and soldiers by the outlawed Kurdish Workers' Party (PKK) have claimed hundreds of lives since 1984.[599]

The consistent policy of the state of Turkey from its inception has been the destruction of Kurdish culture and the forced assimilation of Kurds into a purely Turkish society.[600] Article 14 of the 1982 Constitution prohibits activities which violate "the indivisible integrity of the State with its territory and nation," and article 87 underscores the government's sensitivity on this subject by specifically prohibiting parliament from pardoning prisoners charged with violations of article 14. Article 89 of the Turkish law on political parties states, "No political party may concern itself with the defence, development, or diffusion of any non-

598 Applications Nos. 9940–9944/82. The applications were declared admissible by the Commission on 6 Dec. 1983, but a "friendly settlement" subsequently reached meant that only a pro forma report was adopted by the Commission on 7 Dec. 1985, under art. 30 of the European Convention. The terms of the settlement included a continuing "dialogue" between Turkey and the Commission and informal promises by Turkey that restrictions on individual rights would be progressively removed. Turkey accepted the right of individual petition under art. 25 of the European Convention for a three-year period on 29 Jan. 1987, but its letter of acceptance restricted the right to, *inter alia*, "allegations made in respect of facts, including judgments which are based on such facts[,] which have occurred subsequent to the date of deposit of the present declaration." Declaration by the Government of Turkey, reprinted in Eur. Comm. Human Rights, Minutes of the hundred and eighty-fifth session, Council of Europe Doc. DH (87) 2 (def.), 12 May 1987, at 25.

599 See, e.g., "Turks Pursue Rebel Kurds Into N. Iraq," Wash. Post, 18 Oct. 1984, at A23, col. 1; "Turkey Strikes Rebel Bases in Iraq," *id.*, 16 Aug. 1986, at A16, col. 3; "Turkish Kurds Fight Unheralded," *id.*, 12 Oct. 1986, at A22, col. 1; "A Remote But Bitter War," Newsweek, 30 Mar. 1987, at 45; "Turks Admit Kurd Guerrillas Are Residents," N.Y. Times, 22 Oct. 1987, at A9, col. 1.

600 See, e.g., *Destroying Ethnic Identity, The Kurds of Turkey* (New York and Washington, DC: U.S. Helsinki Watch Committee, 1988), esp. at 1–10.

Turkish language or culture; nor may they seek to create minorities within our frontiers or to destroy our national unity."[601]

Even the United States, a close political and military ally of Turkey, notes that

the [Turkish] Government remains adamantly opposed to any assertion of a Kurdish ethnic identity and has taken a number of steps to suppress it. Publication of books, newspapers, and any other materials in Kurdish is forbidden, as are books or any other materials in Turkish dealing with Kurdish history, culture, or ethnic identity. Use of the Kurdish language is not permitted for any official purposes, e.g., in the courts, nor is it allowed in certain private situations such as receiving visitors in prison.[602]

Indeed, the Turkish government has refused even to acknowledge the existence of the Kurds, referring to them instead as "mountain Turks."[603]

Amnesty International has adopted several Kurdish activists arrested for non-violent promotion of Kurdish culture as "prisoners of conscience."[604] As Turkey is not a party to any of the major human rights conventions (except the European Convention), neither the Human Rights Committee nor the Committee on the Elimination of Racial Discrimination has been able to comment on Turkish treatment of the Kurds.

The eight million Kurds in Turkey remain divided, and many do not support the guerrilla activities of the PKK. Even with greater unity among the Kurds, however, it is unlikely that the Turkish government would be disposed to grant the recognition which it has consistently denied for over 50 years. While it does not exclude the possibility of eliminating discrimination against Kurds and even contemplating the grant of some form of autonomous status, the following pessimistic observation by a European diplomat accurately defines at least part of the problem:

What the Kurds are asking for—an independent state—is simply unacceptable to Turkey and will never even be considered. . . . But the Turks haven't been able to quash Kurdish culture and nationalism in 50 years and there is no

601 Quoted in Kendal, *supra* note 583, at 87.

602 *Country Reports on Human Rights Practices for 1986, supra* note 331 at 1051.

603 There were some indications in 1987 and 1988 that anti-Kurdish policies may be easing, although this seems to be a matter of policy rather than formal amendment of laws. References to Kurds now occasionally appear in the Turkish press, and there has been a relaxation of prohibitions against speaking Kurdish during prison visits. See *Destroying Ethnic Identity, The Kurds of Turkey, supra* note 600, at 4–5; Commission on Security and Cooperation in Europe, CSCE Digest, March 1988, at 6.

604 *See,* e.g., *Amnesty International Report 1988, supra* note 563, at 216.

reason to believe they will be any more successful this time. The sad fact is
there is no solution. . . . The Kurds cannot be simply declared not to exist and
Turkey cannot be expected to give in to their demands."[605]

IRAQ

The history of Kurds in Iraq since 1930 is one of more or less constant,
if sporadic, armed conflict, punctuated by attempts at a negotiated settlement. Despite internal dissension, similar to that in Turkey and Iran,
a single leader, Mullah Mustafa Barzani, did ultimately come to represent the great majority of Iraqi Kurds.

Barzani was a traditional leader who combined both secular and
religious authority as an agha and mullah, respectively. In 1945, after
repelling several attempts by the Iraqi government to defeat him, Barzani was finally pushed over the border into Iran. He returned to Iraq
in 1958, following a successful coup by General Qasim which established
a new Iraqi Republic and recognized the rights of both Arabs and Kurds.

Barzani was unable to use the newly granted constitutional rights
to achieve autonomy for the Kurdish region, and armed conflict resumed. Barzani was supported by Turkey and Iran, so long as he did
not inspire separatist agitation among their own Kurds. Finally, Barzani
and the Iraqi government agreed to a twelve-point program which met
many of the Kurds' demands, but the government fell before the agreement could be implemented.

In 1968, the Ba'th regime resumed power. The longstanding distrust
between Barzani and the Ba'th party made reaching an agreement difficult and hostilities ensued, despite Ba'th pronouncements that settlement of the Kurdish question was a priority. A ceasefire and peace
agreement were reached in 1970, at least temporarily ending a decade
of conflict that may have cost 60,000 casualties and displaced 300,000
people.[606] The Iraqi government considered that the 11 March 1970
agreement constituted "a complete and constitutional settlement of the
Kurdish issue."[607] As the only agreed-upon statement of Kurdish autonomy acceptable (at least for a time) to both sides, the March 1970
agreement is worth citing extensively:

1. The Kurdish language shall be, alongside with the Arabic language, the
official language in areas populated by Kurdish majority. The Kurdish language
shall be the language of instruction in these areas. Arabic language shall be

---

605 Remarks of an unnamed European diplomat, quoted in Wash. Post, 12 Oct.
1986, at A22, col. 4.
606 McDowall, *supra* note 578, at 20.
607 Peace Agreement of 11 Mar. 1970, reprinted in Martin Short and Anthony
McDermott, *The Kurds* (London: Minority Rights Group Report No. 23, 1975) at
25–26.

taught in all schools, where the Kurdish language is the language of instruction while the Kurdish language shall be taught in schools throughout Iraq as a second language within the limits stipulated by law.

2. The sharing of our Kurdish brothers in Government and non-discrimination between the Kurds and others in the assumption of public offices . . . have been and still remain among the important objectives which the Revolutionary Government seeks to achieve. . . . [The government] stresses the necessity of working for its fulfilment in an equitable ratio with due regard to the principle of efficiency the proportionate distribution of inhabitants and the inequities which had befallen our Kurdish brothers in the past.

3. In view of the state of backwardness which in the past afflicted the Kurdish nationality from the cultural and educational standpoints, a plan shall be worked out to make good that backwardness. . . .

4. In the administrative units, populated by a Kurdish majority, officials shall be from Kurds or from among persons well-versed in the Kurdish language provided the required number is available. . . .

5. The Government concedes to the Kurdish people its right to set up student, youth, women and teachers organisations of its own—such organisations to become affiliated in the corresponding national Iraqi organisations. . . . The [national] economic plan shall be drawn up in such a way as to assure equal development to various parts of Iraq with due attention to the Kurdish area. . . .

8. The inhabitants of Arab and Kurdish villages shall be restored to their former places of habitation [or resettled and compensated]. . . .

9. Speedy measures shall be taken to implement the Agrarian Reform law in the Kurdish area and amending it in such a manner as guarantees the liquidation of feudalist relations and the acquisition of appropriate plots of land side by side with waiving for them agricultural taxes accumulating over the years of unfortunate hostilities.

10. It has been agreed to amend the Interim Constitution as follows:

A) The people of Iraq is made up of two principal nationalities; the Arab nationality and the Kurdish nationality. This Constitution confirms the national rights of the Kurdish people and the rights of all minorities within the framework of Iraqi unity.

B) . . . [T]he Kurdish language, alongside with the Arabic language, shall be an official language in the Kurdish area.

C) The above shall be confirmed in the Permanent Constitution. . . .

12. A Kurd shall be one of the vice-presidents [of the Republic].

[Article 13 envisages changes in the law on administrative boundaries "in a manner conforming with the substance of this statement."]

14. . . . [N]ecessary measures shall be taken . . . to unify the governorates and administrative units populated by a Kurdish majority in accordance with official census operations yet to be made. The state shall endeavour to develop this administrative unity and deepen and broaden the exercising by the Kurdish people therein of the sum of its national rights as a guarantee to its enjoyment of self-rule. . . . As the self-rule is to be achieved within the framework of the Iraqi Republic, the exploitation of national riches in the area [i.e., the oil fields] will naturally be under the jurisdiction of the authorities of this Republic.

15. The Kurdish people shall share in the legislative power in a manner proportionate to its population in Iraq.[608]

608 *Id.*; spelling and punctuation are as in the original text, which was taken from

While this agreement was a significant advance over any previous recognition of Kurdish autonomy in Iraq, Turkey, or Iran, full implementation proved impossible. While Iraqi Kurdistan enjoyed four years of relative peace, agreement could not be reached on the boundaries of the Kurdish autonomous region or on the issue of nationalization of the Kirkuk oil fields. The Kurds wanted a proportional distribution of oil revenues, while the Ba'th regime insisted that revenues be allocated by the central government as state assets. Clashes between the Kurds and the government resumed, as the Iraqi military greatly increased its presence along the Iranian border.

In addition to the existence of internal Kurdish divisions and the deep mistrust between Barzani and the Ba'th government, external forces also undermined prospects that the agreement would be implemented. A Soviet-Iraqi agreement in 1972 indicated a lessening of previous Soviet support for Barzani. On the other hand, Iran, the United States, and Israel were interested in reviving the conflict in order to weaken the Iraqi regime, although there was no wish to support establishment of a truly autonomous Kurdish region. The Shah of Iran and Israel provided arms and advisors to the Barzani forces, thus encouraging those who wished to resume the armed struggle.

Without the approval or agreement of Barzani's Kurdistan Democratic Party (KDP), the Iraqi government promulgated Act No. 33 on 11 March 1974, which remains the basic law on autonomy in Kurdistan.[609] Article 1 of Act. No. 33, as subsequently amended, provides that the region of Kurdistan shall enjoy autonomy and shall be regarded as a single administrative unit "within the framework of the legal, political and economic unity of the Republic of Iraq." The autonomous region extends only over those areas with a majority Kurdish population, based on a 1957 census.

Article 2 provides that Arabic and Kurdish are the official languages in the region, and that both languages shall be taught in schools; Arabic is a required subject beginning in the fourth primary grade.[610] Article 3 guarantees the rights of non-Kurdish minorities, including proportional

a translation provided by the Iraqi Ministry of Culture and Information. A summary of the agreement may be found in Vanly, "Kurdistan in Iraq," *supra* note 591, at 168–70.

609 Law for Autonomy in the Area of Kurdistan, excerpts of which are reprinted in Short and McDermott, *supra* note 607, at 27–29. A detailed summary of the law, from which the quotations in this chapter are taken, may be found in various submissions by the Iraqi government to treaty-based human rights monitoring bodies. *See* Iraq, art. 9 CERD Report, UN Doc. CERD/C/107/Add.6 (1984); *id.*, UN Doc. CERD/C/132/Add.2 (1985), Annex II; art. 40 CCPR Report, UN Doc. CCPR/C/1/Add.45 (1979) at 109–16 and Annex; *id.*, UN Doc. CCPR/C/37/Add.3 (1986) at 47–55.

610 Act No. 28 of 1983, cited in Iraq, art. 40 CCPR Report (1986), *supra* note 609, at 50.

representation in all local autonomous institutions. Article 4 states that the judicial system shall conform to the legal system of Iraq; the validity of any autonomous act may be challenged by the Minister of Justice before a special body chosen among members of the Iraqi Court of Cassation, whose decisions are final. Article 5 stipulates that the region shall be "an independent financial unit, within the overall financial unity of the State," and articles 6–9 concern other fiscal issues. There is a Legislative Council with the power to adopt, *inter alia*, "legislative measures needed to develop the region and to improve its local social, cultural and economic facilities within the limits of the general policy of the State," and to approve "detailed planning proposals prepared by the Executive Council . . . in accordance with the requirements of general central planning in the State." An Executive Council is headed by a regional President, appointed by the President of Iraq and subject to approval by the Legislative Council. The autonomous institutions have only those powers specifically delegated to them, and residual authority rests with the central Iraqi government.

The 1974 autonomy law was perceived as weakening the 1970 agreement, and it was rejected by the KDP. The KDP objected, in particular, to the government's use of the outdated 1957 census, as only 60% of what the KDP considered to be Kurdish land was actually included in the autonomous region. Another major KDP objection was to the law's failure to resolve satisfactorily the question of oil and mineral rights in Kirkuk.

The Ba'th Government gave the KDP fourteen days to assent to the law, and the "fifth Kurdistan war"[611] broke out soon after the expiration of the time limit in April 1974. By the end of the summer, the Iraqi army controlled more areas of Kurdistan than it had at any time since 1961. While the Kurdish forces initially received support from Iran, resistance collapsed within a matter of weeks after the March 1975 Algiers Agreement between Iran and Iraq, under which the former agreed to cut off all logistical support to the Iraqi Kurds.

The war had tremendous costs on both sides, with estimates of 50,000 killed and wounded and as many as 600,000 displaced persons. Barzani eventually fled to the United States, where he died of cancer in 1979. The KDP split into various factions, including an "official" KDP and the KDP "Provisional Command," led by two of Barzani's sons. A new party, the Patriotic Union of Kurdistan (PUK) launched the first guerrilla actions against the Iraqi government since the 1975 defeat.[612]

611 Vanly, *supra* note 591.

612 A description of the various Kurdish parties may be found in McDowall, *supra* note 578, at 29–30, and van Bruinessen, *supra* note 619, at 17–18, 22–26.

The Iraqi government attempted to appease the population inside the Kurdish area, granting compensation to displaced families and building over 60,000 new homes in model villages and "strategic hamlets" established in the Iran-Iraq border security zone created after 1975.

> Iraq holds the view that the Kurdish problem has been solved in a legal and democratic manner that is unprecedented in any other country with a Kurdish ethnic minority.
> The political aspect of the problem is merely a result of foreign interference, aimed at prejudicing Iraq's territorial integrity, which constitutes a serious violation of human rights and of the Charter of the United Nations.[613]

Despite the theoretical cultural autonomy which Iraq's three million Kurds enjoy, and which is unknown in neighboring Turkey or Iran, the massacres of Kurdish guerrillas (known as *peshmergas*) and civilians which followed the end of the Iran-Iraq war are perhaps a more significant indicator of Iraqi policies towards the Kurds. Thousands of Kurds were killed by Iraqi army forces, amidst allegations that poison gas had been used; over 100,000 were relocated to government-controlled towns (described by the Iraqi foreign minister as "a reorganization of the urban situation in a mountainous and difficult country"[614]); hundreds of villages were destroyed; and perhaps 100,000 Kurds fled to Turkey.[615] Such massacres cannot be justified, even in the context of a battle against "traitors" who supported Iran during the war.

IRAN

Iranian Kurdistan includes an area of approximately 125,000 square kilometers, and perhaps as much as 16% (five million people) of the population of Iran is Kurdish.[616] As is the case in Turkey, the Iranian

613 Iraq, art. 9 CERD Report (1985), *supra* note 609, Annex II at 7.

614 Tyler, "Iraqi Official Says Kurds Fleeing Army Operation," Wash. Post, 4 Sept. 1988, at A33, at col. 5., also see Tyler, "Iraq Targets Kurds for Relocation," Wash. Post, 30 Apr. 1989, at A34, col. 1.

615 Among many contemporaneous reports, see, e.g., Tyler, *id.*; Dan Oberdorfer, "U.S. Charges Iraq Used Poison Gas on Kurds," Wash. Post, 9 Sept. 1988, at A1, col. 5; Jonathan C. Randal, "'Kurds Have No Friends,'" *id.*, col. 6; Tyler, "Scorched Kurdish Villages Bear Witness to Iraqi Assault," Wash. Post, 17 Sept. 1988, at A1, col. 1; *id.*, "The Kurds: It's Not Genocide," Wash. Post, 25 Sept. 1988, at C5, col. 1. A UN inquiry concluded that Iraq had used chemical weapons against Iranian forces in August 1988, and perhaps hundreds of Kurdish civilians were killed during a mustard, cyanide, and nerve gas attack by Iraq in March 1988. See Physicians for Human Rights, *Winds of Death: Iraq's Use of Poison Gas Against Its Kurdish Population* (Somerville, MA: Physicians for Human Rights, 1989.)

616 A. R. Ghassemlou, "Kurdistan in Iran," in Chaliand, *supra* note 578, at 107–08.

government has generally sought to suppress any Kurdish movement towards autonomy, although the extent of repression has not been as severe as in Turkey.

Following the defeat of Simko in the 1930s, the Kurds in Iran were relatively quiet until the Second World War. Both the Soviets and the British opposed Reza Shah during the war, as the Allies suspected him of pro-German sympathies; Iran was therefore invaded, with the Soviets occupying the northern and the British the southern part of the country.

At the time of their invasion, the Allies pledged that they would withdraw from Iran by March 1946, and, as this deadline approached, both the Kurds and the Azerbaijanis sought to take advantage of the situation. By December 1945, the Azerbaijanis captured Tabriz and founded the Democratic Republic of Azerbaijan. A few days later, the Kurds declared the Republic of Mahabad and, within a month, formed a government under the Presidency of Qazi Muhammad. The Kurds sought complete autonomy within Iran rather than independence, but longstanding divisions among the Kurds began to surface. Some of the chiefs remained non-committal, as they were reluctant to jeopardize their own positions with the government and the tribespeople, while others simply avoided becoming too closely tied to the Mahabad Republic.

The Mahabad Republic lasted only a year, betrayed by internal dissension and lack of support from the Soviet Union, despite the latter's initial encouragement for declaration of the republic.[617] In 1946, Iranian troops entered Azerbaijan and Mahabad unopposed, and both republics collapsed. Qazi Muhammed was executed in March 1947; the expression of Kurdish identity was completely banned; and the nationalist movement in Iran went underground.

Political activism resumed following the Iraqi revolution in 1958 and the struggle by Barzani,[618] and the Kurdish Democratic Party (KDPI) began guerrilla warfare against the Iranian regime. However, when Barzani began receiving aid from the Shah in his battle against the Iraqi government, he refused to assist the Kurds operating inside Iran. Without this support, the movement in Iran began to collapse, culminating in a successful campaign by the Iranian army in 1967–68.

While Barzani's movement in Iraq was traditionally based, the Iranian Kurdish leaders attempted to align themselves with leftist forces opposed to the Shah. The 1979 Islamic revolution in Iran presented the Kurds with yet another opportunity to gain meaningful autonomy, and

617 See generally Archie Roosevelt, Jr., "The Kurdish Republic of Mahabad," in Chaliand, *supra* note 578, at 135–52.
618 See *supra* at 190–92.

there were strong Kurdish nationalist sentiments expressed in the immediate aftermath of the Shah's fall. The KDPI became the major political force in Iranian Kurdistan, and it demanded autonomy from the newly installed Khomeini regime.

Central to the beliefs of Khomeini's revolutionary government was the unity of its Islamic community, and the government therefore rejected all Kurdish demands for autonomy. The government also feared (as had Reza Shah in the 1920s) that, if it ceded autonomy to the Kurds, other minorities would demand similar rights, eventually leading to the disintegration of the state. However, the government's failure to defeat the Kurds militarily in 1979 prompted another attempt at a negotiated settlement.

In December 1979, Tehran set forth its proposals on minority rights in a fourteen-point document. It offered considerable administrative decentralization but not autonomy, and it only recognized the Kurds as a "religious minority."[619] The KDPI rejected the proposals and the fighting continued, with the government reasserting control over the towns and the Kurds in control of the countryside. While internal dissension again hurt the Kurdish cause, the KDPI reportedly exercised governmental powers over large areas of Kurdistan until finally pushed into Iraq by an Iranian offensive in 1983.[620]

THE IRAN-IRAQ WAR

In September 1980, Iraq repudiated the Algiers Agreement and invaded Iran, once again dramatically altering the shifting alliances in one of the most complex areas of the world.

The eight-year war between Iran and Iraq resulted in approximately one million deaths, and its long duration and the resulting instability in the region offered a great opportunity for a unified Kurdish community to try its own hand at the tactics of divide and conquer. However, as has been the case in the past, unity proved elusive, and Kurds were used as proxy pawns by both sides.[621]

Far from taking advantage of the war, the Kurds suffered great losses even before the post-war massacres in Iraq. In 1984, at least 27,500 Kurds were reportedly killed when a Kurdish-controlled region of Iran was virtually eliminated. In a six-month period in 1987, Iraqi forces

619 See Martin van Bruinessen, "The Kurds Between Iran and Iraq," Middle East Report, July-Aug. 1986, at 19–22; Chaliand, "Postscript, 1979," in Chaliand, *supra* note 578, at 230–31; McDowall, *supra* note 578, at 18.

620 Van Bruinessen, *supra* note 619, at 22.

621 See generally McDowall, *supra* note 578, at 24–25; van Bruinessen, *supra* note 619.

destroyed at least 500 Kurdish villages and relocated between 100,000 and 500,000 Kurds, in an effort to deny sanctuaries to the *peshmergas*.[622] Iraqi Kurds included both pro- and anti-government factions fighting each other and the government, and Iraqi-based Turkish Kurds were attacked by Turkish forces.

The fact that much of the fighting occurred in Iraqi Kurdistan suggests that it was not wholly controlled by either of the warring states. By 1983, both Baghdad and the PUK feared possible Iranian breakthroughs in Kurdistan, which neither would welcome. Conceding that they had some interests in common, PUK agreed to discuss a ceasefire with the Ba'th government. It is unclear whether either side was negotiating in good faith, although Baghdad apparently agreed to some of the demands, including repatriation of Kurds settled elsewhere in the country and the release of PUK detainees. In any event, the negotiations broke down in mid-1984.

Convoluted fighting continued until the Iran-Iraq ceasefire in August 1988, as Kurdish guerrillas attacked targets in all three countries, particularly in Iraq and Turkey. However, the Kurds were incapable of turning the tide of the war in either direction, and their position at the war's end was tenuous. The results in Iraq are described above.

SYRIA

Approximately 8% of the population in Syria is composed of Kurds, who are concentrated primarily in three areas along the Syrian-Turkish border. Many may be descendants of medieval military camps of Kurdish troops and have had little real contact with the Kurds of either Iraq or Turkey, while others came to Syria after the collapse of the Ottoman empire. Many of them have become highly Arabicized.

Relations between Syrians and Kurds were generally good under the Ottoman empire, although the latter were recruited into the local French mandatory forces along with other minorities, and separatist tendencies were encouraged by the French. Nevertheless, there was little minority persecution nor a strong desire for separatism, and Syria gained its independence in 1945 without a violent internal struggle comparable to that encountered by other countries in the region.

Beginning in 1958, however, with the establishment by Syria and Egypt of the short-lived United Arab Republic, Kurds began to come under increasing pressure from Syrian authorities. Kurds demanded a more democratic government in Damascus and recognition as an ethnic

622 "Iraqis Are Facing a Growing War From Within," N.Y. Times, 22 Sept. 1987, at A6, col. 1.

group; they also complained of severe economic underdevelopment in Kurdish areas and of the fact that the police and military academies were closed to Kurdish applicants.

The government's response was to increase oppression and harassment, and the situation worsened after the collapse of the United Arab Republic in 1961 and the assumption of power of the Syrian Ba'th party in 1963. A study published in 1963 by the chief of police of Jezireh province, a major Kurdish area, may have reflected then contemporary attitudes:

> [The Kurds] do not constitute a nation . . . [and] the Kurdish people are a people without history or civilization or language or even definite ethnic origin of their own. Their only characteristics are those shaped by force, destructive power and violence, characteristics which are, by the way, inherent in all mountain populations.[623]

In the early 1960s, over 100,000 Kurds considered to be "foreigners" were stripped of their Syrian citizenship, and a plan was adopted to establish a Kurdish-free *cordon sanitaire* along the Syrian border with Turkey.

Ba'th persecution of the Kurds, which seems to have originated primarily in pan-Arabism rather than in response to any Kurdish threat against the state, began to ease in the late 1960s. In 1976, Syrian President Assad officially renounced the policy of population transfers envisaged to create the "Arab belt" along the border of Jezireh. While Syria remains the "Syrian Arab Republic" and does not recognize the Kurds as a separate ethnic group,[624] the Kurdish community does today seem to be relatively safe and free from discrimination.

LEBANON

There are a few thousand Kurds in Lebanon, many of whom originally came seeking employment. Those who are in the country illegally are often exploited, as is the case with illegal or undocumented workers in many countries, but they do not suffer any particular discrimination as Kurds. The widespread violence and civil war in Lebanon in recent years has encouraged many Kurds to leave; most have returned to Syria.

623 Mohamed Talab Hilal, *Study of the Jezireh Province in its National, Social and Political Aspects* (1963), quoted in Mustafa Nazdar, "The Kurds in Syria," in Chaliand, *supra* note 578, at 216.

624 For example, the Syrian government does not mention the Kurds in any of its reports under art. 40 of the Covenant on Civil and Political Rights or art. 9 of the Convention on the Elimination of All Forms of Racial Discrimination.

U.S.S.R.

The Kurds comprise one of the smallest minorities within the Soviet Union, with the most important concentrations found in Soviet Armenia, Azerbaijan, and Georgia. Consistent with the Soviet policy of permitting cultural expression to the various officially recognized "nationalities" in the country, Kurds are permitted to have their own schools, books, press, and radio station.

OBSERVATIONS

The Kurds are the fourth most numerous people in the Middle East. They constitute one of the largest races, indeed nations, in the world today to have been denied an independent state. Whatever the yardstick for national identity the Kurds measure up to it.[625]

The very organization of this chapter, which describes major Kurd-movements in three states and less significant communities in three others, is evidence of the Byzantine complexity of the Kurdish question. The Kurdish people may be the largest geographically separate community in the world not to have achieved either statehood or some form of recognized territorial autonomy; they are certainly the largest among the many "nations" disappointed by the post-World War I territorial realignments in Europe and the Middle East.

At the same time, however, it may be misleading to speak of "the Kurdish people" in the same sense as the Greek, Irish, or Navajo peoples. Kurds do not belong to a single ethnic group, nor do they speak a wholly unified language. They are divided by internal quarrels and disputes rooted in both contemporary ideologies and ancient tribal rivalries. Nevertheless, the Kurds assert with justification that by race, language, lifestyle, and geography, they do form a distinct community.

The lack of unity among the Kurds can be traced to, *inter alia*, the tension which has existed for at least a century between the people of the mountains and those of the plains and urban areas. Differences in economic and social situations have not surprisingly led to support for different political solutions and differing priorities. It is not clear whether traditional Kurdish leaders are as interested in tribal democracy as they are in the constitutional autonomy which they have demanded. Urban and intellectual Kurds have splintered into a plethora of political parties.

It would be a mistake to see the potential for Kurdish unity purely

625 Short, "The Kurdish People," in Short and McDermott, *supra* note 607, at 4.

in terms of traditional tribalism versus modern nationalism, although these divisions certainly exist.

> Tribalism, far from being a matter of a dying breed of village aghas and shaikhs, is reflected in the deep ambivalence of most Kurds between their nationalist and primordial loyalties. So far the latter have proved stronger, being narrower and more directly affecting daily life and relationships.[626]

Nevertheless, such traditional loyalties are likely to be weakened (as are traditional ties in communities throughout the world) by increasing exposure to modern culture; economic development; migration; increased communication across borders; and the contradictory developments, however gradual, of either a sense of pan-Kurdish solidarity or a loss of peculiarly Kurdish identity.

Whatever the level of internal cohesion among the Kurds, it is difficult to escape the conclusion that the primary determining factors in their search for autonomy or independence have been the influence of external forces and the willingness of the states in which the Kurds find themselves to utilize the most extreme forms of repression. If the Allies had maintained the position adopted in the Treaty of Sèvres rather than capitulating to Ataturk three years later, "Kurdistan" would certainly have been no less (and probably more) viable than Czechoslovakia and Yugoslavia. If the Soviet government had supported the Mahabad Republic, meaningful autonomy might have been obtained by the Kurds in Iran. If the United States, Iran, and Israel had not encouraged Barzani's separatism in the early 1970s, a viable modus vivendi might have been established in Iraq. In the Middle Eastern world of oil and geopolitics, the interests of the Kurds have been at the bottom of everyone's list, except insofar as they promoted the strategic goals of weakening one or another of the states in the region.

It is difficult to imagine three governments with more dissimilar political orientations than Turkey, Iran, and Iraq, yet all have generally adopted the same ruthless approach to dealing with the Kurds. None support a separate Kurdish state, and all have opposed meaningful autonomy as fundamentally incompatible with their concept of the secular (Turkey, Iran under the Shah), religious (post-1979 Iran), or socialist (Iraq) state. Other factors, such as strategic security, historical experience, superpower pressures, and the natural resources within Kurdistan, contribute to the desire of each central government to encourage Kurdish separatism in its neighbors while repressing it at home.

The differing political complexions of the states within which the

626 McDowall, *supra* note 578, at 28.

Kurds find themselves also render it extremely unlikely that external forces will intervene on the side of the Kurds, except as part of short-term efforts at temporary destabilization. Few countries will prejudice their relations with the Arab world by supporting Kurdish demands in Iraq or displease the United States and other NATO countries by supporting Kurdish guerrillas in Turkey; neither the United States nor the Soviet Union is likely to support the disintegration of Iran without some idea of what might replace the current regime. The public relations event held in Paris in January 1989—otherwise known as a conference on chemical warfare—totally ignored Iraq's attacks on the Kurds, and France denied visas to Kurdish representatives and prohibited demonstrations outside the conference headquarters.[627]

Unlike some other situations surveyed in the present study, Kurdish demands for autonomy did not arise primarily as a reaction to human rights violations—although such violations have been massive and widespread. For example, while the attempted destruction of Kurdish culture in Turkey violates the most basic norms of internationally recognized human rights and has undoubtedly contributed to Kurdish resistance, Kurdish demands for autonomy predate this repression by the modern Turkish state. Repression of the Kurds is consistent with the repression of other potentially divisive minorities in Turkey and Iran, although the lack of a neighboring Kurdish state has meant the absence of irredentist pressures as they are normally identified.

At the same time, however, any resolution of the "Kurdish question" cannot be divorced from larger human rights issues. It is absurd to pretend that such sensitive issues as minority rights and autonomy can be adequately addressed in a context of widespread killings, torture, and arbitrary detention.

While Iraqi repression of the Kurds is a reality, the Iraqi experience should not be dismissed as entirely irrelevant. Kurdish autonomy in Iraq, unclear though it may be, is constitutionally guaranteed, and the constitution recognizes that "[t]he Iraqi people consists of two main ethnic groups, namely Arabs and Kurds." Among the provisions of the 1974 decree setting forth general guidelines for Kurdish autonomy are requirements that one of the Republic's vice-presidents be a Kurd, that civil servants in majority Kurdish areas be proficient in the Kurdish language, and that there be no discrimination against Kurds with regard to access to public office, including the army.[628] The political and economic powers of the autonomous region are subservient to those of the

---

627 See Jonathan C. Randal, "Chemical War Conference Forgets Kurd Gas Victims," Wash. Post, 7 Jan. 1989, at A16, col. 1.
628 Iraq, art. 9 CERD Report (1985), *supra* note 609.

central government, but the potential significance of linguistic, cultural, and educational guarantees should not be underestimated.

Even if there were a much higher degree of solidarity among Kurds themselves, it is difficult to imagine an independent Kurdish state in the foreseeable future. The reconciliation and accommodation necessary to avoid deterioration of the situation of the Kurds in Iran, Iraq, and Turkey can occur only with the encouragement of allies and neighbors of the states directly concerned. This encouragement must extend not only to resolving the Kurdish situation but to strengthening democratic forms of government and increasing the participation of the entire population in the processes of government. The international community and, in particular, its most powerful members, have not only failed utterly to reduce conflict in this region of the Middle East; they have consciously exacerbated conflict in the pursuit of economic and strategic interests. Until those in and outside the region realize that political stability and respect for human rights are desirable options, the conflicts among Kurds, Turks, Iraqis, and Iranians will continue, and the Kurds will continue to lose.

Chapter 10
The Atlantic Coast of Nicaragua

HISTORICAL BACKGROUND[629]

The Atlantic Coast of Nicaragua, which is separated from the Pacific side of the country by significant geographic barriers, constitutes more than half of Nicaragua's territory but contains only about 10% of the population. The coast is a place of cultural diversity that, throughout its history, has looked more toward the Caribbean and the English-speaking world than toward the seat of central government and the Hispanic heritage of the Pacific side. Much of the history of the Atlantic Coast may be seen as an effort, first by competing colonial powers, then by foreign commercial interests, and, finally, by the Nicaraguan state, to exercise control over the people who live there. Usually, these efforts were unsuccessful.

The Atlantic Coast extends from contemporary Belize to Panama. It is very different physically and culturally from the Pacific part of the region, and it presented different problems to the Spanish conquerors. Reflecting influences from Caribbean and Andean culture, its population was more dispersed. Using the resources of the humid tropical forests, the river banks, and the maritime resources of the littoral, the population lived by farming, fishing, and hunting. Unlike the hierarchical societies of Mesoamerica, political organization never reached the level of large states or chiefdoms, and most of the residents were not subject to any form of indigenous central control. Further, the hot, rainy climate and the virtual impenetrability of the region by land proved to be an insur-

629 Much of the historical material in this chapter is drawn from Martin Diskin, Thomas Bossert, Salomon Nahmad S., and Stéfano Varese, "Peace and Autonomy on the Atlantic Coast of Nicaragua: A Report of the LASA Task Force on Human Rights and Academic Freedom," Part I, 26 LASA [Latin American Studies Association] Forum 1 (No. 4, Spring 1986) and Part II, 27 id. 1 (No. 2, Summer 1986).

mountable obstacle to the Spanish technique of dominating the highland communities. As a result, the Spanish conquerors had no real interest in assimilating the Atlantic Coast into their imperial plan.

During the long period from the early seventeenth through the late nineteenth centuries, patterns were created that persist today. The Atlantic Coast acquired strategic importance because of emergent British expansionism in the Caribbean. British buccaneers, raiding the Caribbean coasts of the Spanish Main, directly challenged Spanish hegemony, and the Atlantic Coast became a boundary between the British sphere of influence in the Caribbean and Spanish interests. The British, however, like the Spanish, were not interested in colonizing the Atlantic Coast so much as in establishing a presence there through coastal trading contacts.

The first people the British met were the Miskitos, who lived mainly on the coast and who were adept in maritime activities. A mutually convenient relationship was quickly established: British privateers could count on refitting and provisioning themselves with fresh water, meat, fruit, and crews, while, in exchange, they provided the Miskitos with muskets and other trade goods. This arrangement assisted the British in extending their effective maritime control in the Caribbean, while the Miskitos began to dominate the other groups in the area, principally the Sumos.

What is now the Atlantic Coast of Nicaragua was largely the home territory of the Sumo people at the moment of European contact, but the alliance with the British permitted the Miskitos (then called Sambo-Miskitu) to expand at the expense of the Sumos. The Miskitos became brokers in the commerce of Sumo slaves, and, through superior force of arms, became the military conquerors of their neighbors in the region.

In the seventeenth century, escaped and shipwrecked African slaves freely intermixed with the indigenous inhabitants of the coast. Through subsequent migration from English-speaking islands, the group now known as Creoles achieved significant proportions, particularly in the southern part of the coast in and around Bluefields, which became the coast's administrative center.

Initially, at least, Catholicism did not penetrate the coast to any significant degree, nor was the Spanish language implanted as it was in the rest of Mesoamerica. The Moravian church, a small German-based Protestant sect, first established missions on the coast in the 1840s and quickly became the dominant religion. Spanish patterns of rural administration and the attendant bureaucracy never developed, and the Atlantic Coast remained a frontier region through most of its history.

In the early nineteenth century, a wave of U.S. adventurers and investors discovered that what could not be accomplished through bribery, force, and their own mercenary forces would in time be supported by the economic and military power of the United States, eventually punctuated by frequent invasions by the Marines. As U.S. influence grew, the British prepared to withdraw through a series of treaties and agreements. The 1860 Treaty of Managua granted Nicaragua sovereignty over all its present territory, including the Atlantic Coast. It also recognized the Rey Mosco, a Miskito monarch created by the British, and stated that he was to be under the sovereignty of Nicaragua. In 1894, the "reincorporation" of the Mosquitia (the Atlantic Coast) was completed, and the Atlantic Coast became the Nicaraguan province of Zelaya. In 1905, the British relinquished their last claims to the coast. The Harrison-Altamirano treaty abrogated earlier provisions recognizing the Miskito monarchy but included certain concessions in favor of the Miskito people, such as respect for Indian land titles, special tax exemptions, and grazing rights.

The period of United States domination began somewhat before the departure of the English and continued until shortly before the fall of Nicaraguan President Somoza in 1979. However, British, Japanese, and European commercial interests were still represented, as Atlantic Coast economic production responded to foreign demands. The wealth provided by the region left no lasting traces in infrastructure or welfare; technology, management, and knowledge were all imported, and the profits exported. What did have a lasting impact was the coast's orientation toward U.S. markets rather than toward Nicaragua's Pacific coast.

The central government in Managua permitted this long period of resource exploitation for several reasons. During this time, the effective exercise of Nicaraguan sovereignty was systematically challenged by U.S. force. There were numerous invasions and occupations by U.S. Marines, and the U.S.-supported Somoza dynasty was formally installed in 1937. The thin pretexts that were used to justify U.S. invasions also served to legitimize U.S. interests on the coast and in other parts of the country.

Increased commercial opportunities during the two decades prior to the 1979 revolution attracted more Spanish-speaking Nicaraguans to the coast and an enlarged presence of the National Guard, especially in the vicinity of the mines. This migration of mestizos (non-Indian, Spanish-speaking peasants) also was encouraged by the expansion of cotton and cattle production on the Pacific side, which drove many peasants off their land.

For the Creole population of southern Zelaya, there was a considerable amount of freedom to trade freely beyond national frontiers. With a fishing industry that sold directly to Honduras, Costa Rica,

Colombia, and the United States, usually for dollars, Bluefields was in effect a free port.

This sporadic economic development on the Atlantic Coast occurred in the absence of state attention. The Atlantic Coast was somewhat isolated from the more brutal aspects of the Somoza regime, although, as an enclave economy, it was subject to a boom-and-bust economic cycle. Politically, the coast depended on Managua, but economically its fate was determined outside of the country.

THE NICARAGUAN REVOLUTION OF 1979 AND THE EARLY SANDINISTA YEARS

The popular revolution led by the Sandinista National Liberation Front (SNLF) that triumphed in 1979 brought a general wave of optimism to the Pacific side of the country, along with the notion that revolution meant overturning the existing social system of privilege. Under the new "logic of the majority," benefits were to go to the most dispossessed groups first. The principle that spreading "Sandinismo" to the entire nation was an absolute good seemed obvious to the broad base of Sandinista supporters.

The population of the Atlantic Coast, with its long history of social and economic distance from the Nicaraguan state, did not embrace this new logic. There had been no major fighting on the coast, and few of the revolutionary organizations had established any presence there prior to 1979. To overcome the historic isolation of the coast, the Sandinista government dedicated itself to incorporating the coast into the new national development process and, among other actions, launched a major literacy campaign.

Rather than welcoming the new Sandinista organizations that were established, the peoples of the Atlantic Coast asked for their own indigenous organization to represent them. MISURASATA (Miskito, Sumo, Rama, Sandinista, Working Together) was formed in 1979, formally designated a "mass organization," and given representation on the national Council of State.

While three indigenous groups are mentioned in the organization's acronym, the leadership continued to be overwhelmingly Miskito. In northern Zelaya, the Miskitos were the most politically sophisticated and energetic in defending community interests and represented at least 80,000 people. The Sumo, Rama, and Garifona (black) communities were quite small, with about 10,000, 800, and 1,500 people, respectively.[630]

---

630 These are Nicaraguan government figures, taken from Nicaragua, art. 9 CERD

The goals of the 30,000 Creoles of Bluefields, in southern Zelaya, differed somewhat from those of the indigenous communities, and the Creoles were never a significant voice in MISURASATA. In addition, there was no organized group that represented the large and growing mestizo community. The latter lived scattered throughout the region as small farmers, miners, merchants, and bureaucrats and represented approximately 65% of the coastal population.

In 1980, when the Sandinista-sponsored literacy campaign began on the coast, MISURASATA insisted that it be conducted in Miskito and English. Although it also represented the Sumos and Ramas, MISURASATA made no major effort to include these languages in the campaign. The literacy campaign facilitated communication between the newly emerged indigenous leadership and the communities, resulting in MISURASATA's quickly acquiring political support. Indigenous demands were formed and pressed on the new government. Among these demands were road construction, health centers, basic grain storage centers, agricultural assistance in the development of crops suitable for the coast, continuation of the literacy campaign in native languages, and bilingual education for children. These demands were similar to those of the mass organizations on the Pacific side and were generally consistent with Sandinista development goals and policies for the nation as a whole.

MISURASATA also pressed for special treatment based on an emerging sense of indigenous rights. The most prominent and problematic of these rights was the recognition of indigenous land ownership. This demand—often expressed in terms of self-determination, sovereignty, or nationhood—seemed to challenge the programs and objectives of the Sandinista government. Against a background of growing counterrevolutionary or "*contra*" forces just across the border in Honduras, supported by the U.S. Central Intelligence Agency (CIA), the Sandinista government feared that MISURASATA could become the vehicle for a separatist movement or an anti-government insurgency.

Prior to 1979, most of the indigenous coastal peoples had exercised de facto control over the lands they used for subsistence. Ocean and riverine resources were freely used by all, and forest products were generally used as needed for house and canoe construction. Access to

Report, UN Doc. CERD/C/128/Add.1 (1986) at 4. These seem to be generally accepted, although some assert that the Miskito figures are understated; one reporter places the Miskito population "in the Atlantic Coast area" at between 120,000 and 170,000, out of a total population of 200,000, but this may also include the Honduras portion of Mosquitia. Shirley Christian, *Nicaragua, Revolution in the Family* (New York: Random House, 1985) at 255.

forests, however, was limited periodically, first by the foreign lumber companies and later by Somoza's forestry agency.

In 1981, MISURASATA produced a background study on indigenous rights, which asserted, *inter alia*, that "the right of indigenous nations over the territory of their communities is preferential to the territorial rights of states."[631] None of the various treaties between Nicaragua and other states was recognized as legitimate, and the extent of indigenous rights to land within Nicaragua was determined to be 76.8% of the territory of the Atlantic Coast or approximately one-third of the total territory of Nicaragua.

In August 1981 the Sandinista government unveiled its own conception of indigenous rights. Article 6 of its "Declaration of Principles" states that

the natural resources of our territory are the property of the Nicaraguan people. The Revolutionary State, representative of the popular will, is the only entity empowered to establish a rational and efficient system of utilization of said resources. The Revolutionary State recognizes the right of the indigenous people to receive a portion of the benefits to be derived from the exploitation of forest resources of the region. These benefits must be invested in programs of community and municipal development in accordance with national plans.[632]

Article 5, dealing with land rights, states:

The Popular Sandinista Revolution will not only guarantee but also legalize the ownership of lands on which the people of the communities of the Atlantic Coast have traditionally lived and worked, organized either as communes or as cooperatives. Land titles will be granted to each community.

The clear implication of these principles is that the state had the exclusive right to decide questions of land ownership and use and that there would be no unique status for indigenous groups. While this attitude is consistent with both Latin American practice vis à vis indigenous peoples and Marxist theory regarding the supremacy of the state, security concerns also strongly contributed to Sandinista fears of special land demands. United States support for the so-called "covert war" had begun in 1981, and any claim for special status for indigenous communities was viewed as a serious threat to national unity.

Throughout 1981, both indigenous and Sandinista leaders contributed toward the heightening of tensions, as the Sandinistas actively

631 MISURASATA, "La tenecia de la tierra de las communidades indígenas y criolla de la costa atlántica," cited in Diskin et al., Part I, *supra* note 629, at 10.

632 Declaración de principios de la revolución popular sandinista sobre las comunidades indígenas de la costa atlántica (Managua: 11 Aug. 1981), cited in *id.* at 11.

recruited supporters on the Atlantic Coast and indigenous leaders attempted to consolidate their own support. In February 1981, shortly before the MISURASATA land study was presented, the Sandinistas arrested many Indian leaders for allegedly hostile activities. One of the three founding leaders of MISURASATA, Steadman Fagoth Muller, became an ardent critic of the government. He was jailed in February 1981 and released in May on condition that he go abroad to study in a socialist country. He immediately left for Honduras and associated himself with the *contra* radio station known as "15th of September."

From mid–1981 through the end of the year, increasing tensions destroyed any hope that a resolution could be found through dialogue. Near the end of the year, the Sandinistas announced discovery of a plot called "Red Christmas," which was designed to attack Sandinista workers on the coast and incite a general uprising. Citing the plot as evidence of an imminent external threat to national integrity, the Sandinistas began a large-scale evacuation of villages on the upper Coco River (which forms the border between Nicaragua and Honduras) and the systematic destruction of houses and livestock there to deny support to the allegedly attacking forces. The approximately 8,500 evacuees were taken 60 kilometers to the south, to a resettlement camp known as Tasba Pri. In addition, perhaps 15,000 people crossed the border into Honduras to live in refugee camps, guerrilla camps, or existing Indian communities.

Squeezed between a growing Indian militancy and a quickly eroding security position on the coast, the Sandinista solution was to try to establish greater control through the imposition of central power. This period of resettlement and turmoil has been subsequently recognized by the government as constituting "errors," and there are well-publicized accounts of human rights abuses on the coast at this time.[633]

The relocation from the Coco River and resulting flight of thousands of Miskitos to Honduras only intensified active Indian resistance to the government. The 1982–1984 period was a time of deepening military conflict between organized Miskito guerrillas and Sandinista forces in the region, and there were evident links between some of the Indian forces and the U.S.-supported *contras*. At the same time, however, the Miskito insurgency that developed was qualitatively different from the *contra* war, which was confined primarily to the Pacific side of the country.

The *contras* were unable to gain shelter and support from the local population on the Pacific side, but the Miskitos were the classic guerrilla fish in water. The sparseness and dispersal of the population and the lack of a strong infrastructure made it more difficult for the government

633 See discussion *infra* at 220–22.

to control territory, allowing the insurgents freer mobility and an ability sporadically to control towns and villages. Government efforts to put down the insurgency often reaped more distrust than military gain for the Sandinistas, and restrictions on the free movement of villagers also engendered hostility.

The failure of the resettlement camps to gain active Miskito support for the government, the partial success of the Indian guerrillas, and the growing perception that the U.S. government might be preparing an invasion, led to a rethinking of Sandinista policy. This meant choosing between the existing policy of central political control and military suppression versus an alternative, more political, solution which might permit a military truce or ceasefire while details were negotiated.

At the same time, Indian groups also were uncertain about continuing the war and suffered from internal conflicts. Some Miskito leaders, notably Steadman Fagoth, were content to strengthen ties with the *contras* or Fuerza Democrática Nicaragüense (FDN); others, such as MISURASATA leader Brooklyn Rivera, resisted these ties under the U.S. umbrella. The FDN had no policy that would respond to Miskito demands concerning land rights or autonomy and was unwilling to incorporate indigenous leaders into its command structure.

THE SEARCH FOR AUTONOMY

MISURASATA—talks and proposals

In September 1984, Nicaraguan President Ortega implicitly invited the leader of MISURASATA, Brooklyn Rivera, to return to Nicaragua and begin a dialogue with the government, and the negotiating process initiated when Rivera accepted the offer in October lasted until May 1985. The respective positions adopted by the government and MISURASATA at the first meeting in December 1984 (held in Bogota, Colombia) indicated the extent of their differences.

The government recognized that "the ethnic groups of the Atlantic Coast must enjoy special rights of autonomy that guarantee their ethnic identity and that must be consigned in the laws of the republic with constitutional rank."[634] All significant issues were said to be open to negotiation, although it was clear that the Sandinistas did not recognize the Indian communities as equal partners.

MISURASATA called upon the government to recognize the Miskitos, Sumos, and Ramas "as indigenous sovereign peoples . . . possessed of the natural right to freely determine their own political,

---

634 Nicaraguan Government Draft Agreement (Bogotá, 8 Dec. 1984), quoted in Diskin et al, *supra* note 629, at 15.

economic, social and cultural development in accord with their values and traditions."[635] It recognized that the autonomous territory would be delimited "within the framework of the sovereignty of the Nicaraguan state and the territorial integrity of the country" and offered an extensive list of issues to be addressed during the negotiations, including defense, territory and land tenure, representation in the national parliament, regional patrimony, and economic and social issues.[636] The MISURASATA proposal also called for demilitarization of the Atlantic Coast, formal recognition of MISURASATA, and eventual replacement of government troops by MISURASATA forces.

The negotiations were attended by a large number of international observers, including North American indigenous organizations and governmental representatives from Canada, the Netherlands, France, Mexico, Sweden, and Colombia.[637] The MISURASATA proposal would have established a tripartite commission to monitor compliance with any agreements, three of whose members would represent unspecified guarantors.[638]

While the two sides did agree at the third meeting in April 1985 to a cessation of all offensive military activities (which has more or less continued in force), no substantive progress in defining autonomy was achieved. At the fourth and final meeting in May, the MISURASATA delegation walked out, in part because it felt that the increasing influence of Interior Minister Tomás Borge, who was chairman of the national autonomy commission and considered to be more hard-line than other members of the Sandinista directorate, signaled that the government was not serious about substantive negotiations.[639]

In April 1987, just days after the government's autonomy proposals (discussed below) were informally approved at a government-organized meeting in Puerto Cabezas, MISURASATA released a proposed Treaty of Peace between the Miskito, Sumo, and Rama nations and the Nicaraguan government.[640] Consistent with MISURASATA's earlier position, the treaty affirms that the Miskito, Sumo, and Rama peoples

635 MISURASATA Draft Agreement (Bogotá, 8 Dec. 1984), §1.1, reprinted in 9 Cultural Survival Quarterly 60 (No. 1, Feb. 1985).

636 *Id.*, §§1.2 and 1.3.

637 UN Commission of Human Rights (statement by Mrs. Casco of Nicaragua), UN Doc. E/CN.4/1985/SR.36 (1985) at para. 22.

638 MISURASATA Draft Agreement, *supra* note 635, §V.

639 See, e.g., "Sandinistas' Talks with Indians Fail," N.Y. Times, 30 May 1985; press release of the Indian Law Resource Center (Washington, DC), "Nicaraguan Indian Peace Talks Stall: No New Talks Set," 10 June 1985.

640 The text of the proposed treaty was subsequently released in an undated document by the Indian Law Resource Center (Washington, DC).

have the "inherent" right to self-determination, although it then specifies that this right "shall be exercised within the framework of the Nicaraguan State."[641]Nevertheless, the scope of authority which would be recognized as belonging to the autonomous territory of "Yapti Tasba" is very close to that of an independent state, joined by a treaty of federation to another.

Residual governmental powers under the proposed treaty rest with Yapti Tasba, and Nicaraguan governmental authority is "strictly limited to those powers that are expressly agreed upon in this Treaty or that may be delegated" to Nicaragua by subsequent agreements.[642] Article VI of the treaty identifies the powers belonging to the central government, which include military defense, foreign relations, customs and international borders, citizenship and immigration, currency and the postal system, and jurisdiction over civil and criminal cases concerning the exercise of delegated national powers within the autonomous territory. However, even these powers are subject to provisos; for instance, a military command is to be established by agreement between the central and autonomous governments, and authority to determine residency rights is within the exclusive jurisdiction of the autonomous government. Disputes over the division of powers between the Nicaraguan and Yapti Tasba authorities are to be resolved by a special joint commission composed of four members appointed by each government and two "respected lawyers or jurists from the international community outside Nicaragua" to be appointed by agreement.[643] The treaty would form part of the "supreme law" of Nicaragua, and Nicaragua would undertake to amend its constitution and laws as necessary to implement the treaty and the constitution of Yapti Tasba.[644]

The government's autonomy process

Just prior to the first meeting with MISURASATA in December 1984, the government named a national commission to develop an autonomy statute for the Atlantic Coast, indicating that the international meetings with MISURASATA were a parallel process to the one taking place within the country. By July 1985, the national commission had produced a general statement of principles of autonomy, within the framework of the Sandinista revolution.[645] While the principles fell far short of the

641 *Id.*, art. I(A).
642 *Id.*, art. IV(A).
643 *Id.*, art. VII.
644 *Id.*, arts. XII and XIV.
645 National Commission on Autonomy for the Atlantic Coast, *Principles and Policies for the Exercise of the Right to Autonomy by the Indigenous Peoples and Communities of the Atlantic Coast of Nicaragua* (Managua, 1985).

1984 MISURASATA proposals, they did represent an advance from the centralist policies espoused in 1979–83.

The principles began with the affirmation that "Nicaragua is one indivisible nation, and the sovereignty of the Revolutionary State extends throughout the national territory."[646] They included recognition of indigenous rights to preservation of culture and historical and religious heritage; free use and development of languages, including the right to education in native languages and Spanish; and "the right to organize their social and economic activity in accordance with their values and traditions."[647]

Individual and collective possession of traditional lands was recognized, along with use of lands, forests, and coastal waters.[648] The coastal peoples were to have the right to determine how apportioned profits from the sale of resources would be reinvested in the regions, and "will determine the rational use of the natural resources of the region."[649]

The principles also envisaged the creation of regional assemblies, although their authority was very limited; all legislative power would remain in the hands of the National Assembly, to which the regional assembly could present bills for adoption.[650] The central government "defines the policies, lines of work, and norms which must be carried out in the entire national territory," including a national economic strategy, and "[g]uarantee[s] that the autonomous regions implement national policies according to the principles and rights of autonomy."[651]

Two regional autonomy commissions were subsequently formed, one for the north and one for the south. They undertook to begin a process of consultation (*"consulta"*) with local residents, based on the principles drafted in 1985. The original timetable of producing a final autonomy statute which could be discussed at the same time as the new Nicaraguan constitution was soon abandoned, and the final statute was not adopted by the National Assembly until September 1987.

The southern regional autonomy commission finished its consultation in November 1985 and identified five major areas of concern: 1) the utilization of natural resources, i.e., the need to return proceeds from resource exploitation to the communities; 2) the nature and functioning of the proposed regional government, especially with respect to ethnic representation; 3) the need to create a center of higher education

646 *Id.*, "Principles and Objectives of Regional Autonomy," §1.
647 *Id.*, §6.
648 *Id.*, §§8 and 9. There is no reference to rights to sub-soil minerals.
649 *Id.*, §10.
650 *Id.*, "Powers of the Regional Assembly."
651 *Id.*, "Powers of the Central Government."

in the Atlantic Coast and to extend bilingual (English) education; 4) the need for regional self-sufficiency through trade within the Caribbean region; and 5) the need for new means of guaranteeing regional security, involving the Indian forces and local people.

The *consulta* in the north proceeded much more slowly, as distrust of the government led many to question the legitimacy of the regional autonomy commission. Several indigenous and other local groups withdrew from the government autonomy process and the regional commission after initially participating in the commission's work. These groups included MISITAN, a Miskito organization created in August 1984 and active in resettling those forcibly removed from the Coco River in 1981, which generally adopts a broad view of autonomy; CEPAD, a Protestant development agency, some of whose leaders had been involved in the MISURASATA negotiations; and the Moravian church, which has a strong grassroots base on the coast.

The autonomy process in the north was also hindered by continuing hostilities between Indian and government forces, despite the ceasefire agreed to in April 1985 by MISURASATA and the government. Honduras-based Miskito forces known as KISAN, allied with the *contras*, tried to destabilize the region and interrupt the return of people to the Coco River, which began in 1985 with government approval and some governmental assistance. This "return to the river" was of great symbolic importance and included not only those relocated by the government but also many who fled to Honduras.[652]

The Miskito-dominated north would probably prefer a single autonomous region for the entire Atlantic Coast rather than two separate regional governments. Their general demands include control of traditionally occupied lands; recognition of Miskito as the official language for the Miskito population, with Spanish as a second language; and bilingual education for the other ethnic groups on the coast. The Sumos and Ramas are understandably concerned that their language and culture not be subsumed by the Miskitos; the Ramas number less than 1,000 (including less than two dozen Rama speakers) and are primarily concerned with living undisturbed on Rama Key (Cay), an island which has been occupied alternately by guerrillas and government troops.

The new Nicaraguan constitution adopted by the National Assembly in November 1986 recognizes that the Nicaraguan people are "multi-ethnic,"[653] provides that "autonomous governments in the regions inhabited by the Communities of the Atlantic Coast" shall be established by law,[654] and defines the rights of the Atlantic Coast communi-

---

652 See generally Diskin et al., Part II, *supra* note 629, at 8–13.
653 Nicaraguan Const., art. 8.
654 *Id.*, art. 181.

ties.[655] These rights include "the right to preserve and develop their cultural identities within the framework of national unity, to be granted their own forms of social organization, and to administer their local affairs according to their traditions."[656] The right to "the free expression and preservation of their languages, art and culture" is recognized;[657] coastal languages "have official use in the cases established by law";[658] and the coastal communities "have access in their region to education in their native language up to the levels set by national plans and programs."[659] The state recognizes communal forms of land ownership and the communities' "enjoyment, use and benefit of the waters and forests of these communal lands."[660] The chapter of the constitution on Atlantic Coast rights also refers to the state's obligation "to enact laws promoting and assuring that no Nicaraguan shall be the object of discrimination for reasons of language, culture or origin."[661]

By mid-1986, pilot autonomy projects had been established in a few communities on the Atlantic Coast, where local indigenous military commanders had agreed to ceasefires and shared security responsibilities with Sandinista army forces. While such local arrangements could bear but little relevance to regional autonomy, they nevertheless increased the momentum for the government's autonomy process.

In April 1987, a "preliminary draft" autonomy statute was adopted at a public assembly called in Puerto Cabezas, the largest town in the northern Atlantic Coast region, which was attended by approximately 2,000 people. Criticisms have been directed towards the unrepresentative nature of the meeting and other problems (such as the lack of full translation into Miskito and the fact that there was no agreement on a name for the autonomous region), but the government-prepared draft approved in Puerto Cabezas nevertheless became the basis of the final autonomy statute adopted by the National Assembly in September 1987.

The 1987 Autonomy Statute

The 1987 Autonomy Statute[662] is generally consistent with the 1985 principles discussed above and could be fairly described as establishing participatory administrative regions on the Atlantic Coast. Two

---

655 *Id.*, arts. 89–91 and 180.
656 *Id.*, art. 89.
657 *Id.*, art. 90.
658 *Id.*, art. 11.
659 *Id.*, art. 121.
660 *Id.*, art. 89.
661 *Id.*, art. 91.
662 Autonomy Statute of the Atlantic Coast Regions of Nicaragua, Law No. 28 of 7 Sept. 1987, published in *La Gaceta* (No. 238, 30 Oct. 1987) at 2833. All translations are unofficial.

"autonomous" regions of the North Atlantic and South Atlantic are created, based respectively in Puerto Cabezas and Bluefields,[663] although no elections for autonomous institutions had been held as of the end of 1988. All regional resolutions and ordinances are subordinate to the Nicaraguan constitution and national laws.[664] Amendments to the Autonomy Statute may be requested by the two regional assemblies and are adopted by the National Assembly according to its normal procedures.[665]

Each region has a directly elected Regional Council,[666] with administrative powers to "participate effectively" in the national development program for the region; administer national health, education, culture, supply, transportation, and community service programs "in coordination with the corresponding State Ministries"; promote the rational use and enjoyment of waters, bays, and communal lands, as well as community and national culture, and "the traditional exchange with Caribbean nations and peoples, in accordance with relevant national laws and procedures"; and set regional taxes.[667] Each Council adopts resolutions and ordinances within its jurisdiction, elects a chief executive known as the Regional Coordinator, prepares a draft budget for the region in conjunction with the national Ministry of Finance, and is to prepare a draft plan for the organization of regional municipalities and determine the boundaries between the various communities in the region.[668]

Communal, collective, and individual ownership of land is recognized; communal lands cannot be sold, seized, taxed, or proscribed;[669] and the inhabitants of the regions have the right "[t]o use, partake of and enjoy the waters, forests and communal lands in accordance with national development plans."[670] The right of the Atlantic Coast communities to promote and develop local languages, religions, and cultures is recognized, as is the right to be educated in their own languages, "through programs that take into account their historical heritage, value system, traditions and the characteristics of their environment, within the framework of the national education system."[671] Spanish is Nica-

---

663 *Id.*, art 6.
664 *Id.*, art. 24.
665 *Id.*, art. 38.
666 *Id.*, arts. 15 and 19. Regional representatives to the National Assembly also are ex officio members of the Regional Councils. *Id.*, art. 20.
667 *Id.*, art. 8.
668 *Id.*, arts. 23 and 32.
669 *Id.*, arts. 11(6) and 36(1).
670 *Id.*, art. 11(3).
671 *Id.*, art. 11(2) and (5).

ragua's official language, but community languages also are recognized for official use within the autonomous regions.[672]

A Regional Coordinator represents the region, may appoint regional executive officials, and may "make representations concerning matters within his/her competence to the national authorities."[673] The Coordinator's primary function seems to be to implement the policies and directives of the national executive branch and to administer a Special Development and Social Promotion Fund earmarked for regional investment, which will include donations and other funds not included in the regular budget.[674]

EXTERNAL INFLUENCES

The initially "covert" and subsequently overt aid given by the Reagan administration in the United States to the armed "counterrevolutionary" forces seeking to overthrow the Sandinista government is well known and need not be detailed here.[675]Financial support of hundreds of millions of dollars and political-logistic support from the U.S. CIA and other bodies to the *contras* ensured the continuation of military conflict in Nicaragua, and the wider Sandinista-*contra* war obviously is the context in which relations between the government and the Atlantic Coast must be seen.

While most of the U.S. financial and other assistance has gone to non-Indian paramilitary and political forces, at least some Indian groups (such as MISURA and KISAN) have been close to the FDN, the main *contra* force based in Honduras. MISURASATA was at one stage close to Eden Pastora's Alianza Revolucionaria Democrática (ARDE), which was based in Costa Rica, although it has attempted to position itself as a pro-Indian but not pro-*contra* organization.

Competition among the various groups for support within the Indian communities has been intense, and one of the most contentious political issues has long been which group, if any, can legitimately claim to represent the bulk of the Indian population of the coast. Personal and political rivalries contributed to a very decentralized military structure, in which local commanders within Nicaragua had a great deal of freedom to conclude or reject ceasefire arrangements with government troops.

672 *Id.*, art. 5.
673 *Id.*, art. 30(4).
674 *Id.*, §5, §6; art. 33.
675 It would serve little purpose to cite the scores of published works on the Sandinista-*contra* war and the U.S. role therein, but one source which might be profitably consulted is the judgment by the International Court of Justice (including the various separate and dissenting opinions) in the suit filed by Nicaragua against the U.S., *Military and Paramilitary Activities in and against Nicaragua, supra* note 46.

However, throughout the period from 1981 to mid-1987, armed encounters between Indian and Sandinista forces in the Atlantic Coast
region (particularly in the north, where the Miskito population is concentrated) were frequent.

The U.S. government actively sought to encourage Indian resistance
to the Nicaraguan government and, if possible, alliance with the larger
contra forces which are most active on the Pacific side of the country.
However, such attempts have not thus far been successful.[676]

U.S. Congressional approval of $100 million in funding for the *con-
tras* in 1986 reportedly included $5 million for Indian fighters, provided
that they would cooperate with the FDN and establish a more unified
command structure, and the availability of such financial support was
said to have "reawaken[ed] an Indian war effort that was nearly dormant
for two years."[677] The CIA effectively controls access to the refugee
and guerrilla camps in Honduras and could thus hinder or promote
support for particular groups or leaders. Since the "Red Christmas"
exodus in late 1981 and early 1982, there have been thousands of Miskito
refugees in Honduras; estimates at various times have ranged from
10,000 to 30,000.

A June 1987 meeting of the major Miskito factions at a Honduran
refugee camp known as Rus Rus was sponsored, financed, and organized
by the United States, in order once again to try to unite competing anti-
Sandinista forces.[678] The organization created at this meeting, named
YATAMA, has pressed for talks with the Nicaraguan government, al-

676 One sign of the failure to achieve any meaningful unification among the *contra*
and Miskito forces is the bewildering succession of organizations and acronyms that
has surfaced since 1982. Fagoth's pro-*contra* organization was known as MISURA in
1982; in mid–1984, ASLA ("unity" in Miskito) temporarily united MISURA and
MISURASATA, but it quickly gave way to the MISURA-dominated KISAN (Indians
and Coast People United in Nicaragua). In the 1985–87 period, many individual KISAN
commanders accepted local ceasefire arrangements with the government, and "pro-peace"
and "pro-war" factions emerged. In early 1987, another "unity" group known as
FAUCON appeared briefly, to be replaced in June 1987 by yet another attempt by the
CIA to unite MISURASATA, MISURA, and KISAN into YATAMA (another acronym
which stands for "united indigenous nations"). While generalizations are difficult because
of the autonomy enjoyed by many individual military commanders and changing tactical
considerations, MISURASATA has generally been more willing to negotiate with the
government and less supportive of the broader *contra* effort to overthrow the Sandinistas,
while MISURA and KISAN were more closely tied to U.S.-supported groups and more
active militarily.

677 "Rivals Compete to Lead Nicaraguan Indian Rebels," Wash. Post, 24 Aug.
1986, at A1, col. 1.

678 "Nicaraguan Indians Reach Unity Accord," Wash. Post, 19 June 1987, at A22,
col. 1.

though it has reserved, at least in theory, the possibility of continuing armed resistance within the Atlantic Coast region.

In September 1987, following adoption of the Esquipulas (Guatemala) II Accords by Nicaragua and the other four Central American governments, YATAMA called for negotiation of a ceasefire with the Nicaraguan government. Some discussions between YATAMA representatives and the government were held in late 1987 and early 1988, but no agreement was reached on changes in the structure of autonomy on the Atlantic Coast.

The regional peace plan promoted by Costa Rican President Oscar Arias and agreed to by Costa Rica, El Salvador, Guatemala, Honduras, and Nicaragua in Esquipulas, Guatemala, in August 1987 does not directly address the issue of autonomy on the Atlantic Coast or the continuing armed conflict between Indian and Sandinista forces. However, a gradual lessening of conflict or a country-wide ceasefire would undoubtedly have a significant impact on the military situation on the coast. Even more relevant may be the effective cessation of U.S. funding for the *contras*, including YATAMA and other Indian groups.

While financial and other support by the U.S. government for Indian (and *contra*) forces may have been the single most important external factor in the Atlantic Coast conflict, both the Nicaraguan government and the indigenous Atlantic Coast communities actively sought international political support for their respective positions. As noted above, MISURASATA invited a number of foreign observers to the 1984–85 talks with the government, although the observers did not actually participate in the negotiating sessions. Brooklyn Rivera and MISURASATA's legal advisers have actively participated in available UN forums concerned with human rights and indigenous issues, including the Working Group on Indigenous Populations of the UN Sub-Commission on Prevention of Discrimination and Protection of Minorities. On a clandestine trip to the Atlantic Coast in January 1986, Rivera was accompanied by leaders of the American Indian Movement, World Council of Indigenous People, and Survival of the American Indian Association.[679]

The Nicaraguan government has been equally active in soliciting outside support and in attempting to demonstrate that its autonomy proposals constitute a progressive response to indigenous demands. A conference held in New York in March 1986, in which Nicaraguan government officials participated, included the issue of autonomy in its

---

679 The World Council of Indigenous Peoples subsequently disavowed its president's participation in the Rivera trip.

discussions of the Nicaraguan constitutional drafting process. An International Symposium on the State, Autonomy, and Indigenous Rights was held in Managua in July 1986, and international observers were invited to observe the April 1987 meeting in Puerto Cabezas at which the draft autonomy statute was approved by those present. The Nicaraguan government also has defended its autonomy plans before relevant UN bodies, where it has been supported by NGOs seeking to counter the interventions of other NGOs highly critical of the Nicaraguan autonomy process.

HUMAN RIGHTS

Allegations of human rights violations have been one of the staple weapons in the arsenals of supporters and opponents of the Sandinista regime since its inception, and purported bias in reporting by human rights and other organizations has been the subject both of external commentary and debate within the human rights community.[680] As the armed conflict between Indian groups and the Sandinistas must be seen in the context of the larger *contra* war, so must indigenous human rights questions be understood within the context of much broader complaints about Sandinista repression of the press and political opposition and *contra* violations of humanitarian law.

Many allegations and counter-allegations of human rights abuses concern military activities in the Atlantic Coast region, although much greater attention has been focused on the situation in Managua and the Pacific side of the country. The Reagan administration labeled the "Red December" relocations in late 1981 as "genocide," and the 1981–82 period focused international attention for the first time on human rights violations committed against the indigenous communities on the Atlantic Coast.

The most thorough and unbiased study of human rights during this period was conducted by the Inter-American Commission of Human Rights, which transmitted its report to Nicaragua in November 1983 and published an updated version in May 1984.[681] The Commission was "not in a position to state that there was loss of life during the relocation" to Tasba Pri, despite the fact that it was carried out "in an atmosphere of fear and severe conflict."[682] It did find that "[h]undreds of Miskitos have been arbitrarily detained without any formalities and under vague

---

680 *See*, e.g., "The Politics of Human Rights Reporting on Nicaragua," 5 Envio [Managua] 14 (No. 60, June 1986); "Nicaragua and Human Rights," Newsweek, 18 Aug. 1986, at 19.

681 IACHR Miskito Report, *supra* note 295.

682 *Id*. at 129.

accusations of carrying out 'counterrevolutionary activities'; many of these detentions have been followed by prolonged periods of incommunicado imprisonment and in some cases the Commission has verified that illegal torture and abuse took place."[683]

The Commission also expressed concern over alleged "disappearances," and a general amnesty for Miskitos was recommended; the latter was accepted by the government and proclaimed on 29 November 1983. Perhaps the most significant and relevant finding of the Commission was that "the greatest obstacles that still confront the Miskito population are due to their lack of participation in the decisions that concern them, resulting from the mutual distrust between that people and the government, all of which exacerbates existing tensions and difficulties."[684]

The Commission also concluded that "the current status of international law does not allow the view that the ethnic groups of the Atlantic zone of Nicaragua have a right to political autonomy and self-determination."[685] However, it went on to observe that

the need to preserve and guarantee the observance of . . . principles [of minority rights to language, religion, and preservation of cultural identity] in practice entails the need to establish an adequate institutional order as part of the structure of the Nicaraguan state. Such an institutional organization can only effectively carry out its assigned purposes to the extent that it is designed in the context of broad consultation, and carried out with the direct participation of the ethnic minorities of Nicaragua, through their freely chosen representatives.[686]

A major concern was the confinement of Miskitos in Tasba Pri and other relocation camps from early 1982 until mid–1985, when they were permitted to return to the Coco River. The "return to the river" continued throughout 1986 and 1987, although large numbers of Miskitos and Sumos remained confined in government camps in the Jinotega and Matagalpa regions of the Pacific Coast, before being gradually allowed to return to the Atlantic Coast in 1988–89.[687] Reconstruction has been extremely difficult, owing to the widespread destruction of villages in 1981–82, sporadic military confrontations between government and guerrilla forces until 1987, and the economic deterioration in Nicaragua as a whole.

An example of the difficulty in analyzing events that occur in the midst of armed conflict and in a highly charged political atmosphere is

683 *Id.* at 130.
684 *Id.* at 131.
685 *Id.* at 81.
686 *Id.* at 82.
687 Statement of Steven M. Tullberg, Indian Law Resource Center, 18 June 1986, at 4 (on file with author).

provided by the "flight" or "kidnapping" of several thousand Miskitos at the end of March 1986 from their villages on the Coco River across the border to Honduras.[688] There seems to be general agreement that the movement across the river was precipitated by a substantial influx of Nicaraguan government forces into the Coco River region, but there is widespread disagreement as to the extent of fighting and/or abuses, if any, by the Sandinista forces and the degree to which the exodus was orchestrated or encouraged by KISAN guerrilla forces based in Honduras. The Nicaraguan government refused permission for an on-site visit by the Inter-American Commission on Human Rights, which prevented the Commission from arriving at any definitive conclusion on the matter.[689]

While Americas Watch concluded that the March 1986 flight was due primarily to the deliberate spreading of fear by KISAN, rather than to major new Sandinista abuses, it also observed that "[t]he Miskitos have suffered more than any other segment of the Nicaraguan population during the past five years. They have endured great abuses at the hands of the Sandinistas and they have every reason to fear and hate the Sandinistas."[690]

This fear and hatred stem from the undenied abuses that occurred in the early 1980s, and, while there is no doubt that the situation has improved since then, there remains a great reservoir of distrust between the Indian population of the Atlantic Coast and the Sandinista government in Managua. The human rights abuses committed in 1981–83 continue to present a fundamental obstacle to a resolution of the conflict, as well as rendering more difficult the good faith necessary to implement any eventual autonomy agreement.

OBSERVATIONS

The conflict between the Miskito, Sumo, and Rama peoples on Nicaragua's Atlantic Coast and the Nicaraguan government is, in many respects, a classic Western Hemisphere confrontation between indigenous peoples and a central government. The long isolation of the coast from the rest of the country, the gradual encroachment on indigenous lands and influx of mestizo settlers, and the attempt to "integrate" indigenous

688 Compare, e.g., Tullberg statement, *supra* note 687, at 6–8, with Americas Watch, *With the Miskitos in Honduras* (New York and Washington, DC: Americas Watch, 11 Apr. 1986).

689 See Inter-American Commission on Human Rights, *Annual Report 1985–1986*, OAS Doc. OEA/Ser.L/V/II.68, doc. 8, rev. 1 (26 Sept. 1986) at 178.

690 *With the Miskitos in Honduras, supra* note 688, at 3. The involuntary nature of the flight was reasserted by Americas Watch in a subsequent report, *Human Rights in Nicaragua 1986* (New York and Washington, DC: Americas Watch, Feb. 1987) at 44–45.

societies into the mainstream (through Marxist socialism rather than Western liberalism) recall earlier confrontations, from Canada to Chile.

While there is no doubt that the United States has attempted to manipulate the situation on the Atlantic Coast to suit its larger goal of overthrowing the Sandinista government, the Indian-Sandinista conflict has nevertheless remained largely separate from the wider *contra*-Sandinista war.[691] The use of havens in Honduras by Miskito and Sumo guerrillas is little different from that of similar facilities which have been available to Tamil guerrillas in India or Kurdish *peshmergas* in Iran or Iraq. In none of these cases can the underlying causes of the conflict be imputed to external influences, even though such influences may have encouraged or exacerbated violence and the growth of armed guerrilla forces.

At the same time, however, the debate over autonomy on the Atlantic Coast may have become more internationalized than is the case with any other similar situation (with the possible exception of Sri Lanka). Anti-Sandinista forces obviously have exploited and emphasized the conflict, and many international pro-indigenous movements view the Nicaraguan Indian cause as an opportunity to set a valuable precedent. Marxist, pro-Sandinista, and generally liberal groups have often been less sympathetic to indigenous demands in Nicaragua than might be the case, for example, with respect to Australia or Paraguay. Indeed, the entire indigenous or "Fourth World" movement has been condemned as yet another capitalist tool,[692] recalling debates over "national" movements earlier this century among European Marxists. As noted by the Nicaraguan Minister of Interior and Coordinator of the National Autonomy Commission, autonomy is viewed as possible only within the context of the Sandinista revolution.[693]

Since late 1984, the response of the Nicaraguan government to demands for autonomy on the Atlantic Coast has been more positive than is often the case in Latin America, although there is clearly a desire to limit autonomy arrangements to the most narrow scope possible. The government's changed attitude in 1984 was due primarily to Indian re-

691 For example, there are only a few scattered references to the Miskitos (and none to the substantive issues of autonomy on the Atlantic Coast) in one of the better known journalistic accounts of the Nicaraguan conflict, Christopher Dickey, *With the Contras* (New York: Simon & Schuster, 1985) and only a single short chapter in another work by a well-known American journalist, Christian, *supra* note 630.

692 See, e.g., Diaz-Polanco, *supra* note 13, at 90–91: "[T]he ideological promoters of neoindigenismo introduced a divisiive factor between the Indians and other exploited sectors of the population by indiscriminately planting the idea that ethnic groups constitute separate nations with 'the right to self-determination.' "

693 Tomás Borge, quoted in Nuevo Diario (Managua), 14 July 1986, at 1, col. 3.

sistance and international pressure, rather than representing a conversion to a pro-indigenous position.

Despite its limitations and whatever the motivations, the autonomy process initiated by the government in late 1984, and, in particular, the consultations with portions of the local population from mid–1985 through early 1987, have been significant. Everyone on the Atlantic Coast now views "autonomy" as essential, although it is unlikely that there is any consensus as to what autonomy might mean. The process itself has fomented greater awareness of ethnic and indigenous identity.

The breakdown of talks between the government and MISURASATA in May 1985 was obviously unfortunate, as was the failure of subsequent discussions in late 1987 and early 1988. The internal Nicaraguan autonomy process challenged the legitimacy and representativeness of MISURASATA (and other Indian guerrilla forces), and the absence of some of the most important Miskito elements from the autonomy process may be problematic. At the same time, the government may be reluctant to negotiate amendments to an Autonomy Statute which it maintains was adopted only after a lengthy process of full consultation with the communities concerned.

A compromise between the present positions of the government and MISURASATA will be difficult, not least due to the fact that, in the midst of armed conflict, there has been no means of judging support for either position. While there has been a significant decrease in tensions and violence since 1987, a free political debate can occur only in the context of peace and respect for human rights, so that all elements of the indigenous and other communities on the Atlantic Coast will be able freely to press their political demands.

Substantively, the demographic complexity of the Atlantic Coast— a Miskito-dominated north and Creole-dominated south, with mestizos nevertheless constituting the single largest ethnic group—will be a challenge to any autonomy plan. Although the 1987 Autonomy Statute adopted by the National Assembly does offer important linguistic and educational guarantees, it does not recognize indigenous or even regional political rights to any meaningful extent. The administrative participation and decentralization it envisages depends almost exclusively on good faith cooperation between the authorities in Managua and the essentially advisory Regional Councils, and the indigenous communities' reluctance to rely on good faith alone is understandable.

On the other hand, the MISURASATA proposals accord essentially no legitimacy to non-Indian inhabitants of the Atlantic Coast, despite references to non-discrimination and apparently equal status for the "native languages" of the Carib (Garifuno) and Creole communities, as well as of the Miskito, Sumo, and Rama. Yet demands for, e.g., complete control over residence in the Atlantic Coast and the exploitation of natural resources, represent understandable efforts to prevent the subjugation of indigenous rights that has occurred throughout the Americas since 1492.

One difficulty with attempts to negotiate an autonomy arrangement acceptable to the major parties is the lack of a strong traditional government or unified position not only among the three indigenous peoples, but within the dominant Miskito community itself. Demands tend to be couched in terms of regaining political and economic power rather than protecting traditional cultural or religious practices, although they are no less legitimate because of this orientation. Nevertheless, this does make indigenous demands less distinguishable from the "minority" demands of, for example, the Creole community.

While the constant international attention paid to Nicaragua since 1979 has undoubtedly played a role in encouraging government acceptance of the concept of autonomy, it also has had some unfortunate consequences. One occasionally has the impression that too many analyses are concerned with precedents or ideological purity rather than responding to the real needs and real fears of those directly affected. A resolution can be found only within the political reality of Nicaragua, despite appeals for international support by both sides, and neither indigenous sovereignty nor centralized socialism offers complete answers.

In 1960, the International Court of Justice decided a long-standing boundary dispute between Honduras and Nicaragua by establishing the Coco River as the frontier, thus dividing historic Mosquitia and the present Miskito community.[694] No mention was made of any rights which might be possessed by the indigenous peoples in the region, nor of the impact of the division upon them. Twenty years later, indigenous rights were being asserted through appeals to international law and recourse to armed force.

It is essential that indigenous rights not be ignored while international attention is directed to wider regional peace plans. Regional peace is a prerequisite to an equitable autonomy agreement on the Atlantic Coast, but arrangements which are more responsive to indigenous survival than the 1987 Sandinista proposals may be necessary if the Atlantic Coast is to share in that peace.

---

694 International Court of Justice, *Arbitral Award Made by the King of Spain on 23 December 1906*, Judgment, I.C.J. Reports 1960, p. 192.

Chapter 11
Northern Ireland[695]

Created by the essentially pragmatic British decision to partition Ireland in 1920, Northern Ireland comprises about one-fifth of the area and one-third of the population of the island of Ireland. It is a divided society in which two separate communities are locked in conflict. The majority community is composed of almost one million Protestants, or unionists, who wish to remain British. The minority community is composed of more than half a million Catholics, or nationalists, who aspire to a united Ireland.[696]

Almost everyone now recognizes these basic facts, with the possible exception of some who believe that Northern Ireland is simply occupied by British troops against the will of the bulk of the population. But there is still a tendency to think that the divisions in Northern Ireland are due wholly to partition and the "fifty years of unionist misrule" that

---

695 This chapter is based upon Kevin Boyle and Tom Hadden, *Ireland: A Positive Proposal* (London: Penquin Books, 1985). However, responsibility for editing, the selection and presentation of materials, and all conclusions and observations rests solely with the author.

696 There are obvious difficulties in using any of these common labels. Calling the two communities Protestant and Catholic suggests, wrongly, that the conflict is primarily religious (though religious intolerance, prejudice and bigotry are widespread in both communities) and ignores the large numbers on either side who do not practice any religion. Calling them unionist and nationalist is equally misleading, in that it suggests that the fairly substantial number of Catholics who are content to remain British have thereby ceased to be part of the minority community. And giving any single label to either community gives a false impression of unity and common purpose. There are huge differences between hard-line unionists—usually called loyalists—and liberal unionists, and between hard-line nationalists—usually called republicans—and other Catholics. Even to talk in terms of majority and minority communities is unsatisfactory in that it suggests that the boundary of Northern Ireland is immutable. Some of these subtle differences are reflected in the choice of one or another label in the text.

followed it. As so often in Ireland, it is not quite as simple as that. The roots of the communal division go back far beyond partition, and the division is maintained by powerful social and economic forces that are too readily ignored by those who seek simple political explanations and solutions.

The peculiar persistence of the communal division in Northern Ireland stems from the fact that the "plantation" of British settlers there succeeded much more thoroughly than elsewhere in Ireland. The Norman invasion of Ireland in the twelfth century merely imposed a foreign nobility on what was already a largely feudal native Irish society. The intention of later plantations was to create more peaceful and stable conditions by excluding the native Irish from large tracts of land and replacing them with loyal British settlers.

In Ulster, which had held out longest against British rule, the process began with an unofficial settlement of Scottish Presbyterians in the thinly populated north-eastern counties of Antrim and Down at the start of the seventeenth century. The Ulster Scots gradually took possession of the whole of these counties, with the exception of the mountainous areas of Moyle in the north and Mourne in the south. Then, after the failure of the Catholic rebellion of 1598–1603 and the eventual flight of the rebel Ulster earls in 1607, James I decided to settle the remaining Ulster counties. His intention was to exclude the native Irish Catholics altogether, but in practice the Protestant settlers from England and Scotland took only the best land, mainly in the river valleys, leaving the Catholic Irish in possession of the hill country and other less desirable tenancies. The Irish remained a threat to the settlers' homesteads, despite reinforcement of the settlement after the victorious British campaigns by Cromwell in 1649 and 1650 and by William of Orange in 1689 and 1690; the last culminated in the famous Battle of the Boyne, which is still celebrated by unionists and members of the Protestant Orange Order on the Twelfth of July each year.

These victories ensured the permanence of the Protestant ascendancy in Ulster. The settlers and the dispossessed Catholics nonetheless continued their skirmishes throughout the seventeenth and eighteenth centuries. Towards the end of the eighteenth century a number of secret societies, notably the Orange Order, were formed on either side for mutual protection and revenge. While physical violence became less common, the struggle for land in rural areas continued at every land sale or inheritance. Farming land even now rarely passes from one community to the other.

In the towns, the balance between the two communities was only slightly more flexible. Catholics were permitted to establish themselves in the cathedral cities of Derry, Armagh, Omagh, Newry, and Down-patrick, where they still predominate. The situation was reversed in a few Protestant-majority towns, like Cookstown and Enniskillen, which were deliberately established in Catholic areas. In Belfast, the proportion of Catholics grew rapidly in the early nineteenth century as the factory system developed, reaching a peak of 34% in 1861.

These patterns may be traced fairly accurately from the mid-nineteenth century, when regular censuses began to be taken, and since then the relative proportions of the two communities have remained remarkably stable. In the counties of Antrim and Down, Protestants have long outnumbered Catholics by four or five to one. In Belfast the proportion has stabilized at about two to one. In the counties of Londonderry and Armagh there has been a continuing small majority of Protestants, and in Tyrone and Fermanagh a small majority of Catholics.

The Proclamation of the Irish Republic in Dublin in 1916 and its Declaration in 1919 were the result of centuries of Irish frustration over unequal treatment under British rule and the conviction that only complete separation achieved by force could ensure justice for the Irish nation. Independence therefore was essential, even if its price was partition.

The Government of Ireland Act of 1920, which was designed to give limited self-government to Ireland while maintaining overall British sovereignty, was rejected by the Irish Sinn Fein movement because it compromised the independence of the Irish Republic. Yet the Act would have created not only two regional parliaments for northern Ireland and southern Ireland, respectively, but also a Council of Ireland that was intended to be a vehicle for eventual political unity. When the subsequent military struggle led to a new offer from Britain, in the Anglo-Irish Treaty of 1921, of dominion status similar to that of Canada, the debates in the Dail (the Irish parliament) focused almost exclusively on the remaining symbols of British rule (such as the oath of allegiance and the status of the Crown as Head of State) and their intrusion on complete independence; partition and the right of Northern Ireland to vote itself out of the Free State were hardly mentioned.

The bitter civil war that was fought over the 1921 treaty led to victory for the pro-treaty party (later Fine Gael) and, in effect, ratified partition. Those who lost the civil war split into a majority determined to fight by political means to undo the settlement of 1921 (through the Fianna Fail party), and a minority committed to re-establishing an all-Ireland Republic by force. It is to this rump of the independence forces of the 1920s that the Provisional Irish Republic Army (IRA) claims today to be the successor.

When Fianna Fail took power in 1932 it adopted a series of measures to move the Irish state towards complete independence. This was finally achieved in 1948, when Ireland left the Commonwealth and declared itself a wholly independent republic. While these efforts to assert identity and statehood blazed a path followed by many other former colonies after the Second World War, they were pursued with little or no regard for their impact on the other national goal of uniting the people of north and south. Unity as a primary goal might well have dictated a very different approach to relationships between Britain and Ireland.

How and why have the two communities in Northern Ireland, in contrast to the Republic, maintained themselves with so little change over the years? The basic answer is that both communities have kept themselves to themselves, and that each is large enough and sufficiently concentrated to sustain its natural growth. The higher birth rate in the Catholic community has been offset by a higher level of emigration, which in turn may be linked to patterns of employment.

The process of segregation begins with education. There are two distinct school systems in Northern Ireland, a state system and an independent Catholic system. Although the state schools are officially and legally non-sectarian, they are in practice Protestant, partly because virtually no Catholics go to most of them and partly because their management committees are composed largely of representatives of the Protestant churches, whose independent schools were in effect taken over by the state system. The Catholic schools, which now receive virtually the same level of state funding as state schools, are expressly committed to educating their pupils in the Catholic faith and ethos and therefore have virtually no Protestant pupils.

The separation of the two communities extends to many other aspects of daily life.[697] Most marriages, of course, are between members of the same community, and considerable family and social pressures are brought to bear against those who dare to embark on a "mixed marriage." Most leisure activities, particularly in rural areas, are arranged by the churches and their associated organizations. There are even two distinct sporting systems: Catholics are encouraged to play Gaelic football and hurley, while Protestants are encouraged to play standard British games, like football, rugby, and cricket. Trades and professions are similarly divided.

These unranked social systems are designed to support as full a range of jobs and services as possible within each community, and they have the effect of minimizing contacts between them. It is perfectly

---

697 The best-known account of communal separation in a rural setting is in R. Harris, *Prejudice and Tolerance in Ulster* (Manchester: Manchester University Press, 1972); for an account of an urban community during the "troubles" see F. Burton, *The Politics of Legitimacy: Struggles in a Belfast Community* (London: Routledge & Kegan Paul, 1978).

possible, and quite normal, to live a full and varied life in Northern Ireland without having any real contact with people from the other community. Of course, the separation cannot be complete, and in larger factories and shops and in public employment there is a good deal of mixing. Even in these sectors, however, there are well established patterns.[698]

These examples—and many more could be given—show the extent to which Northern Ireland really is a divided society. This is not just a question of social segregation and economic differentiation. The two communities have entirely different views of the world in which they live. The nationalist community sees Ireland as a natural geographical and political unit that has a right to be independently governed. The unionist community sees nothing wrong with the partition of Ireland and the continuing link with Britain. The nationalist community thinks of itself as part of the Irish nation, which is regarded as Catholic, Gaelic, and essentially non-British. The unionist community feels excluded from that kind of Irish nation and clings all the harder to its British, or non-Irish, identity.

There are equally different perceptions of what might be thought to be factual matters. Unionists typically deny that there is any real differentiation or discrimination in employment patterns and regard statistics that indicate otherwise as suspect or biased. Many nationalists contest the accuracy of the latest census figures on the relative strength of the two communities. Both communities have entirely different perceptions of the causes of the recent "troubles" and what actually happened in numerous disputed incidents and security operations.

The communal division in Ulster did not begin with partition. Sectarian strife was endemic in rural areas throughout the eighteenth century, and Belfast was notorious for its sectarian employment practices and sectarian riots throughout the nineteenth century. With the exception of a brief period at the end of the eighteenth century when Protestant dissenters and Catholics joined forces as United Irishmen against the British establishment, the Ulster Protestants, like the rest of the Anglo-Irish, could be relied on by the British authorities to assist in suppressing Catholic unrest or rebellion.

The political differences between the two communities became much more important after the creation of Northern Ireland in 1920. While the northern unionists had not originally wanted a separate state, they accepted the 1920 settlement and soon grew to like the power that it gave them. From then on, sectarian divisions were not just a peripheral

698 See Fair Employment Agency, *An Industrial and Occupational Profile of the Two Sections of the Population in Northern Ireland* (Belfast, 1978).

problem in a wider political context; they became the life blood of politics in a state that one side wished to maintain and the other to dismantle.

The first task of the Unionist party government inaugurated in Belfast in 1921 was to establish its authority throughout the six counties of Northern Ireland, in the face of a continuing guerrilla campaign by the IRA and other irregulars. It was given a more or less free hand by the British Government to raise its own local forces to replace the British Army as it withdrew.[699] Three separate special forces were created to supplement the newly formed Royal Ulster Constabulary (RUC), which took over from the all-Ireland Royal Irish Constabulary. Legal authority for the arrest and internment of suspects was provided first under the Restoration of Order in Ireland Act 1920, which continued the wide powers conferred on British forces under the wartime Defence of the Realm Regulations, and then under the Civil Authorities (Special Powers) Act (Northern Ireland) 1922.

The new regime faced a similar challenge on the political front. Most nationalists refused to have anything to do with the institutions of the new state. This caused particular problems in local government districts in which nationalists had a voting majority. Initially, the Unionist government had to make temporary arrangements for the administration of a few such districts in which nationalist councillors voted to secede and refused to carry out their normal duties. In the longer term it sought to resolve this problem by redrawing local government boundaries in sensitive areas so as to produce unionist majorities in areas which nationalists might otherwise have controlled. The most blatant examples of this kind of gerrymandering were in Derry City and County Fermanagh.[700] In most local government areas, however, there were sufficient Unionist Party voters, given the relatively restricted local government franchise at that time and the fact that a higher proportion of the Catholic population has always been below voting age, to make gerrymandering unnecessary.

In elections for the Northern Ireland parliament, Stormont, the Unionist party was content to rely on its natural voting strength, which regularly produced about forty seats out of a total of just over fifty, and to permit the nationalists to hold the remaining seats. The decision by the Unionist government in 1929 to repeal the proportional represen-

---

699 For a general account of security policies and practices in this period see Michael Farrell, *Arming the Protestants: The Formation of the Ulster Special Constabulary and the Royal Ulster Constabulary 1920–1927* (Dingle: Brandon, 1984).

700 For an official account of these and other discriminatory practices, see *Report of the Commission on Disturbances in Northern Ireland* (Cameron Report), Cmd. 532 (Belfast: HMSO, 1969).

tation system of voting, which had been guaranteed under the 1920 settlement for a minimum period of three years, was designed to limit possible fragmentation of the Unionist party vote and the development of any form of alternative opposition, notably the Labour Unionists, rather than to reduce the number of nationalist MPs.

The most serious and continuing political concern of the unionists was the fear that the nationalist population would grow faster than their own. Given the higher Catholic birth rate and the explicit reliance on this prospect by some nationalists, the concern was a real one. In the private sector, most Protestant employers—and most employers were Protestant—favored members of their own community. The resulting lack of job opportunities for Catholics encouraged emigration, which was welcomed by unionists as a way of offsetting the higher Catholic birth rate.

In the public sector, the situation was essentially the same. Any form of legislative discrimination would have been clearly unlawful under the Government of Ireland Act 1920. However, the Unionist party was in a position, at both central and local government levels, to ensure that Protestants were appointed to most jobs and that Catholics were excluded from key positions. The reluctance of many Catholics to apply for or to accept official employment in a state that they preferred not to recognize was an additional advantage from this point of view, which the government did nothing to counteract. It has been estimated that in 1971, after fifty years of Unionist party rule, the unemployment rate among Catholics was more than double that among Protestants.[701]

In other matters, the Unionist government adopted an essentially conservative approach of avoiding state interference in social and economic matters, except for generally keeping in step with British legislation in the areas of social security and welfare benefits. They were encouraged in this approach by an agreement with the British government that any extra costs would be funded by a British subsidy.

The only serious attempt at removing one of the causes of the communal division, a scheme for integrated education which was proposed in the 1920s, was dropped in the face of combined opposition from both Protestant and Catholic churches. On the other hand, measures were adopted from time to time that, though relatively unimportant in themselves, emphasized the illegitimacy of the assertion of any form of Irish identity on the part of the minority. Among the best examples were the prohibition of the naming of streets in Irish in 1949 and the Flags and Emblems (Display) Act 1954, which was intended to prevent the display of the Irish tricolour without formally prohibiting

---

701 *An Industrial and Occupational Profile, supra* note 698.

it. In addition, the Unionist party worked with successive controllers of the British Broadcasting Company (BBC) in Belfast to ensure that the Irish identity of a large section of the community was ignored and a false sense of provincial harmony conveyed to the rest of the United Kingdom.[702]

The effects of this negative and sectarian approach to government on the part of the Unionist party were entirely predictable. The bulk of the Catholic community felt itself excluded from any prospect of sharing in the government of the province and discriminated against both in employment opportunities and in the expression of its aspirations to Irish unity. Most Catholics consequently continued to regard Northern Ireland as an illegitimate state. Their elected representatives either indulged in the politics of abstention or else continued to challenge the very existence of the state. This, in turn, permitted the Unionist party to portray all or most Catholics as inherently disloyal and thus to justify their exclusion from the processes of government and from certain types of employment.

The policies adopted by successive governments in the Irish Republic are also open to serious criticism. While the initial constitution of the Irish Free State "sought to cater for the minority status of Southern Unionists and did so with considerable success,"[703] this does not accurately describe the policies and practices actually pursued in the Republic towards its Protestant minority. Allowing for the different size and circumstances of the minorities in both parts of Ireland after 1920, the record of intolerance and disregard for other than the majority interest was broadly similar both north and south of the border.

On social and religious issues, the policies pursued in the Republic since the 1920s progressively converted what might have been a pluralist state into a confessional or sectarian state. Literature that was offensive to the Catholic church was censored. The possibility of obtaining a divorce was eliminated. An explicitly Catholic constitution was adopted in 1937, and many other laws and practices were adopted to give effect to the views of the Catholic majority, regardless of those of the Protestant minority.

It is sometimes argued that these developments were an inevitable consequence of partition, which created an overwhelming Catholic majority in the south. But that is altogether too charitable a verdict on a state that ignored or overrode the value of the Protestant minority both within the 26 counties of the Republic and within the 32 counties over

---

702 See R. Cathcart, *The Most Contrary Region: The BBC in Northern Ireland 1924–1984* (Belfast: Blackstaff Press, 1984).

703 *New Ireland Forum Report* (Dublin: Stationery Office, 1984), para. 3.2.

which the Republic aspired to rule. While it was natural for a newly formed state to assert its independence from Britain and essential for it to create a distinctive cultural identity, the manner in which these aims were pursued reinforced the prejudices of the northern unionists and made their policies more difficult to criticize from within or outside Northern Ireland. Similar negative consequences of "nation-building" may be observed in the cases of, for example, Nicaragua, the Sudan, and Sri Lanka.

THE CURRENT "TROUBLES"

The challenge that precipitated the fall of the Stormont regime in 1972 came from a somewhat unexpected quarter—not from the traditional nationalists against whom the unionists had prepared their defenses, but from the initially non-sectarian civil rights movement. During the 1960s, economic and social conditions were improving in Northern Ireland, as in the rest of the United Kingdom. An IRA campaign between 1956 and 1962 had not been widely supported and had been easily contained. A new generation of relatively prosperous Catholics was emerging from the schools and universities, and, like many of their Protestant contemporaries, they rejected the barren sectarian politics of the Unionist and Nationalist parties alike. Their basic demand, influenced by the civil rights campaign by blacks in the United States, was for equal political and economic treatment for both communities, within the established constitutional framework. In the Northern Ireland context, attention focused on the continuing existence of the Special Powers Act, the need for an increased number and fairer allocation of jobs and housing, and inequalities in the local government franchise due to the failure of the Unionist government to adopt post-war British reforms.

The Unionist government in Northern Ireland found it difficult to respond to demands of this kind in other than sectarian terms, despite moves towards better relations with the Republic in the mid–1960s. Traditionalists in the party scented a republican plot and reacted accordingly. Marches and demonstrations by the Northern Ireland Civil Rights Association were met by countermarches and demonstrations by extreme loyalists, led by the young Rev. Ian Paisley. The government and police fell back on a policy of attempting to ban civil rights marches. The rest of the story is familiar: escalating violence on the streets between civil rights campaigners and the police; the increasing involvement of loyalist mobs; the eruption of serious sectarian confrontations in the summer of 1969; the introduction of British troops in Derry and Belfast in an attempt to provide a peacekeeping force more acceptable than the local police; and the gradual re-emergence of the IRA in the role of defender of the Catholic community from attacks by loyalists and repression by the security forces.

These events forced the British government to abandon its policy, established in the 1920s, of avoiding involvement in the "Irish question"; Northern Ireland's autonomy had to yield in light of the increasing violence and the desire to reassert order within what was, after all, an integral part of the United Kingdom. The British government first sought to limit its commitment to keeping the peace between the two communities and to pressuring the Unionist government to carry through a reform program, but it gradually became more involved in both political and security matters. Resistance by the conservative wing of the Unionist party to most of the reform program meant that political pressure from London had to be maintained on a more or less constant basis. The increasing level of terrorist activity and continuing rioting in the streets made the integration of police and army operations of increasing importance.

This became particularly obvious when internment without trial was reintroduced in August 1971 at the insistence of the Unionist government.[704] The British Army was used in this operation to assist in the arrest and interrogation of large numbers of republican suspects chosen by the RUC Special Branch from out-of-date and inaccurate files that made little distinction between political and terrorist activists. The result was to unite the entire Catholic community in opposition to the Stormont regime and to increase both IRA recruitment and the level of terrorist activity.

The international outcry following the killing of thirteen Catholic demonstrators in Derry on 30 January 1972, known as "Bloody Sunday," finally led to a decision to impose direct control from London over all aspects of security and the administration of justice. When that was rejected by the Unionist government, the Northern Ireland regime was suspended by the British government in March 1972.

The suspension of Stormont and imposition of direct rule from London were intended only as a temporary expedient. The strategy of the British Government was to "take the border out of politics" by conducting a referendum on whether Northern Ireland was to remain part of the United Kingdom or join the Republic, and then to re-establish a system of regional government in which representatives of the whole community could share in power and influence. The first Border Poll was held in March 1973, and a new Northern Ireland Constitution Act

704 *Cf*. R.J. Spjut, "Internment and Detention without Trial in Northern Ireland 1971–1975: Ministerial Policy and Practice," 49 Modern L. Rev. 712 (1986).

was enacted a few months later. The latter provided for the election of a single-chamber Assembly and the appointment of an Executive of Ministers drawn from the membership of the Assembly, on the condition that the Executive would be likely to be "widely accepted throughout the community" and would form the basis for "government by consent."[705] The Act also made specific provision to invalidate any discriminatory legislation or executive action.[706]

At first, plans went relatively well. Following the Assembly elections in 1973, the British government was able to secure the agreement of the leaders of most of the major Northern Irish parties to the formation of a "power-sharing" Executive. However, the mainstream Catholic party, the Social and Democratic Labour Party (SDLP), conditioned its participation on creation of a meaningful "Irish dimension" within the new arrangements. To negotiate this demand, a summit conference was held in Sunningdale late in 1973, where it was agreed between the British and Irish governments and the major Northern Ireland parties that a Council of Ireland, with representatives from Northern Ireland and the Republic as originally envisaged in 1920, should be established and that there should also be an all-Ireland police authority.

It was this Irish dimension that led to the downfall of the power-sharing Executive soon after it took office in January 1974. Ian Paisley and other Assembly members who had refused to participate in the Sunningdale and other conferences took advantage of an unexpected Westminster election to campaign against the Council of Ireland, which they portrayed as the first step toward unification, and won a clear majority of unionist votes. When large numbers of working-class Protestants joined the Ulster Workers Council strike that brought the whole province to a halt in May 1974, the power-sharing Executive collapsed.

Since 1974, there have been repeated attempts by successive British Secretaries of State to secure agreement among politicians in Northern Ireland on some kind of devolved administration in which representatives of both communities can share power. All have failed. On each successive occasion, the unionist parties have refused to share any executive power with the "republicans," and the nationalist parties have refused to enter into any governmental structure that does not include a substantial Irish dimension. The Northern Ireland Assembly, re-established in 1982 to scrutinize the processes of government, no longer

705 Northern Ireland Constitution Act 1973, §2.
706 *Id.*, §§17–19.

meets and has been boycotted since its creation by both the SDLP and Sinn Fein (the IRA's political wing).

HUMAN RIGHTS AND SECURITY POLICIES

With hindsight, it can be said that the main cause of the continuing violence in Northern Ireland has been the failure of the British government to come to grips with the essentials of the political problem. However, the security policies that it has pursued have undoubtedly made matters worse, particularly the apparent inability of the authorities to recognize and eliminate abuses in the operation of emergency powers. Since these abuses have been experienced mainly by the Catholic community, the result has been to increase the general lack of confidence in the administration of justice felt by many Catholics and to exacerbate their latent antagonism to any form of British rule. Though some of the more serious abuses have eventually been controlled, action has typically been taken after the damage has been done.[707]

Following military security tactics developed in Malaysia, Kenya, and elsewhere, the British army stretched its power to arrest and detain suspects to the limit in a system of mass screening in Catholic areas.[708] Thousands of ordinary people in republican areas were regularly arrested and questioned, and early morning "head counts" were made on a street-by-street basis in order to build up a comprehensive intelligence record. This antagonized even those Catholics who opposed the IRA and made it possible for the IRA to sustain its recruitment and operations despite the arrest and internment of hundreds of its members.

Attempts had been made since the late 1960s to raise various aspects of the Northern Ireland situation under the procedures established by the European Convention on Human Rights, to which the United Kingdom is a party; most concerned alleged violations of human rights by British security forces and the Northern Irish police.[709]

---

707 See generally Kevin Boyle, Tom Hadden and Paddy Hillyard, *Ten Years On in Northern Ireland: The Legal Control of Political Violence* (London: Cobden Trust, 1980).

708 Many of the strategies pursued by the British Army in its early years in Northern Ireland may be traced to Frank Kitson, *Low Intensity Operations: Subversion, Insurgency and Peacekeeping* (London: Faber & Faber, 1971).

709 See Kevin Boyle and Hurst Hannum, "Ireland in Strasbourg: An Analysis of Northern Irish Proceedings before the European Commission of Human Rights," 7 Irish Jurist 329 (new series, 1972); *id.*, "Ireland in Strasbourg: Final Decisions in the Northern Irish Proceedings before the European Commission of Human Rights," 11 *Id.* 243 (new series, 1976); Michael O'Boyle, "Torture and Emergency Powers under the European Convention on Human Rights: Ireland v. United Kingdom," 71 Am. J. Int'l L. 674 (1977).

In 1978, the European Court of Human Rights held that the British had committed "inhuman treatment or punishment" (but not "torture") as part of the practice of "interrogation in depth" in late 1971; it rejected claims of discrimination against the republican Catholic minority in internment and other policies.[710] The failure of the European system to deal with earlier claims of, e.g., discrimination in jobs and housing, left the international community with no way in which to influence the situation in Northern Ireland prior to the outbreak of widespread violence.

A new set of problems soon emerged. The abandonment of internment in 1975 led to increasing reliance on obtaining confessions from suspects during prolonged and intensive interrogation. Numerous complaints about ill-treatment and beatings during interrogation were initially dismissed as mere propaganda. It was not until Amnesty International published a highly critical report in 1978 that the Government responded by appointing a committee of inquiry into interrogation procedures.[711] This led to the imposition of strict internal controls on interrogation practice, and complaints about this kind of ill-treatment declined dramatically.[712]

By 1978, another aspect of the criminalization policy began to create serious problems. Most IRA members convicted in special non-jury "Diplock courts"[713] after 1976 refused either to wear ordinary prison clothes or to work as directed. When they were denied their own clothes they refused to wear prison uniforms and "went on the blanket." When the authorities attempted to retaliate by refusing exercise and other facilities to the protesters, the prisoners resorted to the so-called "dirty protest" —smearing their cells with excrement. Finally, in 1980 and

710 Ireland v. U.K., App. No. 5310/71, Eur. Court of Human Rights Judgment of 18 Jan. 1978, Ser. A No. 25, [1978] Y.B. Eur. Conv. on Human Rights 602; the European Commission of Human Rights had earlier found that these practices did constitute "torture," Report of 25 Jan. 1976, [1976] Y.B. Eur. Conv. on Human Rights 512. *Cf.* O'Boyle, *supra* note 709.

711 *Report of the Committee of Inquiry into Police Interrogation Procedures in Northern Ireland* (Bennett Report), Cmnd. 7497 (London: HMSO, 1979).

712 *Cf.* P. Taylor, *Beating the Terrorists?* (Harmondsworth: Penguin, 1980).

713 These judge-only courts were introduced in the Northern Ireland (Emergency Provisions) Act 1973, based upon the recommendations contained in *Report of the Commission to consider legal procedures to deal with terrorist activities in Northern Ireland* (Diplock Report), Cmnd. 5185 (London: HMSO, 1972). They have remained an often controversial facet of British policies in Northern Ireland; *cf.* Boyle, Hadden, and Hillyard, *supra* note 707, at 57–87; William E. Hellerstein, Robert B. McKay, and Peter R. Schlam, *Criminal Justice And Human Rights in Northern Ireland* (New York: Ass'n of the Bar of the City of New York, 1988) at 40–86.

1981, there was a series of hunger strikes, the traditional and ultimate weapon of Irish protest.

The British government was able to claim a victory of principle over the dirty protest, in that the European Commission of Human Rights rejected the case filed by the protesters,[714] and over the hunger strike, which was eventually abandoned. But the European Commission was highly critical of the "inflexible approach" of the authorities, and many of the prisoners' demands, notably the right to wear their own clothes and a measure of segregation, were eventually conceded.

Another episode in the continuing saga of abuses in Diplock trials has been the systematic use of informers or "supergrasses," as they are popularly called.[715] As with internment and interrogation, a legitimate weapon against terrorism—the use of properly corroborated informers' evidence —has been discredited and devalued by its uncritical use and by the failure on the part of the prosecuting authorities and courts to insist on established safeguards.

Throughout the period of direct rule there also has been sporadic concern about the use of lethal force by members of the security forces. Although some prosecutions have been initiated, almost all have resulted in acquittals. In addition, the law on coroners' inquests in Northern Ireland is interpreted in such a way that, in cases where there is no prosecution, no public scrutiny of the evidence is possible until several years after the event. Members of the minority community and many independent observers simply do not believe that the same rules are applied in cases involving the security forces as in other cases. All of these practices, with the exception of the "supergrass" system, have been directed primarily against members of the Catholic community and have reinforced their instinctive lack of confidence in British security policies and the British judicial system.

The policy of "Ulsterization", that is, the devolution of increasing security responsibility to the Northern Ireland police authorities, has affected the situation in a rather different way. The winding down of the military security system in itself is clearly desirable. The difficulty is that all but some hundreds in the RUC and the paramilitary Ulster Defence Regiment are Protestants, partly because the IRA has pointedly murdered Catholics in the security forces and partly because most Catholics would not wish to join them in any case. The result is that one community has been given the task of

714 McFeeley v. U.K., App. No. 8317/78, Eur. Commission of Human Rights dec. on admissibility of 15 May 1980, 20 Dec. & Rep. 44.

715 See, e.g., Hellerstein, McKay, and Schlam, *supra* note 713, at 76–79.

policing the other, and the antagonism against many aspects of security policy felt by most Catholics has again become a communal and sectarian issue.

OTHER MATTERS

Direct rule from London has proved rather more successful on matters of day-to-day administration than on security and political development. Successive opinion polls in Northern Ireland have indicated that continuing direct rule is the most generally acceptable form of government to both communities, even though it is not the preferred option of either. Considerable progress has been made in eliminating the worst housing conditions and in the fair administration of education and health services.

The same cannot be said about the more important issue of discrimination in employment, and a 1987 report by the governmental Northern Ireland Standing Advisory Commission on Human Rights affirmed that unemployment among Catholics is still more than double that among Protestants.[716] Though poverty and deprivation have long been features of both Protestant and Catholic working-class areas, they remain concentrated in the Catholic community, which also has suffered the worst effects of fifteen years of disorder, terrorist activity, and oppressive action by the security forces. Many more bombs have been planted by the IRA in predominantly Catholic towns than in Protestant towns, and even in Belfast the bombers rarely stray far from the areas in which their own community lives and works. As a result, the physical environment in predominantly Catholic areas is substantially worse than in similar Protestant areas.

All these factors—abuses in the security field and in the operation of emergency powers, the failure of the British Government to make any progress in securing an effective voice for Catholics in the government of Northern Ireland, and the continuing difference in levels of unemployment and deprivation in the two communities—have contributed to a deepening sense of alienation among many Catholics both from Britain and from the majority community. The resulting despair at the prospect of resolving these problems within either a British or a purely Northern Ireland context has been an important factor in the growth of support for Provisional Sinn Fein (the political arm of the Provisional IRA) and in demands for a more radical approach to the whole Northern Ireland problem than has yet been envisaged.

716 "Ulster Report Calls for New Anti-Bias Laws," N.Y. Times, 19 Nov. 1987, at A9, col. 1.

OBSERVATIONS AND FUTURE PROSPECTS

Any settlement of the Northern Ireland problem must be based on the full recognition of the right of a majority of the people in Northern Ireland to determine to which state it belongs. Within that framework, however, the identities and interests of both communities must also be recognized. In particular, the minority nationalist community should be entitled to express its Irish identity in any way that does not conflict with the right of the majority community to remain part of the United Kingdom. If at any time in the future a majority in Northern Ireland were to vote for unification with the Republic, the subsequent unionist minority would be entitled to enjoy corresponding rights within a unitary Irish state.

These assumptions generally underlie the Anglo-Irish Agreement adopted in late 1985 by the Dublin and London governments.[717] In addition to formally recognizing that "any change in the status of Northern Ireland would only come about with the consent of a majority of the people of Northern Ireland...[and] that the present wish of a majority of the people of Northern Ireland is for no change in the status of Northern Ireland,"[718] the agreement creates an "Intergovernmental Conference," serviced by a permanent secretariat based in Belfast, in which high-level British and Irish representatives meet, on a regular basis, to discuss Northern Ireland and relations between Northern Ireland and the Republic. "There is no derogation from the sovereignty of either the Irish Government or the United Kingdom Government, and each retains responsibility for the decisions and administration of government within its own jurisdiction."[719]

The agreement provides that the two governments will work together

i) for the accommodation of the rights and identities of the two traditions which exist in Northern Ireland; and

(ii) for peace, stability and prosperity throughout the island of Ireland by promoting reconciliation, respect for human rights, co-operation against terrorism and the development of economic, social and cultural co-operation.[720]

717 Agreement between Ireland and the United Kingdom, *signed* 15 Nov. 1985 (Dublin: Stationery Office, 1985).
718 *Id.*, art. 1.
719 *Id.*, art. 2.
720 *Id.*, art. 4.

The specific areas to be addressed by the Conference include political matters (including provision of a forum in which the views of the Northern Irish minority can be put forward, if there is no progress towards an acceptable devolved government in Northern Ireland), security matters, legal matters (including possible harmonization of criminal law, extradition, and extra-territorial jurisdiction), and cross-border co-operation on security and other matters.

Unionists have violently objected to even this consultative role for the Irish government in Northern affairs, and Unionist members of the Westminister parliament resigned their seats in order to provoke new elections as a kind of referendum on the agreement. The subsequent elections provided little evidence of any change in voting patterns (either for or against the agreement), and sporadic violence, at times extending to raids by militant unionists into the Republic of Ireland, has continued.

A year after the agreement's adoption, it remained

the subject of deep grievances in the loyalist [unionist] community, which asserts that they [sic] were never fairly consulted and that the pact aims at a united Ireland in which they would become an oppressed minority. The pact also is the subject of mixed hope and skepticism among Catholic nationalists interested in stronger civil rights and tolerance of their identity.[721]

While the Anglo-Irish Agreement has thus failed to win widespread support, it has nevertheless been implemented by the two governments. Its long-term impact is uncertain, but it does permit a certain degree of substantive minority input (via the Irish government) into policies affecting Northern Ireland, the most important of which continue to be formulated in London, in the absence of any agreement on a devolved government in the North.

The political limits of the Anglo-Irish Agreement are illustrated by reactions to a series of British actions in the areas of policing and security in early 1988, which "reinforced the longstanding belief here [in Ireland] that no Irish Catholic, north or south, agreement or no agreement, can ever expect a fair deal from British justice."[722] Nevertheless, the Agreement has survived.

The difficulty that the British have experienced in attempting to establish a system of devolved government in Northern Ireland in which representatives of both communities can participate may be attributable

721 "Britain Proposes Ending Ulster Law," N. Y. Times, 2 Dec. 1986, at A7, col. 1.

722 Karen De Young, "Ireland, Britain Stumbling Over Ulster Obstacles," Wash. Post, 21 Feb. 1988, at A19, col. 2.

to a lack of precision about the respective rights of majority and minority groups in a divided society. The British legal and constitutional tradition within which both Northern Ireland and the Republic evolved identifies democracy with majority rule and ignores the position of minorities. While this may work in relatively homogeneous societies, it is inappropriate in a divided communal society like Northern Ireland, in which the political objectives of two communal groups are fundamentally opposed, and one group is in a position to exercise more or less permanent domination. This is now recognized, to the extent that the British Government has made it clear that power will not be devolved to Northern Ireland on a pure majority-rule basis.

However, the alternative of "power-sharing" is equally impractical. It does not provide any mechanism for resolving differences that are bound to arise within a cabinet or executive, and it encourages brinkmanship in that the ultimate decision about whether a government commands widespread acceptance is left to the discretion of either the Secretary of State (as under the Northern Ireland Constitution Act 1973) or the British Parliament (as under the provisions for "rolling devolution" under the Northern Ireland Act 1982).

Since the government structures within Northern Ireland are crucial to any lasting settlement, a more realistic system than the highly discretionary provisions for "power-sharing" is required. The most practical approach might be to provide that legislation and other governmental decisions concerning matters of particular communal concern (such as education, local government, policing and security, the location of major industrial developments, and all matters of an electoral or constitutional nature) should require a weighted majority of votes in any regional assembly or parliament. The necessary majority could be different for various matters, and a structure of this kind would provide a workable means of involving representatives of all parties in the process of government without requiring the unrealistic degree of consensus that is assumed in the "power-sharing" model. It might also permit the devolution of particular powers to a new Northern Ireland legislature as agreement on the precise majority to be required for each was reached.

Violence and terrorism have diminished somewhat since the Anglo-Irish Agreement, but they have not ceased. There is a long tradition of paramilitary action in all parts of Ireland, and extreme factions on both sides must be expected to do their best to wreck any prospective agreement. However, the activities of the security forces—as well as those of the terrorists—have always been a significant part of the problem. Generally acceptable and workable legal and security arrangements are thus an essential element in any overall settlement, and, as recognized in the 1985 agreement, these must involve not only action within the province but also appropriate cross-border arrangements.[723]

There can be no immediate solution to the problem of making the existing security forces in Northern Ireland more acceptable to the minority. There would be a serious risk in attempting to replace the British Army by an international peacekeeping force, since that would signal to all sides that the constitutional status of Northern Ireland as part of the United Kingdom was in doubt. Nor would it be either practicable or politically acceptable to abolish the Royal Ulster Constabulary and create an entirely new police force, whether within Northern Ireland or on an all-Ireland basis.

There is, in fact, no practical alternative to relying on the RUC as a unitary, non-sectarian police force for the whole of Northern Ireland. That does not mean, however, that nothing can be done to make the RUC more acceptable to the minority community.

The RUC could be made more effectively accountable to representatives of both communities by reconstituting a more directly representative and powerful Northern Ireland Police Authority and establishing a network of local police liaison committees with statutory powers of consultation and scrutiny on issues of local concern.[724] Greater confidence in the RUC and a higher level of recruitment among members of the minority community also could be encouraged by developing links between the RUC and the police forces in the Republic, similar to those that already exist between the RUC and the police in Britain. It should be standard practice for both bodies to advertise and recruit in all parts of Ireland, which would incidentally give some positive meaning to the principle of free movement of labor within the European Community. The ultimate objective should be to dispense with any military support to an unarmed, cross-communal police force, other than that which would be necessary under normal circumstances.

While the current level of terrorist activity persists, the continuation of some emergency powers in Northern Ireland and in the Republic is probably unavoidable. Unfortunately, the authorities have always un-

---

723 *Cf.* Anglo-Irish Agreement, *supra* note 717, arts. 8 and 9.

724 The problem of accountability is only too well exemplified by the so-called "Stalker affair," in which a much-criticized investigation into an alleged RUC "shoot-to-kill" policy eventually concluded that there was "evidence of the commission of offenses of perverting, attempting or conspiring to pervert the course of justice" on the part of the police. However, the British government has refused to prosecute any members of the RUC, nor has the report itself been made public. See De Young, *supra* note 722; John Stalker, *Stalker* (London: Penguin Books, 1988).

derestimated the counter-productive effects of security laws and practices that do not command the general respect of both communities.

Powers of arrest and interrogation must be reformulated to ensure
that they are used only where there is a reasonable suspicion that a
particular person has been involved in serious criminal activity and not,
as is still the case, for the purposes of general intelligence-gathering in
suspect areas. The system of non-jury Diplock courts should be limited
strictly to those cases in which it is shown that there is a real risk of
intimidation of jurors. There is also an urgent need for better means of
dealing with the alleged misuse of lethal force by members of the security
forces. Finally, new procedures are needed to ensure that there is a
speedy public investigation into all disputed shootings and other controversial incidents involving the security forces.

All these reforms are directly linked to two fundamental rules in
dealing with terrorism in a divided society: that any derogation from
the ordinary law must be shown to be strictly necessary for the fair and
effective administration of justice, and that it must be accompanied by
special safeguards to prevent abuse and maintain public confidence.[725]
Those principles have been ignored for far too long in Northern Ireland,
with disastrous results.

No simple "solution" that ignores the identity and commitments of
either of the two communities can be expected to succeed in present
circumstances, and it is not particularly helpful to posit that they might
work in the future if circumstances are different. The essential question
is whether a balanced cross-communal settlement can be made to work
in the 1990s. The answer is that it can work if there is sufficient determination to overcome the initial resistance that must be anticipated from
all sides, if careful attention is paid to demonstrating the general acceptability of the package, and if there are sufficient economic incentives
to induce the two communities in Northern Ireland to give it a try.

There has been a forceful reaction from politicians and paramili-
taries on both sides against every attempt to implement a cross-
communal settlement. The most appropriate response to such challenges
is that thus far adopted by both the British and Irish Governments—a
determination to press forward with those parts of the program that do
not require the active support of all parties in Northern Ireland and to
resist undemocratic challenges on the streets. A serious commitment by
the British government to protecting human rights and implementing
an objectively reasonable solution (if only for the time being) also is

725 *Cf.* sources cited *supra* note 427.

essential in order to maintain legitimacy in the battle against continuing terrorist violence by both the IRA and Protestant-loyalist extremists.

There is an important distinction between the general acceptability of a settlement to both communities and creating a high level of positive support for it. There is no present solution to the Northern Ireland problem that will gain the enthusiastic support of a majority in both communities. It is sometimes even said in Northern Ireland that if a proposal is attacked by both sides, then it must be right. That is clearly absurd. The converse—that if a proposal is enthusiastically supported by one side, it is probably wrong—is nearer to the mark. This means that a straightforward vote on a particular package, whether in a separate referendum or in the context of a general election for a Northern Ireland assembly or for the Westminster Parliament, is unlikely to produce an accurate measure of acceptability. As may also be the case with respect to the Sino-British agreement on Hong Kong[726] and the Gandhi-Jayewardene agreement on devolution in Sri Lanka,[727] the imposition of a *reasonable and responsive* solution from above may be a necessary first step toward a more permanent settlement, as a way of avoiding the "democratic" stalemate that might result from uncompromising political extremes and intimidation.

When autonomy is used to justify bigotry and discrimination, it loses the legitimacy it might otherwise acquire as a mechanism to ensure basic rights to equality and participation in government. It is significant that the foundations of Northern Ireland were finally shaken not by old-fashioned appeals to nationalism and religion, but by modern demands for fundamental human rights and equality. The history of discrimination by the majority in Northern Ireland demonstrates the dangers posed by permanent political, religious, or cultural majorities, while the sectarianism of the Republic of Ireland during the same period leads one to expect that it might have been equally unresponsive to legitimate minority rights of Protestants in a united Ireland. If there are lessons beyond the obvious ones relating to cycles of violence and repression, Northern Ireland might be seen as an example of the limits of autonomy and the difficulties of resolving majority-minority conflicts merely by attempting to carve political entities into the smallest possible pieces.

726 See chap. 7.
727 See chap. 14.

Chapter 12
The Saami (Lapp) People of Norway, Sweden, and Finland

HISTORICAL BACKGROUND

The indigenous people of northern Europe, who inhabit a region much of which is above the Arctic Circle, are variously known as "Lapps" (in the Finnish language), "Finns" (in Norwegian, formerly), or, by their own choice in more recent times, as the "Saami." Their traditional homeland, "Sapmi" (or Lapland), stretches in a great arc from the Soviet Kola peninsula, across the northern third of Finland, and along both sides of the mountain range which separates Norway and Sweden, for a distance of some 1,500 kilometers.

At least one-half of the total estimated Saami population of 60,000 is in Norway, and 15,000–20,000 of this number live in the northernmost Norwegian county of Finnmark. There are 17,000–20,000 Saami in Sweden, approximately 5,000 in Finland, and some 2,000–3,000 in the Soviet Union. However, the Saami constitute a majority in only six Norwegian communes in the heart of Finnmark (out of a total of over 400 in the entire country) and a single commune in Finland; despite the vast territory which they inhabit, they remain a tiny minority in a Nordic sea of over sixteen million people.[728] Nevertheless, one can speak of a generally recognized Saami heartland of some 75,000 square kilometers, which extends from Varanger in northeastern Norway, over inner Finnmark and northern Finland through Swedish Lapland.

Despite their small numbers, the Saami may be divided geograph-

---

728 The five members of the Nordic Council are Norway, Sweden, Finland, Denmark, and Iceland; for convenience, if somewhat inaccurately, "Nordic" in the present chapter will be used as a shorthand reference only to the first three, in which the Saami population is found.

ically and linguistically into four major groups: most of the largest group, the northern Saami, live north of the 68th parallel (Arctic Circle); the small group of eastern Saami are found primarily in what is now the Soviet Union; the central Saami live on both sides of the Norwegian-Swedish border, roughly between the 68th and 66th parallels; and the southern Saami inhabit Norway and Sweden south of the 66th parallel. Another general distinction which is sometimes drawn is between the "mountain" and "sea" Saami.

The Saami language belongs to the Finno-Ugrian group, somewhat related to Finnish and Hungarian but distinct from the Germanic languages which were the foundations of modern Swedish and Norwegian. At least ten different dialects have been recognized, including the four Saami languages which correspond to the four geographic designations mentioned above. Until the twentieth century, Saamish was only a spoken language, although three different orthographies have been recognized by Saami and Nordic bodies since the 1970s. A Saami Literature Committee, funded by the Norwegian government, was established in 1971, and in 1979 a Saami Writers' Union was formed.

The Saami were a people of hunters, trappers, and fishermen and have inhabited what are now the Nordic countries for millennia. In more recent centuries, reindeer herding became known to outsiders as the archetypical Saami enterprise, although most Saami are engaged in farming, crafts, fishing, and other trades. Of course, there are also more assimilated, urban Saami who engage in the whole range of "modern" activities, although their numbers are quite small.

The Saami never established a state in the contemporary sense of the word, although there apparently was a representative Saami assembly on the Kola peninsula. The basic social unit was the *siida*, a small group of families sharing a relatively large, naturally delimited area, often on one side of a watershed. The families were not necessarily related to one another by kinship ties, and the affairs of the *siida* were run by a local council on which each family would be represented. This council would distribute land, fishing rights, etc., and also exercised certain judicial functions.

Within the *siidas*, each family had its own land, and families also would have exclusive grazing areas, often two or three hundred kilometers distant, to which they would bring their reindeer herds during the summer. What have become modern borders obviously had no meaning to the Saami population, and seasonal migration regularly occurred across what are now state frontiers. The sea-saami lived in more permanent villages along the coast.

The Norsemen, Swedes, and Russians established centralized state structures during the twelfth to fourteenth centuries, although none initially extended to the northern Saami territories. Expansion into what were deemed to be "unclaimed" lands soon followed, however, and the Nordic and Russian kingdoms had little trouble establishing areas of control. The Saami offered little armed resistance to this expansion, as there was an abundance of territory and minimal initial interference with their way of life. In 1321, Sweden and the Viking kingdom of Novgorod concluded a treaty which divided the northern territories, although many overlapping claims remained outstanding. For the next several centuries, the Saami were subject to tax collections (for land use) by two or more kingdoms, depending on which controlled a particular area.

The kingdoms gradually asserted greater control over the Saami homeland through trading, taxation, the efforts of Christian missionaries, the establishment of military outposts, and increasing settlement. Nevertheless, the Saami population was essentially left alone (except for the collection of taxes and attempts by missionaries to convert the Saami from their traditional religion), and Saami moved freely throughout the region, regardless of particular land claims by the kingdoms.

By the eighteenth century, the two strong states of Sweden (then including Finland) and Denmark-Norway had emerged, and in 1751 they agreed upon a treaty which established the present border between Norway and Sweden. Annexed to this treaty was what has become known as the Lapp Codicil, which confirmed the right of the Saami to travel freely across the frontiers with their reindeer herds and to use lands and water according to custom.[729] While movement was to be unrestricted, no Saami was allowed to possess land on both sides of the border; thus, families had to choose in which country to live, either by forfeiting land in one country or by transferring from one to the other (normally with the payment of a fee).

The stated purpose of the Lapp Codicil was "the conservation of the Lappish Nation." In some respects, it resembles one of the post-Versailles "minority treaties," in that its primary concern was to ensure that Saami "citizens" of one state were well treated in the other. The Codicil provided for joint tribunals to resolve conflicts between Saami of the two states, and it stipulated that county governors would have a special duty to inquire into the treatment of foreign Saami in their county. The Saami also were guaranteed neutral, non-combattant status in the event of war between the two kingdoms; war also was not to interfere with their freedom of movement.

The Lapp Codicil remained in effect until the entry into force of

---

729 It might be noted that the Saami were only third-party beneficiaries of this agreement and played no part in drafting the boundary treaty or Lapp Codicil.

the 1972 Norwegian-Swedish Reindeer Grazing Convention, and those rights not addressed by the 1972 convention continue to be in force in Norway.[730] The Lapp Codicil allowed the Saami to continue their traditional way of life, but at the same time it extinguished any claims to Saami ownership, as opposed to usufruct rights, of the lands they had inhabited for centuries. Saamis became subjects of one or the other kingdom, so that they were Norwegian Saami or Swedish Saami, and were subject to various formalities and the payment of a fee whenever they crossed the frontier.

In 1809, Sweden was forced to cede Finland to Russia. The Tsar decided to close the frontier between Finland and Norway in 1852 and between Finland and Sweden in 1880, thus further disrupting traditional Saami migration patterns. The Russian border has remained closed throughout Soviet rule.[731] It was only in 1983 that Finland and Norway adopted a treaty which permits "frontier residents" to cross the frontier outside of official border posts, but there have been numerous international agreements between and among the Nordic countries concerning reindeer.[732]

The impact of Nordic settlement on the Saami has been described as signifying the latter's "long retreat" from their traditional homelands.[733] A Royal Resolution adopted in 1775 authorized plots of land to be granted to Norwegian settlers in Finnmark, and the coastal areas of Sapmi (the Saami homeland), in particular, soon became predominantly Norse. There were few instances of the armed attacks that characterized settlement of indigenous land in the Americas, but the encroachment in traditional Saami regions was nonetheless real. Today, Saamis constitute only 25% of the population even in Finnmark.

Denmark was forced to give up Norway in 1814, and Norway and

---

730 *Cf.* Otto Jebens, "Sami Rights to Land and Water in Norway," 55 Nordic J. Int'l L. 46 (1986).

731 There are occasional examples of Finnish or Norwegian Saami visits to the Kola peninsula, and, in 1977, Norway and the Soviet Union entered into an agreement for the repatriation of reindeer, but there is no real freedom of movement across the Soviet frontier. See Mervyn Jones, *The Sami of Lapland* (London: Minority Rights Group Report No. 55, 1982) at 15.

732 Reindeer are closely associated with the traditional economy of the Saami, but it has been estimated that no more than 10% of the Saami population in Norway and Sweden actually make their living from breeding reindeer. Nevertheless, reindeer are central to Saami tradition and culture, and reindeer breeding is closely controlled by the state for the benefit of the Saami. In Norway and parts of Sweden, only Saami may own reindeer, and the reindeer industry seems generally healthy (although the Soviet nuclear accident at Chernobyl could have a devastating impact on the Nordic reindeer herds). Herds are much smaller in Finland, where 60% of the reindeer are owned by non-Saamis. See Jones, *supra* note 731, at 7–9.

733 *Id.* at 6.

Sweden were united under a single crown until 1905. Despite this union, separate legal systems and social policies were maintained, and there were different attitudes towards the Saami. In Sweden, "Lappland" was reserved for traditional Saami culture, but racial theories of "social Darwinism" relegated the Saami to a clearly inferior position.[734]

Norway pursued a much more aggressive assimilationist policy, including the encouragement of Norwegian agricultural settlements in Finnmark and the designation of Saamish- and Finnish-speaking areas of northern Norway as "transitional districts" from which "foreign" languages should be eliminated. From 1880 until after World War II, the official Norwegian policy was that all education should be in Norwegian, with Saamish (and Finnish) used only where absolutely necessary.

In Finland (which was a "grand duchy" within the Russian empire until it declared independence in 1917), there were greater similarities between many Saamis and Finns, and assimilation occurred "almost by default."[735] The Saami population in Finland also is much smaller than that in Norway and Sweden. The 1919 constitution of Finland recognizes two national groups and languages, Finnish and Swedish, although Swedish-speakers constitute only 6% of the population; the Aland Islands also are recognized as an autonomous Swedish-speaking community within Finland.[736] No such special position for the Saami community has been recognized, however.

RECENT DEVELOPMENTS

Norway

The Norwegian policy of assimilation of the Saami people has been gradually abandoned, beginning with the recognition in 1947 that Saamish had to be accepted as the first language of the Saami population.[737] The 1959 report of a Royal Commission on Saami Questions stated that all children had a right to be educated in their mother tongue and marked the definitive end of assimilation. Saami children now generally receive their education in Saamish during the first three years of school, while also learning Norwegian. Since 1979, the government has provided a subsidy to the only Saamish-language newspaper in Norway.

Numerous advisory bodies have been established, including a Nor-

---

734 *Cf.* Tomas Cramer, "Superlawyers and Sami in Sweden," 55 Nordic J. Int'l L. 58 (1986), for examples of anti-Saami Swedish racism in the nineteenth and early twentieth centuries.

735 Jones, *supra* note 731, at 7.

736 *Cf.* discussion *infra* chap. 17, at 370–75.

737 See generally Norges offentilige utredninger, *Samisk kultur og utdanning* (1985:14).

wegian Saami Council created in 1964, which advises national, county, and communal authorities on Saami policy. Its members are appointed by the King upon nomination by Saami and other organizations, as well as by the six counties and nine communes with the largest Saami populations. A Saami Educational Council was established in 1975 as an advisory organ of the Department of Ecclesiastical and Educational Affairs, and, in 1984, a Saami Cultural Committee was created under the Norwegian Cultural Council. The nongovernmental Association of Norwegian Reindeer Herders, established in 1948, works in cooperation with the state on economic and other issues.[738]

In 1980, two bodies, a Saami Rights Committee and a Commission on Saami Cultural and Educational Matters, were appointed by the government. The first report by the Saami Rights Committee, on "the legal status of the Saami population," was delivered in June 1984 and is probably the most significant political-legal development related to the Saami in Norway in recent years.[739] The report addresses a wide range of issues and includes discussions of Norway's obligations to the Saami people under international law.

The 1984 committee report observes that the Saami population "comprises a people in a political and sociological sense" but concludes that articles 1 and 55 of the UN Charter, *inter alia*, were not intended to create a right to self-determination for an "ethnic minority" such as the Saami.[740] It considers that some aspects of indigenous rights have been recognized by international customary law and general principles of international law, but acknowledges that "the degree to which the various states are obligated on this [latter] basis is uncertain."[741]

On the other hand, the report adopts a relatively expansive interpretation of Norway's obligations under article 27 of the Covenant on Civil and Political Rights, which includes a positive obligation to ensure that Saami culture is maintained and provided with opportunities for development.

738 Other significant nongovernmental Saami organizations include the National Organization of Norwegian Saami, founded in 1968, and the Saami National League, established in 1979; the latter is generally in favor of integration, while the former and the Association of Norwegian Reindeer Herders are more concerned with promoting a distinct Saami culture.

739 Norwegian Saami Rights Committee, *Summary of the First Report* (Oslo: n.d.) [hereinafter cited as "Saami Rights Committee Summary"] at 7–9. The full report, in Norwegian only, *The legal status of the Saami population* (1984:18), was submitted to the Norwegian government in June 1984; only the summary is available in English. Also see the government's summary of the report's major recommendations, Norway, art. 9 CERD Report, UN Doc. CERD/C/132/Add.5 (1986) at 2–4.

740 Saami Rights Committee Summary at 14–16.

741 *Id.* at 22–26, 24.

[A]n ethnic minority is entitled [under article 27] in one respect to a certain degree of autonomy (nonintervention on the part of the state), and in another to government support for the maintenance of their cultural activities (positive rights), and in yet another, to be allowed to participate in the rest of community life on an equal footing with the majority population (the principle of non-discrimination). . . .

The Saami people are unquestionably an ethnic group whose culture is protected according to Article 27. Therefore, they are entitled to the support of the Norwegian State in their enjoyment of their own culture. At the same time, the Saami people comprise an ethnic group whose cultural basis lies largely in a traditional utilization of natural resources. Therefore, it is highly likely that their traditional forms of economic activity are also protected to a certain extent by Article 27. . . .

[I]t is not enough to ascertain that the various Norwegian statutes and administrative decisions are not at variance with Article 27. The provision imposes an obligation on the Norwegian State to take active steps to ensure that Saami culture is carried on in Norway.[742]

This interpretation was subsequently adopted by the Norwegian government.[743]

Following the recommendation of a majority of the Saami Rights Committee, a constitutional amendment was adopted in April 1987 to give specific recognition to the Saami people and the government's obligations in their regard.[744]The amendment provides:

It rests on the State authorities to shape conditions so that the Saami ethnic group ["Folkegruppe"] may safeguard and develop its language, its culture and its social life.[745]

The report also recommended establishment of a new central Saami organ to replace the present Norwegian Saami Council, although there was a division of opinon as to how this body should be elected.[746]

The Saami Rights Committee's recommendations were put before the Norwegian parliament in 1984, and legislation to establish a Sa-

---

742 *Id*. at 17, 20.

743 See, e.g., Norway, statement to the Fifth Session of the UN Working Group on Indigenous Populations (n.d. [Aug. 1987]) at 5 (on file with author).

744 See Saami Rights Committee Summary at 34–47. While there was no disagreement with the substance of the recommended provision, a substantial minority of the Committee (7 of the 18 members) felt that a separate constitutional provision concerning the Saami was inappropriate until the position with respect to other minorities in Norway had been clarified.

745 Norwegian Const., sec. 110a (unofficial translation). The term "Folkegruppe" was reportedly used because a reference to the Saami "people" would have inappropriately encompassed the Saami in Sweden, Finland, and elsewhere.

746 Saami Rights Committee Summary at 47–64.

meting, or Saami Parliament, was adopted in May 1987.[747] The 1987 "Saami Act," as it is known, provides that the Sameting will take over the advisory authority presently held by the Saami Council and may have such additional authority as is provided by law. The Sameting is elected directly by all Saami registered on a separate electoral register, as opposed to the present system of appointment of members of the Saami Council. The Saami Act also requires that, at least once during each legislative term, the King (i.e., the Norwegian government) shall present guidelines for the measures which need to be instituted in order to fulfill the intentions of the act.

It also is expected that Saamish will be recognized, along with Norwegian, as an official language of Norway.

Sweden

Recent developments in Sweden parallel those in Norway, although there has not been the same need to reverse early assimilationist policies. For example, Saami children in Sweden have always been taught in Saamish, although under segregated conditions and only through elementary school until the 1950s. Higher education is now available to the Saami on a basis of equality, but (as in all the Nordic countries) there remains a shortage of Saamish materials and qualified teachers. There is an autonomous Saami school system, with a Saami-elected board.[748] Beginning in the 1970s, the Swedish government has made annual grants to a Saami Fund, managed by Saamis, which promotes cultural and other activities.

A Swedish Saami Rights Committee was established in 1982 and submitted a report on "The International Legal Position of the Saami" to the Swedish government in 1986.[749] While the report offered no specific recommendations, it included the following conclusions:

> As we see it, Article 27 [of the Covenant on Civil and Political Rights, to which Sweden is a party] should be taken to require positive discrimination of minorities and indigenous populations. It also implies safeguards for the right to separate cultural identity. The term "culture" should be broadly interpreted in this context, so as also to include the material foundations of culture, e.g. the reindeer-herding activities of the Saami. . . . Article 27 may possibly also be construed as entitling the minority to a certain measure of cultural autonomy. . . .
>
> Summing up, we maintain that under international law, Sweden incurs obligations towards the Saami in a variety of ways. Sweden must refrain from

747 See Statement by Norway to the UN Working Group on Indigenous Populations, *supra* note 743, at 3–4.

748 *Cf.* Sweden, art. 40 CCPR Report, UN Doc. CCPR/C/32/Add.12 (1986) at 18.

749 Delbetäkande av samerättsutredningen, *Samernas Folkrättsliga Ställning* (SOU 1986:36).

interfering with the natural environment in such a way as to jeopardise the natural prerequisites for the survival of reindeer-herding. Furthermore, Sweden must take steps to guarantee the necessary resources for the survival and development of the Saami culture.[750]

The Committee is expected to recommend in a future report that formal Saami participation be required before state authorities grant logging permits that might affect Saami villages and that a Swedish Saami Parliament be created, comparable to those in Finland and Norway.

Finland

The Saami population in Finland is very small, numbering only 5,300 out of a total Finnish population of nearly five million.[751] Of this number, it is likely that no more than one-half actually speak the Saamish language, as Saami are defined in Finland not only as those who speak Saamish but also as persons one of whose parents or grandparents spoke Saamish at the time of a 1962 census.[752] As a result, Saamish has been used in schools only since the 1970s, although a 1985 law expands previous statutes and provides that Saamish can be the language of instruction in the Saami home region. However, curricula are established by local municipalities (in which the Saami have some influence, but which are not controlled by them), and there are difficulties in finding qualified Saami instructors.[753]

Perhaps surprisingly in view of the small Saami population, Finland was the first of the Nordic countries to have an elected Saami political body, the "Delegationen for samearnden" ("Saami Delegation", more popularly known as the Saami Parliament), which was created in 1973. The 20-member body is indirectly elected by Saamis living in the Saami home region;[754] essentially an advisory body, it can propose actions to the government on issues affecting Saami economic, social, and cultural affairs, and it has become an effective spokesperson for the Saami people. There is also a Saami Commission ("Samedelegationen"), originally established in 1960 as an advisory body within the office of the Prime Minister; half of its members represent the government, and half the Saami Parliament.

750 *Id*. at 32, 33.
751 Finland, art. 9 CERD Report, UN Doc. CERD/C/132/Add.1 (1985) at 2; figures are from 1983.
752 Tore Modeen, "The Legal Situation of the Lapp (Sami) Ethnic Group in Finland," 55 Nordic J. Int'l L. 53, 56 (1986).
753 Finland, Art. 9 CERD Report, *supra* note 751, at 3, 4–5.
754 The Parliament is technically appointed by the Finnish cabinet, which selects the 20 candidates who received the highest number of votes, so long as there are at least two members from each of four different Saami communes.

A special committee on Saami land and water rights was established in 1978, and recent Finnish government initiatives include a working group to study problems related to providing social welfare services in minority languages, including Saamish; expanding the availability of state housing and other subsidies to Saami reindeer herders; and creating an independent Saami radio organization unconnected to the state-owned radio.[755]

Joint Nordic initiatives

A Nordic Saami Council was created by various national Saami groups in 1956. In 1973, the Nordic Saami Institute (located in Kautokeino, Norway) was created by the inter-governmental Nordic Council to serve as a center for research concerning Saami economy, law, environment, culture, etc. A 1974 resolution of the Nordic Council invited the Nordic Committee of Ministers to elaborate a common Nordic program to protect and preserve the environment of the main Saami regions. While these bodies have no direct political or decision-making authority, they reinforce the transnational character of Saami life and underscore the need for international solutions to the common problems faced by the Saami in the three countries.[756] The third report by the Norwegian Commission on Saami Cultural and Educational Matters proposed a treaty on Saami culture to be entered into by Norway, Sweden, and Finland.[757]

Although not properly a "joint Nordic initiative," economic and social developments in the Saami homeland have been similar in the three states. The positive and negative aspects of these developments are, to a great extent, those common to other indigenous regions. The extension of social services, roads, modern telecommunications, and electric power to Saami communities has improved the quality of life in many respects. At the same time, increasing contact with "modern" Nordic culture, mining and timber exploitation, the damming of rivers and lakes for hydroelectric production, and the promotion of tourism, have all had significant impacts on the largely rural, migratory, traditional life of the Saami.[758] Also disruptive is the potential exploitation of oil in the North Cape region and restrictions imposed for military reasons in the strategic region of northern Norway.

755 Finland, Art. 9 CERD Report, *supra* note 751, at 2–3.

756 *Cf.* Knut Sverre, "Indigenous Populations and Human Rights: The International Problem from a Nordic Point of View," in Brøsted, Jens et al. (eds.), *Native Power* (Oslo: Universitetsforlaget AS, 1985) at 188–95.

757 *Samisk kultur og utdanning, supra* note 737, at 156.

758 *Cf.* Jones, *supra* note 731, at 9–12.

THE 1985 KAUTOKEINO SEMINAR PROPOSALS

The "small nations of the North"—Aland, the Faroe Islands (Føroyar), Greenland (Kalaallit Nunaat), and the Saami people—convened the third in a series of international seminars to discuss issues of mutual concern in June-July 1985 at Kautokeino, Norway.[759] The main themes of the 1985 meeting were autonomy arrangements, the status of the Saami people, and creation of an "Universitas Borealis."[760]

One of the most interesting proposals at the seminar was for a convention among Finland, Norway, Sweden, and elected representatives of the Saami Nation to establish a transnational, autonomous Saami territory. Although denominated "a first, fumbling attempt . . . [with] absolutely no official status,"[761] the draft "Saami Convention" offers intriguing possibilities for creative constitutional and international legal responses to Saami demands for autonomy.[762]

The basic premise of the draft Saami Convention is that a single autonomous territory should be created in those areas of Finland, Norway, and Sweden in which there is a majority Saami population. This territory ("Saamiid Aednan") would in turn be divided into three communes, corresponding to the areas of Saamiid Aednan which lie within present state frontiers. At the same time, there should be some recognition of the larger Saami nation, which includes those Saami scattered throughout the Nordic countries and U.S.S.R.

Many legislative powers of the proposed Saamiid Aednan are left unspecified, but they would extend, "as a minimum," to those matters currently within the competence of Aland, the Faroe Islands, or Greenland. The most important powers specifically reserved to the Saami authorities would include the ability to restrict the residence of non-Saamis within the territory; ownership of all land not otherwise in private, group, or communal hands, subject to customary rights; and the right to all renewable and non-renewable natural resources in the territory.

Local judges would be appointed by the respective state governments upon the nomination of the Saami legislature, and decisions involving state law could be appealed to the Supreme Court of the state concerned. Disputes concerning the interpretation of the Saami Con-

759 Most of the papers of the seminar are collected as a symposium in 55 Nordic J. Int'l L. (parts 1–2, 1986).

760 Atle Grahl-Madsen, "Introduction", *id.* at 2.

761 *Id.* at 7.

762 The draft text is found at 55 Nordic J. Int'l L. 7–11 and discussed in detail in Atle Grahl-Madsen, *The Peoples of the Twilight Zone* (Bergen: Univ. of Bergen Dept. of Public and International Law, provisional ed. 1988) at 31–74.

vention itself would, at the request of any of the parties, be submitted to a special panel of seven judges, of whom one would be selected by each of the state parties, three by the Saami executive, and the seventh by the President of the International Court of Justice.

Despite the transnational nature of the autonomous territory, there is no suggestion of a formal transfer of sovereignty to Saamiid Aednan. Each of the three state governments would be represented by a High Commissioner, who could participate without a vote in the Saami legislature. The Saami territory could become a party to international human rights and humanitarian treaties and, after consultation with the three High Commissioners, conclude treaties with other states on matters within the competence of the autonomous territory. However, no foreign missions could be established without the consent of all three High Commissioners, except that consulates (whose jurisdiction would extend only to a commune within existing state borders) could be established with the permission of the High Commissioner in whose state the consulate would be located. Saamis would continue to be exempt from compulsory military service in the armed forces of the three states, but could be obliged to serve in an autonomous home guard; normal police powers would be within the jurisdiction of the autonomous authorities. Saamiid Aednan residents would retain their original Finnish, Norwegian, or Swedish citizenship, which could be changed after two years' residence in the commune of another state.

OBSERVATIONS

One of the most striking features of the Saami situation is the absence of violence, although there have been instances of civil disobedience. This absence of violence does not imply an absence of conflict, and the distance between some Saami demands and government responses should not be underestimated. At the same time, all parties do seem to share a sincere commitment to the peaceful resolution of present conflicting demands.

One of the reasons for ongoing attempts to resolve these competing demands peacefully is, no doubt, the democratic nature of the states concerned and their relatively sympathetic responses (even if viewed by many Saamis as insufficient thus far) to Saami assertions of their own dignity and identity. The joint commitment of Finland, Norway, and Sweden to responding to Saami demands rather than repressing them stands in particular contrast to the attitude of Iran, Iraq, and Turkey to the not dissimilar position of the Kurds.[763] Another factor may be the relatively moderate nature of Saami demands; there have as yet

---

763 *Cf.* chap. 9.

been no calls for the Saami equivalent of an independent Khalistan, Kurdistan, or Tamil Eelam.

As is the case with other indigenous peoples, rights to land and natural resources have been in the forefront of Saami concerns, and control over development and the exploitation of natural resources is among the Saamis' fundamental demands. At the same time, none of the three state governments concerned has indicated a willingness to allow control over land to pass from central government authority.

The distinction between Saami rights to use the land and water versus state ownership has been crucial in several court cases in Norway and Sweden.[764] The most favorable to the Saami was a Norwegian case decided in 1862, in which the Supreme Court ruled that "a definite nomadic right for Norwegian Lapps [to use of land and water] ensues from the 1751 Convention," on the basis of reciprocity with rights granted to Swedish Lapps in Norway.[765] The Swedish Supreme Court has denied that the Lapp Codicil vested title to land and water in the Saami, but has adopted a similar view with respect to usufruct rights.[766] A 1981 Swedish case (the "Taxed Mountain" case), while holding against Saami ownership on the particular facts before the Supreme Court, conceded the principle that ownership could be derived from customary use. In 1982, the Norwegian Supreme Court (in the "Alta-Kautokeino" case) rejected Saami (and other) attempts to halt construction of a hydroelectric dam, at least in part on the grounds that the dam interfered only insignificantly with traditional usufruct rights of Saami reindeer herding.[767]

In the areas of language and education, the three Nordic countries have been fairly responsive in recent years, and there is a sincere attempt to promote Saami culture. However, as noted above, development projects in Saami areas and, in particular, the promotion of tourism may have negative impacts on traditional Saami life that could render cultural protection illusory.[768]

State responses to social and cultural issues have not been matched by either symbolic recognition of the unique position of the Saami within Nordic culture or significant political initiatives. For example, the Norwegian Saami Rights Committee refused to recognize that Norway has

764 See generally Otto Jebens, "Sami Rights to Land and Water in Norway," 55 Nordic J. Int'l L. 46 (1988).

765 Quoted in id. at 47.

766 Saami Rights Committee Summary at 7.

767 Cf. Odd Terje Brantenberg, "The Alta-Kautokeino Conflict: Saami Reindeer Herding and Ethnopolitics," in Brøsted et al., supra note 756, at 23–48.

768 See e.g., some of the specific instances mentioned in Jones, supra note 731, at 9–10, 14.

any legal obligations towards the Saami as an indigenous people or a people with a right to political self-determination or autonomy, despite the Committee's fairly expansive view of Norway's positive obligations towards the Saami as an "ethnic minority." On the other hand, Finland and Denmark (a member of the Nordic Council) have had what could be termed generally successful experiences with the autonomous areas of Aland, the Faroe Islands, and Greenland.

This reluctance to grant meaningful political recognition to the Saami people seems to reflect two divisions, one within the Nordic population and one among the Saami. The former can be seen in the disagreement within the Norwegian Saami Rights Committee as to the appropriateness of a constitutional amendment regarding the state's obligations vis à vis the Saami. The primary reservations seem concerned with the possibilities of accentuating differences within societies with many small minorities, both quasi-indigenous and recent immigrants; creating divisions in local communities, where the Saami are commonly in a tiny minority; and unfairly discriminating against the economic and other interests of the Norwegian majority in the northern coastal region.[769]

Divisions among the Saami stem both from inherent disagreements over policies that might be present in any widely scattered community and from the fact that roughly half the Saami population lives outside the northern heartland. While Saami keenly contest local elections where possible, there is no country-wide Saami political party in Norway or Sweden. There also are divisions among Saami (at least in Norway) as to whether designation of the Saami as an identifiable group, through a Saami census which would be a precondition for direct elections to a representative Saami body, would be an integrating or divisive factor.[770]

Elected Saami parliaments will exist in all three countries in the near future. However, the limited advisory role envisaged in, for example, the 1987 Norwegian Saami Act, is unlikely to satisfy those who demand more direct (as well as symbolic) mechanisms for protecting Saami interests. There also is a danger that development of three state-based Saami institutions could inhibit the trans-Nordic character of Saami culture; although it is not necessarily the case that the Saami population would suffer if effective participation in the political process were divided among Finnish, Norwegian, and Swedish institutions, this would seem to detract from the transnational aspects of Saami life that have been recognized by all the states involved for centuries.

769 *Cf.* Sami Rights Committee Summary at 45–46.
770 *Cf.* Sami Rights Committee Summary at 48–53.

[A]ny viable Saami solution must have as its point of departure that Sapmi is One Nation Indivisible, stretching across the territories of three States, and that if Sapmi shall not be reduced from one Nation to three national minorities (or "ethnic groups"), the solution must be Nordic rather than Finnish, Norwegian, or Swedish.[771]

The possibility of a transnational autonomous Saami territory, as an immediate development or following a transitional period in which a separate Saami parliament would exist in each of the three countries, remains intriguing. Certainly the close relationship of the three states within the context of the Nordic Council[772] and the historical and contemporary ties within the Saami population suggest that this option should at least be seriously considered. The possibility of various forms of non-territorial cultural or personal autonomy also is likely to be discussed.

Whether any transnational Saami territory is divided into state-demarcated communes or is "internationalized" more directly through arrangements for some form of joint authority over a unified Saami homeland, it will remain closely tied to the Nordic countries by geography, economy, and inter-cultural tradition. Given the relatively high level of social services available in the Nordic states, some form of continuing subsidy or financial participation by each state in Saami fiscal matters will undoubtedly be required. Military sensitivities are already addressed plausibly in the draft Saami Convention, and other possibilities can be envisaged. Whatever boundary would ultimately be drawn to demarcate Saami territory, as well as existing international frontiers within the Saami region, would be a "soft" border for most purposes, except perhaps for residence and peculiarly territorial matters such as land use and resource exploitation.

The symbolic value to the Saami of establishing an autonomous Saami entity through an international treaty is evident, although the degree to which this is a fundamental demand is not clear. Although none of the states concerned has given any evidence of even considering such a possibility, there certainly would be no international or domestic legal impediment to such an arrangement. One need only recall the membership or representation of many non-state entities in various in-

771 Grahl-Madsen, *supra* note 762, at 73.

772 One complicating factor is the different approaches to strategic and military affairs adopted by the three states, approaches which to some extent reflect the sensitive geo-political character of northern Scandinavia. Norway (with Denmark and Iceland) is a member of the North Atlantic Treaty Alliance (NATO); Sweden is unaligned and neutral; and Finland is also neutral, in the context of its close proximity to and special relationship with the Soviet Union.

ternational organizations, the participation of international organizations themselves in various international agreements, and the obvious precedent of Aland (whose status was originally set forth in an international instrument and is now entrenched in an unalterable [except by mutual consent] provision of the Finnish constitution), to become aware of the flexibility which could govern any ultimate Saami-Nordic agreement.

The situation of the Saami is complex, and the responses of the various governments to Saami demands for cultural and political autonomy reflect the confusion—and, to some extent, artificiality—which results from attempts to justify political conclusions by resorting to purportedly legal distinctions among various categories of rights. It is to be hoped that attention to substantive issues will not be overly distorted by worries about legal precedent, and that the following, relatively optimistic, conclusions reached in 1982 are still valid:

The Saami are among the world's least numerically strong minorities. They are also, thanks to their pacific traditions, one of the most defenceless by the accepted standards of an age given over to violence. They have been subjected to centuries of pressure, to cultural repression, and to the temptations of assimilation. Their physical environment, which is vital to them, is still assaulted and imperilled.

Yet they have succeeded in maintaining their social integrity and their self-confidence; they have made significant gains in their relationship with well-organized nation-states, and can be counted upon to make more in the future; and, as a community, they are in the midst of a period of revival and renewal in which they can take justified pride. If there are lessons here, the lessons must be heartening.[773]

773 Jones, *supra* note 731, at 14.

Chapter 13
Spain—the Basque Country and Catalonia

Modern Spain consists of several distinct ethnic groups, each with its own language and cultural traditions. While Castillian has been recognized as the national language and is what foreigners refer to as "Spanish," most of Spain's wealth lies in regions where Castillian is but a second language. For example, Catalan is the first language of the majority of people in northeastern Spain. The Basques in northwestern Spain also have a well-developed and separate language and culture, as do the Galicians in the region north of Portugal.

The unity of Spain as a single sovereign state dates from the fifteenth century, when Ferdinand of Aragon married Elizabeth of Castile, thus uniting several independent kingdoms. In the seventeenth century, armed opposition to the centralizing projects of King Philip IV's Prime Minister broke out in Catalonia, Andalusia, Aragon, Naples, and Sicily, but the central authorities prevailed. In the early eighteenth century, Philip d'Anjou (subsequently Philip V) defeated forces supportive of the rival claims of Archduke Charles of Austria; the latter forces included Catalonia and Aragon (in addition to England, Portugal, and Holland), and as a result of their defeat Philip abolished many of the still existing local institutions.

The decline of local authority continued throughout the first half of the nineteenth century, and the defeat in 1876 of the Carlist forces (which included the Basques and Catalans) in the third Carlist war reduced regional powers even more.[774] Nevertheless, regional demands contin-

---

774 See generally P. Plans Sanz de Bremond and J. Andres-Gallego, *Historia de España* (Madrid: Editorial Magisterior Español, 3d ed. 1984) at 276–86.

ued, and in 1914 the Madrid government agreed to adopt a plan that did delegate very limited powers to the provinces.

REGIONAL AUTONOMY UNDER THE SECOND REPUBLIC

Basques, Catalans, Galicians, Andalusians, and other regional communities in Spain have long claimed and historically enjoyed the right to autonomy or self-government. The reestablishment of the Spanish Republic in 1931 offered the opportunity to respond to the desire for regional and cultural autonomy felt by large segments of the Spanish population, and the new constitution proclaimed by the Spanish parliament (the Cortes) in 1931 provided for the organization of autonomous regions within the Spanish state out of provinces "with common history, culture and economy."[775] Any proposed autonomy statute had to be approved by the Cortes, following approval by a plebiscite within the proposed autonomous region.

Catalonia was the only region to take advantage of the possibility for autonomy offered under the short-lived Second Republic; the Basque provinces and Galicia proposed autonomy statutes in 1936, but the Spanish Civil War intervened before any action could be taken on the proposals.

The Catalan autonomy statute was approved by the Cortes in September 1932,[776] but the rightist government in power from 1933 to 1935 managed to delay its implementation. From July 1936 until May 1937, Catalonia was a fully functioning autonomous region.

Among those legislative and executive powers specifically reserved to the central government were questions of nationality; church-state relations; national defense; foreign relations; customs and tariff regulation, including commercial treaties; monetary policy and the banking system; and communications.[777] The 1931 constitution also delineates areas of national legislative competence whose execution may be assumed by the autonomous governments.[778] Thus, standard-setting was left to the national government, while administration was the responsibility of the regional government. Catalonia assumed administrative responsibility in all areas permitted under the constitution, including, *inter alia*, penal, social, commercial, and procedural legislation; weights and measures; control over natural resources, including minerals; exercise of the right of eminent domain, except for the central govern-

---

775 1931 Spanish Const., art. 11.
776 Law approving the Statute of Catalonia, No. 1.387 of 15 Sept. 1932.
777 *Id.*, art. 14.
778 *Id.*, art. 15.

ment's reserved right to appropriate property for public purposes; and regulation of the press, associations, meetings, and public performances.

It is unclear what powers the central government retained in order to enforce administration in areas of mixed competence, although provision is made for inspection by the central government of the execution of "social laws" in order "to guarantee their strict fulfillment."[779] In general, national laws were to be implemented by the regional authorities, except those laws "whose enforcement is attributed to special agencies or in whose text some other provision is made."[780]

Executive power in Catalonia was exercised by a president and executive council chosen by the elected regional parliament. The president was the official representative of the region to the national government and to other autonomous regions.

National laws prevailed over regional laws, except in the area of the region's exclusive competence, as set forth in its autonomy statute. Those subjects not specifically recognized in the autonomy statute were reserved to the central government but could later be delegated by law (except for exclusively central powers) to the region. Once the regional autonomy statute had been accepted by the Cortes, there was no provision for national oversight, veto, or other power over the regions in those areas designated as within regional competence. The autonomy statute itself could be modified only by a two-thirds vote of the Cortes, following a request by 25% of the Cortes members or upon the motion of the regional parliament after a regional referendum.

The local Catalan courts had exclusive competence with respect to issues arising under regional laws (except for constitutional challenges) or within any area of administrative competence which had been assumed by the region. Challenges to the constitutionality of any statute, national or regional, were within the exclusive jurisdiction of the national court of constitutional guarantees, and inter-regional conflicts also were to be resolved by the national judiciary.

Both Catalan and Castillian were official languages of Catalonia, and either language could be used in dealing with the regional government. Castillian was to be used in official communications between the Catalan and central governments and among autonomous regions. Catalan was the language of instruction in local (i.e., regional) schools, although the central government was granted the right to fund Castillian-language schools if it so desired.

A complex revenue-sharing formula was provided in the autonomy

779 *Id.*, art. 15(1).
780 *Id.*, art. 20.

statute to assist in funding the regional government.[781] The base figure was determined by the cost of services provided by the regional government, and the actual amount returned to Catalonia from Madrid was a percentage of the national taxes imposed, which could be augmented by local taxes.

The short period during which the autonomous region of Catalonia actually functioned before being abolished by the victorious Franco forces in 1938 makes it difficult to judge the viability of the Second Republic's arrangements for autonomy. Nevertheless, the broad scope of the Catalan and other proposed autonomous statutes indicates that there was a fairly extensive grant of actual as well as theoretical powers of self-government to the autonomous regions. The powers of approval and amendment of autonomy statutes reserved to the national Cortes is significant, but it should be noted that a majority in the 1931 Cortes represented non-Castillian Spain, thus providing a fairly effective political check on discriminatory legislation at the national level and a sympathetic majority for regional autonomy.

The Basque community was more divided than the Catalans, and several early autonomous proposals in the 1930s were unsuccessful.[782] Although a Basque autonomy statute was finally approved in October 1936, it was never implemented. Following Franco's victory, the financial accords (*fueros*) that had been recognized in 1876 were abolished in the Basque provinces of Guipuzcoa and Vizcaya, although they were retained in Alava and Navarra (which had supported Franco during the civil war).

THE FRANCO ERA

The government of General Francisco Franco, which lasted until his death in 1975, suppressed all regional autonomy movements as separatist threats to the state. A total ban was placed on the use of Catalan and Basque outside of the home; teaching of Catalan and Basque was essentially prohibited; educational and cultural institutions were disbanded; and regional government officials commonly came from outside the region and were unversed in local languages or customs.[783]

Both the Basque country (Euzkadi) and Catalonia are among the

781 *Id.* art. 16.

782 See, e.g., E. Orduña y Rebollo, *El Estatuto Autonómico Vasco* (Madrid: Ministerio de Administración Territorial 1979). An early version of a Basque autonomy statute was declared unconstitutional, in part because of the reservation of residual powers to the Basque government and its recognition of a Basque right to negotiate directly with the Vatican. J. Olabarri, "Un conflicto entre Nacionalismos: La 'Cuestión Regional,' 1808–1939," in J. Olabarri, *La España de las Autonomías* (Madrid: Instituto de Estudios de Administración Local, 1985).

783 *Cf.* Kenneth Medhurst, *The Basques and Catalans* (London: Minority Rights Group Report No. 9, rev. ed. 1982) at 6–7.

most developed areas in Spain, despite apparent economic discrimination against the latter during the Franco era. As Spain's principal industrialized regions, both areas also have attracted immigrants from more rural Spanish regions; it is estimated that over half of the Basque and Catalan working class is non-local in origin.[784] While much of this immigration would appear to be economically motivated, allegations have been made that immigration has been encouraged by the state in order to dilute regional distinctiveness.

Opposition to Franco in both the Basque country and Catalonia came from the Catholic church (in varying degrees), illegal political parties, unofficial trade unions, and intellectual movements. In Catalonia, this opposition often was concerned with larger issues of democratization and economic reform, as well as with local autonomy. Catalan nationalism had always been more cohesive than that in the Basque country, in part stemming from the strong cultural and linguistic ties that had been reinforced by a nineteenth-century Catalan literary revival. Catalan socialist and communist parties remained distinct from their Spanish counterparts and organized civil disobedience actions. "Catalonia was the largest single source of opposition to his [Franco's] regime. . . . [M]ass gestures of defiance pointed to the re-emergence of a certain communal self-confidence . . . [which] lay behind a renewed and sometimes spectacular campaign in support of Catalan culture."[785]

Political leadership in the Basque country lay primarily in the hands of the Partido Nacionalista Vasco (PNV), an essentially conservative, Catholic, and nationalist party. The late 1950s and early 1960s saw the emergence of the guerrilla group ETA ("Euskadi Ta Akatasuna," Basque Homeland and Freedom), whose "youthful leaders were dissatisfied with the PNV's inactivity and impatient with its then aging leadership."[786] By the late 1960s, ETA assassinations provoked extreme repression by the Franco regime, which in turn contributed to Basque solidarity and demands for independence. In 1970, the military trial and conviction of several Basque nationalists (including the imposition of six death sentences which were subsequently commuted) in Burgos aroused strong reactions; in 1973, the ETA assassinated the person widely believed to be Franco's chosen successor, Admiral Carrero Blanco.

On the face of it the government seemed to over-react to ETA's challenge and so to play into the opposition's hands. ETA (like the IRA) worked on a theory that action would provoke repression which would provoke increased resistance,

---

784 *Id.* at 8.
785 *Id.* at 10.
786 *Id.* at 10. Similar splits between moderate political elders and more radical youth may be seen among, e.g., Sikhs in India and Tamils in Sri Lanka.

and so on in a continuing upward spiral. In the short run, at least, developments in the Basque area seemed to confirm the theory.[787]

There was no corresponding development of guerrilla violence in Catalonia, although community-wide opposition to the regime was, if anything, even stronger than that in the Basque country. There was some gradual cultural liberalization in the 1950s and 1960s (such as tolerating public use of Basque and Catalan), but this did not portend any real movement towards recognition of local autonomy prior to Franco's death in 1975.

CONTEMPORARY REGIONAL AUTONOMY

Regional autonomy was perhaps nearly as fundamental an issue as democratization in the post-Franco period, and there were strong autonomous movements in the Canary Islands and Navarra as well as in the Basque country and Catalonia.[788] Within this context, however, one should not assume unanimity of opinion. One basic difference is between those who accept the territorial integrity of the Spanish state and seek some form of autonomous/federal solution within it, and those (primarily the Basque ETA) who seek independence and secession. Even within the Basque country, Vizcaya and Guipuzcoa provinces remain more radical than Alava, while Navarra is divided between those in the north who are more sympathetic to Euzkadi and those in the south who feel a stronger Navarra or Navarra-Spanish identity.

Differences between Catalonia and the Basque country are reflected in an opinion survey undertaken in 1982.[789] In the former, 26% of the population considered itself Catalan; 40% felt dual Catalan-Spanish identity; and 30% felt primarily Spanish. In the Basque country, only 13% of the population felt Spanish; 24% felt a dual Basque-Spanish identity; and 60% considered itself Basque.[790] Forty per cent of the Basque working class considered itself Basque, compared with only 14% working class "Catalans" in Catalonia.

Even more dramatic is the difference in preferred solutions to regional issues. A full 35% of the Basque population was in favor of independence (although 40% supported the 1978 constitutional provisions for

787 *Id.* at 11.

788 See generally J. Linz, "De la Crisis de un Estado Unitario al Estado de las Autonomías," in Olabarri, *supra* note 782, at 527–673.

789 The following results are reported in Linz, *id.* at 555.

790 A 1986 poll among the Basque population found that 21% of those surveyed considered themselves primarily Spanish; 36% felt their Spanish and Basque identities equally; and 48% considered themselves moderately or totally "nationalist," i.e., Basque. Cambio 16 (Madrid), 27 Oct. 1986, at 46.

autonomy), compared to only 7% of Catalans who favor independence and 70% who support the constitutional proposals. The referenda to approve the two autonomy statutes had surprisingly identical results, however: in the Basque country, 61% of the eligible voters cast ballots, and 89% of those supported the autonomy statute; approximately 61% also voted in Catalonia, with 88% supporting the statute.

Central (state) – autonomous (regional) relations

Perhaps the major innovation of the contemporary arrangements for regional autonomy is that they apply to the entire country rather than only to certain provinces. While the Basque country, Catalonia, Galicia, and Andalusia are the only four "historic" communities within the terms of article 143 of the constitution, it is anticipated that there will ultimately be no difference between these four regions (which were able to obtain autonomy in a shorter period of time and with the approval of two-thirds rather than three-fourths of those voting in a referendum to approve autonomous status) and the other thirteen regions eligible for autonomy.[791] Thus, to a meaningful extent, the highly centralized Spanish government has become significantly decentralized in less than a decade, and autonomy statutes had been adopted for all seventeen regions by 1983. The present chapter focuses on the first two autonomous regions, Catalonia and the Basque Country, by way of example.

The principle of autonomy is formally recognized in the 1978 Spanish Constitution, which was adopted by the parliament elected in 1977. The Preamble recognizes that one of the goals of the state is to "[p]rotect all Spaniards and peoples of Spain in the exercise of human rights, their cultures and traditions, languages and institutions." Article 2 provides:

The Constitution is based on the indissoluble unity of the Spanish nation, the common and indivisible homeland of all Spaniards, and recognizes and guarantees the right to autonomy of the nationalities and regions which make it up and the solidarity among all of them.

Articles 3 and 4 guarantee the right of the autonomous regions to designate their own regional languages and flags, in addition to Castillian and the national flag. Detailed provisions for attaining autonomous status and the respective powers of the autonomous and central governments are found in articles 143–158.

In 1981, the government (led by the Union del Centro Democratico, UCD) and the major national opposition party, the Spanish Socialist

791 See Rainer Hofmann, "The New Territorial Structure of Spain: The Autonomous Communities," 55 Nordic J. Int'l L. 136, 137–41 (1986) for a summary description of the differences between the two routes to autonomy.

Party (PSOE), agreed on an outline for regional autonomy which would extend throughout Spain.[792] This led to adoption by the Cortes of the Ley Organica de Armonizacion del Proceso Autonomico (LOAPA) in 1982, which codified the 1981 agreement. Pursuant to a constitutional challenge to the LOAPA by the regional parties on grounds, *inter alia*, that the envisaged autonomy statutes could not be subservient to national legislation, the Constitutional Court declared fourteen articles of the law wholly or partially unconstitutional in 1983 and affirmed that only constitutional amendments could modify the fundamental statutes of the autonomous regions.[793]

It is necessary to bear in mind that autonomy requires in principle, for its part, that the actions of the autonomous Administration not be controlled by the State Administration, that [the State] not impugn the validity or efficacy of these actions except through the established constitutional mechanisms. Thus, the power of oversight cannot place the Autonomous Communities in a situation of hierarchical dependence with respect to the State Administration, for, as this Tribunal already has had the occasion to indicate, such a situation is not compatible with the principle of autonomy and the sphere of competence which is derived from it.[794]

The remaining portions of the LOAPA (now known as the "LPA") became law and entered into force in October 1983.[795]

The autonomy statutes are legally subject to the constitution but superior to any state law or administrative order.[796] Once adopted, they can be altered only by the actions of both the regional and central authorities: any amendment must be approved by absolute majorities of the regional autonomous parliament and the Cortes, and by the population concerned through a referendum.[797]

The autonomous governments have exclusive jurisdiction over a wide range of subjects, including, *inter alia*: organization of local gov-

---

792 *Acuerdos Autonómicos Firmados por el Gobierno de la Nacion y el Partido Socialista Obrero Español el 31 de Julio de 1981* (Madrid: Servicio Central de Publicaciones de la Presidencia del Gobierno, Coleccion Informe No. 36, 1981).

793 S.T.C. No. 76/1983 of 5 Aug. 1983, Recursos previos de inconstitucionalidad nums. 311, 313, 314, 315 y 316/1982.

794 *Id.*, quoted in *Jurisprudencia Constitucional en Materia de Autonomías Territoriales, Año 1983* (Madrid: Ministerio de Administración Territorial, 1984) at 71; author's translation.

795 Ley 12/1983, of 14 Oct. 1983, del Proceso Autonómico.

796 See E. Garcia de Enterria, *Curso de Derecho Administrativo* (Madrid: Ed. Civitas S.A., 5th ed. 1984) at 285–91.

797 1978 Spanish Const., art. 152(2); Ley Orgánica 3/1979, of 18 Dec. 1979, de Estatuto de Autonomía para el País Vasco (hereinafter cited as "Basque Autonomy Statute"), arts. 46–47; Ley Orgánica 4/1979, of 18 Dec. 1979, de Estatuto de Autonomía de Cataluña (hereinafter cited as "Catalan Autonomy Statute"), arts. 56–57.

ernment; local civil law; mountains, forests, agriculture, livestock, and fishing in local waters; internal production, distribution, and transportation of energy; urban planning; public works; control over public property which belongs to the autonomous community; control over water resources within the autonomous regions; housing; social welfare; roads, highways, and public works; internal commerce and industry (with some exceptions); and culture.[798] An autonomy statute may grant competence to an autonomous region over any matter not expressly reserved to the central government.[799]

The central state government retains exclusive jurisdiction over, *inter alia*: immigration; foreign relations; national defence and military affairs; the administration of justice; customs; penal and labor legislation; international trade; monetary regulations; coordination of general economic planning; intellectual property; and "basic conditions which guarantee the equality of all Spaniards in the exercise of rights and in the fulfillment of constitutional duties."[800] Article 150 of the constitution permits the central government to delegate to the autonomous regions (jointly or individually) 1) legislative powers to enact laws which would otherwise be under the exclusive jurisdiction of the central state government, and 2) administrative authority to regulate various matters within broad national guidelines;[801] the latter procedure is considered the norm, with the autonomous regions implementing basic national standards.[802]

In case of conflict between national and regional laws not within the exclusive jurisdiction of the autonomous regions, national laws prevail.[803] In addition, national laws are considered to be supplementary to the laws of the autonomous regions.[804]

If an autonomous region does not carry out its obligations under the constitution or relevant laws or "acts in a way which gravely harms the general interest of Spain," an absolute majority of the Senate (which is territorially based and represents the provinces and autonomous regions) may take measures necessary to ensure such compliance or protect

798 1978 Spanish Const., art. 148. The Basque country and Catalonia have assumed essentially the same governmental functions and thus will be discussed as one, except as noted. Basque Autonomy Statute, art. 10; Catalan Autonomy Statute, art. 9.
799 1978 Spanish Const., art. 149(3).
800 *Id*. art. 149(1) [unofficial translation].
801 *Cf*. Garcia de Enterria, *supra* note 796, at 329–35.
802 *Cf*. 1978 Spanish Const., art. 149, paras. (6), (8), (18), (23), & (27), which list numerous central government powers which are to be exercised "without prejudice" to the complementary authority of the autonomous regions.
803 1978 Spanish Const., art. 149(3).
804 *Id*.

the general interest.[805] The Cortes, by an absolute majority of each house, also has the power to harmonize regional laws if necessary in the general interest, even in areas of exclusive regional competence.[806]

Autonomous regions have a local judicial system established in accordance with the constitution, a national organic law on the judiciary, and each region's autonomy statute. Local jurisdiction extends, *inter alia*, to all civil actions and appeals concerning local law and initial criminal and social matters (excluding appeals). There is exclusive jurisdiction over challenges to administrative acts within the exclusive competence of the autonomous authorities and original jurisdiction over other administrative acts.[807] Regional superior courts, whose members are appointed in accordance with the national organic law on the judiciary, are to hear local appeals; presidents of these courts are to be appointed by the King upon the recommendation of the national Council on Judicial Power.[808]

The central government may challenge any regional law or regulation, suspending its application, before the national Constitutional Court, which has exclusive jurisdiction over conflicts between autonomous regions and between an autonomous region and the state.[809]

Autonomous institutions

Legislative authority in the Basque country and Catalonia is exercised by a locally elected legislature, which in the former consists of an equal number of representatives from the three historical territories of Alava, Guipuzcoa, and Vizcaya, and in the latter of a proportional number of representatives from the four Catalan provinces of Barcelona, Tarragona, Lerida, and Gerona. In addition to competence over those areas of exclusive jurisdiction and shared jurisdiction noted above, each regional legislature nominates the Basque and Catalan presidents, respectively; approves the regional budget; and elects the region's representatives to the national Senate.[810]

Executive power is exercised by a collective executive council, headed by a president who serves both as head of the autonomous region

---

805 *Id.* art. 155.

806 *Id.* art. 150(3).

807 Basque Autonomy Statute, art. 14; Catalan Autonomy Statute, art. 20.

808 Basque Autonomy Statute, arts. 34, 35; Catalan Autonomy Statute, arts. 19–23. The national organic law was adopted only in January 1986 and has not yet been fully implemented, so many questions as to jurisdiction cannot be answered with precision until they are addressed by courts in the future.

809 1978 Spanish Const., art. 161.

810 Basque Autonomy Statute, arts. 25–28; Catalan Autonomy Statute, arts. 30–35.

and head of government; the president is named by the King upon the designation of the autonomous legislature.[811] The executive is totally independent from the central authorities (apart from the King's role) and is politically responsible to the autonomous legislature.

In the Basque country, the institutions of the historic territories retain their traditional "foral" powers, and any conflicts between the foral and regional institutions are submitted to an arbitral commission consisting of an equal number of representatives of the Basque government and the concerned foral territory, and presided over by the president of the Basque Superior Court.[812]

The activities of Spanish police and security forces in repressing regional nationalism have historically been the object of great local resentment, and both the Basque and Catalan autonomy statutes provide for an "autonomous police regime" responsible for the maintenance of public order.[813] While ultimate control over the regional police rests with the regional authorities, a "security council" is established to coordinate the activities of the local police and national security forces. Reserved to the national security forces are "police services of an extracommunity or supracommunity character," such as border and customs guards, immigration, regulation of arms and ammunition, and investigation of fraud against the state.

The central security forces retain the right to intervene to maintain public order in the autonomous regions 1) at the request of an autonomous government or 2) unilaterally, with the approval of a majority of the "security council," which is composed of an equal number of local and central government representatives.[814] In cases of "special urgency," and to fulfill their national constitutional responsibilities, the national security forces may intervene on the orders of the central government, subject to the ultimate authority of the Cortes.[815] Finally, in a declared state of emergency, the autonomous police forces are placed under the direct orders of the appropriate authorities, according to Spanish law.[816]

The autonomous regions may enter into agreements with one another, subject to notification to the Cortes or, if the agreement goes beyond matters within the exclusive jurisdiction of the autonomous re-

---

811 Basque Autonomy Statute, arts. 29–33; Catalan Autonomy Statute, arts. 36–39.
812 Basque Autonomy Statute, arts. 37, 39.
813 Basque Autonomy Statute, art. 17; Catalan Autonomy Statute, art. 13.
814 Basque Autonomy Statute, art. 17(6); Catalan Autonomy Statute, art. 14.
815 *Id.*
816 Basque Autonomy Statute, art. 17(7); Catalan Autonomy Statute, art. 14(2).

gions, the Cortes' prior approval.[817] The autonomous regions may request the central government to approve their entry into international agreements in the area of cultural relations.[818]

Spanish and Basque or Catalan, respectively, are designated as official languages in the two autonomous regions; both may be used freely and without discrimination, and the autonomous regions undertake to see that both are taught.[819]

The Spanish Constitution grants "financial autonomy" to the autonomous regions "in conformity with the principles of coordination with the state treasury and of solidarity among all Spaniards."[820] Income to the autonomous regions comes primarily from the collection of national taxes delegated wholly (such as property and inheritance taxes) or partially to the autonomous regions; local taxes; and a portion of the general income of the state, derived from budget allocations from the central government, allocations of non-transferred national taxes, and grants from an interterritorial compensation fund.[821]

In fact, the allocation of funds to the autonomous regions is a major and complex political issue.[822] While the autonomous regions would prefer a more definite law on finances, the central authorities prefer to negotiate financial matters each year. In addition, there are long-standing complaints by Basques and Catalans that they contribute disproportionately to the central government coffers and receive much less in return.

Special financial arrangements exist with respect to the "historic territories" of the three Basque provinces and Navarra, which have entered into *conciertos económicos* with the central government.[823] These agreements provide for collection of all taxes (except customs

817 Basque Autonomy Statute, art. 22; Catalan Autonomy Statute, art. 27. Only one inter-regional agreement had been concluded as of 1986, between Catalonia and Murcia in 1982, concerning cultural relations; that agreement was challenged by the Spanish government before the Constitutional Court.

818 In the case of the Basque country, this authority is granted in the context of protecting and promoting the Basque language, Basque Autonomy Statute, art. 6(5), while it is within the general power of entering into inter-regional agreements in the case of Catalonia, Catalan Autonomy Statute, art. 27(4). No such international agreements had been entered into as of 1986.

819 Basque Autonomy Statute, art. 6; Catalan Autonomy Statute, art. 3. Other dual language autonomous regions are Valencia and the Baleares (Catalan), Navarra (Basque), and Galicia (Gallego).

820 1978 Spanish Const., art. 156(1).

821 *Id.*, art. 157.

822 *Cf.* J. Ferreiro Lapatza and F. Fernandez Rodriguez, "La financiación de las autonomías," in Olabarri, *supra* note 782, at 447–75.

823 Basque Autonomy Statute, arts. 41, 42; Law No. 12/1981 of 13 May 1981.

duties and fiscal monopolies such as tobacco and alcohol) by the foral communities, which then pass on to the central government and the autonomous region the proportion of taxes appropriate to pay for the services received by the community.

As the autonomous regions assume powers formerly exercised by the state, the latter has transferred property rights to the regions through laws or the autonomy statutes.[824] The central government does retain the power of eminent domain, however, which may be exercised for a national public purpose.[825]

OBSERVATIONS

Polls taken in 1982 indicate that implementation of the Basque and Catalan autonomy statutes up to that time had been generally viewed as successful.[826] While only 43% of the Basque population supported the current autonomy arrangements (compared to 42% who preferred more autonomy or independence), 65% believed that autonomy had improved life in the Basque country; only 15% thought that autonomy was a threat to Spanish unity. In Catalonia, 54% supported the current autonomy arrangements, 23% preferred greater autonomy or independence, and 20% were centralists opposed to autonomy; 23% thought that autonomy could pose a threat to Spanish unity.

It was the agreement of the major centrist and leftist political parties, the UCD and PSOE, that made development of the autonomous regimes possible. However, it is the political development of regional Basque and Catalan parties that perhaps gives a clearer indication of recent trends.

In the Basque country, the three major regional parties have been the traditional, relatively conservative Partido Nacionalista Vasco (PNV); the Marxist-oriented Euzkadiko Ezquerra (EE); and the political wing of the ETA, the Herri Batasuna party (HB). While the PNV maintained its position as the largest of the regional Basque parties and won regional elections in 1982 and 1984, it received only 20% of the votes in the June 1986 national elections, while HB received 16%. The Spanish Socialist Party (PSOE) received 44% of the vote.

Cooperation between the PNV and PSOE finally led to a split in the PNV in October 1986, as the former was attacked as insufficiently supportive of Basque nationalism. In the November 1986 Basque elections, seven parties obtained seats in the 81-member Basque parliament: the PSOE became the leading party with 19 seats; the PNV and its rival,

824 Basque Autonomy Statute, art. 43; Catalan Autonomy Statute, art. 43.
825 1978 Spanish Const., art. 33.
826 Linz, *supra* note 788, at 548, 591.

more radical wing which organized itself as "Eusko Alkartasuna" ("Basque Solidarity" or "EA") each received 17 seats; Herri Batasuna increased its representation to 14 seats; a party called "Basque Left" won 11 seats; and two small parties divided the remaining 4 seats.[827] More than 70% of the votes cast were for parties which support, in varying degrees, a greater degree of autonomy. After three months of negotiations, the Socialists and PNV formed a governing alliance.

As noted in other contexts, one sure way to political power seems to be to become increasingly radical and accuse those in power of being "too soft" on the nationalist issue. This is precisely what has happened in the Basque country, and it is perhaps impossible to tell whether increased radicalism is leading or following the feelings of the general public. In this increasingly fragmented atmosphere, it is not surprising that the terrorist activities of the ETA also have continued. A 1982 survey indicated that 38% of the Basque population considered ETA members to be patriots and idealists, while only 31% thought they were fools or criminals.[828] At the same time, however, only 8% of Basques said that they supported ETA, while 77% were opposed to its activities.[829] A 1986 poll confirmed that a majority of Basques consider the ETA harmful to Basque interests and increasingly isolated, although a strong minority continued to believe that the ETA can play a positive role.[830]

While ETA's attacks are often sensational and have included the assassination of prominent military and national security force members, the toll of approximately 600 killed since 1968 is in fact rather modest given the size of Spain and an estimated Spanish Basque population of 2.5 million.[831] Of the total of 1,330 people killed and injured in that period, 45% have been civilians.[832]

The ETA's goals, as articulated by Herri Batasuna, are independence and reunification with the three small Basque provinces across the French border. Their negotiating demands, which have become known as the "KAS alternative," include recognition of the Basques' right to self-determination (including independence); withdrawal of all national security forces and civil guards from Euzkadi; the integration

827 ABC (Madrid), 1 Dec. 1986, at 13.
828 Linz, *supra* note 788, at 614.
829 *Id.*
830 Cambio 16 (Madrid), 27 Oct. 1986. It is likely that anti-ETA feeling has grown since its June 1987 bombing of a shopping mall in Catalonia, in which dozens of people were killed.
831 Compare these figures with the over 2,000 deaths in Northern Ireland, which has approximately 60% of the population of the Basque country, during the same period.
832 ABC (Madrid), 6 Aug. 1986, at 40.

of Navarra into the Basque country;[833] a complete amnesty for all Basque "political prisoners"; and the legalization of all the separatist political parties.[834]

The ETA receives support from various countries, including provision of weapons and training, and traditionally enjoyed an effective right of asylum in France in return for an understanding that no terrorist activities would be undertaken in French territory. Since the assumption of power by a conservative government in France in 1986, however, French authorities have increased cooperation with Spanish authorities and have deported alleged terrorists back to Spain under summary procedures. While Spain has obviously welcomed these developments, even the moderate PNV has alleged that such French actions have "destabilized" the political situation and are "simply fueling the cycle of violence."[835]

Nevertheless, a series of setbacks to the ETA was no doubt partly responsible for a three-month-long truce called by the ETA in early 1989. During the truce, government officials met with ETA representatives in Algiers in order to create what the government called a "framework for dialogue." The ETA called off the truce in April 1989, citing a lack of willingness on the part of the government to negotiate a political solution.

The less volatile political situation in Catalonia is reflected both by the general absence of violence similar to that of the ETA and the lack of electoral support for the more extreme regional parties. The conservative coalition Convergéncia i Unió (CiU, an alliance between Convergéncia Democrática de Catalunya and Unió Democrática de Catalunya), has progressively increased its share of the vote since the late 1970s, while the leftist-separatist party, Esquerra Republicana de Catalunya (ERC), has as steadily lost support. In the 1986 legislative elections, CiU received just over one million votes, while ERC received 84,000,[836] although the latter improved its standing somewhat in the May 1988 general election. The primary political rivalry in Catalonia

833 It might be noted that this is envisaged in the constitution and Basque Autonomy Statute, but only if approved in a referendum in Navarra.

834 ABC (Madrid), 18 Aug. 1986, at 1. Reports in August 1987 indicated that the ETA might be willing to enter into negotiations with the government and had reduced the five "KAS alternative" demands to three: recognition of the right to self-determination, integration of Navarra, and amnesty. "El PNV presiona para que el Gobierno entable negociaciones politicas con ETA," *id.*, 24 Aug. 1987, at 15. However, no negotiations between the government and ETA had occurred as of the end of 1988.

835 "French Antiterror Role Fuels Backlash in Spain," Wash. Post, 27 Aug. 1986, at A22, col. 3.

836 ABC (Madrid), 24 June 1986, at 64.

seems to be between left and right, rather than reflecting divisions over regional or autonomy issues.

The greater discontent in the Basque country as compared to Catalonia (although there do exist small pro-independence movements in Catalonia, such as Terra Lliure and Moviment de Defensa de la Terra) has been explained by the fact that the former has long felt under much greater threat. While one can argue about whether state repression or ETA violence came first, there is no doubt that human rights were violated to a much greater degree in the Basque country, particularly since the late 1960s, than in Catalonia. "[T]he particularly intense nature of recent political repression [in the 1970s] in the Basque area . . . produced an unusually pronounced sense of alienation from the rest of Spain."[837]

Not only have Basque politics been more fragmented, but Basque culture also is more fragile: less than 40% of the Basque population speaks or understands Basque, while in Catalonia nearly 75% speak and over 90% understand Catalan.[838] There was no Basque equivalent to the nineteenth-century Catalan literary revival.

Immigration continues to threaten Basque identity, although there is also a large influx of non-Catalans to Catalonia. Basque industrial power has declined, and the Basque unemployment rate in late 1986 was estimated to be over 25%. Such an environment—"young unemployed people with few horizons, a terrible urbanism, an environment of fear and harassment, that sensation of anger and wrath, that feeling that nothing else exists"[839]—understandably provides a fertile recruiting ground for the ETA, and it may be surprising that its activities have not increased more dramatically in recent years.

While ETA violence and Basque dissatisfaction are the most visible chinks in the armor of autonomy, they are certainly not the only problems. The autonomous structures made possible by the 1978 constitution are only a decade old, and it is to be expected that adjustments will be required. The delimitation of central and autonomous finances appears to be particularly vague, and the competing pressures of well-to-do regions demanding a return of their contributions to the national economy versus poorer regions which expect a redistribution of wealth will be difficult for the Spanish government to balance. It is as yet too soon to judge whether Spain's recent adherence to the European Economic

837 Medhurst, *supra* note 783, at 8.

838 Linz, *supra* note 788, at 572.

839 Interview with Enrique Mugica, Epoca (Madrid), 11 Aug. 1986, at 34, col. 2 [trans.].

Community will have an impact on the politics of autonomy and whether that impact will be positive or negative.[840]

Contemporary Spain has been described as "a State on the threshold of developing into a federal state,"[841] and Basque demands may accelerate that development—although labels of "federal" or "autonomous" will not resolve outstanding conflicts. There can be no justification for continuing terrorist violence by the ETA, particularly given the democratic character of the Spanish central government and the autonomous regions. While the apparent support for greater autonomy on the part of most Basques deserves a response from Madrid, the mere fact that the ETA has access to automatic weapons and plastic explosives does not remove its members from the realm of "normal" criminal activity at this stage. Whatever justification for attacks on government officials and civilians may have been put forward under the Franco dictatorship, the present situation is qualitatively different.

Spain's experiment with decentralization and autonomy may be far from over, but it already deserves to be recognized as innovative and generally responsive to minority demands. However, the experiment also must be completed in an atmosphere of respect for human rights. The lack of success of the ETA may, in part, be attributable to relative restraint on the part of the government. The alleged involvement by the Spanish government and police in the murder of more than 20 Basque activists in France in 1983–87 and the subsequent cover-up are, if true, precisely the kind of activities that can turn terrorists into heroes.[842] Every effort must be made to ensure that the oft-proclaimed "state of law" in Spain and the resulting legitimacy of the post-Franco system are supported, so that the difficult political adjustments yet to come between autonomous and centralist demands can be achieved.

---

840 *Cf.*, e.g., Francese Morata i Tierra, *Autonomía regional i integracio europea* (Barcelona: Generalitat de Catalunya, 1987); P. Perez Tremps, *Comunidades Autonómas, Estado y Comunidad Europea* (Madrid: 1987); Alegria Borràs, "Les relations de Catalunya amb la CEE," in *Comentaris sobre l'Estatut d'Autonomía de Catalunya* (Barcelona: Institut d'Estudis Autonòmies, 1988).

841 Hofmann, *supra* note 791, at 136.

842 See, e.g., David A. Korn, "State Terrorism: A Spanish Watergate?" in Freedom at Issue (Nov.-Dec. 1988) at 15–20; Edward Cody, "Police Accused in Basque Killing Probe," Wash. Post, 22 Jan. 1989, at A30, col. 1.

Chapter 14
Sri Lanka

HISTORICAL BACKGROUND[843]

The present conflict between the Sinhalese and Tamil communities in Sri Lanka (known as Ceylon until 1972) has deep historical roots, dating back to the first century A.D. It is claimed that the Sinhala race was founded in Sri Lanka, an island of 66,000 square kilometers off the southeastern tip of the Indian sub-continent, in the fifth century B.C. by an exiled prince from northern India. The Sinhalese are said to be of Aryan origin, while the Tamils are Dravidians from southern India. Some have suggested, however, that there are no real racial differences between Sinhalese and Tamils, and that the only significant distinctions are cultural, linguistic, and religious.[844] The Tamils and Sinhalese displaced the indigenous Vedic peoples, of whom few remain today.

There are two separate Tamil communities in Sri Lanka: the "Jaffna" or "Ceylon Tamils" and the "Indian" or "estate Tamils." The precise date of arrival in Sri Lanka of the "Ceylon Tamils" is disputed, but there were Tamil incursions from South India at least by the first century A.D. Major Tamil invasions took place from 700 to 1300, culminating in the establishment of a Tamil kingdom in northern Ceylon, and Buddhist historical chronicles note frequent wars between Sinhalese and Tamil kings. The "Indian" or "estate" Tamils are much more recent arrivals, having been brought to Ceylon as indentured laborers by the British in the nineteenth and early twentieth centuries to work on the tea and rubber plantations in the central highlands of the country.

843 Material in this section, up to 1981, is largely drawn from Virginia Leary, *Ethnic Conflict and Violence in Sri Lanka* (Geneva: International Commission of Jurists, 1981) [hereinafter cited as "1981 ICJ Report"] at 7–35.

844 See, e.g., Committee for Rational Development, *Sri Lanka, The Ethnic Conflict* (New Delhi: Navrang, 1984) at 41–44.

The two Tamil communities have remained largely separate. The Ceylon Tamils are concentrated in the northern part of the island, particularly in the Jaffna peninsula, although substantial numbers live in Colombo, the eastern region, and some southern areas. The estate Tamils are found primarily in the hill country in central Sri Lanka. The Ceylon Tamils are, in general, a relatively prosperous and well educated group; the estate Tamils have lived and worked in conditions of misery and poverty. At present, Ceylon Tamils constitute approximately 12.6% of the population of Sri Lanka and estate Tamils 5.5%.[845]

The primary problem faced by the estate Tamils has been that their citizenship was revoked (or denied) by the Ceylon government immediately after independence in 1948, on the grounds that they were in fact Indian citizens who had been brought in by the British to work the tea estates, and that they should be repatriated. Under a 1964 agreement with India, Sri Lanka agreed to repatriate 60% of the estate Tamils and grant citizenship to the remaining 40%, although that agreement was only partially implemented. Subsequent discussions between Sri Lanka and India failed to resolve the situation, until Sri Lanka introduced legislation in early 1986 to grant citizenship to 94,000 stateless Tamils of Indian descent. India, in turn, agreed to grant Indian citizenship to 506,000 applicants then living in Sri Lanka, and these actions appear to have finally resolved this long-standing problem.

There has been little identity of interest or political cooperation between the Ceylon Tamils in the north and east and the Indian or estate Tamils in the central region of the country. The estate Tamils are represented in Parliament by the Ceylon Workers Congress (CWC), their labor union and political party. The CWC leader, S. Thondaman, served as Minister of Rural Affairs in the Jayewardene Cabinet; he is widely respected and has effectively promoted the interests of the estate Tamils. The CWC has not supported the demand of the Ceylon Tamils for a separate state, and this division of interests between estate and Ceylon Tamils continues to play a significant role in Sri Lankan politics. In 1981 and 1983 (and, to some extent, in 1977), however, the estate Tamils also were attacked during communal violence.

The Sinhalese population has historically considered the Tamils to be invaders, and Sinhalese legends frequently celebrate the triumph of Sinhalese kings over rival Tamil rulers. Such myths and symbols are important, and "history and historiography have created an emotive climate of ethnic animosity which often results in violence, preventing compromise and a negotiated settlement of ethnic differences."[846]

845 Sri Lanka, art. 9 CERD Report, UN Doc. CERD/C/101/Add.6 (1984) at 2.
846 1981 ICJ Report at 5.

Sri Lanka is one of the major centers of Buddhism, and the identification of the Buddhist religion with Sinhalese nationalism is a vital element in understanding the conflict in Sri Lanka. It is widely believed that Buddha himself consecrated Sri Lanka; a relic of the Buddha's tooth is enshrined in Kandy in central Sri Lanka. Buddhist temples abound, and the majority Sinhalese population is overwhelmingly Buddhist. The constitution provides that the Republic of Sri Lanka "shall give to Buddhism the foremost place" and that it is the duty of the state to protect and foster the Buddhist faith. The Tamil-speaking population is predominantly Hindu, and there is a substantial minority of Muslims and Christians, but freedom of religion per se (i.e., the right to participate in religious ceremonies or otherwise to practice one's religion) has not been an issue in the Tamil-Sinhalese conflict.

It is frequently noted that, although they are a majority within Sri Lanka, the Sinhalese are very sensitive to their position as a minority ethnic group within the Asian subcontinent. Tamils in Asia outnumber Sinhalese by five to one, and the largest concentration of Tamils is found in the southern Indian state of Tamil Nadu, only a few miles across the Palk Straits from Sri Lanka. The resulting Sinhalese insecurity almost certainly has contributed to ethnic tension in the island.

At the time of independence, the Ceylon Tamils held a disproportionately high percentage of jobs in the prestigious Ceylon civil service and places in the most important higher education faculties. This has been attributed variously to the English education provided by Christian missionary schools in Tamil areas, the relative difficulty of earning a living through agriculture in the more arid north (which encouraged Tamils to seek employment in government service and the professions), and the Tamils' consciousness of their minority status (which increased their interest in education, as opposed to political or family connections, as a means of advancement).

To combat the advantages enjoyed by Tamils after independence, the Sinhalese majority adopted two policies that are the source of much of the subsequent discontent of the Tamils: a "Sinhala only" language policy and a quota system based on race and residence, referred to as "standardization," for entrance to university. The Sinhalese considered these to be affirmative action measures designed to compensate for disadvantages suffered under colonialism; to Tamils, they were discriminatory provisions which placed their language in an inferior position and blocked their access to education. Adoption of Sinhala as the official language also made it more difficult for Tamils to enter government service.

After the disenfranchisement of the estate Tamils in 1948, Tamil voting power in the legislature fell from 33% to 20%. The two-thirds

Sinhalese majority in Parliament made it impossible for the Tamils to oppose Sinhalese policies effectively. The Sinhalese did propose a system of 57% Sinhalese representation to 43% for all other communities, but this was rejected by Tamil leaders, who insisted on an equal division.

The first constitution of Ceylon was drafted by an Englishman, Lord Soulbury, and adopted by a British Order in Council. Section 29 of the "Soulbury Constitution" provided:

No . . . law shall . . . make persons of any community or religion liable to disabilities or restrictions to which persons of other communities or religions are not made liable; or . . . confer on persons or any community or religion any privilege or advantage which is not conferred on persons of other communities or religions.

Despite this provision, the Indian Tamil plantation workers were deprived of their citizenship and disenfranchised; Sinhala was made the only official language; and a quota and standardization system was adopted which drastically curtailed Tamil access to higher education.

When the Sinhala Only Act was adopted, a proposal to include a clause on the use of Tamil was dropped because of pressure from extremist Buddhist groups. Tamil protests led in 1956 to the Bandaranaike-Chelvanayakam Pact, which provided for the use of Tamil in Tamil areas and would have established regional councils with powers in agriculture, education, and colonization schemes; it also included a promise by the government to reconsider the disenfranchisement of the Indian Tamils.[847] The pact was never implemented, again because of strong objections by some Buddhist elements, and in 1958 the first major outbreak of communal violence occurred.

As dissatisfaction with the British-drafted constitution grew during the 1950s and 1960s, the Tamil Federal Party emerged and supported a change from a unitary to a federal structure. This proposal was rejected by the Sinhalese majority, which considered it divisive.[848]

In 1970, the Sri Lanka Freedom Party (SLFP), a strong advocate of Sinhala-Buddhist dominance, came into power in coalition with two Marxist parties. In 1972, legal links with the United Kingdom were severed, and a new constitution established Sri Lanka as a republic. While Tamils had previously accepted Sinhala as the official language, their position changed when section 29 of the Soulbury Constitution (which prohibited discrimination) was dropped from the new constitu-

847 *Id.* at 9 n.5.

848 For a history of proposals for decentralization up to the district councils proposed in 1981, see K. M. de Silva, "Sri Lanka, The Dilemmas of Decentralisation" (Colombo: International Centre for Ethnic Studies, n.d.).

284 Searching for Solutions

tion; the Tamil Federal Party boycotted the Constituent Assembly because the assembly rejected a proposal that both Sinhala and Tamil be declared official languages. Instead, the "Sinhala only" policy was enshrined as a constitutional provision, and "the duty of the state to protect and foster Buddhism" was recognized.[849]

The other major Sinhalese party, the United National Party (UNP), opposed the 1972 constitution and, on coming to power in 1977, drafted the third and present constitution of Sri Lanka. It provides for a modified Presidential-parliamentary system somewhat similar to that of France.

During the SLFP's tenure from 1970 to 1977, the negative effects on Tamils of the "standardized" educational system became increasingly evident, and it also became increasingly difficult for Tamils to obtain government employment.[850] Faced with this perceived discrimination, Tamils began increasingly to support the concept of a separate state of "Tamil Eelam," which would include much of the northern and eastern areas of Sri Lanka.

A resolution adopted in 1976 by the Tamil United Liberation Front (TULF), which had replaced the Federal Party as the dominant Tamil political force, constitutes the first clear commitment of a Tamil party to a separate state of Eelam. Among the complaints cited as supporting a separate state were the deprivation of the estate Tamils' citizenship; the "Sinhala only" language policy; state-planned colonization of Tamil areas; the preeminent place granted to Buddhism under the constitution; denial of equal opportunity to Tamils in employment and education; the systematic isolation of Ceylon Tamils from mainstream Tamil culture in south India; permitting and encouraging Sinhalese violence against Tamils; terrorizing, torturing, and imprisoning Tamil youth; and imposing an unacceptable constitution on the Tamil population.

The resolution also referred to the failure of various other Tamil political parties to win rights through negotiation with successive Sinhalese governments. The resolution concluded with the statement that

[t]he Convention resolves that the restoration and reconstitution of the Free, Sovereign, Secular, Socialist State of TAMIL EELAM based on the right of

849 Buddhist influence on language policy and Sri Lankan nationalism is described in K. M. de Silva, "Nationalism and the State in Sri Lanka," paper presented to the Asian Regional Workshop on Ethnic Minorities in Buddhist Polities (Colombo: International Centre for Ethnic Studies, 1985).

850 See, e.g., K. M. de Silva, "University Admissions and Ethnic Tension in Sri Lanka: 1977–82"; Chandra Richard de Silva, "Sinhala-Tamil Relations and Education in Sri Lanka: The University Admissions Issue—The First Phase, 1971–7"; and S.W.R. de A. Samarasinghe, "Ethnic Representation in Central Government Employment and Sinhala-Tamil Relations in Sri Lanka: 1948–81," in Robert B. Goldmann and A. Jeyaratnam Wilson, *From Independence to Statehood* (London: Frances Pinter, 1984).

self-determination inherent to every nation has become inevitable in order to safeguard the very existence of the Tamil nation in this country.

In the 1977 elections, the TULF received a strong majority in the over-whelmingly Tamil north and a simple majority in the east, demonstrating widespread support for the concept of separation among the Ceylon Tamils.

The theoretical basis for Tamil self-determination is the claim that the sovereignty of the Tamil nation, which existed in 1621 at the time of the Portuguese conquest, reverted to the Tamil community when legal ties with the United Kingdom were severed in 1972. Successive colonial powers administered the Tamil territory separately from the rest of the country until 1833, when the British began administering the island as a common unit. Tamils maintain that they have never given up their sovereignty, as they boycotted the Constituent Assembly which drafted the 1972 constitution, and that the Sinhala nation has never obtained sovereignty over them by conquest or consent.

THE GROWTH OF COMMUNAL VIOLENCE

Nearly 20 years of relative calm followed the May 1958 communal vio-lence in which hundreds of persons, primarily Tamils, were killed. Ten-sions between Tamils and Sinhalese increased during the SLFP rule of Mrs. Bandaranaike from 1970 to 1977, and a major outbreak of violence occurred in August 1977, only a few months after the election of the Jayewardene-led UNP government. According to a government-appointed commission of inquiry (the Sansoni Commission), the violence was a reaction to the shooting of two policemen in the north by Tamil youths, inflammatory speeches by Tamil leaders, and Tamil separa-tism.[851] The Sansoni report details widespread killings, assaults, rapes, and damage to Hindu temples in almost every area of the island during the August-September 1977 events, and over 1,000 people were killed.

The third major outbreak of communal violence occurred in August 1981. Mutual fear and anger had developed as terrorist attacks against police in the north increased, accompanied or followed by the incom-municado detention of Tamil youths and arson and looting by police in Jaffna. The burning by police forces of the Jaffna Public Library, an important Tamil cultural center, was particularly resented and is still referred to as an early example of the lawlessness of the security forces. In the central highlands, subsequent incidents left at least ten estate Tamils dead, numerous Tamil shops and businesses burned, and more than 5,000 estate Tamil refugees. The attacks against the estate Tamils

851 1981 ICJ Report at 20 n.11.

had the effect of internationalizing the conflict, since Indian passport holders were among those attacked.

Unlike the violence in 1958 and 1977, the 1981 attacks appear to have been, in part, the work of organized gangs. It also was claimed that security forces did not intervene to prevent attacks until the declaration of a state of emergency, many days after the attacks began.

On 24 July 1983, the day after thirteen soldiers were killed by Tamil guerrillas in an ambush in north Jaffna, the most serious communal violence to date erupted.[852]

For day after day, Tamils . . . were beaten, hacked or burned to death in the streets, on buses, and on trains, not only in Colombo but in many other parts of the Island. . . . Yet the security forces seemed either unwilling or unable to stop it - indeed, in Jaffna and Trincomalee, some members of the armed forces themselves joined in the fray, claiming an admitted 51 lives. Seen from the Tamil point of view, either the Government had lost control of the situation, or it was deliberately standing by while they were being taught a lesson.[853]

The government acknowledged that the communal killings were pre-planned and well organised. The Minister of State . . . said in a TV broadcast on 29 July 1983: "[A]lthough riots took place, burnings of houses and shops took place in widely different parts of the city (Colombo) and its suburbs, there was a distinct method in every case. The rioters. . . . knew exactly where to go. They didn't search. They looked at a piece of paper, looked at a number and there they were. Therefore, there was pre-planning . . . these names were taken from the Register of Electors, from the Parliamentary Voters Lists, and were prepared very much in advance."[854]

Two massacres of Tamil prisoners held in Walikade jail occurred on 25 and 27 July; no prison officials or inmates were ever charged in connection with the deaths.

The President of Sri Lanka, J.R. Jayewardene, did not appear on national television until the fifth day of the riots. He expressed no sympathy for the victims (apart from a statement that the violence was "very, very distressing"), instead concluding that "[b]ecause of this violence by the [Tamil] terrorists, the Sinhalese people themselves have reacted."[855] He declared that "the government has now decided that

---

852 For a Sinhalese view of the significance of the army deaths, "which will surely go down into the annals of history of the Sri Lanka Army," see T.D.S.A. Dissanayaka, *The Agony of Sri Lanka* (Colombo: Swastika Press, 1983) at 69–73.

853 Paul Sieghart, *Sri Lanka, A Mounting Tragedy of Errors* (London: International Commission of Jurists and Justice, 1984) at 19.

854 International Alert, *Emergency Sri Lanka 1986* (London: International Alert, n.d.) at 25.

855 Text of the President's address quoted in "Laws next week to ban separatism, separatists," Daily News (Colombo), 29 July 1983, at 1.

the time has come to accede to the clamour and the national respect of the Sinhala people that we do not allow the movement for division to grow any more" and announced legislation that would ban any advocacy of separatism.[856]

Soon thereafter, the Sixth Amendment to the constitution was adopted, providing that public office could be held only by persons who took an oath not to support separatism. Since the TULF platform adopted in 1977 included a pledge of support for a separate state of Eelam, the TULF members of Parliament refused to take the oath and thereby lost their seats. Most of the TULF leaders fled to Madras, India, after the riots.

The government has admitted that nearly 400 were killed in the July 1983 riots, but Tamil sources allege as many as 1,500 deaths. Tens of thousands of primarily Tamil refugees were displaced, and there were millions of rupees worth of damage to Tamil businesses and the Sri Lankan economy as a whole.

Tamil militant or guerrilla groups[857] have existed since the mid–1970s, when they grew primarily out of the dissatisfaction of young Tamils with the moderate, established Tamil leadership (such as that of the TULF) in face of what was viewed as increasing human rights violations by the security forces and police.[858] As noted above, killings of

856 *Id.*

857 Tamils normally refer to the various armed Tamil groups and their political leaders as "militants," while the government prefers the term "terrorists." As most of the groups claim to have armed men under their command, "guerrillas" is perhaps the best and most neutral term, although there has been no attempt to make usage in this chapter absolutely consistent. The term "terrorist" certainly can be applied accurately to those who deliberately murder innocent, randomly selected civilians, whatever the ethnic or political identification of the killers.

858 International Alert, a London-based nongovernmental organization, has stated that there are at least 23 armed Tamil groups, although this figure must include those whose existence is known only to close family and friends. The positions of some of these groups are discussed below, and the most important at the time of the 1987 Indo-Sri Lanka Agreement were probably the Liberation Tigers of Tamil Eelam (LTTE), whose base is in the Jaffna Peninsula, and the Eelam Revolutionary Organization [of Students] (EROS), whose strength lies primarily in the east. Other major guerrilla or "militant" groups, which were to a great extent eliminated by the LTTE and army, include the People's Liberation Organization of Tamil Eelam (PLOTE), Tamil Eelam Liberation Organization (TELO), and Eelam People's Revolutionary Liberation Front (EPRLF). Although categorization is difficult, LTTE and TELO are primarily Tamil nationalist, while the others are essentially Marxist in orientation. See generally *Emergency Sri Lanka 1986, supra* note 854, at 26–28; Kumar David, "Sri Lanka After Two Years of Bloodshed What Next?" *Asian Exchange* (Hong Kong)(joint vol. III(4) & IV(1), 1985) at 44–48; and various articles in the Sri Lankan newspaper *The Island* (Colombo), especially interviews with the leaders of LTTE, PLOTE, ERPLF, and EROS, 17 Aug. 1986, and "Tamil militancy in the melting pot," 7 Sept. 1986.

police and security force members, presumably by Tamil guerrillas, sparked (or provided the excuse for) the 1981 and 1983 riots.

The guerrillas' targets were almost exclusively police and army members and Sinhalese or moderate Tamil politicians until late 1984. In attacks which have passed into the collective Sri Lankan memory, hundreds of Sinhalese civilians have since been killed by Tamil terrorists in massacres such as those at the Kent and Dollar farms in November 1984 and in Anuradhapura (a city holy to Buddhists) in May 1985; in the bombing of an Air Lanka jet in Colombo in May 1986; in an attack on three buses in the northeast in April 1987; and in a bomb explosion in Colombo's main bus station only a few days later. Internecine and communal killings, especially by the Liberation Tigers of Tamil Eelam (LTTE or Tigers), continued even after the Indo-Sri Lanka peace agreement of July 1987 and there have been major battles between Indian armed forces and LTTE guerrillas.

The other major components of the spiral of escalating violence have been killings by the Sri Lankan security forces, which are overwhelmingly Sinhalese; mass arrests of hundreds of Tamil youths at a time; and the indefinite detention under emergency laws (which are often ignored) of thousands of suspected Tamil terrorists.[859] Killings by security forces often occur in apparent retaliation for killings of Sinhalese civilians, as do the mass arrests; not a single member of the Sri Lankan security forces had been charged with a crime arising out of such incidents through 1987 (although some were transferred or dismissed from military service). Particularly since 1986, reports have been received that large numbers of civilians have been killed during military operations; since 1987, these reports have included killings by the Indian Peacekeeping Force in Sri Lanka.

Human rights violations have been facilitated by the Prevention of Terrorism (Temporary Provisions) Act, No. 48 of 1979 ["PTA"], which has been described by a prominent English jurist as "an ugly blot on

---

859 Extensive documentation on human rights violations by Sri Lankan forces has been prepared by pro-Tamil groups and independent human rights organizations. See generally Kumar Rupesinghe and Berth Verstappen, *Ethnic Conflict and Human Rights in Sri Lanka: An Annotated Bibliography* (Seven Oaks, England: Butterworth, 1988); Amnesty International, *"Disappearances" in Sri Lanka* (London: Amnesty International, 1986); *id.*, *Amnesty International Report 1986* (London: Amnesty International, 1986) at 256–60; *Amnesty International Report 1988 supra* note 563, at 181–83; P. Raja Nayagam, *Sri Lanka* (London: Centre for Human Rights Documentation and Research, 1986); U.S. State Dept., *Country Reports on Human Rights Practices for 1987* (Washington: Government Printing Office, 1988) at 1300–1312; Tor Skalnes and Jan Egeland (eds.), *Human Rights in Developing Countries 1986* (Oslo: Norwegian Univ. Press, 1986) at 226–59; Sieghart, *supra* note 853; 1981 ICJ Report.

the statute book of any civilised country."[860] The PTA is now a permanent, not temporary, statute, and under its provisions thousands of Tamil young men have been detained and held for extensive periods without trial, often incommunicado. They are frequently detained indiscriminately, following guerrilla or terrorist attacks or during army operations. During the army's assault on the Jaffna peninsula in May 1987, for example, army officials "acknowledged that in their sweep, they had taken 3,500 Tamil youths into custody, virtually the entire young male population of the [20-square-mile] sector that was the target of the offensive."[861] The PTA has been extensively criticized by human rights groups and has promoted a sense of physical insecurity and fear among the Tamil population in the north and east.[862]

Estimates of the number of people who have been killed from 1983 to 1988 as a direct result of the conflict vary widely, but 12,000 would not seem to be an exaggeration.[863] While most of the deaths have occurred in the Tamil areas in the north and east of the country, no part of the population has remained unaffected, and assassinations by militant Sinhalese in the southern part of the country increased dramatically following the July 1987 Indo-Sri Lankan Agreement.

POST-1983 ATTEMPTS TO REACH A NEGOTIATED SETTLEMENT

Sri Lanka lies just 29 miles off India's southern coast, and political leaders in Tamil Nadu in the south of India (whose population is of the same ethnic origin and religion as Sri Lankan Tamils) have continually pressured the central government in India to protest against the treatment of the Tamils in Sri Lanka. In addition, more than 125,000 Tamil refugees from Sri Lanka have fled to Tamil Nadu since 1983, many of whom are maintained by the Indian government at substantial cost. As noted above, the situation of the "Indian" or estate Tamils has been a serious irritant in relations between Sri Lanka and India for many years.

Tamil guerrilla groups maintained bases in Tamil Nadu from which they were able to carry out attacks in the north of Sri Lanka. Diplomatic relations between India and Sri Lanka were seriously strained over the former's willingness to let these militant groups have refuge and sanctuary on its territory, but the support of the Tamil Nadu population for the Sri Lankan Tamils made it politically inexpedient for the central

860 Sieghart, *supra* note 853, at 33–34.
861 "Indian Flotilla Is Turned Back By Sri Lankan Naval Vessels," N. Y. Times, 4 June 1987, at A10, col. 1.
862 See sources cited *supra* note 859.
863 The U.S. Dept. of State notes that estimates of deaths for 1987 alone range from 2,800 to 4,200. *Country Reports for 1987*, *supra* note 859 , at 1301–02.

government to evict them. However, the militants were also a disturbing factor in Tamil Nadu, through internecine fighting and alleged robbery and extortion. Thus, domestic politics in Tamil Nadu and India's geo-political and strategic interests in the Indian Ocean area rendered it virtually impossible for India to remain aloof from events in Sri Lanka.[864]

Soon after the 1983 riots, Indira Gandhi offered the "good offices" of India to assist in resolving the ethnic problem. Fearing more direct military intervention by India, the Sri Lankan government was willing to grant such a role to its more powerful neighbor. Eventually, Sri Lankan President Jayewardene went to New Delhi for discussions with Mrs. Gandhi.

In late 1983, a short document known as "Annexure C" was for-mulated, following discussions among the Sri Lankan and Indian gov-ernments and the TULF. It provided for a substantial devolution of powers to regional councils, rather than the district councils which had been proposed by Sri Lanka in 1979 and 1980. In January 1984, President Jayewardene presented this proposal for regional councils to an "All Party" Conference, at which the most important opposition party, the Sri Lanka Freedom Party (SLFP), was not represented. Its leader, Mrs. Bandaranaike, refused to attend, since she had been deprived of her civic rights by the Jayewardene government after the latter's election in 1977. The Supreme Council of Buddhist clergy did participate, although it is not a political party.

Sinhalese participants in the conference declared their opposition to any form of regional autonomy and claimed that India had forced the Sri Lankan government to accept Annexure C. According to Tamil sources, President Jayewardene made no serious efforts to have An-nexure C accepted, and it was thus dead in the water. The President then proposed increased coordination between districts and a second chamber of Parliament from which district or provincial ministers could be appointed. The TULF rejected these proposals, stating that they did not offer meaningful devolution; India also made it clear that the pro-posals were not acceptable.

The framework of the All Party Conference lasted until the end of 1984, when it was ended by the President, who blamed the TULF for its failure. The TULF insisted that it was interested in continuing ne-gotiations and had not been responsible for the break-up of the Con-ference. In December 1984, President Jayewardene fired his notoriously anti-Tamil Minister of Industry, Cyril Matthew, for his opposition to the proposals —an action many found long overdue.

Rajiv Gandhi became Prime Minister of India in October 1984,

---

864 *Cf.*, e.g., Victor Gunewardena, "Impact of Internal Ethnic Conflicts on the Region: Sri Lanka Case," 8 Marga Q. J. 69 (1986).

following his mother's assassination, and he appeared to be somewhat less sympathetic to Tamil militant demands and more understanding of the Sri Lankan government (perhaps reflecting the deteriorating situation in India's Punjab). Indira Gandhi had felt closer to Mrs. Bandaranaike's socialism than to Jayewardene's capitalism; she also was a personal friend of Mrs. Bandaranaike and resented the decision by the Jayewardene government to deprive Bandaranaike of her civic rights.

The inability or unwillingness of the government to protect Tamils in 1983 encouraged new recruits to join the Tamil militants, and violent attacks by guerrilla groups accelerated. As noted above, direct attacks against Sinhalese civilians by Tamil terrorists began in late 1984. The Tamil guerrillas claimed that the moderate TULF no longer represented the Tamils in the north, and, given the increasing armed attacks by these groups, it soon became clear that a peaceful settlement could not be reached without their participation. In June 1985, through the "mediation and good offices" of India, the Sri Lankan government and the Tamil militant groups agreed to a ceasefire as a preliminary to peace talks.

These talks were held in Thimpu, the capital of Bhutan, in July and August 1985. Thirteen representatives of the Sri Lankan government, led by the President's brother, met with a thirteen-member Tamil delegation consisting of three representatives of the TULF and two representatives from each of the five major Tamil guerrilla groups. Five representatives of the Indian government also attended the talks. The five Tamil militant groups objected to use of the term "Tamil political leadership" to describe the TULF and the term "militants" or "terrorists" to describe their organizations. They claimed that they were "authentic political organizations representing the aspirations of our people."[865] In any event, the Thimpu talks represented the only occasion on which the Sri Lankan government engaged in direct formal negotiations with the "terrorists", prior to negotiations over a cease-fire between the new Premadasa government and the LTTE in mid-1989.

In a joint presentation, the Tamil representatives stated that any meaningful solution to the Tamil question must be based on four basic principles: 1) recognition of the Tamils of Sri Lanka as a nation; 2) recognition of a Tamil homeland in Sri Lanka; 3) recognition of the Tamils' right to self-determination; and 4) recognition of the right to citizenship and the fundamental rights of all Tamils who look upon Sri Lanka as their country (i.e., the enfranchisement of the estate Tamils).

The Sri Lankan government refused to accept any of the Tamils'

---

865 Joint Report dated 18th June 1985, submitted to the authorized representative of the government of India by the United Front of Liberation Organizations, consisting of EPRLF, EROS, LTTE, and TELO, on the Proposals for Ceasefire, reproduced in *At Thimpu* (Cambridge, UK: Tamil International Working Group, 1985) at 6.

four principles. At the second session of the Thimpu talks, it presented what it called "new proposals," but these were rejected by the Tamil delegation as offering nothing beyond proposals which had been rejected by the TULF at the All Party Conference a year earlier.

The government's refusal to accept the Tamils' basic principles and the military excesses by the Sri Lankan army during the ceasefire (in particular, the killing of 200 Tamil civilians in Vavuniya in August 1985) brought the talks to an end. The Tamil groups announced that they were terminating their participation because of this violation of the ceasefire agreement, which had been a pre-condition for the Thimpu talks. The Tamil walk-out was apparently opposed by the Indian delegation, while the militants were offended by India's failure to protest against the massacres which had just occurred in Vavuniya. No direct negotiations between representatives of the Sri Lankan government and the militants had occurred from 1985 to 1989, but diplomatic activity remained intense, with talks among the Sri Lankan government, the Indian government and the TULF, and between the Indian government and the Tamil militant groups.

Between the end of the Thimpu talks in August 1985 and the Indo-Sri Lanka Agreement of July 1987, violence in Sri Lanka increased substantially. In September 1985, Tamil guerrillas murdered two former TULF members of Parliament in Jaffna, underscoring their rejection of moderate Tamil leadership. In May 1986, an Air Lanka jet ready to depart for the Maldives was blown up on the tarmac at Colombo's Katunayake airport, killing sixteen persons and injuring twenty. A few days later, a bomb exploded in the Central Telegraph Office in Colombo, killing fourteen and injuring 100.

During this same period, fighting broke out in Jaffna between the LTTE and other guerilla groups. The LTTE emerged as the dominant group, and, by mid–1986, the Tigers virtually controlled the Jaffna peninsula. Sri Lankan army forces remained generally confined to barracks in the region.

THE JUNE 1986 PROPOSALS

In June 1986, President Jayewardene announced a proposal to devolve powers to new Provincial Councils, which offered significantly greater decentralization than earlier proposals.[866] The military escalation by Tamil guerrillas, the failure of the government's "military solution,"

---

866 The proposals may be found in the Statement by the President to the Political Parties' Conference as Chairman of the Conference on the Proposals for the Devolution of Power to Provincial Councils Announced on Wednesday, 25th June, 1986 (Colombo: Dept. of Gov't Printing, 1986).

and continued pressure from India, no doubt contributed to this formulation of new proposals for local devolution. The announcement also was made one day before a meeting in Paris of the consortium of aid donors to Sri Lanka.[867]

The most important influence was clearly that of the Indian government. The Indian High Commissioner in Sri Lanka issued a statement in connection with the 39th Indian Independence Day, 15 August 1986, in which, after referring to meetings of President Jayewardene and Prime Minister Rajiv Gandhi in the Bahamas and in Dacca and to contacts between ministers of both countries, he stated:

The focus of attention in these contacts naturally was the ethnic problem of Sri Lanka and our shared anxiety to achieve a negotiated solution to it. Discussions ... in May this year and subsequent exchanges of views and suggestions have resulted in the Sri Lankan Government putting forward a package of proposals under the guidance of President Jayewardene which provides a sufficient and practical basis to devise a constitutional framework for Sri Lanka, responsive to the needs and aspirations of all Sri Lankan citizens, regardless of their ethnic, religious or linguistic affinities or identities.[868]

Thus, the Indian government signified that it considered the new proposals as an acceptable basis for a resolution of the conflict.

Several months after the announcement of the Jayewardene proposal for Provincial Councils, the Indian government provided tangible evidence of its ability to exert pressure on the Tamil guerrilla groups. In early November 1986, police raided the houses of Sri Lankan Tamil militants in Tamil Nadu, arresting hundreds and seizing large quantities of arms, in what was believed to be the first major crackdown against Tamil rebel groups in Tamil Nadu.

The proposals made by President Jayewardene in June 1986 do not recognize the principles put forward by the Tamil delegation at Thimpu. Instead, they are based on 1) maintenance of the unity, integrity, and sovereignty of Sri Lanka; 2) maintenance of the unitary character of the Sri Lankan constitution; and 3) the principle of devolution of powers to Provincial Councils within the framework of an amended constitution.

Adoption of a federal system of government based on linguistic units as in the Indian Constitution was not proposed, nor was provision made for any substantial devolution of power to the provinces, although the term "devolution" is used in the proposals. Nevertheless, most observers believed that the proposals could offer a basis for an eventual

867 The Economist, 21 June 1986. A number of human rights organizations had been attempting—generally unsuccessfully—to persuade Western donors to cut off aid to Sri Lanka until a solution was found to the ethnic problem.
868 Quoted in Saturday Review (Sri Lanka), 23 Aug. 1986.

settlement, primarily because of the Indian government's support and a perception that they might have been the maximum which could be obtained from any Sinhalese government without engendering a violent Sinhalese backlash.

The proposals maintained existing provincial and district boundaries and provided for delegation of powers from the central government to the provinces (as opposed to most earlier proposals, which would have devolved powers only to the district council level). A separate "Authority" would govern the important port of Trincomalee and its environs, outside the jurisdiction of any other local government subdivision.

The powers delegated could be withdrawn or added to by a two-thirds majority of the Parliament, after consultation with the provincial council or councils concerned. Since Tamils constitute less than a one-third minority in the country, the provisions thus could be changed and any delegated powers reclaimed without the consent of the Tamil minority.

Members of the Provincial Councils would be elected, with the governor of the province to be appointed by the President. The governor, in turn, would appoint as Chief Minister of the Provincial Council the member "who in his opinion is most likely to command the confidence of the Council."

The central government retained exclusive power in most major areas of government, including defense; internal security; foreign affairs; law and order, subject to whatever police powers may be devolved to the provincial or district councils; justice, "in so far as it relates to the Judiciary and the Courts Structure"; finance, "in relation to National Revenue, Monetary Policy and External Resources"; natural resources; elections at all levels; "National Policy on all subjects and functions"; and "[a]ll subjects and functions not otherwise specifically assigned."

The limited legislative competence of the provincial councils would extend to:

1) Internal law and order, excluding national defence, national security, and the use of any armed forces or other forces under control of the Sri Lankan government in aid of the civil power. The provinces would not have independent police forces, although there would be a separate police division for each province, under the overall control and direction of the Inspector General of the Police of the National Division. The highest officer in each province was to be appointed by the national Inspector General of Police, with the concurrence of the Chief Minister of the Province; if there were no agreement, the President would make the appointment.

2) Land settlement. The criteria for land settlement and irrigation

schemes within the Provincial Councils were not specifically addressed, but it was suggested that "for such schemes the ethnic proportions within the Province would be the best applicable principle." Hence, the proposals did not commit the government to discontinue settling Sinhalese in traditional Tamil areas, a long-standing Tamil grievance, although they represented an advance over criteria based on national rather than regional proportionality.

3) Agriculture and industry. Major subjects concerning agriculture, such as minimum prices, subsidies, inter-district and provincial coordination, national targets, and agricultural research, were reserved to the central government, as was the formulation of national policies of industrial development. State-owned industries would not be transferred to the provinces.

4) Education and culture. The provinces would have "substantial powers" over culture and education up to the secondary level, and they would also have the right to establish and manage private universities without state funds. Public university education would remain in the hands of the central government. National education policy was to be "non-discriminatory," which may have addressed one of the main problems leading to unrest among Tamil youth, i.e., discrimination in higher education through the process of "standardization." However, it was not clear whether this policy referred to access to higher education as well as to primary and secondary education.

5) Finances. The Provincial Councils would have the power to levy local taxes, but their nature would be determined by Parliament. They also could take out local loans, while foreign loans or grants would require approval by the Sri Lankan government. The central government would apportion financial resources (grants, allocations, subventions) to the provinces on recommendations of a committee appointed by the President.

If the President believed that the affairs of any Provincial Council were not being carried on in accordance with the provisions of the Constitution,

he may take such measures or pass such orders as he may deem fit to ensure that they are so carried on, including an order for the dissolution of the Council and for taking such consequential measures as he may deem necessary. Every such order . . . shall be operative for a period of six months at a time but not exceeding one year in all provided however, that Parliament approves of such action within two months of making of the order of dissolution.[869]

The June 1986 proposals were widely perceived as the most far-reaching and significant effort by the Jayewardene government to settle

869 *Id.*, para. 14.

the conflict, and they were the basis of the Indo-Sri Lanka accord a year later. While no Tamil group endorsed the proposals at the time, moderates seemed willing to use them as a foundation for further negotiations.

However, outright opposition to the proposals immediately surfaced, from Mrs. Bandaranaike, leader of the Sri Lankan Freedom Party, from the Senior Buddhist Council, and within the President's own party, the UNP. On the other hand, the small party led by Mrs. Bandaranaike's son-in-law, movie star Vijaya Kumaranatunga, adopted a moderate stance and called for repeal of the Prevention of Terrorism Act and the Sixth Amendment to the constitution (which prohibits advocacy of separatism). Kumaranatunga was assassinated in February 1988.

At least one Sinhalese voice was heard urging a federal solution. Writing in *The Island*, R.N.B. Senanayake criticized the basic concept of the Jayewardene proposals and urged a federal solution rather than decentralization. He suggested autonomy for a Tamil linguistic unit within the Sri Lankan state, with boundaries to be negotiated and with the militants included in the negotiations. He suggested that the Muslims in the Eastern Province should also be involved in the discussions relating to the boundaries of the Province.

It is to these two matters that negotiations should have been directed. Instead we find an elaborate scheme of Provincial Councils being discussed. We seem to be mistaking the wood for the trees. . . . If the Tamil militants agree to join the Sri Lankan state, then it has to be a federal relationship. A division of powers is necessarily a federal solution. Nothing is gained by calling it by other names. . . . Why mix the demand for an autonomous Tamil area with the need for administrative devolution in the rest of the country?[870]

Tamil demands

The primary reason for LTTE rejection of the June 1986 proposals was the Tamil claim to a "homeland," which implied a merger of the Northern and Eastern provinces if some form of provincial councils are established. These claims respond to several fundamental Tamil concerns, including their assertion of the right to self-determination (even within the context of a united Sri Lanka); the perceived need for a territorial sanctuary in order to guarantee their physical safety; and a desire for the greater political and economic power which would accrue to a larger Tamil-dominated province. "The slogan of 'traditional homelands' whatever its objective truth, is first and foremost a political claim meant to

---

870 The Island (Colombo), 24 Sept. 1986.

ensure the security of the Tamils."[871] Recognition of a Tamil homeland also would constitute recognition and acceptance of a distinct Tamil identity within Sri Lanka, an acceptance which many Tamils believe has been rejected by the Sinhalese majority at least since 1956.

The Tamils claim that the area included in the present Northern and Eastern provinces is geographically contiguous and demographically homogeneous, and that the British decision to divide the north and east should not be maintained.[872] At the time of Ceylonese independence in 1948, approximately 90% of the population of the eastern province was Tamil-speaking (this figure includes ethnic Tamils and Tamil-speaking "Moors" or Muslims). While the Sinhala population in the eastern province constituted approximately 25% in 1981, Tamils contend that this is due to state-encouraged settlement on what were traditionally Tamil lands.[873] The 1972 and 1978 Sri Lankan constitutions provide that Tamil shall be the language of administration and the courts in the Northern and Eastern Provinces.

The demand for a Tamil homeland in the north and east is regarded by most Sinhalese as a direct attack on the unity of the Sri Lankan state.

This certainly and implicitly calls for the truncation of the Republic's own territorial integrity as defined by Article 5 of the Constitution. This should not be entertained, let alone considered. We reject this demand as being a violation of the fundamental rights and freedoms of all citizens of Sri Lanka, as its implication is that there is to be a total or partial embargo placed against the settlement of people of other ethnic communities in the areas perceived by the Tamils as their Homeland. We believe that it is the right and freedom of every citizen of Sri Lanka, irrespective of the racial or religious group to which he/she belongs, to settle in any part of Sri Lanka, which has been the homeland of all ethnic communities from a long way back.[874]

[T]here are no "Tamil areas" and "Sinhalese areas" in Sri Lanka. Not to recognise this principle is to give respectability to the principle of apartheid, and the "Tamil homelands" myth of the Tamil racists. . . . The myth of the "Tamil homeland" is one of the persistent myths propagated by the Tamils and given respectability in publications of their fellow travellers. . . . It can be shown

871 S. J. Tambiah, *Sri Lanka: Ethnic Fratricide and the Dismantling of Democracy* (Chicago: Univ. of Chicago Press, 1986) at 80.

872 See generally letter from leaders of the Tamil United Liberation Front to Prime Minister Rajiv Gandhi, 14 Dec. 1986 (on file with author).

873 On similar grounds, Tamils have objected to proposals for the allocation of new land allotments under the Mahaweli development project (a major dam project located in the north of the country) in accordance with national ethnic ratios of approximately 75% Sinhalese and 25% minorities.

874 Letter to Mr. Ernie Epp, M.P., House of Commons, Canada, from Asoka Weerasinghe, on behalf of Project Peace, 18 Feb. 1986. Also see Asoka Weerasinghe, "The Claim for 'Tamil Homelands' in Sri Lanka," in Asoka Yap (ed.), *Sri Lanka Fact Sheet* (Chalk River (Ontario), Canada: Project Peace, 1986).

that there is no basis in history, demography, economics or international law and usage for this homeland. The northern and eastern provinces of Sri Lanka were carved out in 1876 by the British for administrative convenience and has [sic] nothing to do with a "homeland" for Tamils or anybody else.[875]

The Sinhalese also point out that the claimed Tamil homeland covers one-third of the island and includes 60% of the island's coastline, while Tamils, half of whom live outside the claimed homeland, constitute only 18% percent of the total population of the country.[876] Even according to the Tamils' own figures, the Eastern province is divided among three substantial minorities: ethnic Tamils constitute approximately 42%, Tamil-speaking Muslims 32%, and Sinhalese 25%. Historically, Muslims have been more disposed to play off the two major Sinhalese parties against one another in exchange for Muslim electoral support, despite their linguistic affinity with the Tamils. The Tamils naturally assert that language, rather than religion or ethnicity, is the most important factor.

THE INDO-SRI LANKA AGREEMENT OF 29 JULY 1987

The LTTE's rejection of negotiations followed attempts to consolidate its control over the Jaffna peninsula. The militants reportedly set up their own postal service and television station, established a mini-zoo in Nallur with a view to collecting funds, and even had a weapons factory.[877] In mid-December 1986, fighting once again broke out in Jaffna between the LTTE and the EPRLF. The former emerged victorious, and it was announced that an LTTE civil administration—a first step to a unilateral declaration of independence—would be established in Jaffna on 1 January 1987.

The continued refusal of the guerrillas to return to the negotiating table and the announcement by the LTTE that they intended to inaugurate a civil administration in the Jaffna peninsula (which was largely under their military control), galvanized the Sri Lankan government and military into more direct action. On 2 January 1987, the government announced a ban on all fuel shipments to the north; as a result, the threatened LTTE administration was never put into place. A military offensive was launched by the government in spring 1987, following major attacks on Sinhalese civilians by Tamil guerrillas and the guer-

875 Queensland Association for Sri Lankan Unity, *An Analysis of the "Alert International" Report on Sri Lanka* (Yeronga, Australia: Queensland Association for Sri Lankan Unity, Factsheets on Sri Lanka No. 22, 1986) at 18.

876 Compare Nicaraguan objections to the lands claimed by the Miskito population of the Atlantic Coast; *cf.* chap. 10.

877 The Island (Colombo), 8 Sept. 1986; "Tigers make planes and bombs, run farms," Daily News (Colombo), 27 Jan. 1987, at 1, col. 3.

rillas' refusal to respond to government offers for a series of ten-day ceasefires, each of which was, in theory, to be followed by a staged renewal of negotiations. In April 1987, Tamil guerrillas killed over 200 people in separate incidents, including a bomb explosion at the central bus station in Colombo, and the following month the Sri Lankan army began a major offensive to retake the Jaffna peninsula.

The heavy fighting led to numerous casualties on both sides and allegations of widespread civilian suffering in Jaffna. A small flotilla of Indian relief vessels was prevented from landing in the north by Sri Lankan forces, but on 4 June 1987, Indian planes dropped 25 tons of food and other supplies into Jaffna despite Sri Lankan protests over this violation of its sovereignty. With Jaffna city and some other areas surrounded by the Sri Lankan army, but still under the control of the LTTE, and the military offensive stalled, intensive talks between the Indian and Sri Lankan governments led to an agreement between India and Sri Lanka to establish "peace and normalcy."[878]

Adopted by the two governments apparently without the prior approval of any of the Tamil militant groups (or the Sinhalese opposition), the Agreement established a ceasefire which was to be guaranteed by the Indian government. Sri Lanka requested the assistance of Indian troops, several thousand of which immediately landed and took up positions in the north and east; the Sri Lankan army withdrew to barracks. Although the LTTE initially did not accept the Agreement, it ultimately followed the lead of other Tamil groups and agreed to hand over at least the heavy weaponry in its possession; the fact that the LTTE leader was reportedly held in "protective custody" in India during this period no doubt contributed to the LTTE's "cooperation."

Despite the assertion by President Jayewardene that the Agreement "has nothing to do with the concept of autonomy,"[879] the major political concession of the Agreement was the merger of the north and east for an "interim period" into a single province, as had been demanded by the LTTE and others. This "administrative unit" has an elected provincial council and a single governor, chief minister, and board of ministers. Provincial council elections were to be held by the end of 1987, although, in fact, they were not held until late 1988.

With the exception of formal creation of a single province in the north and east, the only substantive provision in the Agreement itself

878 Indo-Sri Lanka Agreement to Establish Peace and Normalcy in Sri Lanka, *signed* 29 July 1987 [hereinafter cited as "Agreement"]. The texts of the agreement, accompanying letters, and a joint press conference held by President Jayewardene and Prime Minister Gandhi on 29 July 1987 are taken from documents provided by the Sri Lankan embassy in Washington, DC.

879 Transcript of press conference, *supra* note 878, at 2.

is that "[t]he official language of Sri Lanka shall be Sinhala. Tamil and English will also be official languages."[880] Other provisions deal with issues such as the resettlement of refugees and displaced persons and the declaration of a general amnesty for combatants and those detained under the Prevention of Terrorism Act and other emergency laws.

The Agreement and an annex thereto make clear that a substantial role for Indian observers and a peace-keeping force is anticipated, and an exchange of letters also annexed to the Agreement addresses several geo-political issues theoretically unrelated to the ethnic conflict in Sri Lanka. Sri Lanka agrees to address several Indian concerns, including the employment by Sri Lanka of "foreign military and intelligence personnel" (presumably including Israeli intelligence advisors and British mercenaries); an agreement not to make the excellent port of Trincomalee available for military use by any country "in a manner prejudicial to India's interests"; and a review of Sri Lanka's agreements with "foreign broadcasting organisations" (a reference to a Voice of America station which broadcasts into India).

Although the Agreement halted the military confrontation between the Sri Lankan army and the Tamil militants, increasing numbers of Indian military forces did not prevent the resumption of serious violence within three months. While most of the Tamil militants (and probably the great majority of the Tamil population) seemed willing to accept the Agreement on at least an interim basis, the LTTE did so only reluctantly. The LTTE had eliminated its Tamil political opposition by murder for years, and additional hundreds of Tamil militants and civilians were killed after the signing of the Agreement, as the LTTE attempted to consolidate its position in the east. The Indian army also was accused of not preventing the massacre by the LTTE of approximately 200 Sinhalese civilians.

When they were not guaranteed control over the new northern-eastern provincial council, the LTTE reversed their earlier acquiescence in the Agreement. In October 1986, the Indian Peacekeeping Force— which had grown to approximately 50,000 troops by late 1988—launched a major operation against LTTE guerrillas in Jaffna, in response to a series of attacks by the LTTE on Sinhalese in the east.[881] After severe

---

880 Agreement, §2.18.

881 One pretext for the renewed LTTE attacks, which included the murder of eight Sri Lankan soldiers held prisoner since March 1987, was the suicide of eleven LTTE members captured by the Indian army. This event was presaged by one of the more irresponsible glorifications of guerrilla chic by the foreign press, in which the *Times* (London) ran a photograph, unrelated to any accompanying story, of three "Tamil militants . . . waging a four-year war for a separate homeland in the Sinhalese-dominaated island, gripping cyanide capsules in their teeth." 16 Feb. 1987, at 9, col. 4.

fighting (during which the Indian army allegedly demonstrated the same disregard for civilians of which the Sri Lankan army had been accused several months earlier), the Indians succeeded in retaking Jaffna, but large numbers of guerrillas escaped into the countryside.

Sinhalese militants, including members of the ruling UNP, also rejected the Agreement, as the highly visible role of India and the presence of the Indian army confirmed their worst fears of Indian domination. An attempted assassination of President Jayewardene in August killed two people, and numerous politicians who publicly supported the Agreement were murdered. Much of the violence from the Sinhalese side has been blamed on the People's Liberation Front (JVP), a Marxist-oriented group which mounted an unsuccessful insurrection in 1971.

Despite the continuing violence, in November 1987 the UNP-dominated legislature adopted, by a vote of 136 to 11 with two abstentions, the necessary constitutional amendment and implementing legislation to create provincial councils in a unified northern and eastern region and seven Sinhalese-majority regions. In September 1988, President Jayewardene issued a formal proclamation merging the northern and eastern provinces, and elections for the new provincial council were held in October and November 1988. The elections were boycotted by the LTTE, which continued its terrorist attacks on civilians and military encounters with the Indian Peacekeeping Force. However, the elections were held as scheduled; 53 of the 71 seats on the provincial council were won by two Tamil parties, the EPRLF and the Eelam National Democratic Liberation Front, while most of the remaining seats (all in the former eastern province) went to the Sri Lanka Muslim Congress.[882]

Violence and assassinations escalated in the south after the 1988–89 presidential and parliamentary elections. An estimated 3,000 people were killed during the first half of 1989, many civilian victims of JVP or LTTE terrorism or security force (Indian or Sri Lankan) excesses.

OBSERVATIONS

Many human rights groups have noted the lack of an effective "early warning system" as a primary impediment to preventing gross abuses and violent conflicts. In Sri Lanka, the warning signs were visible for decades, yet the conflict has inexorably deteriorated as in a Greek tragedy. In fact, Sri Lanka has become one of the most thoroughly studied cases of ethnic conflict in the world (much to the government's displeasure).[883] What went wrong?

882 "EPRLF Gets Absolute Majority," Overseas Tribune (Washington, DC), 26 Nov. 1988, at 1, col. 5.
883 On the academic side, one might cite the activities of Sri Lankan organizations, such as the Marga Institute and the International Centre for Ethnic Studies; the Sri Lanka

Since independence, Sri Lankan politics have been characterized by a lack of generosity or willingness to compromise on the part of both communities. Ceylon, as it was then known, shared with many other former colonies a colonial legacy in which communal differences had been accentuated rather than lessened. The more prosperous Tamil population refused to admit that it held a privileged position out of proportion to its numbers, and it did not seem to understand its delicate position as a minority in a country which itself felt threatened by the looming presence of India.

In the face of what might be termed Tamil arrogance, the Sinhalese reasserted their cultural heritage and assumed power with a vengeance. While many states have adopted dual-language policies to accommodate minorities smaller than the Tamil-speaking minority in Sri Lanka, it was perhaps not unreasonable for a new state to adopt as its official language that spoken by roughly 75% of the population. On the other hand, to enforce such a policy immediately and in a manner that suggested that Sri Lanka was exclusively a Sinhala-speaking Buddhist state *was* unreasonable.

The "standardization" policy for university admissions adopted in the early 1970s was a severe psychological blow to the Tamil community, which had long seen education as its primary means of economic advancement. The obvious discrimination with which the policy was implemented "caused enormous harm to ethnic relations while converting the university admissions issue from a controversial educational problem to a complex, emotionally-charged political issue, the consequences of which will likely persist throughout most of this decade."[884] The university admissions issue offered "an object lesson in how inept policy measures and insensitivity to minority interests can exacerbate ethnic tensions."[885] The 1972 constitution—which gave Sinhala constitutional status as the official language and granted a "foremost place" to Buddhism—was hardly designed to reassure the Tamil minority of its worth in the newly proclaimed republic.

Sri Lankan politicians from both communities attempted to resolve some of the major differences, but Sinhalese militancy (and fears of electoral losses) prevented attempted compromises from even being

Data Base Project of the International Peace Research Institute in Oslo; the London-based Minority Rights Group; and the numerous references to Sri Lanka in books and articles dealing with the subject of ethnic conflict. Human rights organizations, such as Amnesty International and the International Commission of Jurists, also have attempted to monitor and publicize the Sri Lankan situation for several years; see *Ethnic Conflict and Human Rights in Sri Lanka, supra* note 859.

884 K. M. de Silva, *supra* note 850, at 106.

tried: neither the 1957 Bandaranaike-Chelvanayakam Pact[886] nor the 1965 Senanayake-Chelvanayakam Pact[887] was ever implemented, although both would certainly be viewed today as extremely modest "concessions" from the Sinhalese perspective.

Under the Jayewardene government, which was in unchallenged control of parliament from 1977 to 1989, the conflict in Sri Lanka escalated from a serious (if largely non-violent) dispute over discrimination, language rights, and higher education to an all-out communal conflict that by the mid-1980s was virtually indistinguishable from civil war. Responsibility for this escalation (at least prior to the June 1986 proposals) lies primarily, if not wholly, with the government of Sri Lanka.

There are many parallels between Sri Lanka and Northern Ireland, and the period from 1977 to 1983 in Sri Lanka mirrors the cycle of government intransigence, guerrilla terrorism, and security force retribution that occurred in Northern Ireland from the late 1960s to the late 1970s. In each case, the failure to redress basic minority complaints about discrimination was followed by increased repression; this in turn created or revived minority guerrilla groups, whose initially insignificant actions (obviously not insignificant to the relatives of those policemen and soldiers killed, but politically insignificant insofar as they presented no real threat to the state) provided the excuse for governmental overreaction and massive violations of human rights through arbitrary detention without trial, torture, and unpunished killings by members of the security forces.

The government's attempts to resolve the crisis between 1983 and 1987 failed because of its continuing unwillingness to bring criminal charges against even a single member of the security forces, its refusal to permit the International Committee of the Red Cross or other objective groups to have access to detainees, and its inability to secure the political consent of its own supporters and other Sinhalese elements to a meaningful negotiated settlement. It is significant that the original Tamil complaints raised in the 1970s—about language and education—have largely disappeared, and Tamil demands have shifted to much more difficult political issues, such as control over land and substantial alterations in the present political structure of Sri Lanka.[888]

The absence of contested elections for over a decade also may have contributed to the inability of the government to assert political leadership in the absence of any recent electoral mandate—despite its control

885 Chandra Richard de Silva, *supra* note 850, at 134.
886 Reprinted in Dissanayaka, *supra* note 852, at 103–05.
887 *Id.* at 110.
888 A very helpful research document, Sri Lanka Human Rights Data Base Project, *The Negotiations Process in Sri Lanka 1983–1986* (Oslo: International Peace Research

of over 80% of the parliament. Without the looming deadline of elections, there was no political incentive to achieve a settlement, and President Jayewardene had even suggested that the scheduled 1989 elections might be postponed if the security situation did not improve. Well before the December 1988 presidential elections (won by the UNP candidate and out-going Prime Minister, Ranasinghe Premadasa), the opposition SLFP had placed itself firmly on the side of defending Sinhalese militancy rather than joining the government in a unified attempt to seek a resolution to the conflict. Approximately 400 persons were killed during the campaign for parliamentary elections, which were held in February 1989; the UNP received an absolute majority of 125 seats in the 225-seat legislature.

The 1983 constitutional amendment requiring members of Parliament to take an oath against separatism deprived moderate Tamils of a voice in government at a crucial moment. It contributed to discrediting the TULF leadership, and its repeal—along with repeal of the Prevention of Terrorism Act—is seen by many as essential to the success of any future negotiations.

Moderates on both sides were among the earliest casualties of the escalating violence, and Tamil terrorism has given the government an excuse to continue to emphasize the military over the political aspects of the conflict. Until 1984, Tamil guerrilla groups could assert a certain legitimacy of purpose and complain, with at least relatively clean hands, of human rights violations by the government. Since that time, internecine murders and the massacres of at least hundreds of Sinhalese civilians have robbed groups such as the LTTE of that legitimacy.

In few other contemporary situations does another state play as significant a role in potential resolution of a conflict as does India with respect to Sri Lanka. It would be inaccurate to suggest that India is responsible for the underlying conflict in Sri Lanka, but neither does India qualify as a disinterested observer. Toleration of guerrilla camps by Indian authorities in Tamil Nadu can hardly be doubted, and the exchange of letters included as part of the July 1987 Indo-Sri Lanka Agreement makes clear the political price exacted from Sri Lanka in exchange for active Indian opposition to the Tamil guerrillas.

A recurring difficulty may be that each side in Sri Lanka has relied too heavily on the ability of India to bring the other around and enforce a settlement; while India, from the Tamil viewpoint, might have a vital role to play in guaranteeing any eventual agreement, its inability to

Institute, 1986), notes the major areas of dispute between the government and TULF in 1985–86 as internal law and order, land settlement, linkage between the northern and eastern provinces, and the relationship between the central and provincial/regional governments. Appendix 5 at xiii–xvi.

produce meaningful proposals from the Sri Lankan government at Thimpu or to force the LTTE to the negotiating table in 1986 demonstrates the limits of such informal mediation. Secret negotiations between Indian and Sri Lankan government representatives have frequently led to subsequent allegations of betrayal, and mistrust between the two governments is substantial. Indian military forces have not been able to eliminate the LTTE guerrillas, and even military success cannot by itself ensure acceptance of the July 1987 agreement.

In addition, the Indian government has itself been beset with problems, and its will to deal with the difficult issues raised in Sri Lanka— while looking over its shoulder at the Punjab and elsewhere—may be suspect. Indira Gandhi was assassinated in 1984, and three different persons subsequently had primary responsibility for negotiations with Sri Lanka. Domestic politics, particularly the strong pro-Tamil sentiments in Tamil Nadu, no doubt played a large role in Rajiv Gandhi's decision to intervene in Sri Lanka, and it remains to be seen whether the likely long-term role of the Indian army in Sri Lanka will become a domestic political liability.

With the exception of India, there was little public international interest in Sri Lanka until the mid–1980s. Nongovernmental organizations began to raise the human rights situation in Sri Lanka before UN and other forums after the 1983 riots, and the Sri Lankan government exerted formidable efforts to avoid any formal action by UN bodies such as the Commission on Human Rights and its Sub-Commission on Prevention of Discrimination and Protection of Minorities.[889] The Commission finally adopted a resolution concerning Sri Lanka at its 1987 session, in which it called upon all parties to respect the rules of humanitarian law and invited the government to cooperate with the International Committee of the Red Cross.[890]

Sri Lanka has been a major recipient of development assistance funds from Western Europe, and the relationship between human rights and development led Norway to reduce its assistance pending resolution of the conflict. While it is not clear that reducing or ending foreign

889 The Sri Lankan government has made lengthy statements at both the Commission and its Sub-Commission on Prevention of Discrimination and Protection of Minorities, generally denying any human rights abuses and emphasizing the threat to Sri Lanka's territorial integrity supposedly posed by terrorists. See, e.g., statement of Sri Lanka (Dr. H.W. Jayewardene) at the Commission on Human Rights, 4 Mar. 1986 (on file with author). India also has commented on the situation in Sri Lanka, underlining its support for Sri Lanka's territorial integrity but also noting human rights violations, particularly during military activities. See, e.g., statement of India (Dr. G.S. Dhillon) to the Commission on Human Rights, 5 Mar. 1986 (on file with author).

890 Human Rights Commission Res. 1987/61, UN ESCOR, Supp. (No. 5), UN Doc. E/1987/18 (1987) at 134–35.

assistance will necessarily contribute to a solution in a situation such as that in Sri Lanka, the diplomatic pressures (and encouragement) directed towards the Sri Lankan government may have contributed to the significant advance represented by its June 1986 proposals.

A generally pro-government book written in the months immediately following the 1983 riots offered several suggestions as to what each side to the conflict must do "to seek a unity in diversity," and the observations seem (unfortunately) as apt several years later:

> A problem which has bedevilled the nation for twenty five centuries cannot conceivably be solved in twenty five years. However it must be brought within manageable proportions, with no further loss of time and with no further loss of honour.
>
> The Sinhala people, though proud of their heritage, have yet to learn that those who commit atrocities on the Tamil people harm their own people even more than they harm their victims. Indeed the Sinhala people stood condemned before the eyes of the world and before the conscience of mankind for the recent atrocities. . . .
>
> The Tamil people, no less proud of their heritage, have yet to learn that communal harmony can be achieved not merely by the majority not discriminating against the minority, but also by the minority not provoking the majority. . . .
>
> The Sinhala people have yet to understand that by subjecting the Tamils who live in their midst to murder, rape and pillage thus driving them away, they strengthen not weaken the clamour for secession. The Sinhala troops have yet to realise that by rampaging, they strengthen not weaken the hand of the enemy.
>
> The Tamil people have yet to understand that their privileged position prior to Independence stemmed from the insidious colonial policy of divide and rule. The Tamil people have yet to realise that restoring the balance is not perpetrating an injustice on them, but removing the injustice done to the Sinhala people during the period of colonial servitude.
>
> Communal discord . . . is a political problem. The Sinhala people have yet to know that there is no military solution to a political problem. Terrorism however is a military problem. The Tamil people have yet to know that there is no political solution to a military problem.[891]

At the heart of the escalation of Tamil fears and communal violence during the past decade have been violations of human rights, committed or sanctioned by the Sinhalese majority, including a failure adequately to recognize minority rights. Intra-Sinhalese political rivalries have led to increasing polarization, and little attention has been paid to the obligations of a governing majority towards other members of the society or to the initially reasonable demands for autonomy put forward by the Tamil community.

At the same time, there will be no peace in Sri Lanka until the Tamil community recognizes that it is, in fact, a minority—and a rather

891 Dissanayaka, *supra* note 852, at 100–101.

small one at that. No more than one-half of the Tamil population is included in the merged northern and eastern provinces, although Tamil influence has long been disproportionate to mere population size. Nevertheless, Sri Lanka will inevitably be dominated by the Sinhalese, Buddhist culture of 75% of its population; so long as this does not imply discrimination against or denigration of Tamil culture and traditions, that is a reality that cannot be reversed by law or constitutional innovation.

Since 1986, atrocities by Tamil guerrillas and the campaign by the LTTE to achieve political dominance through assassination, have been a major contributing factor in the escalation of the conflict into the full-scale civil war which erupted in 1987. One must question the extent to which the LTTE continues to be committed to Tamil rights, as opposed to its own political aggrandisement. Extremist Sinhalese violence and assassinations in the south of the country since July 1987, attributed primarily to the JVP, mirror those of the LTTE.

That the use of armed force became imperative in a situation in which thousands have been killed is not surprising, and the July 1987 agreement has thus far been imposed by military force rather than through its acceptance by the affected communities. Nevertheless, if the new provincial councils can begin to function in a manner that responds to Tamil needs without threatening the Sri Lankan state, the government may be able to gain the support of a majority of the Tamil and Sinhalese communities.

One of President Premadasa's first actions upon assuming office in January 1989 was to lift the state of emergency which had been in force in Sri Lanka since 1983, although it was reimposed less than six months later. If human rights abuses by government (and Indian) forces can be reduced or eliminated, the government's credibility in isolating and defeating extremist terrorism will be substantially increased. The government's electoral victory in the February 1989 parliamentary elections, in which the UNP won nearly twice as many seats as the SLFP, also should strengthen its hand. However, the suppression of terrorism is only a first step towards the social and political reconciliation within Sri Lankan society which alone can guarantee future peace.

Chapter 15
Sudan

This chapter focuses on the content of southern Sudanese autonomy as embodied in the 1972 Addis Ababa Agreement, which ended a seventeen-year-long civil war, and the constitutional arrangements adopted the following year. The architects of the Agreement no doubt hoped that the cultural, political, and historical differences between northern and southern Sudan could be resolved within a state that offered the southern population a reasonable degree of self-government and participation in national affairs, but structural weaknesses and political manipulation thwarted those hopes. The introduction of religious sectarianism, the resumption of the civil war in 1983, and the fall of President Numeiri in 1985 were only the final signs that the agreement had not worked as intended.

HISTORICAL BACKGROUND[892]

The Sudan is the largest country in Africa, abutting eight sub-Saharan or north African countries and populated by a mosaic of more than 50 ethnic groups. It is estimated that within these groups one can find up to 114 languages.[893] Peoples of Arab extraction, who inhabit the northern and central portions of the country, cover about two-thirds of the country and have traditionally felt their cultural roots to be in the Arab world; most believe in Islam. The southern third of the Sudan is inhabited primarily by Nilotic and Equatorian peoples who speak African languages, are largely Christian or follow traditional African religions, and whose roots are in black Africa. Approximately 70% of the population lives in the north and

---

892 See generally, e.g., R. A. Gray, *History of the Southern Sudan 1839–1889* (London: Oxford Univ. Press, 1961); P. M. Holt and M. W. Daly, *The History of The Sudan* (London: Weidenfeld & Nicholson, 1979).

893 See *Sudan Yearbook* (Khartoum: Ministry of Guidance and National Information, 1983).

30% in the south, although within these two broad geographic categories exist complex tribal, religious, and other social ties beyond the simple distinction between Muslim and non-Muslim.

Turko-Egyptian Rule

The northern and southern regions of the Sudan historically were relatively isolated from one another, although there were, of course, some contacts among the various groups. The southerners were widely dispersed and were mostly cattle herders and agriculturists. They also were involved to some extent in the ivory and gold trade between the Middle East and western and eastern Africa. Southerners generally resisted the Turko-Egyptian invasion in 1821 and subsequent attempts to impose a centralized government on the Sudan. In particular, southerners resented the imposition of forced labor and service in the invader's army, newly imposed taxes, and attempts by northern Arabs to monopolize the ivory trade. Above all, they opposed pressures to convert to Islam and speak Arabic.

Around 1881, an Islamic religious movement led by Mohammed Ahmed al-Mahdi (popularly known simply as "the Mahdi") emerged in the north, with the goal of expelling the Turko-Egyptian regime. Some southerners did support this movement, but there is a general perception that the revolt was primarily a northern one, and southerners opposed Mahdist troops when they attempted to replace the Turko-Egyptian administration.

British rule

The major threat to the Mahdist state came not from the south but from competing European powers (including Italy, France, and Britain) interested in the Sudan. The British prevailed in this competition, joining with Egypt to reconquer the Sudan in 1898; this also marked the first time that the kingdom of the western Sudan had been incorporated into the country.[894] The Sudan constituted a vital link between British territorial interests in southern and eastern Africa and Egypt. The Blue Nile river from Ethiopia joins the White Nile from Uganda at Khartoum, and subjugation of the south was therefore strategically important to the British.

The north and south were essentially administered as two separate entities for over four decades under British rule. British troops had to contend with southern uprisings until the late 1920s, and the British administration prohibited most contacts between the north and south. From 1922, Southerners could not travel to the north without a special permit, and vice versa. Islam and the use of Arabic were banned in the

894 See generally Ann M. Lesch, "Rebellion in the Southern Sudan," *Universities Field Staff International Reports* No. 8 (1985).

south, while the activities of Christian missionaries were encouraged. However, very little was done to develop the south, and there were great economic disparities between the two regions at the time of independence.

The British considered options of granting independence separately to the south or attaching the south to either Kenya or Uganda. However, Egyptian and northern Sudanese pressures succeeded in keeping the two regions together as a united country.[895] A conference was arranged in 1947 at Juba to approve the decision to unify the Sudan, under the assumption that unity was the only desirable solution.

Southern Sudanese representation at the conference was confined to tribal chiefs and administrative officials on the British payroll. There was no response to fears expressed by some southerners of domination by the more politically sophisticated north, and the question put before the conference was simply that of the best way to arrange north-south unity. Southerners were not represented in discussions that followed in 1952 and 1953 to consider whether the Sudan should merge with Egypt, and, in effect, were uninvolved in the preparations for independence. In the transition period between British rule and Sudanese independence, only 6 of 800 junior civil administration posts in the Sudan were filled by southerners.[896]

INDEPENDENCE

At independence, there were two different nationalist visions in the north, divided over whether the Sudan should be completely independent or united with Egypt. This debate was the primary concern of northern politicians, to the exclusion of adequate consideration of the southern Sudanese question. In July 1955, there were political protests in the south, and an order to move southern troops to the north for the independence celebrations sparked off a mutiny on 18 August 1955; several northern officers and several hundred civilians were killed. In November 1955, a month before independence, southern members of the Sudanese Parliament decided to endorse the proclamation of independence only if the south were granted considerable autonomy within a federal state.[897]

Within a year of independence in 1956, there were demands in the north to adopt an Islamic-based constitution. Southerners understand-

895 See Bona Malwal, *People and Power in Sudan - The Struggle for National Stability* (London: Ithaca Press, 1981) at 24–28.

896 Lesch, *supra* note 894, at 17.

897 Abel Alier, "The Southern Sudan Question," in Dunstan M. Wai (ed.), *The Southern Sudan: The Problem of National Integration* (London: Frank Cass, 1973) at 19.

ably viewed these demands with anxiety. In the 1958 elections, the Southern Federal Party won 40 of the 46 southern seats, on a platform which demanded that a federal system of government be established, that English and Christianity have equal status with Arabic and Islam, and that the south have its own military force.[898]

In November 1958, the Sudanese Parliament was abolished in a military coup led by General Ibrahim Abboud, and the new military regime decided to deal forcefully with dissent in the south. It became official government policy that Islam and Arabic would be introduced with all speed into the south, in order to unite the southern people and the Sudan in general and reverse the effects of British attempts to keep the south isolated. African traditional religions and indigenous languages were discouraged, and, in February 1962, all foreign Christian missionaries in the south were expelled. As unrest in the south mounted, northern forces attacked southern villages; as many as half a million southerners fled into exile.

By this time a southern rebel guerilla force known as the Anya-Nya had been established to resist northern dominance. The political wing of the Anya-Nya, the Sudan African National Union (SANU), called for independence for the south. In October 1964, massive general strikes broke out in the north, partly in protest against the government's policies towards the south, and the military government fell.

The 1965 Round-Table Conference

The Prime Minister of the transitional government that replaced the military arranged what has come to be known as the Round Table Conference in March 1965, at which all northern and southern factions were represented. Among the most significant aspects of the conference were the evident divisions among southerners as to whether the south should remain a single political unit and, if so, whether independence was a viable option. The SANU leadership would only discuss how the south was going to become independent, and independence also was supported by the Equatorians. Other factions were willing to discuss some form of federal arrangement, and some wanted the whole issue of the north-south relationship put to a referendum. The northerners initially rejected any discussion of federalism before the elections.

Finally, the conference appointed a twelve-person committee to draw up a working paper on north-south relations. The committee, made up of an equal number of southern and northern members, deliberated for a year before submitting a report, and even then it was unable to

---

898 Lesch, *supra* note 894, at 4.

agree on several key issues. There was no agreement on whether the south should be one region, as most northerners wanted, or three regions. There also were fundamental differences over what relationship would exist between southern and northern troops and how revenue would be allocated.

By the time the committee's report was submitted, the situation in the south had worsened. The government resorted to force to restore order, and, by mid–1965, over 1,400 had died in the south. Notwithstanding the divisions among the various southern factions, the Anya-Nya managed to organize political conventions and established a Sudan Provisional Government which created local councils, courts, schools, and clinics in the areas under its control.

The Addis Ababa Agreement

Against this background, another military coup brought Colonel Ja'far Numeiri into power in May 1969. Numeiri addressed the southern question immediately after the coup, and he took steps towards recognizing "the rights of the southern people to regional autonomy within a United Sudan."[899] Over the next two years, he appointed more southerners to administrative positions in the south. During Numeiri's visit to Ethiopia in 1971, plans were made for a peace conference to be held in Addis Ababa. The accord reached at Addis Ababa received the approval of key rebel leaders, and an agreement was ratified by both sides on 27 March 1972.[900] The National Assembly subsequently adopted a regional self-government law for the south, based on the Agreement, and a ceasefire occurred after the Act's promulgation. The Act was entrenched in the 1973 constitution; it merged the three southern provinces into one region, with a governing council responsible for internal security, local administration, and regional economic development; designated English as the principal language of the south; and recognized the right of southern Sudanese to practice Christianity or indigenous religions.

Attacks on southern autonomy

Divisions among southern politicians became more evident in the post-1973 period. Some, particularly Equatorians who had earlier favored southern independence and had been active in the early days of the civil war, argued that Dinkas were unfairly dominating the amalgamated

---

899 Statement quoted in *Perspective on the South: An Analysis of Trends and events leading to the Final Decree of Regionalization for the Former Southern Region of the Sudan* (Khartoum: Ministry of Guidance and National Information, 1983) at 21–22. *Cf.* Alier, *supra* note 897, at 25–26.

900 The Agreement and the 1973 constitution are discussed in greater detail, *infra* at 317–23.

south. There also was a feeling that the southern region was too large and that it would be more administratively convenient to create several separate provinces. However, redivision was emphatically rejected by the regional assembly.

In December 1980, six new regions were created in northern Sudan, each with a governor appointed by the central government, thus encouraging pro-redivision forces in the south.[901] Nevertheless, a majority of southerners undoubtedly opposed such a division. In October 1981, Numeiri removed the President of the regional council and dissolved the assembly, appointing a military government. In late 1982 and 1983, several southerners opposed to redivision were arrested, and it became clear that Numeiri intended to redivide the south by decree.

The discovery of oil in the south and a proposed canal project, which southerners perceived as a plot to divert needed southern water resources for Egyptian and northern Sudanese use, exacerbated north-south tensions. Numeiri's decision to locate an oil refinery in the North and to create a new province encompassing the southern oil discoveries encouraged increased guerrilla activities.

The President of the Council elected in 1982 was a compromise candidate of the pro-redivision forces, although it was difficult to separate anti-Dinka feelings from pro-redivision politics. In any event, Numeiri suddenly decreed redivision of the south into three provinces on 5 June 1983, circumventing constitutional requirements.

THE SECOND CIVIL WAR

Introduction of Islamic law

Since colonial days, the Sudan had a legal system which reflected the pluralist nature of Sudanese society. There were three recognized sources of law: Islamic law, customary law, and general territorial law.

As would be expected, part of the general territorial law that the newly independent country inherited was derived from the English legal system. In particular, English judge-made law governed "the legal relationships arising from the complexities of modern commercial and industrial society."[902] Islamic *(sharia)* and customary law were essentially personal in nature and covered areas such as marriage and inheritance.

901 For a summary of events in the 1980–83 period, see Charles Meynell, "Sudan—North and South," in Minority Rights Group, *Uganda and Sudan—North and South* (London: Minority Rights Group Report No. 66, 1984) at 24–25; Douglas H. Johnson, *The Southern Sudan* (London: Minority Rights Group Report No. 78, 1988) at 6–8.

902 Natale O. Akolawin, "Islamic and Customary Law in the Sudan: Problems of Today and Tomorrow," in Yusuf Fadl Hassan (ed.), *Sudan in Africa* (Khartoum: Khartoum University Press, 1971) at 279.

The British administration created a judiciary organized into two independent divisions. The *sharia* division administered only Islamic law to Muslims in personal matters. The civil division administered general territorial law and customary law in both civil and criminal matters. This separation of religious law from civil law was confirmed in Sudan's 1956, 1964, and 1973 constitutions.

However, legal pluralism in the Sudan was threatened in the late 1970s and early 1980s, when President Numeiri began to develop close relations with the Muslim Brotherhood movement, which sought the Islamicization of the state.[903] In late summer 1983, Numeiri announced that the Sudan would become an Islamic state and began issuing a series of laws subsequently known as the "September laws."[904] These laws—initially promulgated by Numeiri as provisional orders and subsequently ratified by the reconvened People's Assembly—were sweeping in character, affecting both substance and procedure.

The new laws included the Judiciary Act, the Reorganization of the Attorney-General's Chambers Act, the Advocacy Act, new codes of penal law and civil procedure, and the Judicial Sources of Law Act. In 1984, the government moved to Islamicize the country's commercial law by passing the Civil Transactions Act, the Zakat Tax Act, the Auditor-General Act, and others.

Opposition to Numeiri continued to grow, and Sudanese judges went on strike in 1983 for three months, continuing a series of escalating confrontations between the executive and the judiciary dating back to 1980.[905] On the day before Numeiri announced the re-devision of the southern region in 1983, the southern-based Sudan People's Liberation Movement (SPLM) and its military wing (SPLA) were founded, in reaction against the announced transfer of southern battalions of the Sudanese army to the north. Although its base and primary area of support are in the south, the SPLM/SPLA has consistently claimed to be fighting

903 See generally International Commission of Jurists, *The Return to Democracy in Sudan*, (Geneva: International Commission of Jurists, 1986).

904 Many observers, including the post-Numeiri government, have denied that the laws introduced by Numeiri were, in fact, consistent with or required by *sharia* law; for example, the penal code was not Islamic, defined crimes in an essentially "Western" manner, and included security offenses unrelated to Islam. *Cf.* Sudan, art. 9 CERD Report, UN Doc. CERD/C/114/Add.1/Rev.1 (1987) at 2. It also has been suggested that Numeiri's embrace of Islamic fundamentalism was designed as a purely political move to detract attention from the serious political and economic problems faced by the Sudan in the early 1980s. *Cf.*, e.g., "Identity Crisis, Drive to 'Islamicize' Sudan Deepens Its Ills," Wash. Post, 20 Sept. 1984, at A21, col. 1. A good summary and discussion of the September laws may be found in Cary N. Gordon, "The Islamic Legal Revolution: The Case of Sudan", 19 Int'l Lawyer 797 (no. 3, 1985).

905 International Commission of Jurists, *supra* note 903, at 38–39.

for reform of the entire Sudan and not for secession or simple reassertion of southern autonomy.[906]

By April 1984, talks with southern rebels had broken down, and there had been widespread protests against the September laws in both the north and south, including demonstrations by lawyers, doctors, and academics. Numeiri declared a state of emergency which lasted from April to September 1984, suspended various constitutional rights, and promulgated a set of Emergency Regulations. In May, he established nine Emergency Criminal Courts, which were renamed the Criminal Decisive Justice Courts and incorporated into the regular judicial system after termination of the state of emergency. These courts were created to hear cases involving alleged violations of the State Security Act of 1973, the 1983 Emergency Regulations, and some provisions of the 1983 Penal Code. They also were empowered to hear cases against persons for acts or omissions that impeded the enforcement of the rules of *sharia*.

Numeiri's fall

By March 1985, the renewed civil war had reached such intensity that all three southern governors agreed with Numeiri that it was time for a ceasefire and reconciliation. Numeiri appointed a team to negotiate with the leaders of the Sudan People's Liberation Army (SPLA), but he was too late. On 6 April 1985, following a general strike by various professional groups, the Sudanese military took power and replaced Numeiri with a transitional military government headed by General Abdelraham Sawar-Dhahab. In October 1985, a Transitional Constitution was adopted, which is to remain in force until a constituent assembly drafts a permanent constitution.

The new government revoked the 1983 redivision decree and arranged talks with the rebel troops. In March 1986, the "Koka Dam Declaration" was agreed to by representatives of the SPLM/SPLA and the transitional government, but its provisions—which included repeal of the September laws and the state of emergency—have not been implemented.[907] Article 16(2) of the 1985 constitution provides for re-establishment of regional self-government in the south under the terms of the Southern Provinces Regional Self-Government Act 1972 (discussed below), but article 4 reaffirms that "[t]he Islamic Sharia and custom shall be the main sources of legislation."

906 *Cf.*, Lam Akol, "The Present War and Its Solution," in Francis Mading Deng and Prosser Gifford (eds.), *The Search for Peace and Unity in the Sudan* (Washington, DC: Wilson Center Press, 1987) at 15–26.

907 The Koka Dam Declaration is reprinted in Akol, *supra* note 906 , at 24–26.

The SPLA did not participate in the national elections held in April 1986, which could not be conducted in 37 of the 68 southern districts. However, over 30 political parties fielded approximately 1,500 candidates in the elections. The Umma party won the most seats in the 301-seat constituent assembly, although it did not achieve a majority and governs in coalition with the Democratic Unionist Party. The third most powerful party, with 51 of the 264 seats filled, is the militant National Islamic Front, formerly known as the Muslim Brotherhood.

The head of the new government, Sadiq el Mahdi, made some efforts to come to agreement with the SPLM/SPLA, but his sphere of political action was limited by the Islamic orientation of the three major parties in the north. The National Islamic Front threatened during the election campaign to launch a holy war, or *"jihad,"* if the "September laws" were repealed, thus rejecting a minimum demand of the SPLA.[908]

An observation made at the end of the first year of Mahdi's government remained unfortunately apt through the end of 1988.

Inaction sums up the condition of the Sudan under its first democratic government in seventeen years. The government has not acted on the *sharia*, it has not made any progress towards negotiating with the SPLM or otherwise devising a solution to the problem of the south, and it has not taken any effective steps concerning the economy.[909]

Southern solidarity seems to be increasing, and the SPLA and its allies control much of the southern countryside. Chronic food shortages in the south have increased, as both government and SPLA forces have refused to cooperate with international relief efforts which each fears may aid the other side. Sudan's parliament refused in October 1988 to enact a more stringent *sharia* code, which had been supported by the National Islamic Front, reflecting the growing opposition to further Islamicization in the north, as well as the south.[910] Rejection in late 1988 by the Mahdi-led cabinet of a peace plan agreed to by the Democratic-Unionist Party and the SPLA precipitated a crisis, and, in March 1989, the Sudanese army and a broad coalition of political and labor leaders forced Mahdi to restructure the cabinet. The new one, which did not include the National Islamic Front, immediately endorsed the DUP-SPLA agreement, and the SPLA announced a one-month ceasefire in May 1989. The Mahdi government was overthrown by a military coup in July 1989, with uncertain consequences for the prospects of ending civil war.

908 Marina Ottaway, "Post-Numeiri Sudan: one year on," 9 Third World Q. 891, 893 (1987).

909 *Id.* at 901.

910 See Mary Battiata, "Sudan, Facing Resistance, Shelves Islamic Law Bill," Wash. Post, 6 Oct. 1988, at A40, col. 1; Johnson, *supra* note 901, at 9–10.

THE 1973 CONSTITUTION

The history of the Sudan has been marked since independence by deep suspicion between south and north, as well as by conflicts within the south itself. These suspicions obviously were reinforced and exacerbated by British colonial policies and the decision to maintain the vast territory of the Sudan as a single independent state in 1956. National governments, dominated by northerners, have since independence been concerned with keeping the country united, but the methods used have often supported the conclusion drawn by many southerners that unity is desired only through Islamicizing the south and destroying southern culture.

The only period of relative peace in the Sudan has been during the years following adoption of the 1973 constitution, which purported to provide meaningful autonomy for the south. In the absence of more recent proposals and in light of the civil war which reemerged as the letter and spirit of the constitution were violated, a closer examination of the potential (and failures) of that constitution is warranted.

Part I of the constitution defined the Democratic Republic of the Sudan as a unitary, democratic, socialist, and sovereign republic which forms part of both the Arab and African entities. This section also established the Sudanese Socialist Union as the sole political organization in the Sudan.

Article 7 emphasized the need for the "people's participation in government" and provided for the decentralization of the republic into administrative units. With respect to the southern region, Article 7 called for regional self-government in accordance with the Southern Provinces Regional Self-Government Act of 1972, which was considered an organic law which could not be amended except in accordance with the provisions of the Act. According to Article 9 of the constitution, Islamic law and customs[911] were to be the main sources of legislation, except that personal matters of non-Muslims were to be governed by their own personal laws. Article 10 made Arabic the official language of the Republic.

Parts II and III outlined the political, social, and economic principles of the republic and the fundamental rights and freedoms of Sudanese citizens. Article 16 recognized Christianity and other minority religions in the Sudan, and the state was to "endeavour to express ... [the] values" of both Christianity and Islam; "[h]eavenly religions and the noble aspects of spiritual beliefs" were not to be "insulted or held in

---

911 There is some disagreement as to whether "customs" in art. 9 refers to "Islamic" customs or the general customary law of the country.

contempt."[912] No restrictions were to be imposed on citizens or communities on the grounds of religion. The guarantees of fundamental rights and freedoms in Part III of the constitution included, *inter alia*, equality before the law, freedom of movement and residence, freedom from unlawful search, the right to vote, freedom of opinion, and the rights to education and health. Part IV established an independent judiciary and contained traditional elements of due process rights, standards for dealing with juvenile criminals, and prisoners' rights.

The 1973 constitution created a very powerful presidential system, particularly given the actual situation, in which the President was the driving force behind the only legal political party. The President could appoint or remove the Prime Minister, as well as officers of the armed forces, heads of diplomatic missions, and senior public servants. He could declare a state of emergency for a maximum of thirty days and suspend any of the freedoms and rights guaranteed by the constitution. Within fifteen days, the declaration of a state of emergency had to be considered by the National Assembly. If the President dissolved the Assembly, the matter was to be presented to the newly elected Assembly at its first sitting.

National legislative power was vested in the People's Assembly, along with the President. The Assembly was responsible for the general budget and for the exercise of "supervision and control over the Executive."[913] Members of the Assembly were elected on a geographical basis, with some seats filled by presidential appointment and reserved for "alliances of working forces of the people."[914]

Although safeguards were written into the constitution allowing for the President's removal and legislative checks on his powers, these safeguards were vague and weak. For example, Article 153 gave the People's Assembly the power to assign to any committee of its members the duty to investigate any matter within the authority of the Executive. However, the investigation was subject to the President's approval, thus effectively granting a veto over any such proposed investigation.

Under Article 108, the President, in consultation with the Speaker, could dissolve the Assembly if the President considered that the public interest and circumstances necessitated new elections. In the event of such dissolution, the President had to call new elections within 60 days in order to constitute a new Assembly, which could not be dissolved for at least one calendar year.

When the National Assembly was not in session or following a

912 1973 Sudanese Const., art. 16(c).
913 *Id.*, art. 118.
914 *Id.*, art. 119.

dissolution, the President could issue Provisional Republican Orders which had the force of law.[915] Such an order had to come before the Assembly when it reconvened or when it was reconstituted after elections, and it was this procedure that was utilized to enact the September laws in 1983.

While prohibiting any encroachment by the executive or other authority upon the independence of the judiciary, the constitution made judges solely responsible to the President, who had powers of appointment and removal. The manner in which appointments and removals were to be made was left for "the law" to determine. The extent to which courts could prevent the executive or the legislature from violating the constitution was unclear, and a major concern of many southerners was the allegedly unfair administration of justice by Sudanese courts. One of the early acts of the government which replaced Numeiri in 1985 was to repeal the Summary Law Courts Act; while the courts continue to enforce the *sharia* penalties introduced into the criminal code in 1983, the executive has ceased imposing amputations as a punishment for theft, one of the most visible and widely criticized provisions of the 1983 laws.

The 1973 constitution recognized the "cultural distinction" of different Sudanese peoples and proclaimed the principle of administrative decentralization. In accordance with these aims, the constitution authorized the establishment in each province of a People's Executive Council and a subordinate tier of the People's Local Councils. Article 184 specifically provided that the People's Local Councils in provinces of the southern region would be the basis for the organization of regional self-government.

AUTONOMY UNDER THE ADDIS ABABA AGREEMENT[916]

The 1972 Addis Ababa Agreement was given legal status through enactment of the Southern Provinces Regional Self-Government Act 1972 ["SPRA"] as an organic law of the Sudan.[917] The key provisions of the agreement included creation of a united southern region out of the former provinces of Bahr El Ghazel, Equatoria, and Upper Nile; establishment of a southern regional government; plans for the develop-

915 *Id.*, art. 106.

916 *The Addis Ababa Agreement on the Problem of South Sudan: Draft Organic Law to Organize Regional Self Government in the Southern Provinces of the Democratic Republic of the Sudan* (Khartoum: Ministry of Guidance and National Information, 1972). See generally, e.g., Mohamed Omar Beshir, *The Southern Sudan: From Conflict to Peace* (London: Hurst, 1975).

917 For the text of the Act [hereinafter cited as "SPRA"], see 12 Africa Q. 59–66 (no. 1, 1972).

ment and reconstruction of the south following the civil war; and transitional arrangements for repatriation of refugees and amnesty for southern rebels.

Legislative power

The 1972 Act vested legislative authority in the south in a People's Regional Assembly, which was elected by southern residents. The legislative competence of the Assembly was subject to the reserved powers of the central government, which included national defense; external affairs; currency and coinage; air and inter-regional river transportation; communications and telecommunications; customs and foreign trade, except for border trade and certain commodities which the regional government could identify with the approval of the central government; nationality and immigration; planning for economic development; educational planning; and public audit.[918]

The Regional Assembly could legislate only for the "preservation of public order, internal security, efficient administration, and the development of the southern region in cultural, economic and social fields . . . "[919] The areas within its jurisdiction included the promotion and utilization of regional financial resources for the development and administration of the southern region; local government; legislation on traditional law and native custom; prison and police administration; and regional administration of public schools, health care, cultural activities, land use, and other matters authorized by the (national) President.[920]

The Regional Assembly was expected on request to provide the People's National Assembly with facts and information concerning the administration of the south; the National Assembly had similar obligations. The Regional Assembly could, by a two-thirds majority, request that a national law it deemed detrimental to southern welfare be postponed from entering into force, but the President had discretion to grant or deny such a request. Prior to a national bill's passage, a majority of the Regional Assembly could request the President to withdraw the bill from the National Assembly and then communicate its objections to the bill within fifteen days to the National Assembly. Again, however, such withdrawal was a matter of presidential discretion.

The President could veto any bill of the Regional Assembly that he deemed contrary to the national constitution, and the Assembly could then reintroduce the bill. However, it was not clear whether the bill could become law after its reintroduction, notwithstanding the presi-

918 SPRA, art. 6.
919 *Id.*, art. 10.
920 *Id.*

dential veto. By comparison, article 107 of the 1973 constitution provided specifically that a two-thirds majority of the National Assembly could override a presidential veto.

Executive power

A High Executive Council was established, headed by a President with a mandate to act in the south on "behalf of" the national President. Under article 18, the Council was to act as a cabinet of ministers specifying the duties of the various government departments in the region.

The national President appointed the President of the Council, on the recommendation of the People's Regional Assembly. The Council President in turn recommended members of the Council to the President for appointment; the process was the same for removing appointees from office. As the chief executive, the President of the Council constitutionally had the authority to promulgate administrative regulations, and members of the Council were responsible for their enforcement. The Agreement remained vague on the question of the relationship between the Council and the various ministries of the central government, but ultimate authority for defining the relationship rested in the hands of the national President.[921]

Provisions dealing with the relationship between the southern Council President and the national President left a host of questions unanswered. Article 16 stipulated that the Council acted on behalf of the national President, but article 20 made the Council responsible to the Regional Assembly and the President. Did these provisions together mean that the Council was more responsible to the national President than to the Regional Assembly? What was expected of the southern Council President in situations where the Regional Assembly was in disagreement with the national President over policy?

The national President's constitutional power to regulate the relationship between the southern administration and the central ministries also was problematic.[922] The agreement was not clear on how regional departments should relate to the central ministries, and the role of provincial Commissioners exemplified this confusion. Provincial Commissioners were nominated by the Council President and appointed by the national President. Although their work directly concerned matters assigned by the Act to the regional government, these commissioners reported to the central government authorities in Khartoum. The Re-

---

921 *Id.*, art. 22.

922 For a good analysis of the relationship between the national government and the regional government, see Nelson Kasfir, "Southern Sudanese Politics Since the Addis Ababa Agreement," 76 African Affairs 143–66 (Jan. 1977).

gional Assembly resented its lack of control and, as a result, politicized the selection of Provincial Commissioners in an effort to ensure that appointees were not agents of the Khartoum government. Control over the regional public service system in the south exhibited a similar confusion of authority, as there were numerous instances in which public officials found themselves accountable to the regional government yet reporting directly to Khartoum.[923]

Southern economic development

The 1972 agreement was very specific about the southern government's responsibility for the south's economic development.[924] The implementing Act gave the southern government the power to impose taxes, and the National Assembly was required to vote funds "in accordance with the requirements of the Region."[925] However, the regional government's budget had to be approved by the National Assembly.

Given the ravages of the war, the regional government was not able to raise the necessary tax money to fund development projects. In its 1974–75 budget, for example, the regional government sought 88% of its necessary income from the National Assembly.[926] Thus, the south was dependent on the central government for its economic survival, but the latter could not provide what was needed. At the time of the Agreement, the National Assembly established a "Special Fund" for the south, with a goal of $50 million; two years later, there was only $4.7 million in the fund.[927]

Although the 1972 arrangements envisaged economic cooperation between the regional and central governments, in fact the south became very dependent on the north at a time when the country was in economic difficulties. With the National Assembly holding the purse strings, the southern development envisaged in the Addis Ababa Agreement did not materialize.

Against this background, southerners viewed with suspicion many development schemes proposed by the central government. The proposed Jonglei Canal, for example, in which Sudan and Egypt were to share the costs and benefits, was thought to benefit Egypt at the expense of the southern Sudan. The SPLM asserted that 2.5 million southern peasants would become landless as a result of the project.[928] Numeiri's decision to create a new province to encompass oil discovered in south-

923   *Id*. at 152.
924   Addis Ababa Agreement, *supra* note 916, art. 6(viii).
925   SPRA, art. 25(1)(v).
926   Kasfir, *supra* note 922, at 156.
927   *Id*. at 157.
928   Lesch, *supra* note 894, at 9.

ern territories was seen as another example of northern efforts to thwart southern development efforts.[929]

OBSERVATIONS

The 1972 Addis Ababa Agreement was concluded in the context of very deep cleavages between the north and the south. The two sides were forced together by an awareness of the destructiveness of the civil war and an understanding that there would be no peace without some degree of autonomy in the south. A decade later, however, the Agreement was in serious trouble, and Numeiri's attempts to Islamicize the entire country signaled the end of even theoretical southern autonomy.

The 1972 Act which implemented the Agreement could be amended only by the joint approval of three-fourths of the National Assembly and a two-thirds majority of the citizens of the southern region voting in a referendum, thus rendering its provisions more entrenched than even the constitution itself. However, there was no attempt to square the Act with the wide powers enjoyed by the Sudanese President, which might well have caused insurmountable difficulties even within the context of a functioning Sudanese democracy. Given the dictatorial powers in fact wielded by Numeiri, it was perhaps inevitable that a democratic, autonomous regional government would be seen as a threat which the non-democratic center would seek to control.

Although the national President never directly vetoed southern bills, the Regional Assembly was clearly subservient to the central government. For example, President Numeiri dissolved the Assembly on three different occasions within a five-year period from 1978 to 1983, even though the Assembly was required under law to have a life span of four years. While neither the Addis Ababa Agreement nor the implementing Act provided the President with specific authority to dissolve the Regional Assembly, the President was granted such power with respect to the National Assembly under Article 108 of the constitution. It is perhaps not surprising that Numeiri felt that he had equivalent powers over the Regional Assembly.

The regional President was also seriously constrained in his actions by the influence of the national government. Immediately after the Addis Ababa conference, a pattern of presidential interference in southern politics began to emerge, and President Numeiri regularly influenced selection of the southern Council President. Such intervention in the election process created a southern perception that the Council President was under the control of the national government, fueling the well-

929 *Id*. at 9–10.

entrenched suspicion that northern politicians were unwilling to leave the south in charge of its own affairs.

The 1972 arrangements created an executive whose loyalty to both the national President and the regional body impeded his effectiveness. Presidential interference in the selection process created animosities between former rebel comrades and exacerbated existing political differences within the south. So long as there were no major issues over which the regional Council and the national President differed, the arrangements seemed to work. However, whenever the southern executive took independent stands, the President came down with a heavy hand and usually dissolved the Regional Assembly, disrupting the stability of the south.

To a certain extent, some of the administrative ambiguities and jurisdictional conflicts that plagued the operation of the 1972 Act were unavoidable, and some ambiguities must be expected in any such partially decentralized system of government. As Kasfir has pointed out, the history of the United States shows that the successful resolution of administrative conflicts in decentralized political systems can indeed strengthen the capacity of institutions to handle future disputes.[930] In the case of the Sudan, however, these conflicts, far from providing a framework within which disputes could be resolved, fueled existing political disagreements and suspicions and threatened the whole agreement. In the absence of conflict resolution mechanisms, the Agreement was perhaps doomed to fail in its mission of guaranteeing southern autonomy within the Sudanese Republic.

While the Agreement envisaged an increasingly self-sufficient south, the country could not supply the resources needed to boost the southern economy. A feeling of economic neglect therefore persisted in the south and increased existing feelings of economic discrimination.

Finally, the creation of a single southern region did not eliminate suspicions that existed among different southern ethnic groups. Despite attempts to balance the representation of different groups in the Regional Assembly, southern self-government allowed the maintenance of ethnic and geographically based divisions that were subsequently exploited by the central government.

Four years after Numeiri's fall, the new Sudanese government had not yet repealed the "September laws," and the civil war had intensified. In late 1987, Prime Minister Mahdi described the war as "an afterthought" for his government, "fought with a minimum kind of exer-

---

930 Kasfir, *supra* note 922, at 152.

tion."[931] Conditions in the south worsened, as food shortages added to the "normal" ravages of war.

By arming Arab tribal militia with an unprecedented level of modern firepower, Mahdi's government appears to have exacerbated rather than reduced north-south hatreds. The fruit of this policy includes tribal massacres, the theft of millions of head of cattle and large-scale resumption of the ancient practice of inter-tribal slavery.[932]

The SPLM continues to insist that the so-called "southern problem" is linked to reviving national political and economic democracy, not just to regional autonomy.[933] A ten-point memorandum issued in April 1985 reaffirmed the SPLM's commitment to national unity and called for, *inter alia*, a return to the 1956 constitution; reunification of the south into a single region; the immediate repeal of the "September laws"; adequate representation for southerners in all government institutions; and the release of all political prisoners and the restoration of civil rights.[934]

In contrast, the "Sudan Charter" proposed by the National Islamic Front emphasizes the numerical majority of Muslims in the Sudan and states that "Islamic jurisprudence shall be the general source of law."[935] While freedom of religion is to be guaranteed in private, family, and social matters, "[i]n common [legal] matters, where it is not feasible to enforce but one option or system, the majority [i.e., Muslim] option shall be determinative, with due respect to the minority expression."[936] At the same time, the Sudan Charter also calls for creation of a federal system of government with autonomous regions and a central government leadership which incorporates elements from all regions.

While the tentative agreement reached in spring 1989 and the subsequent ceasefire declared by the SPLA give reason for hope, the failure of the National Islamic Front thus far to support the agreement is ominous. Fundamental differences between militant Muslims and much of

---

931 Quoted in Blaine Harden, "Hopes for Bold Moves in Sudan Are Fading," Wash. Post, 21 Nov. 1987, at A14, col. 1.

932 *Id.* at A20; also see "Slavery regains foothold in regions of Sudan," Christian Science Monitor, 31 Aug. 1987, at 9, col. 1; "New Guns Revive Slavery in Sudan," Wash. Post, 29 Nov. 1987, at A1, col. 1.

933 *Cf.* Mansour Khalid, ed., *John Garang Speaks* (London: KPI, 1987).

934 This summary is taken from Ottaway, *supra* note 908, at 897.

935 Sudan Charter, adopted by the National Islamic Front (Jan. 1987), reprinted in Deng and Gifford, *supra* note 906, at 78–89, at 81.

936 *Id.* at 81.

the rest of Sudanese society remain, and significant compromises will be necessary to reconcile those opposing views.

Foreign aid to both sides has enabled the war to continue and increased the death toll through modernizing the available weaponry.[937] Libya and the United States have supported the government, while Ethiopia, Israel, Kenya, and Uganda have reportedly aided the SPLA. As in other similar situations, such foreign intervention did not create the conflict, but it has arguably made it more difficult to resolve, as each side is assured of sufficient material and logistic support to avoid military defeat. At the same time, however, the massive economic problems faced by the Sudan will undoubtedly require that any political solution is accompanied by positive foreign financial support.

Formal division of the Sudan would not necessarily resolve its ethnic and other conflicts; the south, in particular, is far from homogeneous, and there are long-standing differences among Equatorians, Dinkas, and other southerners. If division did occur, presumably through agreement between both sides, it would run the risk of encouraging other secessionist movements in Africa and elsewhere (although it might also encourage more flexible responses to regional demands for autonomy or federalism).

Any future agreement within a united Sudan will need to include specific guarantees which will both preserve any division of powers between the central and regional governments and encourage democratic structures at the national and regional levels. For example, guarantees of religious and cultural rights will need to be firmly entrenched in a national constitution, along with any new autonomous structural arrangements—although such entrenchment did not prevent the violation of fundamental rights under Numeiri. A process for resolving conflicts between the regional and central governments should be established, as part of the revitalization of an independent judiciary. Certain regional-central relationships might be clarified in a new agreement, leaving less room for unilateral manipulation by the central authorities.

In the end, however, technical adjustments to the 1956 or 1973 or 1985 constitution or even new compromises on fundamental issues cannot ensure reconciliation without a good faith commitment to the processes of democracy. Despite its flaws, the 1972 Addis Ababa Agreement did offer a framework for political development within the Sudan. While some problems (such as lack of economic development at the national or regional levels) were perhaps beyond the control of the parties, the Agreement failed primarily because Numeiri increasingly refused to

937 *Cf.*, Mansour Khalid, "External Factors in the Sudanese Conflict," in Deng and Gifford, *supra* note 906, at 109–25.

accept its basic premise, that is, meaningful southern autonomy beyond the manipulation of the central government. Some southern politicians no doubt also saw political rewards in the failure rather than the success of the arrangements.

At the same time, candor requires the recognition that the Sudan has never effectively existed as a state unified by culture, politics, or economics; it remains perhaps one of the most difficult tests for the post-colonial credo of territorial integrity above all else. "What matters after all is not the Sudan, but the Sudanese. . . . With peace can come a new unity, but in the Sudan, as elsewhere, wanting peace means working for justice."[938]

938 M. W. Daly, "Conclusions and Reflections," in Deng and Gifford, *supra* note 906, at 183.

Part III Other Examples of Autonomous Arrangements

Man has a right, in this our brief existence,
To call some fleeting happiness his own,
Partake of worldly pleasures and subsistence
And have bread on his table rather than a stone.
Such are the basic rights of man's existence.
But do we know of anything suggesting
That man enjoys his basic rights, or no?
To have one's rights would be most interesting,
But in our present state this can't be so.

Now please remain all standing where you're standing
And join in the hymn of the poorest of the poor,
Whose most arduous life you have seen portrayed here today.
For, in fact, the poor come to very sticky ends.
The saviors on horseback are far from frequent in practice.

Bertold Brecht, *Three Penny Opera* (1928)
trans. Mannheim/Willett, 1976)

INTRODUCTION

The scope of arrangements which provide for some degree of "autonomy" is almost unlimited, and the case studies which follow furnish a glimpse of some of the many unique structures which have been developed to respond to geographic, political, ethnic, linguistic, or other differences within a single sovereignty. The examples are historical and contemporary, successful and unsuccessful, but most evidence creative legal and constitutional thought.

Even though classifications of rights or political status rarely contribute to problem-solving or provide automatic answers to complex issues, a certain degree of categorization may make analyses more meaningful. The structures summarized in the following studies have therefore been grouped into three very broad categories.

The first group, of federal or quasi-federal arrangements, includes situations in which cultural or ethnic differences provided one of the motivating factors for the adoption of a federal, confederal, consociational, or similar structure. Thus, the classic federations of Australia and the United States (information about which may be easily found elsewhere) are not discussed, as ethnic divisions played little role in their formation. With the exception of the former Danish colony of Greenland and the Netherlands Antilles, which exist in a context which might be more appropriately described as devolution rather than classic federalism, it is notable that federations tend to be created only in the early stages of independence; there are no examples of an essentially unitary state dividing and then reintegrating as a federation (although the regional autonomy developing in Spain, discussed in Chapter 13, exhibits some of the characteristics of a federal system).

The second group consists of "internationalized" territories or territories of particular international concern. While there has not been direct international or multilateral participation in the actual government of each of the entities surveyed, there was a greater international component in situations such as the Saar, Memel, Danzig, Aland Islands, Trieste, and in the process of decolonizing New Zealand's former colonies than was the case where structures were developed to respond to almost entirely internal concerns. Many of these "international" entities also involved competing claims or conflicting political concerns of two or more states. Even within this category, however, one should not search too closely for consistency: for example, Eritrea is discussed with other federal or quasi-federal arrangements, even though its short-lived autonomous status was based on a United Nations resolution.

A final miscellaneous group includes, *inter alia*, attempts to address ethnic differences through preferential policies rather than territorial autonomy arrangements (e.g., Fiji and Malaysia); contemporary developments in Brazil with respect to indigenous peoples; assertions of cultural autonomy and linguistic rights in Western Europe; and the vast multicultural state of China.

Within the necessary time and space restrictions of any work such as the present one, these studies have been selected to present as wide a range of "autonomy" arrangements as is feasible. At the same time, an attempt has been made to discuss situations whose historical and legal context is not so different or unusual as to lessen their value as precedents in contemporary situations in which autonomy may be at issue. For this reason, the historical anomalies of Monaco, San Marino, Andorra, and Liechtenstein have been omitted, as has the uniquely situated Holy See. Similarly, there is no discussion of the unique set of cultural, historical, and political ties between Great Britain and members of the British Commonwealth or empire, whose gradual constitutional development was rarely expressed in formal legal arrangements; several (such as India and Canada) now are faced with their own problems of regional autonomy and devolution.

There are, of course, dozens of other situations that might profitably be studied as either positive or negative examples of attempts to deal with issues of autonomy, but the present work does not pretend to be an encyclopedic compilation of all such examples. Among those situations to which further attention might be directed are aboriginal/indigenous issues in Australia, Canada, and the United States; Yugoslavia; Cyprus; historical arrangements in Lebanon; New Caledonia; U.S.-territorial relations (e.g., Guam, Puerto Rico, and the U.S. Virgin Islands); Quebec; the future of such small yet sensitive territories as the Falkland (Malvinas) Islands and Gibraltar; Cameroon; Nigeria; and Uganda.

In view of the wide variation in the governmental structures considered, no single term adequately encompasses every relationship discussed. The terms "central," "national," and "principal" all describe the sovereign or superior entity; "autonomous," "regional," "provincial," and "local" are used to describe the dependent or inferior entity. The use of different terms does not necessarily imply any difference in the degree or type of autonomy under discussion.

A final caveat with respect to the case studies concerns the highly summary nature of many of the comments and observations. The primary purpose of this section is to survey some of the many different kinds of autonomy found in past or current power-sharing structures, not to define "autonomy" or "self-government" per se. The studies highlight the most distinctive aspects of the arrangements discussed, rather than offering detailed statutory or case-law interpretations of every nuance in such arrangements. In most cases, reference should be made to the constituent documents themselves and to cited sources in order to make more detailed comparisons. Because of the summary nature of the descriptions, footnote references have generally been kept to a minimum, except for direct quotations. As in Part II, most of the contemporary situations are described as of mid-1988 to early 1989.

Most of the entities surveyed are described by a straightforward summary of their basic constitutional structure, i.e., the division of executive, legislative, and judicial powers between the central and local governments. Any particular or noteworthy arrangements to deal with specific issues—such as control of police, land use, exploitation of natural resources, or economic issues—are then summarized. A brief section of "observations" highlights the most salient features of each entity, occasionally distinguishing it from similar arrangements.

While no single situation is likely to offer a precedent directly applicable to a specific contemporary conflict, many may suggest possible resolutions. The great variety of constitutional arrangements, the detailed provisions occasionally developed to resolve particularly difficult local problems, and the flexibility in addressing issues such as revenue-sharing or participation in international organizations, demonstrate that neither "sovereignty" nor "self-determination" need stand in the way of innovative political solutions.

Chapter 16
Federal or Quasi-Federal Structures

Eritrea (1952–1962)

HISTORICAL BACKGROUND

The region now known as Eritrea became an Italian colony in 1890 and was probably first recognized as a distinct entity at that time. That period of Italian domination lasted until 1941, during which that a sense of Eritrean national identity began to develop. Following Italy's defeat by Anglo-American forces in 1941, Britain assumed administration over Eritrea and restored Emperor Haile Selassie to his throne in Ethiopia. In 1949, the British proposed to partition Eritrea between Ethiopia and the Sudan, but this plan was rejected by the United Nations (and the Eritreans). Both Ethiopia and Sudan had historical and cultural claims to the region known as Eritrea, and the former was particularly desirous of ensuring access to the Red Sea through Eritrea.

After the failure of the British partition plan, a United Nations commission was established, and its 1950 report formed the basis for a General Assembly resolution which set forth in unusual detail a proposed act of federation between an autonomous Eritrea and Ethiopia.[939] While the compromise was not universally applauded, the Eritreans and Ethiopians ratified the Federal Act and the constitution subsequently adopted by the Eritrean Assembly.

By the late 1950s, a serious independence movement was developing in Eritrea, and the Eritrean Liberation Front began an armed revolution in western Eritrea in 1961. In 1962, Eritrea was annexed by Ethiopia, and, in 1967, it was placed under direct military administration. Eritrea

---

939 G.A. Res. 390(V), 5 UN GAOR, Supp. (No. 20), UN Doc. A/1775 (1950) at 20 [hereinafter cited as "Federal Act"].

remains part of Ethiopia, but guerrilla fighting has continued between Ethiopian and Eritrean forces, both before and after the overthrow of Emperor Haile Selassie and the establishment of a revolutionary Marxist regime in 1974.

The following comments relate to the period of Eritrean autonomy from 1952 to 1962.

EXECUTIVE POWERS

The executive power of Eritrea was exercised by a Chief Executive elected at the beginning of each legislative session by two-thirds of the members of the Eritrean Assembly. The cabinet secretaries selected by the Chief Executive were not approved by the Assembly, but were to represent the principal population groups and geographical areas of the territory. The Chief Executive could be impeached by a two-thirds vote of the Assembly for a grave violation of the constitution or for failing to dismiss any department secretary who committed such a grave violation; he also could be removed from office upon conviction by the Supreme Court.

The powers of the Chief Executive were those normally associated with a president, head of state, or governor: enforcement of the constitution and laws and direction of executive and administrative departments and public services. The constitution also provided specific authority for, *inter alia*, control over local police, preparation of an annual budget, and the temporary suspension of certain constitutional provisions in an emergency.

The constitution provided for a Representative of the Ethiopian Emperor in Eritrea whose duties and responsibilities were primarily ceremonial. The Representative's one substantive power was the authority to ask that the Assembly reconsider any legislation that the Representative considered encroached upon national (Ethiopian) jurisdiction or involved the international responsibility of the federation; legislation so returned was, in effect, vetoed, unless the Assembly overrode the action by a two-thirds majority vote.

There also was provision in the Federal Act for an "Imperial Federal Council," composed of an equal number of Eritrean and federal representatives, which met at least once a year "to advise upon the common affairs of the Federation."[940]

LEGISLATIVE POWERS

The legislative power of Eritrea was vested in a unicameral Assembly, whose jurisdiction extended "to all matters not vested in the Federal

---

940 *Id.*, para. 5; Eritrean Const., art. 7.

Government by the Federal Act."[941] In addition to this general grant
of residual power, the Assembly was given explicit jurisdiction over,
inter alia, legal matters, such as the criminal and civil codes; organization
of public services, including internal police, communications, and public
utilities; public assistance, social security, health, education, and protection of labor; internal commerce and trade; exploitation of natural
resources and agriculture; and taxation.[942]

The Federal Act is adopted and ratified by reference in the constitution, and the former set forth the jurisdiction of the federal Ethiopian
government. That federal jurisdiction included defense, foreign affairs,
currency and finance, foreign and interstate commerce, and external
and interstate communications (including ports). In addition, the federal
government was granted the power "to maintain the integrity of the
Federation."[943]

The Federal Act also provided that the federation would constitute
a single customs unit, with duties on goods originating from or with a
final destination in Eritrea being assigned to Eritrea. The assessment
and collection of federal taxes was to be delegated to the government
of Eritrea. Finally, there was a single nationality throughout the Federation, including Eritrea.

JUDICIAL POWERS

The Eritrean government possessed judicial power in the field of domestic affairs. The constitution mandated that this power "shall be exercised by a Supreme Court and by other courts which will apply the
various systems of law in force in Eritrea," and the Supreme Court was
given specific jurisdiction over disputes involving the constitutionality
of laws and orders.[944]

There was no provision for appeals from the Eritrean judicial system
to the federal system, although federal questions would presumably be
decided in the federal court system. Neither was there provision for the
settlement of jurisdictional disputes that might arise over the respective
competencies of the Eritrean and federal governments; one assumes
that such conflicts would have been dealt with by the courts under normal
processes of constitutional interpretation.

OTHER MATTERS

Both the federal and Eritrean governments undertook to "ensure to
residents in Eritrea, without distinction of nationality, race, sex, lan-

941 Eritrean Const., art. 5(1).
942 *Id.*, art. 5(2).
943 Federal Act, para. 3.
944 Eritrean Const., arts. 85, 90.

guage or religion, the enjoyment of human rights and fundamental liberties."[945] Special rights were accorded the various population groups in Eritrea, including "the right to respect for their customs and their own legislation governing personal status and legal capacity, the law of the family and the law of succession."[946] Ethnic languages were "permitted to be used in dealing with the public authorities, as well as for religious or educational purposes and for all forms of expression of ideas."[947]

The Eritrean constitution was subordinate to the provisions of the Federal Act, which, in effect, contained unamendable constitutional articles dealing with the fundamental structure of government. The constitution only entered into effect, according to its own terms, following approval by a UN Commissioner appointed to assist in the transition from British administration to Ethiopian federation.

OBSERVATIONS

Eritrea was established as "an autonomous unit federated with Ethiopia under the sovereignty of the Ethiopian Crown," and its government possessed "legislative, executive and judicial powers in the field of domestic affairs."[948] The Federal Act represented a very broad grant of authority within a federal context, particularly in that residual powers rested with Eritrea, despite Ethiopia's underlying sovereignty. Eritrea did not, however, retain the right to withdraw unilaterally from the federation.

Although there was intensive and wide-ranging United Nations participation in the formation of the Eritrean-Ethiopian federation, this participation effectively ended upon adoption of the Federal Act and constitution by both parties. There was no provision for international dispute settlement or international supervision once the federation was established.

The extent of international involvement in the development of Eritrea's political status and Ethiopia's proclaimed need for access to the Red Sea invite comparison with the Free City of Danzig and the Memel Territory in the post-World War I period. Danzig is perhaps the less similar, as its status as an international city under the sovereignty of the League of Nations, the continuing presence of the League's High Commissioner, and the dispute-settling mechanism under the League's authority provided an international involvement that was lacking in Eritrea. While the Memel Territory was placed under Lithuanian sov-

945 Federal Act, para. 7; Eritrean Const., art. 22.
946 Eritrean Const., art. 36.
947 *Id.*, art. 38.
948 G.A. Res. 390(V), *supra* note 939, at paras. 1, 2.

ereignty, the Port of Memel was declared to be a matter "of international concern," and disputes between Lithuania and any of the Principal Allied Powers were to be submitted to the Permanent Court of International Justice.

The extent of autonomy enjoyed by the Memel Territory was considerably less than that mandated by the Eritrean Federal Act. In Memel, for example, residual power rested with Lithuania; local legislation was subject to the Lithuanian constitution; and the Lithuanian Governor appointed Memel's chief executive officer (with the concurrence of the Memel legislature). The Memel Territory was established to protect the rights of a German minority enclave of strategic significance; in Eritrea, the purpose of granting a large measure of political autonomy and self-government was to respond to the principle of self-determination, insofar as that was politically feasible.

Despite these differences, the fate of Danzig, Memel, and Eritrea was the same: absorption or annexation into the larger political entity. It remains to be seen whether "autonomy" imposed by the international community can be a viable long-term solution, and the UN-sponsored federation reflected geopolitical and strategic interests as much as it represented a response to Eritrean demands for self-determination. As the then U.S. Secretary of State observed, "From the point of view of justice, the opinions of the Eritrean people must receive consideration. Nevertheless, the strategic interest of the United States ... [makes] it necessary that the country has to be linked with our ally, Ethiopia."[949]

The 1950 UN compromise remains a basis upon which some agreement might be reached, as many Eritreans would favor autonomy rather than independence as an ultimate solution. However, there is no evidence of an agreement between the Ethiopian government and Eritrean guerrillas in the near future, and the latter continue to view their fight against Ethiopia in anti-colonial terms. In the meantime, at least a quarter of a million lives have been lost on the battlefield alone, without taking into account the massive starvation in Eritrea and Tigray in recent years.[950]

Greenland

HISTORICAL BACKGROUND

Greenland is the largest island in the world, totaling over 2,000,000 square kilometers, of which fewer than 350,000 are not covered by the

949 John Foster Dulles, quoted in Robert D. Kaplan, "The Loneliest War," Atlantic Monthly (July 1988) at 61.
950 Colin Legum, "Eritrea," in Minority Rights Group, *Eritrea and Tigray* (Report No. 5, 1983 ed.) at 4.

permanent ice-cap. Its population today is approximately 53,000, of which 41,000 are ethnically Inuit people, born in Greenland. Greenland was attached to the Danish-Norwegian kingdom until 1814 and was a Danish colony until its formal integration with metropolitan Denmark in 1953.

There was very little contact between Greenland and the rest of the world until after World War II, when an industrialization and modernization program was begun. Local advisory councils had been established in the mid-nineteenth century, and two elected provincial councils were created in 1911. However, Greenland was essentially administered as a Danish colony throughout this period and was declared to be a non-self-governing territory by the United Nations in 1947.

In 1953, Denmark unilaterally adopted a new constitution which integrated Greenland and its residents into the Danish Kingdom on a basis of full equality with other Danish citizens. Danish laws therefore automatically applied to Greenland unless specific exceptions were made. The constitution did contain certain special provisions with respect to Greenland—concerning representation in the Danish parliament (the Folketing), referenda, the rights of an accused to be brought before a judge within 24 hours, and age qualifications for voting in local elections—but in general it did not establish any special status of home rule or autonomy. As a result of these constitutional changes, Greenland was dropped from the non-self-governing territory list by the UN General Assembly in 1954.

During the 1960s and 1970s, Greenlanders expressed a growing desire for greater local autonomy, although secession from Denmark does not seem to have been seriously considered.[951] In 1967 and 1970, Danish laws expanded the democratic, elective nature of Greenland's local government institutions. Following Denmark's entry into the European Economic Community in 1972, a move strongly opposed in Greenland, a Commission on Home Rule in Greenland was created in 1975 in order, *inter alia*, "to determine the areas within which and the measures by which the influence and responsibility at present resting with the Greenland Provincial Council may be increased" and to draft recommendations "for Home Rule in Greenland within the framework of national unity."[952]

The Home Rule Commission's report formed the basis for the

951 See generally Jens Dahl, "Greenland: Political Structure of Self-Government," 23 Arctic Anthropology 315 (1986).

952 See generally Jens Dahl, "New Political Structure and Old Non-Fixed Structural Politics in Greenland," in Brøsted et al. *supra* note 756, at 172–86; Isi Foighel, "Home Rule in Greenland," 1 Man & Society (1980), reprinted in Denmark, art. 9 CERD Report, UN Doc. CERD/C/106/Add.9 (1983), Annex I.

Greenland Home Rule Act, which was adopted by the Folketing in November 1978 and approved in a referendum in Greenland the following year.[953] As discontent with EEC membership continued, another referendum was held in 1982, in which 52% of those voting in Greenland voted in favor of withdrawal from the EEC. Following negotiations to amend the EEC Treaty, Greenland was accorded "overseas countries and territories" status in 1984, and agreement also was reached on various aspects of Greenland fisheries, including payment of compensation to Greenland for EEC access to fishing.[954] Greenland withdrew from the EEC in February 1985.

EXECUTIVE POWERS

The Home Rule Act establishes a quasi-parliamentary system in Greenland in which the elected assembly, the Landsting, elects the Chairman and other members of the executive cabinet, the Landsstyre. The Chairman and a majority of the other members of the Landsstyre must be members of the Landsting, and the Landsting may delegate those powers that it determines are appropriate to the executive.

The "chief representative" of the Danish central government in Greenland is known as the Rigsombudsmand (High Commissioner) and replaces the former governor. The Rigsombudsmand may be invited to participate in Greenland executive or legislative debates, but his primary role appears to be one of liaison between the Greenland and central authorities. He has no veto or other power over internal Greenland affairs.

"[Q]uestions affecting the foreign relations of the Realm" are specifically reserved to the central Danish authorities, and the supremacy of international treaties over local powers is set forth explicitly.[955] The Greenland authorities may comment on proposed treaties which would affect Greenland's interests, and, in the commercial area, Greenland may (with the approval of the central authorities) negotiate directly with foreign governments, participate in international negotiations, and demand that Danish diplomatic missions employ officers specifically to attend to Greenland's interests in countries of special commercial importance to Greenland. Greenland and the Faroe Islands have separate membership, under the aegis of Denmark, in the North Atlantic Salmon Conservation Organization, Northwest Atlantic Fisheries Organization,

953 Act No. 577 of 29 Nov. 1978 [hereinafter cited as "Home Rule Act"], reprinted in Denmark, art. 9 CERD Report, *supra* note 952, at Annex II; also see, e.g., Denmark, art. 40 CCPR Report, UN Doc. CCPR/C/1/Add.51 (1978) at 32–34.

954 Denmark, art. 9 CERD Report, UN Doc. CERD/C/131/Add.6 (1985), Annex V at 8–9.

955 Home Rule Act, §§10, 11.

and North East Atlantic Fisheries Commission.[956] Greenland recently assumed control over the activities of the Royal Greenland Trade Department (KGH), which regulates the Greenland fishing industry.

LEGISLATIVE POWERS

The legislative competence of the Landsting extends to 1) those areas listed in the Schedule to the Home Rule Act as within local competence, and 2) other matters as subsequently agreed by the Greenland and central governments. All of the specific areas listed in the Schedule (except health) had been transferred gradually to the local Greenland authorities by 1989 and include, *inter alia*, organization of home rule and local government; direct and indirect taxation;[957] internal transportation; fishing, hunting, agriculture, reindeer breeding, conservation, environmental protection, and country planning; commercial matters, including trade and competition, labor market affairs, and support and development of economic activities; and social welfare, education, cultural affairs, health services, and housing matters.[958]

In areas where legislative competence has not yet been transferred to the local authorities, the Danish government may, after negotiation, transfer administrative and regulatory authority to Greenland.

Greenland authorities must be given the opportunity to comment on proposed domestic Danish legislation and administrative orders which concern Greenland exclusively or which are of particular importance to Greenland. However, the Greenland authorities have no veto or other power over such legislation or orders.

JUDICIAL POWERS

There is no special provision in the Home Rule Act relating to separate Greenland courts, but local courts have been established to consider local statutes and other local matters.

OTHER MATTERS

Dispute settlement

The Home Rule Act provides that, in the event of a dispute concerning the respective jurisdiction of the Greenland and central authorities, the question shall be laid before a special mediation/arbitration board. This board consists of two central government members, two Greenland

---

956 1985 CERD Report, *supra* note 954, at 9.

957 Income and corporate taxes collected from Greenland are returned to Greenland, although the annual block grant to Greenland from Denmark is decreased by an amount equal to the latter.

958 Home Rule Act, Schedule.

members, and three Supreme Court judges. Should the four local and central government representatives agree on a settlement, the issue is deemed resolved; if there is no agreement, the Supreme Court judges decide. In practice, there are annual meetings of the Premiers of Denmark, Greenland, and the Faroe Islands to discuss matters of mutual interest.

Natural resources

Approximately one-third of Greenland's population is directly or indirectly involved in the fishing industry, and both the report of the Home Rule Commission and the Home Rule Act recognize the particular importance of natural resources to Greenland. Another impetus for the Commission's creation was the awarding of the first concession for oil exploitation on the Greenland continental shelf in 1975. The Home Rule Act states that "[the] resident population of Greenland has fundamental rights in respect of Greenland's natural resources" and requires that study, prospecting, and exploitation of those resources be regulated by joint agreement between the Danish government and the Greenland Landsstyre.[959] Thus, both governments seem to retain a veto over general development policy or specific proposals concerning Greenland's natural resources. The government describes mineral exploitation as being administered "in accordance with the principles of equality, joint decision-making and practical co-operation between Denmark and Greenland."[960]

Language

Greenlandic is recognized as the "principal" language in Greenland, and either Greenlandic or Danish may be used for official purposes. Danish is required to be "thoroughly taught," although in other respects education is a matter within local competence.[961] Because of the large number of Danes employed in the public sector, Danish remains the most widely used language in the administration.

OBSERVATIONS

The Greenland home rule provisions recognize local autonomy in a manner similar to that in many federal states, although it would be inaccurate to describe the Greenland-Denmark relationship as a federation. Nevertheless, Greenland does seem to have the possibility of achieving meaningful self-government, beyond the assumption of the

959 *Id.*, §8.
960 1985 CERD Report, *supra* note 954, at 9.
961 Home Rule Act, §9.

specific grants of power set forth in the Home Rule Act. "A major principle behind Greenlandic self-government is that the Home Rule authorities . . . are in a position to assume political responsibility in *all national* Greenlandic matters, provided they can create the economic foundation."[962] However, the fact that approximately 75% of Greenland's public expenditures are dependent upon economic aid from Denmark, suggests that the possibility for greater political independence remains remote.

There may be other inherent limitations on Greenlandic self-government, as well. Although only foreign relations are specifically reserved to the Danish government by the Home Rule Act, the Chairman of the Home Rule Commission has observed:

It follows from the principle of national unity that certain fields cannot be transferred to home rule authorities. This applies particularly to such fields as constitutional law (including . . . the adminstration of justice, constitutional rights), external relations (including the treaty-making power), national finances (including the Central Bank and its functions), financial-, monetary-, and currency policy, defence policy, criminal proceedings and imprisonment, as well as fundamental principles regarding the law of persons, family law, inheritance law, and the law of contracts.

The fact that these fields cannot be transferred to home rule authorities does, however, not prevent continuing the adoption of specific provisions . . . , having due regard to Greenland conditions, but it is up to national authorities to adopt such provisions.[963]

The Danish constitution "in its entirety" continues in force for Greenland, and sovereignty rests with the Danish government.

In addition to grants of authority over such "normal" local matters as, for instance, education and social legislation, the Home Rule Act addresses areas of particular concern to Greenland, such as natural resources. The joint local-national control to be exercised over mineral and oil resources is noteworthy, as are the negotiations which made Greenland's withdrawal from the EEC possible. Thus, while the theoretical scope of the act is rather narrow, it does offer the possibility of substantial autonomy for Greenland in those areas which are most significant. Ultimately, the Home Rule Act depends for its implementation on political and administrative cooperation between Greenland and Denmark, based on a general presumption of equality in those areas over which jurisdiction is shared.

962 Dahl, *supra* note 951, at 321; emphasis in original.
963 Foighel, *supra* note 952, at 5.

Netherlands Antilles

HISTORICAL BACKGROUND

The Netherlands Antilles consist of two separate island groups in the Caribbean Lesser Antilles: one, off the northern coast of Venezuela, consists of the islands of Curaçao and Bonaire (and Aruba, until 1985), and the other group includes the much smaller islands of St. Eustatius, Saba, and the southern part of St. Maartens. All form part of a single governmental district and were formerly administered as colonies jointly with Suriname. The larger islands have been under the political control of the Netherlands since 1634, and the entire Antilles group has been under Dutch rule since 1790.

The Netherlands Antilles were administered as colonies until 1937, when they became "territories"; this brought little political change, although a representative body that had been first created in the mid-nineteenth century was expanded, and an Advisory Council to the Dutch Governor was established. At the end of World War II, advisory committees were created in the Netherlands, Netherlands Antilles, and Suriname to develop new political arrangements. This coincided with the expansion of local suffrage to include women and to eliminate minimum income requirements, as well as the establishment of administrative councils responsible to local representative bodies. However, formal control remained in the hands of the Governor.

During the post-war period, distinctions were drawn between internal and external affairs, with the gradual devolution of power to the islands with respect to the former. In 1954, the three countries agreed on a Charter for the Kingdom of the Netherlands, which was designed to permit internal autonomy in the Netherlands Antilles and Suriname (and the Netherlands itself), while maintaining a link under the Dutch crown to conduct "common interests on the basis of equality."[964] As a result of this new political situation, arrived at "by mutual consent," the UN General Assembly removed the Netherlands Antilles and Suriname from its list of non-self-governing territories and ended the Netherlands' reporting obligations under article 73 of the UN Charter.[965]

Suriname became fully independent in 1975, and the Charter was revised so that it referred only to the Netherlands and the Netherlands Antilles. A further revision occurred when separate status was sought

964 Charter for the Kingdom of the Netherlands (1954), reprinted in Albert P. Blaustein and Phyllis M. Blaustein (eds.), *Constitutions of Dependencies and Special Sovereignties* (Dobbs Ferry, NY: Oceana, 1988), Preamble.

965 G.A. Res. 945(X), 10 UN GAOR, Supp. (No. 19), UN Doc. A/3116 (1955) at 25; for a critical appraisal of this process, see Clark, *supra* note 44, at 46–49.

and obtained by Aruba in 1985, although the following description is of the pre–1985 arrangements, based on the Charter and the constitution of the Netherlands Antilles as amended through 1966.

"Kingdom affairs" are essentially within the province of the Netherlands government, which automatically becomes the Kingdom government when considering Kingdom affairs. The Netherlands Antilles are represented at both the executive (Council of Ministers and Council of State) and legislative (States-General) levels by a Minister Plenipotentiary.

Although the terminology is somewhat confusing, internal affairs are dealt with by the Netherlands Antilles legislature and the Governor, who together adopt "federal ordinances." Thus, "federal" matters are local matters within the competence of the Netherlands Antilles, while "Kingdom" affairs are within the competence of the Netherlands government, sitting as the Kingdom government with Netherlands Antilles participation.

There is no provision for the unilateral termination of the Kingdom relationship by any of the parties, and both the Netherlands and Netherlands Antilles agreed to Suriname's withdrawal in 1975.

EXECUTIVE POWERS

Executive powers with respect to Kingdom affairs are exercised by the Governor, the King's representative in the Netherlands Antilles. The Governor's powers and duties in this representative capacity are determined by Kingdom statutes or ordinances, and include promulgation of Kingdom laws and overseeing "the general interests of the Kingdom" in the Netherlands Antilles.[966] The Governor may not promulgate a federal (local) ordinance "if he is of the opinion that the ordinance or the resolution is in conflict with the Statute [Charter], an international regulation, a Kingdom law or a Royal resolution containing general enactments, or is in conflict with the interests of which the protection or guarantee is a matter of the Kingdom."[967] The King (i.e., the Netherlands government) also may suspend federal legislation or administrative measures on similar grounds, but such suspension must be confirmed within a year by a Kingdom resolution. The Charter provides that any amendment to a federal statute relating to the powers of the Governor must be approved by the Kingdom government.

The Governor also acts as head of state of the Netherlands Antilles government. In this capacity, the Netherlands Antilles constitution out-

---

966 Regulation for the Governor of the Netherlands Antilles, Netherlands Off. Gazette 1955, No. 137.
   967 *Id.*, art. 24.

lines his powers and obligations, which include appointment and discharge of civil servants, administration of local finances, pardon powers, and the promulgation of federal ordinances. The Governor is assisted by a Government Advisory Council, appointed by and responsible to him, and he also appoints the members of the Netherlands Antilles Council of Ministers, after consultation with the legislature.

The Governor may veto proposed federal ordinances and, unless that veto is overruled by the King, no federal ordinance can take effect without the Governor's approval. He also may promulgate federal regulations ("resolutions"), after consultation with the Advisory Council.

An Explanatory Memorandum which accompanies the Charter states that, as head of state of one of the constituent countries of the Kingdom,

the Governor, in exercising his functions is bound by the decisions of a parliamentary Cabinet [the Netherlands Antilles Council of Ministers] and has to act in full agreement with its members, who in their turn are bound by their responsibility to the States. . . . Consequently, his powers and duties are not determined by Kingdom Statute, but by Country legislation which, in this instance is subject to the concurrence of the Government of the Kingdom [under article 454 of the Charter].[968]

Although there is specific provision for replacement of a minister who no longer enjoys the confidence of the Legislative Council, there is no similar provision with respect to the Governor.

As noted above, the Netherlands Antilles are represented in the Netherlands by a Minister Plenipotentiary, who has the right to participate in meetings of the Kingdom Council of Ministers and may demand a continuance of any discussion, thus preventing a decision being taken, if he objects to any action. Consultations are then required between the Minister Plenipotentiary and Kingdom ministers, and the Council of Ministers is required to abide by any decision reached during these deliberations. If the opportunity for deliberation is not utilized after a period of time which may be specified by the Council of Ministers, the Council of Ministers may proceed with its consideration of the question.

The Minister Plenipotentiary also may participate in debates of the Netherlands States-General (legislature) and may similarly request a postponement of any vote until the following meeting. Debate on a matter so objected to must be suspended unless it is adopted by a three-fifths vote.

968 Explanatory Memorandum to the Charter, *supra* note 964, at 23.

350 Other Autonomous Arrangements

LEGISLATIVE POWERS

The legislative power of the Netherlands Antilles is exercised by a uni-cameral Legislative Council, which is elected by universal suffrage. It adopts federal ordinances for the regulation of "subjects concerning the internal affairs of the Netherlands Antilles" and "other subjects which must be regulated by federal ordinance in accordance with a law or a decree of the Realm."[969] The assent of both the Legislative Council and the Governor is required to enact a local law.

The Netherlands Antilles constitution restricts "federal ordinances" to those subjects not superseded by the Charter, applicable international agreements, applicable Kingdom laws or resolutions, or the constitution itself. Designated as Kingdom affairs and therefore beyond the competence of the Legislative Council are, *inter alia*, defense; foreign relations; nationality; immigration; and the observance of fundamental human rights and freedoms, the rule of law, and the integrity of administration.[970] Kingdom laws are enacted by the Netherlands legislature, but they must be simultaneously submitted to the Netherlands Antilles Legislative Council. The latter may then forward any comments on the proposed legislation to the States-General.

While the Charter declares that the Netherlands Antilles and the Netherlands "conduct their internal affairs autonomously," any proposed amendment to the Netherlands Antilles constitution which relates to the powers of the Legislative Council, the distribution of seats on the Council, the regulation of island territories, or fundamental human rights, must also be approved by the Kingdom government.[971] Other amendments to the constitution may be adopted by a two-thirds vote of the Legislative Council.

JUDICIAL POWERS

The jurisdiction of the Supreme Court of the Netherlands over cases arising in the Netherlands Antilles is determined by Kingdom statute, although the Netherlands Antilles may request the addition to the court of an advisory or extraordinary member. The Netherlands Antilles judiciary consists of a Supreme Court of Justice and such other courts as may be established by federal ordinance. The justices of the Netherlands Antilles Supreme Court and the Attorney General are appointed by the King after consultation with the Governor.

Private and commercial law, civil procedure, criminal law and pro-

969 Netherlands Antilles Const., art. 18.
970 Charter, *supra* note 964, art. 3.
971 Netherlands Antilles Const., art. 189.

cedure, and other specific matters are governed by federal ordinance, "as much as possible corresponding with the existing laws in the Netherlands."[972] Any proposal for the "drastic amendment" of such laws must first be sent to the Netherlands government for its comments.

OTHER MATTERS

International economic and financial agreements

Although foreign relations are within the realm of Kingdom affairs, the Charter specifically provides that the King may neither enter into nor denounce international economic and financial agreements which bind the Netherlands Antilles without the latter's consent.[973] The Kingdom government also "shall cooperate in concluding such an agreement" upon the request of the Netherlands Antilles, "unless this would be inconsistent with the partnership of the Country in the Kingdom."[974] The Netherlands Antilles may be bound by treaties and international agreements concluded by the Kingdom in other spheres, for example, political or military.

Defense

The Kingdom may acquire property for defense purposes, pursuant to Kingdom statutes, although "whenever possible" execution of such statutes is entrusted to the local authorities. The King also may declare any part of the territory of the Kingdom to be in a state of war or siege, with Kingdom statutes setting forth the manner of transferring civil power to other civil or military authorities in such a situation. While the Netherlands Antilles contribute to the expense of defending the Kingdom, Netherlands Antilles residents cannot be compelled to serve in the armed forces or perform compulsory civil duty except pursuant to federal (local) ordinance. The constitution further provides that conscripts serving in the ground forces cannot be sent abroad without their consent, in the absence of an authorizing federal ordinance.

OBSERVATIONS

During the debate in the United Nations on the question of relieving the Netherlands of its reporting obligations under article 73 of the UN Charter, doubts were expressed as to the actual extent of autonomy obtained by the Netherlands Antilles and Suriname. The final vote to

972 *Id.*, art. 98.
973 Charter, *supra* note 964, art. 25.
974 *Id.*, art. 26.

permit the Netherlands to cease reporting was only 21 to 10, with 35 abstentions.

This hesitancy on the part of the General Assembly seems justified, as in the area of Kingdom affairs the powers of the Netherlands Antilles are indeed sparse. In effect, Kingdom affairs are determined by the Netherlands, and it is doubtful whether the participation of the Minister Plenipotentiary of the Netherlands Antilles is particularly influential. The King, that is, the Netherlands government, also appoints the Netherlands Antilles Governor and justices of its Supreme Court.

With respect to internal autonomy, the Netherlands-appointed Governor retains substantial powers of veto and appointment within the Netherlands Antilles. In addition, determination of the scope of internal affairs is made by the Netherlands, acting through the Governor, King, and Council of Ministers.

Nevertheless, there has been little suggestion that the present arrangements within the Kingdom of the Netherlands do not represent the wishes of the people of the Netherlands Antilles. There is a fairly broad degree of autonomy in matters such as education, social services, and the local economy. The Netherlands Antilles also have a certain degree of independence with respect to international economic and financial agreements and, in accordance with international agreements entered into by the Kingdom, the Netherlands Antilles may accede to membership in international organizations. If real power reposes in the locally elected Netherlands Antilles Council of Ministers (as suggested in the memorandum accompanying the Kingdom Charter), the de facto autonomy of the Netherlands Antilles may be much greater than suggested by the theoretical limitations imposed upon it, thus lending support to the principle that substance is more relevant than formal structures.

Switzerland (1848–1874)[975]

Prior to 1848, the Old Swiss Confederation was in essence a series of alliances among thirteen small sovereign states, bound together by a common desire for security. Of the thirteen cantons, six were pure democracies; four were urban aristocracies; and three were commercial oligarchies. The Diet, a periodic meeting of the representatives of the thirteen cantons, was the only body for the coordination of the activities of the Confederation. Each decision reached by the Diet had to be

---

975 See generally George A. Codding, *The Federal Government of Switzerland* (Boston: Houghton Mifflin, 1961).

unanimous, and each had to be ratified by the member governments. Thus, no central government as such existed to make binding decisions. Furthermore, the Diet had no authority over such matters as citizenship, money, and tariffs.

There were several attempts at Swiss federation or confederation in the early nineteenth century, but none was particularly successful. A Confederated Treaty between 22 cantons was signed in 1815, and several draft constitutions were subsequently proposed. In 1845, seven Catholic cantons seceded from the Confederation, but they were defeated by confederation forces, and unity was restored. One draft constitution was defeated in a popular referendum in May 1848, leading to the adoption and promulgation of the constitution considered in the present study in September 1848.

The 1848 constitution was seen as a compromise between the unitarists and the "particularists," and, while it was greatly admired by foreign observers, it was criticized by both Swiss conservatives and radical democrats. Particularly after the adoption of fairly liberal cantonal constitutions by Basel and Zurich in the 1860s, pro-unity and pro-democracy tendencies increased in Switzerland. A major revision of the 1848 constitution which would have, *inter alia*, centralized the army and unified the civil and penal law, was narrowly defeated in 1872, after minor amendments to articles 41 and 48 had been adopted in 1866. Another major revision was proposed and ratified in a referendum in 1874, and it is that 1874 constitution that remains in force (as amended) today.

The 1874 constitution retained Switzerland's federal structure, bicameral legislature, and collegiate executive, but otherwise increased the powers of the central federal government in relation to the cantons. The Confederation gained new powers with respect to the military, railways, private law, hunting and fishing, dams and forests, protection of factory workers, currency, weights and measures, civil status, and deprivation of political rights. The Federal Tribunal became permanent and more powerful; suffrage was expanded; and the possibility for optional referenda was introduced. The process for amending the constitution was basically unchanged.

The powers of the Swiss central government have continued to expand, in much the same way as the U.S. federal government has gradually assumed a greater role in national affairs. Recent amendments have, for example, granted to the Swiss federal government the right to legislate in order to eliminate unemployment, protect the family, and provide for social security—powers that were not clearly within the federal government's competence in 1874 or 1848.

Even today, however, Switzerland remains a federal rather than a unitary state. The cantons retain all residual governmental powers not delegated by the constitution to the federal government, and the canton remains the base for party political organization. In addition, the cantons exercise primary responsibility over certain matters, such as public works, education, health and sanitation, and the maintenance of law and order; they also are primarily responsible for the execution and administration of federal laws. Finally, the cantons possess certain "defensive" powers with which to check the growth of the federal government, including equal representation in the upper house of the legislature and use of the initiative and referendum. Thus, cantonal government remains an active force in the political lives of most Swiss citizens.

The 1848 constitution is the foundation upon which the Swiss federal system was built, and it was also the most decentralized of the Swiss "federal," as opposed to merely "confederated," structures. The following description will focus on the 1848 constitution (as amended in 1866), and all references to the "constitution" mean that constitution adopted in 1848, unless otherwise indicated.

EXECUTIVE POWERS

Federal executive power was vested in a seven-person collegiate executive, the Federal Council, whose members were appointed by the Federal Assembly (in joint session) for three-year terms; no more than one member could be chosen from any one canton. The President of the Union, who was the titular head of state and served as chairman of the Council, was elected by the Assembly every year from among the Council members.

The Federal Council was responsible for the administration and execution of the constitution, federal laws and regulations, and the sentences of the Federal Tribunal; it could issue administrative orders, suggest laws to the Federal Assembly, conduct foreign affairs, and was responsible for defense, the "preservation of quiet and order" within the confederation, and the confederation's finances.[976] The Council's de facto powers have increased in the twentieth century, and it is now responsible for the initiation and drafting of most legislation passed by the Federal Assembly.

The constitution refers to the 22 cantons as "sovereign," but only "so far as their sovereignty is not limited by the Federal Constitution."[977] The central government under the 1848 constitution easily fit within the classic definition of a federation, as there was a division of powers

976 1848 Swiss Const. (as amended in 1866), art. 90.
977 *Id.*, art. 3.

between the central and cantonal governments based on a superior authority, the constitution, which could not be changed by either party unilaterally. Thus, there is a clear distinction between the 1848 central government and its predecessor, the Diet.

Article 5 of the constitution provided, "The Union guarantees to the Cantons their territory, their sovereignty . . . , their constitutions, the liberty and rights of the people and the constitutional rights of the citizens, as well as the rights and powers which the people have conferred upon the authorities." Article 16 authorized the federal government to take any measures within its power to enforce these guarantees. This authority has been utilized on several occasions, for example, when federal government troops put down an insurrection in Ticino in 1890 which had actually overthrown the cantonal government.

While the confederation was not permitted "to maintain standing armies,"[978] this wording has been interpreted to mean a mercenary army independent of the federal army described in articles 19 and 20. A federal military force was therefore constitutionally permissible, but it was composed only of cantonal contingents, based on population. No canton could maintain a standing force of more than 300 troops without federal permission, although this restriction did not apply to cantonal police forces.

The conduct of foreign affairs was specifically delegated to the federal government, and article 7 prohibited "special alliances and treaties of a political character between Cantons." Other foreign affairs powers vested in the confederation government included the right to declare war and conclude peace and to make treaties, "especially such as relate to customs and commerce."[979]

Cantonal conventions "for matters of legislation, justice or administration" were authorized and were utilized to permit joint cooperation in such areas as the exploitation of water resources, maintenance of welfare programs, and coordination of police activities.[980] A canton also could enter into agreements with a foreign power concerning such matters as "public economy, neighbourly intercourse, and police." However, any such agreement (between cantons or between a canton and a foreign country) had to be brought to the attention of the federal authorities, which could prevent its execution if it were found that the agreement was contrary to the Union or to the rights of other cantons. The cantonal treaty-making power still exists, although it has been exercised only rarely in recent times.

978 *Id.*, art. 13.
979 *Id.*, art. 8.
980 *Id.*, art. 7.

LEGISLATIVE POWERS

The Federal Assembly was a bicameral legislature similar to the U.S. system: the National Council was composed of representatives based on population, with each canton or half-canton guaranteed at least one representative, and the States Council consisted of two representatives from each full canton and one from each divided or half-canton. Each canton was considered to be a single electoral district for the purpose of Assembly elections.

While article 3 reserved to the cantons those powers not delegated to the federal government, the powers delegated to the Federal Assembly even under the 1848 constitution were considerable. These areas of exclusive federal concern included, *inter alia*, foreign affairs in general; defense; construction of public works and the power to prohibit the erection of public works "which would be detrimental to the military interests of the Confederation"; customs duties and related matters (although cantons were to be indemnified under the 1848 provisions for losses due to the abolition by the central government of cantonal customs, tolls, and similar taxes); postal service; coinage of money; uniformity of weights and measures; the expulsion of foreigners and the determination of the citizenship of stateless persons; extradition between cantons, with the restriction that extradition for political offenses or misuse of the press could not be mandatory; laws and decrees to implement the constitution, e.g., voting and election laws; the manufacture and sale of gunpowder, arms, and ammunition; and certain legal disputes, including those among cantons, as to whether a subject was within cantonal or federal jurisdiction, and as to whether a question was within the jurisdiction of the Federal Council or Federal Tribunal.[981] The federal government also had broad powers to regulate inter- and intra-cantonal commerce.

The Federal Assembly was specifically granted the power to guarantee the cantonal constitutions, including intervention if necessary, and to adopt "measures for domestic security [and] for the maintenance of tranquility and order."[982] The guarantee of cantonal constitutions was interpreted to require the approval of the federal government of all amendments to those constitutions, to ensure that they contained nothing contrary to the federal constitution, that they secured the exercise of political rights according to republican forms, and that they were accepted by the people of the canton.

Under the 1874 constitution, the cantons were given "primary"

981 *Id.*, art. 74.
982 *Id.*, art. 74(7).

authority over health and sanitation, public works, education, and the maintenance of law and order, while under the 1848 provisions they had exclusive authority at least over health, sanitation, and education. In addition, since 1874, the cantons have been responsible for the execution of laws within the cantons, within the limits fixed by federal legislation.

JUDICIAL POWERS

The 1848 constitution established a Federal Tribunal, whose eleven members were appointed by the Federal Assembly for three-year terms, as Switzerland's highest court. In civil cases, the Tribunal had jurisdiction over appeals involving federal issues "of considerable importance"; disputes, not pertaining to public law, between cantons and between the Union and a canton; disputes between the Union, as defendant, and private individuals or corporations, when there was a federal question "of considerable importance"; and cases concerning stateless persons.[983] In disputes involving a canton, the Federal Council had the authority to proclaim a case to be beyond the jurisdiction of the Tribunal, in which case the Federal Assembly decided the controversy. The Tribunal also could decide alleged violations of federal constitutional rights, but only if such complaints were referred to it by the Federal Assembly.

As noted above, provisions in the 1874 constitution considerably strengthened the role of the Federal Tribunal, which was relatively weak with respect to deciding basic constitutional issues under the 1848 constitution.

OTHER MATTERS

Language

The constitution provided that German, French, and Italian were the "national languages" of Switzerland, but it did not further define under which conditions each or all could be used. Language use is, in fact, territorial, and each canton determines its official language(s).

Land

Discrimination against non-cantonal citizens and rights of redemption exercised by citizens of one canton to the detriment of other citizens were specifically abolished. All Swiss citizens were guaranteed "the right of free settlement" within the Confederation, provided that they possessed birth certificates, citizenship, and "good moral conduct."

---

983 *Id.*, arts. 101, 102.

OBSERVATIONS

Despite the reserved powers of the cantons and their "sovereignty," the 1848 Swiss constitution accorded moderately broad powers to the federal government in most matters one would normally consider to be "national" in scope. Among those matters *not* delegated to the Union and therefore within exclusive cantonal competence were education; health and welfare; local police powers; criminal laws; the protection and exploitation of natural resources; and, in general, what might be termed cultural or social matters, including regulation of social and personal status. The federal government's powers in the areas necessary to maintain a viable union—national defense, foreign affairs, a national customs union, guarantee of a republican form of local government, control over currency—were sufficient, but the reservoir of powers available to the cantonal governments clearly placed severe restrictions on the ability of the central government to expand its power.

As noted above, Switzerland has become more and more centralized, beginning with the constitutional revision adopted in 1874. While it would be inaccurate to suggest that cantonal rights have been extinguished, it is unlikely that a nineteenth-century Swiss citizen would recognize the vast powers wielded by his or her central government in the late twentieth century.

In 1848, Switzerland was a true federal state, with substantial powers reserved to the cantons. The cantons enjoyed autonomy with respect to most civil, penal, cultural, and social matters. At the same time, the rights of the federal government to preserve the union were reasonably substantial, and the federal government was much more than a mere alliance of autonomous regions. In addition to the federal government's power in the national defense and foreign affairs areas, the general guarantees of non-discrimination by the cantons against any Swiss citizen should be noted and contrasted, for example, to the "discriminatory" autonomy retained by the Aland Islands with respect to non-resident Finnish citizens.

Union of Soviet Socialist Republics

The 1979 Soviet census enumerated 92 different national groups within a total Soviet population of 262,000,000 people; Russians constitute the largest ethnic group, with approximately 52% of the population, followed by Ukrainians (16.2%), Uzbeks (4.7%), Byelorussians (3.6%), Kazakhs (2.5%), Tatars (2.4%), and Azerbaijanis (2.1%).[984] Five other

984 Teresa Rakowska-Harmstone, "The Soviet Union," in Robert G. Wirsing (ed.), *Protection of Ethnic Minorities* (New York: Pergamon Press, 1981) at 120–21.

groups (Tadzhiks, Armenians, Georgians, Moldavians, and Lithuanians) comprise 1–2% of the population each, while the remaining 80 have less than 1% each.[985]

HISTORICAL BACKGROUND

The common interests of the proletariat that are the basis of Marxist philosophy should in theory transcend "national" interests of ethnic or other groups, but it was evident during the period of consolidation of the Bolshevik Revolution in 1917–1922 that a unified Soviet state could be created only by recognizing the equality and national identity of non-Russian peoples formerly within the Russian empire. Most of these peoples sought to achieve self-determination, and between January and May 1918, Finland, Lithuania, Latvia, Estonia, Siberia, Ukraine, Moldavia, Oirot, Byelorussia, North Caucasia, Azerbaijan, Armenia, and Georgia declared their independence. The Russian Socialist Federative Soviet Republic (RSFSR), the nucleus of the subsequent U.S.S.R., was founded in January 1918, and it soon established eight "autonomous republics" within its borders.

As the Bolshevik army gradually emerged victorious from the civil war, it conquered or intimidated all the minority republics except Finland, Lithuania, Latvia, and Estonia.[986] In 1922, the Union of Soviet Socialist Republics was formed through the federation of the RSFSR, Ukraine, Byelorussia, and the Transcaucasian Republic, which had been formed earlier that year by the merger of Armenia, Azerbaijan, and Georgia.

The 1924 U.S.S.R. Constitution adopted by the four republics formally established a federal system, although in fact it more closely resembled an incorporation of the other three republics into the RSFSR. Nevertheless, the constitution did include clauses allocating certain powers to the federal government and reserving other powers to the constituent republics, and it formally recognized the right of the "sovereign" republics to secede from the Union. Provision was made for "autonomous republics" and "autonomous regions," which were granted cultural rights and had direct representation at the federal level. One house of the bicameral legislature was designated the Soviet of Nationalities

---

985 *Id.*

986 Only Finland escaped the further consolidation of the U.S.S.R. that occurred in the post-World War II period, and the 1978 area of the Soviet state (22.4 million square kilometers) almost precisely equaled that of the Russian empire in 1913 (22.3 million square kilometers). Ilya Levkov, "Self-Determination in Soviet Politics," in Alexander and Friedlander, *supra* note 163, at 133. *Cf.*, e.g., Hugh Seton-Watson, "Russian Nationalism in Historical Perspective," in Robert Conquest, ed., *The Last Empire* (Stanford, CA: Hoover Institution Press, 1986) at 14–29; Alexandre Benningsen, "Soviet Minority Nationalism in Historical Perspective," in *id.* at 131–50.

and consisted of five delegates from each Union or autonomous republic and one delegate from each autonomous region.

Matters of civil rights and existing penal, civil, labor, land, and other codes were essentially left within the domain of the union republics, although they could be overridden by federal laws within federal competence. The federal Union was granted authority over the entire state economy, including the use and development of all natural resources.

The second Soviet constitution was adopted in 1936 and "significantly expanded the central authority and moved the Soviet state closer to complete centralization,"[987] although the constituent republics were still referred to as "sovereign" and retained the right to secede under article 17. Article 14 of the constitution listed 23 areas within the exclusive jurisdiction of the central authorities, while the republics retained authority over the ministries of education, local industry, collective economy (excluding state farms), and social welfare.

Two amendments in 1944 expanded the rights of the republics, allowing each to establish and maintain a military force and to enter into direct diplomatic relations with foreign states and conclude international agreements. No republic availed itself of the first right (which is absent from the 1977 constitution), and the latter competence was utilized primarily to justify separate membership in the United Nations for the U.S.S.R., Ukrainian S.S.R., and Byelorussian S.S.R. The exercise of both powers was, in any event, under the supervision of the federal government, and the conduct of foreign relations in all the republics except the Ukraine and Byelorussia has been limited to ceremonies pertaining to relations with neighboring states.[988]

Autonomous republics and regions were altered at various times by the federal authorities, and one author has likened the theoretically "autonomous" status of the republics to a "capricious privilege rather than . . . a prescribed constitutional right which stems from the political development of a given nation."[989]

THE 1977 CONSTITUTION

The current Soviet constitution was adopted in 1977 and, while there are several changes from previous constitutions, it does not represent a radical departure from previous policies vis à vis the federal structure

987 Levkov, *supra* note 986, at 150.
988 John N. Hazard, *The Soviet System of Government* (Chicago & London: Univ. of Chicago Press, 1957, rev. 5th ed. 1980) at 104.
989 Levkov, *supra* note 986, at 152.

of the state. The U.S.S.R. is deemed to be "an integral, federal, multi-national state formed on the principle of socialist federalism as a result of the free self-determination of nations and the voluntary association of equal Soviet Socialist Republics."[990] It "embodies the state unity of the Soviet people and draws all its nations and nationalities together for the purpose of jointly building communism."[991] The U.S.S.R. consists of fifteen Union Republics, which include within their boundaries 20 Autonomous Republics and seven Autonomous Provinces; the RSFSR contains an additional ten National Districts.

Legislative powers

The competence granted to the central Soviet government in article 73 of the constitution is sufficient to ensure a centralized political system within the U.S.S.R., despite its formal federal structure. The Union government has jurisdiction over, *inter alia*, the "establishment of the general principles for the organisation and functioning of republican and local bodies of state authority and administration; . . . the ensurance of uniformity of legislative norms throughout the USSR and establishment of the fundamentals of the legislation of the Union of Soviet Socialist Republics and [individual] Union Republics; . . . direction of the country's economy; . . . drafting and approval of state plans for the economic and social development of the USSR; . . . [and] drafting and approval of the consolidated Budget of the USSR."[992] The central government is responsible for the "ensurance of conformity of the Constitutions of Union Republics to the Constitution of the USSR" and "settlement of other matters of All-Union importance."[993]

The 1977 constitution requires that the two chambers of the bi-cameral Supreme Soviet (one of which continues to be based on "nationality"[994]) be equal. However, the Soviet of Nationalities has never disagreed with any program proposed by the Communist Party of the Soviet Union (CPSU), and the constitutional provisions for re-conciling differences between the two chambers have never been utilized.[995]

---

990 1977 U.S.S.R. Const., art. 70. (This and other quotations are taken from the translation reprinted in Hazard, *supra* note 988, at 247–85.)

991 *Id.*

992 *Id.*, art. 73, §§3–6.

993 *Id.*, §§10, 11.

994 The Soviet of Nationalities currently consists of 32 deputies from each Union Republic, 11 deputies from each Autonomous Republic, five deputies from each Autonomous Region, and one deputy from each Autonomous Area. 1977 U.S.S.R. Const., art. 110.

995 Hazard, *supra* note 988, at 102; 1977 U.S.S.R. Const., art. 115.

As noted below, effective power in the U.S.S.R. is wielded by the CPSU rather than by the Supreme Soviet per se.

Except for its symbolic value, membership in the Supreme Soviet is virtually meaningless, because this body's primary role, notwithstanding the constitution, is not to make laws but to socialize the electorate and build support for party decisions in elections. It meets for only a few days each year.[996]

Day-to-day governmental authority is exercised by the 39-member Presidium of the Supreme Soviet; each of the Presidium's fifteen Vice-Chairmen must be from a different Union Republic.[997] It is the Presidium which has the obligation to "ensure observance of the Constitution of the USSR and conformity of the Constitutions and laws of Union Republics to the Constitution and laws of the USSR" and "interpret the laws of the USSR."[998] Between the short sessions of the Supreme Soviet, the Presidium also may amend existing legislation.

Each Union Republic and Autonomous Republic is headed by its own Supreme Soviet, and the former retains residual power "to deal with all matters within the jurisdiction of the Republic under the Constitutions of the USSR and the Republic."[999] As noted by the broad grant to the central authorities, however, the authority of the republics is much more limited than this language might suggest. Article 113 grants to the Union Republics the right to initiate legislation in the Supreme Soviet.

Executive powers

The government or "cabinet" of the U.S.S.R. is the Council of Ministers, which is elected by the Supreme Soviet; corresponding bodies exist at the level of the republics. The Council of Ministers is subordinate to the Presidium, and the former's members may be replaced by the latter. The Council of Ministers "shall coordinate and direct" the work of both Union and joint Union-Republic ministries; may issue decisions and ordinances which are binding throughout the country; and has the right to suspend implementation of republic Councils of Ministers "in matters within the jurisdiction of the Union of Soviet Socialist Republics."[1000]

---

996 Rakowska-Harmstone, *supra* note 984, at 132.
997 1977 U.S.S.R. Const., art. 120.
998 *Id.*, art. 121.
999 *Id.*, art. 137.
1000 *Id.*, art. 134.

Judicial powers

The Soviet Union does not follow the principle of "separation of powers" familiar to most Western systems, but it has adopted what some have termed a "separation of functions."[1001] Higher courts, including the Supreme Court of the U.S.S.R., are elected by the corresponding Supreme Soviet (legislature); lower courts are elected by direct or indirect suffrage. The U.S.S.R. Supreme Court supervises the administration of justice by Soviet and Union Republic courts. Jurisdiction between federal and republic courts is divided along functional lines: all civil matters are heard before republic (or lower level) courts, while there is shared jurisdiction in criminal matters. As noted above, statutory interpretation is within the jurisdiction of the Presidium.

OTHER MATTERS

Language

Linguistic policy, and, in particular, the relationship between Russian and other "national" languages, have been extremely delicate and important issues throughout the history of the Soviet Union. Over 90% of the Soviet population considers their national language to be their first language, and only 23.4% of the non-Russian population speak Russian as a second language.[1002]

The inherent tension between development of a Soviet consciousness and recognition of the reality of a multi-linguistic and multi-ethnic society is evident throughout the constitution.

Citizens of the USSR of different races and nationalities have equal rights.
Exercise of these rights is ensured by a policy of all-round development and drawing together of all the nations and nationalities of the USSR, by educating citizens in the spirit of Soviet patriotism and socialist internationalism, and by the possibility to use their native language and the languages of other peoples of the USSR.[1003]

Linguistic rights are referred to in several provisions of the 1977 constitution, such as the provision that judicial proceedings be conducted in the language "spoken by a majority of people in the locality."[1004] Article 34 of the constitution prohibits discrimination on the basis of language, and article 45 guarantees "the opportunity to attend a school where teaching is in the native language."

1001 See, e.g., Hazard, *supra* note 988, at 192–94.
1002 1979 figures, taken from Rakowska-Harmstone, *supra* note 984, at 123.
1003 1977 U.S.S.R. Const., art. 36.
1004 *Id.*, art. 159.

The policy "to promote the Russian language as a second native tongue which would serve as a cultural framework for the development of one socialist culture"[1005] has been a major source of complaints regarding "Russification" of non-Russian cultures. For example, a 1985 revision to the Soviet statute setting forth the fundamental principles of public education added a requirement that the "necessary conditions" be created to ensure that all schools teach Russian, "which has been voluntarily adopted by the Soviet people as the means of communication between different nationalties, . . . due account being taken of the national characteristics of the population of the Union Republics."[1006]

Of the non-Russian republics, only Georgia, Armenia, and Azerbaijan include in their constitutions a guarantee that the national language of the republic also is the state or official language; attempts to alter this formulation in 1978 resulted in public protests in Georgia, and the "state language" designation was retained. While bilingualism has increased throughout the Soviet Union, use of national languages has become "the key instrument of national self-assertion and a vehicle for the expression of newly found pride."[1007]

Education and culture

As noted, education in national languages is constitutionally guaranteed, although this right is available only within the relevant autonomous republic or province. At the same time, article 25 of the constitution provides that there shall be "a uniform system of public education" throughout the U.S.S.R., and there is little or no variation in the substantive content of education in the autonomous areas.

While the Soviet Union emphasizes the cultural diversity of its citizenry,[1008] there are no specific constitutional protections for national or minority cultures. Rather, the concern seems to be to promote culture at the state level:

> The state concerns itself with protecting, augmenting and making extensive use of society's cultural wealth for the moral and aesthetic education of the Soviet people, for raising their cultural level.

1005 Levkov, *supra* note 986, at 162.
1006 See U.S.S.R. art. 9 CERD Report, UN Doc. CERD/C/149/Add.8 (1986) at 3–4.
1007 Rakowska-Harmstone, *supra* note 984, at 129.
1008 For example, almost every issue of the government-produced periodical, *Soviet Life*, includes an article on one of the autonomous republics or provinces; see, e.g., "Tajik Culture —Alive," Nov. 1985, No. 11 (350); "Armenia, An Introduction to the Republic," June 1986, No. 6 (357); and several articles on the Baltic Republics, Aug. 1986, No. 8 (359).

In the USSR development of the professional, amateur and folk arts is encouraged in every way.[1009]

The state helps enhance the social homogeneity of society, namely the elimination of class differences and of the essential distinctions between town and country and between mental and physical labour, and the all-round development and drawing together of all the nations and nationalities of the USSR.[1010]

Foreign relations

Article 18-A of the 1936 constitution stated: "Each union republic has the right to enter directly into diplomatic relations with foreign states, to conclude agreements with them and to exchange diplomatic and consular representatives." The 1977 formulation in article 80 is slightly weaker and omits the salient word "directly": "A Union Republic has the right to enter into relations with other states, conclude treaties with them, exchange diplomatic and consular representatives, and take part in the work of international organisations."

The right of the republics to conduct foreign relations is limited by the federal power to represent the U.S.S.R. in international relations and establish "the general procedure for, and co-ordination of, the relations of Union Republics with other states and with international organisations"; the federal authorities also have jurisdiction over "foreign trade and other forms of external economic activity on the basis of state monopoly."[1011] The procedures referred to are outlined in a 1978 law which further restricts the republics' role in foreign policy.[1012]

Article 72 of the constitution declares that "[e]ach Union Republic shall retain the right freely to secede from the USSR." This article has never been invoked, and persons advocating secession have, in fact, been imprisoned for anti-state activities.

"GLASNOST" AND "PERESTROIKA" UNDER GORBACHEV

The "openness" and "restructuring" which became identified with the policies of General Secretary and President Mikhail Gorbachev may have played a significant role in the reassertion of minority nationality rights which became evident in the late 1980s. While the adoption of several amendments to the Soviet constitution in December 1988 was generally thought to bring somewhat greater democracy to the Soviet

---

1009 1977 U.S.S.R. Const., art. 27.

1010 *Id.*, art. 19.

1011 *Id.*, art. 73(10).

1012 Law concerning the Order of Signature, Implementation, and Withdrawal of International Agreements by the USSR, adopted on 6 July 1978, cited in Levkov, *supra* note 986, at 154.

system, it also offered delegates from the Baltic republics of Estonia, Latvia, and Lithuania, in particular, the opportunity to voice their fears that the amendments undesirably concentrated power in Moscow at the expense of the republics.[1013]

The development of "Popular Front" political organizations in the Baltic republics during 1988 presented the most serious constitutional challenge in recent years to central government hegemony. In November 1988, the Estonian legislature declared its "sovereignty" vis à vis the central authorities and the supremacy of its laws over those of Moscow. Despite an immediate rebuff from Moscow, on the grounds that the Estonian actions were incompatible with the Soviet constitution, Estonia reaffirmed its decision in December 1988 and subsequently adopted a law making Estonian the sole official language in the republic.

Similar political movements developed in Latvia and Lithuania, although neither republic's government had asserted its independence from Moscow quite as directly as Estonia by the end of 1988. In February 1989, however, the Lithuanian mass movement known as Sajudis overwhelmingly approved a manifesto calling for "legal, political, economic and cultural independence for Lithuania," citing a speech by President Gorbachev to the United Nations in which he called for all nations to be allowed to exercise "freedom of choice."[1014] Because of ethnic Russian immigration, Latvians may now constitute only a minority of the population in Latvia, while Estonians and Lithuanians still form a majority of approximately 60% and 80%, respectively, in their own republic.

A somewhat more "traditional" conflict, perhaps also inspired by a hope that the Gorbachev regime would be more sympathetic, erupted in the Nagorno-Karabakh region of Azerbaijan in February 1988.[1015] After clashes between Armenians and Azerbaijanis in which over 30 Armenians were killed, scores of thousands of Armenian demonstrators demanded the reincorporation of the Azerbaijani-surrounded enclave

---

1013 Attempts by the Baltic republics to require approval of the constitutional amendments by each of the 15 constituent republics or to reserve the right to retain single-chamber rather than bicameral legislatures were rebuffed. The latter proposal was said to "contradict the principle of uniformity of institutions across the nation." A special plenum of the CPSU's Central Committee in 1989 was to address the second stage of constitutional reform, which includes the question of the division of power between the republics and the central government. See Michael Dobbs, "Soviet Legislators Adopt Gorbachev Reform Plan," Wash. Post, 2 Dec. 1988, at A1, col. 5.

1014 Michael Dobbs, "Lithuanian Mass Movement Calls for Independence," Wash. Post, 17 Feb. 1989, at A1, col. 2.

1015 A convenient chronology of events between February and September 1988 may be found in Tamara Dragadze, "The Armenian-Azerbaijani conflict: structure and sentiment," 11 Third World Q. 55, 55–57.

of Nagorno-Karabakh (whose population is approximately 75% Armenian) with Armenia, from which it was severed in 1923 when the autonomous region of Azerbaijan was created.

The central government refused to alter Nagorno-Karabakh's status, despite formal requests for reincorporation of the enclave into Armenia by the Nagorno-Karabakh and Armenian legislatures (rejected by Azerbaijan) and a two-month long general strike in Nagorno-Karabakh. In January 1989, a "special form of administration" by a Moscow-based committee was imposed on Nagorno-Karabakh by the Presidium, although the province remains legally a part of Azerbaijan.

OBSERVATIONS

Despite the Gorbachev reforms and the opening of the Soviet system to greater diversity of views, no analysis of the policy of the U.S.S.R. towards minorities and "nationalities" is meaningful without recognition of the pervasive influence and control of the Communist Party. It is perhaps significant that the description of the "federal" structure in the Soviet Union does not begin until article 70 of the 1977 constitution, while the initial chapter (articles 1–9) makes clear the primacy of the central state and party:

The Soviet state is organised and functions on the principle of democratic centralism. . . . [which] combines central leadership with local initiative and creativity. . . . [1016]

The leading and guiding force of Soviet society and the nucleus of its political system, of all state organisations and public organisations, is the Communist Party of the Soviet Union. . . . The Communist Party . . . determines the general perspectives of the development of society and the course of the home and foreign policy of the USSR, directs the great constructive work of the Soviet people, and imparts a planned, systematic and theoretically substantiated character to their struggle for the victory of communism. [1017]

It is within this context of actual, centralized party control that the degree of effective autonomy by the 37 autonomous republics, regions, or areas must be understood.

Whatever cultural, linguistic, or other autonomy is present, it is clear that there has been no meaningful political autonomy or power-sharing within the U.S.S.R.—despite the theoretical federal structure and article 72's right to secede. An early and generally sympathetic observer of the Soviet "un-national" state concluded:

1016 1977 Constitution, art. 3.
1017 *Id.*, art. 6.

For those who do not accept the doctrine of the dictatorship of the proletariat the "self-determination" promised to the nationalities has, admittedly, been a farce, and often a tragic farce at that, if we mean by self-determination the right of a nationality to decide, by the will of its numerical majority, what its political and social constitution shall be, and whether or no it shall adhere to the Soviet Union. Even local autonomy in political and economic questions has been reduced to-day to a shadow.[1018]

The actual recognition of "national" cultural and political rights has varied tremendously according to the shifting winds of politics in Moscow. It has been estimated that one million Ukranians died during the Stalinist purges of the 1930s, and other national groups also suffered greatly. While the CPSU Congress in 1961 stated that "[t]he boundaries between the constituent republics of the U.S.S.R. are increasingly losing their former significance," it also recognized that "the obliteration of national distinctions, and especially of language distinctions, is a considerably longer process than the obliteration of class distinctions."[1019] Another crackdown on "local nationalism" in the Ukraine occurred in 1972–73, and Georgian nationalism also increased during the 1970s. As noted above, in 1988 the Baltic states and the question of Nagorno-Karabakh presented the most serious assertions of nationalism in decades.

Soviet policy in largely Muslim central Asia has been to accentuate differences among "nationalities" (primarily on the basis of language) as a means of discouraging pan-Islamic or pan-Turkic identity. The result, however, often has been to reinforce nationalist feelings rather than to increase a sense of solidarity with the larger Soviet society. For example, replacement of the Communist Party leader in Kazakhstan by an ethnic Russian in December 1986 touched off serious riots, although there were no doubt political as well as "nationalist" motives for this violent reaction; normal practice in the Soviet Asian republics is for a member of the dominant nationality to be in charge, with a Russian as second in command.

Serious complaints about Russian immigration into autonomous or ethnically distinct areas and "Russification" of local languages and cultures continue. However, even pre-Gorbachev Soviet policy was undoubtedly an advance over the aggressive Russification practices of the Tsar in the late nineteenth century, when national languages were essentially prohibited and large-scale ethnic Russian emigration to non-Russian areas encouraged. There has been a cultural and literary resurgence in recent years in, for example, Georgia and the Ukraine, and

1018 Macartney, *supra* note 79, at 463.
1019 Quoted in Hazard, *supra* note 988, at 289.

most nationalities (the Kazakhs and Latvians are notable exceptions) retain a fairly stable majority in their own republic.[1020] On the other hand, political conformity ordered from Moscow often seems to be anti-national, as any reaffirmation of autonomous identity may be interpreted as a political as well as cultural threat to communist hegemony.

Soviet willingness to tolerate at least cultural nationalism within the U.S.S.R. stands in sharp contrast to the attempted eradication of ethnic or linguistic minorities by many of its neighbors. It would be incorrect to consider the linguistic and cultural autonomy enjoyed by most of the Soviet nationalities even in the pre-Gorbachev era as illusory, despite attempts to impose an overlay of Russian language and culture. At the same time, the dominance and centralized structure thus far character-istic of the CPSU has made a sham of theoretical political autonomy and limits the value of the Soviet model with respect to other situations in which ethnic and cultural differences exist.

1020 Rakowska-Harmstone, *supra* note 984, at 121. *Cf.* Mikhail S. Bernstam, "The Demography of Soviet Ethnic Groups in World Perspective," in Conquest, *supra* note 986, at 314–68.

Chapter 17
Territories of International Concern

Aland Islands

HISTORICAL BACKGROUND[1021]

The Aland Islands are located in the Baltic Sea between Sweden and Finland and, because of their location, have been considered to be of prime strategic importance by Sweden and Russia for centuries. The islands are inhabited by persons of Swedish language, culture, and traditions, stemming from the period from 1157 to 1809, when they were under Swedish control. Following Sweden's defeat by Russia, the Treaty of Frederiksham ceded Finland (including the Aland Islands) to Russia, and Finland became an autonomous Grand Duchy within the Russian empire. Following attempts at the Russification of Finland in the late nineteenth and early twentieth centuries and the March 1917 Russian Revolution, Finland declared its independence in December 1917. The question presented to the international community was whether the Aland Islands were a part of the new Finnish state or whether they should be permitted to reunite with their cultural motherland, Sweden.

The islands had been demilitarized pursuant to an 1858 treaty among the United Kingdom, France, and Russia,[1022] although they were re-fortified by Russia during World War I. Because of the Aland Islands's threatening position vis à vis Stockholm and their strategic importance in the Baltic Sea, all parties seem to have agreed that the continued demilitarization or neutrality of the islands was a necessity.

1021 See generally James Barros, *The Aland Islands Question: Its Settlement by the League of Nations* (New Haven, CT: Yale Univ. Press, 1968); League of Nations Off. J., Spec. Supp. No. 1 (1920).

1022 Convention of 30 Mar. 1858, 25 Martens Nouveau Recueil 788.

The dispute over which country Aland rightly belonged to went on for several years. The Alanders rejected initial Finnish offers of autonomy, and the Finish government subsequently arrested two of the most prominent pro-Swedish Aland leaders. Finally, the League of Nations was called upon to determine the islands' status.

The League appointed two commissions to examine the Aland Islands question. The first decided that the matter was one of international concern and therefore within the League's competence, since Finland had not acquired sovereignty over Aland during the period when the Russian empire was disintegrating and prior to the Alanders' expressed wishes to be reunited with Sweden.[1023] The second commission rejected Aland claims to self-determination and proposed the solution eventually adopted by the Council of the League of Nations in 1921, that of according the islands autonomy under Finnish sovereignty.[1024]

Aland autonomy was assured by Finland in the "Guarantee Law" of 6 May 1920 and was reinforced by a 27 June 1921 resolution of the League Council, which was accepted by both Finland and Sweden; under the terms of that resolution, Finland agreed to guarantee to the Alanders "the preservation of their language, of their culture, and of their local Swedish tradition."[1025] Subsequent measures expanded the extent of Aland autonomy after World War II, and the most recent statement of Aland's relationship with Finland is found in the Finnish Autonomy Act of 28 December 1951, which was approved by both the Finnish and Aland parliaments. While the formal status of the 1921 international guarantees is now somewhat unclear,[1026] the 1951 law can only be amended with the mutual consent of the Aland parliament and the Finnish government.

EXECUTIVE POWERS

The executive powers of the province are vested in an Executive Council chosen by the Aland parliament. The administration of most central government laws and regulations has been delegated to the Aland gov-

---

1023 *Report of the International Committee of Jurists, supra* note 86.

1024 *Report presented to the Council of the League by the Commission of Rapporteurs, supra* note 87.

1025 League of Nations Off. J., Supp. 5, *Resolutions adopted by the Council of the League of Nations at its Thirteenth Session* (1921) at 24; statement by M. Hymans, *id.* at 25. One authority has termed the agreement "the most radical form of international guarantee for a national minority ever to have been drawn up." Tore Modeen, "The International Protection of the National Identity of the Aland Islands," in *Scandinavian Studies in Law* (1973) at 177, 184.

1026 *Cf.* Modeen, *supra* note 1025; *Study of the Legal Validity of the Undertakings Concerning Minorities,* UN Doc. E/CN.4/367 (1950) at 69.

ernment by the central authorities. Before the central government can issue administrative provisions within its legislative competence which are to be applied solely within Aland, the provincial government has the right to comment on the proposals.

The Finnish central government is represented in the Aland Islands by a County Governor appointed by the President of Finland, either with the agreement of the chairman of the provincial Aland parliament or, if there is no agreement, from among a list of five persons nominated by the provincial parliament. If none of the five are considered suitable by the President, further nominations may be requested. In every case, provincial agreement must be obtained. The County Administrative Board, which is headed by the County Governor, has primarily fiscal responsibilities; a County Administrative Court considers appeals against local administrative decisions.

LEGISLATIVE POWERS

Article 13 of the 1951 law enumerates the matters in which the unicameral Aland legislature is competent, which include education, social affairs, police and health services, and promotion of local industry. Provincial taxes may be levied, and Aland also receives a "fiscal adjustment" of state funds to cover services that would be the responsibility of the central government if responsibility had not been delegated to Aland; Alanders receive social benefits equal to those received by other Finnish citizens. This "adjustment" is apportioned to Aland according to the recommendations of the "Aland Delegation," which is discussed below.

The President may veto provincial laws, but only if, after having heard the opinion of the Finnish Supreme Court, he is of the opinion that the provincial law concerns matters within the legislative competence of the central government or concerns its internal or external security.

Exclusive national legislative competence extends under section 11 to, *inter alia*, the "basic laws" of the country (excluding laws relating to self-government in Aland, which may be amended only with the joint consent of the national and Aland authorities), human rights, foreign relations, national defense, customs, the penal code, and most aspects of civil law.

JUDICIAL POWERS

Section 21 of the Autonomy Act provides simply, "Justice in the Province shall be administered by the national courts of law." The succeeding section designates the County Administrative Council as responsible for the administration of justice insofar as it is not, in fact, exercised by the courts and is not otherwise provided for by the provincial authorities with respect to matters within their jurisdiction.

OTHER MATTERS

Regional citizenship

In order to acquire real estate, practice certain trades, or vote in provincial elections, a person must have acquired regional citizenship of the Aland Islands. Those not born in Aland must have resided in Aland for a continuous period of five years prior to acquiring this citizenship, and it may be lost if a person has permanently resided outside the islands for five years. A company or other business entity is considered to have the citizenship of its directors. An Aland regional citizen is exempt from compulsory Finnish military service, although he or she may be required to serve in a civilian capacity.

Restrictions on land alienation

Without the permission of the Provincial Executive Council, only those with Aland regional citizenship may own land in Aland; all companies (even wholly Aland-owned) must have such permission in order to acquire or lease real estate. If land is conveyed to a person not having a domiciliary right, any private person with the right, the local community, or the province itself is entitled to "redeem" the property at an agreed-upon price or at a fair market price determined by the courts.

Education and language

Both Finnish and Swedish are official languages throughout Finland, with individual communes designated as unilingual or bilingual. In Aland, the language of instruction in all provincially-supported schools is exclusively Swedish, unless the commune within which the school is located requests otherwise. In no event can a county council or commune be required to contribute to the support of a school in which the language of instruction is not Swedish.

Not only is Swedish the official language within Aland, but communication between provincial officials and state officials serving within the province and between such state officials and other central government authorities also must be in Swedish. Provincial civil servants must have complete mastery of spoken and written Swedish, and opinions of the Supreme Court in all matters affecting the province must be given in Swedish.

The Aland Delegation

The Aland Delegation is a body of legal experts comprised of two members appointed by the Finnish government, two members appointed by the Aland parliament, and a chairman appointed by the President of Finland, with the agreement of the Speaker of the Aland parliament.

As noted above, it plays a crucial role in the economic administration of the province, and it also advises the Finnish President as to whether a bill adopted by the Aland parliament exceeds provincial competence. While the Delegation is only an advisory body to the President, it appears to have a significant legal and political role in resolving potential conflicts between the central and Aland governments.

Foreign affairs

Foreign agreements entered into by Finland do not apply to Aland if they concern matters within the competence of the Aland parliament, unless the latter agrees. Since 1970, the Aland parliament has elected a representative, who participates as part of the Finnish delegation, to meetings of the Nordic Council. This representation was increased in 1984 to two members, as part of changes to facilitate participation by all the Nordic autonomous regions (i.e., the Faroe Islands and Greenland, in addition to Aland).

OBSERVATIONS

Swedish-speakers occupy a position of equality within Finland proper, despite the fact that they constitute less than 10% of the population, and they "see themselves not as a cultural minority but as co-founders of the Finnish state."[1027] This status has undoubtedly made it more acceptable for a peculiarly Swedish region to be established, and unilingual Swedish-speaking (and Finnish-speaking) administrative communes also are found in mainland Finland.

While the extent of Aland's theoretical political autonomy is, in many respects, fairly limited, the effective cultural independence of the Aland Islands is secure. The overwhelming majority of Aland residents are native Swedish-speakers, and there is no intra-island tension with respect to linguistic or cultural matters. The central Finnish government retains sovereignty and general legislative authority over Aland, but the matters reserved to the islands in the areas of education, language, and restrictions on land alienation seem to be sufficient to maintain Aland's cultural distinctiveness.

After several years of deliberations, a new autonomy statute was proposed in 1987 by a joint provincial-central government committee. Since amendments to the autonomy statute have the status of constitutional laws, any changes will take effect only in 1993, following the law's adoption by two successive sessions of parliament. The primary effects of the revision are likely to be to define more clearly the respective

---

1027 Antony Alcock, "The Swedish Community in Finland," in *Co-existence in some plural European societies* (London: Minority Rights Group Report No. 72, 1986) at 10.

leglislative competences of the Aland and state authorities; gradually to transfer additional competence to Aland in areas such as social insurance, housing, and postal services; to make the requirements for land ownership somewhat more restrictive; and to expand the scope of Aland's autonomy in economic matters.

While no one thinks of the Aland islands as a scene of conflict today, the contribution of the League of Nations to peaceful resolution of the dispute between Finland and Sweden over Aland in the early 1920s should not be underestimated. The League's primary goals, to ensure the cultural autonomy of the Swedish-speaking residents and to maintain the islands as unfortified, neutral territory, have been accomplished. While the present consensus regarding Aland autonomy may reflect, in part, its small size and lack of contemporary strategic or economic importance, it also represents agreement by all concerned that recognition of two equally valid cultural identities need not detract from the stability and integrity of a single state.

Free City of Danzig[1028]

HISTORICAL BACKGROUND

The Free City of Danzig was established by the Treaty of Versailles, in order to respond to one of Woodrow Wilson's "Fourteen Points" and ensure access to the sea for the newly recreated state of Poland.[1029] Danzig (Gdansk) was an ethnically German city, although Germany renounced its rights over Danzig after the war; the surrounding hinterland was primarily Polish. Neither Danzigers nor Poles were in favor of the establishment of a "free city"; the former wished to be sovereign or at least completely autonomous, in order eventually to reunite with Germany, while the latter wished outright cession of the city to Poland. However, article 100 of the Versailles Treaty placed the city and surrounding territory directly "under the protection of the League of Nations."

The respective rights of Danzig and Poland were detailed in two treaties,[1030] and the Free City's constitution was drafted and adopted by

1028 See generally Christoph M. Kimmich, *The Free City: Danzig and German Foreign Policy 1919–1934* (New Haven, CT: Yale Univ. Press, 1968); John B. Mason, *The Danzig Dilemma* (Stanford, CA: Stanford Univ. Press, 1946); Ydit, *supra* note 35, at 185–230.

1029 Treaty of Versailles, signed 28 June 1919, 11 Martens Nouveau Recueil 3d, 323, sec. IX, arts. 100–108.

1030 Treaty of Paris, Poland-Danzig, signed 9 Nov. 1920, 6 L.N.T.S. 190; Treaty of Warsaw, Poland-Danzig, signed 24 Oct. 1921, 116 L.N.T.S. 6.

Danzig citizens with the approval of the League of Nations' High Commissioner in Danzig and, after certain amendments, by the Council of the League of Nations.[1031] Danzig remained a constant source of tension between Germany and Poland, and it was eventually invaded and annexed by Germany in 1939. At the end of World War II, Danzig was committed to Polish administration and has remained part of Poland since that time.

EXECUTIVE POWERS

The executive power under the Free City's constitution was vested in a twelve-member Senate, which was in turn elected by and from the parliament, the Volkstag. The Senate was thus a parliamentary executive, dependent on the Volkstag for its powers and responsible for implementing the laws of Danzig. At the same time, however, the Senate participated in the legislative process: its assent was required before laws were adopted, and it could veto legislation. In the latter event, if the Volkstag insisted on a law's adoption, the Senate was required to submit the measure to a popular referendum. The President of the Senate acted as the head of state.

Among the specific powers and duties of the Senate were the promulgation of laws, conduct of public administration, drafting the budget, determining revenues and expenditures, supervising the state authorities, nominating public servants, and providing public security (police).[1032] The League of Nations' executive representative, the High Commissioner, had no direct authority over the internal affairs of Danzig; his primary functions were those of conciliation and mediation, discussed below.

LEGISLATIVE POWERS

Legislative authority in Danzig was vested in the 120-member Volkstag, which was elected every four years under a system of proportional representation. The subject-matter competence of the Volkstag was not limited by the constitution, although certain special rights were granted to Poland by the terms of the treaties referred to above. These special rights included, *inter alia*, a guarantee to Poland of free and secure access to the sea; creation of a customs union between Danzig and Poland, subject to Polish legislation and tariffs; creation of a harbor Board, staffed equally by Poles and Danzigers, to administer the port; the right of Poland to establish postal and telegraphic services from the

1031 Constitution of the Free City of Danzig, League of Nations O.J., Spec. Supp. 7 (1922).
    1032 *Id.*, art. 39.

port to Poland and from Poland abroad, via the port; certain guarantees with respect to the civil rights of the Polish minority in Danzig; and a grant to Poland of the right and obligation to conduct Danzig's foreign relations, including the establishment of a Polish commissioner-general in Danzig to facilitate communications.[1033] Danzig retained control over its own police force, including the branch which policed the harbor, and it had its own postal service and currency.

The Volkstag could propose amendments to the constitution by a two-thirds vote on two separate readings, but such amendments were specifically subject to approval or veto by the League of Nations Council.

JUDICIAL POWERS

The judicial branch of the Danzig government has been called the only independent branch of administration; its territorial jurisdiction was comprehensive, and it was subject only to the laws of Danzig. The courts had jurisdiction even over "special" entities such as the Polish Railway Administration in Danzig and the Port of Danzig, since by-laws issued by the jointly administered Harbor Board were given legislative effect by the Senate. Organizationally, the judicial system consisted of Police Courts for minor infractions, Courts of First Instance, a Court of Appeal, a Public Prosecutor's Office, and a Supreme Court.

Disputes between Danzig and Poland were subject to a special procedure set forth in article 103 of the Versailles Treaty and article 39 of the Paris Treaty, pursuant to which disputes were submitted to the original and exclusive jurisdiction of the League's High Commissioner, who also acted as arbitrator and mediator. While it is generally agreed that the High Commissioner performed a valuable function in mediating between Danzig and Polish interests, 54 of the 66 formal decisions he rendered were nevertheless appealed to the Council of the League of Nations.[1034] While the Council sustained the Commissioner in the great majority of cases, in six instances the Council requested an Advisory Opinion from the Permanent Court of International Justice;[1035] the

1033 Treaty of Versailles, *supra* note 1029, art. 104; Treaty of Paris, *supra* note 1030.

1034 Ydit, *supra* note 35, at 212–13.

1035 Polish Postal Service in Danzig, Advisory Opinion, 1925, P.C.I.J., Series B, No. 11; Jurisdiction of the Courts of Danzig, Advisory Opinion, 1928, P.C.I.J., Series B, No. 15; Free City of Danzig and the ILO, Advisory Opinion, 1930, P.C.I.J., Series B, No. 18; Access to, or Anchorage in, the Port of Danzig, of Polish War Vessels, Advisory Opinion, 1931, P.C.I.J., Series A/B, No. 43, p. 128; Treatment of Polish Nationals and Other Persons of Polish Origin or Speech in the Danzig Territory, Advisory Opinion, 1932, P.C.I.J., Series A/B, No. 45, p. 68; and Consistency of Certain Danzig Legislative Decrees with the Constitution of the Free City, Advisory Opinion, 1935, P.C.I.J., Series A/B, No. 65, p. 41.

Council also had recourse to specially appointed commissions of jurists to assist it in its decisions.

The Court generally upheld the rights and autonomy of the Free City in these cases and often treated Danzig as a separate state, despite the powers with respect to Danzig affairs exercised by the League of Nations and Poland. Danzig was bound by and had the benefit of "the ordinary rules governing relations between States.... With regard to Poland, the Danzig Constitution, despite its peculiarities, [was] ... the Constitution of a foreign State."[1036]

The Court interpreted the right of Poland to conduct Danzig's foreign relations as a kind of agency relationship with a right of veto:

[T]he rights of Poland as regards the foreign relations of the Free City are not absolute. The Polish Government is not entitled to impose a policy on the Free City nor to take any step in connection with the foreign relations of the Free City against its will. On the other hand, the Free City cannot call upon Poland to take any step in connection with foreign relations of the Free City which are [sic] opposed to her own policy.[1037]

ROLE OF THE LEAGUE OF NATIONS

In addition to the dispute-settling function described above, the League was responsible for guaranteeing the democratic constitution of Danzig and the territorial integrity of the city. The original constitution was subject to the approval of the League of Nations Council, and the Council also could request the Volkstag to adopt amendments to the constitution (which the Volkstag was not required to accept).

The League's guarantee of Danzig's territorial integrity was in theory accomplished by a guarantee of Danzig's neutrality: article 5 of the constitution stated, "The Free City of Danzig cannot without the previous consent of the League of Nations, in each case: 1) serve as a military or naval base; 2) erect fortifications; 3) authorize the manufacture of munitions or war material on its territory." The Council rejected a request to delegate its responsibility for the defense of Danzig to Poland, noting only that Poland would be "particularly fitted" to undertake such a role were the Council to request it.

OBSERVATIONS

The Free City of Danzig is perhaps the purest example of an "internationalized territory" in which, despite almost complete autonomy and various attributes of statehood, sovereignty resided in an international

---

1036 Treatment of Polish Nationals, *supra* note 1035, at 23–24.
1037 Free City of Danzig and the ILO, *supra* note 1035, at 13.

organization, the League of Nations. Within the confines of its constituent documents, Danzig enjoyed complete autonomy over its internal affairs both de jure and de facto, despite the restriction that changes in Danzig's constitution required the approval of the League. Danzig exercised all of the normal functions of an independent state—police, currency, public administration, criminal and civil jurisdiction, etc.— with the exceptions noted above concerning the port, the customs union with Poland, and the conduct of foreign affairs and defense.

While the twenty-year history of the Free City must be considered at least a qualified success, due in large part to the mediation efforts of the League, it must nevertheless be remembered that its structure was imposed upon it by the Great Powers, in spite of the opposition of the two groups most directly concerned, the Poles and the Danzigers. It has been suggested that Poland constantly stretched the limits of the relevant treaties and increasingly violated Danzig's quasi-sovereignty; the eventual reunification of Danzig with Germany as a result of the invasion of Poland in 1939 doubtless reflected the wishes of most Danzigers.

Given the constant tension among Danzig, Poland, and Germany, the mediation role of the League of Nations assumed primary importance. Insofar as the High Commissioner and the League were able to defuse potential sources of more serious conflict, this form of international oversight (including reference of disputes to an international tribunal) should perhaps be viewed as the most distinctive innovation of the Danzig governmental structure.

Memel Territory

HISTORICAL BACKGROUND

The Memel Territory, consisting of some 1,700 square kilometers and 145,000 inhabitants, was part of Germany until Germany renounced its sovereignty in favor of the Allied and Associated Powers, pursuant to article 99 of the Treaty of Versailles.[1038] After three years of negotiations in which various forms of "international" status for Memel were discussed, Lithuania militarily seized the territory from the French administration in January 1923. Proposals that Poland and Lithuania both have guaranteed access to the sea through Memel and Danzig were rejected by the Lithuanians, who were then at war with Poland over the latter's seizure of Vilna.

Faced with the fait accompli of Lithuanian occupation, the "Conference of Ambassadors" which had been considering the situation

[1038] *Supra* note 1029.

agreed to recognize Lithuanian sovereignty over Memel, provided that the local, ethnically German population was granted full cultural autonomy. In addition, the Port of Memel was to be placed under the administration of an "International Harbour Board" and was to be considered a "port of international concern." After appointment of a special commission of experts by the League of Nations Council, a convention and statute were agreed upon by the Four Powers (United Kingdom, France, Italy, and Japan) and Lithuania; the convention was signed in May 1924.[1039]

Memel was to constitute, "under the sovereignty of Lithuania, a unit enjoying legislative, judicial, administrative and financial autonomy within the limits prescribed by the Statute" annexed to the convention.[1040] Article 15 further stipulated that sovereignty over Memel could not be transferred without the consent of the High Contracting Parties.

The Memel Territory continued under Lithuanian sovereignty until Germany invaded Poland in 1939, and after the war Memel became an integral part of Lithuania/the U.S.S.R.

EXECUTIVE POWERS

The executive authority of Memel was exercised by a Directorate of not more than five Memel citizens and a Governor appointed by Lithuania. The Governor appointed the President of the Directorate, who in turn appointed the remaining members. Once appointed, however, the Directorate was required to receive the confidence of the Memel Chamber of Representatives; it thus constituted a parliamentary-style cabinet responsible to the local legislature, despite its initial appointment by the Lithuanian Governor. The Directorate and the Chamber shared the right to initiate legislation.

Primary responsibility for the maintenance of public order was assigned to a local police force, although Memel could apply to the Lithuanian government for assistance. The harbor police were from Memel but served under Lithuanian authorities; the frontier, customs, and railway police were Lithuanians under the direct authority of the Lithuanian central government.

LEGISLATIVE POWERS

Legislative power was exercised by the unicameral Chamber of Representatives, whose members were elected by universal suffrage, served

---

1039 Convention and Transitory Provision concerning Memel, signed 8 May 1924, 29 L.N.T.S. 87 [hereinafter cited as "Memel Convention"]; the Statute of the Memel Territory [hereinafter cited as "Memel Statute"] is included as Annex I to the Convention.
1040 Memel Convention, art. 2.

for three-year terms, and had to be citizens of the territory. The Representatives enjoyed legislative immunity throughout Lithuania. Special legislative sessions could be called or the Chamber dissolved by the Governor in agreement with the Directorate; after dissolution, new elections were required within six weeks.

The legislative competence of the local Memel authorities is set forth in detail in article 5 of the Statute, which lists fifteen areas of local competence, including, *inter alia*, administration and organization of local government; public worship, education, and health; social welfare and labor legislation; police powers, subject to restrictions regarding the harbor, frontier, customs, and railway police; civil, property, criminal, agrarian, forestry, and commercial legislation; and direct and indirect taxation within the territory, excluding customs and excise duties, commodity taxes, and taxes on alcohol, tobacco, and other luxury article monopolies. This legislative competence could be extended by Lithuanian legislation.

Residual legislative competence not within the jurisdiction of the Memel authorities under the Statute was reserved to the exclusive jurisdiction of Lithuania. In addition, local Memel laws were subject to the Lithuanian constitution, in the absence of any contrary provisions in the Statute.

The Governor had the right to veto laws adopted by the Chamber "if these laws exceed the competence of the authorities of the Territory as laid down by the present Statute, or if they are incompatible with the provisions of Article 6 [conformity of local laws with the Lithuanian constitution] or with the international obligations of Lithuania."[1041] Otherwise, the Governor was obliged to promulgate laws passed by the Chamber.

With respect to international obligations, article 4 provided that treaties and conventions entered into by Lithuania applied to Memel unless they were contrary to the Statute or within the realm of local affairs reserved to the territory under article 5. In the latter case, the local Memel authorities were to implement the agreements.

The Statute itself could be amended only with the approval of the Legislative Assembly of Lithuania, after an amendment had been adopted by three-fifths of the Memel Chamber of Representatives and, in certain circumstances, a popular referendum of Memel citizens.

JUDICIAL POWERS

Article 24 provided that the jurisdiction of the Supreme Court of Lithuania extended over the whole territory of Lithuania, including the

---

1041 Memel Statute, art. 16.

Memel Territory, although a special section for Memel affairs was to be created, composed "mainly" of Memel magistrates. There was reciprocity for judgments and warrants emanating from courts throughout Lithuania, including Memel. Subject to Lithuanian Supreme Court supremacy, judicial organization and jurisdiction were local matters. In 1935, Lithuania established a court with jurisdiction over cases involving the compatibility of acts of the Memel government with the Statute.[1042]

There was no provision comparable to that found in the Treaty of Versailles with respect to Danzig-Polish relations for resolution of Memel-Lithuania disputes by an international tribunal. However, article 17 of the Convention provided that any League member "shall be entitled to draw the attention of the Council to any infraction" of the Convention's provisions. In case of a dispute between Lithuania and one of the Principal Allied Powers, Lithuania agreed to submit the dispute (if requested by the other party) for final resolution to the Permanent Court of International Justice.[1043]

OTHER MATTERS

Port of Memel

As noted above, the port was declared to be "of international concern," and the recommendations of the 1921 Barcelona Convention on Navigable Waterways[1044] were intended to be applied to Memel. Expenses in connection with the port were to be borne by Lithuania, but the "administration, operation, upkeep, and development" of the port was entrusted to a Harbour Board consisting of one member appointed by Lithuania, one member appointed by Memel, and one member (not a citizen of a Niemen riparian state) appointed by the Chairman of the Advisory and Technical Committee for Communications and Transit of the League of Nations. After a period of five years, the system of port administration could be modified upon the proposal of Lithuania and the approval of the League of Nations Council, including all four of the other parties to the Convention. Similar League approval was required for any modification of various guarantees relating to transit traffic, set forth in Annex III to the Convention.

1042 Amtsblatt des Memelgebietes (1935) at 207.

1043 Such reference to the P.C.I.J. occurred on one occasion, in Interpretation of the Statute of the Memel Territory, Preliminary Objection, Judgment, 1932, P.C.I.J., Series A/B, No. 47, p. 243, and Merits, Judgment, 1932, P.C.I.J., Series A/B, No. 49, p. 294.

1044 Barcelona Convention and Statute on the Regime of Navigable Waterways of International Concern, signed 20 Apr. 1921, 7 L.N.T.S. 36.

Minority rights

Several provisions of the Statute guaranteed individual and minority rights within Memel, such as the rights proclaimed under the terms of the declaration made by Lithuania to the League Council; the right to private property; and freedom of association, conscience, and education. Lithuanian and German were designated as equal and official languages. Future civil servants were to be recruited, "as far as possible," from among Memel citizens, and foreigners could be employed as teachers, without permission of the Lithuanian government, only during a transitional period. Even within the transitional period, no alien "against whom the Governor adduces proof that he is engaged in political agitation contrary to the interests of Lithuania" could be employed.[1045]

Shared powers

Several provisions in the statute provided for powers to be shared between the local Memel authorities and the central Lithuanian government. Perhaps the most complex was the organization of the various police functions, mentioned above, set forth in article 20 of the Statute. The Harbour Board also involved shared authority. In addition, the Lithuanian-appointed Governor participated in the Memel legislative process; there was a special section within the Lithuanian Supreme Court for Memel affairs; the employment of foreign teachers was subject to Lithuanian approval; and passports were delivered by the Memel government on behalf of Lithuania, noting the joint Lithuanian nationality and Memel citizenship of the bearer.

OBSERVATIONS

The Memel Territory was established as an autonomous unit within the sovereign state of Lithuania because of the fact of Lithuanian occupation; it was not a truly international territory in the same sense as the Free City of Danzig. Memel had no international personality and no control or influence over Lithuanian foreign relations or defense, for which purposes Memel was considered to be an integral part of Lithuania. Memel can perhaps be most aptly described as an area of formally recognized international concern, evidenced by the right of the Principal Allied Powers to take disputes concerning the Convention or Statute to the Permanent Court of International Justice, and by the authority of the League Council over proposed changes with respect to the port. In

---

1045 Memel Statute, art. 31.

other respects, the Memel Territory was essentially an autonomous province similar to a sub-division within a federal system.

The autonomy enjoyed by Memel was certainly narrower than, for example, that which would be possessed by a "self-governing territory" in United Nations terms. Local competence extended only to enumerated powers, although these included such important matters as education, police, and taxation. Residual power and sovereignty rested with Lithuania, which also retained ultimate authority to approve or disapprove any change in the territory's Statute. The Governor also enjoyed significant formal and informal influence within the Memel government.

The purpose of the Memel Statute was not to grant *political* autonomy to the territory, but rather to preserve "the traditional rights and culture of its inhabitants."[1046] This can be seen from the provisions devoted to education, the recognition of two official languages, and the references to minority rights. The level of international involvement was certainly less than that with respect to Danzig or in the 1947 Trieste proposals, although it was greater than, for example, in Eritrea after its federation with Ethiopia. Despite the somewhat antagonistic nature of the Memel-Lithuanian relationship, the system seems to have encountered fewer problems than other similar situations. However, Memel's subsequent absorption by Germany and then Lithuania indicates the fragile nature of such small autonomous enclaves.

New Zealand—The Associated States of the Cook Islands and Niue and the Territory of Tokelau

HISTORICAL BACKGROUND

The former New Zealand dependencies of the Cook Islands and Niue are the only examples of decolonization by means of free association to have been formally "approved" by the United Nations since the adoption of General Assembly Resolutions 1514[1047] and 1541[1048] in 1960. The Cook Islands, which today consist of fifteen islands in the southwest Pacific with a total population of approximately 20,000, were placed under British protection between 1888 and 1901 and transferred to New Zealand administration in 1901. Following the gradual development of institutions of self-government, including creation of a popularly-elected Legislative Assembly in 1946, discussions between the Cook Islands and New Zealand governments resulted in the attainment of full self-

---

1046 Memel Statute, Preamble.
1047 *Supra* note 104.
1048 *Supra* note 38.

governing status by the Cook Islands in 1965 and their removal from the UN list of non-self-governing territories.[1049] As discussed below with respect to Niue, the Cook Islands remain in "free association" with New Zealand, and the latter is responsible for the foreign relations and defense of the islands.

The island of Niue (with a population of approximately 2,500) has followed a pattern very similar to that of the Cook Islands, and the present arrangement of free association with New Zealand is essentially the same as that concluded between the Cook Islands and New Zealand in 1965. The Niue Island Assembly was recognized in 1966, and executive authority for internal affairs was transferred to a local Executive Committee in 1972. The status of free association with New Zealand was attained in 1974, with the adoption of the Niue constitution by both the Niue and New Zealand parliaments; the General Assembly subsequently agreed unanimously to drop Niue from the list of non-self-governing territories.[1050]

Tokelau consists of three small atolls (Atafu, Nukunonu, and Fakaofo), whose total population is approximately 1,700. They are situated north of Apia, Western Samoa, and were formerly part of the Gilbert and Ellice Islands Colony under British protection. Tokelau has been under New Zealand administration since 1925, and it is presently included within the territorial boundaries of New Zealand pursuant to the Tokelau Islands Act 1948.[1051] The islands are governed by a New Zealand Administrator responsible, since 1974, to the Ministry of Foreign Affairs. Tokelauans have been encouraged to resettle in New Zealand to relieve the islands' over-population, and there has been slow movement towards greater self-government over the past decade.

The following comments focus on a comparison of Niue and Tokelau; as noted earlier, the status of Niue and that of the Cook Islands are essentially identical.

EXECUTIVE POWERS

As a member of the Commonwealth, Niue vests its executive authority in the Queen, represented in Niue by a Governor-General appointed by New Zealand. In fact, executive authority is exercised by the Niue Cabinet, which is responsible for "the general direction and control of the executive government of Niue, and shall have such other functions

1049 See G.A. Res. 1064, 20 UN GAOR, Supp. (No. 14), UN Doc. A/6014 (1965) at 56.

1050 G.A. Res. 3285, 29 UN GAOR, Supp. (No. 31), UN Doc. A/6131 (1974) at 98.

1051 New Zealand Act No. 24 of 29 Oct. 1948.

and powers as are conferred on it by law."[1052] The Cabinet is appointed by and responsible to the Niue Assembly.

Article 6 of the Niue Constitution Act reserves control over Niue's external affairs and defense to New Zealand. In addition, residents of Niue retain their status as British subjects and New Zealand citizens. New Zealand also specifically recognizes its "continuing responsibility ...to provide necessary economic and administrative assistance to Niue,"[1053] an obligation that was only implicit in the earlier arrangement with the Cook Islands. The Act provides that effect is to be given to the above-mentioned provisions after consultation between the Prime Minister of New Zealand and the Premier of Niue.

All civil servants in Niue are appointed by a Niue Public Service Commission established in the constitution. The Commission is composed of three members: the Chairman of the New Zealand State Services Commission acts as the ex officio Chairman of the Niue Commission; the second member is appointed by and must also be a member of the New Zealand Commission; the third member is also appointed by the New Zealand Commission, but with the concurrence of the Niue Cabinet. While this de facto delegation of power to new Zealand with respect to government employment runs counter to the notion of full internal self-government, it might provide a certain independence or expertise unavailable in Niue itself; in any event, as noted below, Niue retains the power to amend its constitution unilaterally, including those provisions concerning the Public Service Commission.

Tokelau forms part of New Zealand and is governed directly by an Administrator who has full authority to "make all such regulations as he thinks necessary for the peace, order, and good government of the Tokelau Islands."[1054] Actual administration of and supervision over Tokelau is carried out by a staff based in Western Samoa, with the permission of that government. De facto administration of the three Tokelau atolls is the responsibility of local officials on each island, who are selected in accordance with traditional custom, and each island retains wide administrative autonomy within a quasi-traditional structure.

LEGISLATIVE POWERS

The Niue Assembly consists of fourteen members elected from village constituencies and six members elected at-large, thus offering an interesting combination in a unicameral system of representatives of both

---

1052 Niue Const., set forth in the Schedule to the Niue Constitution Act 1974, New Zealand Act No. 42, §2.

1053 Niue Const., §7.

1054 Tokelau Islands Act 1948, New Zealand Law No. 24 of 29 Oct. 1948 (as amended through 1974), §4.

national and more parochial concerns. Subject only to the constitution, "the Niue Assembly may make laws for the peace, order, and good government of Niue," including "the power to repeal or revoke or amend or modify or extend, in relation to Niue, any law in force in Niue."[1055]

This last clause includes not only local laws of Niue but also any New Zealand laws applicable to Niue. Thus, Niue has full power to repeal the provisions of the New Zealand Act which reserves to New Zealand responsibility for Niue's foreign relations and defense, as well as other laws. Niue also retains the unilateral power to terminate its relationship of free association with New Zealand at any time, although amendment of the basic "free association" principles of the constitution or the Constitution Act requires both a two-thirds affirmative vote in the Niue Assembly and approval by two-thirds of those voting in a popular referendum.

The New Zealand Governor-General has no power over the enactment of Niue legislation. In addition, article 36 of the constitution provides that no New Zealand Act of Parliament or subordinate legislation may apply to Niue without the specific request and consent of Niue and a declaration to that effect in the legislation itself. Existing New Zealand laws extended to Niue on the effective date of the constitution continued in force, subject to repeal or amendment by the Niue Assembly.

New Zealand legislation does not apply to Tokelau unless expressly provided, although there are no formal constitutional or other restrictions on New Zealand's authority to legislate for Tokelau. Over the past decade, however, the General Fono (Council), Tokelau's customary representative body, composed of fifteen persons from each island, has assumed a growing role in Tokelauan political life.[1056] "The General Fono as yet has no legislative authority in its own right. It continues, however, to initiate or be fully consulted regarding all legislation that is to be made for Tokelau and is currently considering the nature of some legislative authority that it may exercise in its own right."[1057]

JUDICIAL POWERS

The High Court of Niue has "all . . . jurisdiction (both civil and criminal) as may be necessary to administer the law in force in Niue."[1058] Article 51 of the constitution provides for the right of appeal from a final High

---

1055 Niue Const., §28.

1056 See generally New Zealand, art. 40 CCPR Report, UN Doc. CCPR/C/10/Add.11 (1983) at 2–6, *id.*, UN Doc. CCPR/C/37/Add. 12 (1989).

1057 UN Doc. CCPR/C/37/ADd. 12 (1989), *supra* note 1056, at 2.

1058 Niue Const., §37.

Court judgment to the Court of Appeal of New Zealand in three instances: where the High Court certifies that the case involves "a substantial question of law as to the interpretation or effect of any provision of this Constitution"; following any serious criminal conviction; and, in civil cases, where the amount in dispute is $400 or more. Discretionary appeals may be granted by the High Court in other cases. There is currently only one judge of the High Court, who serves as Chief Justice and is appointed by the New Zealand Governor-General on the advice of the Niue Cabinet.

There is a three-tiered judicial system in Tokelau.[1059] The primary judicial authority is exercised by a local Commissioner appointed by the Governor-General for each of the three Tokelau atolls. The traditional island head, or Faipule, currently serves as Commissioner on each island, and his jurisdiction extends to minor civil and criminal proceedings. Appeals from a Commissioner's decision, serious criminal cases, and civil cases involving more than $1,000 are heard by the High Court of New Zealand, acting as the High Court of Tokelau. Final appeals may be taken to the New Zealand Court of Appeal.

OTHER MATTERS

Land alienation in Tokelau

All land not privately held in fee simple is vested in the Crown, subject to the customary title or beneficial ownership of the land as determined by the customs and usages of Tokelau.[1060] While the Governor-General may expropriate such land for public purposes and vest absolute title in the Crown, in other respects the land is held in trust for the people of Tokelau. No Tokelauan may alienate or dispose of any Tokelauan land vested in the Crown except according to local custom, and then only to another Tokelauan.

OBSERVATIONS

The legal distinctions between the self-governing, associated state of Niue (and the Cook Islands) and the non-self-governing territory of Tokelau are clear: the former possesses unlimited legislative competence over its own affairs, subject only to such restrictions (which Niue may unilaterally alter) as are contained in its constitution and the 1974 Niue Constitution Act; the latter is wholly subject to the plenary legislative authority of the New Zealand Parliament and the discretionary administrative powers of the Tokelau Administrator.

1059 See Tokelau Islands Amendment Act 1986.
1060 Tokelau Islands Amendment Act 1967, New Zealand Act No. 38 of 26 Oct. 1967, Part II, Tokelau Islands Amendment Act 1986.

In fact, however, there is much greater local participation in To-kelauan affairs than the purely legal status of the territory would indi-cate. As noted, New Zealand legislation is applied to Tokelau only after consultation with the Tokelauan General Fono, and primary judicial authority is wielded by traditional island chiefs.

Three UN missions have visited Tokelau at the invitation of New Zealand, in 1976, 1981, and 1986, and each has noted the desire of the people of Tokelau to maintain their present status and relationship with New Zealand.[1061] While the General Assembly has reiterated that "such factors as territorial size, geographical location, size of population and limited natural resources should in no way delay" Tokelau's exercise of its right to self-determination, it noted at the same time "the special problems facing Tokelau by virtue of its isolation, small size, limited resources and lack of infrastructure."[1062]

These factors make the precedents of small Pacific islands of dubious relevance to other regions, but the successful operation of associated statehood for the Cook Islands and Niue (and, one assumes, for Tokelau at some future stage) should not be entirely ignored even in non-colonial, non-island contexts. However, the former New Zealand territories do not present the same strategic or emotional problems for the adminis-tering powers and indigenous populations as are present in, for example, Palau, Guam, or Gibraltar, and it remains to be seen whether such arrangements of free association can be successfully implemented in those and other non-self-governing territories.

The Saar (1920–1935)

HISTORICAL BACKGROUND[1063]

As defined in the Treaty of Versailles, the Saar Basin consisted of an area of approximately 1,900 square kilometers (slightly larger than the Free City of Danzig) and a population of 820,000. It is a densely populated, coal-producing region, situated on the present Franco-German border just north of Lorraine, and has been a source of Franco-German conflict for centuries. The French claims stem in some degree from the Saar's reliance on Lorraine for coke and other trade; in ad-

1061 See, e.g., G.A. Res. 41/26, 41 UN GAOR, Supp. (No. 53), UN Doc. A/ 41/53 (1986) at 227, para. 5.

1062 *Id.*, Preamble.

1063 See generally Laing G. Cowan, *France and the Saar, 1680–1948* (1950; re-printed, New York: ABS Press, 1966); Michael T. Florinsky, *The Saar Struggle* (New York: Macmillan, 1934); Frank M. Russell, *The Saar, Battleground and Pawn* (New York: Russell & Russell, 1951).

dition, the Saar was under French control during the reign of Louis XIV, who founded Saarlouis. There has always been a French minority in the Saar, although the general view seems to be that this minority, if it existed at all, is now extremely small, despite French references to the "200,000 Frenchmen" in the Saar during World War I.

The Congress of Vienna in 1815 gave the Saar region to the two German states of Prussia and Bavaria. Under German influence for the next century, the region became overwhelmingly Germanic culturally, ethnically, and linguistically. Nevertheless, France continued to press its claims to the region and maintained its desire for "return" of the Saar along with Alsace and Lorraine, which were lost to Germany in the Franco-Prussian war of 1870. After Germany's defeat in World War I, France wanted sovereignty over the Saar and reparations for the destruction of France's northern coal fields. As outlined below, France was given exclusive rights to work the Saar coal fields for a period of fifteen years; government over the Saar for that period was assumed by the League of Nations, but formal sovereignty remained with Germany.[1064]

The Treaty of Versailles provided for a plebiscite to be held in the Saar at the end of the fifteen-year period of League governance to determine the region's future. This plebiscite, in 1935, resulted in an overwhelming vote in favor of reunion with Germany, which duly occurred on 1 March 1935. At the end of World War II, after the Saar had been reintegrated with Germany for only ten years, France again asserted control over the region. This period, from 1945 through 1956, is discussed separately in the immediately following case study.

FRENCH POSSESSION OF THE SAAR COAL FIELDS

Under article 45 of the Versailles Treaty, Germany agreed to cede to France "in full and absolute possession, with exclusive rights of exploitation, unencumbered and free from all debts and charges of any kind, the coal-mines situated in the Saar Basin." If the plebiscite mandated by the treaty led to reunion of the Saar with Germany, Germany agreed to repurchase France's ownership rights in the mines.

French control over the Saar's coal resources—and, by extension, over the entire economy of the Saar—was in effect total and was specified in detail in the Versailles Treaty provisions. All coal deposits became "the complete and absolute property of the French State," whether publicly or privately owned (in fact, the great majority of the mines were state-owned, thus minimizing possible problems of expropriation of private property). This ownership extended to all accessories and

---

1064 See Treaty of Versailles, *supra* note 1029, sec. IV, arts. 45–50 and Annex.

subsidiaries of the mines, and France had the right to install necessary communication, transportation, and other facilities incidental to exploitation of the mines, including French-language schools, hospitals, etc. No restriction was placed on the importation of French workers into the Saar, and no discriminatory tariffs could be established by Germany on any items concerned with exploitation of the mines. The Saar Basin was subject to the French customs regime, and a customs union with France was established in 1925. No restrictions could be placed on circulation of the French franc, and by 1923 the franc had become the Saar's only official currency.

LEAGUE OF NATIONS GOVERNMENT OF THE SAAR

Executive Powers

The Versailles Treaty provided that government of the Saar Basin was to be entrusted to a League of Nations Governing Commission, which "shall have all the powers of government hitherto belonging to the German Empire, Prussia, or Bavaria, including the appointment and dismissal of officials, and the creation of such administrative and representative bodies as it may deem necessary."[1065] Formal or residual sovereignty, however, remained with Germany, and German courts considered the Saar to be part of the Reich for various purposes. Saar residents also retained German nationality. However, the Saar was a wholly autonomous regime during the fifteen-year period of League administration, and all governmental ties with Germany were severed during this time.

   The Governing Commission consisted of five members, appointed for one-year terms by the League Council. One member was a citizen of France; one was a native inhabitant of the Saar Basin, but not a French citizen; and the other three members were from three different countries other than France or Germany. In practice, the Commission was strongly pro-French, and the French member acted as Chairman.

   The Governing Commission had plenary powers in both the executive and legislative areas, including "full powers" to operate public services; conduct foreign relations "to ensure . . . the protection abroad of the interests of the inhabitants of the . . . Saar Basin"; protect persons and property; and establish a local police force. Military service and the construction of fortifications within the territory were prohibited. In the course of its activities, the Saar Government had its own stamps and flag and was a member of the Universal Postal Union and the Universal Telegraphic Convention. While Saar residents retained German citi-

1065 *Id.*, Annex, art. 19.

zenship, passports were issued by the Saar government to "inhabitants of the Saar."

It has been suggested that the Governing Commission became increasingly repressive during its fifteen years of governance. Following the Franco-Belgian occupation of the Ruhr region in 1923, for example, the Commission promulgated an ordinance that made it a criminal offense to cast discredit on the Versailles Treaty or defame the League of Nations, although the ordinance was repealed and replaced by one less draconian. As Nazi influence grew in the 1930s, the Commission's police powers were expanded; direct control over trade unions was imposed; and publication of some pro-German newspapers was suspended. In 1934, the League authorized an international police force in the Saar (French garrison troops had been withdrawn in 1927), but the force was never created. It should be remembered, however, that there was generally unified opposition on the part of the Saarlanders to French (and League of Nations) rule throughout the relevant period; only with the rise of the Nazis did some minimal support for the status quo arise.

LEGISLATIVE POWERS

The laws in force in the Saar on the armistice date (except those enacted because of the state of war) remained in force. However, the Governing Commission had the authority to modify those laws and regulations "after consultation with the elected representatives of the inhabitants in such a manner as the Commission may determine."[1066] Local assemblies were elected, but they generally refused to cooperate with the Commission or rejected its decisions. Laws and/or regulations were enacted in any event, as there was no requirement for local consent to the Commission's acts. In 1922, an Advisory Council was elected to give advice on changes in existing laws and matters relating to taxation; it, too, generally rejected ordinances proposed by the Commission, which were then promulgated anyway. A Technical Committee of eight local members also was appointed by the League Council to assist the Commission.

The only real restrictions on the legislative power of the Commission related to the mines. Given the fact that the French member usually served as the Commission's Chairman, it is not surprising that there do not seem to have been any serious disputes between the Commission and the French government.

JUDICIAL POWERS

The existing civil and criminal courts in the Saar were retained. The Governing Commission did establish a Saar Supreme Court, however,

1066 *Id.*, art. 23.

which had jurisdiction to hear all appeals from the local courts. While some cases were reversed, it does not seem that the Supreme Court had much influence on the activities of the lower courts. The French representative on the Commission proposed the establishment of a special political court, but the proposal was not implemented.

The Governing Commission itself retained the power to decide all questions arising from the interpretation of the Treaty provisions. Ultimate League control could be exercised through removal of Commission members by the League Council.

THE PLEBISCITE

The Treaty of Versailles provided that three alternatives would be offered to the Saar population at the end of the fifteen-year period of League administration: maintenance of the international regime created by the treaty; union with France; or union with Germany. Following the plebiscite, the League was to "decide on the sovereignty under which the territory is to be placed, taking into account the wishes of the inhabitants as expressed by the voting."[1067] Germany and the League further agreed to take whatever steps might be necessary to effect any required transfer of sovereignty.

The vote was taken by commune or district, and partition of the territory was clearly within the range of possible decisions on sovereignty. It might also be noted that the League was not directly bound by the plebiscite results; it had only to take into account the wishes of the population "as expressed by the voting." In fact, the results of the plebiscite left no doubt as to the only possible course: out of 528,105 votes cast, over 90% opted for union with Germany; 8.8% favored maintenance of the status quo; and only 0.4% wanted union with France. In addition, there was a pro-German vote of at least 83% in each voting district, so there was no question of partition. The Saar was formally returned to German administration on 1 March 1935.

OBSERVATIONS

The government of the Saar Basin from 1920 to 1935 is primarily of interest as an example of a temporary regime which was conceived as an interim rather than a permanent solution to a particular problem.[1068] The problem was primarily that of ensuring French access to and exploitation of the Saar coal mines, without interference by the German

1067 *Id.*, art. 35.

1068 Of course, the option of continuing under international administration was available to the Saarlanders in the plebiscite, but this option does not seem to have been seriously anticipated by any of the parties to the arrangement.

authorities, but also without permitting French annexation of the territory. Direct administration by the League of Nations was the solution. The League's control over the Saar was absolute and, while the Saar was certainly autonomous with respect to the central German government and, to a lesser extent, France, the Saarlanders themselves cannot be said to have enjoyed any meaningful degree of self-government. The only functioning local institutions were the lower courts, which were subject to the jurisdiction of the Commission-established Supreme Court, and the purely advisory local assemblies and Advisory Council. While such advice might have been persuasive or have represented meaningful participation in the decision-making process, the non-cooperation of the local Advisory Council with the French-dominated Governing Council effectively precluded such participation. With the rise of the Nazis in the 1930s and the anti-Nazi response of the Governing Council, the situation in the Saar was essentially one of purely foreign administration, if not occupation, by 1935.

The Saar Basin is the only entity to have been directly governed by either the League of Nations or the United Nations,[1069] although the UN proposal for the Free Territory of Trieste would have involved direct UN participation in at least the executive branch of the Trieste government.[1070] The international presence was devoted to guaranteeing French rights to coal exploitation rather than to protecting or responding to the wishes of the local inhabitants, and it is hardly surprising that the Saarlanders resented the League presence rather than viewing it as a neutral caretaker which would permit them eventually to decide their own status free from undue French or German pressures. In fact, the period of League government could be seen as offering France the opportunity to "Frenchify" the Saar; in light of the plebiscite results, the opportunity was clearly lost.

The Saar (1945–1956)[1071]

HISTORICAL BACKGROUND

At the end of World War II, the Saar was placed within the French zone of occupation by the Potsdam Agreement among the four Allied

---

1069 The UN Council for Namibia might be an exception, although the de facto administration of Namibia by South Africa makes it quite a different situation.

1070 See the discussion of Trieste, *infra* at 400–06.

1071 See generally Jacques Freymond, *The Saar Conflict 1945–1955* (Westport, CT: Greenwood Press, 1960); Russell, *supra* note 1063, 1070; 3 Whiteman, *supra* note 35, at 392–425.

powers.[1072] France almost immediately undertook unilateral action to integrate the Saar region economically with France, and in December 1946 France set up a customs barrier between the Saar and the rest of Germany. The Saar's frontiers were expanded to the north, and moves towards integrating the Saar with France continued. The French franc was made legal tender in late 1947, and in January 1948 it became the only legal currency.

In 1947, the French appointed a Constitutional Commission of twenty Saarlanders, in consultation with the Saar political parties (which had been prohibited from having any ties with their German counterparts). The constitution drafted by the commission was ratified by the subsequently elected parliament, the Landtag, by a vote of 48–1–1. There was no direct referendum on the constitution itself, and it is not clear what proportion of the Saarlanders supported its provisions, although 95% of the eligible voters participated in the 1947 Landtag election. After the constitution came into force, the French military administration was replaced by a civilian administration, although a French High Commissioner retained extensive powers over the local government.

The legal status of the Saar remained unsettled, although the Saar received greater autonomy in a series of 1950 agreements with France.[1073] A reply from the Allied High Commission in 1951 to a complaint from German Chancellor Adenauer concerning alleged French repression of pro-German groups in the Saar stated that Allied approval of the Franco-Saar economic union in 1948 concerned only technical matters, and that the final status of the Saar would be determined by a peace treaty or similar instrument. In 1953, the Saar's autonomy was again expanded in an agreement with France, although the latter retained exclusive authority in the areas of defense and foreign affairs, and French laws concerning monetary and customs matters continued to apply to the Saar.

In 1954, France and the Federal Republic of Germany reached an

1072 Potsdam Agreement, France–U.S.S.R.–United Kingdom–United States, signed 2 Aug. 1945, 1 Amtsblatt Des Kontrollrats in Deutschland 13.

1073 There were five separate agreements between France and the Saar Territory, all of which were signed 3 Mar. 1950, and which are set forth in Amtsblatt des Saarlandes, 5 Jan. 1951. The first was a General Convention between France and the Saar Territory (hereinafter cited as "General Convention"). The others dealt respectively with the economic union between France and the Saar; the operation of Saar railways; the working of the Saar mines; and the settlement of nationals of the two countries and conduct of professional activities. The last agreement included general provisions prohibiting discrimination against either Saarlanders or French nationals with respect to travel and domicile (subject to unspecified police and security regulations) and with respect to real and personal property rights.

agreement with respect to an autonomous Saar territory within the context of a Western European Union.[1074] However, the Saar Statute included in this agreement was soundly rejected by 67% of the Saar voters in a referendum in 1955. One year later, France and Germany agreed (with subsequent U.S. and U.K. assent) that the Saar should be returned to Germany as an integral part of the Federal Republic, "in the endeavour to regulate this question with due regard to the feelings and interests of both sides, and thereby to contribute to a general and final state of peace."[1075] The Saar formally entered the Federal Republic of Germany on 1 January 1957, although the Franco-Saar customs and monetary union continued for a transitional period of three years.

The status of the Saar and its relationship with France during the decade after the war were in a state of constant evolution, and a detailed examination of the gradual development of government in the Saar during this period is beyond the scope of the present study. However, the basic outlines of Saar autonomy are set forth in the 1947 Saar constitution[1076] and the 1950 agreements between France and the Saar;[1077] it is with reference to these documents that the following observations are made.

EXECUTIVE POWERS

The 1947 constitution describes the Saar as an "autonomous, democratic and social" territory "economically attached to France," and it states that supreme power emanates from the Saar people.[1078] The 1950 General Convention reiterated that the Saar "is autonomous in all legislative, administrative and jurisdictional matters" and that such autonomy "shall be exercised within the limits of the Constitution, including the Preamble, and of the agreements entered into by the Saar Territory and the French Republic."[1079]

The Preamble is perhaps the most significant part of the constitution, at least with respect to the relationship between the Saar Territory and France. It provided that, *inter alia*, the Saar was founded on its economic attachment to and monetary and customs union with France; the Saar was independent from Germany; France would exercise all powers of

---

1074 Agreement between the Federal Republic of Germany and France on the Saar Statute, signed 23 Oct. 1954, reprinted in 3 Whiteman, *supra* note 35, at 412.

1075 Treaty between the Federal Republic of Germany and France for the Settlement of the Saar Question, signed 27 Oct. 1956, excerpts reprinted in 3 Whiteman, *supra* note 35, at 415.

1076 Entered into force 15 Dec. 1947, Amtsblatt des Saarlandes, 17 Dec. 1947.

1077 *Supra* note 1073.

1078 This and all other translations of the constitution are unofficial.

1079 General Convention, art. 1.

defense and foreign relations; French monetary and customs laws would apply in the Saar; the Saar judicial system would be compatible with that of France; and a French government representative (the High Commissioner) had the authority to issue decrees in order to safeguard the monetary and customs union and had a "general right of control" in order to guarantee respect for the Saar's status. These provisions were reinforced by article 63, which provided that economic integration with France, the rules of international law, and current and future international agreements "are an integral part of the law of the country and override domestic State law."

Pursuant to the High Commissioner's "right of control," subsequent French decrees empowered the High Commissioner to issue decrees necessary for the functioning of the economic and customs union; required that the Commissioner approve all laws adopted by the Saar government and appointments of all high Saar officials; permitted the Commissioner to insert expenditures into the Saar budget which were necessary for the normal functioning of the public services essential to the life of the Saar; and retained the Commissioner's right to take all necessary measures to maintain public order.

The 1950 General Convention reduced the High Commissioner's power somewhat, specifying that he could veto laws and regulations only if they "constitute a menace to the monetary and customs union; or disregard an international obligation of the Saar Territory; or are of a nature to infringe the political independence or the external security of the Saar Territory."[1080]

The maintenance of peace and order in the territory was transferred to the responsibility of the Saar police, except for matters which related to the French army or officials or French monetary and customs laws. Short of the declaration of a state of siege by the French government (in consultation with the Saar government), the convention also declared that the French armed forces could be deployed only with the consent of the Saar Government. France retained exclusive control over defense and foreign relations, although ratification by the Saar government began to be required in 1953 for international agreements concluded by France on behalf of the Saar.

In the administrative sphere, several agreements adopted at the same time as the 1950 General Convention provided for joint Franco-Saar action in certain specific areas. These included the establishment of a Franco-Saar Economic Commission, a joint Board of Directors to administer the Saar Railways, and an advisory Saar Mines Council; responsibility for operation of the Saar coal fields was specifically en-

1080 *Id.*, art. 3.

trusted to France. French and Saar representation on all of these bodies was equal, but the French Chairman of the Economic Commission had a casting vote in case of disputes relating to either the economic convention or the Saar Railways.

LEGISLATIVE POWERS

Subject to the High Commissioner's veto power, his right to issue decrees, and the direct application of French customs and monetary laws, the popularly-elected Saar Assembly enjoyed full legislative competence. As noted above, the primary restrictions on its jurisdiction were in the Preamble of the constitution, to which specific reference is made in article 1 of the 1950 General Convention.

The 1950 General Convention granted the Saar authorities "the power to repeal ordinances and regulations promulgated by the French Representative [High Commissioner] prior to the enforcement of the present convention, by means of laws and ordinances clearly and explicitly stating such repeal," excluding war-related ordinances.[1081] Such repeal remained, of course, subject to the general restrictions on the Assembly's legislative competence noted above.

The constitution could be amended by a three-fourths majority of the Assembly, but any proposed amendment contrary to the fundamental principles contained in the constitution "must be rejected"— although it is not clear by whom. Presumably, the French Representative could veto such an amendment as being contrary both to the constitution itself and to the Saar's international agreements.

JUDICIAL POWERS

The constitution provided for an independent Saar judicial system, but a special Franco-Saar Chamber within the Saar Court of Appeal was created to hear appeals, where French law was directly applicable, and other matters, where there was a conflict between Saar and applicable French laws. The Chamber also had jurisdiction over criminal cases involving French officials or members of the French military. The decisions of the Franco-Saar Chamber could be appealed to the French Cour de Cassation. The French Conseil d'Etat had jurisdiction over appeals from the local Saar administrative tribunals and also over all claims against the French administration in the Saar.

The judiciary was reorganized in 1953 under various agreements, so that both administrative and judicial appeals were heard by, first, the newly established Court of the Franco-Saar Union and, ultimately, the Supreme Court of the Franco-Saar Union. The former consisted of three

1081 *Id.*, art. 4.

Saarlanders and two French members; the latter had three French members and two Saarlanders. The system established in 1953 eliminated all appeals to French courts.

OBSERVATIONS

One of the most respected studies of the Saar Territory in the post-World War II period concludes that "it was not possible [for France] to escape from the initial confusion between autonomy and protectorate,"[1082] and the brief history of French control did see substantial changes in the governmental structure of the Saar. From an all-encompassing military government in 1945–47, France gradually expanded the scope of Saar autonomy to the point of agreeing, in the unimplemented 1954 Franco-German agreement, to replace the French Representative or High Commissioner with a European Commissioner (who would be neither French, German, nor Saarlander) and to grant to the Saar "exclusive competence" in all fields expressly reserved to the Commissioner. All the French proposals, however, reserved defense and foreign affairs to the French government (or, in the 1954 accords, to the European Commissioner). The 1954 proposals also would have returned administration of the coal fields to the Saar and encouraged the gradual establishment of a German-Saar customs union similar to that in force between France and the Saar.

In addition to the reservation of foreign affairs and defense powers, the economic, customs, and monetary links between France and the Saar were consistently outside the competence of the Saar authorities. The broad exceptions to local authority in the area of guaranteeing observance of the constitution and the various Franco-Saar agreements severely curtailed the actual autonomy of the Saarlanders; the fact that French actions in these areas could be taken by decrees issued by the High Commissioner or by vetoes of local legislation, rather than by a more complex process, reinforced French oversight and control.

While the Saar government seems in general to have been much more cooperative with the French authorities than had been the case in 1920–35, it is worth noting that the first popular referendum on the Saar's political status rejected, by a margin of 2 to 1, autonomy under even European, rather than French, oversight. Clearly, the Saar retained its desire to reunite with Germany.

Perhaps the least clear aspect of Franco-Saar relations concerns the many "agreements" entered into by the two governments. Given French control over foreign relations, the idea of Franco-Saar agreements based on equality seems untenable. The agreements clearly constituted a se-

1082 Freymond, *supra* note 1071, at 319.

rious restriction on local freedom of action, yet there is no indication that they were merely shams dictated by the French authorities.

A contemporaneous U.S. State Department opinion summarizes the confusion over the Saar's precise status:

> The status of the Saar in relation to France reveals a number of legal ambiguities which neither the constitution nor the French decrees eliminate. . . . France hopes to secure *de jure* confirmation of the present *de facto* status through an international charter, but at present it is not at all certain that such approval will be forthcoming. Such a charter might conceivably reduce present French controls in the interest of a genuinely autonomous Saar state.[1083]

It is difficult to conclude that a genuinely autonomous Saar ever came into existence, although the trend until the Saar's reintegration with Germany in 1955 was clearly in the direction of greater local control. France was more persuasive in encouraging ties between the Saar and France than it had been in the inter-war period, but the Saar's long-standing affinity with Germany prevented any permanent shift of allegiance.

Free Territory of Trieste[1084]

HISTORICAL BACKGROUND

Trieste has been an important port since the Roman empire and was often a source of conflict between Italy and Austria. It was ruled by the Kingdom of Venice from 997 to 1382, then for more than four centuries by the Hapsburg monarchy. After a brief period of integration into the Napoleonic Kingdom of Italy (1809–1815), the Congress of Vienna returned Trieste and what are now parts of northern Italy to the Austro-Hungarian empire. Trieste became the most important port of the Hapsburg empire during the century of Austro-Hungarian rule from 1815 to 1918.

Italy joined the Allies against the Central Powers of Germany and Austria-Hungary in 1915, and the redemption of Trieste became an emotional symbol for Italy during the war. After the collapse of Austria, the Treaty of Rapallo awarded Trieste and the Istrian Peninsula to Italy, while Yugoslavia obtained the Dalmatian coast up to, but excluding, the cities of Fiume and Zara (Zadar).[1085]

1083 U.S. Dept. of State, "The Present Status of the Saar," (1948), quoted in 3 Whiteman, *supra* note 35, at 396.

1084 See generally, Bogdan C. Novak, *Trieste 1941–1954* (Chicago: Univ. of Chicago Press, 1970); Ydit, *supra* note 35.

1085 Italy-Yugoslavia, signed 12 Nov. 1920, 18 L.N.T.S. 388.

The port of Trieste became increasingly Italian in the inter-war period, with an Italian majority by the late 1930s of perhaps 80% or more. The suburbs and surrounding area, however, were largely inhabited by Slavs, with a smaller proportion of German-speaking Austrians. Economically and commercially, the port of Trieste remained dependent on the Austrian hinterland, as both Italy and Yugoslavia had an abundance of other seaports.

As World War II drew to an end, both Yugoslavian and New Zealand troops invaded and occupied Trieste. The disputed city and its surrounding territory were divided into two zones of military occupation, Zone "A" under British-American control and Zone "B" under Yugoslav control. The next several years were spent in efforts to reconcile the competing interests of Italy, supported by the Western powers, and Yugoslavia, initially supported by the Soviet Union.

On the basis of a French proposal, the United States, United Kingdom, France, and U.S.S.R. agreed in 1946 to a formula that would internationalize Trieste as an autonomous entity under the United Nations Security Council. Despite objections from both Italy and Yugoslavia to this compromise solution, the Statute of Trieste was approved by the Security Council in January 1947 and agreed to a month later in the Peace Treaty with Italy.[1086] The Permanent Statute for Trieste and matters relating to a provisional government, the free port of Trieste, and technical and economic provisions were set forth as Annexes VI–X of the treaty.

Because of continuing political differences and, in particular, the onset of the "cold war" and the consolidation of Soviet influence in eastern Europe, the Security Council was unable to agree on the selection of a governor for Trieste as mandated by the Permanent Statute. The Soviet Union's support for the Yugoslav position evaporated in the aftermath of Tito's expulsion from the Comintern in 1948; the Western powers then became more sympathetic to Tito's claims, as a way of widening the gap between Yugoslavia and the U.S.S.R. Following the failure of direct Italian-Yugoslav negotiations, the Allied Military Government relinquished its administration over Zone A to Italy in 1953, but riots in Trieste soon thereafter provided greater urgency to arrive at a final settlement.

In October 1954, the proposed Free Territory of Trieste was definitively abandoned under the London Agreement among Italy, Yugoslavia, the United States, and the United Kingdom, which provided for the annexation of Zone A (including Trieste) by Italy and Zone B by

---

1086 Signed 10 Feb. 1947, 49 U.N.T.S. 3, art. 21.

Yugoslavia (with certain minor border adjustments).[1087] Both Italy and Yugoslavia agreed to respect the rights of each other's minorities, and Italy undertook to maintain the free port at Trieste "in general accordance" with the provisions relating to the free port set forth in the Peace Treaty (excluding the proposed international port commission).

The following description is of the ultimately unimplemented "Free Territory of Trieste" proposed by the Security Council.

EXECUTIVE POWERS

The Free Territory of Trieste was to be a neutral, independent entity under the direct control of the UN Security Council. The Security Council was to ensure the "integrity and independence" of Trieste, the observance of the Statute, the protection of basic human rights, and the maintenance of public order and security.[1088] The Security Council's administrative arm in Trieste was the Governor, who was to be appointed by the Council, after consultation with Italy and Yugoslavia, for a term of five years. The Governor could not be a citizen of Italy or Yugoslavia, reported directly to the Council, and was prohibited from seeking or receiving instructions "from any other authority."

The Governor had primary responsibility for the observance of the Statute and the maintenance of public order. He had the authority to veto legislation passed by the Trieste Assembly which he considered contrary to the Statute; to suspend administrative regulations contrary to the Statute; to exercise the powers of pardon and reprieve; to approve or disapprove international treaties and agreements; to appoint the head of the Territory's police force, the Director of Public Security (although the Director was "normally" to be "under the immediate authority" of the local Trieste Council of Government); and, in emergency situations, to order that "appropriate measures" be taken and to assume control of the security services. The Governor's actions could be appealed to the Security Council by the Trieste government, but it is clear that his powers of direct administration were substantial.

Subject to the powers and responsibilities of the Governor, the remaining executive power was vested in the Council of Government, chosen by the Trieste Assembly. The Council of Government was to suggest appointees for the positions of Director of Public Safety and Director of the Free Port (neither of whom could be an Italian or Yugoslav national); refer disputed actions of the Governor in suspending

1087 Signed 5 Oct. 1954, 235 U.N.T.S. 99.
1088 Peace Treaty with Italy, *supra* note 1086, Annex VI, Permanent Statute of the Free Territory of Trieste [hereinafter cited as "Permanent Statute"], art. 2.

administrative measures to the Security Council; be jointly responsible with the Governor for entering into international agreements, which were limited to economic, technical, cultural, social, and health questions; and normally oversee the police and security forces, with the exceptions noted above.

LEGISLATIVE POWERS

The legislative power of Trieste was vested in a popularly-elected, unicameral Assembly, which had the right "to consider and discuss any matters affecting the interests of the Free Territory."[1089] However, this broad grant of competence was subject to the superior status of the Statute and its many specific restrictions. The Assembly could not override the Governor's veto of legislation, although the UN Security Council could promulgate laws over such a veto. In the economic sphere, the Assembly adopted the Trieste budget and could levy local taxes; however, economic union or other exclusive associations with any other country were specifically prohibited by the Statute. Trieste was to have its own monetary system.

Trieste was to receive all Italian state and para-statal property within the Territory, without compensation being paid to Italy. There were no explicit restrictions on the alienation of public lands or resources, although security considerations might have given the Governor some power in this area. No restrictions could be placed on the transfer of property to Italy by those who opted for Italian citizenship.

JUDICIAL POWERS

Only general guidelines for the Trieste judiciary were set forth in the Statute; details were left to be determined by a future Trieste constitution and laws. The Governor was given the power to appoint judges from among candidates proposed by the Trieste Council of Government "or from among other persons," after consultation with the Council of Government; the Governor also had the power to remove judges, "subject to safeguards to be established by the Constitution."[1090]

With respect to interpretation of the Permanent Statute, any dispute not resolved by direct negotiations or by a mutually agreed upon means of settlement was to be referred to an ad hoc commission, composed of one representative of each party to the dispute and a third party selected by mutual agreement or, if agreement were impossible, by the UN Secretary-General. Decisions by this commission were final.

1089 *Id.*, art. 18.
1090 *Id.*, art. 16.

OTHER MATTERS

Provisional government

Annex VII to the Peace Treaty provided for a provisional regime to govern Trieste until the institutions established under the Statute came into effect. Essentially, administrative and, to some extent, legislative power was vested in the Governor, whose "first concern" was "to ensure the maintenance of public order and security."[1091] Troops of the occupying countries were to remain at the Governor's disposal for 90 days after his assumption of office and were to be withdrawn at the end of that time unless the Governor requested that some or all of them remain.

The Governor was to appoint a Provisional Council of Government, after consultation with Italy and Yugoslavia, which would act as a transitional advisory body. While the Governor had the power to suspend or revoke existing laws and regulations, new or amended laws and regulations required the approval of a majority of the Provisional Council.

A constitution for Trieste was to be drafted by a popularly-elected Constituent Assembly; elections to this body were to be held within four months after appointment of the Governor.

Free Port of Trieste

A free port was to be established, somewhat similar to that of Danzig, under the supervision of an International Commission.[1092] The Commission consisted of one representative of Trieste, who would serve as Chairman, and representatives of eleven other states. Administration of the port would be entrusted to a Director, appointed by the Governor from among persons recommended by the Council of Government. Disputes would be settled by an ad hoc commission, and proposed amendments could be submitted for approval to the Security Council either by the Trieste Council of Government or by any three members of the International Commission.

Water and electricity

Specific provision was made for the continuing supply of water and electricity to Trieste by both Italy and Yugoslavia, and a mixed commission of Trieste, Italian, and Yugoslav representatives was to be created to supervise execution of the agreements regarding hydroelectric supply.[1093]

1091 Peace Treaty with Italy, *supra* note 1086, art. 4.
1092 *Id.*, Annex VIII.
1093 *Id.*, Annex IX.

Minority rights

Both the Permanent Statute and the 1954 London Agreement protect ethnic minorities from discrimination in Trieste or, after 1954, Italy and Yugoslavia. Among the rights guaranteed in the 1954 agreement are civil and political rights, access to public administration, non-discriminatory taxation, and protection of the use of ethnic languages.[1094]

OBSERVATIONS

Perhaps the first point to underscore in relation to the Free Territory of Trieste is that it never came into being. While neither Italy nor Yugoslavia supported internationalization of the territory, the ultimate collapse of the UN proposal was due more to East-West rivalry than to Italian or Yugoslav intransigence. In any event, one is unable to judge how the Permanent Statute would have worked in practice, and no local constitution was ever drafted.

Trieste would have been a true internationalized territory, with its own citizenship and a de facto head of state (the Governor) responsible directly to the UN Security Council. Unlike the Memel Territory, Trieste was not placed under the sovereignty of another state; unlike Danzig, it was forbidden rather than encouraged to enter into special relationships with another country. While the League of Nations High Commissioner in Danzig acted primarily as a mediator, the Trieste Governor would have participated directly in the territory's government.

In effect, the Free Territory approached the status of what might have been termed a "guaranteed state" in the nineteenth century. Trieste was to be independent, but demilitarized and neutral, and it was prohibited from entering into relationships which might jeopardize that neutrality. The major difference between Trieste and a nineteenth-century guaranteed state is that the former would have been under the protection of a multilateral international organization rather than a small group of the "Great Powers" (although, of all the UN organs, the Security Council most closely reflects the Great Power system).

It might be noted that, while popular participation in drafting the constitution and choosing the subsequent government of Trieste was anticipated, no such participation was afforded the residents of the Trieste region in adopting the Permanent Statute itself. "Self-determination" was not deemed relevant, perhaps because Trieste—

1094 Under art. 7 of the Permanent Statute, Italian and Slovene were to be the official languages of Trieste, with the constitution to determine "in what circumstances Croat may be used as a third official language."

whatever its status—clearly did not fall within the scope of decolonization.

As with most examples of shared sovereignty or less-than-independent autonomy, the actual success or failure of the Free Territory's government would have depended largely on the relationship between the elected Trieste government and the appointed Governor, as well as on the respective political goals of Italy and Yugoslavia. There is certainly no reason to prefer the unusual resolution proposed in 1947 to the ultimate solution of partition which was agreed to by Italy and Yugoslavia in 1954; whatever the initial difficulties, Trieste has ceased to be a source of international tension.

Finally, the annexes to the Statute that deal with technical, economic, and financial matters are interesting examples of the kind of detailed treatment that can be given to particular problems, such as guaranteeing water and electricity supply from outside the territory or property rights. While it is difficult to extrapolate from the specifics addressed in the Trieste context, the technical annexes do offer a precedent for the resolution of very specific items of concern, irrespective of larger political determinations.

Chapter 18
Other Situations of Interest

Belgium

HISTORICAL BACKGROUND

Belgium became an independent state in 1830, following earlier attachment to Holland and France and unification with Holland in 1815 as part of the Kingdom of the Netherlands. After declaring its independence, Belgium was recognized by the major European powers as an independent and "perpetually neutral" state.

Belgium has been home to at least two distinct ethnic groups since the sixteenth century: the Dutch-speaking, Protestant, Flemish community in the north, and the French-speaking, Catholic, Walloon community in the south. In addition, there is a small German-speaking minority, dating from a period of Austrian control in the sixteenth and seventeenth centuries.

The 1830 revolution was in large part dictated by Walloon dissatisfaction with rule by the Dutch, and friction between Flemish and Walloons was not diminished by independence. The minority French-speaking community dominated the majority Dutch-speaking population economically and politically, and the first linguistic reforms aimed at establishing at least legal equality between Dutch and French were not adopted until the 1930s.

Tensions continued, particularly in the area of education. In the early 1960s, a complaint was filed before the European Commission of Human Rights by French-speaking parents alleging that the effective denial of French-language instruction to their children violated the European Convention on Human Rights. The complaint eventually was appealed to the European Court of Human Rights, which in 1968 found that the challenged statute, insofar as it prevented certain children from having access to French language schools near Brussels on the basis of their parents' residence, did violate the Convention.[1095] The expansion of French-speaking university faculties into Flemish areas and resultant rioting in Flanders led to the resignation of the Flemish members of the Belgian cabinet in 1968.

A declaration of intent to revise the constitution was proclaimed following the fall of the government in 1968, and the newly elected parliament reconvened as a Constituent Assembly to propose the revisions. In 1970, agreement was reached on a series of amendments which attempted to recognize and safeguard the integrity of the three cultural communities in Belgium, the Flemish, Walloon, and German. The universities of Brussels and Louvain were divided along linguistic lines, and three linguistic regions were recognized: the French-speaking Walloon region, the Dutch-speaking Flemish region, and the bilingual (Dutch and French) region of Brussels. Members of parliament were divided into Dutch- and French-speaking groups, which constituted "cultural councils" with certain powers to deal with cultural, educational, and other matters as set forth in the constitution and in subsequent enabling legislation.

The general provisions of the 1970 constitutional amendments left the details of regionalization to be determined by subsequent legislation, and successive governments have found it difficult to reconcile the demands by Walloons for full regional status for Brussels (primarily French-speaking though located in the Flemish region) with Flemish fears that loss of the capital would leave them in an an inferior position, as two of the three regions would then be controlled by French-speakers. Establishment of regional institutions in Brussels continued to be an insurmountable stumbling block, and "every government from 1968–80 fell as a direct result of the community problem."[1096]

There was another major constitutional revision in 1980, which put into effect "the most profound institutional reform in Belgian history."[1097] There are now three linguistic communities (Dutch, French,

1095 *Case Relating to Certain Aspects of the Laws on the Use of Languages in Education in Belgium, supra* note 404. It should be noted that, while the Court found that the children's right of education was violated, it did not find that the territorially-based Belgian educational system was impermissibly discriminatory.

1096 R. E. M. Irving, *The Flemings and Walloons of Belgium* (London: Minority Rights Group Report No. 46, 1980) at 12. A long-standing dispute concerning the election of a French-speaking mayor in the small town of Fourons, which had become part of the Flemish region after territorial adjustments, led to another government resignation in October 1987.

1097 Marc J. Bossuyt, "Belgium: Part I," in *Co-existence in some plural European Societies, supra* note 1027, at 11. Additional amendments were adopted in July 1988. A helpful chronology may be found in the April 1989 supplement on Belgium in Albert P. Blaustein and Gisbert H. Flanz, 2 *Constitutions of the Countries of the World* (Dobbs Ferry, NY: Oceana, 1989).

and German) and four regions (Dutch-, French-, and German-speaking, and bilingual Brussels);[1098] the communities have personal jurisdiction over their members, while the regions have territorial competence. The Flemish community and region are co-extensive and share a common executive and legislature, while the French community and Walloon region have different government structures; all are distinct from the national government.

EXECUTIVE POWERS

The national executive authority of Belgium is vested in the King, who acts through a parliamentary cabinet of ministers. The King has the power to issue regulations and decrees necessary to implement legislation passed by parliament but does not have any veto or suspensive power. The 1970 amendments provided that, with the exception of the Prime Minister, the cabinet must consist of an equal number of French-speaking and Flemish-speaking ministers.

There is a separate executive linked to each of the three linguistic community councils.

LEGISLATIVE POWERS

Legislative power at the national level is exercised collectively by the cabinet and the bicameral parliament, which consists of a House of Representatives and a Senate. The 1970 constitutional amendments provided that, except in the case of budgets and laws requiring a special majority for passage, the members of each house of parliament are divided into a French-language group and a Dutch-language group, determined by the region from which the member is elected or, in the case of members from Brussels, by the language in which a member takes his or her oath of office; however, legislators are to "represent the Nation, and not only the province . . . which elected them."[1099]

A motion by three-fourths of the members of either linguistic group may suspend consideration of any bill for thirty days, if the proposed bill is "of such a nature as to have a serious effect on relations between the communities."[1100] The cabinet reconsiders the bill during the thirty-day period, offers its opinion as to the objections to the bill, and may then resubmit the bill to parliament. The bill may subsequently be

---

1098 While art. 3b of the constitution refers to four regions, art. 107d mentions only three regions, excluding the German-speaking. Authority over German-speakers is exercised by the German-speaking community council established in 1983; that authority may extend to German-speaking areas within the Dutch-speaking region, with the agreement of the Dutch regional council.

1099 Belgian Const., art. 32 (this and other translations are unofficial).

1100 *Id.*, art. 38b.

adopted, in the same manner as other bills, by an absolute majority of the votes cast.

The three community councils have authority over cultural matters, education (with certain exclusions), cooperation between the communities, "international cultural cooperation," and "personal matters."[1101] Decrees adopted by the cultural councils are effective within the respective linguistic regions and also apply to institutions in Brussels whose activities or organization are such that they "should be considered as belonging exclusively to one or the other community."[1102]

The powers of the territorially-based regional institutions are determined by law and include environmental matters; planning; housing; and regional economic, energy, and employment policies. The constitution provides that the community councils may assume the powers of the regional institutions, which the Dutch council has done. The community and regional authorities have limited powers of taxation and receive most of their budget through appropriations from the national legislature.

All laws establishing the community and regional institutions and their competence must be adopted by a majority of each of the linguistic groups in parliament and must also receive two-thirds of the total votes cast by the two groups combined. Regional and community legislators continue to be drawn from members of the national parliament, although this was originally envisaged only as a transitional arrangement.

The 1980 and 1988 reforms established a complex structure for governing Brussels, providing for a regional council divided into linguistic groups, with the latter exercising authority over community matters.

JUDICIAL POWERS

The 1970 constitutional revisions provided that all preliminary draft decrees by a cultural council be submitted to the legislation section of the Council of State, but this requirement was eliminated by subsequent amendments. A new Court of Arbitration was created in 1983 to assume jurisdiction over conflicts among community, regional, and national laws, although the 1988 constitutional amendments authorize a future law to govern the court's composition and jurisdiction. Federal legislation does not prevail over inconsistent regional or community decrees, provided that the latter are within the competence granted by the constitution and relevant laws.

1101 *Id.*, arts. 59b, §2 and 2b.
1102 *Id.*, art. 59b, §§4 and 4b.

Language use in Belgian courts is still governed largely by a 1935 law which operates on the basis of territoriality.[1103] A single language is adopted for most court proceedings, although the parties in a civil case and the accused in a criminal case retain the right to testify in the language of their choice regardless of the language of the proceedings. Appeals are normally heard in the language of the challenged decision, and most judges are not required to be bilingual. The Cour de Cassation is composed of an equal number of Dutch- and French-speaking members, and cases are usually heard by unilingual chambers.

OTHER MATTERS

Language

While the thrust of the 1970 constitutional amendments was to grant a certain degree of cultural autonomy to the three linguistic groups, no official language or languages were mandated. The bill of rights provides that the use of languages spoken in Belgium "is optional" and "may only be regulated by law and only for acts of public authorities and judicial matters."[1104]

Foreign affairs

As clarified in the 1988 constitutional amendments, each region has foreign affairs powers commensurate with its substantive internal powers. Thus, regions may enter into international agreements with foreign states concerning, for example, cultural exchanges, and such agreements are not subject to approval by the central government. This may well lead to problems of representation in international organizations such as Unesco, since there is no national body responsible for educational or cultural affairs.

OBSERVATIONS

While Belgium under the 1970 revisions to its constitution was termed a "communal state," it is clear that the degree of autonomy reserved to the various linguistic communities in Belgium was very limited. Nevertheless, within the areas of culture, education, and language, each of the three cultural groups identified in the constitution possessed fairly extensive authority.

The 1980 revisions granted greater autonomy to the respective com-

---

1103 See generally Kenneth D. McRae, *Conflict and Compromise in Multilingual Societies: Belgium* (Waterloo, Ontario: Wilfrid Laurier Univ. Press, 1986) at 203–09.
1104 Belgian Const., art. 23.

munities, although "[i]t has to be confessed that the actual state structure is somewhat confused due to a lack of clarity in the terms of the law and to the incomplete character of the reform. No homogeneous policy-packages have been transferred to the communities or the regions and the limits between the several fields of competence are far from clear-cut."[1105] There does seem to be an increasing trend towards regional devolution, and Belgium may be in the process of transforming itself into a federal state.

Despite the continuing tension and conflicts over the status of Brussels, there have been no serious calls (at least in the post-World War II era) for division of Belgium along linguistic lines. Extreme positions on both sides have generally been rejected by the voters, and the purely linguistic parties never received more than 22% of the total vote.[1106] It appears that an acceptable, if still rather vague, compromise is being reached, and the complex political and social distinctions which characterize Belgian society have not been replaced by those based primarily on ethnicity or language. Nevertheless, the continuing significance of language and cultural questions in Belgian political life evidences the extreme difficulty of resolving such deeply emotional and often technically complex issues.

Indian Peoples in Brazil

HISTORICAL BACKGROUND

When Europeans arrived in Brazil in 1500, it is estimated that there were from one to six million indigenous Indian inhabitants, divided among a myriad of tribes. The story of deliberate genocide and exploitation, coupled with deaths from European illnesses, is perhaps best illustrated by the fact that Brazil's Indian population today is approximately 220,000, or 0.15% of the total Brazilian population. There are over 230 separate tribes and languages, with most tribes concentrated in the Amazon basin.[1107] The average population of each tribe is less than 2,000 and ranges from a membership of only 13 to approximately 15,000.[1108]

The earliest colonial legislation adopted a paternalistic attitude towards the indigenous populations, and in 1532 conversion of the Indians

1105 Bossuyt, *supra* note 1097, at 12.
1106 Dick Leonard, "Belgium: Part II," in *Co-existence in some plural European societies*, *supra* note 1027, at 13.
1107 "O Brasil tem 220 mil indios," Jornal da Funai (Brasilia), Aug. 1986, at 7.
1108 Greg Urban, "Developments in the Situation of Brazilian Tribal Populations from 1976 to 1982," 20 Latin American Research Rev. 7, 21 (no. 1, 1985).

was affirmed as being the main reason for settlement of the new colony. At the same time, however, war against Indian "enemies" also was sanctioned. The Catholic orders, particularly the Jesuits, adopted a generally protective attitude towards the Indians vis à vis secular colonists, but they also attempted to "civilize" indigenous culture. In 1758, Indians were freed from their status as virtual slaves under the guardianship of the Catholic church, and the Jesuits were expelled from Brazil the following year.

Brazil achieved independence from Portugal in 1822, but this event had little impact on the continued penetration of Brazilian-European settlers and explorers into central Brazil and other Indian-inhabited regions. In 1850, Brazil first distinguished between public land, which belonged to the state, and private land. Indigenous land was theoretically private, but Indians normally had neither the documentation nor the legal understanding needed to legitimize their rights; as elsewhere in the hemisphere, the acquisition of Indian land by whites was a characteristic of nineteenth century settlement.

Where products in demand on the international market might be found, Indian tribes were soon driven out, decimated, or brought into peonage or outright slavery. This was particularly true, for example, in the Amazon Valley, where the increasing demand for rubber during the late nineteenth century attracted Brazilians into the headwaters of Amazon tributaries still inhabited by tribal groups. In the rubber forests, the process of detribalization and assimilation which took place along the coast of Brazil was again enacted. . . . Perhaps the only reason that any Brazilian Indian tribes persisted into the twentieth century was the indolent expansion of Brazilian civilization into the interior of the country; poor communications allowed many Indian tribes to survive in distant and isolated parts of the country.[1109]

The Brazilian Indian Protection Service (SPI) was founded in 1910 by a group of military officers; their mission was to protect indigenous tribes through pacification rather than conquest. This policy was remarkably successful for a time, permitting initial Brazilian economic penetration of Indian lands and some settlement, but its humanitarian goals were irrelevant to the actual impact on the Indians. Disease destroyed vast numbers of Indians, and the constant pressures for economic development soon reduced most tribes to "marginalized ethnic populations on minuscule parcels of land."[1110]

Whatever the protective policy adopted, whether it tried to guarantee an honest wage or attempted to set aside lands for the Indian, it always seemed

1109 Wagley and Harris, *supra* note 170, at 30.
1110 Shelton H. Davis, *Victims of the Miracle* (Cambridge: Cambridge Univ. Press, 1977) at 5.

to run counter to the economic interests of the Brazilian frontiersmen. . . . [D]espite the humanitarian and idealistic efforts and policies of the Indian Service, the process of acculturation and assimilation of the Indian groups in Brazil has continued to be disastrous to them.[1111]

The final push into central Brazil began in the 1940s and accelerated following the military coup of 1964. "Operation Amazon," a plan to spend US$2 billion in developing transport, power, communications, and natural resources in the Amazon Basin, was announced in 1966. In 1970, plans to build the Trans-Amazon Highway and encourage settlement in the region were announced, and the new government agency FUNAI (National Indian Foundation)—which had replaced the SPI in 1967, following revelations of corruption and massacres—was given the task of ensuring that Amazonian Indians would not obstruct the government's development plans. Forced assimilation became the goal, and construction of a network of roads through Indian parks and reserves in order to make lands accessible for mineral and other exploitation had a devastating effect on the indigenous tribes.[1112]

Current battles between developers, particularly miners, and Indians are reminiscent of those of the nineteenth century and earlier. In 1975, the Amazonian homeland of the Yanomami tribe was invaded by hundreds of independent prospectors (*"garimpeiros"*), who were eventually expelled by the government. A second invasion in 1985 was initially turned back by federal troops, but it has been estimated that at least 20,000 and perhaps as many as 100,000 miners have inundated the region since 1987.[1113] Hydroelectric and other development projects continue to threaten the traditional peoples of the Amazon region.[1114]

1111   Wagley and Harris, *supra* note 170, at 36.

1112   See generally, e.g., Davis, *supra* note 1110; M. L. Margolis and W. E. Carter (eds.), *Brazil: Anthropological Perspectives* (1979); Marc Pallemaerts, "Development, Conservation, and Indigenous Rights in Brazil," 8 Human Rights Q. 374 (1986); and the many publications of nongovernmental organizations, such as Survival International and Cultural Survival. It might be noted in passing that Brazil ratified ILO Convention No. 107 (on indigenous peoples) in 1965, which is a generally pro-integrationist or assimilationist treaty; *cf.* discussion in chap 5, at 77–78.

1113   A complaint against Brazil's treatment of the Yanomami was filed with the Inter-American Commission on Human Rights by several NGOs in 1980. In 1985, the Commission recognized that Brazil had taken "important measures" to protect the Yanomami since 1983, but concluded that the government's earlier failure to take "timely and effective measures" had led to violations of Yanomami rights to life, liberty, personal security, residence and movement, and health. Case No. 7615 (Brazil), *supra* note 295; also see Davis, *supra* note 295, at 41–62; statement by the National Conference of Brazilian Bishops, "CNBB denuncia genoc dio dos Yanomami," Correio Braziliense, 16 Dec. 1988, at 15.

1114   See, e.g., Dave Treece, *Bound in Misery and Iron* (London: Survival International, 1987) (concerning the impact of Brazil's Grande Carajás program).

The approximately 20,000 Yanomami who inhabit the region along the Brazil-Venezuela frontier (of whom approximately 12,000 are in Brazil) are perhaps the largest tribe in the region. Although their homeland, an area twice the size of Switzerland, was provisionally closed to outsiders in 1981, no formal steps were taken until late 1988 to protect the area as an Indian park or reserve. Even then, the area proposed in August 1988 to be demarcated included only 30% of the traditional Yanomami lands, divided into nineteen separate areas. Brazil apparently has adopted a new plan, "Calha Norte" or "Northern Headwaters," to establish a string of frontier posts with airstrips to form nuclei for new economic development and the integration of Brazilian forest-dwellers into the state.

CONTEMPORARY LEGAL SITUATION

Article 8 of the 1969 Brazilian Constitution provided that the central government may legislate on the "incorporation of the forest-dwelling aborigines into the national community." While article 4 includes within the national patrimony "the lands occupied by forest-dwelling aborigines," article 198 of the constitution nevertheless guarantees the inalienability of lands inhabited by Indians, "under the terms that federal law may establish." The federal government has *dominio* or ownership of the lands, but both *posse* (legal occupation) and *propriedade* (legal right of possession) are guaranteed to the Indians. Article 198 further provides that Indians have the exclusive right to use natural resources within their lands, but this provision seems to be contradicted by the distinction between sub-soil and other resources made in the 1973 Indian Statute.[1115] The latter revised FUNAI's mandate and is the basic law which governs Indian affairs today.

Personal status

Article 6 of Brazil's Civil Code defines Indians, along with persons between the ages of 16 and 21, as "relatively incapable." Indians are citizens but are under the guardianship or tutelage of the central government, which has delegated that responsibility to FUNAI. FUNAI "has complete responsibility for them in law and control over all aspects of their lives."[1116] An Indian individual or tribe may acquire a more independent status by being declared *integrado* or emancipated, although none has yet requested formal emancipation.[1117]

1115 Law 6001, 19 Dec. 1973.

1116 UN Indigenous Study, *supra* note 276, at 198.

1117 Brazil, art. 9 CERD Report, UN Doc. CERD/C/149/Add.3 (1986) at 11. Brazil's basic policies towards its indigenous populations are summarized in its sixth periodic report, UN Doc. CERD/C/66/Add.1 (1980).

Political autonomy

Article 6 of the Indian Statute recognizes the customs and traditions of Indian peoples in organizing their internal affairs, including traditional leadership systems. There is, however, no provision for external autonomy vis à vis the federal government and no Indian representatives as such in FUNAI.[1118] Thus, while various policies have been implemented in order to protect Indian lands and culture, all of the policies are the responsibility of the federal government; there is no Indian self-government per se.

Land rights

The 1973 Indian Statute recognizes three kinds of Indian lands: those inhabited or occupied by Indians and over which they have unquestionable rights pursuant to article 198 of the constitution; reserved areas (usually called parks or reserves) established for Indians by FUNAI or SPI; and other areas in which Indians have acquired property rights under the normal provisions of civil law.

The first category is fully protected, at least in theory, by article 22 of the Statute, which provides, "Indians and forest-dwellers are fully entitled to permanent possession of the land they live on and to exclusive usufruct of the natural wealth and all the utilities existing on that land." Article 25 states that recognition of these rights "shall be independent of the delimitation thereof and shall be assured by [FUNAI]." Prior dispossession would seem also to be illegal, under article 62:

Any acts whatsoever that aim to exert dominion, tenure, or occupation over Indian communities or lands inhabited by Indians are hereby annulled and declared void of legal effect.
(1) This article also applies to land which has been abandoned by Indians or Indian communities due to illegal acts by officials or private citizens.
(2) No one shall have the right to sue the State or the Indians themselves for damages incurred as a consequence of the annulment mentioned above or its economic consequences.[1119]

However, article 20 of the Statute permits the government to "intervene" even in these constitutionally protected areas, "if there is no alternative solution," in order:

1118 The government has stated that 25% of FUNAI's employees are Indians, of whom 55 occupy senior positions, although these figures are not accepted by anthropologists and other experts on the Brazilian situation. Art. 9 CERD Report (1986), *supra* note 1117, at 12.

1119 Section 3 of art. 62 does permit the continuation "for a reasonable timespan" of leases of Indian land which were in force in 1973.

(a) To put an end to fighting between tribal groups.
(b) To combat serious outbreaks of epidemics. . . .
(c) For the sake of national security.
(d) To carry out public works of interest to national development.
(e) To repress widespread disorder or pillaging.
(f) To work valuable subsoil deposits of outstanding interest for national security and development.

Intervention may include the removal of tribal groups, which "shall be assigned an area equivalent to the former one, ecological conditions included," and Indians are to be compensated for any damages arising from the removal.[1120]

While the protection of indigenous lands theoretically does not depend on their identification, such a task is obviously essential to define a frontier between indigenous and exploitable land. Thus, FUNAI has been charged since 1973 with a three-stage process of identifying, delimiting, and demarcating Indian lands. By the end of 1984, over 67 million hectares of Indian lands (approximately 8% of the total land area of Brazil) had been identified for demarcation, but, in over a decade, only 15% had been "delimited" and only 8% fully demarcated.[1121] This lack of progress is lamentable, despite the difficulties inherent in identifying hitherto isolated groups whose likely territory can only be guessed; whose culture, even language, is unknown; and whose lands already may have been invaded by rubber tappers, squatters, and miners.

Exploitation of surface resources (including minerals) is reserved to Indians under article 44 of the Indian Statute, but the following article exempts subsoil wealth, which may be exploited under whatever terms are established by law. Revenue from such exploitation is to revert to the Indians. A controversial 1983 decree established more detailed regulations for subsoil exploitation; among its provisions is that FUNAI may require mining companies to adopt "precautionary measures aimed at preserving the Indians' culture, mores and traditions," including the possibility of suspending mining activities.

1120 Law 6001, *supra* note 1115, §§3, 4.
1121 Art. 9 CERD Report (1986), *supra* note 1117, at 12. As of November 1985, Indian lands identified for demarcation had increased to 75.2 million hectares, in 400 separate areas. The government claims that the process of demarcation has been accelerated since 1985, and the attention given to the subject by FUNAI's monthly newspaper is evidence of its importance and sensitivity. See, e.g., Jornal da Funai, Sept. 1986 at 3; Oct. 1986 at 7; Jan. 1987 at 6. The last-noted article indicates that 85 areas were demarcated under the new civilian government in 20 months, compared to 174 demarcated in the previous 74 years.

OBSERVATIONS

To the surprise of many, the new Brazilian constitution adopted by the Constituent Assembly in June 1988 contains several positive references to Indian rights, although it remains to be seen whether these provisions reflect a new commitment to the effective protection of Brazil's indigenous peoples. The status of Indians as original settlers and their rights to social organization, customs, language, religion, and traditions are recognized. Indians are to have permanent posession, including the "exclusive enjoyment" of products of the soil, rivers, and lakes, of those lands they have "traditionally occupied," those "inhabited by them in a permanent manner, utilized for productive activities, [and] vital to the preservation of the environmental resources necessary to their physical and cultural reproduction."[1122] The most significant amendments may be those which place responsibility for exploitation of water and mineral resources, as well as possible removal of indigenous communities from their lands, directly under the control of the Brazilian Congress, rather than an administrative agency; this should at lest ensure a wider political debate over destructive intrusions into indigenous lands.[1123]

Even a generally pro-government, Unesco-sponsored study was forced to conclude (in 1964):

It is a strange paradox that Brazil, a country known throughout the world for its democratic policy and practice in race relations, has not been successful in providing equal rights and conditions for its tribal Indians. The fact is that most Brazilian Indian tribes suffer serious disabilities. Contact with Brazilian civilization continues to be highly disastrous to most groups. Many tribes have lost, or are in the process of losing, their land.[1124]

This pessimistic conclusion is no less true today, and, in fact, development plans had a much greater negative impact on indigenous life in Brazil in the 1960s, immediately after the conclusion of the study just cited.

Most of the funding for Brazilian development projects is from external sources, such as the World Bank. In 1985, the Bank suspended disbursements to Brazil for a major project in the Amazon because the government had not applied an earmarked $26 million to protect Indian lands and forest-dwellers. Another suspension of funding for a road project in the Amazon region was threatened in 1987, on grounds of Brazil's failure to protect the rain forest and its inhabitants from envi-

1122 1988 Brazilian Const., art. 234(1) and (2); unofficial translation.
1123 *Id.*, art. 234(3) and (5).
1124 Wagley and Harris, *supra* note 170, at 44.

ronmental degradation. However, such external actions have been rare, despite frequent expressions of international concern.

> The initial and fundamental contradiction [in Brazilian indigenous policies] is that FUNAI is an organization within the Ministry of the Interior and thus dependent on the Ministry for its budget and subordinate to its policy decisions. As the interests of the large private and government economic groups currently conducting the activity known as development are protected by the Ministry and clash with the interests of the Indians whose territories fall within the ambit of this development, it is clear that the interests of the Indians have no real representative.[1125]

These internal conflicts of interest; the lack of recognized indigenous political autonomy; and the isolated location, small size, and technologically primitive nature of many of the indigenous tribes in Brazil have all contributed to the fundamental problems arising out of the confrontation between modern Brazilian and traditional indigenous societies. Much of this conflict is inevitable, and the real question is on what terms it will be resolved in coming years and decades.

Even with the best of intentions, cultural confrontations are likely to be extremely disruptive to the less "advanced" of two societies. In Brazil, the perceived interests of national security and the riches in natural resources that the government and private interests hope to find in the Amazon Basin make it less likely that the confrontation will be gradual or disinterested. In addition to the profit motives of Brazilian entrepreneurs and transnational corporations, the government has viewed the "Indian problem" in geopolitical terms similar to those of many other states in which there are cross-border minority or indigenous groups. For example, the governor of the province in which the Yanomami are largely located has stated that, while he does not oppose creation of a Yanomami reserve, "there are ideological problems. There is nothing to stop those who today defend the preservation of Indians like creatures in a zoo from one day trying to declare an independent Yanomami state in this land of great mineral riches. As Brazilians, we cannot accept this calmly."[1126]

Thus, in addition to inevitable cultural conflicts, nation-building and sovereignty have come to the rain forests of the Amazon.

1125 Anna Presland, "Reconquest, an account of the contemporary fight for survival of the Amerindian peoples of Brazil," 4 Survival Int'l Rev. (Spring 1979), quoted in 4 UN Indigenous Study, *supra* note 276, at 43.

1126 Getulio Cruz, quoted in "Brazil's Miners, Military Eye Amazon Tribal Lands," Wash. Post, 17 Apr. 1987, at A25, col. 1. A government report refers to "foreign pressures to create a Yanomami state out of Brazilian and Venezuelan territory." *Id.*

China

HISTORICAL BACKGROUND

The 55 recognized minority groups in China constitute less than 7% of the population, but the areas they have traditionally inhabited account for more than half of the territory of the People's Republic. There are presently five Autonomous Regions in China (Nei Monggol [Inner Mongolia], Ningxia Hui, Guangxi Zhuang, and the two vast regions of Xinjiang Uighur and Tibet), all of which are situated in border areas. Lower administrative subdivisions include autonomous prefectures (currently numbering 31) and counties. Article 31 of the 1982 constitution also provides for the establishment of Special Administrative Regions, although this status apparently will not be utilized until the return of Hong Kong to China in 1997.[1127]

Without entering into the complex web of relationships between some of the now "autonomous" regions (such as Tibet and Mongolia) and various invaders and Chinese dynasties, the situation that faced the Chinese Communist Party (CCP) in 1949 was somewhat similar to that faced by the Bolsheviks in 1922: a very diverse, multi-ethnic, and vast territory was brought under the control of a government dedicated to sweeping social, economic, and political change through, *inter alia*, "democratic centralism."

Before coming to power, the CCP took a position similar to that of the Soviets with respect to minorities, and the 1931 constitution of the Chinese Soviet Republic specified that national minorities had the right to secede from China. But while the Soviets have continued to adhere to the principle (if not the practice) of self-determination for the constituent republics of the Union of Soviet Socialist Republics,[1128] the CCP, once it assumed power, rejected both the principle of national self-determination and the concept of federation.

Although in many domains of political and economic work a high degree of decentralization, or of devolution of power and responsibility, has prevailed in China during most of the period since 1949, the unitary nature of the Chinese state has been forcefully asserted, and any hint of the federalism which prevails (in theory) in the Soviet Union utterly repudiated.[1129]

Nevertheless, there was a concern for national, i.e., cultural or linguistic, minorities within China, and the 1949 Common Programme

1127 See chap. 7.

1128 See discussion *supra* chap. 16, at 358–69.

1129 Stuart R. Schram, "Decentralization in a Unitary State: Theory and Practice, 1940–1984," in Stuart R. Schram (ed.), *The Scope of State Power in China* (London: School of Oriental and African Studies, 1985) at 81.

of the Chinese People's Political Consultative Conference (which served as the provisional constitution until 1954) provided:

> Regional autonomy shall be carried out in areas where national minorities are aggregated and autonomous organs of the various nationalities shall be set up according to their respective population and size of the region. . . .
> All national minorities have the right freely to develop their dialects and languages and to preserve or reform their customs, habits, and religious beliefs. The People's Government shall help the masses of the people of all national minorities to develop their political, economic, cultural and educational construction work.[1130]

The initial governmental structure of the People's Republic consisted of six Great Administrative Areas and a separate Autonomous Region of Inner Mongolia. Smaller Autonomous Areas came into existence in 1950, and the 1954 constitution introduced additional subdivisions for small minority groups. The four other Autonomous Regions were established between 1955 and 1965, and the "Great Leap Forward" in the late 1950s, which was in part designed to standardize Chinese life throughout the state, brought the power and philosophy of the state much closer to minority groups. Communalization, literacy programs, and similar state campaigns inevitably tended to ignore minority cultures and societies.

As many of the more coercive aspects of the Great Leap Forward were abandoned, there was less pressure on minority populations in the early 1960s. However, the "Cultural Revolution" in 1966–71 had a devastating impact on minority religions, in particular, although the upheavals in autonomous regions were perhaps of no greater (or lesser) importance than in the country as a whole.

> Since 1949, . . . the tendency has been for the national minorities to be absorbed into the Chinese mainstream, often by the emigration of Han Chinese to the national minority areas, or by including administrative areas inhabited by Han Chinese into autonomous units, thus diluting the concentration of national minority groups. Thus, when Suiyuan was incorporated into Inner Mongolia there were then more Chinese than Mongols in the area. The Inner Mongolian Autonomous Region lost much of its territory to the surrounding provinces in about 1970.[1131]

The 1975 constitution was less protective of minority rights than the 1954 constitution, although the system of autonomous regions, prefec-

---

1130 Arts. 51, 53, quoted in Israel Epstein, *Tibet Transformed* (Beijing: New World Press, 1983) at 488.

1131 Derek J. Waller, *The Government and Politics of the People's Republic of China* (New York & London: New York Univ. Press, 1981) at 94.

tures, and areas was retained. The 1978 constitution represented in some ways a reversion to 1954,[1132] and the late 1970s saw a greater tolerance of and even encouragement for minority cultures and languages. Past repression of minorities has recently been formally recognized by the CCP as mistaken, and there seems to be a general consensus among outside observers that minority policies in the 1980s have been more benign.

In the past, particularly during the "cultural revolution", we committed, on the question of nationalities, the grave mistake of widening the scope of class struggle and wronged a large number of cadres and masses of the minority nationalities. In our work among them, we did not show due respect for their right to autonomy. We must never forget this lesson. . . . We must take effective measures to assist economic and cultural development in regions inhabited by minority nationalities, actively train and promote cadres from among them and resolutely oppose all words and deeds undermining national unity and equality.[1133]

THE CURRENT POSITION

Minority rights

The current Chinese constitution, adopted in 1982, reaffirms the equality of all nationalities and prohibits "[d]iscrimination against or oppression of any nationality,"[1134] and notes that, "[i]n the struggle to safeguard the unity of the nationalities, it is necessary to combat big-nation chauvinism, mainly Han chauvinism, and also necessary to combat local-national chauvinism."[1135] Article 4 also states that "[t]he people of all nationalities have the freedom to use and develop their own spoken and written languages, and to preserve or reform their own ways and customs." Government organs in autonomous areas are to employ the languages commonly used in the area, "in accordance with the autonomy regulations of the respective areas."[1136]

"Normal" religious activities are protected, but "[n]o one may make use of religion to engage in activities that disrupt public order, impair the health of citizens or interfere with the educational system of the

1132 For example, art. 4 of the 1978 constitution restored the right of the nationalities "to preserve or reform their own customs and ways," which had been omitted from the 1975 constitution.

1133 Resolution on certain questions in the history of our party since the founding of the People's Republic of China, adopted by the 6th Plenary Session of the 11th Central Committee of the CCP (1981), quoted in Epstein, *supra* note 1130, at 510.

1134 1982 Chinese Const., art. 4.

1135 *Id.*, Preamble.

1136 *Id.*, art. 121.

state."[1137] No right to education in minority languages is recognized. There are several "nationalities institutes" in China, but most seem to serve the purpose of socializing minority students rather than promoting minority cultures; teaching at these institutes (and in secondary schools in China) is in Chinese.

Political autonomy

The Preamble to the 1982 constitution describes China as "a unitary multi-national state built up jointly by the people of all nationalities. Socialist relations of equality, unity and mutual assistance have been established among them and will continue to be strengthened." Acts "that undermine the unity of the nationalities or instigate their secession" are prohibited, but regional autonomy "is practised in areas where people of minority nationalities live in compact communities."[1138]

Section VI of the constitution describes the various organs of "self-government" of the autonomous regions, prefectures, and counties, and it is clear that the centralized, hierarchical structure of the state is supreme. The autonomous entities exercise the same powers as local organs of the state; in addition, "they exercise the right of autonomy within the limits of their authority as prescribed by the constitution, the law of regional national autonomy and other laws, and implement the laws and policies of the state in light of the existing local situation."[1139]

Statutes adopted by the autonomous regions must be approved by the Standing Committee of the National People's Congress before they take effect; similarly, laws adopted by the autonomous prefectures and counties must be approved by higher provincial or regional legislatures and are reported to the Standing Committee for the record. Autonomous organs do have authority to administer finances and economic development plans, while the state is to give "due consideration" to the interests of autonomous areas in exploiting natural resources.[1140] The autonomous areas may "independently administer educational, scientific, cultural, public health and physical culture affairs in their respective areas, protect and cull through the cultural heritage of the nationalities and work for the development and prosperity of their cultures."[1141]

TIBET[1142]

Tibet, whether considered in its current form as the Tibet Autonomous Region (TAR) or in its much larger historic sense, is undoubtedly the

1137 *Id.*, art. 36.
1138 *Id.*, art. 4.
1139 *Id.*, art. 115.
1140 *Id.*, art. 118.
1141 *Id.*, art. 119.
1142 The diametrically opposed views of Tibet's history and contemporary status

most well-known of all the areas inhabited by "minority nationalities" in China. Covering a vast area whose average altitude is 12,000 feet and which is bounded by the Himalayan and other mountains, the Tibet Autonomous Region has a population of approximately two million people; another two to four million inhabit areas not included within the TAR.

The deeply religious, traditional Tibetan Buddhist culture, headed by the Dalai Lama, has a world-wide influence out of proportion to its numbers, and one observer has commented that "[i]n a way, it is unfair to concentrate on Tibet because it has been without doubt the least successful example of relations between the Chinese communists and a minority people. On the other hand, it does encapsulate everything that has gone wrong with the Chinese government's policy towards minorities."[1143]

In many respects, the legal debate about the status of Tibet is over self-determination in the classic sense rather than minority (or indigenous) rights. Certainly, the Tibetans' claim to self-determination and independence is at least as strong as that of any other recognized national group, although Tibet is unfortunately not alone in having been denied this right by a more powerful neighbor.

The Chinese invasion (or liberation, from the Chinese perspective) of Tibet in 1950 and China's suppression of the 1959 Tibetan rebellion represented the nadir of Han-minority relations. Commenting after the flight of the Dalai Lama in 1959, Chinese Premier Zhou Enlai perhaps unintentionally articulated the conflicting aspects of theoretical "autonomy" in China and the inevitability of "reform" along communist lines:

[W]e have always adhered to the principle of the unity of all the nationalities of our country and the unity of the Tibetan people themselves, and have stood for the institution of local autonomy in Tibet. . . .

[T]he local government of Tibet should unite the people and drive the aggressive forces of imperialism out of Tibet; and the backward social system of Tibet must be reformed.[1144]

from the Chinese government's and exiled Tibetan viewpoints, respectively, are perhaps best seen by comparing Epstein, *supra* note 1130, with John F. Avedon, *In Exile from the Land of Snows* (New York: Alfred A. Knopf & London: Michael Joseph, 1984), and Michael van Walt van Praag, *The Status of Tibet* (Boulder, CO: Westview Press, 1987); also see Chris Mullin and Phuntsog Wangyal, *The Tibetans* (London: Minority Rights Group Report No. 49, rev. ed. 1983).

1143 Mullin, in Mullin and Wangyal, *supra* note 1142, at 5.

1144 Excerpted from Premier Zhou Enlai's Report on the Work of the Government to the First Session of the National People's Congress (1959), quoted in Epstein, *supra* note 1130, at 504.

The 1951 agreement between China and the Tibetan government promised that "[t]he central authorities will not alter the existing political system in Tibet,"[1145] including the functions and powers of the Dalai Lama, and the 1959 revolt was in response to Chinese violations of this accord. Approximately 100,000 Tibetans, including the Dalai Lama and his closest advisers, fled Tibet after this second Chinese invasion. Most settled in India, and the Dalai Lama's de facto government in exile is based in Dharamsala, although it has not been granted formal recognition as a government by the international community.

The UN General Assembly addressed the situation in Tibet in three resolutions adopted in 1959, 1961, and 1965.[1146] While only the 1961 resolution directly addressed the issue of self-determination, all expressed grave concern in similar terms over "the continued violation of the fundamental rights and freedoms of the people of Tibet and the continued suppression of their distinctive cultural and religious life."[1147]

The Cultural Revolution had a devastating impact in Tibet and effectively destroyed the physical manifestations of the Tibetan religion and centuries of Tibetan culture. Shrines, temples, monasteries, and religious artifacts were destroyed, and communal life was forcibly introduced. The Cultural Revolution "appears to have alienated irrevocably many who until then may have been able to live with the changes that had overtaken their homeland."[1148]

There have been significant improvements in Tibet during the 1980s: some monks have been allowed to return to their monasteries; freedom of religious worship is more or less guaranteed, although there are allegations that recent religious tolerance is more for show than substantive and that serious religious study and teaching are prohibited; there are no longer public attacks on Tibetan culture. Nevertheless, standards of education and health care remain low; the Tibetan administration remains dominated by Han Chinese; and Tibet has become an essential part of China's strategic defense system.

Allegations continue to be raised by Tibetan exiles and human rights organizations of blatant discrimination against Tibetans in housing, jobs, and other areas. Particularly since 1983, the major issue has been the

1145 Agreement of the Central People's Government and the Local Government of Tibet on Measures for the Peaceful Liberation of Tibet, signed 23 May 1951, quoted in Epstein, *supra* note 1130, at 489–91, art. 4.

1146 UN G.A. Res. 1353 (XIV), 14 UN GAOR, Supp. (No. 16), UN Doc. A/4354 (1959) at 61; Res. 1723 (XVI), 16 UN GAOR, Supp. (No. 17, vol. 1), UN Doc. A/5100 (1961) at 66; Res. 2079 (XX), 20 UN GAOR, Supp. (No. 14), UN Doc. A/6014 (1965) at 3.

1147 G.A. Res. 2079 (XX), *supra* note 1146.

1148 Mullin, in Mullin and Wangyal, *supra* note 1142, at 9.

massive immigration by Han cadres into Tibet, as part of continuing attempts to "Sinocize" the region. It has been estimated that there are now 7.5 million Han Chinese compared to 6 million Tibetans within the traditional region of Tibet (over half of which has been incorporated into the neighboring Chinese provinces of Tsinghai, Kansu, Szechwan, and Yunnan), and 2 million Han to 1.8 million Tibetans in the TAR; in the capital of Lhasa, Chinese are said to outnumber Tibetans by three to one. While other estimates of the numbers of Chinese in the TAR are lower, there is agreement that the Chinese control political and economic life in the region.

In September 1987, March 1988, and March 1989, anti-Chinese and pro-independence demonstrations by Tibetan Buddhist monks sparked off the most violent confrontations in decades.[1149] Approximately a dozen people were killed by Chinese police in the first clash, at least 30 and proably many more died in 1989. Martial law was declared in March 1989, for the first time in 30 years; hundreds were arrested; communications between Tibet and the outside world were cut; and tourism, which was promoted by the Chinese as a means of drawing hard currency to Tibet, was curtailed. The long-term impact of these events—clearly damaging to the more tolerant image the Chinese government has attempted to project in recent years—remains unclear.

OBSERVATIONS

Minority cultures within China have been caught up in the political upheavals in the country at large in recent decades, and it is difficult to separate minority policies from broader questions related to the impact of, for example, the Great Leap Forward, the Cultural Revolution, or the more pragmatic economic and social policies which seemed to emerge in the 1980s. The mid-1989 suppression of the pro-democracy movement does not suggest a more tolerant attitude towards minority autonomy. The fact that state-wide political struggles have had such a direct impact on China's minorities is in itself an indication of the centralized nature of the system that has been in place since the founding of the People's Republic.

Despite the designation of territories inhabited by ethnic or linguistic minorities within China as "autonomous" regions, prefectures, or counties, the present Chinese system does not grant meaningful political autonomy to these entities. The CCP exercises effective political control over the entire state, and even the formal constitutional provisions

1149 See, e.g., Asia Watch, *Human Rights in Tibet* (Washington, DC: Asia Watch, Feb. 1988); *id.*, *Evading Scrutiny* (Washington, DC: Asia Watch, July 1988), Daniel Southerland, "Chinese Open Fire in Tibet," Wash. Post, 6 Mar. 1989, at A1, col. 1; *id.*, "Police, Rioters Clash in Tibet for 2nd Day, "Wash. Post, 7 Mar. 1989, at A16, col. 3.

relating to autonomous regions offer little opportunity for true self-government. While there is some room for local variations in implementing national plans, China remains a centralized, unitary state.

Introduction of the concept of "one country, two systems" with respect to the projected Special Administrative Regions of Hong Kong and Macao has not, thus far, led to any change in minority policies with respect to those regions already integrated into China. As recent events in Tibet demonstrate, Beijing appears to have chosen repression as the means of imposing its view of progress on China's minority peoples. One can only hope that the Chinese government will develop a more flexible attitude, so that meaningful cultural, religious, and political authority can be devolved to regions such as Tibet, within the context of the unified state that the CCP is unlikely to abandon.

Fiji

HISTORICAL BACKGROUND

Fiji is a small state in the Southwest Pacific, consisting of some 320 islands and atolls, about 700 miles north of New Zealand. Its population in 1986 of 714,548 was composed of 48.6% Indians, 46.2% native Fijians, and the remainder primarily Europeans and Chinese.[1150] As in Malaysia, the immigrant population has long been the dominant economic force, while political power traditionally has rested with the indigenous Fijians.

Although Fiji was "discovered" by the Dutch in 1643, the first European settlement was not established until the early nineteenth century. Political rivalries among the indigenous peoples in the islands facilitated European use of classic "divide and conquer" tactics, and alliances were formed with various Fijian chiefs in order to set up a centralized government. Eventually, the chief of a shaky Fiji-wide government offered to cede dominion to Britain in return for protection of Fijian political and economic interests. Britain accepted, and in 1874 the Fijian high chiefs signed a Deed of Cession, making Fiji a possession of the Crown.

In the succeeding half-century, the composition of the islands' population changed dramatically. Exposure to European diseases such as measles and influenza took a heavy toll on the Fijians, whose population dropped from approximately 115,000 in 1881 to 84,000 in 1921.[1151] During the same period, the colonial government imported Indian workers, primarily to work the sugar plantations, either as indentured laborers

---

1150 Fiji Visitors Bureau, *1987/88 Fiji Islands Travel Guide* (1987) at 17.

1151 David Murray, "Fiji," in Georgina Ashworth (ed.), *World Minorities in the Eighties* (Sunbury, UK: Quartermaine House, 1980) at 42.

or sponsored immigrants; the Indian population increased from a negligible number in the late nineteenth century to 61,000 in 1921, constituting 39% of the total population.[1152] Even after the end of the importation of labor, varying birth rates meant that the Indian proportion of the population continued to increase, and it reached a 51% majority in the last census before independence.[1153] Greater emigration by Indians in recent years has led to the present situation of rough equivalence between Indian and Fijian communities.

British colonial policy in Fiji was to encourage indirect rule and preserve traditional Fijian village society and leadership. A separate system of administration was established to protect Fijians from the competition of other racial groups; the basic structure at the time of independence was created in 1944, with adoption of the Fijian Affairs Ordinance.[1154]

The heart of this system of native administration was the Fijian Affairs Board, which could make orders binding on all Fijians. Its regulations covered every aspect of Fijian life, from the structure of administrative and judicial machinery to customary rights, social services, health, education, and economic activity. The Board advised the British Governor on the appointment of all Fijian officials except the highest provincial officials. It had its own central treasury, independent from that of the central government, and controlled all native revenue and expenditure.

Regulations were enforced through Fijian courts presided over by Fijian magistrates. Appeals were heard by the provincial court, which was composed of three magistrates—two Fijians and one district officer; appeals from this court went to the Supreme Court of the colony.

An organization of district administrations overlapped the indigenous Fijian government. The Fijian chief of a province was responsible to a (British) District Commissioner, although the latter's civil servants, the District Officers, had no direct authority over indigenous Fijian structures. District Officers made regular inspections of accounts and presided at provincial courts but did not have authority over Fijian officials. Most Fijians thus lived in relative isolation from the rest of the colony, within their own framework of social, economic, and legal institutions.

Preparations for self-government began in the early 1960s. Many Fijians initially opposed plans for self-government, for they viewed co-

---

1152 *Id.*
1153 *Id.*
1154 Fijian Affairs Ordinance, No. 3 of 1944.

lonial rule as a defense against political and economic domination by the Indian community, which had been the largest single ethnic group in the islands since the mid-1940s. While most of the special Fijian administration was phased out prior to independence, the special Fijian rights recognized in the Deed of Cession and the Fijian Affairs Ordinance were preserved in the independence constitution, which entered into force in 1970.

GOVERNMENTAL STRUCTURE (PRIOR TO 1989)

The Fijian government is based on the Westminster model, but with several particular provisions designed to ensure Fijian representation. There is a two-chamber legislature, and the House of Representatives is elected according to a complex formula which includes four separate electoral rolls.[1155] Equal numbers of representatives (twelve) are elected from separate Fijian and Indian electoral rolls by Fijians and Indians, respectively; an additional ten seats each are allotted to ethnic Fijians and Indians, elected by all those inscribed on the national electoral roll (which includes all electors of whatever ethnic background); and there are eight non-Fijian, non-Indian members, three of whom are elected by the non-Fijian, non-Indian electoral roll and five of whom are elected at-large by the national electorate.

The Senate is more firmly controlled by native Fijians, as the Great Council of Fijian Chiefs nominates eight of the 22 members; the Council of Rotuma (an island traditionally treated separately) nominates one member; and the Prime Minister and leader of the opposition nominate seven and six members, respectively. Assuming that Fijians are represented by either the government or opposition, they are thus assured of a Senate majority.

Nine pre-independence ordinances establishing the separate indigenous administration and reserving approximately 85% of the land for native ownership are entrenched in the constitution. No changes to this body of law can be made without the concurrence of an absolute three-fourths majority of the House and (with respect to Fijian land, customs, and customary rights) six of the eight Senate members appointed by the Great Council of Fijian Chiefs. While racial discrimination is prohibited in article 15 of the constitution, the prohibition does not apply to the existing preferential laws establishing Fijian land and other rights. Civil servants are to be appointed in a manner which will ensure fair treatment to each ethnic community in Fiji.

1155 Fijian Const., art. 32.

RECENT EVENTS

There had been little serious ethnic violence between the communities in Fiji until the 1987 elections (discussed below), but ethnic tensions nevertheless existed. The government remained firmly in Fijian hands (particularly those of the traditional chiefs) through the Alliance Party, a coalition of ethnic-based associations dominated by the Fijian chiefs. Most Indian political support was given to the National Federation Party (NFP). In the 1977 general election, discrimination against Indian citizens in the awarding of university scholarships was a major issue, and at the same time the Alliance Party was challenged by the new and more militant Fijian National Party.[1156] As a result of the split within the Fijian community, the Indian-based NFP actually elected more representatives in the March 1977 elections, but the Governor General dissolved the newly elected legislature in light of apparent weakness or difficulty in forming a government on the part of the NFP leader; in the ensuing September elections, the Fijian-based Alliance Party received a clear majority.

In 1985, a new Labour Party was formed, primarily by younger Fijians and Indians who were dissatisified with the traditional political parties. In April 1987, the Labour Party won a majority in the legislature and assumed office. Although the Prime Minister was a native Fijian, the specter of Indian domination and the implicit rejection of the authority of the Fijian chiefs by Fijian members of the Labour Party led to the first major incidents of racial violence in the country's history. While there were no deaths, scores of Indians were attacked by Fijian mobs, and unrest continued for weeks. Despite the entrenched nature of the laws protecting ethnic Fijian privileges, fears were expressed that an Indian-dominated government would seek to repeal them.

These tensions led to a non-violent military coup a month after the new government took office. While there were some East-West political elements to the coup, its leader, Lt. Col. Sitivini Rabuka, told reporters that "he acted primarily out of concern for the rights of ethnic Fijians."[1157] The coup, which had been supported by the Great Council of Chiefs, soon unraveled, but the Labour government nevertheless was dismissed by the Governor General. When constitutional changes were not forthcoming sufficiently rapidly, Rabuka led a second coup in September 1987 and declared Fiji a republic.

1156 *See* Murray, *supra* note 1151, at 45–46.
1157 "Fijian Claims Coup Restored Pro-West Stance," Wash. Post, 17 May 1987, at A1, col. 6. *Cf.* Gwen Ifill, "Fiji: Paradise Lost?" *id.*, at C2, col. 1.

As noted by a journalist in the period between the election and the first coup,

[t]he tensions that have arisen here [in Fiji] frame a question of importance throughout the Pacific: How should self-determination be reconciled with the special claims of a native people?

Ethnic Fijians already have some rights guaranteed in the country's Constitution, but some want a new constitutional amendment: a guarantee that only Fijians could run the government.

"This is not their country," a historian and member of the Great Council of Chiefs, Fiau Tabakaucoro, said of the Indians. "They still speak Hindi. They still eat curry. They are not Christians.". . . .

Miss Tabakaucoro stressed the difficulties that ethnic Fijians have in wresting economic and political power from Indians.

"How do you compete with a race that has thousands of years of what we call civilization?" she asked.[1158]

The indigenous Fijian demands—to control "their" country—are similar to those of indigenous peoples elsewhere. At the same time, however, the coup also reflects serious disagreements within the Fijian community; support for the coup by traditional Fijian chiefs was perhaps directed as much against the younger, better educated, urban Fijians who joined the Labour Party as it was against the latter's Indian allies. Certainly, it would be incorrect to ignore the realities of political power and describe the conflict in purely ethnic terms.

Nevertheless, the draft constitution expected to be adopted by presidential decree in 1989 focuses on increased ethnic representation in order to secure the political dominance of native Fijians. The new 67-member parliament will be comprised of 22 Indians, 28 Fijians, one Rotuman, and eight others (neither Indian nor Fijian), elected by their respective communities; four additional members, one of whom is to serve as commander of the Fijian military and Minister of Home Affairs, are to be appointed by the Grand Council of Chiefs, and a final four members will be appointed by the Prime Minister. The President, Prime Minister, military commander, and Commissioner of Police all must be native Fijians. Provisions relating to land ownership remain essentially unchanged, except that the veto power of the Great Council of Chiefs over certain legislative changes has been removed, in light of increased Fijian domination in the legislature. A transitional provision grants immunity to all members of the security forces involved in the 1987 coups.

1158 Nicholas D. Kristof, "In a South Seas Eden, a First Taste of Race Strife," N.Y. Times, 1 May 1987, at A4, col. 2.

OBSERVATIONS

While Fijians may be the indigenous population, Fiji also is very much the country of its ethnic Indian citizens, most of whom have lived in Fiji for generations and many of whom were essentially involuntary pawns in the economic plans of the British colonial empire. The situation that arose in Fiji in 1987 also reflects the problems inherent in attempting to maintain traditional or indigenous structures while, at the same time, neighboring societies develop along "modern" (i.e., urban) lines, and segments of the indigenous community itself are increasingly exposed to non-traditional life.

One answer, of course, is to halt the initial penetration or settlement of indigenous areas and attempt to keep out "foreign" or non-indigenous influences, although such isolation is impossible in a small state such as Fiji. The other obvious option—encouraging assimilation or acculturation while offering no protection to the more vulnerable traditional indigenous society—has been clearly rejected by indigenous peoples themselves.

Fiji often has been cited as a model of racial harmony, and political control by indigenous Fijians and economic dominance by Indians seemed to have created a viable balance of power. The 1987 election temporarily upset that balance, as the traditional indigenous community saw itself being deprived of all power. Whether or not Fijian fears of becoming subordinated to other ethnic groups are objectively reasonable, Fiji's image of a balanced, racially harmonious society seems to have been irretrievably shattered. One must hope that the new structures can provide sufficient protection for both major communities, without artificially reinforcing communalism and racial distinctions.

Italy—The South Tyrol

HISTORICAL BACKGROUND[1159]

The South Tyrol, an integral part of the Habsburg Empire until the end of World War I, was severed from the rest of Tyrol by the 1919 Peace Treaty of Saint Germain. Although overwhelmingly inhabited by German-speakers, the area was incorporated into an enlarged Italian state and subjected to enforced acculturation. By executive decree and legislation, the Italian government under Mussolini repressed the German presence and influence in all spheres of cultural, economic, and

1159 See generally Antony E. Alcock, *The History of the South Tyrol Question* (London: Michael Joseph, 1970); Alain Fenet, *La Question du Tyrol du Sud* (Paris: Pichon & Durand-Auzias, 1968).

political life, and German schools, trade unions, political parties, and names were prohibited. This policy in fact reinforced German nationalism, particularly in the previously apolitical rural German settlements, and created a deep-seated distrust of all future Italian policies and motives.

After Austria was annexed by Nazi Germany, Hitler concluded an agreement with Mussolini which offered German-speaking South Tyrolese the option of resettlement in Germany or, if they chose to remain in Italy, of acceptance of the Italian policy of assimilation. However, of the 80% who chose to emigrate to Germany, only about one-third actually left during World War II, and many of these returned after 1945. Today, the province consists of approximately 64% German-speakers, 30% Italian-speakers, and 4% Ladin-speakers.[1160]

In September 1946, the Foreign Ministers of Austria and Italy reached an agreement on ensuring to the German-speaking community "complete equality of rights with the Italian-speaking inhabitants within the framework of special provisions to safeguard the ethnical character and the cultural and economic development of the German-speaking element."[1161] The agreement guaranteed autonomy to South Tyrol in many spheres of economic and cultural life and promised that the German-speaking community would be consulted on the form that autonomy would take.

Italy violated at least the spirit of the agreement almost immediately when, in the First Autonomy Statute, the province of South Tyrol (known in Italy as the province of Bolzano or Bozen) was included within a larger region which also encompassed the more populous and overwhelmingly Italian province of Trentino.[1162] The German-speaking population thus found itself outnumbered by Italians in the regional government, which controlled all important political and economic authority.

From 1955, after the signing of the Austrian State Treaty and full restoration of Austria's sovereignty, Austria played an increasingly larger role in South Tyrolean efforts to gain greater autonomy. After several fruitless years of bilateral talks, Austria brought the problem to the United Nations General Assembly and filed an interstate complaint against Italy under the European Convention on Human Rights. Although the General Assembly did adopt two resolutions in the early

---

1160 Provincial Government of South Tyrol, *Statistisches Jahrbüch für Südtirol, Annuario Statistico* (1987) at 74–75.

1161 This agreement, known as the De Gasperi-Gruber Accord, was included as Annex IV of the Treaty of Peace with Italy, *supra* note 1086.

1162 Special Statute for the Trentino-Alto Adige, Constitutional Law of 2 Feb. 1948, reprinted in Alcock, *supra* note 1159, at 475–92.

1960s, they said little beyond urging the parties to resume negotiations.[1163] The European Commission on Human Rights concluded that there had been no violation of the Convention in the case raised by Austria, which was concerned with the fairness of the trial and sentencing of several South Tyrolean youths for murder.[1164]

Pressures to reach a solution intensified, and there were several terrorist bombings during the 1960s. In 1961, a Mixed Commission of eleven Italians and eight South Tyrolese convened to conduct an inquiry and draw up proposals for a solution to the problem. Its report, released in 1964, was considered insufficient, but it did lead to subsequent negotiations which ultimately resulted in adoption in 1969 of an agreement known simply as "the Package."[1165]

The Package consists of 137 administrative and legislative measures the Italian government was to undertake to improve and expand South Tyrolean autonomy. Among the basic principles in the Package were: 1) the province of Bolzano/Bozen was granted broad legislative and administrative powers previously reserved to the state or region; 2) the principles of ethnic proportionality and linguistic parity were to be applied to employment in all state and semi-state bodies in the province, with the exception of the Ministry of Defense and the national police forces; and 3) the provincial government could challenge state laws which allegedly violated the equality of linguistic groups before the constitutional court, a power formerly reserved to the region.

The Package was not a treaty, however. Under the so-called Operational Calendar, negotiated concurrently with the Package, Italy and Austria agreed to a series of alternate steps to implement the Package, including submission of future disputes to the jurisdiction of the International Court of Justice and conclusion of an Austrian-Italian Treaty of Friendship and Co-operation.[1166] The Package and Operational Calendar were informally approved by the Italian and Austrian Parliaments in December 1969, and an amended Autonomy Statute entered into force in 1972.[1167]

1163 G.A. Res. 1497 (XV), 15 UN GAOR, Supp. (No. 16, vol. 1), UN Doc. A/4684 (1960) at 131; GA Res. 1661 (XVI), 16 UN GAOR, Supp. (No. 17, vol. 1), UN Doc. A/5100 (1961) at 242. *Cf.* Alcock, *supra* note 1159, at 330–49; Fenet, *supra* note 1159, at 227–62.

1164 European Comm. Human Rights, Report of 30 Mar. 1963, 4 Yearbook Eur. Conv. on Human Rights 138 (1963). *Cf.* Fenet, *supra* note 1159, at 279–96.

1165 9 *Osterreichische Zeitschrift fur Aussenpolitik* 317 (1969), reprinted in Alcock, *supra* note 1159, at 434–48.

1166 9 *Osterreichische Zeitschrift fur Aussenpolitik* 345 (1969), reprinted in *id.* at 448–49.

1167 Law No. 670 of 31 Aug. 1972, 1 *Raccolta Ufficiale delle Leggi* 3136 (1972) [hereinafter cited as "Autonomy Statute"].

THE 1972 AUTONOMY STATUTE

The Regional Council for Trentino-Alto Adige/South Tyrol is composed of members elected separately from the two provinces of Trento and Bolzano/Bozen (South Tyrol). In order to participate in an election, a voter must have four years of uninterrupted residence in the region. The Presidency alternates between a member of the Italian group for half of the term and a member of the German group for the other half. The Regional and Provincial Councils may be dissolved by the President of Italy, following deliberation by the national Council of Ministers; in that event, a three-member committee (one of whose members must be from the German language group) exercises the functions of the dissolved council until new elections can be held within three months.

The region's relatively limited competence extends to, *inter alia*, regulations for regional offices; municipal boundaries; establishment and maintenance of land records; fire services; regulation of health services, hospitals, chambers of commerce, public charitable institutions, and credit agencies; and community order.[1168]

Executive powers

The province is governed by three organs: the Provincial Council, the Provincial Government, and its President. The Provincial Government is elected by the Council, and its composition must be proportional to the linguistic groups in the Council.

The President and Provincial Government exercise administrative powers in the areas of competence set forth in the Autonomy Statute, including the implementation of many national laws. Absent from this competence is overall responsibility for public order, which remains an Italian state concern, although local city and rural police fall within the jurisdiction of the province. The President does, however, have certain emergency powers and may participate in meetings of the Italian Cabinet, whenever it deals with questions affecting the province.

The central government is represented in each province by a commissioner, who is responsible for, *inter alia*, maintaining order and supervising provincial administration of duties delegated to them by the state.

Legislative powers

The Provincial Council's legislative powers were significantly expanded at the expense of both the region and the state. The Autonomy Statute lists 29 areas where this legislative power is primary (i.e., subject only

1168 *Id.*, arts. 4, 5.

to the Constitution, international obligations, and basic principles of the Italian legal order) and eleven areas where provincial powers are secondary (i.e., also subject to the principles contained in ordinary statutes).[1169] The powers are quite diverse, but are primarily concerned with economic, social, and cultural matters. For example, the Provincial Council has primary competence over place names, local customs and usages, town and country planning, the environment, mining, agriculture, communications, and transport, and secondary competence over elementary and secondary education, commerce, and public health.

Laws adopted by a provincial or regional council may be returned by the central government, on the grounds that "they go beyond their respective competences or are in contrast with national interests or with those of one of the two Provinces in the Region."[1170] An absolute majority vote of a council will override such a veto, although the government also may challenge a law before the Constitutional Court, thus suspending its effect for up to several years while the Constitutional Court reaches a decision.

Judicial powers

There is a Regional Administrative Court which includes a separate section for the South Tyrol, whose members are appointed by the Bolzano/Bozen Provincial Council and must be drawn equally from the German- and the Italian-speaking communities. Provincial Council members may challenge before the South Tyrol section any administrative act "deemed to be in violation of the principle of equality among citizens belong to different language groups."[1171]

Provincial or regional legislation can be challenged before the national Constitutional Court by a majority of the Council members of one linguistic group, on the grounds that a law violates "the equal rights of the citizens of the different language groups or the ethnic and cultural characteristics of those groups," although this challenge does not have the effect of suspending the law.[1172] The Constitutional Court also has jurisdiction over challenges by the provincial or central government to provincial or regional acts which allegedly violate the Autonomy Statute.

Judgments of the Constitutional Court are binding on the South Tyrol, and many of the court's decisions in recent years have tended to undermine the province's autonomy by holding that inherent national powers of "direction and coordination" (*l'indirizzo e coordinamento*) take precedence over regional and provincial competence. In broad

1169 *Id.*, arts. 8, 9.
1170 *Id.*, art. 55.
1171 *Id.*, art. 92.
1172 *Id.*, art. 56.

terms, the court has upheld state action where a sufficiently important "national interest" has been identified or where an interest is inherently incapable of being divided; no deference has been shown to the special autonomous status of South Tyrol.[1173]

OTHER MATTERS

Language

In the Trentino-Alto Adige region, German is recognized as having "equal standing" with Italian, which is the "official language" of the state.[1174] Either language may be used before all courts and authorities in the region, although the inability of all officials to achieve fluency in both languages prevented full application of this principle for many years. All regional and provincial laws are published in Italian and German, and public officials must use the mother tongue of any person with whom they are dealing.[1175] Article 100 of the Autonomy Statute recognizes the "separate use of one or the other of the two languages," and a dispute has arisen as to whether that should require single-language court proceedings (in the language of the accused or parties), as opposed to bilingual or mixed proceedings.

Education

A fundamental principle of the 1946 De Gasperi-Gruber Accord was that elementary and secondary education be in the mother tongue of the child, and instruction in the South Tyrol is given in separate German and Italian schools. Language instruction in the other language of the province is obligatory, and all teachers must be native speakers of the primary language of the school in which they teach. Special provision is made for using Ladin in kindergartens and elementary schools in the Ladin-speaking areas, with German and Italian taught equally as additional languages. School administration is under the authority of the province, but teachers are state employees.

Representation in the civil service

The Autonomy Statute provides for proportional linguistic representation in public office, and this principle has been consistently upheld by the Italian Constitutional Court.[1176] Every person must make a formal

---

1173 See, e.g., Italian Const. Court Judgments No. 177 of 1988, No. 294 of 1986, and No. 340 of 1983.

1174 Autonomy Statute, art. 99.

1175 The principle of bilingualism also applies to those offering services of interest to the public; see Italian Const. Court Judgment No. 312 of 1983.

1176 See, e.g., Italian Const. Court Judgment No. 678 of 1988 (privatization of railways did not affect applicability of principle of proportionality).

declaration at the time of the census as to his or her language group, and failure to make the declaration will lead to loss of rights to stand for public office, be employed in the public administration or as a teacher, or be given housing.[1177] Positions which are vacant because of lack of qualified applicants from one lingusitic group can only be filled by members of the other linguistic group for a non-renewable twelve-month period, which has caused some resentment among under-employed Italian speakers.

Taxation

The province has the right to levy taxes only within the limits allowed by regional law, while the region may levy taxes "in keeping with the principles of the State taxation system."[1178] However, the province's share of state expenditures in the areas of economy and social welfare represents a substantial and regularly available source of revenue which seems to be sufficient for the province's needs. In addition, the provinces receive 90% of state taxes collected in areas such as power and gas usage, real property taxes, and personal income taxes, as well as a portion (determined annually by agreement between the provincial and central governments) of the value-added tax and other national taxes collected within the region.

Foreign relations

While only the central government may enter into international agreements, the Italian Constitutional Court has held that "promotional activities" with foreign governments (e.g., tourism) can be carried out by the regions so long as they do not imply the assumption of international obligations.[1179] Pursuant to a 1980 European convention on trans-border cooperation, frontier regions (or provinces or communal authorities) can conclude agreements on trans-border issues with neighboring states provided that the central government has 1) concluded a treaty with that state on the content of the cross-border cooperation, and 2) approved the agreement itself.[1180]

OBSERVATIONS

1177 However, a 1984 decision by the Italian Council of State declared the law requiring such a declaration illegal, on the grounds that it did not offer an opportunity for persons to declare themselves as "other language" or "mixed language." See Antony Alcock, "South Tyrol," in *Co-existence in some plural European societies, supra* note 1027, at 6.

1178 Autonomy Statute, art. 73.

1179 See Natalino Ronzitti, "Cross-border Relations between Italy/Yugoslavia, Italy/Austria and Italy/Switzerland," in S. Ercmann (ed.), *Cross-Border Relations: European and North American Perspectives* (Zurich: Schulthess Polygraphischer Verlag, 1987) at 84.

1180 *Id.* at 85

OBSERVATIONS

Italy includes 20 autonomous regions, five of which enjoy "special" status, and two of which (Trentino-Alto Adige and Friuli-Venezia Giulia, surrounding Trieste) have certain treaty-based protections. Autonomy generally takes the form of protecting linguistic rights through provision for, e.g., bilingual or separate education and preferential government hiring policies for regional residents.[1181] There is a French-speaking community in the Val d'Aosta, and other linguistic minorities include the Friulians, Sardinians, Slavs, and Ladins. Thus, South Tyrol is not unique in Italian politics, although it has been perhaps the most contentious situation.

While it would be incorrect to assume that the present autonomy arrangements are universally satisfactory, the 1972 amendments resulted in a system that enjoys general acceptance and has proved workable in practice. Some South Tyroleans would ideally prefer an independent state, perhaps along the lines of San Marino or Liechtenstein, but few would confuse this ideal with reality. It is significant that most contemporary complaints concern the failure of Italian government to implement the 1969 Package or respect the 1972 Autonomy Statute fully, rather than demands for more extensive powers.

While no veto power over legislation is available to the minority Italian-speaking community in the South Tyrol, provincial governments have thus far been formed by coalitions among the dominant German-speaking Südtiroler Volkspartei (SVP) and provincial wings of the Italian Social Democrats and Socialists. Thus, politics have not acquired a wholly linguistic-ethnic cast, and there is a degree of bipartisanship even though the SVP effectively controls provincial political power.

The reassertion of German cultural and political dominance has been sufficiently successful that the Italian-speaking proportion of the province has been slowly, if steadily, declining. Mixed marriages have increased, and the next stage in the South Tyrol question may be how the Italian community reacts to its increasingly minority role; right-wing Italian-speakers have called for revision of the 1972 Autonomy Statute, and the neo-fascist Movimento Sociale Italiano became the largest party on the Bolzano city council in the 1984 local elections. At the same time, however, the strong desire of both Austria and Italy to prevent a resurgence of conflict over the South Tyrol, as well as the recognition by Tyrolean political leaders that the present arrangements are a clear advance over previous situations, suggests that future changes are more

---

1181 *Cf.* Fabio Lorenzoni, "Italian Accommodation of Cultural Differences," in Daniel J. Elazar (ed.), *Governing Peoples and Territories* (Philadelphia: Institute for the Study of Human Issues, 1982) at 89–99.

likely to come about as a result of normal political processes rather than violence or open conflict.

Finally, the role of Austria in guaranteeing the autonomy of the South Tyrol should not be underestimated, although Italy has consistently maintained its position that Tyrolean autonomy is a purely internal matter (with the exception of the broad obligations included in the 1946 De Gasperi-Gruber Accord). Austria has not yet declared (as it is required to do under the Operational Calendar) that the Package has been fulfilled, and this remains a significant factor in Austro-Italian relations. In this respect, the situation of the South Tyrol resembles one of the classic post-Versailles examples of minority protection, and Austrian support was perhaps decisive in obtaining the relatively broad autonomy granted in 1972.

Malaysia

HISTORICAL BACKGROUND[1182]

Malaysia is a federation of thirteen states, comprised of the nine original Malay states, the former British colonial settlements of Malacca and Penang, and the former British Crown Colonies of Sarawak and Sabah (North Borneo). There are three major racial or ethnic groups in Malaysia: Malays (approximately 47% of the entire population and a slim majority of peninsular Malaysia), Chinese (approximately 35%), and Indians (9%).[1183] The balance of the population is composed of a small number of other indigenous groups, Europeans, and others. The different groups are not concentrated in separate geographical areas, although there has traditionally been a division between urban Chinese and Indians, on one hand, and rural Malays. In addition, the groups themselves are not homogenous. "Indians," for example, include Muslim Pakistanis, Hindu South Indians (largely Tamils), and Sri Lankans. Similar linguistic, religious, and cultural distinctions can be found among the Chinese and Malays, although the latter are overwhelmingly Muslim.

The territory which is now Malaysia has been a crossroads of trade for centuries. In 1511, the Portuguese captured the town of Malacca, which it controlled for the next 130 years before yielding it to the Dutch. Over the next century, struggles to control the area's trade continued

---

1182 This summary is drawn from the *Report* of an International Mission of Lawyers to Malaysia (London: Marram Books, rev. ed. 1983), in which the author participated.

1183 A distinction should be made among "Malay," a person of the Malay ethnic group and an indigenous inhabitant of the state of Malaysia; "Malayan," a citizen of the former Federation of Malaya; and "Malaysian," a citizen of present-day Malaysia.

between the Dutch and local rulers. The first British trading post was established on the island of Penang in 1786.

British influence gradually increased, and, in response to warfare over tin mines in the 1870s, Britain began asserting greater control over the internal affairs of the Malay states, often with the consent of well-rewarded local nobility. As rubber plantations and tin mines proliferated, the number of Chinese immigrants continued to grow.

The Japanese conquest and occupation of Malaya for three years during World War II devastated the country and also tended to increase racial divisions between the Malay and Chinese. Following the war, there was resistance to British attempts to impose a more centralized system of government, partly in reaction to plans for the incorporation of Penang and Malacca, both of which had large Chinese and Indian populations, into the proposed "Malayan Union." Finally, the Malay States and the British colonial settlements were unified under the British Crown as the "Federation of Malaya" in 1948.

The individual states within the federation retained important authority in areas such as education and land, but each state ruler undertook to accept the advice of the British High Commissioner for Malaya in all matters, except issues relating to Islam or Malay customs. The High Commissioner was obligated to safeguard "the special position of the Malays" and the legitimate interests of other communities. This special position was reinforced by strict provisions with respect to citizenship. Most Chinese and Indians could qualify for citizenship only after meeting a long list of requirements, including birth in the Federation, their father's birth and long residence in the Federation, good character, adequate knowledge of Malay or English, and declared intention to reside permanently in the Federation. Only a few could meet these requirements.

The Alliance Party, a multi-racial coalition of the United Malay's National Organization (UMNO), Malayan Chinese Association (MCA), and Malayan Indian Congress (MIC), dominated elections in the early 1950s, and Malaya achieved independence in 1957. The 1957 constitution incorporated many features common to British parliamentary government: a non-political head of state; a legislature composed of two houses, one of which is directly elected; and an independent judiciary. It also contained some unique features which further entrenched the special position of Malays and established the framework within which the various racial groups would operate. In return for recognition of the special status of the Malays, acceptance of Islam as the state religion, and designation of Malay as the sole official language (after a transition period), non-Malays were granted full participation in the activities of the Federation, and citizenship requirements were eased.

The Federation was expanded in 1963 to include Sabah, Sarawak, and Singapore. Singapore and Malaysia parted in 1965, following a period of increasing disagreement concerning the extent of Chinese participation in the Malaysian government. The Alliance, still the dominant political party, showed signs of weakening, and riots broke out in Penang in 1967.

New elections were called in 1969, from which the Alliance emerged with a bare majority. A few days after the elections, communal riots broke out in Kuala Lumpur in which several hundred people were killed or injured. A state of emergency was declared, and normal constitutional government was not restored until February 1971. Certain additional measures protective of the Malays (and other indigenous groups) were introduced, and preventing a recurrence of the ethnic violence of 1969 has been a constant preoccupation of the Malaysian government.

The former Alliance was enlarged to form the National Front, which encompasses the three original parties, much of the major opposition party to the Alliance, and Gerakan, a predominantly Chinese party based in Penang. This ethnically based coalition is dominated by UMNO, and the primary opposition is from the Chinese-based Democratic Action Party and a more right-wing, pro-Islamic party, PAS (a descendent of the former opposition Pan-Malayan Islamic Party).

THE SPECIAL POSITION OF THE MALAYS

Much like the situations in Sri Lanka and Fiji, the indigenous (predominantly Malay) population of Malaysia has long been economically subordinate to a numerically smaller ethnic group, in this case the Chinese.

Aside from foreign dominance of the economy, there were at the time of independence in 1957 three important groups in Malaya—the politically powerful Malays, the economically dominant Chinese and the ambiguously situated Indians. With relatively few exceptions, each group operated in separate economic enclaves of the economy. Throughout the colonial period, the Malay masses were treated as outside the mainstream of the commercial and industrial life of the country. . . .

By the time of independence, the ethnic division of labour had been accentuated, which was reflected in sharp inequalities in income, asset ownership, skills, schooling and living standards. In the context of post-independence communal politics, deep-rooted fears of Chinese encroachment on Malay rights and fears of Malay threats to Chinese economic freedom grew.[1184]

The Malayan constitution has recognized the special position of the *Bumiputra* (indigenous) population of the country since 1957. Article

1184 Tai Yoke Lin, "Inter-Ethnic Restructuring In Malaysia, 1970–80: The Employment Perspective," in Goldmann and Wilson, *supra* note 850, at 44, 45.

153 states that the head of state shall "safeguard the special position of the Malays and the natives of the states of Sabah and Sarawak and the legitimate interests of other communities." Members of these groups may have reserved for them a "reasonable" proportion of positions in the civil service, scholarships, other educational or training privileges or special facilities accorded by the federal government, and business permits or licenses. However, a person cannot be deprived of an existing position, license, or other privilege.

Land

Article 89 of the constitution preserves land reserved for Malays prior to independence, in accordance with existing law. The state also may acquire additional reserved lands in undeveloped or uncultivated areas for the settlement of Malays or other communities. The law creating the pre-independence reservation can now be amended only by a difficult process requiring the votes of two-thirds of the total members of the state legislative assemblies and a resolution of each House of Parliament, passed by a two-thirds majority.

Language

Malay is constitutionally recognized as the national language of Malaysia, but the use (other than for official purposes), teaching, or learning of any other language is guaranteed. English may be used in the legislature and courts, until Parliament provides otherwise. Although special provision is made for the use of English and native languages in Sabah and Sarawak, there are no similar provisions for Chinese, apart from the general guarantee of free use of language.

Recent government decisions suggest that a new linguistic nationalism may be developing in Malaysia, to the detriment of non-Malay groups. In June 1987, the government indicated that it was reviewing the National Education Act, with the intention of giving Malay primacy. While Malay has been the primary classroom language for required courses at the University of Malaya for some time, in 1987 the university also began to require that elective courses in the English, Chinese, and Indian studies departments be taught in Malay. In August 1987, officials in Jahore Bahru decreed that signs displayed at a local festival had to include Malay words, in addition to any other languages.

Religion

Islam is the state religion, but individual freedom of religion is guaranteed. Article 11(4) of the constitution distinguishes between "professing and practicing" and "propagating" a religion; the latter may be restricted by state and federal law if proselytizing is attempted among the Muslim community. In a controversial decision taken in 1987, the University of Technology of Malaysia began to require that all students wear the traditional Malay *songkok* cap during official functions; Chinese students protested that the cap had Muslim religious overtones.[1185]

POST–1969 POLICIES

The absence of any time limit on the exercise of special or affirmative-action provisions has been criticized by non-Malay politicians as granting a permanent advantage to Malays. At the same time, Malay fears and dissatisfaction with economic progress were at the root of the 1969 riots. The case for expanding the protections available for Malays was made in a controversial 1970 book by Mahathir bin Mohamad, Prime Minister of Malaysia since 1981.

> Removal of all protection would subject the Malays to the primitive laws that enable only the fittest to survive. . . .
> Malaysia has far too many non-Malay citizens who can swamp the Malays the moment protection is removed. The frequent suggestion that the only way to help the Malays is to let them fight their own battles cannot therefore be seriously considered. The answer seems to lie somewhere in between; in a sort of "constructive protection" worked out after a careful study of the effects of heredity and environment. Until this is done, the deleterious effect of heredity and environment on the Malays is likely to continue.[1186]

The government determined that the primary causes of the riots in 1969 were 1) discontent and fear encouraged by challenges to the special constitutional provisions relating to the Malays; and 2) the increasing economic disparity between Malays and non-Malays, despite the "special position" of the former, which led to resentment and, ultimately, violence directed against the Chinese and, to a lesser extent, Indian communities.

The response to the first problem was to limit certain types of political debate, initially through an Emergency Ordinance, and subsequently by constitutional amendment. Article 10 was amended to permit laws (which were subsequently adopted) "prohibiting the questioning of any matter, right, status, position, privilege, sovereignty, or prerogative" established or protected by constitutional provisions dealing with

---

1185 "Malaysia's Ethnic Chinese, Indians Fear Cultural Domination by Malays," Wash. Post, 22 Sept. 1987, at A17, col. 1.

1186 Mahathir bin Mohamad, *The Malay Dilemma* (Kuala Lumpur: Federal Publications, 1970, 1980 ed.) at 31. Mahathir was expelled from UMNO in 1969, and his book was banned for several years because of its criticisms of the ruling UMNO elite and suggestions of inherent or hereditary inferiority of the Malays.

citizenship, language, the special position of the Malays, or the sovereignty of the state Rulers. No amendment to any of the above-mentioned provisions of the constitution can be passed without the consent of the Conference of Rulers, an assembly consisting of the rulers of the nine Malay states.

Perhaps even more significant was adoption by the government of a "New Economic Policy" (NEP) to stimulate development and increase Malayan participation in the economy.[1187] The twin goals of the NEP were to reduce and eventually eradicate poverty in all racial groups, by raising income levels and increasing employment, and to restructure Malaysian society in order to correct economic imbalances by increasing Malay participation and ownership in the economy. The New Economic Policy seeks to create a Malay commercial and industrial community (with a goal of 30% *Bumiputra* ownership of the total commercial and industrial wealth of the country), modernize rural life, and encourage growth in all urban activities. In the context of a rapidly expanding economy, these goals were to be accomplished without depriving any group of current possessions.

The NEP has been implemented primarily by extensive government involvement in the economy, and Malaysia's impressive economic growth during the 1970s "made it possible for the state to redistribute income and restructure society without openly resorting to discriminatory measures against particular ethnic groups."[1188] The Malay share of the economy has increased, although some have questioned whether development under the NEP will, in fact, reduce ethnic tensions.

> It appears from all available data that progress towards achievement of NEP employment targets is well under way. On closer examination, however, one cannot be sure that all is as well as it seems. . . . Although [the generation of employment primarily through government intervention] . . . may be a defensible strategy in the short run,. . . . [t]here is a danger that the Bumiputra community may, in the face of continued government protection, be spared the need to constantly upgrade and compete with other segments of the population.[1189]

The economic pie has turned out to be more limited than the government originally predicted. Indians, in particular, have been forced out of civil service jobs by pro-Malay policies and have been unable to

---

1187 See generally, e.g., Tai Yoke Lin, *supra* note 1184; Mavis Puthucheary, "Public Policies Relating to Business and Land, and Their Impact on Ethnic Relations in Peninsular Malaysia," in Goldmann and Wilson, *supra* note 850, at 147.

1188 Puthucheary, *supra* note 1187, at 161.

1189 Tai Yoke Lin, *supra* note 1184, at 56.

compete commercially with the Chinese, thus losing ground vis-à-vis both other groups.

OBSERVATIONS

The different ethnic groups of Malaysia are so intermingled that territorially based political "autonomy" has never been considered as an option. Instead, the Malay-dominated government has adopted a series of affirmative action measures to redress the economic balance, which has traditionally favored the Chinese and Indians. As a result, ethnicity has become the most significant factor in most people's lives. The ruling National Front government is a coalition of ethnically based political parties, rather than a non-ethnic or pan-ethnic party.

So long as Malaysia enjoyed a rapidly expanding economy, the attempt to favor ethnic Malays without discriminating against the vested interests of other ethnic groups seemed relatively successful. However, while the National Front remains a powerful force, it is coming under increasing pressures on economic, political, and ideological fronts.

Economically, the boom days of the 1970s are over. In many ways, attempts to raise the relative position of the Malays have been successful, although they also may have contributed to increasing rather than decreasing ethnic tensions. For example, the composition of the armed forces and police shifted from 70% Malay in 1969–70 to 86% Malay in 1979–80; a 53.5% Bumiputra enrollment in higher education in 1970 had become 73.4% in 1980.[1190] That degree of dominance in two extremely sensitive areas could well detract from the proclaimed Malaysian goal of equality. New ethnic pressures also have arisen from the presence of as many as 300,000 illegal Indonesian migrants in the state of Jahore.

The NEP also has come under attack as creating a small, wealthy Malay capitalist class but failing to do enough to reduce the poverty of the Malay masses.

[T]he NEP has done little to reduce income inequalities, either between ethnic groups or within an ethnic group. To be sure, the incidence of poverty has fallen, especially among the poorest sections of society; but the country has a long way to go towards reducing or eradicating poverty. . . . [I]n emphasising the ethnic differences between the races, it [the NEP] has tended to provide benefits and privileges to Malays whether they are poor or not while denying assistance to members of other ethnic groups even when they are poor and need assistance. . . . Thus there is the danger that the NEP may succeed in its short-term policy of achieving the target of 130 [sic] per cent Bumiputra ownership and wealth in the modern sectors of the economy while failing in its long-term policy designed to achieve inter-ethnic harmony and national unity.[1191]

1190 *Id*. at 48, 49.
1191 Puthucheary, *supra* note 1187, at 169.

Politically, the National Front has suffered from widespread allegations of corruption; in 1986, for example, the leader of the Malaysian Chinese Association was charged in Singapore with stock-market fraud. In addition, there are long-standing restrictions on political activity, and many political opponents resent the total dominance of politics by the National Front (which enjoys a two-thirds majority in parliament and can thus amend the constitution at will). In 1986, the National Front won 148 of the 177 seats in the House of Representatives.

Malaysia has technically remained under a state of emergency since 1969; administrative detention is permitted under the 1960 Internal Security Act; and limits on normal fair-trial guarantees are permitted under the 1975 Essential (Security Cases) (Amendment) Regulations.[1192] These and other derogations from the normal judicial process are justified as necessary to combat communist insurgents (who mount occasional actions in border areas but have not presented a serious threat since a major insurgency in the late 1940s and early 1950s) and drug traffickers, and to maintain communal harmony.

Ideologically, the present government is under pressure from Islamic fundamentalists, many of whom support the opposition PAS party. However, this increased religious activism has not been translated into widespread political support, and many activist Muslims have been co-opted into the Mahathir government.[1193] An increasingly militant Islamic movement obviously could increase fears among the Chinese and Indian communities. However, recent manifestations of Malay nationalism in the areas of language and education, two particularly sensitive areas to any minority, are disquieting. In the face of increasing tensions within UMNO and Chinese resentment over pro-Malay language policies, the government detained several Chinese opposition leaders and other critics without trial in late 1987, and ethnic tensions were probably at their highest level since 1969.

Malaysia's ethnic and other divisions were contained fairly successfully from 1969 until the mid-1980s, through a difficult combination of emphasizing ethnicity and tolerance at the same time. Attempts to impose the majority culture on well-defined minorities in, for example, Sri Lanka and Sudan, have led to bitter conflicts, and one can only hope that recent assertions of Malay dominance and intolerance do not presage a similar fate for Malaysia.

The difficulties of maintaining an ethnically balanced state through

1192 *Cf. Report, supra* note 1182; Amnesty International, *Report 1986, supra* note 561, 859, at 141–42.

1193 See "Malaysia's Muslims: Two Images, One Spirit," Far Eastern Economic Review, 22 Jan. 1987, at 20–25.

a formal system of ethnic preferences and apportionment of political power are demonstrated only too well by Cyprus, Lebanon, and, more recently, Fiji. Where such differences exist, and it is impossible to devise autonomous community structures which will give each ethnic group access to some relevant political power, the Malaysian version of a one-party state is an option that will continue to be attractive—so long as a true commitment to pluralism in the context of Malay political dominance does not yield to extremist demands for Malay exclusivity.

Part IV **Conclusion**

When parties in a state are violent, he offered a wonderful contrivance to reconcile them. The method is this: you take a hundred leaders of each party; you dispose them into couples of such whose heads are nearest of a size; then let two nice operators saw off the occiput of each couple at the same time, in such a manner, that the brain may be equally divided. Let the occiputs, thus cut off, be interchanged, applying each to the head of his opposite party-man. It seems indeed to be a work that requires some exactness, but the professor assured us that if it were dexterously performed, the cure would be infallible. For he argued thus: that the two half brains, being left to debate the matter between themselves within the space of one skull, would soon come to a good understanding, and produce that moderation, as well as regularity of thinking, so much to be wished for in the heads of those who imagine they come into the world only to watch and govern its motion: and as to the difference of brains, in quantity or quality, among those who are directors in faction, the doctor assured us, from his own knowledge, that it was a perfect trifle.

Jonathan Swift, Gulliver's Travels (1727)

Chapter 19
Conclusion

Much of history has been concerned with efforts by those without power to assert greater control over their own lives. Designation as a "minority" or "majority" has had little meaning in many of these struggles, as the territory in which dissident or anti-state forces find themselves is generally defined (by them) in a manner which ensures that the principle of "majority rule" can be used to justify their rejection of the ruling authorities.[1194] In the nineteenth century, those groups which obtained international recognition as constituting a new state became majorities; unsuccessful aspirants to statehood remained minorities.

There has been great concern in the twentieth century with "nation building," but a more accurate view of recent history would be that of nations being destroyed (or at least diminished) by states. The spread of empires—from the Egyptian, Greek, and Roman to the British, French, Ottoman, and Russian—reflected political and legal theories that separated ethnicity, religion, and "nationhood" from the authority of government. While the government of the empire was often itself closely tied to a particular culture, non-settler empires did not always seek to impose more than political and economic control over their subjects (with the exception of missionaries' attempts at religious conversion).

The identification of "state" with "nation" in the late nineteenth

---

1194 "[I]n the most refractory cases, the conduct of a 'fair and free election' is no panacea. Rather, it raises in a most acute form the question of which population belongs to which territory—a question which . . . is often inextricably bound up with the issue of the critical date. Preconceived notions of who the 'real' population of a territory is; of the significance to be given to movements of population, in the recent and more remote past; and, above all, of *whose* rights should prevail over whose—ineluctably influence the stand taken on the illusorily neutral issue of the conditions for holding a 'fair' referendum." Pomerance, *supra* note 103, at 29.

and twentieth centuries dramatically reversed the course of the empires. As democracy and social contract theory became central to European concepts of government, multi-ethnic states became more difficult to sustain. States-in-waiting utilized ethnic or linguistic homogeneity to justify their separation from the empire to which they were subject, as well as to legitimize peripheral territorial expansion. Contiguous empires, such as the Ottoman and Austro-Hungarian, disintegrated under the pressures of ethnic nationalism (aided and abetted by rival powers), while the new overseas empires could be justified only with respect to peoples whose level of development did not entitle them, in the European view, to assert their "nationhood" against European domination.

As noted in chapter 3, nineteenth-century "national" self-determination gave way to twentieth-century "territorial" self-determination. The new states were all too aware of the power of appeals to "national" self-determination, and the preservation of territorial integrity—no matter how artificial—was enforced by a general rejection of minority rights. In some instances, the new state "nationalism" was ideological; in others, attempts to transform the majority or dominant culture into that of the state as a whole paralleled similar efforts in postwar Europe. Coerced assimilation of minority groups and indigenous peoples was state policy in both the developed and developing world, as the centralization of state power became a hallmark of political activity in the 1950s and 1960s.

However, "[i]f there is no logical, philosophical, or sociological limit to nationalism, then the point at which one states the process of national liberation has proceeded far enough is a matter of political choice."[1195] For many minorities and indigenous groups today, that choice is to return to the rhetoric of the ethnic-linguistic state of the nineteenth century. Yet minorities and indigenous peoples, too, may need to abandon the "nation-state" as an ideal, so long as their "nation" can otherwise be preserved. Political loyalty to an existing state does not necessarily imply national or cultural disloyalty, any more than the recognition of diversity by a central or majority government need engender disunity or fragmentation.[1196]

Full exercise of ethnic self-determination, grounded on linguistic, religious, or other self-defining criteria, might better protect current incarnations of "nationalities," "minorities," and "indigenous peoples". Nevertheless, the prospect of 5,000 homogeneous, independent statelets which define themselves primarily in ethnic, religious, or linguistic terms

---

1195 Barnett, *supra* note 272, at 314–15.

1196 *Cf.* Alain Fenet, "La question des minorités dans l'ordre du droit," in Chaliand, *supra* note 72, at 58–68.

is one that should inspire at least as much trepidation as admiration. As frontiers are shifted and minorities displaced to make way for greater purity, a new age of intolerance is more likely to follow than is an era of mutual respect and tolerance for all.

Some people romanticise their real or supposed ancestral community, and at the same time oppose ethnic prejudice and wish to be fair to everyone. But you can't really have it both ways. The cosy old community *was* ethnocentric, and if you wish to love and perpetuate it as it truly was, prejudice against outsiders must be part of the romantic package-deal. The trouble about the Nazis was that they were only too consistent on this point.[1197]

Self-determination does not give the resulting majority the right to impose its will in such a way that the rights of others are violated—and this is true whether that majority is a modern, secular, pluralistic society which forces the assimilation of its minorities and the incorporation of indigenous peoples, or whether it is a traditional, homogeneous society which seeks to exclude dissenting or different minorities under the guise of national, ethnic, or religious purity. Individuals and minorities will continue to exist no matter how carefully borders are drawn, and forcing the individual to conform to any majority's conception of the perfect society is as inadmissible as destruction of so-called "backward" societies by dominant invaders.

Yet the potential dangers of ethnic unity combined with the power available to an ethnically homogeneous state should not lead one to dismiss the legitimacy or importance of responding to deeply felt needs for group identity and dignity. The modern, particularly Western, emphasis on the individual has undervalued and often undermined the fundamental importance of the group, and maintenance of smaller, more homogeneous societies (as opposed to the creation of small, homogeneous states) is an appropriate goal of central state governments.[1198]

Conflict is at the heart of political life, and not every minority-majority conflict in which some form of autonomy is an issue has been accompanied by violence. "The issue is not why the differentials [in the relative development of different ethnic groups] exist—successes and failures have a thousand causes—but how people and their governments respond to these differences and the fears and demands that accompany them."[1199] A common characteristic of those ethnic conflicts which *have* led to serious violence is the violation of fundamental human rights.

1197 Gellner, *supra* note 18, at 88; emphasis in original.
1198 *Cf.*, e.g., Vernon Van Dyke, "The Individual, The State, and Ethnic Communities in Political Theory," in Kommers and Loescher, *supra* note 23, at 36–62.
1199 Weiner, *supra* note 526, at 17.

Human rights violations are neither constant nor uniform, and they are more often responsible for exacerbating existing conflicts than for creating divisions where there were none before. Nevertheless, it is these violations which often escalate political or economic differences to the status of open and violent conflict. Among the major case studies examined in the present work, several offer instances of obvious human rights violations: for example, decades of blatant discrimination against Northern Irish Catholics in housing and jobs, and denial of the right to speak Kurdish freely or even refer to one's self as a Kurd in Turkey. At the same time, minority or guerrilla terrorism and murder also escalate conflicts (usually deliberately), although most such incidents begin only after state violence has reached a relatively high level.

Colonialism has influenced many situations of ethnic conflict, as colonial policies exacerbated existing ethnic divisions and introduced new minorities to formerly homogeneous territories. While colonial powers attempted to some degree to transform loosely organized Asian and African societies into structures closer to the Western "state," there was rarely any concern to develop a sense of nationhood among those colonized (although opposition to colonial rule itself became a rallying point for those within colonial boundaries).[1200] Indeed, the reinforcement of tribal divisions often formed part of the classic "divide and rule" policies of all the European colonizers.

However, colonialism rarely created ethnic conflict where none existed previously (with some exceptions, as where foreign labor was imported into a formerly homogeneous society or where colonial borders or policies may have created conflicts between groups which formerly had little contact with one another). European history certainly offers ample evidence that colonialism is not a necessary ingredient for the existence of violent ethnic or religious conflict.

Outside intervention also is a factor in many contemporary conflicts, and it is frequently sought by the dissident or minority group concerned. Although intervention may occasionally greatly influence (or even determine) the outcome of struggles for autonomy, it has more frequently repressed than encouraged minority or secessionist movements. "Ceasefires, amnesties, and concessions far short of autonomy or secession are all recurrent effects of international involvement on the side of the separatists. . . . By opting for foreign help, secessionists risk losing control over their destiny to states that have different, usually more limited, objectives."[1201]

1200 *Cf.*, e.g., Christopher C. Mojekwu, "Self-Determination: The African Perspective," in Alexander and Friedlander, *supra* note 163, at 221–23.

1201 Horowitz, *supra* note 5, at 277.

Outside intervention often takes the form of permitting territory to be used as a safe haven by dissident groups or providing weapons or training to guerrillas, and the limited destabilization of a neighboring or rival state may be welcomed by the minority-supporting state. Minorities which are ethnically linked to a neighboring state may, in particular, draw support from that state, but active pro-minority intervention, such as that of Turkey in Cyprus, the U.S. in Nicaragua, or India in Bangladesh, is rare. Where outside support is present, the legitimacy of a minority's claim may be tainted by suspicions that minority grievances are merely being used as a pawn in larger geopolitical struggles.

International, as opposed to extra-national, intervention may hold more promise for some minority and indigenous groups, although multilateral support will certainly fall short of recognizing a right to secession. As noted in chapter 4, post-1919 attempts to guarantee minority rights through international oversight were not altogether ineffective. Contemporary initiatives in the United Nations, with respect both to rights of minorities and indigenous peoples and to human rights generally, also may contribute to better understanding of and greater protection for less powerful communities. Many conflicts by their very nature concern more than one state, and, in some situations, multilateral mediation or involvement may be preferable to unilateral pressure from a single neighboring state.[1202]

At the same time, however, the limits of international powers of persuasion—generally the most potent weapon that international bodies possess—need to be kept in mind. Intergovernmental human rights bodies are extremely uncomfortable whenever the discussion turns to questions of autonomy or minority political rights (although expert bodies such as the Human Rights Committee and the Committee on the Elimination of Racial Discrimination are increasingly willing to question states about their treatment of ethnic and other minorities). Often, more effective pressure may be brought to bear through attention from the international media and nongovernmental organizations than through the formal action of intergovernmental bodies.

Regional bodies may offer somewhat more potential, as states often are more responsive when such delicate issues as minority rights are discussed *"en famille."* Efforts such as those by the Organization of

---

1202 Query whether imposition of a solution by "parties" to the conflicts in Sri Lanka and Northern Ireland would be more likely to succeed if the initiatives were wholly bilateral or much more broadly international? Certainly any resolution of the conflicts in Kurdistan, the Atlantic Coast of Nicaragua, and the Saami region requires an international or multinational component. *Cf.* Ryan, *supra* note 6.

African States to mediate in the Western Sahara dispute should be encouraged. On the other hand, no European country has challenged Turkish treatment of the Kurds under the provisions of the European Convention on Human Rights, and Latin American states may be reluctant to question their neighbors about indigenous rights when their own territories include numerous indigenous communities.

THE CONTENT OF AUTONOMY

While each situation is unique, the conflicts in which autonomy is viewed by one party as essential to the guarantee of its survival concern some or all of the following basic issues: language; education; access to governmental civil service, including police and security forces, and social services; land and natural resources; and representative local government structures.

Language is perhaps the most distinctive feature of a culture. There are thousands of languages in the world, and linguistic variation is much greater than differences in ethnicity, religion, political and economic structures, or social mores. Self-determination, as that concept developed in the nineteenth and early twentieth centuries in Europe, was based primarily on linguistic groups, rather than on religion, politics, or economics.

"The reality is that languages are now dying at an alarming rate and this process will presumably continue."[1203] The process of linguistic extinction has many causes, ranging at the extremes from the active repression of minority languages by the state to the "natural" disappearance of language through acculturation or assimilation. Among the most serious threats to the survival of minority languages are the tremendous influence of the mass media, immigration, tourism, and the increasingly international and multinational character of the world economy and communications.[1204]

Language not only has a real function as the glue which holds a culture together but also has a symbolic role vis à vis the larger community or state. Designation of a language as "official" or "national" is a recognition of the role that those who speak the language play as co-founders or essential partners in the state. Withdrawal of that status, as occurred in Sri Lanka, is a visible and direct rejection of that cooperative role.

1203 Terence O'Brien, "Economic Support for Minority Languages," in Alcock, Taylor, and Welton, *supra* note 7, at 84.

1204 *Cf.*, e.g., Glanville Price, "The Present Position and Viability of Minority Languages," in *id.* at 30–43.

Language . . . is a symbol of domination. . . . Claims for official status for a language are typically demands for an authoritative indication "that some people have a legitimate claim to greater respect, importance, or worth in the society than have some others." . . . As the demand for a single official language reflects the desire for a tangible demonstration of preeminence, so linguistic parity is transparent code for equality more generally.[1205]

There is disagreement as to whether the right of minorities "to use" their own language implies a positive obligation on the part of the state to support such use,[1206] but prohibiting use of a language is clearly impermissible under international human rights norms. The right to use one's own language was a fundamental aspect of the guarantees included in the various post-World War I "minorities treaties"; it is basic to the political structures of, for instance, Belgium, Canada, Finland, India, Spain, and Yugoslavia; and it is an inextricable component of freedom of expression and association.

Even where a minority language is not sufficiently important to the country as a whole to merit special constitutional recognition, statutory or administrative provisions for the use of minority languages in certain circumstances may be essential to the smooth functioning of government. Human rights norms require, for example, that judicial proceedings be conducted in a language the accused understands (or that a translator be provided).[1207] Multilingual ballots are common in many states, and social services should be available in a manner understandable to the potential recipients.[1208]

Multilingual states often seem more adaptable in their linguistic policies than bilingual states. In the latter, political dominance often leads to linguistic dominance and the rejection of equality. More diverse societies, such as Yugoslavia and India, may contain larger proportions of the population to whom linguistic flexibility is seen as desirable. Indeed, this may be true for minority rights generally, as multiple minorities obviously have much greater reason to be tolerant of one another than does a majority which dominates a single minority.[1209]

1205 Horowitz, *supra* note 5, at 219, 220 (citation omitted).
1206 See discussion in chap. 6, *supra* at 111–12.
1207 See, e.g., Covenant on Civil and Political Rights, art. 14; American Convention on Human Rights, art. 14; European Convention on Human Rights, art. 6.
1208 Of course, the majority may wish to resist this manifestation of multiculturalism, as was the case with the "Sinhala only" policy in Sri Lanka and recent drives for "English only" in the United States.
1209 For this reason, pluralist models such as Switzerland, Yugoslavia, Mauritius, and the U.S.S.R. may not provide helpful models for minority "autonomy" in countries with only one or two small minority groups.

There is no formula for recognition or support of non-majority languages that is appropriate for all situations.[1210] It is certainly not required or necessarily helpful to draw political boundaries precisely according to linguistic divisions, although a sufficiently large linguistic community may feel that it needs at least one local or regional unit in which its language is officially recognized.

The appropriate balance to be struck between the legitimate needs of the state for some degree of linguistic uniformity and of minorities for the practical and/or symbolic recognition of their languages may be difficult to determine, but good faith efforts to arrive at such a balance are essential to the maintenance of intra-state harmony. One also should ensure that linguistic exclusivity does not become a vehicle for unfairly maintaining traditional social and political control within a minority community, to the detriment of (particularly younger) members of that minority who may be more open to bilingualism or multilingualism.

Recent immigrants who speak a language other than that of the majority have a weaker claim for positive support or recognition than do those groups indigenous to the larger society, and it is legitimate for a state to pursue a goal of unilingualism or at least linguistic primacy for the majority (or a "neutral") language. But where repression or denial of linguistic rights reflects political and economic discrimination as well, ethnic resurgence will almost invariably be the response of the beleaguered minority.

Education is, along with language, the primary vehicle through which culture is transmitted, and it has long been a basic demand of minorities that they be permitted to establish and maintain their own schools. This right was commonly recognized in the post-1919 minority treaties, but it is not among those directly guaranteed to minorities under article 27 of the Covenant on Civil and Political Rights. In fact, contemporary human rights instruments speak primarily of the right to education as a state obligation to provide education on a universal basis, although there also are references to parental rights to ensure that their children's education is in conformity with their own religious or moral values.[1211] The Covenant on Economic, Social and Cultural Rights does

1210 See, e.g., K. D. McRae, "The Constitutional Protection of Linguistic Rights in Bilingual and Multilingual States," in Gotlieb, *supra* note 177, at 211–27.

1211 See, e.g., Covenant on Civil and Political Rights, art. 18(4); Covenant on Economic, Social and Cultural Rights, art. 13(3) and (4); Protocol No. 1 to the European Convention on Human Rights, art. 2; American Convention on Human Rights, art. 12(4). But compare art. 17(3) of the African Charter on Human and Peoples' Rights, which states that "promotion and protection of morals and traditional values recognized by the community shall be the duty of the State." *Cf.* Eur. Court Human Rights, *Case Relating*

refer to "the liberty of individuals and bodies to establish and direct educational institutions . . . [which] shall conform to such minimum standards as may be laid down by the State," but there is no affirmative state obligation to promote or assist such non-state institutions.

Disputes over education may focus on access or content (or both). At the primary school level, ensuring education in the minority language and in a manner consistent with local traditions is perhaps the major concern of many minority communities; control over broader aspects of the curriculum and teaching personnel may be essential to indigenous and other groups whose cultures differ markedly from that of the dominant society. The state naturally views the educational system as the primary vehicle for inculcating its own values, and it is unlikely to grant exclusive control over education to any non-state entity.

Educational policies can be extremely divisive even within a majority group, and minorities are not immune from similar disagreements over the content of education.[1212] However, in conflicts in which education is only one area in which autonomy is sought, there is likely to be a consensus within the minority community that greater local control over the direction and staffing of schools is essential. In many cases, this would not necessarily exclude a "state" component as part of the curriculum (such as a requirement that the majority language or history be taught), but establishment of educational priorities might remain in the hands of the autonomous region or community.[1213]

Access to higher education is often linked to questions of language and non-discrimination, and it is more appropriately seen as a reflection of broader opportunities for minorities to participate in the dominant society than as an issue in and of itself. Conflicts most often arise over the adoption of preferential or "affirmative action" policies which favor an allegedly disadvantaged group, rather than overt discrimination against a particular group.[1214]

Particularly in developing countries, **access to government civil ser-**

to *Certain Aspects of the Laws on the Use of Languages in Education in Belgium, supra* note 404.

1212 *Cf.* Margaret B. Sutherland, "Comparative Perspectives on the Education of Cultural Minorities," in Alcock, Taylor, and Welton, *supra* note 7, at 44–62.

1213 Of course, the major problem in many developing countries is the lack of sufficient resources to ensure *any* level of schooling. In such circumstances, it will be important to avoid duplication in educational efforts, and the state may be more likely to support schools under its direct control than to provide funds to autonomous entities.

1214 An excellent summary of some of the philosophical and political problems posed by "affirmative action" in educational and other fields may be found in Myron Weiner, "The Pursuit of Ethnic Equality through Preferential Policies: A Comparative Public Policy Perspective," in Goldmann and Wilson, *supra* note 850, at 63–81.

vice employment and social services is a fundamental issue that determines the economic, social, and political influence of minority group
members. The government is often a (if not the) primary employer, and
preferential employment or other economic policies are most easily
administered through government intervention. Again, the mirror issues
of non-discrimination versus preferential policies arise frequently; the
former may be exercised indirectly through language or education requirements that minority members are unable to meet.

State-directed or tolerated discrimination—and discrimination in
employment is one of the most visible manifestations—is one of the
most divisive factors in majority-minority relations. At best, the state
must be seen as the impartial arbiter of fundamental governmental policies, the "gatekeeper of the contradictions and the controller of the
conflict."[1215] If minorities are deliberately excluded from the process of
government decision-making at the administrative level, they may legitimately conclude that the political process is equally biased. Perceived
bias in the provision of government services is a major cause of ethnic
friction; where a highly centralized government is represented in an
ethnically or culturally distinct region by "outsiders," local resentment
is likely to develop. In such situations, some form of preferential policies
to encourage the employment of local residents (which might be possible
through geographical rather than ethnic or linguistic classifications)
seems almost essential.

Of course, "discrimination" in the distribution of government services, benefits, and employment is precisely the reward sought by political parties.

By appealing to electorates in ethnic terms, by making ethnic demands on
government, and by bolstering the influence of ethnically chauvinist elements
within each group, parties that begin by merely mirroring ethnic divisions help
to deepen and extend them. . . . Since the party aspires to control the state, and
in conflict-prone polities ethnic groups also attempt to exclude others from state
power, the emergence of ethnic parties is an integral part of this political
struggle.[1216]

The identification of the state with a single ethnic group, to the
detriment of other ethnic groups and/or peripheral regions, makes
it even more essential that fundamental human rights be respected.
Freedom of expression and association and the principle of non-
discrimination may not prevent the unwarranted domination of the ma-

1215 Rothschild, *supra* note 8, at 4.
1216 Horowitz, *supra* note 5, at 291, 294

chinery of the state by a single group, but their violation will ensure that conflict increases rather than subsides.

If conflict and violence do increase, discrimination by the central authorities is likely to intensify, as members of the minority will be viewed as potentially disloyal. Minorities are commonly under-represented in the police and security forces, and reduction of their numbers in a time of crisis will, from the minority's perspective, reinforce the image of the state's security forces as an ethnic or sectarian army rather than an impartial arbiter of the law. As conflict worsens, minority extremists often view those who continue to work for the state as traitors to the minority cause, and assassination and intimidation will contribute to the increasingly communal nature of state institutions.

The resulting imbalance in state administrators, employees, and security forces makes even the technical aspects of conflict resolution more difficult. For example, the police and/or army in Northern Ireland, Sri Lanka, Fiji, Spain, and Malaysia are overwhelmingly composed of members of only one group; dominance by a single tribal group in Africa also is common. In such a situation, particularly where violence has led to well-founded fears on the part of minority members for their personal safety, the absence of a neutral policing force can be a major stumbling block in attempts to negotiate a settlement. Ethnic imbalance and re-sulting mistrust are commonly reflected in demands for autonomous or regional control over local police, as well as some local control over the use of state security forces in the autonomous region.

Land is the literal and figurative foundation of the state and of every community that aspires to political autonomy. While the exercise of certain forms of personal jurisdiction or autonomy in the areas of religion and civil status does not require a territorial base, the wide range of autonomous powers discussed in the present book presumes a minority population which is sufficiently numerous, concentrated, and/or isolated from the dominant society so that an autonomous territory would be feasible.

Control over territory is essential for the creation of the normal organs of local or regional government and may also be important in terms of economic viability or development, but it is the symbolic aspect of controlling one's "homeland" that is the primary motivation under-lying demands for an autonomous territory. At the same time, the ter-ritorial integrity of the state has attained an equally mythical status often inseparable from that of self-determination.

Less clear is the rationale for equating territorial integrity with a unitary or centralized form of government. It is certainly possible that a government's emphasis on territorial integrity is merely a smokescreen to cover up its unwillingness to share political power; the specter of secession and geographic disintegration is a much more powerful symbol around which to organize support than the "threat" of administrative decentralization, local control over police, or even the regional devolution of power. However, it cannot seriously be doubted that federal or consociational states, or those in which substantial powers have been devolved to local governments, are any less sovereign or stable than unitary states; in fact, the reverse may be true.

Territory can be seen as a primary guarantor of two fundamental human needs, identity and security.[1217] Territory or land as an identifying force is a very complex concept, and it may be difficult to distinguish between the socio-political organization which controls a territory and the territory itself. Herein lies a fundamental distinction between indigenous and other peoples, as the former have a much closer, more spiritual link to their traditional lands than do many other groups.[1218]

It would be incorrect, however, to assume that lack of spiritual ties to the "earth" necessarily reduces the attachment of a people to a particular piece of land. Without questioning the unique nature of traditional indigenous relationships with the earth (as distinguished from geopolitical "territory"), one can also note that the psychological link between many people and the land of their ancestors is often undervalued both by those with a more spiritual relationship with the earth and by those who are products of modern, cosmopolitan, essentially landless cultures. For example, the attachment of Christians, Jews, and Muslims to Jerusalem and other religious-historic sites in the Middle East and even of the English to the island on which they have lived for centuries, goes beyond mere habit or "state" identity.[1219]

The necessity of territory in order to secure physical security is a universal need among threatened groups. The perceived need for Armenians and Jews to have respective territories (arguably more important than a state) to prevent future genocide is an obvious example of the reaction of a community which fears for its survival. Where members of minority groups are dispersed throughout a state (for example, Sikhs

---

1217 *Cf.* Ronan Paddison, *The Fragmented State*, (New York: St. Martin's Press, 1983) at 14–18.

1218 See chap. 5, *supra* at 91–95.

1219 *Cf.*, e.g., William Shakespeare, *King Richard the Second*, Act III, scene 2:
> . . . I weep for joy
> To stand upon my kingdom once again.—
> Dear earth, I do salute thee with my hand,
> Though rebels wound thee with their horses' hoofs:
> As a long-parted mother with her child
> Plays fondly with her tears and smiles in meeting,
> So, weeping, smiling, greet I thee, my earth,
> And do thee favours with my royal hands.

in India and Tamils in Sri Lanka), attacks on those dispersed members and subsequent displacement and population shifts intensify the need for a defined territory in which community members can be physically secure.

Again, it is gross violations of human rights that commonly create a minority's need, which may not be present in earlier stages of a conflict, for a specific territorial base or homeland. Ethnic riots in which the minority are the primary victims, invasions of indigenous lands by armed settlers or security forces, or even peaceful incursions by an overwhelmingly dominant community, all give rise to demands for control over territory that go beyond economic or political participation in the larger polity.

Control over natural resources is a somewhat more complex issue and, in many instances, is more entwined with modern (or old-fashioned) greed than with the preservation of culture or the assertion of "rights" in their traditional sense. Many states which recognize various forms of territorial autonomy or are dedicated to private ownership of property nevertheless view sub-soil (or ocean or river) resources as part of statal patrimony, to be exploited as the central government deems best in the interests of state economic development.

In the case of mineral or other underground resources which need to be extracted before they can be used, it is difficult to concede the existence of a cultural attachment to such resources. However, there is frequently intense opposition to central government plans for developing unexploited natural resources, whether those plans call for hydroelectric projects, timber harvesting, mining, or drilling. In some cases, such exploitation may only be the most recent example (from the minority or regional perspective) of discrimination in economic development; in others, a strong regional stand on retention of natural resource wealth may simply be the normal attempt of every community to see that it receives a fair share of the economic pie. In all cases, the exploitation of natural resources is almost certain to heighten conflicts between local/regional communities and central authorities, even where state identity is strong; where divided loyalties already exist, it should not be surprising that ethnic, religious, or other divisions that coincide with geographic lines will be reinforced.

Many disputes over natural resources are simply examples of the innumerable conflicts which political systems are designed to resolve, but some represent deeper antagonisms which lead to demands for autonomy. If those most directly affected by a development project have not been involved to a significant degree in the decision as to whether and how such resources will be utilized, the feelings of isolation or irrelevance on the part of those who live in peripheral areas of an increasingly centralized state will be reinforced. Indeed, it is this lack of local input into economic development projects (including those involving natural resources) that prompted international concern over "popular participation" in decision-making.[1220]

A distinction should be made between the apportionment of wealth which may arise from natural resource exploitation and the physical impact of exploitation on the communities involved. In this context, one can again identify particular dangers to indigenous communities: new discoveries of untapped natural resources are most likely to occur in peripheral or relatively unpopulated areas, which are precisely those in which traditional indigenous peoples commonly live. As indigenous peoples also tend to be politically powerless, their interests will be either ignored or unheard amidst demands of developers who will benefit from unfettered exploitation.

The relationship between indigenous peoples and their physical environment suggests that decisions as to resource exploitation must respect the imperatives of indigenous societies, whose social and cultural life, as well as economic well-being, depends on that environment. At a minimum, recognition that exploitation of natural resources on indigenous lands can be undertaken only with the joint agreement of the indigenous community and central government would ensure that indigenous cultures would not, as is presently the case, automatically yield to so-called economic imperatives of the state. At the same time, joint use would reflect the reality that few states will abandon their claims to natural resources, which they assert not only against indigenous peoples but against other states and private enterprises.

The creation of **representative local government structures** is fundamental to most demands for autonomy, although, particularly in small states, effective representation at the state or national level may be a more important goal. However, just as it is unnecessary for political analyses always "to indulge in elaborate definitional distinctions among an ethnic group, a nation, a nationality, a people, a tribe, and the like,"[1221] it is not the intent of the present work to catalog the various types of unitary, devolved, federal, quasi-federal, confederal, consociational, or other constitutional systems.[1222] Rather, the purpose is to

---

1220 *Cf.* chap. 6, *supra* at 113–17.

1221 Rothschild, *supra* note 8, at 8.

1222 *Cf.*, e.g., Claire Palley, "The Role of Law in Relation to Minority Groups," in Alcock, Taylor, and Welton, *supra* note 7, at 120–60; it distinguishes among federalism, regionalism or devolution, administrative decentralization, local government, and community development authorities, and discusses various electoral and legislative arrangements for providing minority representation; Daniel J. Elazar, "Arrangements For

identify what, if any, guidance may be found in international legal principles towards identifying a core of values which might be included in a "right to autonomy."

International law places essentially no restrictions on the internal constitutional arrangements that any state may adopt, pursuant to its "sovereign" independence, as evidenced in the case studies in Parts II and III. "Self-determination" may be exercised by a people in any manner it freely chooses, from full integration with an existing state to total independence; a choice of autonomy, federalism, or any other sub-sovereign status is *ipso facto* equally appropriate. Many new actors—from individuals to transnational corporations to sub-state and inter-state entities—have acquired varying degrees of international personality, and international law is developing, if with some hesitation, sufficient flexibility to accommodate them.

More autonomy is not necessarily better, from the perspective of either the subordinate entity or the state. For purposes of comparison, however, one might expect a "fully autonomous" territory to possess most of the following powers:

1) There is a locally elected legislative body with some independent legislative authority, limited by a constituent document. Unless the exercise of this authority exceeds the local legislature's competence as defined in the constituent document, it should not be subject to veto by the principal/sovereign government. Local competence should generally include control or influence over primary and secondary education, the use of language, the structure of local government, and land use and planning.

2) There is a locally selected chief executive, who may be subject to approval by the central government; the executive may have responsibility for the administration and enforcement of state (national) as well as local laws. While the executive may be jointly responsible to the local and central authorities, this structural confusion is probably best avoided in circumstances where strong local identity is asserted.

3) There is an independent local judiciary with full responsibility for interpreting local laws. Disputes over the extent of local authority or the relationship between the autonomous and central governments may be within the original jurisdiction of local courts, but final decisions are commonly within the competence of either the state judiciary or a joint dispute-settling body.

4) Areas of joint concern may be the subject of power-sharing arrangements between the autonomous and central governments, in which

Self-Rule and Autonomy in Various Countries," in Elazar, *supra* note 1181, at 153–68; Enloe, *supra* note 18; Sigler, *supra* note 170, at 111–31; Horowitz, *supra* note 5, at 601–52.

local flexibility is permitted within the broad policy parameters set by the central government. In addition to local implementation and administration of state norms, joint authority is frequently exercised over such matters as ports and communication facilities, police, and exploitation of natural resources.

The above summary of "full autonomy" is applicable to Western-oriented democracies based on separation of powers, but this is evidently not the only appropriate model. For example, most indigenous societies are characterized by the continued existence of a government structure which predates their contact with the surrounding or encroaching society, and the preservation of such traditional structures may be the best means of guaranteeing effective autonomy. So long as members of indigenous communities desire to maintain their form of government, those structures should normally be immune from the intervention of an outside authority.

An autonomous region should enjoy effective control over matters which are primarily of local concern, within the overall framework of the fundamental norms of the state. Autonomy is not equivalent to independence, and autonomous governments should not expect to be immune from the influence of central governments. At the same time, however, the state must adopt a flexible attitude which will enable the autonomous region to exercise real power, precisely when that exercise of power runs counter to the state's inherent preference for centralization and uniformity.

THE RIGHT TO AUTONOMY

At the end of a struggle that approaches or achieves the status of civil war, answers to fundamental questions concerning the very legitimacy of political authority may be essential to a settlement. Where possible, however, compromises or agreements on specific, less weighty issues—e.g., representation in the civil service or control over development projects—are likely to be much easier if addressed before the structure of the state itself is called into question. The following observation is apt, although made in the context of international rather than domestic disputes:

[W]hat is needed is a way of breaking up political disputes and differences—before they become crises—into pieces sufficiently small so that if they are dealt with one at a time a state will have a greater interest in keeping the game going than it will in winning what is involved in any particular piece. . . . The single most important step in winning an international [or domestic] dispute lies in formulating an objective which is attainable. Once a state [or minority group] commits itself to the pursuit of an unattainable objective, there is nothing that legal techniques or anything else can do to produce success.[1223]

Many of the issues noted above (language, education, access to employment and social services, land, natural resources, and local government) can be resolved on an ad hoc basis, particularly where they involve recognized rights, such as language use or a free press. Even where it is difficult to identify a direct "right," e.g., to adequate representation on a police force, reasonably articulated demands may be satisfied by a responsive government that wishes to avoid exacerbating ethnic or regional tensions. If conflicts have not become overly violent, various forms of administrative decentralization may offer solutions to complaints of geographical or economic marginalization.

Where most or all of these demands are at issue, however, the question becomes one of autonomy or less-than-sovereign self-determination. It should first be underscored that a political demand for autonomy—even without assertion of an underlying "right"—should be given serious consideration by any responsible government. State sovereignty does not imply retention of any particular political or economic system, and responsiveness to legitimate minority grievances is the hallmark of a government that respects the human rights of its entire population, as well as the principle of self-determination.

Where demands for autonomy and self-determination are asserted as a matter of right, they are often founded on the illegitimacy of the government or the state itself.

The concept of the illegitimate *state* underlies the right to self-determination in its anti-colonial manifestation. Because the governing authority is deemed by the international community to have no right to govern, the territory in question has the right to independence (or to any other status it freely chooses); the issue is not one of autonomy or secession, but of the internal self-determination of an entire nascent state.

Statehood also may be denied by the international community where recognition would imply sanctioning secession or otherwise interfering with the principles of national unity and territorial integrity, as is the case with the various "independent" South African bantustans, the Turkish Republic of Northern Cyprus, and the historical examples of Biafra and Katanga/Shaba.

1223 Roger Fisher, *Points of Choice* (Oxford: Oxford Univ. Press, 1978) at 25–26, 54. *Cf. id.*, *Improving Compliance with International Law* (Charlottesville: Univ. Press of Virginia, 1981).

The most common reason for denying the legitimacy of the *govern-ment* of a state is that it is a puppet regime under the control of a foreign power. A domestic government may be treated as if it were foreign if it denies self-determination to the majority, as was the case in Southern Rhodesia[1224] or is presently in South Africa.

The only example of withdrawal by the international community of recognition of the legitimacy of a government on human rights grounds seems to be the remarkable resolution adopted by Organization of American States, concerning the status of the Somoza government in Nicaragua.[1225] The OAS Meeting of Consultation of Ministers of Foreign Affairs declared, *inter alia*, that there should be

1. Immediate and definitive replacement of the Somoza regime.
2. Installation in Nicaraguan territory of a democratic government... which reflects the free will of the people of Nicaragua.
3. Guarantee of the respect for human rights of all Nicaraguan [sic] without exception.
4. The holding of free elections as soon as possible, that will lead to the establishment of a truly democratic government that guarantees peace, freedom and justice.[1226]

The resolution also observed that "[t]he inhumane conduct of the dictatorial regime governing the country . . . is the fundamental cause of the dramatic situation faced by the Nicaraguan people."[1227]

Although there was no equivalent intergovernmental declaration of illegitimacy, the immediate recognition of the governments which re-placed the regimes of Amin in Uganda, Bokassa in the Central African Republic, Duvalier in Haiti, and Marcos in the Philippines was moti-vated primarily by the illegitimate nature of and gross human rights violations committed by the former regimes. In these instances, there was no question of the legitimacy of the state itself; the only issue was whether a successor government had a legitimate claim to replace its predecessor by extra-constitutional means.

A government may become partially illegitimate if effective partic-ipation by minority or indigenous groups or their members has been rendered impossible by either deliberate discrimination or a political

---

1224 *Cf.* Crawford, *supra* note 27, at 103–06.

1225 One might contrast this action by the OAS with the lack of any international action with respect to, e.g., the Pol Pot government of Democratic Kampuchea or the Idi Amin regime in Uganda.

1226 OAS Res. of 23 June 1979, *reprinted in* Inter-American Commission on Human Rights, *Report on the Situation of Human Rights in the Republic of Nicaragua* (Washington, DC: OAS General Secretariat, 1981), OAS Doc. OEA/Ser.L/V/II.53, doc. 25, at 2–3.

1227 *Id.*

situation which permanently excludes such groups. A government may not demand the denial of one's group identity as the price of political participation, even where (as in Northern Ireland) the technical forms of democracy may be observed. "One person, one vote" may not be sufficient to ensure the effective participation in the political and cultural life of the state required under international human rights norms.

In such situations, the "right" of self-determination and the possibility of secession are automatically raised wherever such groups are sufficiently separate geographically from the rest of the country. The controversy over secession is likely to remain a fundamental reality in the twentieth century and beyond, and appeals to theories of sovereignty offer little assistance in resolving the dispute. No author has asserted that international law currently recognizes a right of secession, although several scholars have sought to develop criteria for determining when secession *should* be deemed legitimate.[1228]

[T]he conviction that the legitimacy of a claim to self-determination [by a separatist group] can be tested by the degree of success that attends the claimants' undertaking is probably the prevailing view among most international jurists. ... [A]t the present time there is neither an international consensus regarding the status of secession within this doctrine [of self-determination] nor (should it be conceded such a status) is there an accepted teaching regarding the nature of a legitimate secessionist movement.[1229]

In the search for a means of determining whether a particular secessionist movement is legitimate or illegitimate, one common denominator is the violation of fundamental rights by the state; only where such violations occur can secession be justified. While not confirming or implying a right to secession, even the League of Nations, during its consideration of the Aland Islands, seemed to suggest that what would now be called human rights were a legitimate concern.[1230]

1228 Perhaps the only suggestion that there currently exists a "relatively fragile" right to secession is found in Daniel Turp, "Le droit de sécession en droit international public," 20 Canadian Yearbook of Int'l L. 24, 76 (1982).
1229 Buchheit, *supra* note 90, at 45, 216.
1230 In the context of its discussion of self-determination and the rights of peoples, the first League committee declined to give an opinion "concerning the question as to whether a manifest and continued abuse of sovereign power, to the detriment of a section of the population of a State, would, if such circumstances arose," give rise to an international dispute within the competence of the League. *Report of the International Committee of Jurists* (1920), *supra* note 86, at 5.
The second commission noted that one could not compare the right of self-determination of Aland with that of Finland, for the latter had been oppressed and persecuted by Russia, while Aland had not been so treated. *Report presented to the Council of the League by the Commission of Rapporteurs* (1921), *supra* note 87, at 28.

The idea of justice and of liberty, embodied in the formula of self-determination, must be applied in a reasonable manner to the relations between States and the minorities they include. It is just that the ethnical character and the ancient traditions of these minorities should be respected as much as possible, and that they should be specially authorised to practise freely their religion and to cultivate their language. . . . [W]hat reasons would there be for allowing a minority to separate itself from the State to which it is united, *if this State gives it the guarantees which it is within its rights in demanding, for the preservation of its social, ethnical or religious character?* Such indulgence, apart from every political consideration, would be supremely unjust to the State prepared to make these concessions.

The separation of a minority from the State of which it forms a part and its incorporation in another State can only be considered as an altogether exceptional solution, a last resort *when the State lacks either the will or the power to enact and apply just and effective guarantees.*[1231]

Some modern commentators have expressed similar attitudes. In the context of Bangladesh, Crawford notes that genocide is "a clear case of abuse of sovereignty" and concludes that East Bengal was a "self-determination unit" analogous to a non-self-governing territory under the terms of UN General Assembly Resolution 1541.[1232] Others have asserted more generally that the violation of minority rights might create a right to self-determination and secession. "What seems to be required is a denial of political freedom and/or human rights as a sine qua non for a legitimate separatist claim."[1233] The "only reliable test for determining the reasonableness of self-determination has to be the nature and extent of the deprivation of human rights of the subgroup claiming the right."[1234]

One state is not to be condemned for its diversity of language, religion, or descent, nor another for its homogeneity. The state is only to be condemned, and secession approved, where it does not protect and promote, in reasonable measure, the rights of the individual citizens, included among which are their interests as members of a national community.[1235]

This view is given support by the 1970 Declaration on Friendly Relations, which proclaims the fundamental importance of the territorial

1231 *Report presented to the Council of the League by the Commission of Rapporteurs* (1921), *supra* note 87, at 28; emphasis added.

1232 Crawford, *supra* note 27, at 116–17. It might be noted that Res. 1541 requires, *inter alia*, that a non-self-governing territory be geographically separate and ethnically distinct from the country administering it, conditions which also were fulfilled by East Bengal.

1233 Buchheit, *supra* note 90, at 94.

1234 Ved P. Nanda, "Self-Determination Outside the Colonial Context: The Birth of Bangladesh in Retrospect," in Alexander and Friedlander, *supra* note 163, at 204.

1235 Cobban, *supra* note 67, at 140.

integrity and political unity "of sovereign and independent States conducting themselves in compliance with the principle of equal rights and self-determination of peoples as described above and thus possessed of a government representing the whole people belonging to the territory without distinction as to race, creed or color."[1236] The word "thus" may be somewhat problematic in utilizing this resolution to justify secession, as may be the rather limited requirement of non-discrimination only on the grounds of race, creed, or color. Nevertheless, the concept of the representativeness of a government is important.

While it is appropriate to focus on secession as the ultimate expression of the right to self-determination, it is precisely this focus that has led states to reject categorically any suggestion of "self-determination" for minority or indigenous peoples within their jurisdiction. One need not accept the view that states are the only entities which should influence the development of international law, in order to understand their reluctance to agree to their own legal dismemberment. Nevertheless, the continued refusal of the international community to apply self-determination norms when they conflict with the statist norm of territorial integrity only underscores to sub-state groups the perceived irrelevance of international law to the problems faced by minorities and indigenous peoples throughout the world.

At the same time, however, it is difficult to see how more precise legal norms regarding a situation which almost invariably culminates in civil war would be helpful in preventing such wars. "It would be uselessly pedantic . . . to draw up rules for when secession is a right. It is enough to say that no minority is likely to attempt anything like this unless it or a substantial section of it has been driven desperate by events."[1237]

It is the suggestion of the present book that a new principle of international law can be discerned in the interstices of contemporary definitions of sovereignty, self-determination, and the human rights of individuals and groups, which will support creative attempts to deal with conflicts over minority and majority rights before they escalate into civil war and demands for secession.[1238] This right to autonomy recognizes the right of minority and indigenous communities to exercise meaningful internal self-determination and control over their own affairs in a manner

---

1236 G.A. Res. 2625, *supra* note 107, at 121.

1237 Conor Cruise O'Brien, "Preface," in Georgina Ashworth (ed.), *World Minorities* (Sunbury, UK: Quartermaine House, 2 vols., 1977, 1978) at xv.

1238 At least one other author has found that the linkage of respect for the territorial integrity of a state to respect for minority rights to equality and self-identity is "slowly emerging at the international level." Giorgio Sacerdoti, "New Developments in Group Consciousness and the International Protection of the Rights of Minorities," 13 Israeli Yearbook on Human Rights 116 (1983) at 144–45.

that is not inconsistent with the ultimate sovereignty—as that term is properly understood—of the state.[1239]

In a sense, autonomy lies at the end of a progression of rights. While it is perhaps of greatest importance to indigenous peoples and ethnic or other minorities, it may respond to purely regional needs, as well. It cannot replace or subvert the rights of individuals of either the minority or majority community, however, and recognition of minority rights should not be an excuse for abandoning the fundamental principles of non-discrimination and equality before the law. Territorially based autonomy arrangements are neither incompatible with, nor do they require, other preferential or "affirmative action" policies to enable disadvantaged groups to achieve effective, as opposed to only theoretical, equality.

Nor is autonomy an end in itself—it is a political tool to ensure that other rights and needs are appropriately addressed. The mere achievement of "autonomy" will not guarantee development or preserve a threatened culture, and the form which any particular manifestation of autonomy takes must be consciously related to the goals of the community which seeks it, as well as to the requirements of the larger state polity.

Autonomy has both a permissive and a somewhat more coercive side. Even in a democratic, participatory state in which human rights are generally protected, groups may demand autonomy as a means of reinforcing their own identity beyond that of being merely citizens of the state. While in such circumstances one may not recognize a "right" to a particular form of devolved or federal political structure, opposition to such demands by the central government should be founded on a demonstration that the regional or minority demands are unreasonable or are being met in practice, rather than on irrelevant incantations of state sovereignty or even majority rule.

The right to autonomy may be asserted more aggressively in situations where regional, ethnic, or economic disparities are shown to exist; where there is discrimination against minority groups as such; or where the marginalization of certain groups prevents their effective participation in society (where such participation is desired by them). Even in these situations, differences within minority groups must be recognized; many minority members wish only to participate on an equal basis in the majority society, without being forced to abandon their own identity, and not to be forced into a segregated "autonomous" community.

The full and effective implementation of existing international hu-

1239 Accord, Alexandre Kiss, "The Peoples' Right to Self-Determination," 7 Human Rights L. J. 165 (1986).

man rights norms would resolve the vast majority of contemporary "minority" complaints. In this context, it should be emphasized that rights of particular concern to minority groups are found not only in article 27 of the Covenant on Civil and Political Rights, but also in articles 22 (freedom of association), 25 (the right to participate in government), and 26 (the right to equality before the law). Many groups seeking to protect their culture, land, or physical integrity are victims of gross violations of "traditional" human rights, and redress could be provided by actions as unimaginative as halting state and private theft, torture, and murder.

Nevertheless, it is clear that in many instances true group rights must be recognized in order to satisfy deeply felt needs. These will be more extensive than purely social or cultural rights—including fundamental issues such as linguistic and educational rights, control over land and natural resources, and the opportunity for local group authority to address primarily local concerns—yet they need not necessarily pose a challenge to the underlying sovereignty or integrity of the state. What should be sought in such situations is a kind of flexible intermediary status which will enable parties to negotiate solutions to particular grievances on the basis of pragmatic creativity.

The balance to be found between territorial states as they are presently constituted and the legitimate expressions of national or cultural identity upon which smaller groups will continue to insist cannot be found by resorting to simplistic formulas of federalism or decentralization, although these concepts may contain the seeds of potential solutions in many situations. The case studies of autonomous and other structures outlined in Parts II and III are merely illustrative, and solutions will be unique to each situation. What is important is that both subordinate and dominant groups begin to worry less about precedents (either establishing or following them) than about creative solutions to the problems at hand.

As international actors—states, liberation movements, international organizations, transnational corporations, non-sovereign entities, etc.— become more diverse, appropriate responses to demands for group identity and recognition should become more common. As domestic constitutional arrangements become more inventive and flexible—as demonstrated from Greenland to Hong Kong—the securing of meaningful autonomy should respond more effectively to demands for self-determination.

While the sovereign state is far from becoming an anachronism, there can be no question that modern communication and transportation, combined with the intrusive pervasiveness of modern consumer societies, present new problems to those who wish to determine for themselves how much "progress" is appropriate. Both the state as a whole and its constituent parts often feel threatened by social and economic stresses, and one natural reaction is to turn inward, to resist rather than confront change. These fundamentally conservative postures are taken by minority and indigenous groups whose cultures are under attack, as well as by majority communities and state elites, who fear that regional or ethnic dissension will subvert an often tenuous political identity. Both minority and majority elites also fear threats to their own political and economic status, and they may oppose creative change out of narrow personal interest as well as the altruistic community concern they claim. Those in power rarely yield it voluntarily.

Yet no society is static, and it is absurd to think that any particular form of government structure now extant will survive unchanged. "[W]hatever the model of the nation may be when it is first translated into an ideology designed to guide a country's first faltering steps toward the future, it must necessarily undergo many modifications as the future becomes the present."[1240] International law does a disservice to this necessary evolution, if it is predicated on an unchanging system of states whose boundaries, competence, and role in international affairs are immutable.

Conflict and tension are inherent in society; so are differences in individuals and cultures. A fundamental state obligation under international human rights norms is to eliminate discrimination, not to destroy all differences. Recognition of the right to personal autonomy and group identity is essential to ensure that the principles of self-determination, participation, and tolerance are allowed to flourish. At the same time, majority democratic rule also is a fundamental principle, and the ability of groups to veto or reject majority decisions can be exercised only to protect legitimate group rights.

"[T]he question of whether an arrangement of autonomy is to be crowned with success or doomed to failure depends, in the final analysis, on the state of mind of the parties. The legal or procedural intricacies of the arrangement cannot guarantee the outcome."[1241] In those intricacies, however, one can perhaps find structures that will respond to the mosaic of internal social, cultural, economic, and political tensions

---

1240 Aristide R. Zolberg, "Patterns of National Integration," 5 J. Modern African Studies 449, 467 (1967). One might cite as recent positive examples the flexibility in devising new political structures evidenced in Spain, Denmark (with respect to Greenland), Hong Kong, the Swiss Jura, Canada (Quebec), and India (the Punjab remaining an unfortunate exception), as well as the creativity evidenced in some of the short-lived post-Versailles arrangements.

1241 Yoram Dinstein, "Autonomy," in Yoram Dinstein (ed.), *Models of Autonomy* (New Brunswick, NJ: Transaction Press, 1981) at 295.

that exist among groups and individuals within the state. Law also is a symbol, and it can be used to give a framework to that diversity which is a fact of modern society, promoting mutual respect rather than coercing obedience.

If self-determination and human rights are to contribute to a better life for a greater number of people in the twenty-first century, it will be as the joint guarantors of tolerance and justice. These two principles, reflecting to some extent the inherent tension between minority rights and majority rule, must guide society's constant attempts to find an appropriate balance among the interlocking identities of the individual, the group, and the state.

Selected Bibliography

This selective listing includes general works which consider the major issues of autonomy, self-determination, sovereignty, and minority rights discussed in the present book. Reference should be made to individual chapters for country-specific works.

Alcock, Antony E., Brian K. Taylor, and John M. Welton (eds.). *The Future of Cultural Minorities*. London: Macmillan, 1979.

Alexander, Yonah, and Robert A. Friedlander. *Self-Determination: National, Regional, and Global Dimensions*. Boulder, CO: Westview Press, 1980.

Ashworth, Georgina (ed.). *World Minorities*. Sunbury, UK: Quartermaine House, 2 vols., 1977, 1978.

————. *World Minorities in the Eighties*. Sunbury, UK: Quartermaine House, 1980.

Bernier, I. *International Legal Aspects of Federalism*. Hamden, CT: Archon Books, 1973.

Blaustein, Albert P., and Dana Blaustein Epstein. *Resolving Language Conflicts: A Study of the World's Constitutions*. Washington, DC: U.S. English, 1986.

Blaustein, Albert P., and Phyllis M. Blaustein. *Constitutions of Dependencies and Special Sovereignties*. Dobbs Ferry, CT: Oceana, looseleaf, various dates.

Bokor-Szegő, Hanna. *New States and International Law*. Budapest: Akadémiai Kiadó, 1970.

Bossuyt, Marc J. *Guide to the "Travaux Préparatoires" of the International Covenant on Civil and Political Rights*. Dordrecht, Boston, Lancaster: Martinus Nijhoff, 1987.

Breuilly, John. *Nationalism and the State*. New York: St. Martin's Press, 1982.

Brøsted, Jens et al. (eds.). *Native Power*. Oslo: Universitetsforlaget AS, 1985.

Brownlie, Ian. *Principles of Public International Law*. Oxford: Clarendon Press, 3d. ed. 1979.

Buchheit, Lee C. *Secession*. New Haven, CT: Yale Univ. Press, 1978.

Calogeropoulos-Stratis, S. *Le Droit des peuples à disposer d'eux-mêmes*. Paris: Bruylant, 1973.

Cappelletti, Mauro, Monica Seccombe, and Joseph Weiler. *Integration Through Law*. Berlin & New York: Walter de Gruyter, 3 vols. 1985, 1986.

Caratini, Roger. *La Force des faibles*. Paris: Larousse, 1987.

Carey, John. *UN Protection of Civil and Political Rights*. Syracuse, NY: Syracuse Univ. Press, 1970.

Chaliand, Gérard (ed.) *Les Minorités à l'âge de l'état-nation*. Paris: Fayard & Minority Rights Group, 1985.

Chowdhuri, R. N. *International Mandates and Trusteeship Systems*. The Hague: Martinus Nijhoff, 1955.

Claude, Inis L., Jr. *National Minorities*. Cambridge, MA: Harvard Univ. Press, 1955.

Cobban, Alfred. *The Nation State and National Self-Determination*. New York: Thomas Y. Crowell, rev. ed. 1969.

Council of Europe. *Digest of Strasbourg Case-Law relating to the European Convention on Human Rights*. Cologne: Carl Heymanns, 6 vols. 1984–1985.

Crawford, James. *The Creation of States in International Law*. Oxford: Clarendon Press, 1979.

——— (ed.). *The Rights of Peoples*. Oxford: Clarendon Press, 1988.

Delupis, Ingrid. *International Law and the Independent State*. New York: Crane Russak, 1974.

Dickinson, Edwin Dewitt. *The Equality of States in International Law*. Cambridge, MA: Harvard Univ. Press, 1920; New York: Klaus Reprint Co., 1972.

Dinstein, Yoram. *Models of Autonomy*. New Brunswick, NJ: Transaction Press, 1981.

Djordjevic, Dimitrije, and Stephen Fischer-Galati. *The Balkan Revolutionary Tradition*. New York: Columbia Univ. Press, 1981.

Dofny, Jacques and Akinsola Akiwowo (eds.). *National and Ethnic Movements*. (Beverly Hills, CA and London: Sage Productions, 1980.

Le Droit des Peuples à Disposer d'Eux-Mêmes, melanges offerts à Charles Chaumont. Paris: Pedone, 1984.

Elazar, Daniel J. (ed.). *Governing Peoples and Territories*. Philadelphia: Institute for the Study of Human Issues, 1982.

El-Ayouty, Yassin. *The United Nations and Decolonization: The Role of Afro-Asia*. The Hague: Martinus Nijhoff, 1971.

Enloe, Cynthia H. *Ethnic Conflict and Political Development*. Boston: Little, Brown, 1973.

Falch, Jean. *Contribution à l'étude du statut des langues en Europe*. Quebec: Presses de l'Univ. Laval, 1973.

Fall, Ibou Ibrahima. *Contribution à l'étude du Droit des Peuples à Disposer d'Eux-Mêmes en Afrique*. Paris: Univ. de Paris I, doctoral thesis 1972.

Fenwick, Charles G. *Wardship in International Law*. Washington, DC: U.S. Gov't. Printing Office, 1919.

Gellner, Ernest. *Culture, Indentity, and Politics*. Cambridge: Cambridge Univ. Press, 1987.

Goldmann, Robert B. and A. Jeyaratnam Wilson. *From Independence to State-hood*. London: Frances Pinter, 1984.

Gotlieb, Allan (ed.) *Human Rights, Federalism and Minorities*. Toronto: Canadian Institute of International Affairs, 1970.

Guilhaudis. *Le Droit des Peuples à Disposer d'Eux-Mêmes*. Grenoble: 1976.

Harden, Sheila (ed.) *Small is Dangerous*. London: Frances Pinter, 1985.

Hassan, Farooq. *The Concept of State and Law in Islam*. Lanham, MD, and London: University Press of America, 1981.

Held, David et al. (eds.). *States and Societies*. New York and London: New York Univ. Press, 1983.

Henkin, Louis (ed.). *The International Bill of Rights, The Covenant on Civil and Political Rights*. New York: Columbia Univ. Press, 1981.

Hinsley, F. H. *Sovereignty*. New York: Basic Books, 1966.

Horowitz, Donald L. *Ethnic Groups in Conflict*. Berkeley: Univ. of California Press, 1985.

Independent Commission on International Humanitarian Issues. *Indigenous Peoples, A Global Quest for Justice*. London and New Jersey: Zed Books, 1987.

International Court of Justice. *Reservations to the Convention on the Prevention and Punishment of the Crime of Genocide*. Advisory Opinion. I.C.J. Reports 1951, p. 15

————. *Case concerning the Northern Cameroons (Cameroon v. United Kingdom)*. Preliminary Objections, Judgment of 2 December 1963. I.C.J. Reports 1963, p. 15

————. *Barcelona Traction, Light and Power Company, Limited*. Second Phase, Judgment. I.C.J. Reports 1970, p. 3

————. *Legal Consequences for States of the Continued Presence of South Africa in Namibia (South West Africa) notwithstanding Security Council Resolution 276 (1970)*. Advisory Opinion. I.C.J. Reports 1971, p. 16

————. *Western Sahara*. Advisory Opinion. I.C.J. Reports 1975, p. 12

————. *Military and Paramilitary Activities in and against Nicaragua (Nicaragua v. United States of America)*. Judgment, I.C.J. Reports 1986, p. 14

International Labour Organization. *Partial revision of the Indigenous and Tribal Populations Convention, 1957 (No. 107)*. Geneva: ILO (Reports VI(1) and VI(2) to the 1988 International Labour Conference) 1987.

James, Alan. *Sovereign Statehood*. London: Allen & Unwin, 1986.

Jankovic, Branimir M. *Public International Law*. Dobbs Ferry, NY: Transnational Publishers, 1984.

Janowsky, Oscar I. *Nationalities and National Minorities*. New York: Macmillan, 1945.

Kann, Robert A. *A History of the Habsburg Empire 1526–1918*. Berkeley: Univ. of California Press, 1974.

Knight, David B., and Maureen Davies. *Self-Determination: An Interdisciplinary Annotated Bibliography*. New York and London: Garland Publishing, 1987.

Kohn, Hans, *Nationalism: Its Meaning and History*. Princeton, NJ: Van Nostrand, rev. ed. 1965.

Larson, Arthur, C. Wilfred Jenks, et al. *Sovereignty Within the Law.* Dobbs Ferry, NY; Oceana, 1965.

Lenin, Vladimir I. *Questions of National Policy and Proletarian Internationalism.* Moscow: Foreign Languages Publishing House, n.d.

Lijphart, Arend. *Democracy in Plural Societies.* New Haven, CT: Yale Univ. Press, 1977.

Macartney, C.A. *National States and National Minorities.* London: Oxford Univ. Press, 1934.

Makonnen, Yilma. *International Law and The New States of Africa: A Study of the International Legal Problems of State Succession in the Newly Independent States of Eastern Africa.* Paris: Unesco, 1983.

Mazrui, Ali A., and Michael Tidy. *Nationalism and New States in Africa.* London: Heinneman, 1984.

McRae, Kenneth D. *Conflict and Compromise in Multilingual Societies.* Waterloo, Ontario: Wilfrid Laurier Univ. Press; vol. 1, Switzerland, 1983; vol. 2, Belgium, 1986.

Minority Rights Group. *Co-existence in some plural European societies.* London: MRG Report No. 72, 1986.

Okeke, Chris N. *Controversial Subjects of Contemporary International Law.* Rotterdam: Rotterdam Univ. Press, 1974.

Paddison, Ronan. *The Fragmented State.* New York: St. Martin's Press, 1983.

Pearson, Raymond. *National Minorities in Eastern Europe 1848–1945.* London: Macmillan, 1983.

Permanent Court of International Justice. *Minority Schools in Albania.* Advisory Opinion, Series A/B, No. 64 (1935), p. 4.

Plishke, Elmer. *Microstates in World Affairs.* Washington, DC: American Enterprise Institute, 1977.

Pomerance, Michla. *Self-Determination in Law and Practice.* The Hague: Martinus Nijhoff, 1982.

Poulter, Sebastian M. *English Law and Ethnic Minority Customs.* London: Butterworths, 1986.

Rigo Sureda, A. *The Evolution of the Right of Self-Determination.* Leiden: Sijthoff, 1973 .

Ronen, Dov. *The Quest for Self-Determination.* New Haven, CT: Yale Univ. Press, 1979.

Rothschild, Joseph. *Ethnopolitics.* New York: Columbia Univ. Press, 1981.

———. *East Central Europe between the Two World Wars.* Seattle: Univ. of Washington Press, 1974.

Said, Abdul, and Luiz R. Simmons (eds.). *Ethnicity in an International Context.* New Brunswick, NJ: Transaction Books, 1976.

Seton-Watson, Hugh. *Nations and States.* London: Methuen, 1977.

Sigler, Jay A. *Minority Rights, A Comparative Analysis.* Westport, CT: Greenwood Press, 1983.

Smith, Anthony D. *State and Nation in the Third World.* New York: St. Martin's Press, 1983.

Société Belge de Droit International. *Les États fédéraux dans les relations internationales.* Brussels: Ed. Bruylant & Univ. of Bruxelles, 1984.

Sohn, Louis B., and Thomas Buergenthal. *International Protection of Human Rights*. Indianapolis, IN: Bobbs-Merrill, 1973.

Soroos, Marvin S. *Beyond Sovereignty*. Columbia: Univ. of South Carolina Press, 1986.

Stalin, Josef. *Marxism and the National and Colonial Question*. London: Lawrence & Wishart, Eng. ed. 1936.

Stavenhagen, Rodolfo. *La legislación indígena y los derechos humanos de las poblaciones indígenas en America Latina*. San Jose, Costa Rica: Interamerican Institute of Human Rights, 1987.

Steiner, Henry J. (ed.). *Ethnic Conflict and the U.N. System*. Papers and proceedings of a conference held at Oxford University in March 1989, forthcoming.

Stephens, Meic. *Linguistic Minorities in Western Europe*. Llandysol: Gomer Press, 1976.

Sugar, Peter F. *Southeastern Europe under Ottoman Rule, 1354–1804*. Seattle: Univ. of Washington Press, 1977.

Thornberry, Patrick. *Minorities and Human Rights Law*. London: Minority Rights Group Report No. 73, 1987.

Tivey, Leonard (ed.). *The Nation-State*. New York: St. Martin's Press, 1981.

Tunkin, G. I. *Theory of International Law*. Cambridge, MA: Harvard Univ. Press, Butler trans. 1974.

Turi, Giuseppe. *Les Dispositions juridico-constitutionnelles de 147 états en matière de politique linguistique*. Quebec: Int'l Center for Research on Bilingualism, 1977.

Umozurike, Umozurike Oji. *Self-Determination in International Law*. Hamden, CT: Archon Books, 1972.

United Nations. *Popular Participation in Decision Making for Development*. UN Sales No. E.75.IV.10 (1975).

———. *Protection of Minorities*. UN Sales No. 67.XIV.3 (1967).

———. *Racial Discrimination* (Hernan Santa Cruz, Special Rapporteur). UN Sales No. E.76.XIV.2 (rev. ed. 1977).

———. *Study by the Secretary-General on Popular Participation in its Various Forms as an Important Factor in Development and in the Full Realization of Human Rights*. UN Doc. E/CN.4/1985/10 (1984).

———. *Study of the Problem of Discrimination Against Indigenous Populations* (Jose R. Martinez Cobo, Special Rapporteur). UN Doc. E/CN.4/Sub.2/1986/7 & Adds.1–4, UN Sales No. (Add.4 only) E.86.XIV.3 (1986).

———. *Study on the rights of persons belonging to ethnic, religious and linguistic minorities* (Francesco Capotorti, Special Rapporteur). UN Sales No. E.78.XIV.1 (1978).

———. *The Right to Self-Determination, Historical and Current Developments on the Basis of the United Nations Instruments* (Aurelieu Cristescu, Special Rapporteur). UN Sales No. E.80.XIV.3 (1981).

———. *The Right to Self-Determination, Implementation of United Nations Resolutions* (Hector Gros Espiell, Special Rapporteur). UN Sales No. E.79.XIV.5 (1980).

————. *United Nations Action in the Field of Human Rights*. UN Sales No. E.88.XIV.2 (1988).

————. Committee on the Elimination of Racial Discrimination. *Annual Reports* (issued as supplements to the Official Records of the General Assembly).

————. Sub-Commission on Prevention of Discrimination and Protection of Minorities. *Activities of the United Nations Relating to the Protection of Minorities*. UN Doc. E/CN.4/Sub.2/194 (1958).

————. Sub-Commission on Prevention of Discrimination and Protection of Minorities. *Treaties and international instruments concerning the protection of minorities 1919–1951*. UN Doc. E/CN.4/Sub.2/133 (1951).

Van Dyke, Vernon. *Human Rights, Ethnicity, and Discrimination*. Westport, CT and London: Greenwood Press, 1985.

Vasak, Karel (gen. ed.), and Philip Alston (Eng. ed. ed.). *The International Dimensions of Human Rights*. Paris: Unesco and Westport, CT: Greenwood Press, 2 vols. 1982.

Verdoodt, Albert. *La protection des droits de l'homme dans les états plurilingues*. Paris: Nathan and Bruxelles: Labor, 1973.

Whitaker, Ben (ed.). *Minorities: A Question of Human Rights?* Oxford: Pergamon Press, 1984.

Williams, Colin H. (ed.). *National Separatism*. Vancouver and London: Univ. of British Columbia Press, 1982.

Willoughby, W. W., and C. G. Fenwick. *Types of Restricted Sovereignty and of Colonial Autonomy*. Washington, DC: U.S. Gov't. Printing Office, 1919.

Wirsing, Robert G. (ed.). *Protection of Ethnic Minorities*. New York: Pergamon Press, 1981.

Ydit, Méir. *Internationalised Territories from the "Free City of Cracow" to the "Free City of Berlin"*. London: Sithoff, 1961.

Index

Shipping, 140, 141, 147
Shiromani Gurdwara Prabhandak Committee (SGPC), 157, 162
Siberia, 359
Sicily, 263
Siida, 248
Sikhs, 70, 124; Akali Dal, 157, 158, 160, 161–66; Akal Takht, 166; Anandpur Sahib Resolution, 161, 162–63; autonomy struggle, 173–76; grievances with Indian government, 160–61, 166–69; fundamentalists, 161–62, 163; and Indian partition, 157–60, 174–75; Khalsa brotherhood, 156; nationalism of, 156–57; Nirankari sect, 162; in Punjab empire, 155–56; seek independent state, 160, 162, 163, 166, 171, 173–74; Temple Management Committee (SGPC), 157, 162; terrorism, 163, 164, 171, 176, 177; violence against, 163–64, 170, 175
Sikkim (India), 22, 151, 172
Simko, Isma'il Shakkah, 185, 195
Sindhi (language), 68
Singapore, 442
Singh (lion), 156
Sinhala (language), 282, 283, 284, 299–300, 302, 459 n. 1208
Sinhalese: attacks on, 291, 298–99; People's Liberation Front (JVP), 301, 307; and Tamil autonomy, 290, 293–94, 296, 297–98; and Tamil conflict, 280–85, 302–03, 306–07; United National Party (UNP), 284, 285, 296, 301, 304, 307; violence against Tamils, 286–87, 301
Sinn Fein, 228, 236–37, 240
Sinti gypsies, 65
Slavery, 75, 78, 108, 204, 413
Slavs, 67, 401, 439
Slovaks, 67
Slovene: language, 405 n. 1094; Slovenes, 57–58, 68
Smith, Ian, 16
Smuts, Jan Christiaan, 52 n. 177
Social contract theory, 71, 71 n. 272, 454
Social Darwinism, 251
Socialist internationalism, 21
Somalia, 47 n. 159
Somoza Debayle, Anastasio, 205, 206, 207–08, 470
Sorbs, 67

Soulbury Constitution (Ceylon), 283
South Africa, 38–39, 394 n. 1069
Southern Rhodesia, 16
South Tyrol, 57, 68, 432–40
Sovereignty, 5, 26; defining, 14–16; Hong Kong, 136–37; limits on, 19–23; minorities and, 71, 71 n. 272; and self-determination, 48
Soviet Life, 364 n. 1008
Soviet Union, 89, 115 n. 420, 195, 250 n. 731, 380; Communist Party (CPSU), 361–62, 366 n. 1013, 367, 368, 369; Constitution, 359–61, 362, 363, 364, 365, 366 n. 1013, 367; Council of Ministers, 362; ethnic populations, 358–59; federal government powers, 359–60, 361–63, 365; and Kurds, 179, 192, 199, 200, 201; language and cultural policies, 363–65; nationality conflicts, 365–69; religious intolerance in, 111; Saami in, 247, 248–49, 250; secession rights in, 32–33, 43, 420; Soviet of Nationalities, 359–60, 361, 361 n. 994; Supreme Court, 363; Supreme Soviet, 361–62, 363; and Yugoslavia, 401. *See also* Russia
Space, 19
Spain, 38, 125–26, 263–64; autonomous regions of, 264–66, 268–72, 272–79; Civil War, 264, 266; colonialism, 203–04; Constitution, 269, 270, 271, 273; Cortes, 264, 265, 266, 270, 272, 273–74; Council on Judicial Power, 272; under Franco, 266–68; Ley Organica de Armonizacion del Proceso Autonomico (LOAPA), 270; minorities in, 65; Senate, 271–72; Socialist Party (PSOE), 269–70, 275
Spanish (language), 204, 214, 216–17, 273. *See also* Castillian
Sports, Northern Ireland, 229
Sri Lanka, 4, 126, 149, 175, 176–77; All Party Conference, 290; Constituent Assembly, 283–84, 285; Constitution, 282, 283–84, 287, 293, 296, 297, 302; history, 280–85; human rights violations, 288–89, 288 n. 859, 303, 304, 305 n. 889, 307; India agreement (1987), 287 n. 858, 288, 289, 292, 295–96, 298–301; Indian Peacekeeping Force in, 288,